images of women in literature

images of women in literature

mary anne ferguson

university of massachusetts

houghton mifflin / boston

atlanta   dallas   geneva,ill.   hopewell,n.j.   palo alto

preface

This anthology contains 26 short stories, 8 poems, and a playlet, all on the subject of women, more than half of them written by women. With the addition of some of the novels, plays, and criticism chosen from the Suggestions for Further Reading, the book can serve as the central text for a course on "Images of Women in Literature." Organized around female stereotypes and archetypes, the selections contain both negative and positive views of women as wives, mothers, sex objects, seductresses, old maids, and free women.

The Introduction, which is both theoretical and historical, attempts to explain the psychological and sociological bases for the images of women and the uses to which literature has put them. The book may therefore be useful in courses on the history and sociology of women and in American Studies programs, as well as in literature courses focusing on the short story as a genre or on modern or American literature. Twenty of the short stories are by 20th-century American authors, two by 20th-century British, and one each by 20th-century French and Italian authors. Three 19th-century stories (two American and one Russian) as well as poems by Blake, Keats, and Heine indicate the relationship between modern images and the past.

The stories are varied enough technically to be useful in teaching literary sophistication. Both male and female authors use men, women, and children as central consciousnesses. Some stories are written with a first-person narrator, others in dramatic style with little authorial presence. A consideration of such technical aspects is necessary in order to discover the stereotypes and to help students understand the futility of separating form and content in a work of art.

The varied milieux of the stories—urban, rural, small-town; high society, working class; France, London, New York, Ohio, New England—enable students to consider the pervasiveness of the stereotypes and to come to grips with their power. The range of characters, from an infant crying in the night, a black boy of nine, an idealistic young girl, and middle-aged wives, to a dying grandmother, documents the similarity among literary views of women.

In order to avoid dictating interpretation of the stories and poems in the anthology, the Introduction analyzes at length works which do not appear in the book. These works, most of which are readily available, are included in the Index and in the Suggestions for Further Reading at the end of the book. It is hoped that the suggested readings will prove useful in expanding the range of each stereotype. Students may find many of the selections depressing, particularly those in Section I, "The Submissive Wife," and in Section V, "The Sex Object." An antidote for such depression is to read widely in order to understand modifications of the stereotypes and ways of transcending them. The autobiographies listed in suggested reading for "The Liberated Woman" are particularly useful in showing the limitations of literary images.

I am indebted for ideas in the Introduction to many of the authors listed in the suggested readings; to my students, who have served as guinea pigs, friends, and advisors; and to colleagues in Women's Studies who have generously shared their experience.

Mary Anne Ferguson

University of Massachusetts / Boston

contents

introduction

A famous surgeon was a passenger in a car driven by his teenage son. "I'll drop you at the hospital, Dad," said the young man.

"Fine, son," said his father. Those were his last words; a wildly careening convertible crossed the center strip and ran headlong into the car. At the emergency room the father was pronounced dead on arrival; the son was taken for emergency surgery. The surgeon called to the scene reached for a scalpel but paused: "I can't operate," the surgeon said; "this is my son."

This story is being presented as a riddle at cocktail parties in 1971; listeners are asked to explain the surgeon's remarks in the emergency room. Answers reported by a young man who had asked the riddle fifty-three times recently suggested that the father wasn't really dead or even injured; that the father had been thrown clear and the dead man was the driver of the other car; that the uneasy ghost of the father had appeared in the emergency room to fulfill his role. Only two people proposed the correct answer to the riddle; one of the two had heard it before and the other was a surgeon. "That's easy," said both; "the surgeon was his mother."

The fifty-one people bewildered by this riddle undoubtedly represent the majority today who cling to the long-held belief that surgeons should be male and that women's place—or certainly mothers' place—is in the home. A recent book showing the outmoded oversimplification of this myth, Elizabeth Janeway's *Man's World, Woman's Place* (1971), was greeted by a reviewer with the headline "Witch, bitch, goddess, or human being?" We are living in a time when the images of women in life and in literature are undergoing both analysis

1

and change. Adjectives used by sociologists to describe real women and by literary critics to describe their reflections—or models—in literature include such baffling pairs of opposites as passive–aggressive, intuitive–logical, possessive-self-sacrificing, materialistic-spiritual, frigid-lustful. The only common factor among these contradictory descriptions is that they all use the same standard of measurement: the characteristics of men are the norm, those of women subsidiary.

Women are thought to be passive when compared to men who assume the initiative in the sexual act, in business, in politics; passivity has a lower value since assertiveness is needed for success, and it is men who succeed. Aggressive women who succeed in male spheres are considered unfeminine and unnatural. When women are considered intelligent, their kind of intelligence, their mysterious intuition, is equated with flightiness and fuzzy thinking; male logicality is the norm few women achieve. The other opposing pairs of characteristics are extremes both of which are applicable to women; the norm is a happy medium reached by men. Possessiveness in men is associated with protectiveness and responsibility, in women with narrowness and selfishness; self-sacrifice in men is marvelled at, taken for granted in women. Women are seen paradoxically as highly materialistic and as devout and pious; but they carry these traits to undesirable extremes, whereas men exemplify admirable restraint when it comes to lovingly polishing furniture or putting on church bazaars. A woman may be less or more desirous of sex than a man; either frigidity or lust in a woman is a negative characteristic because the male appetite is the norm. Because of the conflicts among these images, women are bewildered about their identity; they feel damned if they do and damned if they don't.

Even for physical measurements the male is accepted as the standard; women are smaller, weaker, digitally more adept, capable of longer periods of continuous effort than men. Smallness and weakness are considered inferior, even in situations where size and strength are irrelevant.

Moreover, so universal is the association of masculinity with superiority that even women's "good" qualities make them suitable for inferior positions: their skilled fingers and ability to withstand monotony fit them admirably for menial jobs in industry and business and for the unpaid job of housewife. As Simone de Beauvoir has said, the image of women has been that of the second sex, the Other for man. This view has emphasized sexual differences instead of human similarities, to women's disadvantage. Even when exalted as a model of purity and generosity, woman has been considered strange and mysterious—superhuman or super-male. All the adjectives used to describe woman make it apparent that she is not the equal of man: she may be supernatural, she may be childlike—she is both more and less than man. This sexist image of women has prevailed in myth and literature for so long that it seems inevitable and true in spite of the obvious logical impossibilities.

A witch, a bitch, and a goddess may actually be the same person; the difference in the image is in the eye of the beholder. A beautiful woman is despised as a bitch if she uses her "weapons" of tongue and sex to diminish a man's sense of worth. Such a woman may be seen as deserving death: in Norman Mailer's *An American Dream* (1964), Stephen Rojack feels that mere murder is not enough for his wife, upon whose dead body he wants to inflict further indignities. In the Middle Ages and well into the 17th century in this country, a woman with mysterious powers—the witch—was thought to deserve death by fire. Arthur Miller has demonstrated the irrational forces leading to witch-hunting in his play *The Crucible* (1953). If the influence of a powerful woman was considered benign, she was thought to be a goddess, the muse of poetry and music, bestower of inspiration, and worthy of worship. These three views of beautiful women are all male views; the prevailing images of women are male pictures, often internalized by women as well as men.

How have such images come to prevail both in life and in literature? If we try to understand what happens when a single individual forms an image of a particular woman, we begin to comprehend the process at work in history and in literature. Imagine that you are looking through a family album. You stop at a picture of your mother holding you in her arms the day she brought you home from the hospital. Is that slender girl in the too-long skirt really the same person as the matronly woman sitting beside you now? Which one do you *see* when you think the word *mother*?

Your image of your mother may be kaleidoscopic, a merging of past memories and present reality. You may see her primarily as she used to be, obscuring the present because the changes in her remind you of your own mortality. A deep need to think well of your mother in order to bolster your own self-esteem may transmute your image of an actually cold, selfish woman into a warm, loving one; conversely, a need to avoid facing your own faults may reverse this process and turn your image of an ordinary, well-meaning person into a monster of greed and selfishness, like Portnoy's mother in Philip Roth's *Portnoy's Complaint* (1969). Your vision of your mother is shaped by your own self-image and by your dreams for the future. If you are ambitious to become a doctor, say, you may credit your mother's tenderness with giving you the desire to serve mankind; but if you cannot stand the sight of blood and must change your goal, you will blame her squeamishness. Your sex too, as Freud has emphasized, influences your attitude toward your mother: if you are male, you may see your father as a rival; whereas if you are female, you will see your mother as a threat to your relationship with your father. Our images of others may be a good deal more subjective than objective. Our pictures of the external world must fit our own pattern of memory, desire, and dream. When we look out, we look into a mirror.

Furthermore, to a degree we are only now becoming aware of, each person's images of others are colored by the ideas of society as a whole, of family, peers, country, the age. In a time and place in which women are expected to stay home and care for children, the image of a mother who does not is tarnished by her failure; she herself is likely to feel guilty no matter how valid her reason for absenting herself and no matter how many other women actually do not fulfill society's expectations. In spite of the fact that 40 percent of all women in this country go out of their homes to work, the current image is that most women are to "stay in their place," the home. Images have a curious way of being distorted, like those in the mirrors at carnivals, because they are tied so closely to the emotions. Every person absorbs through the process of acculturation or socialization the concepts of his society; through role-playing begun long before the age of reason, the individual attempts to shape himself or herself into the image expected. This process is necessary for human development, however full of dangers it may be for the individual psyche.

Society's images are called *stereotypes,* a term taken by sociologists from printing which refers to metal plates used to make exact copies. Character stereotypes differ in one major way from metal ones: they need not duplicate the pattern exactly. As long as some aspects of the stereotype are present, the observer supplies the others from previous experience. To the pattern "beautiful and blonde" the observer adds "dumb," whether it applies to the specific person or not. Jumping to such conclusions constitutes "prejudging" or prejudice. The beautiful blonde herself may play dumb in order to fulfill the stereotype and to win social approval. Thus the stereotypes which shape our personalities are even more rigid than heavy metal ones. The configuration of characteristics is held together by mental patterns harder to escape than factory-formed ones; the mind so quickly fills in the blanks that individual differences are lost sight of and the observer is likely to prejudge. A person who deliberately departs from a socially approved stereotype by playing a new role—developing a new life style—usually must pay a heavy cost in guilt, alienation, or psychosis; tendencies toward schizophrenia may be aggravated by the person's sense of his divided self. One wonders about the mental health of an Ivy League honor graduate in Russian who, according to a Boston newspaper, became a Playboy Bunny.

According to some psychologists, certain stereotypes are particularly strong because they are formed not by a single society but by the entire experience of mankind; they are the images of myths, stories told in every society to impose order upon and explain the inexplicable and chaotic aspects of experience. Jungian psychology teaches that our image of mother, for example, stems from deep within our minds in the realm of the Collective Unconscious, where images common to all mankind and perhaps also to animals are found. These images are too deeply imbedded to be available to any individual's conscious mind, but they find expression through symbol and art. The figures in myths, which Jung called *archetypes,* are recognizable in art because they correspond to the images in the Collective Unconscious.

Sociologists who do not share Jung's theories about the genetic and universal structure of the psyche nonetheless testify that the archetypes, grounded in emotion, are strong; they represent man's desires and fears about his nature and the structure of the world. A myth of creation must explain both man's presence in the world (his beginning) and his knowledge of death (his ending). The images of good and evil embodied in the Great Mother so widespread among primitive societies reflects man's love for the giver of life but also his fear of the inescapable death that the gift brings with it. Archetypes strongly resist modification by facts and logic and are often fortified by religion, which inevitably involves a large measure of myth.

One peculiarity of the images of women throughout history is that social stereotypes have often been reinforced by archetypes. Another way of putting this would be to say that in every age woman has been seen primarily in her biological, primordial role, as the mysterious source of life. Women have been viewed as mother, wife, mistress, sex object—their roles in relationship to men. Of course, men also are viewed in their biological roles, but not to the same degree as women; men are neither defined by nor limited to these roles. Cave drawings which show men casting a spear or running after a boar also show women pregnant, their secondary sexual characteristics grossly exaggerated so that they seem all bosom, belly, and butt. Man has been defined by his relationship to the outside world—to nature, to society, indeed, to God—whereas woman has been defined in relationship to man: Milton described Adam and Eve, "He for God only; she for God in him." The word *defined* means "having a limit around," "fenced in." Women have been fenced into a small place in the world.

Since this biological restriction is assumed to have existed forever, the tendency is to believe that it is part of the nature of things, that it is innate; because it has "always" been thus, it must ever be. It is upon this assumption that the dangers of departing from their biological roles have been impressed upon women. Perhaps more than anyone else, Sigmund Freud in our own century reinforced the idea that an unwillingness to accept fully her biological role was the cause of woman's hysteria, neurosis, and psychosis; if women are to be healthy, they should remain "natural."

identifying the stereotypes

It is obvious from this preliminary view that to discuss the images of women in literature intelligently, we must know something about women in history, about the psychological and sociological views which have existed; and we must know something about the process by which literature makes use of these views. Literature both reflects and helps to create reality. It is through their preservation in works of art that we know what the stereotypes and archetypes have been and are; in turn, knowing the images influences our view of reality and even our behavior. The famous lovers Paolo and Francesca in Dante's *Inferno* were reading about those famous lovers Lancelot and Guenevere when they yielded to the passion which led to their damnation; it was largely from reading that Emma in Flaubert's *Madame Bovary* (1856) got the romantic dreams which drove her to dissatisfaction and suicide. How many of us today are subliminally affected by advertising that specifies that we must be young, slender, and beautiful to be lovable? And do we realize that a further reinforcement of this image may be found in so-called "highbrow" literature? The media absorb and adapt literary suggestions today with very little cultural lag; Norman Mailer writes for *Life,* Fitzgerald was published by the *Saturday Evening Post.* The process is even reversed: a professor of classics at Yale writes a movie scenario which he later turns into the best-selling book *Love Story.*

The popularization of literary images has increased their influence so that the distinction between imaginary characters and real people has become blurred in the minds of many readers. The term *stereotype* used in its sociological sense is merely descriptive of a mental image arrived at by making characteristics of some individuals into a pattern which is then assumed to apply to other individuals exhibiting several of the characteristics. Stereotypical thinking is necessary in the socialization process of finding role models. But when stereotypes become so rigid that individual variations are ignored or denigrated, they act as barriers to recognizing the complexity of human beings. For this reason the word *stereotype* is commonly used in literary criticism pejoratively to apply to underdeveloped or "flat" characters or caricatures recognizable in outline.

Yet even characters presented sketchily are often useful for legitimate literary purposes. A flat character may serve as a contrast or foil to a more rounded one; character types used in comedy and satire make readers who recognize them feel superior and hence in a position to laugh. Furthermore, behind even the most fully developed characters lie the sociological stereotypes we have been discussing. Any character that a reader can identify with, in which he sees himself, must possess a recognizable pattern of characteristics into which personal idiosyncrasies can fit. The method by which the best literature communicates is to present specific characters in concrete circumstances; a reader is able to extract from the specifics a generalization, a theme, which he sees as relevant to other specific situations.

Take for example Lady Macbeth in Shakespeare's tragedy. In the character of Lady Macbeth, who plotted the death of Duncan and later went mad, the reader can see on one level the stereotype of a woman who in assuming male aggressiveness loses her natural femininity and ultimately her sanity. Unless the reader recognizes such a stereotype, the story of Lady Macbeth is perhaps entertaining but hardly an occasion for experiencing and transcending fear felt personally. By recognizing in Lady Macbeth one's own ruthless ambitions—or those of one's wife or mother-in-law—one participates in her fate, is drawn into the play. But in recognizing that her fate is fictional the reader is able to transcend his emotional involvement; he does not forget the specifics of Lady Macbeth's character which Shakespeare has vividly presented. Remembering that she is a highly unusual woman—one who is gifted in intellect and drive and who is in a position to profit from her schemes—the reader is prevented from accepting the stereotype as being rigidly applicable to his circumstances and from seeing in every aggressive woman a potential murderess. To identify with Lady Macbeth requires from the reader an imaginative leap, an ability to perceive the general— the stereotype—within the specific. It is when an author presents only the stereotype as if it were specific (like the oversimplified "bitch" Maggie in the comic strip "Maggie and Jiggs") that art disappears and we enter the realm of propaganda. In studying literary stereotypes we should not be content with discovering one level of meaning; in the most individualistic characters we should look for universality of meaning, and in apparently superficial characters we should expect to find complexity.

The Mother   Images of women in literature have always been ambivalent; for every biological role there has been both a negative and a positive view. In the Biblical creation myth, Eve, the mother of us all, is the temptress who brought sin and death into the world. But the Virgin Mary, passively acted upon by the

Holy Ghost, pondering in her heart the experience of her Son, is the Queen of Heaven, the Mother of God and, through Him, of us all. Eve could be tolerated as a necessary evil; Mary was worshipped as a model for all womankind. In Greek mythology, Pandora, sent to earth by the gods to marry and establish the human race, brings with her a magic box or vial; opening it, she releases not only all evil but the greatest gift man can have, hope. Both Eve and Pandora act in defiance of divine law. If they had passively obeyed (experienced the world vicariously, as Mary did), man would have been spared the particular kind of life known as human. In both myths, except for the action of a woman mankind would have been godlike. Because of woman, man is condemned to be mortal; he must die. Yet every human being in his early years sees his mother as the bringer of life, the nurturer, the source of pleasure and comfort. He soon learns that she also takes away pleasure; she says no, and he blames her for denying satisfaction, no matter what her reasons may be. The role of mother is ambiguous. Myths about woman's dual nature are attempts to explain primordial reactions to her double role as the giver of life and death, of pleasure and pain.

The Wife Both in myth and in life the roles of mother and wife overlap; the difficulty for even a husband to separate the roles in his mind is reflected in the common American custom of a man's referring to his wife as "Mother." A wife performs many of the functions of the mother; not only her children but her husband require her attentions as cook and nurse. But when she extends to her husband her motherly role of disciplinarian, scolding, nagging, or withholding her services, her husband reacts as negatively as a child. For him the very qualities desirable in a good mother—firmness, decisiveness, ability to organize time—seem undesirable in a wife. A submissive wife, happy to be supportive and to "stay in her place" is the ideal; a dominating wife is ridiculed or hated.

The Mistress-Seductress Although public acknowledgment of extramarital relationships has in many societies been disapproved of, the mistress has been admired for her power, her ability to seduce; her overwhelming attractiveness exonerates the male for succumbing to her. Frequently the effect of the seductress is disastrous. In the *Iliad,* Helen of Troy's decision to run away with Alexandros (Paris) brought death to thousands of men, the destruction of Troy, and the enslavement of the Trojan women. Though objectively Alexandros' weakness and disregard of the mores might seem to have been equally at fault, it was Helen's face "that launched a thousand ships and burnt the topless towers of Ilium" in Marlowe's *Dr. Faustus* (1588). Similarly, Guenevere, married to King Arthur, causes her lover Lancelot to betray his king and start a civil war. Both Malory (15th century) and Tennyson (19th century) put the blame squarely on Guenevere for seducing the noble Lancelot.

Yet other beautiful women are seen as ennobling to men who loved them: Dante is led through Purgatory by the vision and guidance of Beatrice; Petrarch worships Laura even though he can never possess her. Perhaps it is significant that Beatrice and Laura, both in life apparently happy as the wives of other men, are exalted by the poets more after death than before; inconvenient facts must not interfere with mythical roles. In stories of extramarital love the lack of children in pre-birth-control days among goddess-like women can be ascribed only to literary convenience, the fictitiousness of their roles. Yet real women accept exalted roles as self-images, feeling that to inspire a man outside marriage is a high calling. The power of such a self-image is shown in Ibsen's play *Hedda Gabler* (1890) in which the beautiful Hedda commits suicide not because of marriage to a stodgy professor but because of her failure to inspire a creative writer to his best work.

The Sex-Object and Sexual Politics   In another biological role the woman is the opposite of the all-powerful seductress: the sex object is man's prey. The stereotype of woman as sex object is both broader and narrower than that of the wife or the mistress. A woman may be a sex object before, during, and outside marriage; in this role she is seen as the fulfiller of man's sexual needs, a receptacle for his passions. It is difficult for a woman to be viewed in this single role for a long time. A virgin obviously changes when as a sex object she yields her virginity. If she becomes a wife, she assumes the complex role of nurse, friend, guardian of comfort, mother of children, as well as that of sex object; if she becomes a "fallen" woman, she is callously discarded to become human garbage like the young girl in Stephen Crane's *Maggie, A Girl of the Streets* (1893).

It is impossible to consider women as sex objects without discussing what Kate Millett has called "sexual politics," the system by which men have kept women subordinate. It is their usefulness to men that has determined women's value in society. Virgins have been valued not only because of youth, possible beauty, and freedom from venereal disease but also because they could become wives and mothers, the legitimacy of whose children would not be questioned; through their offspring, property could be lawfully transferred. Virgins have been exalted not only because of myths about their special powers over beasts like the unicorn but because of their value as commodities. As late as the 18th century Dr. Samuel Johnson remarked about chastity: "Upon that all the property in the world depends." The primitive practice of the bride-price, the careful negotiation of dowry, and the vesting of all property rights in the husband are aspects of the economics of marriage; until the late 19th century and in many parts of the world even today, economic and social considerations have been the primary basis of marriage. For both men and women marriage has been a way of obtaining comfort and status as well as sexual service. But this avenue was closed to women who lost their virtue; their disgrace meant living somehow on the fringes of society as servant or governess, seamstress or washerwoman, "kept woman" or prostitute—or it could result in being stoned to death. Sexual politics have kept women (whether married or not) as men's dependents, often literally their chattels, properly to be kept locked into a chastity belt—as rigid as any stereotype can be.

The Old Maid   The roles we have considered so far—those of mother, wife, mistress, and sex object—have received more literary treatment than any others, though women as daughters, sisters, grandmothers, and aunts have appeared frequently in drama, fiction, and poetry. An examination of their images would show just as much ambivalence as in women's major roles (those more explicitly connected with sex). Yet throughout history many women have not been wives or mothers or sex objects; many have remained single. Unlike the other stereotypes, the image of the single woman has not been at all ambivalent; with very few exceptions the old maid—a single woman beyond the marriageable age of, say, 30—has been either pitied or ridiculed in literature. The exception is the nun, admired for giving herself to a supernatural cause as bride of the church. But a single woman who remains in society is seen as queer, frequently thin and emaciated to symbolize withdrawal from life, prim, highly conventional, excessively curious, and quarrelsome. Seldom does she function as a main character; normally she acts in a subordinate role reflecting her marginal position in society. Earlier centuries used to give single women the title of "mistress" or "madame" after they had passed the age of consent, but the now universal "miss" is an ironically apt reflection of the opinion that they have missed out on living; the term "old maid" is always pejorative in our society.

The Educated Woman In addition to these stereotypes of women as defined by their biological roles, there have been other images of women. For example, whether married or single, young or old, a learned woman has usually been suspect and the butt of ridicule in literature. Particularly mocking is the picture Byron gives in *Don Juan* (1819) of Donna Inez, who flaunts her little Latin and less Greek and henpecks her husband; one does not know whether Byron despises her more for her learning or her domination, but he sees them as part of the same pattern. Even now the stereotype of a highly educated woman is of an unattractive female in sturdy oxfords and tailored suit; when Germaine Greer, a professor at Warwick University in England and author of *The Female Eunuch* (1971), appeared in television interviews in this country, reviewers invariably expressed amazement at her attractiveness as a woman. Beginning in puberty, American girls become afraid of success in school, hiding their learning as much as possible or deliberately failing. Even women do not expect high intellectual achievement from other women. Asked to "grade" the performance of scholars, a group of college women rated as inferior articles to which women's names were attached and rated the same articles as superior when men's names were attached to them. Perhaps this tendency accounts for the fact that many successful women downgrade women in general; these women see themselves as successful *and* feminine but share the stereotype when they view other women.

The Lady Another stereotype, dependent more upon social class than biology, is that of the *grande dame* or lady; special rules for her behavior were prescribed by rigid social systems including that of the antebellum South in this country. A gentlewoman truly gentle, such as Melanie in *Gone with the Wind* (1936), has been a part of the romantic exaltation of women; but the view of D. H. Lawrence in *Lady Chatterley's Lover* (1926), that *gentilesse* diverts women from their true role as sexual creatures, has prevailed in modern literature. Lady Chatterley realized that her place in life was not presiding at a tea table but being serviced by her gardener; since the sexual liberation of the 1920's, ladies have removed themselves from their pedestals.

Role-Conflict in Women   Until recently, literature has not focused on the problem for women of the ambiguity of their overlapping roles. Homer only hints at how Helen felt about her husband and her lover; Dante never raises the question of how the real Beatrice might have felt about his worship of her. Yet recent sociological studies have emphasized that role-conflict causes women great anguish; to be simultaneously wife, mother, and mistress to one's own husband, causes stress for women that male role-conflict does not. As Elizabeth Janeway has pointed out, men are not expected to play their multiple roles full-time; it is expected that a man will spend most of his time not as husband, father, and lover, but as a worker. Hence multiplicity of roles is a minor problem for men, while a major one for women. Even in the kitchen the demands of being wife and mother cause strain; pablum for the baby, chopped liver for the toddler, and a steak for the husband demand decisions and triple labor. The shift in role-playing symbolized by changing from an apron into a black chiffon nightgown may cause great stress without involving the rejection of a feminine role to which Freud attributed women's neurosis and hysteria.

Much contemporary literature deals with the stress on women of role-playing. For example, Joan Didion's novel *Play It As It Lays* (1970) shows a woman who has been rejected as a wife; she cannot find another role to play and spends most of her time driving aimlessly around when not in a drugged or drunken sleep. In *The Diary of a Mad Housewife* (1967) Sue Kaufman depicts the reaction of a wife and mother who learns that her husband has been unfaithful; she adds adulteress to her roles in order to cope with his infidelity. In *A Woman of My Age* (1967) Nina Bawden shows a middle-aged wife disoriented by the "empty nest" syndrome; once her children have gone, she tries the role of adulteress to fill her emptiness. When her one night of love results in pregnancy, she happily resumes the role of mother; her husband, happy that she has found a role, accepts the child as his.

It is significant that these recent works which show the difficulties of women's role-playing are written by women; but with very few exceptions the literature of the western world has been written by men. Sappho, Marie de France, Marguerite of Navarre, and Lady Mary Wortley Montagu are among the very few women authors known to us before the 19th century. We must remember in discussing the history of the images of women in literature that they reflect the masculine angle of vision; masculine images have established our literary tradition and have controlled both male and female authors. Even among female authors—who have no distinctively feminine literary tradition—male attitudes persist. Both Sue Kaufman and Nina Bawden see women's dilemma but suggest as a solution only an escape from one biological role to another. And it is reportedly a woman author, Pauline Réage, who has created one of the most explicitly pornographic books of our time, *The Story of O,* in which O delights in finding new ways of becoming completely submissive to men's sexual desires. Even such admittedly great female writers as Emily Brontë and Emily Dickinson have been viewed condescendingly both by their contemporaries and by male critics today because they wrote like women. Brontë's fictional world is seen as limited; "woman's place" is inferior, not to be compensated for by depth of insight. Emily Dickinson's individuality is ascribed as often to her old-maid status as to genius. No wonder women on the whole have attempted to write like men!

images in this anthology

In this collection of readings only a few of the many stereotypes of women can be represented. The widow, the young unmarried girl, the bawd who traffics in women, the lady, the learned woman, and many others will not be treated here. Instead, we shall concentrate upon the primary stereotypes in literature, those associated with a woman's biological role: wife, mother, seductress, and sex object. For these roles, archetypes also exist, so that their literary history is both old and widespread. The old maid, who has denied her biological role, will be included. Finally, examples of liberated women who have transcended their traditional roles will illustrate the beginning of a new stereotype, the free woman. Now we will turn to a fuller examination of the literary treatment of these selected stereotypes.

The Submissive Wife   In patriarchal societies the woman who willingly and happily submits to her husband—and father—is an ideal, the submissive wife. One of the clearest and oldest embodiments of this stereotype is the Patient Griselde in Chaucer's *Canterbury Tales* (1389). The pilgrims who hear the tale told by the celibate Clerk bemoan the fact that no wives like Griselde can be found in their own times; though they recognize her as a fantasy, they hold her up as a model to be imitated. The universal appeal of this fantasy is clear; an ancient folktale known in many countries, it was retold in the 14th century by Boccaccio in *The Decameron,* and put into Latin by Petrarch. Chaucer got the story either from Petrarch or from a French version. In the 16th century both French and English versions appeared, usually with the words "pleasant" and "comedy" in the title: the story is an enjoyable one with a happy ending.

   In Chaucer's version, Griselde is a serf with no property of her own; she sees her marriage to a noble husband, Count Walter, as a great condescension on his part and never questions his right to the absolute obedience he exacts as the condition of marrying her. Her meekness makes her a peacemaker throughout the land, as well as a model of "wyfly hoomlinesse." She passes her husband's acid test of assenting to his proposal to kill their daughter and then their son; she consents, after he has put her aside, to become the servant of his new bride. Her abject obedience is rewarded when her husband tells her that the years of testing have been just that, and she is reunited with him and her children whom he had only pretended to murder.

   In this story the characteristics of the submissive wife are beauty, passivity, acknowledged inferiority to the husband, complete obedience to his commands, and above all, willingness; Griselde does not rebel even when giving up her children. She sees no conflict between her roles as mother and wife; she accepts the legal dictum which prevailed well into the 19th century that a woman has no right either to her own body or its fruit; her children and she herself are equally the property of her lord and master. Like children, women had no choice but to submit to their husbands' will; being childlike is an additional characteristic of the submissive wife. In Chaucer's poem and in society this view has been sanctioned by religious dogma; women have been expected by Islam, Judaism, and Christianity to submit to the will of their husbands. In Chaucer's poem the pilgrims see Griselde's obedience, though impossible to achieve, as an analog to the obedience every Christian owes to God. Chaucer is probably making a little gentle fun of the worldly, bookish Clerk and of the pilgrims for taking seriously the idea that a woman can fulfill this noble ideal; but Chaucer's satire is evidence that the idea was entertained in several strata of 14th-century society.

One explanation for the persistence of the stereotype of the submissive wife is that it is grounded in myth: Griselde represents an archetypal attempt to explain the mystery of love. The 14th-century literary versions reflect the myth of Cupid and Psyche, a folktale extant in many cultures; it no doubt reached the Middle Ages through the Latin version of Apuleius in the 2nd century, but its wide diffusion as an oral tale indicates its mythic force. The Middle Ages were truly mediary in passing on to us the culture familiar to them, only a small part of which has ever been written down. In the Cupid and Psyche myth, Psyche is a beautiful maiden whose name means *breath, life, soul.* Cupid, the God of Love, falls in love with her but can visit her only at night; she is expressly forbidden ever to see him or try to find out his identity. When Psyche disobeys and takes a lamp so that she can look at her lover, a drop of hot oil falling on his shoulder awakens him; he flees and she is condemned to be the slave of Venus, Cupid's mother. Eventually she and Cupid are happily reunited.

The relation of this story to the Griselde stereotype is obvious; a beautiful woman who obeys her lord absolutely will be supremely happy, the mate of a god. Disobedience exposes her to all the miseries of love, symbolized by her enslavement to the Goddess of Love. This myth explains much of the mystery of love: the old adage that love is—or ought to be—blind; the anti-rational nature of love which depends upon *not*-seeing, *not*-knowing the beloved, except in the Biblical sense of the word *know* as applied to women, "to have carnal knowledge of." In the myth the prohibitions apply only to Psyche; Cupid has seen her, knows who she is, knows the penalty for disobeying. The double standard is embodied in the archetype.

The "feminine mystique" of the 1950's acquired much power from its grounding in this myth. If we look at other literary versions, we can see how the myth has been passed on, maintaining its basic power. In Shakespeare's *The Taming of the Shrew,* the happy ending is achieved by the rebellious, shrewish Kate's apparent conversion to the Griselde ideal. The beautiful Kate is wooed and won by the impecunious Petrucchio who needs a wife in order to retrieve his fortunes; Kate's father is happy to give her a large dowry to get her off his hands, no questions asked. Petrucchio succeeds in taming her by forcing her to submit to tests only somewhat less cruel than Griselde's: he torments her on a long cold journey by horseback, starves her, humiliates her in front of servants. Though Shakespeare does not explicitly say so, her sexual submission is the primary means which Petrucchio uses to convert her to the role of willing slave; the shrew in her is "killed with kindness," a saying which illustrates the hostility inherent in "love." At the end of the play, Petrucchio shows her off to her family and friends, and Kate wins the prize as the best wife present when she recommends to all wives that they joyfully accept the dominance of their husbands:

> Thy husband is thy lord, thy life, thy keeper,
> Thy head, thy sovereign; one that cares for thee,
> And for thy maintenance commits his body
> To painful labour both by sea and land,
> To watch the night in storms, the day in cold,
> Whilst thou liest warm at home, secure and safe;
> And craves no other tribute at thy hands
> But love, fair looks, and true obedience;
> Too little payment for so great a debt.
> Such duty as the subject owes the prince,
> Even such a woman oweth to her husband;
> And when she's forward, peevish, sullen, sour,
> And not obedient to his honest will,
> What is she but a foul contending rebel,
> And graceless traitor to her loving lord?

Kate goes on to make clear that woman's subservient position is part of the order not only of the state but also of nature:

> Why are our bodies soft, and weak, and smooth,
> Unapt to toil and trouble in the world,
> But that our soft conditions and our hearts
> Should well agree with our external parts?

To be complete and integrated, she tells other women, "place your hands below your husband's foot."

Shakespeare satirizes the Griselde ideal by placing it in the context of farce; he implies that Kate's meekness is assumed by letting us see how false was the submissiveness of Bianca, Kate's sister, who becomes shrewish after marriage. But the moral remains that docility in a wife leads to happiness for all—husband, wife, father; and that upsetting the domestic order may lead to disrupting social and cosmic order. Woman in her place is the cornerstone of society.

In the 20th century the sexual basis of male dominance in marriage is made more explicit than in Shakespeare. D.H. Lawrence has spelled out the condition for women's happiness—and indeed for men's salvation—as their eager submission to the sexual partner. Through sex, Lawrence wrote, men may acquire the intuition needed to cure "the deep psychic disease of modern men." In *The Rainbow* (1915) the relationships between couples of three generations are strikingly like those of the Psyche myth. Repeatedly Lawrence emphasizes the mystery of love; his characters fall most deeply in love with those about whom they know nothing at all. Tom Brangwen falls in love with a foreign woman whom by chance he has seen walking along the road; the marriage is happy only when the wife gives up attempting to understand or communicate verbally with her husband, a taciturn farmer. Lawrence emphasizes that the couple do not understand each other; they accept each other, probing in their sexual union the meaning of life. If Lawrence did not present all this with high seriousness, one could not help equating it with the relationship between Tarzan the ape man and the English girl he meets and mates with in the forest: "Me Tarzan, you Jane" is as much speech as they need. Ursula in the third generation of the Brangwens recapitulates Tom's experience by falling in love with a foreigner; but because their relationship is more intellectual than passionate Ursula does not marry him. In *Women In Love* (1920) a continuation of *The Rainbow,* Ursula finds true love in marrying a man to whom she can submit completely, happy because of his superiority. All her arduous pursuit of education is shown to be irrelevant to the pursuit of happiness that can be achieved only through sex.

Lawrence's anti-intellectual approach to life is made strongly attractive in his works by the aura of mysticism he gives to love. Men and women are drawn to each other in response to an inexplicable force—by their very difference and otherness for each other; to deny this force is to die. Ursula's sister Gudrun, a sculptor, resists her passion for Gerald Crich because she wants to express herself through art; her resistance, caused by her inability to love, *i.e.,* to yield completely, brings about Gerald's suicide. Like Freud, Lawrence felt that for women artistic creativity conflicted with natural creativity. Like Freud, Lawrence believed that "anatomy is destiny"; woman's role is to save mankind by sexual submission.

While writers often point out that both Freud and Lawrence were reflecting the stereotypes of their times, their image of women, reinforced by the Griselde-Psyche myth, has continued with undiminished attractiveness into the 1960's and 70's. The popularity of the musical *Kiss Me, Kate* (based on Shakespeare's *The Taming of the Shrew*) and the beautiful movie version of Lawrence's *Women in Love* adds new appeal to the age-old stereotype and is evidence of its strength. Such widespread acceptance of the feminine mystique even in the 1970's is understandable when we consider all the devices used to make it attractive. An ancient prescription for literature was that it should "teach by pleasing." Certainly this formula applies to Shakespeare's farcical treatment and the magic of his language, as well as Lawrence's subtle mysticism as a substitute for the religious sanction of previous times—all illustrated with clever music and lyrics, beautiful scenarios, and skillful acting. How can these delights be resisted, when to their psychological influence are added the force of custom and tradition, religious sanction, and economic need?

The economic usefulness of the stereotype is perhaps the main reason for the persistently attractive rendering of the submissive wife in literature. Significantly Griselde, child of a serf, comes to her marriage totally dependent upon Count Walter. Economic dependence is part of the motivation for the otherwise incredible willingness of Griselde to submit. Kate gives as one reason for submissiveness the luxury of women's lives while their men work hard. Yet the notion that wives are economic drones has been shown to be a myth. Elizabeth Janeway has shown that until the Industrial Revolution the work of both men and women, in and out of the home, was necessary to survival. Even upper-class women like Griselde and Kate probably worked hard; life on a medieval or Renaissance manor, as on a Southern plantation, required supervision by women of many workers and activities. The fact that their labor was unpaid and could seldom result in the accumulation of wealth for anyone but males required submissiveness.

As much of the work formerly done at home was removed to factories, the myth that being "just a housewife" was legitimately subordinate acquired renewed force. It is a convenient myth when the economic situation demands that women work in factories, as in World War II; since their work at home has no economic validity, they can drop it when needed and return to it when the need has gone. The feminine mystique of the 1950's was a reaction to the end of the need for women in military production; when the boys came marching home, women were bumped. Highly educated women responded by happily exalting unpaid housework as a woman's role; lower-class women left comparatively well-paid jobs making weapons to become low-paid service workers, in areas where the majority of women workers remain today – maids, laundry workers, nurses' aides, clerical "help." In 1972 women's insistence on their right to equal work and equal pay is blamed for persistently high unemployment rates more often than is the lack of planning for conversion to a peacetime economy. Just as in *The Taming of the Shrew,* it would be convenient if women would accept a secondary role. One does not need to be a Marxist to recognize that women have been economically exploited and to see that literature has facilitated their exploitation by encouraging their willingness. Economic goals have been accomplished at least partly through the persuasiveness of art: the Griselde stereotype has been used as propaganda to blind women to the nature of their oppression. Love is indeed blind.

Incorporated in the Griselde story, in addition to the Psyche legend, is another widespread folktale, the Cinderella story, showing how a lower-class woman may be exalted by marriage. Though the daughter of a serf, Griselde is perfectly comfortable as the chatelaine of a count and knows how to perform her wifely duties. Unlike the heroine of "My Fair Lady," she does not have to be taught an upper-class accent. This fairy tale reflects the reality that in a patriarchal society women, powerless in a system rigidly based on power, belong to no class. As Kipling put it in the late 19th century, "Judy O'Grady and the Colonel's Lady are sisters under the skin." But this sisterhood is not a democracy; it is a caste system which separates women from men in every class. The symbol of their caste is the apron, as a recent survey of illustrations for children's books demonstrates. Of fifty-eight pictures of adult female characters, all but four were wearing aprons. One of the four exceptions was a queen; she was knitting. Lacking either the moats of a medieval castle or the stone walls of towns, men still keep women in their sphere. William Blake, the poet of freedom and revolution in the late 18th century, understood that the strongest agent of oppression is "mind-forged manacles"; stereotyped self-images explain the otherwise incomprehensible willingness of women to be victims.

The Mother: Angel or "Mom"?   Closely related to the submissive wife is the stereotype of the mother. In the 19th century John Stuart Mill insisted that not only children but also women were spineless and meek because of their domination by men. Freud's psychology half a century later emphasized the danger of dominance by the mother. Unless a male child could overcome his innate Oedipus complex, his desire to murder his father and marry his mother, he would be an emotional cripple. For female children Freud considered the difficulty of outgrowing jealousy of the mother to be the cause of women's inferiority to men in moral character and creativity. The difference between Freud's and Mill's views is less important than their similarity in placing great responsibility for child-rearing upon the mother. Traditionally the mother has been presented as the source of all tenderness and love, the only force in a child's life enabling him to resist the competitiveness of the external, masculine world; maternal tender loving care has been seen as necessary to a child's self-love and ability to accept himself. The father's love, conditionally given and dependent upon good behavior and conformity to expectations, has been regarded as the source of insecurity and alienation. But along with the rampant sentimentality of Mother's Day has grown a new stereotype, the "Mom" whom Philip Wylie described in *The Generation of Vipers* (1942).

Wylie wholeheartedly accepted Freud's theory of sex as the dominant instinct and attributed Americans' problems to their insistence on believing in the myth of maternal goodness. Almost hysterically, Wylie painted Mom as destructive of her sons, purposely preventing them from maturing because she wants them to be her willing slaves. As early as 1927, in a play titled *The Silver Cord,* Sidney Howard had shown the crippling effect of being tied to mother's apron strings, as strong as the Biblical silver cord, to be loosed only at the end of the world. More significant are the plays of Eugene O'Neill, the greatest American dramatist. Influenced by Freud, O'Neill adapted Greek myths to New England landscapes to obtain a sense of timelessness and inevitability for his characters. In *Desire Under the Elms* (1924), a woman smothers her child in order to gain her husband's love, much as Medea in the Greek play murdered her children to punish her husband. In *Strange Interlude* (1928), the heroine has an abortion in order to deprive her husband of the satisfaction of a child; later she passes off the child of her lover as her husband's. The "Jewish mother" of contemporary literature is usually presented humorously, but her effect is nonetheless serious. In Philip Roth's *Portnoy's Complaint* (1969), his mother's domination makes Portnoy unable to enjoy heterosexual sex; he must resort to masturbation though desiring intercourse. A "Wasp" mother is shown in Dan Wakefield's *Going all the Way* (1970) as responsible for her son's ineptness not only in sex but in any decision-making situation; and in D.H. Lawrence's *The Virgin and the Gypsy* (1930), a mother not only rules her son but causes her daughter to become a sour old maid, "eating" both children as the female spider eats her mate.

The Dominating Wife   Freud, in labeling a fixation upon the mother and consequent immaturity the "Oedipus complex," enlisted a literary archetype to explain what he thought were observed facts about the human psyche. Maternal dominance he saw as unnatural and leading to neurosis and psychosis. He saw as equally unnatural the wife who departed from the Psyche-Griselde archetype. The dominating wife, viewed with a certain amused tolerance as a shrew in earlier centuries, has in the 20th century been hated as the bitch who because of her own emotional problems castrates her husband by making him feel inadequate. But the dominating wife also has archetypes. Xantippe, the nagging wife of Socrates, is proverbial. In the Middle Ages, Mrs. Noah became a stock feature of comedy as she ordered her husband around, ranting and raving at his slightest attempts to disobey. A more subtle medieval version is Chaucer's Wife of Bath in *The Canterbury Tales*. The Wife, both in her autobiography (the Prologue to her Tale) and in her Tale, reveals herself as a woman who exults in her ability to rule men. So realistic has Chaucer made the Wife that scholars consider her drawn from life, rather than evoked from literary sources. The verisimilitude of her first-person narrative is an indication that Chaucer was presenting her as realistic, unlike the idealized Griselde presented through the erudite Clerk as a literary figment. The Wife contrasts with Griselde in every respect; almost every trait she exhibits was held up by medieval antifeminists (such as St. Jerome) as a fault all too prevalent among women of the time. Not only does the Wife of Bath dominate all five of her husbands; she is physically ugly, sexually insatiable, materialistic, selfish, assertive, and deceitful. She marries three times for money, keeping her elderly husbands in line (making them "swink") by doling out or oversupplying sexual privileges and trapping them with her lying tongue. Having inherited their estates, she can afford to indulge her tastes by marrying a lusty "revelour" whom she keeps reluctantly faithful by making him jealous; she becomes his "purgatorie," because, unlike Griselde, she controls the purse strings. Before the fourth husband dies, she has her eye on a young clerk. When she is widowed and marries him, it seems at first that she has reversed her role, for she cannot resist his sexual advances even after he has beaten her. But she manages to dominate him too by preying on his sympathy: pretending to be dying, she swears she loves him, although it is his blow which has "killed" her—and in remorse he gives her the "governaunce."

All the Wife's traits are undesirable in a time when the sole purpose of marriage was thought to be procreation. Chaucer seems to be stacking the deck against her even more when he mentions that she is skilled in her craft of weaving while not emphasizing this as a "virtue." Chaucer also allows her to reveal her weaknesses not only as a wife but as a woman. She is satirized as the "learned lady" when she tries to rationalize her attitudes and behavior by reference to learned sources, misquoting them to support her illogical arguments. Thus when she tells her Tale, her reliability as a narrator is suspect, if not to the Canterbury pilgrims who are the fictional audience, certainly to the sophisticated courtly audience to whom Chaucer's work was read aloud or to the modern reader equipped with voluminous footnotes. Even though her Tale of the Loathly Lady who tricks her husband into willing submission is a folktale with archetypal overtones as ancient as the Griselde story, it strikes us less as authoritative than as expressive of her character. One of the pilgrims, the Friar, reacts to it as a boring example of preaching better left to the clergy, and offers to make up for her "scole-matere" by telling a racy story. Even so, Chaucer has made the Wife more than a stereotype. Though her self-revelation has dramatic irony, in that it reveals as undesirable the traits which she is proud of, the Wife is not repulsive; her frank enjoyment of life, her pleasure in her triumphs, her broad experience make her attractive as a human being. Simone de Beauvoir points out that modern Western man prefers a good battle before the final submission; Chaucer was perhaps anticipating the modern reality in portraying the Wife as a lively partner, in contrast to the meek Griselde.

The Loathly Lady of the Wife's story is shown to be very definitely worth submitting to. An ugly old hag, she offers to save the life of a desperate knight if he will consent to give her the "Soverainte" in their relationship. He reluctantly agrees because he despairs of saving himself by answering correctly the question "What do women value most?"—a question similar to Freud's baffled "What do women want?" after many years of psychoanalyzing them. After she has saved him and he has married her, he longs to escape the bargain. She then gives him a further choice: he can have her ugly, old, and faithful, or young, beautiful, and unfaithful. When he wisely chooses the former, she rewards him by becoming young and beautiful while remaining faithful—as striking a fairy-tale ending as the happy conclusion of the Griselde story. Both the Wife's Prologue and her Tale show her belief that happiness is possible only if the wife dominates. But by his literary treatment Chaucer shows that the opposite belief is the one which the pilgrims—and most people—accept.

Shakespeare understood very well the popular antipathy towards dominating women: *The Taming of the Shrew* focuses on the absurdity of Kate's assertiveness. Bianca, Kate's meek younger sister, is the ideal emphasized by contrast with the cantankerous Kate. The shrew who can be tamed can be laughed at, but dominating women who do not change their ways are shown by Shakespeare to cause tragedy. Shakespeare's late tragedies are deeply rooted in myth, and much of the strength of his characterization stems from the universality gained from this rooting.

In *Macbeth,* for example, Shakespeare evokes the unnaturalness of the dominating wife. Realizing that Macbeth is hesitant about taking the necessary steps to achieve his ambition to become king, Lady Macbeth resolves that she will "chastise [him] with the valour of . . . [her] tongue"; she begs supernatural spirits "to unsex me here/ And fill me from the crown to the toe top-full/ Of direst cruelty . . . ; come to my woman's breasts/ And take my milk for gall." She pleads with her husband to "put/ This night's great business into my dispatch"; when he demurs at her proposal to murder Duncan, she goads him with the accusation of being less than a man until he decides to do her bidding. He is so unnerved after the deed that she must murder the servants who are to be the scapegoats. Macbeth's weakness in following his wife's orders is paralleled in the rest of the play by his inability to rule himself and his kingdom, but his weakness does not stem from supernatural sources. His fault is in being human, "too full of the milk of human kindness." The kingdom is destroyed, and Macbeth dies because of his human errors. Lady Macbeth's madness is an appropriate price for one who has subverted the natural order; Macbeth is allowed to die heroically, fighting against overwhelming odds, and is redeemed from his error.

Even as villains, women are not considered equal to men. In another tragedy, *Antony and Cleopatra,* Shakespeare places the blame for Antony's fall from greatness largely upon Cleopatra's deliberate seduction of him. Shakespeare allows Cleopatra the nobility of death by suicide from a painless asp's sting, but Octavius Caesar sees it as a "noble weakness," the result of her search for "easy ways to die." Antony takes the harder way to die of falling on his sword, worthy of a Roman stoic. Caesar interprets his death as world-shaking in its implications and honors Antony as a worthy opponent. Woman's failure to be subordinate and to fill her "natural place" is the nail whose lack causes kingdoms to fall. In all three of the plays discussed here, Shakespeare reflects the Elizabethan world view that disorder in the microcosm of man—or specifically here, woman—is paralleled by disaster in the macrocosm of the world.

Without the willfulness of Kate, the trickiness of Lady Macbeth, or the seductive wiles of Cleopatra, a wife simply by her very existence may dominate her husband and subvert his manliness. In a 12th-century French romance by Chrétien de Troyes, *Erèc and Enide,* Erèc is so enamored of his bride that he becomes uxorious: "But Erèc loved her with such a tender love that he cared no more for arms, nor did he go to tournaments, nor have any desire to joust; but he spent his time in cherishing his wife." All his friends regret this state of affairs, and, ironically, Enide herself weeps so over his loss of knightly reputation that she inadvertently awakens him and tells him what his friends are saying. Unable to stand this insult to his honor, he undertakes a series of adventures to restore his princely reputation. Only when his wife spurs him on to be his true self, completely submerging herself as an individual, wife, and lover by becoming his page, can Erèc achieve true manhood.

Similarly, in Milton's *Paradise Lost* (1667), Adam is worried because Eve's beauty interferes with his rational knowledge that she is his inferior; he complains to the Angel Raphael,

> . . . yet when I approach
> Her loveliness, so absolute she seems
> And in herself complete, so well to know
> Her own, that what she wills to do or say
> Seems wisest, virtuosest, discreetest, best;
> All higher knowledge in her presence falls
> Degraded, wisdom in discourse with her
> Loses discount'nanced, and like folly shows.

Raphael advises him not to let Eve's beauty delude him, nor sensual delight:

> . . . if the sense of touch whereby mankind
> Is propagated seem such dear delight
> Beyond all other, think the same vouchsafed
> To cattle . . .

He should be no more willing to be subdued by Eve than he would be by beasts.

He must not yield to passion which might delude him, but only to love which "hath his seat in reason, and is judicious" and knows that she was made for him to control.

In the 20th century, the attitude toward female dominance as a threat to virility and the cause of men's alienation and self-hatred has taken on a new virulence—probably because the sexual revolution allows overt exposure of the techniques of dominance which the Wife of Bath used to keep her elderly husbands in line.

Martha in Edward Albee's *Who's Afraid of Virginia Woolf?* (1962) is shown as deliberately undermining her husband George's confidence as a man and scholar. She flaunts her power over him by openly sleeping with a younger man of whose sexual and intellectual prowess she is also contemptuous. Albee gives Martha a sympathetic motive for her bitchiness—her inability to have a child. This motive emphasizes that her destructive behavior is unnatural and would never have occurred had she been able to fill her "inner space" (the remedy advocated by the contemporary psychologist Erik Erikson for feminine psychological ills). That Martha's behavior is as destructive to herself as to her husband is evidence of her irrationality, her "sickness." Her pathetic "game" of creating an imaginary child is further proof that she is neurotic. In constantly singing "Who's afraid of Virginia Woolf?" to the tune of "Who's afraid of the big bad wolf?" (recalling the falsely brave three little pigs), she gives us another indication of her abnormal emotional condition. *She* is afraid of Virginia Woolf— that is, of committing suicide, as did the famous author, or perhaps of facing reality.

In spite of the grimness of the play, Albee allows a glimmer of hope for both George and Martha to remain at the end: it seems that George's apparently cruel destruction of Martha's illusion of having a son may be the therapeutic stroke that will return both of them to rationality. The fact that they had created the mythical son together may symbolize the hope that basically they love each other. Now that George has taken the initiative—the "normal" situation, with Martha accepting his lead in interpreting reality—happiness may ensue. Just as in the Renaissance, only a submissive wife is regarded as rational and whole.

Albee's play shares with many other 20th-century works the identification of the castrating bitch with the forces of society. Martha's goal for George is success as defined in the academic world in which her father has been a dominant person (a college president). Martha views George's sexual failures as resulting from his lack of success in his work. The 20th-century polarization of women's place as the home and men's as the world has put upon men the entire burden of economic support; in rebelling against this kind of slavery, men must rebel against the women for whose sake it has occurred. The comic strip character Andy Capp whose wife supports him but tries to deprive him of all his masculine prerogatives of bars and blondes, the proverbial Caspar Milquetoast, James Thurber's famous Walter Mitty—all ineffectually try to assert themselves against their wives, each of whom is presented as an ugly battleaxe, the ball-and-chain that prevents men's dreams from coming true. In Strindberg's *The Father* (1888), the wife conspires to get her husband committed to an asylum so that she can control their daughter. The witty arguments and "smiling" satire of Chaucer's "Marriage Group," to which the Clerk's and the Wife of Bath's tales belong, have in the 20th century been exchanged for the battle of the sexes, a war with no holds barred.

The Sex Object   As Diana Trilling has shown, many 20th-century male authors, involved mostly in a quest for self-identity, have justified men's treatment of women as sex objects to be used instead of loved on the grounds that modern women are all bitches and castrators who interfere with or deny men's search for identity. Women are seen as reinforcing society's pressures for conformity to its cultural patterns and hence as denigrating individuality. Any "red-blooded American male" must resist women's encroachment on his inalienable right to be himself; he feels justified in protecting himself by having only temporary liaisons with women and by having sex without love.

The main characteristic of the sex object as a stereotype is the passivity she is supposed to share with all women; the myth of women's sexual apathy, documented by Germaine Greer in *The Female Eunuch,* has afforded the rationale for prostitution, for group sex, and for casual sexual encounters. Once again, "anatomy is destiny." Because women are *capable* of sexual intercourse without being aroused, using them against their will is possible and therefore justifiable: like Mt. Everest, women are climbed simply because they are there. By the curious workings of masculine logic, a woman's unlimited capacity for sexual performance—documented by Kinsey and Masters and Johnson—is seen not as admirable but as frightening. Male fantasy adds to the stereotype the characteristic of willingness: the famous heroines of pornography, such as Fanny Hill and the mysterious O are so conditioned to pleasing that they share in or even exult in their own exploitation and thus invite brutality. Women are seen as the legitimate prey of men, who like primitive hunters achieve status by the number of bodies they collect. In adolescent bragging and in the posturing of such heroes as Mailer's Steven Rojacks, women function as statistics, not as human beings.

Not all writers have been callous about the plight of the prostitute. The view that women might as well relax and enjoy rape when it is inevitable has been paralleled by the view that they are to be pitied as victims of society. William Blake's picture of London shows the prostitute as an extreme example of man's inhumanity:

> I wander through each chartered street,
> Near where the chartered Thames does flow,
> And mark in every face I meet
> Marks of weakness, marks of woe.
>
> In every cry of every Man,
> In every Infant's cry of fear,
> In every voice, in every ban,
> The mind-forged manacles I hear.

How the Chimney-sweeper's cry
Every black'ning Church appalls;
And the hapless Soldier's sigh
Runs in blood down Palace walls.

But most through midnight streets I hear
How the youthful Harlot's curse
Blasts the new-born Infant's tear,
And blights with plagues the Marriage hearse.

Blake points to prostitution as the support, even the price, of marriage. In "An Attack of Nerves," Chekhov shows a sensitive student's horror on a round of brothels with his friends; but a doctor convinces him that his repulsion is abnormal, that prostitution is a logical necessity of civilized life. That it bolsters not only the sanctity of the home but also the economic system is shown in Maxim Gorky's "A Pair of Blue Eyes," in which a mother applies for the yellow license of a prostitute in order to send her children to the proper schools.

One of the first glimpses afforded us of a prostitute's life as it actually is appeared in an anthology called *Women in Sexist Society* (1971). In "Quartet," by Kate Millett, four women—two prostitutes, two not—discuss prostitution and their experience with it. Millett records extensive interviews with a white prostitute who later earned a Ph.D., a black prostitute still in the business, a woman lawyer who has worked extensively with prostitutes in New York City, and finally adds her own responses. These real experiences give us a way of measuring the stereotypical prostitute of fiction. Though victims of society, in the sense that all of us are at least partially determined by forces over which we have no control, the two prostitutes were certainly not "innocent"; both went into prostitution knowingly, because it afforded them the highest profit for the least effort. One needed to support a drug habit; the other not only preferred her work to menial low-paid jobs but, after getting a Ph.D. in psychology, realized that one of her motives had been hatred of men. Far from being "the misled innocent with a heart of gold," she recognized her motivation as contempt for men who had to pay for what they should have found through love. The lawyer's experience supports the image of prostitutes as passive, but it adds insight as to the cause. Prostitutes accept the contempt of policemen and judges and internalize it as a negative self-image which makes a desire to change most unlikely. Their apparent reluctance to change stems from the numbness of self-hatred.

Kate Millett emphasizes the ways in which amateur sex objects prostitute themselves for the price of a dinner or for professional advantage; women sharing the views of their oppressors see themselves as commodities. A fictional version of such a self-image appears in Doris Lessing's short story, "Notes for a Case History," in which the good-looking Maureen uses all her sexual charms in order to marry into a higher class than she was born into. Calculating every move, she permits increasing intimacy in order to entrap an eligible male, holding out for marriage as the price of intercourse. She has a bleak moment of insight into what this technique really costs her when, appearing without make-up and in an old dress, she frightens her fiancé away; not only has she given up the man she loved for him, but she has renounced her own identity and condemned herself to a life of role-playing in which she can never relax. This story illustrates the profound truth that women who accept society's definition of them have no self-definition as individuals; they have nothing to withstand the strength of the stereotype's molding. Calculating females like Maureen have been portrayed often in literature, ever since Samuel Richardson's *Pamela* in the 18th century spelled out how to sell "virtue" for marriage. Pamela's techniques were necessary for her survival; a woman with no choice but marriage must use every device to achieve it. Richardson's heroine in *Clarissa* is harassed by her family to marry a repulsive rich man in order to augment her brother's fortune. The Marquis de Sade tells of women forced to become nuns so that their families can keep their dowries. To trap a rich husband might be preferable to being bartered by father or husband.

The Seductress–Goddess   Few unmarried girls, especially in America today, are as calculating as Maureen and Pamela about themselves as sex objects; instead they see themselves as adored for their beauty and worth, protected and looked up to by their suitors. This romantic self-image of the seductress-goddess has prevailed since the 12th century, as Denis de Rougemont has shown in *Love in the Western World*. The fantasy of the young girl is that she will be the object of a "grand passion," a supreme and irresistible love like that which motivated Tristan and Lancelot. The myth of the irresistible power of women over men usually has involved royal or supernatural force, or both. Today, using the right mouthwash or haircolor may be the requisite magic.

Tristan and Isolde by mistake drink a magic potion which compels them to love. They are excused from guilt in betraying King Mark because no one can be expected to resist magic. The evil Morgan La Fay, half sister of the king in Arthurian romances, is a shape-changer; in T. H. White's modern version of the legend, *The Once and Future King,* Morgan is shown as a witch brewing magic drinks. Guenevere wins Lancelot's unswerving devotion merely by being beautiful. In romance, beauty is itself bewitching, and the responsibility for its effects lies with the woman. According to the code of courtly love, a woman should respond with pity to the suit of any man who falls in love with her; she owes him compassion because she has "entrapped" him—regardless of her own feelings. The passion of Guenevere and Lancelot is mutual, but Lancelot never feels that he is the Queen's equal. At her command he fights badly, sacrificing even his precious honor for her whims. In the famous "night of love" scene recorded in Chrétien de Troyes' version of the story, when Lancelot approaches the Queen's bed he kneels before her, "holding her more dear than the relic of any saint"; ready to leave, he "suffered a real martyr's agony," and when he actually departs, "he bows and acts precisely as if he were before a shrine." Andrew Marvell in "To his Coy Mistress" (1681) admits that his beloved deserves such worship as Lancelot's, saying "Lady, you deserve this state"; but because in the real world necessity forbids endless courtship, he urges her to be willing to forego it, to stop being coy.

Most medieval grand passions were adulterous, but today popular romances and advertising depict perpetual courtship as part of marriage. A husband and wife are to remain lovers, the prime responsibility for the necessary attractiveness being the woman's. He may acquire a pot belly and still be desirable, while she must retain her adolescent dimensions. The cult of youth and beauty in our society is a direct descendant of the stereotype of the seductress. Like the Griselde story, the modern love story emphasizes the classlessness of women; grand passions once reserved for queens and "the fairest of them all" are now supposed to be the right of every woman. Erich Segal's *Love Story* (1970) portrays this stereotype in the heroine, Jenny, who inspires her husband to be the best law student—almost. Even on her deathbed Jenny is able to exert her will, reconciling her husband and his father. *Love Story* is a democratized version of high romance: Jenny is from a lower class than Oliver. The story keeps one of the major aspects of its original formula: the price of grand passion is death, though only for the woman. Significantly, the modern version of the seductress has earmarks of the stereotype of the submissive wife: Jenny has sacrificed her musical scholarship to Paris with the same grace as, in dying, she concentrates on sparing Oliver's feelings. The domestication of the seductress makes her as harmless as a wolf without fangs.

The strength of the romantic ideal is not limited to popular literature; it underlies such an artistically perfect story as Katharine Anne Porter's "The Jilting of Granny Weatherall," justly admired because of the skill with which the author focuses the angle of narration in a character who dies. Granny's recollection of a long life as wife and partner of her husband, mother, and matriarch, is colored by her memory of the pain and humiliation of having been jilted by her first fiancé. The persistence of this memory shows her dominant self-image to be that of the all-powerful seductress; no amount of success in her other roles can compensate for the shattering of this image.

The seductress stereotype has persisted not only as every stenographer's self-image but as the sex goddess, the pinup of lonely males. The movie queen, Miss America, and Miss Universe have the supreme beauty—expressed in precise measurements of secondary sexual characteristics—that justifies male worship. If they also have a little talent and intelligence, that is an added bonus, but the essentials are girth of bosom and butt, length of legs. Though on a pedestal, these goddesses are sex objects in the dreams of their devotees; their true debasement is attested to by their commercial exploitation or by being referred to as a "38D," as in the movie *Carnal Knowledge*. Even less exalted women, such as models or any young well-endowed female, are used to sell products from cars to cigars. The psychic cost of being both exalted and debased as a sex goddess has been movingly portrayed in the play *After the Fall* (1964), by Arthur Miller. Miller was the husband of Marilyn Monroe, the epitome of the stereotype who found playing the role so unsatisfying that she committed suicide.

The Old Maid   Unlike the willing wife or sex object, the old maid is rarely seen as choosing her role; an old maid must have been jilted or had her lover die or somehow been deprived of an opportunity to marry. No story illustrates this view more forcibly than William Faulkner's "A Rose for Emily." Emily Grierson is prevented from marrying because her tyrannical father requires her services, and because in the rigid Southern class system of her environment, no suitor is considered good enough for her. One suitor, a traveling salesman who arrives on the scene after Emily's father's death, is her last hope. The shocking denouement of the story shows Emily's desperate need to keep him: at her death, the towns-people find his bones carefully preserved in the double bed which might have been the marriage bed. Emily murdered her suitor and has kept his body for thirty years. We do not learn whether he had tried to escape because of her unattractiveness or whether she could not bring herself to marry him because it would make her "déclassée." Emily has most of the characteristics of the old maid stereotype. She is physically unattractive ("What would have been merely plumpness in another was obesity in her"), pitiful, irrational, queer, finally crazy. Almost all old maids in fiction share these characteristics, as Dorothy Deegan has shown in *The Single Woman in American Literature*. The images in Flaubert's novella "The Simple Heart," in De Maupassant's "Miss Harriet," in D. H. Lawrence's *The Virgin and the Gypsy,* indicate that the stereotype knows no national boundaries. Strangely, it does have a limitation in time: before the 18th century, literature seldom showed a single woman at all. Marginal to the continuation of the species, she existed as if invisible.

Deegan points out the curious lack of realism involved in the literary stereo-type of the old maid. Many single women have led happy lives as schoolteachers, missionaries, nurses, doctors, lawyers, and businesswomen. Quite a few have been listed in *Who's Who*. However, one would never know this from reading our literature. Yet such women as Florence Nightingale, Clara Barton, the beautiful Hamilton sisters (Alice the first woman on the Harvard medical faculty, Edith the famous analyst of Greek culture) found fulfillment in the single life. The fact that the stereotype of the frustrated old maid continues in the 1970's is the best indication that literature is not necessarily an accurate reflection of life.

A New Image: The Liberated Woman   Elizabeth Janeway points out that because myths represent the hopes and dreams of mankind, they must claim to be universally true. This claim makes them persist long after actual experience has begun to change, but a myth cannot indefinitely withstand too many excep-tions. As soon as its universality is thoroughly challenged, its emotional appeal is diminished. New myths begin to evolve and to create new role-models. The ratio of divorce to marriage today—1 out of 3—is an indication of the death of the romantic stereotype of marriage as "made in heaven," strong enough to last a lifetime. The old pattern for divorcées was an immediate attempt to remarry; failure meant the same kind of banishment to the fringes of society to which the old maid was condemned. Today many divorcées cherish their liberty. Like Nora, in Ibsen's *A Doll's House,* they want to be independent in order to find themselves. Among those who stay married, many do not fulfill the old role of the double standard; it is reported that perhaps a million couples in the United States today are "swingers," arranging swaps of marital partners with other couples or practicing group sex. The picture of "happily ever after" among those who are monogamous is dimmed by the increase in schizophrenia and suicide among women who find role-conflict intolerable. When the old stereotypes are recognized as destructive, the creative force of society helps to develop viable new ones.

Yet the emotional force of the old stereotypes remains strong and they continue to influence behavior. It was because of the seductive power of poetry that Plato recommended its abolition from his ideal Republic. A similar fear is behind the recurrent attempts to censor literature which paints the new images of women so attractively. This fear also explains the intense hostility toward the Women's Liberation Movement which is creating new stereotypes.

One of the main emphases of the Women's Movement is on "consciousness-raising," which takes place in leaderless groups where women share their experiences openly and learn that their problems are not unique. As they realize that they are not alone in finding the old roles intolerable, women gain the strength to question not their own sanity but the validity of the stereotypes. Literature by reflecting the new stereotypes contributes to consciousness-raising and helps women to overcome the sense of isolation, which has been one of the main instruments of their oppression in patriarchal society. The analogy between women and other oppressed groups is valid in that they live with and serve their oppressors; divided, they can be easily ruled. The analogy breaks down because women in general have loved their oppressors. Liberation for women begins with an understanding of the oppressiveness of role-playing based on stereotypes. Women must separate in their minds the stereotypical image a beloved person may have of them from the person himself. Women's Liberation hopes that in becoming full human beings, women will liberate not only themselves but men.

Perfect freedom is a goal that no human being has achieved. What women want (to answer Freud) is the same degree of freedom of choice that men have— no more, no less. Significantly, one of the best literary examples of freedom of choice for women, Willa Cather's *My Ántonia* (1918), is a story of pioneers who seek freedom without any illusions that it is easily found. Just like men on the American frontier, the "hired girls" in a Nebraska agricultural town have the world before them. One, the heroine Ántonia, after being seduced and abandoned, marries happily and has eleven children by a man who loves her. It is Ántonia who really runs their large and thriving farm as well as the children. Ántonia, who as a girl had hitched herself to a plow, has weathered disillusionment and disgrace; she has chosen her life, and like a man, she has paid the penalty for her mistakes. Two of the other "hired girls" become successful businesswomen. Both choose not to marry, one because she remembers what constant childbearing and poverty did to her mother. She prefers freedom so that she can give to her parents and siblings.

It is significant that Willa Cather chose a male narrator to tell these women's stories. As a boy who shared many of their experiences and later as a Harvard-educated lawyer, he has the authority to make their stories credible. Daniel Boone, Davy Crockett, and Paul Bunyan became the myths of the American frontier; the women who shared the rigors of building a continent have not become myths, and Cather must present their story as realistic. Only as more and more women pioneers' lives are written about will a new stereotype emerge, someday to replace that of women who sought husbands rather than a pot of gold in the West.

The search for alternative life styles among the young—such as the establishment of both heterosexual and monosexual communes—indicates that an old myth may be returning to prominence, the ancient search for the perfect cooperative society or Utopia. The effort to establish day-care centers as a means for childhood socialization, rather than as custodial depositories serving economic purposes, is another aspect of the search of women for freedom from their traditional roles. Only women can give birth, but no evidence exists that only they can rear children. Another life style characteristic of Americans and some preindustrial societies—the sharing of childcare and housework—has been curiously overlooked in literature. Yet highly virile men put on aprons to cook outdoors and even to wash dishes. In *The Prisoner of Sex* (1971), Norman Mailer rephrases Freud's question "What do women want?" into "Who will wash the dishes?" His answer is that the woman should, when a man of genius is around. Women's answer is that any real man will do the dishes, half the time.

In spite of the common stereotype of women in their "place" (the home), the fact is that 40 percent of American women are in the labor market. To one who has been working in the often boring and dehumanizing world of business and industry, women's equating liberation with the right to work seems like further evidence of their mental softness; what person in his right mind wants to face the fatigue and boredom of commuting, long hours, tyrannical bosses and ever-increasing demands for productivity? Yet the fact is that even the most boring job represents freedom for women; like the men of our age, women have internalized economic values and they, too, gain self-respect from earning their own money. Not every medical technician is looking for a doctor to marry; today she may be working toward becoming a surgeon. Both work and the education which will prepare them for better jobs are major goals of Women's Liberation. A play by J.E. Franklin, *Black Girl*, which played on Broadway in 1971, shows the poignant struggle of a Texas teenager who escapes her environment to go North to college. The audience knows the kind of ghetto she may become lost in, but her very expectation of freedom may enable her to find a larger measure of it than she would have otherwise. All Americans are having to face the reality that the frontier is gone, that education is not the "open sesame" which until very recently represented our best hopes. Women want to share in the search for new avenues that will offer hope and a better life for all.

Women's achievement of sexual freedom has aroused the greatest hostility toward the Women's Movement. The tendency of myth toward universalizing has made the most prominent image of the liberated woman that of the Lesbian; fear of any change has made the most extreme danger into a horrifying bogyman. Although recent studies have shown that only 3 percent of women are practicing Lesbians and not more than 10 percent exhibit a tendency toward homosexuality, any aggressive woman is viewed not only as bitchy but as a "butch," the masculine partner in a Lesbian union. Yet the facts of female sexuality are that neither partner need be "masculine"; since women experience orgasm much more from sensual stimulation and clitoral excitation than from vaginal penetration, life-long Lesbian unions need no masculine overtones. These unions also are more likely to be permanent and happy than male homosexual relations.

Yet the modern literary image of Lesbians is of cold, quarrelsome, catty, unattractive women rejected by men. D. H. Lawrence's *The Fox* (1923) fully illustrates the stereotype in two ineffectual women past their prime who have chosen each other because they have no alternative. As soon as one of them becomes desired by a man, their union is over and the man kills his unworthy and dangerous rival. Radclyffe Hall's *The Well of Loneliness* (1944) shows Lesbian desires from the female view. Like all human attempts to find love, Lesbianism is an attempt to find and transcend the self, to overcome the dehumanizing sense of isolation.

The new stereotype of the "sensuous woman" is, like the old images, viewed ambiguously: men both want and fear women's sexual desires, now openly acknowledged. A much more realistic fear than that all women will become Lesbians is that sexually free women will simply reverse old masculine-feminine roles by becoming the dominant partners, casting off the sexually maladroit or boring as "used" sex objects. In *The Golden Notebook* (1962) Doris Lessing has shown the difficulties faced by women who want to be mothers but not wives. Both heroines in the story bring up their children alone, functioning as house-wife, mother, and wage-earner as well as facing isolation because they refuse to fill accepted social roles. Each has the consolation of the other, a close friend who makes the isolation bearable. The friendship endures, whereas the sexual relationships do not. This novel reflects the agonies that accompany times of great social change: in seeking their own freedom women may well "use" men as ruthlessly as they themselves have been used. But Lessing's book makes it clear that it is the men's resistance to new ideas that causes the women to reject them. If men cannot envision women as their equals, women will be driven to the companionship of other women. The fear that "sisterhood is powerful" is realistic; the best way to encourage monosexual relationships is to keep women the prisoners of heterosexual sex. The old dream of love as mutually liberating, as a partnership conducive to the greatest happiness human beings can know, can become viable again only when women as well as men are free. A great work of the Middle Ages, Wolfram von Eschenbach's *Parzival*—revived in Wagner's opera of love transcending mortality—offers us a model. Parzival is shown not as the conquering hero, like Tristan and Lancelot, but as a simpleton who interprets all instructions too literally. He learns from his wife the value of loyalty and from two other women, the wisdom of following the demands of compassion. By asking the right question about the cause of suffering, he achieves knightly greatness by liberating the Fisher King of the Grail and finds human happiness by being reunited with his wife. This image, which has coexisted with those of the submissive wife, the bitch, and the beautiful woman as evil, has all the appeal of myth: Eve was given to Adam as a helpmeet, Pandora was envisioned by Prometheus as worthy of the same gift of life as man.

The liberated woman is aware of the choices open to her. This awareness frees her from the compulsiveness of traditional role-playing and at the same time awakens her to the complexity of living and loving. To be fully human is to face the hardness of life with strength. Intellectual recognition of the old confining images is not enough; one must react emotionally toward them, because that is their mode of operation. To respond with anger to restricting stereotypes and with eagerness and hope toward liberating ones will make dream approach reality.

I. the submissive wife and the feminine mystique

Like Griselde of the *Canterbury Tales,* the submissive wife ideally is willing to be subordinate to her husband. She chooses her role and is often unaware that she has given up her freedom to be herself. In Sally Benson's "Little Woman," Penny Loomis emphasizes her smallness and childishness by her language and her choice of clothes. She refuses to maintain friendships or leave her home more often than necessary, delighting in her captivity. It is this willingness of a woman to lose her own identity which has been labeled the "feminine mystique" and which constitutes the primary attribute of the submissive wife stereotype. In Chekhov's "The Darling," Olenka all her life wishes to be dominated by someone—first her father, then her two husbands, and finally the schoolboy whom out of loneliness she adopts. She feels hardly alive in interludes when she is free and reassumes a supportive role as quickly as possible. The extent to which Olenka carries her subordination is shown by Chekhov to be ridiculous: she parrots her second husband's opinions which are exactly opposite those of the first husband (whom she also parroted), and later she repeats as words of wisdom the schoolboy's report on his daily activities. Just as absurd are the efforts of Alice Waythorn, in Edith Wharton's "The Other Two," to please each of three successive husbands. She gets confused about how they like their coffee and muffs her role as the adoring doll.

Yet what is important in these three stories is the reaction of the other characters and of the reader to the attempts of these three women to approach the Griselde ideal. Penny's husband soon wearies of the littleness he had once found so attractive and longs for a wife who is a full human being. All of Olenka's neighbors think her a "darling" when she so meekly and fervently echoes each husband; yet the reader sees her as pitiful, giving herself away so completely that she has no resources to face the inevitable abandonment of the schoolboy. Chekhov asks us to see the absurdity of a society which accepts the sacrifice of a person's identity as "darling" and which values a woman who is less than fully human, a mere puppet. Edith Wharton may have intended her story to illustrate that divorce leads to the futile repetition of patterns, but the story also shows the diminishment of life for a woman who sees her role as always subordinate. Alice's final husband senses the hypocrisy of her devotion to him but refuses to face a reality that might disrupt his comfort; he prefers Alice as a role-fulfiller to her identity as a person.

In Dorothy Parker's "Big Blonde" and Sherwood Anderson's "Death in the Woods," the wives are less willingly submissive. Hazel, the big blonde, is happy to marry because she is tired of playing the role of the good sport, oblivious to her own needs in order to be popular with men; she learns to her sorrow that marriage involves a continuation of that role. In spite of her efforts to be herself, neither her husband nor any of the succession of lovers she takes after he abandons her is willing to accept her naturally melancholy self; she must either be the gay drinking partner they want or remain alone. Mrs. Grimes, in "Death in the Woods," marries the brutal Jake because he represents an escape from the farmer who tries to rape her; becoming Jake's servant and the feeder of all the farm animals is a role she must assume because she has no alternative. Anderson's narrator finds Mrs. Grimes' dead body beautiful, lying naked in the snow; but the reader realizes that her lonely life and death were not beautiful to her: she has been brutally treated and dehumanized, and it is sheer romanticism for the male narrator to see her life as a thing of beauty; it is rather his own reaction which gives him a "mystical feeling."

The male right to be exalted by woman's submission is supported by religion as well as romanticism. Like the big blonde and Mrs. Grimes, the Jewish bride traditionally has been expected to submerge her identity completely when she marries. Symbolically, when the bride in Ruth Whitman's poem has her hair cut off, she has given herself completely to her husband.

In all the readings of this section, the stereotype of the submissive wife is shown as a sterile image resulting in emptiness or death for the woman. Yet the women in the stories themselves accept this stereotype as their own self-image; they have internalized the image and act out a role which in reality cheats them of selfhood and happiness. All of the stories show the tenacity of this mythical image. Olenka and Alice do not learn from experience that their self-chosen roles are a fraud; Penny cannot accept the idea that her husband might prefer to have her grow up and be a real person. The big blonde is driven to attempt suicide when she realizes the limitations of her role, but both she and Mrs. Grimes envision no alternative. The feminine mystique is the product of a society which stunts the imagination of women so that only one self-image prevails. By amputating their own identities and remaining incomplete human beings, submissive wives "shift the balance of the universe," in Ruth Whitman's words—to men's advantage.

Sally Benson

(1900–1948) Sally Benson began her career as a journalist in New York and ended it writing for motion pictures. She is best known for her short stories, many of which, including "Little Woman," appeared first in The New Yorker.

Little Woman

Penny Loomis liked to look back to the day when Ralph had first seen her. It was the day she had first seen Ralph, too, but she didn't think of that. She remembered only the delighted, incredulous look in Ralph's eyes when he caught sight of her sitting in the large wing chair in the Matsons' living room. In the short skirts and long waists of ten years ago, she had seemed just like a doll. Later in the evening he had told her so. "I can't get over you!" he exclaimed. "You're so tiny!"

"Oh, I know! And I hate it!" she answered. "It's dreadful, really! About clothes, I mean. Why, I wear size eleven!"

"You could look taller," Louise Matson said. "Naturally, those flat-heeled shoes make you look awfully little. If you *wanted* to look taller, you could wear high heels."

Penny Loomis had surveyed her strapped, patent-leather shoes thoughtfully and then her eyes had rested for a rather long instant on Louise's substantial Size 7 brocade slippers. "It's all very well for you to talk," she replied ruefully. "Your feet are a decent size, not disgraceful little Chinese feet like mine. You have nice, *big* feet."

Taking her home that night, Ralph had commented on Louise's attitude. "She was just trying to be catty," he said. "And you were swell about it. You may be little, but you aren't *small*!"

There was nothing to it after that first evening. It was as though Ralph never knew what hit him. There were three months of being engaged, of dancing night after night, attracting attention because Ralph was so tall—over six feet—and she was so tiny. He was enchanted with her daintiness and made jokes about it. "Now where," he would ask, looking over her head and pretending he couldn't see her, "did I put that woman I had with me?"

Everybody would laugh, especially Penny. "Big silly!" she would say. "Take me home!"

Everything she did pleased and amazed him. When, the Christmas before they were married, she presented him with a scarf she had knitted, he was genuinely overwhelmed. "I don't believe it," he said, smoothing it over and over with his hands. "You're not big enough to hold the needles."

He made so much fuss about the scarf at home that his mother, who had knitted scarves, sweaters, and socks for him all his life, was inclined to be bitter. "You act as though she'd knitted that scarf with her feet," she said acidly. "And, by the way, I put those golf stockings I just finished for you in your bottom bureau drawer."

His enchantment lasted long after they were married. It amused him to see her childish, round-toed shoes lying on the floor, to see her diminutive dresses hanging in the closet. Their house was full of company, too, those first months, men mostly, who marvelled with Ralph at the sight of Penny in an apron actually being able to get dinner, carrying platters of food almost bigger than she was.

They had no children, which was a pity, as Penny had fancied the idea of herself surrounded by tall, stalwart sons, but she had Ralph to flutter over and take care of. She made few friends and was content in their small apartment. Once Ralph asked her why she didn't go out more. "Do you good," he said, "to get out and play bridge or something in the afternoon. Why don't you look up Louise? You and she used to be pretty good friends."

Penny replied scornfully. Women were all right, she supposed. But she hated bridge, really. It was such a silly game. And she felt so funny going out with Louise, who was so tall. They looked ridiculous walking together.

Ralph had laughed at that. "Say, listen," he said, "I'm taller than Louise."

"You are a man," she answered. "Men are supposed to be big."

She looked so little and so pretty that Ralph agreed with her. "Louise is kind of a horse," he said.

They spent their vacations in Canada, where Ralph liked to fish. And Penny, dressed enchantingly in boy's denim trousers, checked shirt, and felt hat, lounged against cushions in the canoe while he paddled. She would scream a little, hiding her head, as he took the fish off the hooks. When they walked, Ralph carried her over the rough spots and took her arm up the hills, so that finally, although he insisted she was no trouble, he took to fishing nearer the Lodge.

Sometimes he was surprised at the number of things a man who was married to a little thing like Penny had to think of. There was the question of theatre tickets, for instance; he had to make an effort to get seats in the first row so that Penny wouldn't have to crane her neck or sit on her coat to see the stage; he must also remember to shorten his steps when they walked together or Penny got tired and out of breath; things must be left where Penny could reach them without having to stand on a chair.

Once he had spoken to her about it. "Gosh," he said, "it is kind of tough to be as little as you are! I never thought how it must be for you, not being able to do things that other people do."

The instant the words were out of his mouth, he knew he had said the wrong thing. "I'd like to know what I can't do that other women can!" she told him indignantly. "I think I manage to keep busy!"

He had to admit she did keep busy. In fact, she was never still. She was as busy, he thought, as a canary in a cage, fluttering, picking, keeping up an incessant chirping. "Sure you keep busy," he said. "Busy as a bird."

When they had been married almost ten years, he went on a business trip to Chicago. The thought of being left all alone frightened Penny and she made a great deal of it. He must put a chain lock on the front door and write down where he would be every night so that she could call him in case anything happened. Her anxious fluttering depressed him, and his depression lasted until he was safely on the train and seated in the warm, noisy dining car.

His second night in Chicago, the man he had come to see, a Mr. Merrick, asked him out for dinner. Mrs. Merrick went with them. She was a plain-looking woman, a little too stout, but there was something pleasing in the monotony of her solid brown hair that had no disturbing highlights, in her soft, friendly brown eyes, and her uninteresting brown felt hat. She had the appearance of a woman who had contemplatively set aside all personal vanity and turned to other things.

Ralph was surprised to find himself having a rather hilarious evening with them, and delighted to learn that Mr. Merrick had about decided to go back to New York with him and wind up their business for good and all. "And take me," Mrs. Merrick said.

"Oh, sure, take you," Mr. Merrick agreed.

And Ralph had added, "You bet!"

That night at the hotel, he wrote to Penny. It was a long, enthusiastic letter, and he wrote everything he could think of to please her. "They asked all about you," he wrote. "And I told them you were no bigger than a minute and as pretty as a picture. So we'll take them to dinner, when I get back, which should be about Friday. I'll wire exactly when. I miss you."

As he wrote "I miss you," he stopped and put his pen down on the desk. It struck him that he hadn't missed Penny at all, while she—well, he supposed that she was rattling around in the apartment not knowing what to do with herself. It occurred to him that she ought to have something to do, something better than fussing around with things at home. Not that he wanted her to work, he thought. Penny was far too helpless and little to be able to cope with a job. His heart softened when he remembered their evenings together with Penny curled up on his lap as he sat in the big chair, talking to him a mile a minute in her rather high, clear voice. He was ashamed of the many times he had wished she would read more, and recalled one dreadful evening when he had looked up from his paper at the sound of her nervous wandering about the room to say, "For the love of Pete, *light,* can't you?"

Thinking of these things and of the fine evening he had had with the Merricks, he picked up his pen again and underlined "I miss you."

The trip back to New York with the Merricks was great, but Penny was not at the station to meet him. "Unless we've missed her," he said gaily. "She's so darned little, she's easy to miss."

He assured the Merricks that he would just dash home, change his clothes, pick up Penny, and meet them at their hotel.

Penny was waiting for him at home. She was almost hysterically glad to see him, and he noticed that the house was shining and spotless, with fresh flowers in the vases and a wood fire burning in the grate. She was already dressed for the evening in a pale-pink taffeta dress with many ruffles, and stubby satin shoes tied with large bows. She wore a ribbon around her hair, and in the shaded lights of the living room she looked very young. It was only when she followed him to the bathroom to talk to him while he shaved that he noticed her more closely; the line of her mouth, always too thin, looked set and unhappy; the skin on her face looked drawn; and there was more than a sprinkling of gray in her black hair. The pink taffeta dress looked suddenly absurd on her, and he wished that she had worn something more suitable, something more her age. Why, Penny must be thirty-five!

She was curious about the Merricks, she said. "I never heard you make so much fuss over any two people in my life. What's she like?"

"Mrs. Merrick?" he asked, struggling with his stiff white shirt. "Oh, she's darned nice."

"Oh, I *know* that," Penny answered impatiently. "I know you think she's nice. What does she look like? Is she pretty?"

"No," he told her. "You couldn't call her pretty."

"Well, is she big, little, fat, thin?"

"She's not little," he said. "Why, she'd make two of you."

This seemed to satisfy her and she asked no more about the Merricks.

At the hotel they were told that Mr. and Mrs. Merrick were waiting for them in the main dining room. Walking through the lobby and down the long corridor, Penny was pleasantly conscious of the stir they created. She even shortened her steps a little, so that she appeared to be keeping up with Ralph by tripping at his side.

Mrs. Merrick's first words to her were what she expected. "Why, you're tiny!"

Penny laughed sweetly and looked up at Ralph. "Yes, isn't it silly?" she said. "I must look perfectly absurd beside Ralph, who is so enormous."

Mrs. Merrick's eyes took in every detail of Penny, her dress, her shoes, and the ribbon around her hair, and then she said, in almost the exact words that Louise had used so many years ago, "Do you know, with heels you'd look much taller. Why, you must be five feet one or so, and with good, high heels you'd look three inches taller. That would make you five feet four, which is a nice height. A great many movie actresses are five feet four."

Penny laughed again, but she flushed slightly.

"Now, Nellie," Mr. Merrick said, "don't go to making people over the first minute you see them. Maybe Mrs. Loomis *likes* to look small."

"Nonsense!" Mrs. Merrick exclaimed heartily. "No one wants to look like a midget! That is, no one wants to look *too* different. I know I was awfully tall for my age when I was about fifteen and I felt terribly about it. I was a sight, I can tell you."

And you're a sight now, Penny thought furiously. She chose a seat next to Mrs. Merrick and during dinner she rested her small, thin hand next to Mrs. Merrick's large, square one. She picked at her food daintily and exclaimed pleasantly when the other woman ordered ice cream with chocolate sauce for dessert. "Not that I wouldn't love it, but I just haven't *room*," she said.

Later, when the music started, she was surprised to see Ralph spring eagerly to his feet and ask Mrs. Merrick to dance.

"I haven't danced much lately," he said. "But let's go!"

He put one arm around Mrs. Merrick's waist and they started off. It was pleasant to have her face so near his own, to feel her soft, straight hair brush his forehead. She wore a dark-brown velvet dress, not very new and not very smart, but she had dignity and she moved smoothly with him across the dance floor. Over her shoulder he saw Penny dancing with Mr. Merrick. She was looking up into his face and talking brightly and animatedly. Mr. Merrick was bending down to catch what she was saying, smiling a frozen sort of smile, but he didn't look very happy.

The rest of the evening was not especially successful. Ralph tried in vain to recapture the spirit of hilarity he had felt with the Merricks in Chicago. But there was a sort of uneasiness in the air, even though Penny showed them several match tricks.

He was a little relieved, as they said good night, to learn that the Merricks had bought theatre tickets for the following evening and were leaving the day after for Chicago.

All the way home, Ralph sat in one corner of the taxi watching Penny as she talked. Her head was bent slightly to one side in the birdlike way she affected, and the white street lights flashing through the window were not kind to her. As he looked at her, she seemed to grow smaller and smaller until there was nothing much left of her but a pink taffeta dress and a pink ribbon. It had started to rain and the drops on the glass cast black dots on the pink taffeta dress, and he had the impression that it, too, might eventually disappear.

He did not notice that the cab had stopped in front of their apartment until Penny's voice gaily brought him back to earth. It was habit that made him pick her up and carry her across the wet, slippery pavement. And for such a little woman, she felt surprisingly heavy in his arms.

Anton Chekhov

*(1860–1904) The grandson of a Russian
serf, Anton Chekhov was a physician
as well as an author of many famous
short stories and plays. Though not a
revolutionary, he was ahead of his time
in his acceptance of the need for
change. He was particularly concerned
with education for women and the
hypocrisy of the existing class
structure.*

The Darling

Olenka, the daughter of the retired collegiate assessor, Plemyanniakov, was
sitting in her back porch, lost in thought. It was hot, the flies were persistent and
teasing, and it was pleasant to reflect that it would soon be evening. Dark rain-
clouds were gathering from the east, and bringing from time to time a breath of
moisture in the air.

Kukin, who was the manager of an open-air theatre called the Tivoli, and
who lived in the lodge, was standing in the middle of the garden looking at the
sky.

"Again!" he observed despairingly. "It's going to rain again! Rain every day,
as though to spite me! I might as well hang myself! It's ruin! Fearful losses every
day."

He flung up his hands, and went on, addressing Olenka:

"There! that's the life we lead, Olga Semyonovna. It's enough to make one
cry. One works and does one's utmost; one wears oneself out, getting no sleep at
night, and racks one's brain what to do for the best. And then what happens?
To begin with, one's public is ignorant, boorish. I give them the very best
operetta, a dainty masque, first-rate music-hall artists. But do you suppose that's
what they want! They don't understand anything of that sort. They want a
clown; what they ask for is vulgarity. And then look at the weather! Almost
every evening it rains. It started on the tenth of May, and it's kept it up all May

and June. It's simply awful! The public doesn't come, but I've to pay the rent just the same, and pay the artists."

The next evening the clouds would gather again, and Kukin would say with an hysterical laugh:

"Well, rain away, then! Flood the garden, drown me! Damn my luck in this world and the next! Let the artists have me up! Send me to prison!—to Siberia!—the scaffold! Ha, ha, ha!"

And next day the same thing.

Olenka listened to Kukin with silent gravity, and sometimes tears came into her eyes. In the end his misfortunes touched her; she grew to love him. He was a small thin man, with a yellow face, and curls combed forward on his forehead. He spoke in a thin tenor; as he talked his mouth worked on one side, and there was always an expression of despair on his face; yet he aroused a deep and genuine affection in her. She was always fond of someone, and could not exist without loving. In earlier days she had loved her papa, who now sat in a darkened room, breathing with difficulty; she had loved her aunt who used to come every other year from Bryansk; and before that, when she was at school, she had loved her French master. She was a gentle, soft-hearted, compassionate girl, with mild, tender eyes and very good health. At the sight of her full rosy cheeks, her soft white neck and a little dark mole on it, and the kind, naïve smile, which came into her face when she listened to anything pleasant, men thought, "Yes, not half bad," and smiled too, while lady visitors could not refrain from seizing her hand in the middle of a conversation, exclaiming in a gush of delight, "You darling!"

The house in which she had lived from her birth upwards, and which was left her in her father's will, was at the extreme end of the town, not far from the Tivoli. In the evenings and at night she could hear the band playing, and the crackling and banging of fireworks, and it seemed to her that it was Kukin struggling with his destiny, storming the entrenchments of his chief foe, the indifferent public; there was a sweet thrill at her heart, she had no desire to sleep, and when he returned home at daybreak, she tapped softly at her bedroom window, and showing him only her face and one shoulder through the curtain, she gave him a friendly smile. . . .

He proposed to her, and they were married. And when he had a closer view of her neck and her plump, fine shoulders, he threw up his hands, and said:

"You darling!"

He was happy, but as it rained on the day and night of his wedding, his face still retained an expression of despair.

They got on very well together. She used to sit in his office, to look after things in the Tivoli, to put down the accounts and pay the wages. And her rosy cheeks, her sweet, naïve, radiant smile, were to be seen now at the office window, now in the refreshment bar or behind the scenes at the theatre. And already she used to say to her acquaintances that the theatre was the chief and most important thing in life, and that it was only through the drama that one could derive true enjoyment and become cultivated and humane.

"But do you suppose the public understands that?" she used to say. "What they want is a clown. Yesterday we gave 'Faust Inside Out,' and almost all the boxes were empty; but if Vanitchka and I had been producing some vulgar thing, I assure you the theatre would have been packed. To-morrow Vanitchka and I are doing 'Orpheus in Hell.' Do come."

And what Kukin said about the theatre and the actors she repeated. Like him she despised the public for their ignorance and their indifference to art; she took part in the rehearsals, she corrected the actors, she kept an eye on the behaviour of the musicians, and when there was an unfavourable notice in the local paper, she shed tears, and then went to the editor's office to set things right.

The actors were fond of her and used to call her "Vanitchka and I," and "the darling"; she was sorry for them and used to lend them small sums of money, and if they deceived her, she used to shed a few tears in private, but did not complain to her husband.

They got on well in the winter too. They took the theatre in the town for the whole winter, and let it for short terms to a Little Russian company, or to a conjurer, or to a local dramatic society. Olenka grew stouter, and was always beaming with satisfaction, while Kukin grew thinner and yellower, and continually complained of their terrible losses, although he had not done badly all the winter. He used to cough at night, and she used to give him hot raspberry tea or limeflower water, to rub him with eau-de-Cologne and to wrap him in her warm shawls.

"You're such a sweet pet!" she used to say with perfect sincerity, stroking his hair. "You're such a pretty dear!"

Towards Lent he went to Moscow to collect a new troupe, and without him she could not sleep, but sat all night at her window, looking at the stars, and she compared herself with the hens, who are awake all night and uneasy when the cock is not in the hen-house. Kukin was detained in Moscow, and wrote that he would be back at Easter, adding some instructions about the Tivoli. But on the Sunday before Easter, late in the evening, came a sudden ominous knock at the gate; someone was hammering on the gate as though on a barrel—boom, boom, boom! The drowsy cook went flopping with her bare feet through the puddles, as she ran to open the gate.

"Please open," said someone outside in a thick bass. "There is a telegram for you."

Olenka had received telegrams from her husband before, but this time for some reason she felt numb with terror. With shaking hands she opened the telegram and read as follows:

"Ivan Petrovich died suddenly to-day. Awaiting immate instructions fufuneral Tuesday."

That was how it was written in the telegram—"fufuneral," and the utterly incomprehensible word "immate." It was signed by the stage manager of the operatic company.

"My darling!" sobbed Olenka. "Vanitchka, my precious, my darling! Why did I ever meet you! Why did I know you and love you! Your poor heart-broken Olenka is all alone without you!"

Kukin's funeral took place on Tuesday in Moscow, Olenka returned home on Wednesday, and as soon as she got indoors she threw herself on her bed and sobbed so loudly that it could be heard next door, and in the street.

"Poor darling!" the neighbours said, as they crossed themselves. "Olga Semyonovna, poor darling! How she does take on!"

Three months later Olenka was coming home from mass, melancholy and in deep mourning. It happened that one of her neighbours, Vassily Andreitch Pustovalov, returning home from church, walked back beside her. He was the manager at Babakayev's, the timber merchant's. He wore a straw hat, a white waistcoat, and a gold watchchain, and looked more like a country gentleman than a man in trade.

"Everything happens as it is ordained, Olga Semyonovna," he said gravely, with a sympathetic note in his voice; "and if any of our dear ones die, it must be because it is the will of God, so we ought to have fortitude and bear it submissively."

After seeing Olenka to her gate, he said good-bye and went on. All day afterwards she heard his sedately dignified voice, and whenever she shut her eyes she saw his dark beard. She liked him very much. And apparently she had made an impression on him too, for not long afterwards an elderly lady, with whom she was only slightly acquainted, came to drink coffee with her, and as soon as she was seated at table began to talk about Pustovalov, saying that he was an excellent man whom one could thoroughly depend upon, and that any girl would be glad to marry him. Three days later Pustovalov came himself. He did not stay long, only about ten minutes, and he did not say much, but when he left, Olenka loved him—loved him so much that she lay awake all night in a perfect fever, and in the morning she sent for the elderly lady. The match was quickly arranged, and then came the wedding.

Pustovalov and Olenka got on very well together when they were married.

Usually he sat in the office till dinner-time, then he went out on business, while Olenka took his place, and sat in the office till evening, making up accounts and booking orders.

"Timber gets dearer every year; the price rises twenty per cent," she would say to her customers and friends. "Only fancy we used to sell local timber, and now Vassitchka always has to go for wood to the Mogilev district. And the freight!" she would add, covering her cheeks with her hands in horror. "The freight!"

It seemed to her that she had been in the timber trade for ages and ages, and that the most important and necessary thing in life was timber; and there was something intimate and touching to her in the very sound of words such as "baulk," "post," "beam," "pole," "scantling," "batten," "lath," "plank," etc.

At night when she was asleep she dreamed of perfect mountains of planks and boards, and long strings of wagons, carting timber somewhere far away. She dreamed that a whole regiment of six-inch beams forty feet high, standing on end, was marching upon the timber-yard; that logs, beams, and boards knocked together with the resounding crash of dry wood, kept falling and getting up again, piling themselves on each other. Olenka cried out in her sleep, and Pustovalov said to her tenderly: "Olenka, what's the matter, darling? Cross yourself!"

Her husband's ideas were hers. If he thought the room was too hot, or that business was slack, she thought the same. Her husband did not care for entertainments, and on holidays he stayed at home. She did likewise.

"You are always at home or in the office," her friends said to her. "You should go to the theatre, darling, or to the circus."

"Vassitchka and I have no time to go to theatres," she would answer sedately. "We have no time for nonsense. What's the use of these theatres?"

On Saturdays Pustovalov and she used to go to the evening service; on holidays to early mass, and they walked side by side with softened faces as they came home from church. There was a pleasant fragrance about them both, and her silk dress rustled agreeably. At home they drank tea, with fancy bread and jams of various kinds, and afterwards they ate pie. Every day at twelve o'clock there was a savoury smell of beetroot soup and of mutton or duck in their yard, and on fast-days of fish, and no one could pass the gate without feeling hungry. In the office the samovar was always boiling, and customers were regaled with tea and cracknels. Once a week the couple went to the baths and returned side by side, both red in the face.

"Yes, we have nothing to complain of, thank God," Olenka used to say to her acquaintances. "I wish everyone were as well off as Vassitchka and I."

When Pustovalov went away to buy wood in the Mogilev district, she missed him dreadfully, lay awake and cried. A young veterinary surgeon in the army, called Smirnin, to whom they had let their lodge, used sometimes to come in in the evening. He used to talk to her and play cards with her, and this entertained her in her husband's absence. She was particularly interested in what he told her of his home life. He was married and had a little boy, but was separated from his wife because she had been unfaithful to him, and now he hated her and used to send her forty roubles a month for the maintenance of their son. And hearing of all this, Olenka sighed and shook her head. She was sorry for him.

"Well, God keep you," she used to say to him at parting, as she lighted him down the stairs with a candle. "Thank you for coming to cheer me up, and may the Mother of God give you health."

And she always expressed herself with the same sedateness and dignity, the same reasonableness, in imitation of her husband. As the veterinary surgeon was disappearing behind the door below, she would say:

"You know, Vladimir Platonitch, you'd better make it up with your wife. You should forgive her for the sake of your son. You may be sure the little fellow understands."

And when Pustovalov came back, she told him in a low voice about the veterinary surgeon and his unhappy home life, and both sighed and shook their heads and talked about the boy, who, no doubt, missed his father, and by some strange connection of ideas, they went up to the holy ikons, bowed to the ground before them and prayed that God would give them children.

And so the Pustovalovs lived for six years quietly and peaceably in love and complete harmony.

But behold! one winter day after drinking hot tea in the office, Vassily Andreitch went out into the yard without his cap on to see about sending off some timber, caught cold and was taken ill. He had the best doctors, but he grew worse and died after four months' illness. And Olenka was a widow once more.

"I've nobody now you've left me, my darling," she sobbed, after her husband's funeral. "How can I live without you, in wretchedness and misery! Pity me, good people, all alone in the world!"

She went about dressed in black with long "weepers," and gave up wearing hat and gloves for good. She hardly ever went out, except to church, or to her husband's grave, and led the life of a nun. It was not till six months later that she took off the weepers and opened the shutters of the windows. She was sometimes seen in the mornings, going with her cook to market for provisions, but what went on in her house and how she lived now could only be surmised. People guessed, from seeing her drinking tea in her garden with the veterinary surgeon, who read the newspaper aloud to her, and from the fact that, meeting a lady she knew at the post-office, she said to her:

"There is no proper veterinary inspection in our town, and that's the cause of all sorts of epidemics. One is always hearing of people's getting infection from the milk supply, or catching disease from horses and cows. The health of domestic animals ought to be as well cared for as the health of human beings."

She repeated the veterinary surgeon's words, and was of the same opinion as he about everything. It was evident that she could not live a year without some attachment, and had found new happiness in the lodge. In anyone else this would have been censured, but no one could think ill of Olenka; everything she did was so natural. Neither she nor the veterinary surgeon said anything to other people of the change in their relations, and tried, indeed, to conceal it, but without success, for Olenka could not keep a secret. When he had visitors, men serving in his regiment, and she poured out tea or served the supper, she would begin talking of the cattle plague, of the foot and mouth disease, and of the municipal slaughterhouses. He was dreadfully embarrassed, and when the guests had gone, he would seize her by the hand and hiss angrily:

"I've asked you before not to talk about what you don't understand. When we veterinary surgeons are talking among ourselves, please don't put your word in. It's really annoying."

And she would look at him with astonishment and dismay, and ask him in alarm: "But, Voloditchka, what *am* I to talk about?"

And with tears in her eyes she would embrace him, begging him not to be angry, and they were both happy.

But this happiness did not last long. The veterinary surgeon departed, departed for ever with his regiment, when it was transferred to a distant place— to Siberia, it may be. And Olenka was left alone.

Now she was absolutely alone. Her father had long been dead, and his arm-chair lay in the attic, covered with dust and lame of one leg. She got thinner and plainer, and when people met her in the street they did not look at her as they used to, and did not smile to her; evidently her best years were over and left behind, and now a new sort of life had begun for her, which did not bear think-ing about. In the evening Olenka sat in the porch, and heard the band playing and the fireworks popping in the Tivoli, but now the sound stirred no response.

She looked into her yard without interest, thought of nothing, wished for nothing, and afterwards, when night came on she went to bed and dreamed of her empty yard. She ate and drank as it were unwillingly.

And what was worst of all, she had no opinions of any sort. She saw the objects about her and understood what she saw, but could not form any opinion about them, and did not know what to talk about. And how awful it is not to have any opinions! One sees a bottle, for instance, or the rain, or a peasant driving in his cart, but what the bottle is for, or the rain, or the peasant, and what is the meaning of it, one can't say, and could not even for a thousand roubles. When she had Kukin, or Pustovalov, or the veterinary surgeon, Olenka could explain everything, and give her opinion about anything you like, but now there was the same emptiness in her brain and in her heart as there was in her yard outside. And it was as harsh and as bitter as wormwood in the mouth.

Little by little the town grew in all directions. The road became a street, and where the Tivoli and the timber-yard had been, there were new turnings and houses. How rapidly time passes! Olenka's house grew dingy, the roof got rusty, the shed sank on one side, and the whole yard was overgrown with docks and stinging-nettles. Olenka herself had grown plain and elderly; in summer she sat in the porch, and her soul, as before, was empty and dreary and full of bitterness. In winter she sat at her window and looked at the snow. When she caught the scent of spring, or heard the chime of the church bells, a sudden rush of memories from the past came over her, there was a tender ache in her heart, and her eyes brimmed over with tears; but this was only for a minute, and then came emptiness again and the sense of the futility of life. The black kitten, Briska, rubbed against her and purred softly, but Olenka was not touched by these feline caresses. That was not what she needed. She wanted a love that would absorb her whole being, her whole soul and reason—that would give her ideas and an object in life, and would warm her old blood. And she would shake the kitten off her skirt and say with vexation:

"Get along; I don't want you!"

And so it was, day after day and year after year, and no joy, and no opinions. Whatever Mavra, the cook, said she accepted.

One hot July day, towards evening, just as the cattle were being driven by, and the whole yard was full of dust, someone suddenly knocked at the gate. Olenka went to open it herself and was dumbfounded when she looked out: she saw Smirnin, the veterinary surgeon, grey-headed, and dressed as a civilian. She suddenly remembered everything. She could not help crying and letting her head fall on his breast without uttering a word, and in the violence of her feeling she did not notice how they both walked into the house and sat down to tea.

"My dear Vladimir Platonitch! What fate has brought you?" she muttered, trembling with joy.

"I want to settle here for good, Olga Semyonovna," he told her. "I have resigned my post, and have come to settle down and try my luck on my own account. Besides, it's time for my boy to go to school. He's a big boy. I am reconciled with my wife, you know."

"Where is she?" asked Olenka.

"She's at the hotel with the boy, and I'm looking for lodgings."

"Good gracious, my dear soul! Lodgings! Why not have my house? Why shouldn't that suit you? Why, my goodness, I wouldn't take any rent!" cried Olenka in a flutter, beginning to cry again. "You live here, and the lodge will do nicely for me. Oh dear! how glad I am!"

Next day the roof was painted and the walls were whitewashed, and Olenka, with her arms akimbo, walked about the yard giving directions. Her face was beaming with her old smile, and she was brisk and alert as though she had waked from a long sleep. The veterinary's wife arrived—a thin, plain lady, with short hair and a peevish expression. With her was her little Sasha, a boy of ten, small for his age, blue-eyed, chubby, with dimples in his cheeks. And scarcely had the boy walked into the yard when he ran after the cat, and at once there was the sound of his gay, joyous laugh.

"Is that your puss, auntie?" he asked Olenka. "When she has little ones, do give us a kitten. Mamma is awfully afraid of mice."

Olenka talked to him, and gave him tea. Her heart warmed and there was a sweet ache in her bosom, as though the boy had been her own child. And when he sat at the table in the evening, going over his lessons, she looked at him with deep tenderness and pity as she murmured to herself:

"You pretty pet! . . . my precious! . . . Such a fair little thing, and so clever."

" 'An island is a piece of land which is entirely surrounded by water,' " he read aloud.

"An island is a piece of land," she repeated, and this was the first opinion to which she gave utterance with positive conviction after so many years of silence and dearth of ideas.

Now she had opinions of her own, and at supper she talked to Sasha's parents, saying how difficult the lessons were at the high schools, but that yet the high school was better than a commercial one, since with a high school education all careers were open to one, such as being a doctor or an engineer.

Sasha began going to the high school. His mother departed to Harkov to her sister's and did not return; his father used to go off every day to inspect cattle, and would often be away from home for three days together, and it seemed to Olenka as though Sasha was entirely abandoned, that he was not wanted at home, that he was being starved, and she carried him off to her lodge and gave him a little room there.

And for six months Sasha had lived in the lodge with her. Every morning Olenka came into his bedroom and found him fast asleep, sleeping noiselessly with his hand under his cheek. She was sorry to wake him.

"Sashenka," she would say mournfully, "get up, darling. It's time for school."

He would get up, dress and say his prayers, and then sit down to breakfast, drink three glasses of tea, and eat two large cracknels and half a buttered roll. All this time he was hardly awake and a little ill-humoured in consequence.

"You don't quite know your fable, Sashenka," Olenka would say, looking at

him as though he were about to set off on a long journey. "What a lot of trouble
I have with you! You must work and do your best, darling, and obey your
teachers."

"Oh, do leave me alone!" Sasha would say.

Then he would go down the street to school, a little figure, wearing a big cap
and carrying a satchel on his shoulder. Olenka would follow him noiselessly.

"Sashenka!" she would call after him, and she would pop into his hand a
date or a caramel. When he reached the street where the school was, he would
feel ashamed of being followed by a tall, stout woman; he would turn round and
say:

"You'd better go home, auntie. I can go the rest of the way alone."

She would stand still and look after him fixedly till he had disappeared at
the school-gate.

Ah, how she loved him! Of her former attachments not one had been so
deep; never had her soul surrendered to any feeling so spontaneously, so disinterestedly, and so joyously as now that her maternal instincts were aroused.
For this little boy with the dimple in his cheek and the big school cap, she would
have given her whole life, she would have given it with joy and tears of tenderness. Why? Who can tell why?

When she had seen the last of Sasha, she returned home, contented and
serene, brimming over with love; her face, which had grown younger during the
last six months, smiled and beamed; people meeting her looked at her with
pleasure.

"Good-morning, Olga Semyonovna, darling. How are you, darling?"

"The lessons at the high school are very difficult now," she would relate at
the market. "It's too much; in the first class yesterday they gave him a fable to
learn by heart, and a Latin translation and a problem. You know it's too much
for a little chap."

And she would begin talking about the teachers, the lessons, and the school
books, saying just what Sasha said.

At three o'clock they had dinner together: in the evening they learned their
lessons together and cried. When she put him to bed, she would stay a long time
making the cross over him and murmuring a prayer; then she would go to bed
and dream of that far-away misty future when Sasha would finish his studies and
become a doctor or an engineer, would have a big house of his own with horses
and a carriage, would get married and have children. . . . She would fall asleep
still thinking of the same thing, and tears would run down her cheeks from her
closed eyes, while the black cat lay purring beside her: "Mrr, mrr, mrr."

Suddenly there would come a loud knock at the gate.

Olenka would wake up breathless with alarm, her heart throbbing. Half a
minute later would come another knock.

"It must be a telegram from Harkov," she would think, beginning to tremble
from head to foot. "Sasha's mother is sending for him from Harkov. . . . Oh,
mercy on us!"

She was in despair. Her head, her hands, and her feet would turn chill, and
she would feel that she was the most unhappy woman in the world. But another

minute would pass, voices would be heard: it would turn out to be the veterinary surgeon coming home from the club.

"Well, thank God!" she would think.

And gradually the load in her heart would pass off, and she would feel at ease. She would go back to bed thinking of Sasha, who lay sound asleep in the next room, sometimes crying out in his sleep.

"I'll give it you! Get away! Shut up!"

Edith Wharton

(1862–1937) A major American writer of fiction, Edith Wharton frequently satirized the New York high society of which she was a member until she moved to Europe in 1907. Her finest work is perhaps the atypical novel, Ethan Frome, *about the tragedy of a New England farm wife.*

The Other Two

1 Waythorn, on the drawing-room hearth, waited for his wife to come down to dinner.

It was their first night under his own roof, and he was surprised at his thrill of boyish agitation. He was not so old, to be sure—his glass gave him little more than the five-and-thirty years to which his wife confessed—but he had fancied himself already in the temperate zone; yet here he was listening for her step with a tender sense of all it symbolised, with some old trail of verse about the garlanded nuptial door-posts floating through his enjoyment of the pleasant room and the good dinner just beyond it.

They had been hastily recalled from their honeymoon by the illness of Lily Haskett, the child of Mrs. Waythorn's first marriage. The little girl, at Waythorn's desire, had been transferred to his house on the day of her mother's wedding, and the doctor, on their arrival, broke the news that she was ill with typhoid, but declared that all the symptoms were favourable. Lily could show twelve years of unblemished health, and the case promised to be a light one. The nurse spoke as reassuringly, and after a moment of alarm Mrs. Waythorn had adjusted herself to the situation. She was very fond of Lily—her affection for the child had perhaps been her decisive charm in Waythorn's eyes—but she had the perfectly balanced nerves which her little girl had inherited, and no woman ever wasted less tissue in unproductive worry. Waythorn was therefore quite prepared to see her come in presently, a little late because of a last look at Lily, but as serene and well-appointed as if her good-night kiss had been laid on the brow of health. Her

From The Descent of Man, *New York, Charles Scribner's Sons, 1904.*

composure was restful to him; it acted as ballast to his somewhat unstable sensibilities. As he pictured her bending over the child's bed he thought how soothing her presence must be in illness; her very step would prognosticate recovery.

His own life had been a gray one, from temperament rather than circumstance, and he had been drawn to her by the unperturbed gaiety which kept her fresh and elastic at an age when most women's activities are growing either slack or febrile. He knew what was said about her; for, popular as she was, there had always been a faint undercurrent of detraction. When she had appeared in New York, nine or ten years earlier, as the pretty Mrs. Haskett whom Gus Varick had unearthed somewhere—was it in Pittsburgh or Utica?—society, while promptly accepting her, had reserved the right to cast a doubt on its own indiscrimination. Enquiry, however, established her undoubted connection with a socially reigning family, and explained her recent divorce as the natural result of a runaway match at seventeen; and as nothing was known of Mr. Haskett it was easy to believe the worst of him.

Alice Haskett's remarriage with Gus Varick was a passport to the set whose recognition she coveted, and for a few years the Varicks were the most popular couple in town. Unfortunately the alliance was brief and stormy, and this time the husband had his champions. Still, even Varick's stanchest supporters admitted that he was not meant for matrimony, and Mrs. Varick's grievances were of a nature to bear the inspection of the New York courts. A New York divorce is in itself a diploma of virtue, and in the semi-widowhood of this second separation Mrs. Varick took on an air of sanctity, and was allowed to confide her wrongs to some of the most scrupulous ears in town. But when it was known that she was to marry Waythorn there was a momentary reaction. Her best friends would have preferred to see her remain in the rôle of the injured wife, which was as becoming to her as crape to a rosy complexion. True, a decent time had elapsed, and it was not even suggested that Waythorn had supplanted his predecessor. People shook their heads over him, however, and one grudging friend, to whom he affirmed that he took the step with his eyes open, replied oracularly: "Yes—and with your ears shut."

Waythorn could afford to smile at these innuendoes. In the Wall Street phrase, he had "discounted" them. He knew that society has not yet adapted itself to the consequences of divorce, and that till the adaptation takes place every woman who uses the freedom the law accords her must be her own social justification. Waythorn had an amused confidence in his wife's ability to justify herself. His expectations were fulfilled, and before the wedding took place Alice Varick's group had rallied openly to her support. She took it all imperturbably; she had a way of surmounting obstacles without seeming to be aware of them, and Waythorn looked back with wonder at the trivialities over which he had worn his nerves thin. He had the sense of having found refuge in a richer, warmer nature than his own, and his satisfaction, at the moment, was humourously summed up in the thought that his wife, when she had done all she could for Lily, would not be ashamed to come down and enjoy a good dinner.

The anticipation of such enjoyment was not, however, the sentiment expressed by Mrs. Waythorn's charming face when she presently joined him.

Though she had put on her most engaging teagown she had neglected to assume the smile that went with it, and Waythorn thought he had never seen her look so nearly worried.

"What is it?" he asked. "Is anything wrong with Lily?"

"No, I've just been in and she's still sleeping." Mrs. Waythorn hesitated. "But something tiresome has happened."

He had taken her two hands, and now perceived that he was crushing a paper between them.

"This letter?"

"Yes—Mr. Haskett has written—I mean his lawyer has written."

Waythorn felt himself flush uncomfortably. He dropped his wife's hands. "What about?"

"About seeing Lily. You know the courts—"

"Yes, yes," he interrupted nervously.

Nothing was known about Haskett in New York. He was vaguely supposed to have remained in the outer darkness from which his wife had been rescued, and Waythorn was one of the few who were aware that he had given up his business in Utica and followed her to New York in order to be near his little girl. In the days of his wooing, Waythorn had often met Lily on the doorstep, rosy and smiling, on her way "to see papa."

"I am so sorry," Mrs. Waythorn murmured.

He roused himself. "What does he want?"

"He wants to see her. You know she goes to him once a week."

"Well—he doesn't expect her to go to him now, does he?"

"No—he has heard of her illness; but he expects to come here."

"Here?"

Mrs. Waythorn reddened under his gaze. They looked away from each other.

"I'm afraid he has the right. . . . You'll see. . . . " She made a proffer of the letter.

Waythorn moved away with a gesture of refusal. He stood staring about the softly lighted room, which a moment before had seemed so full of bridal intimacy.

"I'm so sorry," she repeated. "If Lily could have been moved—"

"That's out of the question," he returned impatiently.

"I suppose so."

Her lip was beginning to tremble, and he felt himself a brute.

"He must come, of course," he said. "When is—his day?"

"I'm afraid—to-morrow."

"Very well. Send a note in the morning."

The butler entered to announce dinner.

Waythorn turned to his wife. "Come—you must be tired. It's beastly, but try to forget about it," he said, drawing her hand through his arm.

"You're so good, dear. I'll try," she whispered back.

Her face cleared at once, and as she looked at him across the flowers, between the rosy candle-shades, he saw her lips waver back into a smile.

"How pretty everything is!" she sighed luxuriously.

He turned to the butler. "The champagne at once, please. Mrs. Waythorn is tired."

In a moment or two their eyes met above the sparkling glasses. Her own were quite clear and untroubled: he saw that she had obeyed his injunction and forgotten.

2 Waythorn, the next morning, went down town earlier than usual. Haskett was not likely to come till the afternoon, but the instinct of flight drove him forth. He meant to stay away all day—he had thoughts of dining at his club. As his door closed behind him he reflected that before he opened it again it would have admitted another man who had as much right to enter it as himself, and the thought filled him with a physical repugnance.

He caught the "elevated" at the employes' hour, and found himself crushed between two layers of pendulous humanity. At Eighth Street the man facing him wriggled out, and another took his place. Waythorn glanced up and saw that it was Gus Varick. The men were so close together that it was impossible to ignore the smile of recognition on Varick's handsome overblown face. And after all—why not? They had always been on good terms, and Varick had been divorced before Waythorn's attentions to his wife began. The two exchanged a word on the perennial grievance of the congested trains, and when a seat at their side was miraculously left empty the instinct of self-preservation made Waythorn slip into it after Varick.

The latter drew the stout man's breath of relief. "Lord—I was beginning to feel like a pressed flower." He leaned back, looking unconcernedly at Waythorn. "Sorry to hear that Sellers is knocked out again."

"Sellers?" echoed Waythorn, starting at his partner's name.

Varick looked surprised. "You didn't know he was laid up with the gout?"

"No. I've been away— I only got back last night." Waythorn felt himself reddening in anticipation of the other's smile.

"Ah—yes; to be sure. And Seller's attack came on two days ago. I'm afraid he's pretty bad. Very awkward for me, as it happens, because he was just putting through a rather important thing for me."

"Ah?" Waythorn wondered vaguely since when Varick had been dealing in "important things." Hitherto he had dabbled only in the shallow pools of speculation, with which Waythorn's office did not usually concern itself.

It occurred to him that Varick might be talking at random, to relieve the strain of their propinquity. That strain was becoming momentarily more apparent to Waythorn, and when, at Cortlandt Street, he caught sight of an acquaintance and had a sudden vision of the picture he and Varick must present to an initiated eye, he jumped up with a muttered excuse.

"I hope you'll find Sellers better," said Varick civilly, and he stammered back: "If I can be of any use to you—" and let the departing crowd sweep him to the platform.

At his office he heard that Sellers was in fact ill with the gout, and would probably not be able to leave the house for some weeks.

"I'm sorry it should have happened so, Mr. Waythorn," the senior clerk said with affable significance. "Mr. Sellers was very much upset at the idea of giving you such a lot of extra work just now."

"Oh, that's no matter," said Waythorn hastily. He secretly welcomed the pressure of additional business, and was glad to think that, when the day's work was over, he would have to call at his partner's on the way home.

He was late for luncheon, and turned in at the nearest restaurant instead of going to his club. The place was full, and the waiter hurried him to the back of the room to capture the only vacant table. In the cloud of cigar-smoke Waythorn did not at once distinguish his neighbours: but presently, looking about him, he saw Varick seated a few feet off. This time, luckily, they were too far apart for conversation, and Varick, who faced another way, had probably not even seen him; but there was an irony in their renewed nearness.

Varick was said to be fond of good living, and as Waythorn sat despatching his hurried luncheon he looked across half enviously at the other's leisurely degustation of his meal. When Waythorn first saw him he had been helping himself with critical deliberation to a bit of Camembert at the ideal point of liquefaction, and now, the cheese removed, he was just pouring his *café double* from its little two-storied earthen pot. He poured slowly, his ruddy profile bent above the task, and one beringed white hand steadying the lid of the coffee-pot; then he stretched his other hand to the decanter of cognac at his elbow, filled a liqueur glass, took a tentative sip, and poured the brandy into his coffee-cup.

Waythorn watched him in a kind of fascination. What was he thinking of—only of the flavour of the coffee and the liqueur? Had the morning's meeting left no more trace in his thoughts than on his face? Had his wife so completely passed out of his life that even this odd encounter with her present husband, within a week after her remarriage, was no more than an incident in his day? And as Waythorn mused, another idea struck him: had Haskett ever met Varick as Varick and he had just met? The recollection of Haskett perturbed him, and he rose and left the restaurant, taking a circuitous way out to escape the placid irony of Varick's nod.

It was after seven when Waythorn reached home. He thought the footman who opened the door looked at him oddly.

"How is Miss Lily?" he asked in haste.

"Doing very well, sir. A gentleman—"

"Tell Barlow to put off dinner for half an hour," Waythorn cut him off, hurrying upstairs.

He went straight to his room and dressed without seeing his wife. When he reached the drawing-room she was there, fresh and radiant. Lily's day had been good; the doctor was not coming back that evening.

At dinner Waythorn told her of Seller's illness and of the resulting complications. She listened sympathetically, adjuring him not to let himself be over-worked, and asking vague feminine questions about the routine of the office. Then she gave him the chronicle of Lily's day; quoted the nurse and doctor, and told him who had called to inquire. He had never seen her more serene and unruffled. It struck him, with a curious pang, that she was very happy in being with him, so happy that she found a childish pleasure in rehearsing the trivial incidents of her day.

After dinner they went to the library, and the servant put the coffee and liqueurs on a low table before her and left the room. She looked singularly soft and girlish in her rosy pale dress, against the dark leather of one of his bachelor armchairs. A day earlier the contrast would have charmed him.

He turned away now, choosing a cigar with affected deliberation.

"Did Haskett come?" he asked, with his back to her.

"Oh, yes—he came."

"You didn't see him, of course?"

She hesitated a moment. "I let the nurse see him."

That was all. There was nothing more to ask. He swung round toward her, applying a match to his cigar. Well, the thing was over for a week, at any rate. He would try not to think of it. She looked up at him, a trifle rosier than usual, with a smile in her eyes.

"Ready for your coffee, dear?"

He leaned against the mantelpiece, watching her as she lifted the coffee-pot. The lamplight struck a gleam from her bracelets and tipped her soft hair with brightness. How light and slender she was, and how each gesture flowed into the next! She seemed a creature all compact of harmonies. As the thought of Haskett receded, Waythorn felt himself yielding again to the joy of possessorship. They were his, those white hands with their flitting motions, his the light haze of hair, the lips and eyes. . . .

She set down the coffee-pot, and reaching for the decanter of cognac, measured off a liqueur-glass and poured it into his cup.

Waythorn uttered a sudden exclamation.

"What is the matter?" she said, startled.

"Nothing; only—I don't take cognac in my coffee."

"Oh, how stupid of me," she cried.

Their eyes met, and she blushed a sudden agonised red.

3 Ten days later, Mr. Sellers, still house-bound, asked Waythorn to call on his way down town.

The senior partner, with his swaddled foot propped up by the fire, greeted his associate with an air of embarrassment.

"I'm sorry, my dear fellow; I've got to ask you to do an awkward thing for me."

Waythorn waited, and the other went on, after a pause apparently given to the arrangement of his phrases: "The fact is, when I was knocked out I had just gone into a rather complicated piece of business for—Gus Varick."

"Well?" said Waythorn, with an attempt to put him at his ease.

"Well—it's this way: Varick came to me the day before my attack. He had evidently had an inside tip from somebody, and had made about a hundred thousand. He came to me for advice, and I suggested his going in with Vanderlyn."

"Oh, the deuce!" Waythorn exclaimed. He saw in a flash what had happened. The investment was an alluring one, but required negotiation. He listened quietly while Sellers put the case before him, and, the statement ended, he said: "You think I ought to see Varick?"

"I'm afraid I can't as yet. The doctor is obdurate. And this thing can't wait. I hate to ask you, but no one else in the office knows the ins and outs of it."

Waythorn stood silent. He did not care a farthing for the success of Varick's venture, but the honour of the office was to be considered, and he could hardly refuse to oblige his partner.

"Very well," he said, "I'll do it."

That afternoon, apprised by telephone, Varick called at the office. Waythorn, waiting in his private room, wondered what the others thought of it. The newspapers, at the time of Mrs. Waythorn's marriage, had acquainted their readers with every detail of her previous matrimonial ventures, and Waythorn could fancy the clerks smiling behind Varick's back as he was ushered in.

Varick bore himself admirably. He was easy without being undignified, and Waythorn was conscious of cutting a much less impressive figure. Varick had no experience of business, and the talk prolonged itself for nearly an hour while Waythorn set forth with scrupulous precision the details of the proposed transaction.

"I'm awfully obliged to you," Varick said as he rose. "The fact is I'm not used to having much money to look after, and I don't want to make an ass of myself—" He smiled, and Waythorn could not help noticing that there was something pleasant about his smile. "It feels uncommonly queer to have enough cash to pay one's bills. I'd have sold my soul for it a few years ago!"

Waythorn winced at the allusion. He had heard it rumoured that a lack of funds had been one of the determining causes of the Varick separation, but it did not occur to him that Varick's words were intentional. It seemed more likely that the desire to keep clear of embarrassing topics had fatally drawn him into one. Waythorn did not wish to be outdone in civility.

"We'll do the best we can for you," he said. "I think this is a good thing you're in."

"Oh, I'm sure it's immense. It's awfully good of you—" Varick broke off, embarrassed. "I suppose the thing's settled now—but if—"

"If anything happens before Sellers is about, I'll see you again," said Waythorn quietly. He was glad, in the end, to appear the more self-possessed of the two.

The course of Lily's illness ran smooth, and as the days passed Waythorn grew used to the idea of Haskett's weekly visit. The first time the day came round, he stayed out late, and questioned his wife as to the visit on his return. She replied at once that Haskett had merely seen the nurse downstairs, as the doctor did not wish any one in the child's sick-room till after the crisis.

The following week Waythorn was again conscious of the recurrence of the day, but had forgotten it by the time he came home to dinner. The crisis of the disease came a few days later, with a rapid decline of fever, and the little girl was pronounced out of danger. In the rejoicing which ensued the thought of Haskett passed out of Waythorn's mind, and one afternoon, letting himself into the house with a latch-key, he went straight to his library without noticing a shabby hat and umbrella in the hall.

In the library he found a small effaced-looking man with a thinnish gray beard sitting on the edge of a chair. The stranger might have been a piano-tuner, or one of those mysteriously efficient persons who are summoned in emergencies to adjust some detail of the domestic machinery. He blinked at Waythorn through a pair of gold-rimmed spectacles and said mildly: "Mr. Waythorn, I presume? I am Lily's father."

Waythorn flushed. "Oh—" he stammered uncomfortably. He broke off, disliking to appear rude. Inwardly he was trying to adjust the actual Haskett to the image of him projected by his wife's reminiscences. Waythorn had been allowed to infer that Alice's first husband was a brute.

"I am sorry to intrude," said Haskett, with his over-the-counter politeness.

"Don't mention it," returned Waythorn, collecting himself. "I suppose the nurse has been told?"

"I presume so. I can wait," said Haskett. He had a resigned way of speaking, as though life had worn down his natural powers of resistance.

Waythorn stood on the threshold, nervously pulling off his gloves.

"I'm sorry you've been detained. I will send for the nurse," he said; and as he opened the door he added with an effort: "I'm glad we can give you a good report of Lily." He winced as the *we* slipped out, but Haskett seemed not to notice it.

"Thank you, Mr. Waythorn. It's been an anxious time for me."

"Ah, well, that's past. Soon she'll be able to go to you." Waythorn nodded and passed out.

In his own room he flung himself down with a groan. He hated the womanish sensibility which made him suffer so acutely from the grotesque chances of life. He had known when he married that his wife's former husbands were both living, and that amid the multiplied contacts of modern existence there were a thousand chances to one that he would run against one or the other, yet he found himself as much disturbed by his brief encounter with Haskett as though the law had not obligingly removed all difficulties in the way of their meeting.

Waythorn sprang up and began to pace the room nervously. He had not suffered half as much from his two meetings with Varick. It was Haskett's presence in his own house that made the situation so intolerable. He stood still, hearing steps in the passage.

"This way, please," he heard the nurse say. Haskett was being taken upstairs, then: not a corner of the house but was open to him. Waythorn dropped into another chair, staring vaguely ahead of him. On his dressing-table stood a photograph of Alice, taken when he had first known her. She was Alice Varick then— how fine and exquisite he had thought her! Those were Varick's pearls about her neck. At Waythorn's instance they had been returned before her marriage. Had

Haskett ever given her any trinkets—and what had become of them, Waythorn wondered? He realised suddenly that he knew very little of Haskett's past or present situation; but from the man's appearance and manner of speech he could reconstruct with curious precision the surroundings of Alice's first marriage. And it startled him to think that she had, in the background of her life, a phase of existence so different from anything with which he had connected her. Varick, whatever his faults, was a gentleman, in the conventional, traditional sense of the term: the sense which at that moment seemed, oddly enough, to have most meaning to Waythorn. He and Varick had the same social habits, spoke the same language, understood the same allusions. But this other man . . . it was grotesquely uppermost in Waythorn's mind that Haskett had worn a made-up tie attached with an elastic. Why should that ridiculous detail symbolise the whole man? Waythorn was exasperated by his own paltriness, but the fact of the tie expanded, forced itself on him, became as it were the key to Alice's past. He could see her, as Mrs. Haskett, sitting in a "front parlour" furnished in plush, with a pianola, and a copy of "Ben Hur" on the centre-table. He could see her going to the theatre with Haskett—or perhaps even to a "Church Sociable"—she in a "picture hat" and Haskett in a black frock-coat, a little creased, with the made-up tie on an elastic. On the way home they would stop and look at the illuminated shop-windows, lingering over the photographs of New York actresses. On Sunday afternoons Haskett would take her for a walk, pushing Lily ahead of them in a white enamelled perambulator, and Waythorn had a vision of the people they would stop and talk to. He could fancy how pretty Alice must have looked, in a dress adroitly constructed from the hints of a New York fashion-paper, and how she must have looked down on the other women, chafing at her life, and secretly feeling that she belonged in a bigger place.

For the moment his foremost thought was one of wonder at the way in which she had shed the phase of existence which her marriage with Haskett implied. It was as if her whole aspect, every gesture, every inflection, every allusion, were a studied negation of that period of her life. If she had denied being married to Haskett she could have hardly have stood more convicted of duplicity than in this obliteration of the self which had been his wife.

Waythorn started up, checking himself in the analysis of her motives. What right had he to create a fantastic effigy of her and then pass judgment on it? She had spoken vaguely of her first marriage as unhappy, had hinted, with becoming reticence, that Haskett had wrought havoc among her young illusions. . . . It was a pity for Waythorn's peace of mind that Haskett's very inoffensiveness shed a new light on the nature of those illusions. A man would rather think that his wife had been brutalised by her first husband than that the process has been reversed.

4 "Mr. Waythorn, I don't like that French governess of Lily's."

Haskett, subdued and apologetic, stood before Waythorn in the library, revolving his shabby hat in his hand.

Waythorn, surprised in his armchair over the evening paper, stared back perplexedly at his visitor.

"You'll excuse my asking to see you," Haskett continued. "But this is my last visit, and I thought if I could have a word with you it would be a better way than writing to Mrs. Waythorn's lawyer."

Waythorn rose uneasily. He did not like the French governess either; but that was irrelevant.

"I am not so sure of that," he returned stiffly; "but since you wish it I will give your message to—my wife." He always hesitated over the possessive pronoun in addressing Haskett.

The latter sighed. "I don't know as that will help much. She didn't like it when I spoke to her."

Waythorn turned red. "When did you see her?" he asked.

"Not since the first day I came to see Lily—right after she was taken sick. I remarked to her then that I didn't like the governess."

Waythorn made no answer. He remembered distinctly that, after that first visit, he had asked his wife if she had seen Haskett. She had lied to him then, but she had respected his wishes since, and the incident cast a curious light on her character. He was sure she would not have seen Haskett that first day if she had divined that Waythorn would object, and the fact that she did not divine it was almost as disagreeable to the latter as the discovery that she had lied to him.

"I don't like the woman," Haskett was repeating with mild persistency. "She ain't straight, Mr. Waythorn—she'll teach the child to be underhand. I've noticed a change in Lily—she's too anxious to please—and she don't always tell the truth. She used to be the straightest child, Mr. Waythorn—" He broke off, his voice a little thick. "Not but what I want her to have a stylish education," he ended.

Waythorn was touched. "I'm sorry, Mr. Haskett; but frankly, I don't quite see what I can do."

Haskett hesitated. Then he laid his hat on the table, and advanced to the hearth-rug, on which Waythorn was standing. There was nothing aggressive in his manner, but he had the solemnity of a timid man resolved on a decisive measure.

"There's just one thing you can do, Mr. Waythorn," he said. "You can remind Mrs. Waythorn that, by the decree of the courts, I am entitled to have a voice in Lily's bringing up." He paused, and went on more deprecatingly: "I'm not the kind to talk about enforcing my rights, Mr. Waythorn. I don't know as I think a man is entitled to rights he hasn't known how to hold on to; but this business of the child is different. I've never let go there—and I never mean to."

The scene left Waythorn deeply shaken. Shamefacedly, in indirect ways, he had been finding out about Haskett; and all that he had learned was favourable. The little man, in order to be near his daughter, had sold out his share in a profitable business in Utica, and accepted a modest clerkship in a New York manufacturing house. He boarded in a shabby street and had few acquaintances. His passion for Lily filled his life. Waythorn felt that this exploration of Haskett was like groping about with a dark-lantern in his wife's past; but he saw now that there were recesses his lantern had not explored. He had never enquired into the exact circumstances of his wife's first matrimonial rupture. On the surface all had been fair. It was she who had obtained the divorce, and the court had given her the child. But Waythorn knew how many ambiguities such a verdict might cover. The mere fact that Haskett retained a right over his daughter implied an unsuspected compromise. Waythorn was an idealist. He always refused to recognise unpleasant contingencies till he found himself confronted with them, and then he saw them followed by a spectral train of consequences. His next days were thus haunted, and he determined to try to lay the ghosts by conjuring them up in his wife's presence.

When he repeated Haskett's request a flame of anger passed over her face; but she subdued it instantly and spoke with a slight quiver of outraged motherhood.

"It is very ungentlemanly of him," she said.

The word grated on Waythorn. "That is neither here nor there. It's a bare question of rights."

She murmured: "It's not as if he could ever be a help to Lily—"

Waythorn flushed. This was even less to his taste. "The question is," he repeated, "what authority has he over her?"

She looked downward, twisting herself a little in her seat. "I am willing to see him—I thought you objected," she faltered.

In a flash he understood that she knew the extent of Haskett's claims. Perhaps it was not the first time she had resisted them.

"My objecting has nothing to do with it," he said coldly; "if Haskett has a right to be consulted you must consult him."

She burst into tears, and he saw that she expected him to regard her as a victim.

Haskett did not abuse his rights. Waythorn felt miserably sure that he would not. But the governess was dismissed, and from time to time the little man demanded an interview with Alice. After the first outburst she accepted the situation with her usual adaptability. Haskett had once reminded Waythorn of the piano-tuner, and Mrs. Waythorn, after a month or two, appeared to class him with that domestic familiar. Waythorn could not but respect the father's tenacity. At first he had tried to cultivate the suspicion that Haskett might be "up to" something, that he had an object in securing a foothold in the house. But in his heart Waythorn was sure of Haskett's single-mindedness; he even guessed in the latter a mild contempt for such advantages as his relation with the Waythorns might offer. Haskett's sincerity of purpose made him invulnerable, and his successor had to accept him as a lien on the property.

Mr. Sellers was sent to Europe to recover from his gout, and Varick's affairs hung on Waythorn's hands. The negotiations were prolonged and complicated; they necessitated frequent conferences between the two men, and the interests of the firm forbade Waythorn's suggesting that his client should transfer his business to another office.

Varick appeared well in the transaction. In moments of relaxation his coarse streak appeared, and Waythorn dreaded his geniality; but in the office he was concise and clear-headed, with a flattering deference to Waythorn's judgment.

Their business relations being so affably established, it would have been absurd for the two men to ignore each other in society. The first time they met in a drawing-room, Varick took up their intercourse in the same easy key, and his hostess's grateful glance obliged Waythorn to respond to it. After that they ran across each other frequently, and one evening at a ball Waythorn, wandering through the remoter rooms, came upon Varick seated beside his wife. She coloured a little, and faltered in what she was saying; but Varick nodded to Waythorn without rising, and the latter strolled on.

In the carriage, on the way home, he broke out nervously: "I didn't know you spoke to Varick."

Her voice trembled a little. "It's the first time—he happened to be standing near me; I didn't know what to do. It's so awkward, meeting everywhere—and he said you had been very kind about some business."

"That's different," said Waythorn.

She paused a moment. "I'll do just as you wish," she returned pliantly. "I thought it would be less awkward to speak to him when we meet."

Her pliancy was beginning to sicken him. Had she really no will of her own—no theory about her relation to these men? She had accepted Haskett—did she mean to accept Varick? It was "less awkward," as she had said, and her instinct was to evade difficulties or to circumvent them. With sudden vividness Waythorn saw how the instinct had developed. She was "as easy as an old shoe"—a shoe that too many feet had worn. Her elasticity was the result of tension in too many different directions. Alice Haskett—Alice Varick—Alice Waythorn—she had been each in turn, and had left hanging to each name a little of her privacy, a little of her personality, a little of the inmost self where the unknown god abides.

"Yes—it's better to speak to Varick," said Waythorn wearily.

5 The winter wore on, and society took advantage of the Waythorns' acceptance of Varick. Harassed hostesses were grateful to them for bridging over a social difficulty, and Mrs. Waythorn was held up as a miracle of good taste. Some experimental spirits could not resist the diversion of throwing Varick and his former wife together, and there were those who thought he found a zest in the propinquity. But Mrs. Waythorn's conduct remained irreproachable. She neither avoided Varick nor sought him out. Even Waythorn could not but admit that she had discovered the solution of the newest social problem.

He had married her without giving much thought to that problem. He had fancied that a woman can shed her past like a man. But now he saw that Alice was bound to hers both by the circumstances which forced her into continued relation with it, and by the traces it had left on her nature. With grim irony Waythorn compared himself to a member of a syndicate. He held so many shares in his wife's personality and his predecessors were his partners in the business. If there had been any element of passion in the transaction he would have felt less deteriorated by it. The fact that Alice took her change of husbands like a change of weather reduced the situation to mediocrity. He could have forgiven her for blunders, for excesses; for resisting Haskett, for yielding to Varick; for anything but her acquiescence and her tact. She reminded him of a juggler tossing knives; but the knives were blunt and she knew they would never cut her.

And then, gradually, habit formed a protecting surface for his sensibilities. If he paid for each day's comfort with the small change of his illusions, he grew daily to value the comfort more and set less store upon the coin. He had drifted into a dulling propinquity with Haskett and Varick and he took refuge in the cheap revenge of satirising the situation. He even began to reckon up the advantages which accrued from it, to ask himself if it were not better to own a third of a wife who knew how to make a man happy than a whole one who had lacked opportunity to acquire the art. For it *was* an art, and made up, like all others, of concessions, eliminations and embellishments; of lights judiciously thrown and shadows skillfully softened. His wife knew exactly how to manage the lights, and he knew exactly to what training she owed her skill. He even tried to trace the source of his obligations, to discriminate between the influences which had combined to produce his domestic happiness: he perceived that Haskett's commonness had made Alice worship good breeding, while Varick's liberal construction of the marriage bond had taught her to value the conjugal virtues; so that he was directly indebted to his predecessors for the devotion which made his life easy if not inspiring.

From this phase he passed into that of complete acceptance. He ceased to satirise himself because time dulled the irony of the situation and the joke lost its humour with its sting. Even the sight of Haskett's hat on the hall table had ceased to touch the springs of epigram. The hat was often seen there now, for it had been decided that it was better for Lily's father to visit her than for the little girl to go to his boarding-house. Waythorn, having acquiesced in this arrangement, had been surprised to find how little difference it made. Haskett was never obtrusive, and the few visitors who met him on the stairs were unaware of his identity. Waythorn did not know how often he saw Alice, but with himself Haskett was seldom in contact.

One afternoon, however, he learned on entering that Lily's father was waiting to see him. In the library he found Haskett occupying a chair in his usual provisional way. Waythorn always felt grateful to him for not leaning back.

"I hope you'll excuse me, Mr. Waythorn," he said rising. "I wanted to see Mrs. Waythorn about Lily, and your man asked me to wait here until she came in."

"Of course," said Waythorn, remembering that a sudden leak had that morning given over the drawing-room to the plumbers.

He opened his cigar-case and held it out to his visitor, and Haskett's acceptance seemed to make a fresh stage in their intercourse. The spring evening was chilly, and Waythorn invited his guest to draw up his chair to the fire. He meant to find an excuse to leave Haskett in a moment; but he was tired and cold, and after all the little man no longer jarred on him.

The two were enclosed in the intimacy of their blended cigar-smoke when the door opened and Varick walked into the room. Waythorn rose abruptly. It was the first time that Varick had come to the house, and the surprise of seeing him, combined with the singular inopportuneness of his arrival, gave a new edge to Waythorn's blunted sensibilities. He stared at his visitor without speaking.

Varick seemed too preoccupied to notice his host's embarrassment.

"My dear fellow," he exclaimed in his most expansive tone, "I must apologise for tumbling in on you in this way, but I was too late to catch you down town, and so I thought—"

He stopped short, catching sight of Haskett, and his sanguine colour deepened to a flush which spread vividly under his scant blond hair. But in a moment he recovered himself and nodded slightly. Haskett returned the bow in silence, and Waythorn was still groping for speech when the footman came in carrying a tea-table.

The intrusion offered a welcome vent to Waythorn's nerves. "What the deuce are you bringing this here for?" he said sharply.

"I beg your pardon, sir, but the plumbers are still in the drawing-room, and Mrs. Waythorn said she would have tea in the library." The footman's perfectly respectful tone implied a reflection on Waythorn's reasonableness.

"Oh, very well," said the latter resignedly, and the footman proceeded to open the folding tea-table and set out its complicated appointments. While this interminable process continued the three men stood motionless, watching it with a fascinated stare, till Waythorn, to break the silence, said to Varick: "Won't you have a cigar?"

He held out the case he had just tendered to Haskett, and Varick helped himself with a smile. Waythorn looked about for a match, and finding none, proffered a light from his own cigar. Haskett, in the background, held his ground mildly, examining his cigar-tip now and then, and stepping forward at the right moment to knock its ashes into the fire.

The footman at last withdrew, and Varick immediately began: "If I could just say half a word to you about this business—"

"Certainly," stammered Waythorn; "in the dining-room—"

But as he placed his hand on the door it opened from without, and his wife appeared on the threshold.

She came in fresh and smiling, in her street dress and hat, shedding a fragrance from the boa which she loosened in advancing.

"Shall we have tea in here, dear?" she began; and then she caught sight of Varick. Her smile deepened, veiling a slight tremor of surprise.

"Why, how do you do?" she said with a distinct note of pleasure.

As she shook hands with Varick she saw Haskett standing behind him. Her smile faded for a moment, but she recalled it quickly, with a scarcely perceptible side-glance at Waythorn.

"How do you do, Mr. Haskett?" she said, and shook hands with him a shade less cordially.

The three men stood awkwardly before her, till Varick, always the most self-possessed, dashed into an explanatory phrase.

"We—I had to see Waythorn a moment on business," he stammered, brick-red from chin to nape.

Haskett stepped forward with his air of mild obstinacy. "I am sorry to intrude; but you appointed five o'clock—" he directed his resigned glance to the time-piece on the mantel.

She swept aside their embarrassment with a charming gesture of hospitality.

"I'm so sorry—I'm always late; but the afternoon was so lovely." She stood drawing off her gloves, propitiatory and graceful, diffusing about her a sense of ease and familiarity in which the situation lost its grotesqueness. "But before talking business," she added brightly, "I'm sure every one wants a cup of tea."

She dropped into her low chair by the tea-table, and the two visitors, as if drawn by her smile, advanced to receive the cups she held out.

She glanced about for Waythorn, and he took the third cup with a laugh.

Dorothy Parker

(1893–1967) Dorothy Parker is best known for her witty, satiric poems and stories about love and hypocrisy in human relations. She was a drama critic for Vanity Fair *and* The New Yorker *and was an active part of New York literary life for many years.*

Big Blonde

1 Hazel Morse was a large, fair woman, of the type that incites some men when they use the word "blonde" to click their tongues and wag their heads roguishly. She prided herself upon her small feet and suffered for her vanity, boxing them in snub-toed, high-heeled slippers of the shortest bearable size. The curious things about her were her hands, strange terminations to the flabby white arms splattered with pale tan spots—long, quivering hands, with deep and convex nails. She should not have disfigured them with little jewels.

She was not a woman given to recollections. At her middle thirties her old days were a blurred and flickering sequence, an imperfect film dealing with the actions of strangers.

In her twenties, after the deferred death of a hazy, widowed mother, she had been employed as a model in a wholesale dress establishment—it was still the day of the big woman, and she was then prettily coloured and erect and high-breasted. Her job was not onerous, and she met numbers of men and spent numbers of evenings with them, laughing at their jokes and telling them she loved their neckties. Men liked her, and she took it for granted that the liking of many men was a desirable thing. Popularity seemed to her to be worth all the work that had to be put into its achievement. Men liked you because you were fun, and when they liked you they took you out, and there you were. So, and successfully, she was fun. She was a good sport. Men liked a good sport.

No other form of diversion, simpler or more complicated, drew her attention.

She never pondered if she might not be better occupied doing something else. Her ideas—or, better, her acceptances—ran right along with those of the other substantially built blondes in whom she found her friends.

When she had been working in the dress establishment some years she met Herbie Morse. He was thin, quick, attractive, with shifting lines about his shiny, brown eyes and a habit of fiercely biting at the skin around his finger-nails. He drank largely; she found that entertaining. Her habitual greeting to him was an allusion to his state of the previous night.

"Oh, what a peach you had," she used to say, through her easy laugh. "I thought I'd die, the way you kept asking the waiter to dance with you."

She liked him immediately upon their meeting. She was enormously amused at his fast, slurred sentences, his interpolations of apt phrases from vaudeville acts and comic strips; she thrilled at the feel of his lean arm tucked firm beneath the sleeve of her coat; she wanted to touch the wet, flat surface of his hair. He was as promptly drawn to her. They were married six weeks after they had met.

She was delighted at the idea of being a bride; coquetted with it, played upon it. Other offers of marriage she had had, and not a few of them, but it happened that they were all from stout, serious men who had visited the dress establishment as buyers; men from Des Moines and Houston and Chicago, and, in her phrase, even funnier places. There was always something immensely comic to her in the thought of living elsewhere than New York. She could not regard as serious proposals that she share a western residence.

She wanted to be married. She was nearing thirty now, and she did not take the years well. She spread and softened, and her darkening hair turned her to inexpert dabblings with peroxide. There were times when she had little flashes of fear about her job. And she had had a couple of thousand evenings of being a good sport among her male acquaintances. She had come to be more conscientious than spontaneous about it.

Herbie earned enough, and they took a little apartment far up-town. There was a Mission-furnished dining-room, with a hanging central light globed in liver-coloured glass; in the living-room were an over-stuffed suite, a Boston fern and a reproduction of the Henner *Magdalene* with the red hair and the blue draperies; the bedroom was in grey enamel and old rose, with Herbie's photograph on Hazel's dressing-table and Hazel's likeness on Herbie's chest of drawers.

She cooked—and she was a good cook—and marketed, and chatted with the delivery boys and the coloured laundress. She loved the flat, she loved her life, she loved Herbie. In the first months of their marriage she gave him all the passion she was ever to know.

She had not realized how tired she was. It was a delight, a new game, a holiday, to give up being a good sport. If her head ached or her arches throbbed she complained piteously, babyishly. If her mood was quiet she did not talk. If tears came to her eyes she let them fall.

She fell readily into the habit of tears during the first year of her marriage. Even in her good-sport days she had been known to weep lavishly and disinterestedly on occasion. Her behaviour at the theatre was a standing joke. She could weep at anything in a play—tiny garments, love, both unrequited and mutual, seduction, purity, faithful servitors, wedlock, the triangle.

"There goes Haze," her friends would say, watching her. "She's off again."

Wedded and relaxed, she poured her tears freely. To her who had laughed so much, crying was delicious. All sorrows became her sorrows; she was Tenderness. She would cry long and softly over newspaper accounts of kidnapped babies, deserted wives, unemployed men, strayed cats, heroic dogs. Even when the paper was no longer before her, her mind revolved upon these things and the drops slipped rhythmically over her plump cheeks.

"Honestly," she would say to Herbie, "all the sadness there is in the world, when you stop to think about it!"

"Yeah," Herbie would say.

She missed nobody. The old crowd, the people who had brought her and Herbie together, dropped from their lives, lingeringly at first. When she thought of this at all, it was only to consider it fitting. This was marriage. This was peace.

But the thing was that Herbie was not amused.

For a time he had enjoyed being alone with her. He found the voluntary isolation novel and sweet. Then it palled, with a ferocious suddenness. It was as if one night, sitting with her in the steam-heated living-room, he would ask no more; and the next night he was through and done with the whole thing.

He became annoyed by her misty melancholies. At first, when he came home to find her softly tired and moody, he kissed her neck and patted her shoulder and begged her to tell her Herbie what was wrong. She loved that. But time slid by, and he found that there was never anything really, personally, the matter.

"Ah, for God's sake," he would say; "crabbing again. All right, sit here and crab your head off. I'm going out."

And he would slam out of the flat and come back late, and drunk.

She was completely bewildered by what happened to their marriage. First they were lovers; and then, it seemed without transition, they were enemies. She never understood it.

There were longer and longer intervals between his leaving his office and his arrival at the apartment. She went through agonies of picturing him run over and bleeding, dead and covered with a sheet. Then she lost her fears for his safety and grew sullen and wounded. When a person wanted to be with a person he came as soon as possible. She desperately wanted him to want to be with her; her own hours only marked the time till he would come. It was often nearly nine o'clock before he came home to dinner. Always he had had many drinks, and their effect would die in him, leaving him loud and querulous, and bristling for affronts.

He was too nervous, he said, to sit and do nothing for an evening. He boasted, probably not in all truth, that he had never read a book in his life.

"What am I expected to do—sit around this dump on my tail all night?" he would ask rhetorically. And again he would slam out.

She did not know what to do. She could not manage him. She could not meet him.

She fought him furiously. A terrific domesticity had come upon her, and she would bite and scratch to guard it. She wanted what she called "a nice home." She wanted a sober, tender husband, prompt at dinner, punctual at work. She wanted sweet, comforting evenings. The idea of intimacy with other men was terrible to her; the thought that Herbie might be seeking entertainment in other women set her frantic.

It seemed to her that almost everything she read—novels from the drug-store lending library, magazine stories, women's pages in the papers— dealt with wives who lost their husbands' love. She could bear those, however, better than accounts of neat, companionable marriage and living happily ever after.

She was frightened. Several times when Herbie came home in the evening he found her determinedly dressed—she had had to alter those of her clothes that were not new to make them fasten—and rouged.

"Let's go wild tonight; what do you say?" she would hail him. "A person's got lots of time to hang around and do nothing when they're dead."

So they would go out, to chop-houses and the less expensive cabarets. But it turned out badly. She could no longer find amusement in watching Herbie drink. She could not laugh at his whimsicalities, she was so tensely counting his indulgences. And she was unable to keep back her remonstrances—"Ah, come on, Herb, you've had enough, haven't you? You'll feel something terrible in the morning."

He would be immediately enraged. All right, crab; crab, crab, crab, crab, that was all she ever did. What a lousy sport *she* was! There would be scenes, and one or the other of them would rise and stalk out in fury.

She could not recall the definite day that she started drinking herself. There was nothing separate about her days. Like drops upon a window-pane, they ran together and trickled away. She had been married six months; then a year; then three years.

She had never needed to drink formerly. She could sit for most of a night at a table where the others were imbibing earnestly and never droop in looks or spirits, nor be bored by the doings of those about her. If she took a cocktail it was so unusual as to cause twenty minutes or so of jocular comment. But now anguish was in her. Frequently, after a quarrel, Herbie would stay out for the night, and she could not learn from him where the time had been spent. Her heart felt tight and sore in her breast, and her mind turned like an electric fan.

She hated the taste of liquor. Gin, plain or in mixtures, made her promptly sick. After experiment she found that Scotch whisky was best for her. She took it without water, because that was the quickest way to its effect.

Herbie pressed it on her. He was glad to see her drink. They both felt it might restore her high spirits, and their good times together might again be possible.

"Atta girl," he would approve her. "Let's see you get boiled, baby."

But it brought them no nearer. When she drank with him there would be a little while of gaiety, and then, strangely without beginning, they would be in a wild quarrel. They would wake in the morning not sure what it had all been about, foggy as to what had been said and done, but each deeply injured and bitterly resentful. There would be days of vengeful silence.

There had been a time when they had made up their quarrels, usually in bed. There would be kisses and little names and assurances of fresh starts. . . . "Oh, it's going to be great now, Herb. We'll have swell times. I was a crab. I guess I must have been tired. But everything's going to be swell. You'll see."

Now there were no gentle reconciliations. They resumed friendly relations only in the brief magnanimity caused by liquor, before more liquor drew them into new battles. The scenes became more violent. There were shouted invectives and pushes, and sometimes sharp slaps. Once she had a black eye. Herbie was horrified next day at sight of it. He did not go to work; he followed her about, suggesting remedies and heaping dark blame on himself. But after they had had a few drinks—"to pull themselves together"—she made so many wistful references to her bruise that he shouted at her and rushed out, and was gone for two days.

Each time he left the place in a rage he threatened never to come back. She did not believe him, nor did she consider separation. Somewhere in her head or her heart was the lazy, nebulous hope that things would change and she and Herbie settle suddenly into soothing married life. Here were her home, her furniture, her husband, her station. She summoned no alternatives.

She could no longer bustle and potter. She had no more vicarious tears: the hot drops she shed were for herself. She walked ceaselessly about the rooms, her thoughts running mechanically round and round Herbie. In those days began the hatred of being alone that she was never to overcome. You could be by yourself when things were all right, but when you were blue you got the howling horrors.

She commenced drinking alone, little, short drinks all through the day. It was only with Herbie that alcohol made her nervous and quick in offence. Alone, it blurred sharp things for her. She lived in a haze of it. Her life took on a dream-like quality. Nothing was astonishing.

A Mrs Martin moved into the flat across the hall. She was a great blonde woman of forty, a promise in looks of what Mrs Morse was to be. They made acquaintance; quickly became inseparable. Mrs Morse spent her days in the opposite apartment. They drank together to brace themselves after the drinks of the nights before.

She never confided her troubles about Herbie to Mrs Martin. The subject was too bewildering to her to find comfort in talk. She let it be assumed that her husband's business kept him much away. It was not regarded as important; husbands, as such, played but shadowy parts in Mrs Martin's circle.

Mrs Martin had no visible spouse; you were left to decide for yourself whether he was or was not dead. She had an admirer, Joe, who came to see her almost nightly. Often he brought several friends with him—"The Boys," they were called. The Boys were big, red, good-humoured men, perhaps forty-five, perhaps fifty. Mrs Morse was glad of invitations to join the parties—Herbie was scarcely ever at home at night now. If he did come home, she did not visit Mrs Martin. An evening alone with Herbie meant inevitably a quarrel, yet she would stay with him. There was always her thin and wordless idea that, maybe, this night, things would begin to be all right.

The Boys brought plenty of liquor along with them whenever they came to Mrs Martin's. Drinking with them, Mrs Morse became lively and good-natured and audacious. She was quickly popular. When she had drunk enough to cloud her most recent battle with Herbie she was excited by their approbation. Crab, was she? Rotten sport, was she? Well, there were some that thought different.

Ed was one of The Boys. He lived in Utica—had "his own business" there was the awed report—but he came to New York almost every week. He was married.

He showed Mrs Morse the then current photographs of Junior and Sister, and she praised them abundantly and sincerely. Soon it was accepted by the others that Ed was her particular friend.

He staked her when they all played poker; sat next her and occasionally rubbed his knee against hers during the game. She was rather lucky. Frequently she went home with a twenty-dollar bill or a ten-dollar bill or a handful of crumpled dollars. She was glad of them. Herbie was getting, in her words, something awful about money. To ask him for it brought an instant row.

"What the hell do you do with it?" he would say. "Shoot it all on Scotch?"

"I try to run this house half-way decent," she would retort. "Never thought of that, did you? Oh no, his lordship couldn't be bothered with that."

Again, she could not find a definite day to fix the beginning of Ed's proprietorship. It became his custom to kiss her on the mouth when he came in, as well as for farewell, and he gave her little quick kisses of approval all through the evening. She liked this rather more than she disliked it. She never thought of his kisses when she was not with him.

He would run his hand lingeringly over her back and shoulders.

"Some dizzy blonde, eh?" he would say. "Some doll."

One afternoon she came home from Mrs Martin's to find Herbie in the bedroom. He had been away for several nights, evidently on a prolonged drinking-bout. His face was grey, his hands jerked as if they were on wires. On the bed were two old suitcases, packed high. Only her photograph remained on his bureau, and the wide doors of his closet disclosed nothing but coat-hangers.

"I'm blowing," he said. "I'm through with the whole works. I got a job in Detroit."

She sat down on the edge of the bed. She had drunk much the night before, and the four Scotches she had had with Mrs Martin had only increased her fogginess.

"Good job?" she said.

"Oh, yeah," he said. "Looks all right."

He closed a suitcase with difficulty, swearing at it in whispers.

"There's some dough in the bank," he said. "The bank-book's in your top drawer. You can have the furniture and stuff."

He looked at her, and his forehead twitched.

"God damn it, I'm through, I'm telling you," he cried. "I'm through."

"All right, all right," she said. "I heard you, didn't I?"

She saw him as if he were at one end of a canyon and she at the other. Her head was beginning to ache bumpingly and her voice had a dreary, tiresome tone. She could not have raised it.

"Like a drink before you go?" she asked.

Again he looked at her, and a corner of his mouth jerked up.

"Cock-eyed again for a change, aren't you?" he said. "That's nice. Sure, get a couple of shots, will you?"

She went to the pantry, mixed him a stiff highball, poured herself a couple of inches of whisky, and drank it. Then she gave herself another portion and brought the glasses into the bedroom.

He had strapped both suitcases and had put on his hat and overcoat. He took his highball.

"Well," he said, and he gave a sudden, uncertain laugh. "Here's mud in your eye."

"Mud in your eye," she said.

They drank. He put down his glass and took up the heavy suitcases.

"Got to make a train around six," he said.

She followed him down the hall. There was a song, a song that Mrs Martin played doggedly on the phonograph, running loudly through her mind. She had never liked the thing:

> Night and daytime,
> Always playtime.
> Ain't we got fun?

At the door he put down the bags and faced her.

"Well," he said. "Well, take care of yourself. You'll be all right, will you?"

"Oh, sure," she said.

He opened the door, then came back to her, holding out his hand.

"'Bye, Haze," he said. "Good luck to you."

She took his hand and shook it.

"Pardon my wet glove," she said.

When the door had closed behind him she went back to the pantry.

She was flushed and lively when she went in to Mrs Martin's that evening. The Boys were there, Ed among them. He was glad to be in town, frisky and loud and full of jokes. But she spoke quietly to him for a minute.

"Herbie blew to-day," she said. "Going to live out west."

"That so?" he said. He looked at her and played with the fountain-pen clipped to his waistcoat-pocket.

"Think he's gone for good, do you?" he asked.

"Yeah," she said. "I know he is. I know. Yeah."

"You going to live on across the hall just the same?" he said. "Know what you're going to do?"

"Gee, I don't know," she said. "I don't give much of a damn."

"Oh, come on, that's no way to talk," he told her. "What you need—you need a little snifter. How about it?"

"Yeah," she said. "Just straight."

She won forty-three dollars at poker. When the game broke up, Ed took her back to her apartment.

"Got a little kiss for me?" he asked.

He wrapped her in his big arms and kissed her violently. She was entirely passive. He held her away and looked at her.

"Little tight, honey?" he asked anxiously. "Not going to be sick, are you?"

"Me?" she said. "I'm swell."

2 When Ed left in the morning he took her photograph with him. He said he wanted her picture to look at, up in Utica.

"You can have that one on the bureau," she said.

She put Herbie's picture in a drawer, out of her sight. When she could look at it, she meant to tear it up. She was fairly successful in keeping her mind from racing around him. Whisky slowed it for her. She was almost peaceful in her mist.

She accepted her relationship with Ed without question or enthusiasm. When he was away she seldom thought definitely of him. He was good to her; he gave her frequent presents and a regular allowance. She was even able to save. She did not plan ahead of any day, but her wants were few, and you might as well put money in the bank as have it lying around.

When the lease of her apartment neared its end it was Ed who suggested moving. His friendship with Mrs Martin and Joe had become strained over a dispute at poker; a feud was impending.

"Let's get the hell out of here," Ed said. "What I want you to have is a place near the Grand Central. Make it easier for me."

So she took a little flat in the Forties. A coloured maid came in every day to clean and to make coffee for her—she was "through with that housekeeping stuff," she said, and Ed, twenty years married to a passionately domestic woman, admired this romantic uselessness and felt doubly a man of the world in abetting it.

The coffee was all she had until she went out to dinner, but alcohol kept her fat. Prohibition she regarded only as a basis for jokes. You could always get all you wanted. She was never noticeably drunk and seldom nearly sober. It required a larger daily allowance to keep her misty-minded. Too little, and she was achingly melancholy.

Ed brought her to Jimmy's. He was proud, with the pride of the transient who would be mistaken for a native, in his knowledge of small, recent restaurants occupying the lower floors of shabby brown-stone houses; places where, upon mentioning the name of an habitué friend, might be obtained strange whisky and fresh gin in many of their ramifications. Jimmy's place was the favourite of his acquaintances.

There, through Ed, Mrs Morse met many men and women, formed quick friendships. The men often took her out when Ed was in Utica. He was proud of her popularity.

She fell into the habit of going to Jimmy's alone when she had no engagement. She was certain to meet some people she knew, and join them. It was a club for her friends, both men and women.

The women at Jimmy's looked remarkably alike, and this was curious, for, through feuds, removals and opportunities of more profitable contacts the personnel of the group changed constantly. Yet always the newcomers resembled those whom they replaced. They were all big women and stout, broad of shoulder and abundantly breasted, with faces thickly clothed in soft, high-coloured flesh. They laughed loud and often, showing opaque and lustreless teeth, like squares of crockery. There was about them the health of the big, yet a slight unwholesome suggestion of stubborn preservation. They might have been thirty-six or forty-five, or anywhere between.

They composed their titles of their own first names with their husband's surnames—Mrs Florence Miller, Mrs Vera Riley, Mrs Lilian Block. This gave at the same time the solidity of marriage and the glamour of freedom. Yet only one or two were actually divorced. Most of them never referred to their dimmed spouses; some, a shorter time separate, described them in terms of great bio-logical interest. Several were mothers, each of an only child—a boy at school somewhere, or a girl being cared for by a grandmother. Often, well on towards morning, there would be displays of kodak portraits and of tears.

They were comfortable women, cordial and friendly and irrepressibly matronly. Theirs was the quality of ease. Become fatalistic, especially about money matters, they were unworried. Whenever their funds dropped alarmingly, a new donor appeared; this had always happened. The aim of each was to have one man, permanently, to pay all her bills, in return for which she would have immediately given up other admirers and probably would have become exceed-ingly fond of him; for the affections of all of them were, by now, unexacting, tranquil, and easily arranged. This end, however, grew increasingly difficult yearly. Mrs Morse was regarded as fortunate.

Ed had a good year, increased her allowance and gave her a sealskin coat. But she had to be careful of her moods with him. He insisted upon gaiety. He would not listen to admissions of aches or weariness.

"Hey, listen," he would say, "I got worries of my own, and plenty. Nobody wants to hear other people's troubles, sweetie. What you got to do, you got to be a sport and forget it. See? Well, slip us a little smile, then. That's my girl."

She never had enough interest to quarrel with him as she had with Herbie, but she wanted the privilege of occasional admitted sadness. It was strange. The other women she saw did not have to fight their moods. There was Mrs Florence Miller who got regular crying jags, and the men sought only to cheer and comfort her. The others spent whole evenings in grieved recitals of worries and ills; their escorts paid them deep sympathy. But she was instantly undesirable when she was low in spirits. Once, at Jimmy's, when she could not make herself lively, Ed had walked out and left her.

"Why the hell don't you stay home and not go spoiling everybody's evening?" he had roared.

Even her slightest acquaintances seemed irritated if she were not conspic-uously light-hearted.

"What's the matter with you, anyway?" they would say. "Be your age, why don't you? Have a little drink and snap out of it."

When her relationship with Ed had continued nearly three years he moved to Florida to live. He hated leaving her; he gave her a large cheque and some shares of a sound stock, and his pale eyes were wet when he said good-bye. She did not miss him. He came to New York infrequently, perhaps two or three times a year, and hurried directly from the train to see her. She was always pleased to have him come and never sorry to see him go.

Charley, an acquaintance of Ed's that she had met at Jimmy's, had long admired her. He had always made opportunities of touching her and leaning close to talk to her. He asked repeatedly of all their friends if they had ever heard such a fine laugh as she had. After Ed left Charley became the main figure in her life. She classified him and spoke of him as "not so bad." There was nearly a year of Charley; then she divided her time between him and Sydney, another frequenter of Jimmy's; then Charley slipped away altogether.

Sydney was a little, brightly dressed, clever Jew. She was perhaps nearest contentment with him. He amused her always; her laughter was not forced.

He admired her completely. Her softness and size delighted him. And he thought she was great, he often told her, because she kept gay and lively when she was drunk.

"Once I had a gal," he said, "used to try to throw herself out of the window every time she got a can on. Jee-*zuss,*" he added feelingly.

Then Sydney married a rich and watchful bride, and then there was Billy. No—after Sydney came Ferd, then Billy. In her haze she never recalled how men entered her life and left it. There were no surprises. She had no thrill at their advent nor woe at their departure. She seemed to be always able to attract men. There was never another as rich as Ed, but they were all generous to her, in their means.

Once she had news of Herbie. She met Mrs Martin dining at Jimmy's, and the old friendship was vigorously renewed. The still admiring Joe, while on a business trip, had seen Herbie. He was settled in Chicago, he looked fine, he was living with some woman—seemed to be crazy about her. Mrs Morse had been drinking vastly that day. She took the news with mild interest, as one hearing of the sex peccadilloes of somebody whose name is, after a moment's groping, familiar.

"Must be damn' near seven years since I saw him," she commented. "Gee. Seven years."

More and more her days lost their individuality. She never knew dates, nor was sure of the day of the week.

"My God, was that a year ago?" she would exclaim, when an event was recalled in conversation.

She was tired so much of the time. Tired and blue. Almost everything could give her the blues. Those old horses she saw on Sixth Avenue—struggling and slipping along the car-tracks, or standing at the curb, their heads dropped level with their worn knees. The tightly stored tears would squeeze from her eyes as she teetered past on her aching feet, in the stubby, champagne-coloured slippers.

The thought of death came and stayed with her and lent her a sort of drowsy cheer. It would be nice, nice and restful, to be dead.

There was no settled, shocked moment when she first thought of killing herself; it seemed to her as if the idea had always been with her. She pounced upon all the accounts of suicides in the newspapers. There was an epidemic of self-killings—or maybe it was just that she searched for the stories of them so eagerly that she found many. To read of them roused reassurance in her; she felt a cosy solidarity with the big company of the voluntary dead.

She slept, aided by whisky, till deep into the afternoons, then lay abed, a bottle and glass at her hand, until it was time to dress to go out for dinner. She was beginning to feel towards alcohol a little puzzled distrust, as toward an old friend who has refused a simple favour. Whisky could still soothe her for most of the time, but there were sudden, inexplicable moments when the cloud fell treacherously away from her, and she was sawn by the sorrow and bewilderment and nuisance of all living. She played voluptuously with the thought of cool, sleepy retreat. She had never been troubled by religious belief and no vision of an after-life intimidated her. She dreamed by day of never again putting on tight shoes, of never having to laugh and listen and admire, of never more being a good sport. Never.

But how would you do it? It made her sick to think of jumping from heights. She could not stand a gun. At the theatre, if one of the actors drew a revolver, she crammed her fingers into her ears and could not even look at the stage until after the shot had been fired. There was no gas in her flat. She looked long at the bright blue veins in her slim wrists—a cut with a razor blade and there you'd be. But it would hurt, hurt like hell, and there would be blood to see. Poison—something tasteless and quick and painless—was the thing. But they wouldn't sell it to you in drugstores, because of the law.

She had few other thoughts.

There was a new man now—Art. He was short and fat and exacting, and hard on her patience when he was drunk. But there had been only occasionals for some time before him and she was glad of a little stability. Also, Art must be away for weeks at a stretch, selling silks, and that was restful. She was convincingly gay with him, though the effort shook her.

"The best sport in the world," he would murmur, deep in her neck. "The best sport in the world."

One night, when he had taken her to Jimmy's, she went into the dressing-room with Mrs Florence Miller. There, while designing curly mouths on their faces, with lip-rouge, they compared experiences of insomnia.

"Honestly," Mrs Morse said, "I wouldn't close an eye if I didn't go to bed full of Scotch. I lie there and toss and turn and toss and turn. Blue! Does a person get blue lying awake that way!"

"Say, listen, Hazel," Mrs Miller said impressively, "I'm telling you I'd be awake for a year if I didn't take veronal. That stuff makes you sleep like a fool."

"Isn't it poison, or something?" Mrs Morse asked.

"Oh, you take too much and you're out for the count," said Mrs Miller. "I just take five grains—they come in tablets. I'd be scared to fool around with it. But five grains and you cork off pretty."

"Can you get it anywhere?" Mrs Morse felt superbly Machiavellian.

"Get all you want in Jersey," said Mrs Miller. "They won't give it to you here without you have a doctor's prescription. Finished? We'd better go back and see what the boys are doing."

That night Art left Mrs Morse at the door of her apartment; his mother was in town. Mrs Morse was still sober, and it happened that there was no whisky left in her cupboard. She lay in bed, looking up at the black ceiling.

She rose early, for her, and went to New Jersey. She had never taken the tube, and did not understand it. So she went to the Pennsylvania station and bought a railroad ticket to Newark. She thought of nothing in particular on the trip out. She looked at the uninspired hats of the women about her and gazed through the smeared window at the flat, gritty scene.

In Newark, in the first drug-store she came to, she asked for a tin of talcum powder, a nail-brush and a box of veronal tablets. The powder and the brush were to make the hypnotic seem also a casual need.

The clerk was entirely unconcerned. "We only keep them in bottles," he said, and wrapped up for her a little glass vial containing ten white tablets, stacked one on another.

She went to another drug-store and bought a face-cloth, an orange-wood stick and a bottle of veronal tablets. This clerk also was uninterested.

"Well, I guess I got enough to kill an ox," she thought, and went back to the station.

At home she put the little vials in the drawer of her dressing-table and stood looking at them with a dreamy tenderness. "There they are, God bless them," she said, and she kissed her finger-tip and touched each bottle.

The coloured maid was busy in the living-room.

"Hey, Nettie," Mrs Morse called. "Be an angel, will you? Run around to Jimmy's and get me a quart of Scotch."

She hummed while she awaited the girl's return.

During the next few days whisky ministered to her as tenderly as it had done when she first turned to its aid. Alone, she was soothed and vague, at Jimmy's she was the gayest of the groups. Art was delighted with her.

Then, one night, she had an appointment to meet Art at Jimmy's for an early dinner. He was to leave afterward on a business excursion, to be away for a week. Mrs Morse had been drinking all the afternoon; while she dressed to go out she felt herself rising pleasurably from drowsiness to high spirits. But as she came out into the street the effects of the whisky deserted her completely and she was filled with a slow, grinding wretchedness, so horrible that she stood swaying on the pavement, unable for a moment to move forward. It was a grey night, with spurts of mean, thin snow, and the streets shone with dark ice. As she slowly crossed Sixth Avenue, consciously dragging one foot past the other, a big, scarred horse, pulling a rickety express-wagon, crashed to his knees before her. The driver swore and screamed and lashed the beast insanely, bringing the whip back over his shoulder for every blow, while the horse struggled to get a footing on the slippery asphalt. A group gathered and watched with interest.

Art was waiting when Mrs Morse reached Jimmy's.

"What's the matter with you, for God's sake?" was his greeting to her.

"I saw a horse," she said. "Gee, I—a person feels sorry for horses. I—it isn't just horses. Everything's kind of terrible, isn't it? I can't help getting sunk."

"Ah, sunk, me eye," he said. "What's the idea of all the bellyaching? What have you got to be sunk about?"

"I can't help it," she said.

"Ah, help it, me eye," he said. "Pull yourself together, will you? Come on and sit down, and take that face off you."

She drank industriously and she tried hard but she could not overcome her melancholy. Others joined them and commented on her gloom and she could do no more for them than smile weakly. She made little dabs at her eyes with her handkerchief, trying to time her movements so they would be unnoticed, but several times Art caught her, and scowled and shifted impatiently in his chair.

When it was time for him to go to his train she said she would leave too, and go home.

"And not a bad idea, either," he said. "See if you can't sleep yourself out of it. I'll see you Thursday. For God's sake try and cheer up by then, will you?"

"Yeah," she said. "I will."

In her bedroom she undressed, with a tense speed wholly unlike her usual slow uncertainty. She put on her nightgown, took off her hair-net and passed the comb quickly through her dry, vari-coloured hair. Then she took the two little vials from the drawer and carried them into the bathroom. The splintering misery had gone from her and she felt the quick excitement of one who is about to receive an anticipated gift.

She uncorked the vials, filled a glass with water, and stood before the mirror, a tablet between her fingers. Suddenly she bowed graciously to her reflection and raised the glass to it.

"Well, here's mud in your eye," she said.

The tablets were unpleasant to take, dry and powdery and sticking obstinately half-way down her throat. It took her a long time to swallow all twenty of them. She stood watching her reflection with deep, impersonal interest, studying the movements of the gulping throat. Once more she spoke aloud.

" 'For God's sake try and cheer up by Thursday, will you?' " she said. "Well, you know what he can do. He and the whole lot of them."

She had no idea how quickly to expect effect from the veronal. When she had taken the last tablet she stood uncertainly, wondering, still with a courteous, vicarious interest, if death would strike her down then and there. She felt in no way strange, save for a slight stirring of sickness from the effort of swallowing the tablets, nor did her refelected face look at all different. It would not be immediate, then; it might even take an hour or so.

She stretched her arms high and gave a vast yawn.

"Guess I'll go to bed," she said. "Gee, I'm nearly dead."

That struck her as comic, and she turned out the bathroom light and went in and laid herself down in her bed, chuckling softly all the time.

"Gee, I'm nearly dead," she quoted. "That's a hot one!"

3 Nettie, the coloured maid, came in late the next afternoon to clean the apartment, and found Mrs Morse in her bed. But then, that was not unusual. Usually, though, the sounds of cleaning waked her, and she did not like to wake up. Nettie, an agreeable girl, had learned to move softly about her work.

But when she had done the living-room, and stolen in to tidy the little square bedroom, she could not avoid a tiny clatter as she arranged the objects on the dressing-table. Instinctively she glanced over her shoulder at the sleeper, and, without warning, a sickly uneasiness crept over her. She came to the bed and stared down at the woman lying there.

Mrs Morse lay on her back, one flabby, white arm flung up, the wrist against her forehead. Her stiff hair hung untenderly along her face. The bed-covers were pushed down, exposing a deep square of soft neck and a pink nightgown, its fabric worn uneven by many launderings; her great breasts, freed from their tight confiner, sagged beneath her armpits. Now and then she made knotted, snoring sounds, and from the corner of her opened mouth to the blurred turn of her jaw ran a lane of crusted spittle.

"Mis' Morse," Nettie called. "Oh, Mis' Morse! It's terrible late."

Mrs Morse made no move.

"Mis' Morse," said Nettie. "Look, Mis' Morse. How'm I goin' get this bed made?"

Panic sprang upon the girl. She shook the woman's hot shoulder.

"Ah, wake up, will yuh?" she whined. "Ah, please wake up."

Suddenly the girl turned and ran out into the hall to the elevator-door, keeping her thumb firm on the black, shiny button until the elderly car and its negro attendant stood before her. She poured a jumble of words over the boy, and led him back to the apartment. He tiptoed creakingly in to the bedside; first gingerly, then so lustily that he left marks in the soft flesh, he prodded the unconscious woman.

"Hey, there!" he cried, and listened intently, as for an echo.

"Jeez. Out like a light," he commented.

At his interest in the spectacle, Nettie's panic left her. Importance was big in both of them. They talked in quick, unfinished whispers, and it was the boy's suggestion that he fetch the young doctor who lived on the ground floor. Nettie hurried along with him. They looked forward to the limelit moment of breaking their news of something untoward, something pleasurably unpleasant. Mrs Morse had become the medium of drama. With no ill wish to her, they hoped that her state was serious, that she would not let them down by being awake and normal on their return. A little fear of this determined them to make the most, to the doctor, of her present condition. "Matter of life and death" returned to Nettie from her thin store of reading. She considered startling the doctor with the phrase.

The doctor was in, and none too pleased at interruption. He wore a yellow-and-blue striped dressing-gown, and he was lying on his sofa, laughing with a dark girl—her face scaly with inexpensive powder—who perched on the arm. Half-emptied highball glasses stood beside them, and her coat and hat were neatly hung up with the comfortable implication of a long stay.

"Always something," the doctor grumbled. "Couldn't let anybody alone after a hard day." But he put some bottles and instruments into a case, changed his dressing-gown for his coat, and started out with the negroes.

"Snap it up there, big boy," the girl called after him. "Don't be all night."

The doctor strode loudly into Mrs Morse's flat and on to the bedroom, Nettie and the boy right behind him. Mrs Morse had not moved; her sleep was as deep, but soundless now. The doctor looked sharply at her, then plunged his thumbs into the lidded pits above her eyeballs and threw his weight upon them. A high, sickened cry broke from Nettie.

"Look like he tryin' to push her right on th'ough the bed," said the boy. He chuckled.

Mrs Morse gave no sign under the pressure. Abruptly the doctor abandoned it, and with one quick movement swept the covers down to the foot of the bed. With another he flung her nightgown back and lifted the thick, white legs, cross-hatched with blocks of tiny, iris-coloured veins. He pinched them repeatedly, with long, cruel nips, back of the knees. She did not awaken.

"What's she been drinking?" he asked Nettie, over his shoulder.

With the certain celerity of one who knows just where to lay hands on a thing, Nettie went into the bathroom, bound for the cupboard where Mrs Morse kept her whisky. But she stopped at the sight of the two vials, with their red and white labels, lying before the mirror. She brought them to the doctor.

"Oh, for the Lord Almighty's sweet sake!" he said. He dropped Mrs Morse's legs and pushed them impatiently across the bed. "What did she want to go taking that tripe for? Rotten yellow trick, that's what a thing like that is. Now we'll have to pump her out, and all that stuff. Nuisance, a thing like that is; that's what it amounts to. Here, George, take me down in the elevator. You wait here, maid. She won't do anything."

"She won't die on me, will she?" cried Nettie.

"No," said the doctor. "God, no. You couldn't kill her with an axe."

4 After two days, Mrs Morse came back to consciousness, dazed at first, then with a comprehension that brought with it the slow, saturating wretchedness.

"Oh, Lord; oh, Lord," she moaned, and tears for herself and for life striped her cheeks.

Nettie came in at the sound. For two days she had done the ugly, incessant tasks in the nursing of the unconscious, for two nights she had caught broken bits of sleep on the living-room couch. She looked coldly at the big, blown woman in the bed.

"What you been tryin' to do, Mis' Morse?" she said. "What kine o' work is that, takin' all that stuff?"

"Oh, Lord," moaned Mrs Morse again, and she tried to cover her eyes with her arms. But the joints felt stiff and brittle, and she cried out at their ache.

"Tha's no way to ack, takin' them pills," said Nettie. "You can thank you' stars you heah at all. How you feel now?"

"Oh, I feel great," said Mrs Morse. "Swell, I feel."

Her hot, painful tears fell as if they would never stop.

"Tha's no way to take on, cryin' like that," Nettie said. "After what you done. The doctor, he says he could have you arrested, doin' a thing like that. He was fit to be tied, here."

"Why couldn't he let me alone?" wailed Mrs Morse. "Why the hell couldn't he have?"

"Tha's terr'ble, Mis' Morse, swearin' an' talkin' like that," said Nettie, "after what people done for you. Here I ain' had no sleep at all for two nights, an' I had to give up goin' out to my other ladies!"

"Oh, I'm sorry, Nettie," she said. "You're a peach. I'm sorry I've given you so much trouble. I couldn't help it. I just got sunk. Didn't you ever feel like doing it? When everything looks just lousy to you?"

"I wouldn't think o' no such thing," declared Nettie. "You got to cheer up. Tha's what you got to do. Everybody's got their troubles."

"Yeah," said Mrs Morse. "I know."

"Come, a pretty picture card for you," Nettie said. "Maybe that will cheer you up."

She handed Mrs Morse a post-card. Mrs Morse had to cover one eye with her hand in order to read the message; her eyes were not yet focusing correctly.

It was from Art. On the back of a view of the Detroit Athletic Club he had written: "Greeting and salutations. Hope you have lost that gloom. Cheer up and don't take any rubber nickels. See you on Thursday."

She dropped the card to the floor. Misery crushed her as if she were between great smooth stones. There passed before her a slow, slow pageant of days spent lying in her flat, of evenings at Jimmy's being a good sport, making herself laugh and coo at Art and other Arts; she saw a long parade of weary horses and shivering beggars and all beaten, driven, stumbling things. Her feet throbbed as if she had crammed them into the stubby champagne-coloured slippers. Her heart seemed to swell and harden.

"Nettie," she cried, "for heaven's sake pour me a drink, will you?"

The maid looked doubtful.

"Now you know, Mis' Morse," she said, "You been near daid. I don' know if the doctor he let you drink nothin' yet."

"Oh, never mind him," she said. "You get me one, and bring in the bottle. Take one yourself."

"Well," said Nettie.

She poured them each a drink, deferentially leaving hers in the bathroom to be taken in solitude, and brought Mrs Morse's glass in to her.

Mrs Morse looked into the liquor and shuddered back from its odour. Maybe it would help. Maybe, when you had been knocked cold for a few days, your very first drink would give you a lift. Maybe whisky would be her friend again. She prayed without addressing a God, without knowing a God. Oh, please, please, let her be able to get drunk, please keep her always drunk.

She lifted the glass.

"Thanks, Nettie," she said. "Here's mud in your eye."

The maid giggled. "Tha's the way, Mis' Morse," she said. "You cheer up, now."

"Yeah," said Mrs Morse. "Sure."

Sherwood Anderson

*(1876–1941) Sherwood Anderson is
an important American novelist
and short story writer. In* Winesburg,
Ohio *and other short story collections
he probed beneath the surface of
smalltown life, often focusing on
sexual frustration as the cause
of wasted lives. In* Perhaps Women
*(1931), an essay on the evils of
industrialization, he wrote about
women as men's hope of salvation in a
technological society.*

Death in the Woods

1 She was an old woman and lived on a farm near the town in which I lived.
All country and small-town people have seen such old women, but no one knows
much about them. Such an old woman comes into town driving an old worn-
out horse or she comes afoot carrying a basket. She may own a few hens and
have eggs to sell. She brings them in a basket and takes them to a grocer. There
she trades them in. She gets some salt pork and some beans. Then she gets a
pound or two of sugar and some flour.

Afterwards she goes to the butcher's and asks for some dog-meat. She may
spend ten or fifteen cents, but when she does she asks for something. Formerly
the butchers gave liver to any one who wanted to carry it away. In our family
we were always having it. Once one of my brothers got a whole cow's liver
at the slaughter-house near the fairgrounds in our town. We had it until we were
sick of it. It never cost a cent. I have hated the thought of it ever since.

The old farm woman got some liver and a soup-bone. She never visited with
any one, and as soon as she got what she wanted she lit out for home. It made
quite a load for such an old body. No one gave her a lift. People drive right
down a road and never notice an old woman like that.

There was such an old woman who used to come into town past our house
one Summer and Fall when I was a young boy and was sick with what was
called inflammatory rheumatism. She went home later carrying a heavy pack on
her back. Two or three large gaunt-looking dogs followed at her heels.

The old woman was nothing special. She was one of the nameless ones that hardly any one knows, but she got into my thoughts. I have just suddenly now, after all these years, remembered her and what happened. It is a story. Her name was Grimes, and she lived with her husband and son in a small unpainted house on the bank of a small creek four miles from town.

The husband and son were a tough lot. Although the son was but twenty-one, he had already served a term in jail. It was whispered about that the woman's husband stole horses and ran them off to some other county. Now and then, when a horse turned up missing, the man had also disappeared. No one ever caught him. Once, when I was loafing at Tom Whitehead's livery-barn, the man came there and sat on the bench in front. Two or three other men were there, but no one spoke to him. He sat for a few minutes and then got up and went away. When he was leaving he turned around and stared at the men. There was a look of defiance in his eyes. "Well, I have tried to be friendly. You don't want to talk to me. It has been so wherever I have gone in this town. If, some day, one of your fine horses turns up missing, well, then what?" He did not say anything actually. "I'd like to bust one of you on the jaw," was about what his eyes said. I remember how the look in his eyes made me shiver.

The old man belonged to a family that had had money once. His name was Jake Grimes. It all comes back clearly now. His father, John Grimes, had owned a sawmill when the country was new, and had made money. Then he got to drinking and running after women. When he died there wasn't much left.

Jake blew in the rest. Pretty soon there wasn't any more lumber to cut and his land was nearly all gone.

He got his wife off a German farmer, for whom he went to work one June day in the wheat harvest. She was a young thing then and scared to death. You see, the farmer was up to something with the girl—she was, I think, a bound girl and his wife had her suspicions. She took it out on the girl when the man wasn't around. Then, when the wife had to go off to town for supplies, the farmer got after her. She told young Jake that nothing really ever happened, but he didn't know whether to believe it or not.

He got her pretty easy himself, the first time he was out with her. He wouldn't have married her if the German farmer hadn't tried to tell him where to get off. He got her to go riding with him in his buggy one night when he was threshing on the place, and then he came for her the next Sunday night.

She managed to get out of the house without her employer's seeing, but when she was getting into the buggy he showed up. It was almost dark, and he just popped up suddenly at the horse's head. He grabbed the horse by the bridle and Jake got out his buggy-whip.

They had it out all right! The German was a tough one. Maybe he didn't care whether his wife knew or not. Jake hit him over the face and shoulders with the buggy-whip, but the horse got to acting up and he had to get out.

Then the two men went for it. The girl didn't see it. The horse started to run away and went nearly a mile down the road before the girl got him stopped. Then she managed to tie him to a tree beside the road. (I wonder how I know all this. It must have stuck in my mind from small-town tales when I was a boy.)

Jake found her there after he got through with the German. She was huddled up in the buggy seat, crying, scared to death. She told Jake a lot of stuff, how the German had tried to get her, how he chased her once into the barn, how another time, when they happened to be alone in the house together, he tore her dress open clear down the front. The German, she said, might have got her that time if he hadn't heard his old woman drive in at the gate. She had been off to town for supplies. Well, she would be putting the horse in the barn. The German managed to sneak off to the fields without his wife seeing. He told the girl he would kill her if she told. What could she do? She told a lie about ripping her dress in the barn when she was feeding the stock. I remember now that she was a bound girl and did not know where her father and mother were. Maybe she did not have any father. You know what I mean.

Such bound children were often enough cruelly treated. They were children who had no parents, slaves really. There were very few orphan homes then. They were legally bound into some home. It was a matter of pure luck how it came out.

2

She married Jake and had a son and daughter, but the daughter died.

Then she settled down to feed stock. That was her job. At the German's place she had cooked the food for the German and his wife. The wife was a strong woman with big hips and worked most of the time in the fields with her husband. She fed them and fed the cows in the barn, fed the pigs, the horses and the chickens. Every moment of every day, as a young girl, was spent feeding something.

Then she married Jake Grimes and he had to be fed. She was a slight thing, and when she had been married for three or four years, and after the two children were born, her slender shoulders became stooped.

Jake always had a lot of big dogs around the house, that stood near the unused sawmill near the creek. He was always trading horses when he wasn't stealing something and had a lot of poor bony ones about. Also he kept three or four pigs and a cow. They were all pastured in the few acres left of the Grimes place and Jake did little enough work.

He went into debt for a threshing outfit and ran it for several years, but it did not pay. People did not trust him. They were afraid he would steal the grain at night. He had to go a long way off to get work and it cost too much to get there. In the Winter he hunted and cut a little firewood, to be sold in some nearby town. When the son grew up he was just like the father. They got drunk together. If there wasn't anything to eat in the house when they came home the old man gave his old woman a cut over the head. She had a few chickens of her own and had to kill one of them in a hurry. When they were all killed she wouldn't have any eggs to sell when she went to town, and then what would she do?

She had to scheme all her life about getting things fed, getting the pigs fed so they would grow fat and could be butchered in the Fall. When they were

butchered her husband took most of the meat off to town and sold it. If he did
not do it first the boy did. They fought sometimes and when they fought the
old woman stood aside trembling.

She had got the habit of silence anyway—that was fixed. Sometimes, when
she began to look old—she wasn't forty yet— and when the husband and son
were both off, trading horses or drinking or hunting or stealing, she went around
the house and the barnyard muttering to herself.

How was she going to get everything fed?—that was her problem. The dogs
had to be fed. There wasn't enough hay in the barn for the horses and the cow.
If she didn't feed the chickens how could they lay eggs? Without eggs to sell
how could she get things in town, things she had to have to keep the life of the
farm going? Thank heaven, she did not have to feed her husband—in a certain
way. That hadn't lasted long after their marriage and after the babies came.
Where he went on his long trips she did not know. Sometimes he was gone from
home for weeks, and after the boy grew up they went off together.

They left everything at home for her to manage and she had no money. She
knew no one. No one ever talked to her in town. When it was Winter she had
to gather sticks of wood for her fire, had to try to keep the stock fed with very
little grain.

The stock in the barn cried to her hungrily, the dogs followed her about. In
the Winter the hens laid few enough eggs. They huddled in the corners of the
barn and she kept watching them. If a hen lays an egg in the barn in the Winter
and you do not find it, it freezes and breaks.

One day in Winter the old woman went off to town with a few eggs and the
dogs followed her. She did not get started until nearly three o'clock and the
snow was heavy. She hadn't been feeling very well for several days and so she
went muttering along, scantily clad, her shoulders stooped. She had an old grain
bag in which she carried her eggs, tucked away down in the bottom. There
weren't many of them, but in Winter the price of eggs is up. She would get a
little meat in exchange for the eggs, some salt pork, a little sugar, and some
coffee perhaps. It might be the butcher would give her a piece of liver.

When she had got to town and was trading in her eggs the dogs lay by the
door outside. She did pretty well, got the things she needed, more than she had
hoped. Then she went to the butcher and he gave her some liver and some dog-
meat.

It was the first time any one had spoken to her in a friendly way for a long
time. The butcher was alone in his shop when she came in and was annoyed
by the thought of such a sick-looking old woman out on such a day. It was bitter
cold and the snow, that had let up during the afternoon, was falling again. The
butcher said something about her husband and her son, swore at them, and
the old woman stared at him, a look of mild surprise in her eyes as he talked. He
said that if either the husband or the son were going to get any of the liver
or the heavy bones with scraps of meat hanging to them that he had put into the
grain bag, he'd see him starve first.

Starve, eh? Well, things had to be fed. Men had to be fed, and horses that weren't any good but maybe could be traded off, and the poor thin cow that hadn't given any milk for three months.

Horses, cows, pigs, dogs, men.

3 The old woman had to get back before darkness came if she could. The dogs followed at her heels, sniffing at the heavy grain bag she had fastened on her back. When she got to the edge of town she stopped by a fence and tied the bag on her back with a piece of rope she had carried in her dress-pocket for just that purpose. It was hard when she had to crawl over fences and once she fell over and landed in the snow. The dogs went frisking about. She had to struggle to get to her feet again, but she made it. The point of climbing over the fences was that there was a short cut over a hill and through a woods. She might have gone around by the road, but it was a mile farther that way. She was afraid she couldn't make it. And then, besides, the stock had to be fed. There was a little hay left and a little corn. Perhaps her husband and son would bring some home when they came. They had driven off in the only buggy the Grimes family had, a rickety thing, a rickety horse hitched to the buggy, two other rickety horses led by halters. They were going to trade horses, get a little money if they could. They might come home drunk. It would be well to have something in the house when they came back.

The son had an affair on with a woman at the county seat, fifteen miles away. She was a rough enough woman, a tough one. Once, in the Summer, the son had brought her to the house. Both she and the son had been drinking. Jake Grimes was away and the son and his woman ordered the old woman about like a servant. She didn't mind much; she was used to it. Whatever happened she never said anything. That was her way of getting along. She had managed that way when she was a young girl at the German's and ever since she had married Jake. That time her son brought his woman to the house they stayed all night, sleeping together just as though they were married. It hadn't shocked the old woman, not much. She had got past being shocked early in life.

With the pack on her back she went painfully along across an open field, wading in the deep snow, and got into the woods.

There was a path, but it was hard to follow. Just beyond the top of the hill, where the woods was thickest, there was a small clearing. Had some one once thought of building a house there? The clearing was as large as a building lot in town, large enough for a house and a garden. The path ran along the side of the clearing, and when she got there the old woman sat down to rest at the foot of a tree.

It was a foolish thing to do. When she got herself placed, the pack against the tree's trunk, it was nice, but what about getting up again? She worried about that for a moment and then quietly closed her eyes.

She must have slept for a time. When you are about so cold you can't get any colder. The afternoon grew a little warmer and the snow came thicker than ever. Then after a time the weather cleared. The moon even came out.

There were four Grimes dogs that had followed Mrs. Grimes into town, all tall gaunt fellows. Such men as Jake Grimes and his son always keep just such dogs. They kick and abuse them, but they stay. The Grimes dogs, in order to keep from starving, had to do a lot of foraging for themselves, and they had been at it while the old woman slept with her back to the tree at the side of the clearing. They had been chasing rabbits in the woods and in adjoining fields and in their ranging had picked up three other farm dogs.

After a time all the dogs came back to the clearing. They were excited about something. Such nights, cold and clear and with a moon, do things to dogs. It may be that some old instinct, come down from the time when they were wolves and ranged the woods in packs on Winter nights, comes back into them.

The dogs in the clearing, before the old woman, had caught two or three rabbits and their immediate hunger had been satisfied. They began to play, running in circles in the clearing. Round and round they ran, each dog's nose at the tail of the next dog. In the clearing, under the snow-laden trees and under the wintry moon they made a strange picture, running thus silently, in a circle their running had beaten in the soft snow. The dogs made no sound. They ran around and around in the circle.

It may have been that the old woman saw them doing that before she died. She may have awakened once or twice and looked at the strange sight with dim old eyes.

She wouldn't be very cold now, just drowsy. Life hangs on a long time. Perhaps the old woman was out of her head. She may have dreamed of her girlhood at the German's, and before that, when she was a child and before her mother lit out and left her.

Her dreams couldn't have been very pleasant. Not many pleasant things had happened to her. Now and then one of the Grimes dogs left the running circle and came to stand before her. The dog thrust his face to her face. His red tongue was hanging out.

The running of the dogs may have been a kind of death ceremony. It may have been that the primitive instinct of the wolf, having been aroused in the dogs by the night and the running, made them somehow, afraid.

"Now we are no longer wolves. We are dogs, the servants of men. Keep alive, man! When man dies we become wolves again." When one of the dogs came to where the old woman sat with her back against the tree and thrust his nose close to her face he seemed satisfied and went back to run with the pack. All the Grimes dogs did it at some time during the evening, before she died. I knew all about it afterward, when I grew to be a man, because once in a woods in Illinois, on another Winter night, I saw a pack of dogs act just like that. The dogs were waiting for me to die as they had waited for the old woman that night when I was a child, but when it happened to me I was a young man and had no intention whatever of dying.

The old woman died softly and quietly. When she was dead and when one of the Grimes dogs had come to her and had found her dead all the dogs stopped running.

They gathered about her.

Well, she was dead now. She had fed the Grimes dogs when she was alive, what about now?

There was the pack on her back, the grain bag containing the piece of salt pork, the liver the butcher had given her, the dog-meat, the soup-bones. The butcher in town, having been suddenly overcome with a feeling of pity, had loaded her grain bag heavily. It had been a big haul for the old woman.

It was a big haul for the dogs now.

4 One of the Grimes dogs sprang suddenly out from among the others and began worrying the pack on the old woman's back. Had the dogs really been wolves that one would have been the leader of the pack. What he did, all the others did.

All of them sank their teeth into the grain bag the old woman had fastened with the ropes to her back.

They dragged the old woman's body out into the open clearing. The worn-out dress was quickly torn from her shoulders. When she was found, a day or two later, the dress had been torn from her body clear to the hips, but the dogs had not touched her body. They had got the meat out of the grain bag, that was all. Her body was frozen stiff when it was found, and the shoulders were so narrow and the body so slight that in death it looked like the body of some charming young girl.

Such things happened in towns of the Middle West, on farms near town, when I was a boy. A hunter out after rabbits found the old woman's body and did not touch it. Something, the beaten round path in the little snow-covered clearing, the silence of the place, the place where the dogs had worried the body trying to pull the grain bag away or tear it open—something startled the man and he hurried off to town.

I was in Main Street with one of my brothers who was town newsboy and who was taking the afternoon papers to the stores. It was almost night.

The hunter came into a grocery and told his story. Then he went into a hardware-shop and into a drugstore. Men began to gather on the sidewalks. Then they started out along the road to the place in the woods.

My brother should have gone on about his business of distributing papers but he didn't. Every one was going to the woods. The undertaker went and the town marshal. Several men got on a dray and rode out to where the path left the road and went into the woods, but the horses weren't very sharply shod and slid about on the slippery roads. They made no better time than those of us who walked.

The town marshal was a large man whose leg had been injured in the Civil War. He carried a heavy cane and limped rapidly along the road. My brother and

I followed at his heels, and as we went other men and boys joined the crowd.

It had grown dark by the time we got to where the old woman had left the road but the moon had come out. The marshal was thinking there might have been a murder. He kept asking the hunter questions. The hunter went along with his gun across his shoulders, a dog following at his heels. It isn't often a rabbit hunter has a chance to be so conspicuous. He was taking full advantage of it, leading the procession with the town marshal. "I didn't see any wounds. She was a beautiful young girl. Her face was buried in the snow. No, I didn't know her." As a matter of fact, the hunter had not looked closely at the body. He had been frightened. She might have been murdered and some one might spring out from behind a tree and murder him. In a woods, in the late afternoon, when the trees are all bare and there is white snow on the ground, when all is silent, something creepy steals over the mind and body. If something strange or uncanny has happened in the neighborhood all you think about is getting away from there as fast as you can.

The crowd of men and boys had got to where the old woman had crossed the field and went, following the marshal and the hunter, up the slight incline and into the woods.

My brother and I were silent. He had his bundle of papers in a bag slung across his shoulder. When he got back to town he would have to go on distributing his papers before he went home to supper. If I went along, as he had no doubt already determined I should, we would both be late. Either mother or our older sister would have to warm our supper.

Well, we would have something to tell. A boy did not get such a chance very often. It was lucky we just happened to go into the grocery when the hunter came in. The hunter was a country fellow. Neither of us had ever seen him before.

Now the crowd of men and boys had got to the clearing. Darkness comes quickly on such Winter nights, but the full moon made everything clear. My brother and I stood near the tree, beneath which the old woman had died.

She did not look old, lying there in that light, frozen and still. One of the men turned her over in the snow and I saw everything. My body trembled with some strange mystical feeling and so did my brother's. It might have been the cold.

Neither of us had ever seen a woman's body before. It may have been the snow, clinging to the frozen flesh, that made it look so white and lovely, so like marble. No woman had come with the party from town; but one of the men, he was the town blacksmith, took off his overcoat and spread it over her. Then he gathered her into his arms and started off to town, all the others following silently. At that time no one knew who she was.

5 I had seen everything, had seen the oval in the snow, like a miniature race-track, where the dogs had run, had seen how the men were mystified, had seen the white bare young-looking shoulders, had heard the whispered comments of the men.

The men were simply mystified. They took the body to the undertaker's, and when the blacksmith, the hunter, the marshal and several others had got inside they closed the door. If father had been there perhaps he could have got in, but we boys couldn't.

I went with my brother to distribute the rest of his papers and when we got home it was my brother who told the story.

I kept silent and went to bed early. It may have been I was not satisfied with the way he told it.

Later, in the town, I must have heard other fragments of the old woman's story. She was recognized the next day and there was an investigation.

The husband and son were found somewhere and brought to town and there was an attempt to connect them with the woman's death, but it did not work. They had perfect enough alibis.

However, the town was against them. They had to get out. Where they went I never heard.

I remember only the picture there in the forest, the men standing about, the naked girlish-looking figure, face down in the snow, the tracks made by the running dogs and the clear cold Winter sky above. White fragments of clouds were drifting across the sky. They went racing across the little open space among the trees.

The scene in the forest had become for me, without my knowing it, the foundation for the real story I am now trying to tell. The fragments, you see, had to be picked up slowly, long afterwards.

Things happened. When I was a young man I worked on the farm of a German. The hired-girl was afraid of her employer. The farmer's wife hated her.

I saw things at that place. Once later, I had a half-uncanny, mystical adventure with dogs in an Illinois forest on a clear, moon-lit Winter night. When I was a schoolboy, and on a Summer day, I went with a boy friend out along a creek some miles from town and came to the house where the old woman had lived. No one had lived in the house since her death. The doors were broken from the hinges; the window lights were all broken. As the boy and I stood in the road outside, two dogs, just roving farm dogs no doubt, came running around the corner of the house. The dogs were tall, gaunt fellows and came down to the fence and glared through at us, standing in the road.

The whole thing, the story of the old woman's death, was to me as I grew older like music heard from far off. The notes had to be picked up slowly one at a time. Something had to be understood.

The woman who died was one destined to feed animal life. Anyway, that is all she ever did. She was feeding animal life before she was born, as a child, as a young woman working on the farm of the German, after she married, when she grew old and when she died. She fed animal life in cows, in chickens, in pigs, in horses, in dogs, in men. Her daughter had died in childhood and with her one son she had no articulate relations. On the night when she died she was hurrying homeward, bearing on her body food for animal life.

She died in the clearing in the woods and even after her death continued feeding animal life.

You see it is likely that, when my brother told the story, that night when we got home and my mother and sister sat listening, I did not think he got the point. He was too young and so was I. A thing so complete has its own beauty.

I shall not try to emphasize the point. I am only explaining why I was dissatisfied then and have been ever since. I speak of that only that you may understand why I have been impelled to try to tell the simple story over again.

Ruth Whitman

(b. 1922)   Ruth Whitman graduated
from Radcliffe College in 1944 with
honors in Greek and English. She
has published several volumes of trans-
lations as well as two volumes of
poetry, Blood and Milk Poems *(1963)*
and The Marriage Wig and Other
Poems *(1968). A new volume of*
poems, The Passion of Lizzie Borden,
and a new translation, The Selected
Poems of Jacob Glatstein, *are in press.*
Ms. Whitman has won many awards
and is currently an instructor in
poetry at the Radcliffe Seminars.

Cutting the Jewish Bride's Hair

It's to possess more than the skin
that those old world Jews
exacted the hair of their brides.
>Good husband, lover of the Torah,
>does the calligraphy of your bride's hair
>interrupt your page?

Before the clownish friction of flesh
creating out of nothing
a mockup of its begetters,
a miraculous puppet of God,
you must first divorce her from her vanity.

She will snip off her pride,
cut back her appetite to be devoured,
she will keep herself well braided,
her love's furniture will not endanger you,
>but this little amputation
>will shift the balance of the universe.

II. the mother: angel or "mom"?

Often in literature a single character may embody the contrasting Mother's Day vision of "the one that means the world to me" and the image of the all-powerful "Mom," a character to be both loved and feared. In Ernest J. Gaines' "The Sky is Gray" and Kay Boyle's "His Idea of a Mother," even a child's view of mother is shown to be ambivalent. In Gaines' story, to the oldest son in a home temporarily fatherless, "Mama" is not only a strong brave adult who can cope with reality but also a pitiful woman overburdened by poverty and loneliness. The son accepts her authority and aid but at the same time wants to protect her. Through his desire to help her and his fear of punishment, he is able to put aside his fear of the dark and to pretend not to be hungry. What might have been a negative attitude toward her for denying him his childish comforts and forcing him into adulthood is sublimated as a sense of dignity at being able to live up to her expectations.

The young orphan in Kay Boyle's story has similar ideas of what a mother might be. He sees her as the opposite of a father, whom he imagines as a source of punishment, stern and unyielding. The child's primordial image of mother as a source of both comfort and discipline is expressed vividly in his love for a cow which he fears from a distance. When in the dark he cuddles up against her like a calf, she licks him both caressingly and roughly. His despair when she leaves him abruptly is existential and archetypal, in contrast to the later "human fear" he has when in the moonlight he is able to "see" and comprehend his surroundings. The use of the metaphor of sight as insight, in the specifically human sense, emphasizes the prerational nature of his response to the unseen cow through touch and smell and hearing. In both these stories, deprived children are shown as knowing what children under more normal circumstances may only sense: the mother who loves is also the mother who punishes.

Adrienne Rich in "The Crib" focuses on a mother's understanding of what her image is to her child. Though she is fulfilling her role as comforter, the mother in the poem realizes that the child's nightmare may be caused by an image of her as the enemy, the bringer of death and fate. She weeps as she realizes that such an attitude is inevitable and will cause the child to see her as woman, not mother—that is, it will cause him to grow up.

All three images emphasize the bonds between mother and child as having mythical reinforcement. Gaines' story deals with a child old enough to verbalize his feelings, but his mother discourages communication except for practical reasons: "She don't like for you to say something just for nothing." She refuses to explain to him why he must become a man, willing to kill for food. Urged by her sister to explain, she just beats the child. Her image of herself as mother does not involve reason but necessity, which it is the child's role to accept; their bond is too deep for logic. Kay Boyle shows how wrong is the boy's image of a father, gained from explanations by adults. The implication is that his image of a mother, gained from much more primitive sources, is accurate. Adrienne Rich interprets a child's scream, his nightmare without words.

In these selections the ambivalence of the mother image is presented as a mystery but also as a fact of life to be accepted as part of the human condition. "No villain need be," in spite of Philip Wylie's readiness to blame women for the hold they have over their sons. It is the relationship and its rooting in emotion that make the role of mother complex and fraught with dangers to all.

Ernest J. Gaines

(b. 1933) Born in Oscar, Louisiana,
Ernest J. Gaines was educated in
California, where he now lives. His
novel Catherine Carmier *appeared in*
1964, and three of his novellas have
been published in Negro Digest,
Sewanee Review, *and* The Texas
Quarterly. *In his most recent novel,*
The Autobiography of Miss Jane
Pittman *(1971), Gaines tells the story*
of a slave woman's quest for freedom.

The Sky is Gray

1   Go'n be coming in a few minutes. Coming round that bend down there full
speed. And I'm go'n get out my handkerchief and wave it down, and we go'n
get on it and go.

I keep on looking for it, but Mama don't look that way no more. She's
looking down the road where we just come from. It's a long old road, and far's
you can see you don't see nothing but gravel. You got dry weeds on both
sides, and you got trees on both sides, and fences on both sides, too. And you
got cows in the pastures and they standing close together. And when we was
coming out here to catch the bus I seen the smoke coming out of the cows's
noses.

I look at my mama and I know what she's thinking. I been with Mama so
much, just me and her, I know what she's thinking all the time. Right now
it's home—Auntie and them. She's thinking if they got enough wood—if she left
enough there to keep them warm till we get back. She's thinking if it go'n
rain and if any of them go'n have to go out in the rain. She's thinking 'bout the
hog—if he go'n get out, and if Ty and Val be able to get him back in. She
always worry like that when she leaves the house. She don't worry too much if
she leave me there with the smaller ones, 'cause she know I'm go'n look after
them and look after Auntie and everything else. I'm the oldest and she say
I'm the man.

93

I look at my mama and I love my mama. She's wearing that black coat and that black hat and she's looking sad. I love my mama and I want to put my arm round her and tell her. But I'm not supposed to do that. She say that's weakness and that's crybaby stuff, and she don't want no crybaby round her. She don't want you to be scared, either. 'Cause Ty's scared of ghosts and she's always whipping him. I'm scared of the dark, too, but I make 'tend I ain't. I make 'tend I ain't 'cause I'm the oldest, and I got to set a good sample for the rest. I can't ever be scared and I can't ever cry. And that's why I never said nothing 'bout my teeth. It's been hurting me and hurting me close to a month now, but I never said it. I didn't say it 'cause I didn't want act like a crybaby, and 'cause I know we didn't have enough money to go have it pulled. But, Lord, it been hurting me. And look like it wouldn't start till at night when you was trying to get yourself little sleep. Then soon's you shut your eyes—ummm-ummm, Lord, look like it go right down to your heartstring.

"Hurting, hanh?" Ty'd say.

I'd shake my head, but I wouldn't open my mouth for nothing. You open your mouth and let that wind in, and it almost kill you.

I'd just lay there and listen to them snore. Ty there, right 'side me, and Auntie and Val over by the fireplace. Val younger than me and Ty, and he sleeps with Auntie. Mama sleeps round the other side with Louis and Walker.

I'd just lay there and listen to them, and listen to that wind out there, and listen to that fire in the fireplace. Sometimes it'd stop long enough to let me get little rest. Sometimes it just hurt, hurt, hurt. Lord, have mercy.

2 Auntie knowed it was hurting me. I didn't tell nobody but Ty, 'cause we buddies and he ain't go'n tell nobody. But some kind of way Auntie found out. When she asked me, I told her no, nothing was wrong. But she knowed it all the time. She told me to mash up a piece of aspirin and wrap it in some cotton and jug it down in that hole. I did it, but it didn't do no good. It stopped for a little while, and started right back again. Auntie wanted to tell Mama, but I told her, "Uh-uh." 'Cause I knowed we didn't have any money, and it just was go'n make her mad again. So Auntie told Monsieur Bayonne, and Monsieur Bayonne came over to the house and told me to kneel down 'side him on the fireplace. He put his finger in his mouth and made the Sign of the Cross on my jaw. The tip of Monsieur Bayonne's finger is some hard, 'cause he's always playing on that guitar. If we sit outside at night we can always hear Monsieur Bayonne playing on his guitar. Sometimes we leave him out there playing on the guitar.

Monsieur Bayonne made the Sign of the Cross over and over on my jaw, but that didn't do no good. Even when he prayed and told me to pray some, too, that tooth still hurt me.

"How you feeling?" he say.

"Same," I say.

He kept on praying and making the Sign of the Cross and I kept on praying, too.

"Still hurting?" he say.

"Yes, sir."

Monsieur Bayonne mashed harder and harder on my jaw. He mashed so hard he almost pushed me over on Ty. But then he stopped.

"What kind of prayers you praying, boy?" he say.

"Baptist," I say.

"Well, I'll be—no wonder that tooth still killing him. I'm going one way and he pulling the other. Boy, don't you know any Catholic prayers?"

"I know 'Hail Mary,'" I say.

"Then you better start saying it."

"Yes, sir."

He started mashing on my jaw again, and I could hear him praying at the same time. And, sure enough, after while it stopped hurting me.

Me and Ty went outside where Monsieur Bayonne's two hounds was and we started playing with them. "Let's go hunting," Ty say. "All right," I say; and we went on back in the pasture. Soon the hounds got on a trail, and me and Ty followed them all 'cross the pasture and then back in the woods, too. And then they cornered this little old rabbit and killed him, and me and Ty made them get back, and we picked up the rabbit and started on back home. But my tooth had started hurting me again. It was hurting me plenty now, but I wouldn't tell Monsieur Bayonne. That night I didn't sleep a bit, and first thing in the morning Auntie told me to go back and let Monsieur Bayonne pray over me some more. Monsieur Bayonne was in his kitchen making coffee when I got there. Soon's he seen me he knowed what was wrong.

"All right, kneel down there 'side that stove," he say. "And this time make sure you pray Catholic. I don't know nothing 'bout that Baptist, and I don't want know nothing 'bout him."

3 Last night Mama say, "Tomorrow we going to town."

"It ain't hurting me no more," I say. "I can eat anything on it."

"Tomorrow we going to town," she say.

And after she finished eating, she got up and went to bed. She always go to bed early now. 'Fore Daddy went in the Army, she used to stay up late. All of us sitting out on the gallery or round the fire. But now, look like soon's she finish eating she go to bed.

This morning when I woke up, her and Auntie was standing 'fore the fireplace. She say: "Enough to get there and get back. Dollar and a half to have it pulled. Twenty-five for me to go, twenty-five for him. Twenty-five for me to come back, twenty-five for him. Fifty cents left. Guess I get little piece of salt meat with that."

"Sure can use it," Auntie say. "White beans and no salt meat ain't white beans."

"I do the best I can," Mama say.

They was quiet after that, and I made 'tend I was still asleep.

"James, hit the floor," Auntie say.

I still made 'tend I was asleep. I didn't want them to know I was listening.

"All right," Auntie say, shaking me by the shoulder. "Come on. Today's the day."

I pushed the cover down to get out, and Ty grabbed it and pulled it back.

"You, too, Ty," Auntie say.

"I ain't getting no teef pulled," Ty say.

"Don't mean it ain't time to get up," Auntie say. "Hit it, Ty."

Ty got up grumbling.

"James, you hurry up and get in your clothes and eat your food," Auntie say. "What time y'all coming back?" she say to Mama.

"That 'leven o'clock bus," Mama say. "Got to get back in that field this evening."

"Get a move on you, James," Auntie say.

I went in the kitchen and washed my face, then I ate my breakfast. I was having bread and syrup. The bread was warm and hard and tasted good. And I tried to make it last a long time.

Ty came back there grumbling and mad at me.

"Got to get up," he say. "I ain't having no teefes pulled. What I got to be getting up for?"

Ty poured some syrup in his pan and got a piece of bread. He didn't wash his hands, neither his face, and I could see that white stuff in his eyes.

"You the one getting your teef pulled," he say. "What I got to get up for. I bet if I was getting a teef pulled, you wouldn't be getting up. Shucks; syrup again. I'm getting tired of this old syrup. Syrup, syrup, syrup. I'm go'n take with the sugar diabetes. I want me some bacon sometime."

"Go out in the field and work and you can have your bacon," Auntie say. She stood in the middle door looking at Ty. "You better be glad you got syrup. Some people ain't got that—hard's time is."

"Shucks," Ty say. "How can I be strong."

"I don't know too much 'bout your strength," Auntie say; "but I know where you go'n be hot at, you keep that grumbling up. James, get a move on you; your mama waiting."

I ate my last piece of bread and went in the front room. Mama was standing 'fore the fireplace warming her hands. I put on my coat and cap, and we left the house.

4 I look down there again, but it still ain't coming. I almost say, "It ain't coming yet," but I keep my mouth shut. 'Cause that's something else she don't like. She don't like for you to say something just for nothing. She can see it ain't coming, I can see it ain't coming, so why say it ain't coming. I don't say it, I turn and look at the river that's back of us. It's so cold the smoke's just raising up from the water. I see a bunch of pool-doos not too far out—just on the other side the lilies. I'm wondering if you can eat pool-doos. I ain't too sure, 'cause I ain't never ate none. But I done ate owls and blackbirds, and I done

ate redbirds, too. I didn't want kill the redbirds, but she made me kill them. They had two of them back there. One in my trap, one in Ty's trap. Me and Ty was go'n play with them and let them go, but she made me kill them 'cause we needed the food.

"I can't," I say. "I can't."

"Here," she say. "Take it."

"I can't," I say. "I can't. I can't kill him, Mama, please."

"Here," she say. "Take this fork, James."

"Please, Mama, I can't kill him," I say.

I could tell she was go'n hit me. I jerked back, but I didn't jerk back soon enough.

"Take it," she say.

I took it and reached in for him, but he kept on hopping to the back.

"I can't, Mama," I say. The water just kept on running down my face. "I can't," I say.

"Get him out of there," she say.

I reached in for him and he kept on hopping to the back. Then I reached in farther, and he pecked me on the hand.

"I can't, Mama," I say.

She slapped me again.

I reached in again, but he kept on hopping out my way. Then he hopped to one side and I reached there. The fork got him on the leg and I heard his leg pop. I pulled my hand out 'cause I had hurt him.

'Give it here," she say, and jerked the fork out of my hand.

She reached in and got the little bird right in the neck. I heard the fork go in his neck, and I heard it go in the ground. She brought him out and helt him right in front of me.

"That's one," she say. She shook him off and gived me the fork. "Get the other one."

"I can't, Mama," I say. "I'll do anything, but don't make me do that."

She went to the corner of the fence and broke the biggest switch over there she could find. I knelt 'side the trap, crying.

"Get him out of there," she say.

"I can't, Mama."

She started hitting me 'cross the back. I went down on the ground, crying.

"Get him," she say.

"Octavia?" Auntie say.

'Cause she had come out of the house and she was standing by the tree looking at us.

"Get him out of there," Mama say.

"Octavia," Auntie say, "explain to him. Explain to him. Just don't beat him. Explain to him."

But she hit me and hit me and hit me.

I'm still young—I ain't no more than eight; but I know now; I know why I had to do it. (They was so little, though. They was so little. I 'member how I picked the feathers off them and cleaned them and helt them over the fire.

Then we all ate them. Ain't had but a little bitty piece each, but we all had a little bitty piece, and everybody just looked at me 'cause they was so proud.) Suppose she had to go away? That's why I had to do it. Suppose she had to go away like Daddy went away? Then who was go'n look after us? They had to be somebody left to carry on. I didn't know it then, but I know it now. Auntie and Monsieur Bayonne talked to me and made me see.

5 Time I see it I get out my handkerchief and start waving. It's still 'way down there, but I keep waving anyhow. Then it come up and stop and me and Mama get on. Mama tell me go sit in the back while she pay. I do like she say, and the people look at me. When I pass the little sign that say "White" and "Colored," I start looking for a seat. I just see one of them back there, but I don't take it, 'cause I want my mama to sit down herself. She comes in the back and sit down, and I lean on the seat. They got seats in the front, but I know I can't sit there, 'cause I have to sit back of the sign. Anyhow, I don't want sit there if my mama go'n sit back here.

They got a lady sitting 'side my mama and she looks at me and smiles little bit. I smile back, but I don't open my mouth, 'cause the wind'll get in and make that tooth ache. The lady take out a pack of gum and reach me a slice, but I shake my head. The lady just can't understand why a little boy'll turn down gum, and she reach me a slice again. This time I point to my jaw. The lady understands and smiles little bit, and I smile little bit, but I don't open my mouth, though.

They got a girl sitting 'cross from me. She got on a red overcoat and her hair's plaited in one big plait. First, I make 'tend I don't see her over there, but then I start looking at her little bit. She make 'tend she don't see me, either, but I catch her looking that way. She got a cold, and every now and then she h'ist that little handkerchief to her nose. She ought to blow it, but she don't. Must think she's too much a lady or something.

Every time she h'ist that little handkerchief, the lady 'side her say something in her ear. She shakes her head and lays her hands in her lap again. Then I catch her kind of looking where I'm at. I smile at her little bit. But think she'll smile back? Uh-uh. She just turn up her little old nose and turn her head. Well, I show her both of us can turn us head. I turn mine too and look out at the river.

The river is gray. The sky is gray. They have pool-doos on the water. The water is wavy, and the pool-doos go up and down. The bus go round a turn, and you got plenty trees hiding the river. Then the bus go round another turn, and I can see the river again.

I look toward the front where all the white people sitting. Then I look at that little old gal again. I don't look right at her, 'cause I don't want all them people to know I love her. I just look at her little bit, like I'm looking out that window over there. But she knows I'm looking that way, and she kind of look at me, too. The lady sitting 'side her catch her this time, and she leans over and says something in her ear.

"I don't love him nothing," that little old gal says out loud.

Everybody back there hear her mouth, and all of them look at us and laugh.

"I don't love you, either," I say. "So you don't have to turn up your nose, Miss."

"You the one looking," she say.

"I wasn't looking at you," I say. "I was looking out that window, there."

"Out that window, my foot," she say. "I seen you. Everytime I turned round you was looking at me."

"You must of been looking yourself if you seen me all them times," I say.

"Shucks," she say, "I got me all kind of boyfriends."

"I got girlfriends, too," I say.

"Well, I just don't want you getting your hopes up," she say.

I don't say no more to that little old gal 'cause I don't want have to bust her in the mouth. I lean on the seat where Mama sitting, and I don't even look that way no more. When we get to Bayonne, she jugg her little old tongue out at me. I make 'tend I'm go'n hit her, and she duck down 'side her mama. And all the people laugh at us again.

6 Me and Mama get off and start walking in town. Bayonne is a little bitty town. Baton Rouge is a hundred times bigger than Bayonne. I went to Baton Rouge once—me, Ty, Mama, and Daddy. But that was 'way back yonder, 'fore Daddy went in the Army. I wonder when we go'n see him again. I wonder when. Look like he ain't ever coming back home. . . . Even the pavement all cracked in Bayonne. Got grass shooting right out the sidewalk. Got weeds in the ditch, too; just like they got at home.

It's some cold in Bayonne. Look like it's colder than it is home. The wind blows in my face, and I feel that stuff running down my nose. I sniff. Mama says use that handkerchief. I blow my nose and put it back.

We pass a school and I see them white children playing in the yard. Big old red school, and them children just running and playing. Then we pass a café, and I see a bunch of people in there eating. I wish I was in there 'cause I'm cold. Mama tells me keep my eyes in front where they belong.

We pass stores that's got dummies, and we pass another café, and then we pass a shoe shop, and that bald-head man in there fixing on a shoe. I look at him and I butt into that white lady, and Mama jerks me in front and tells me stay there.

We come up to the courthouse, and I see the flag waving there. This flag ain't like the one we got at school. This one here ain't got but a handful of stars. One at school got a big pile of stars—one for every state. We pass it and we turn and there it is—the dentist office. Me and Mama go in, and they got people sitting everywhere you look. They even got a little boy in there younger than me.

Me and Mama sit on that bench, and a white lady come in there and ask me what my name is. Mama tells her and the white lady goes on back. Then I hear somebody hollering in there. Soon's that little boy hear him hollering, he starts hollering, too. His mama pats him and pats him, trying to make him hush up, but he ain't thinking 'bout his mama.

The man that was hollering in there comes out holding his jaw. He is a big old man and he's wearing overalls and a jumper.

"Got it, hanh?" another man asks him.

The man shakes his head—don't want open his mouth.

"Man, I thought they was killing you in there," the other man says. "Hollering like a pig under a gate."

The man don't say nothing. He just heads for the door, and the other man follows him.

"John Lee," the white lady says. "John Lee Williams."

The little boy juggs his head down in his mama's lap and holler more now. His mama tells him go with the nurse, but he ain't thinking 'bout his mama. His mama tells him again, but he don't even hear her. His mama picks him up and takes him in there, and even when the white lady shuts the door I can still hear little old John Lee.

"I often wonder why the Lord let a child like that suffer," a lady says to my mama. The lady's sitting right in front of us on another bench. She's got on a white dress and a black sweater. She must be a nurse or something herself, I reckon.

"Not us to question," a man says.

"Sometimes I don't know if we shouldn't," the lady says.

"I know definitely we shouldn't," the man says. The man looks like a preacher. He's big and fat and he's got on a black suit. He's got a gold chain, too.

"Why?" the lady says.

"Why anything?" the preacher says.

"Yes," the lady says. "Why anything?"

"Not us to question," the preacher says.

The lady looks at the preacher a little while and looks at Mama again.

"And look like it's the poor who suffers the most," she says. "I don't understand it."

"Best not to even try," the preacher says. "He works in mysterious ways—wonders to perform."

Right then little John Lee bust out hollering, and everybody turn they head to listen.

"He's not a good dentist," the lady says. "Dr. Robillard is much better. But more expensive. That's why most of the colored people come here. The white people go to Dr. Robillard. Y'all from Bayonne?"

"Down the river," my mama says. And that's all she go'n say, 'cause she don't talk much. But the lady keeps on looking at her, and so she says, "Near Morgan."

"I see," the lady says.

7 "That's the trouble with the black people in this country today," somebody else says. This one here's sitting on the same side me and Mama's sitting, and he is kind of sitting in front of that preacher. He looks like a teacher or somebody that goes to college. He's got on a suit, and he's got a book that he's been reading. "We don't question is exactly our problem," he says. "We should question and question and question—question everything."

The preacher just looks at him a long time. He done put a toothpick or something in his mouth, and he just keeps on turning it and turning it. You can see he don't like that boy with that book.

"Maybe you can explain what you mean," he says.

"I said what I meant," the boy says. "Question everything. Every stripe, every star, every word spoken. Everything."

"It 'pears to me that this young lady and I was talking 'bout God, young man," the preacher says.

"Question Him, too," the boy says.

"Wait," the preacher says. "Wait now."

"You heard me right," the boy says. "His existence as well as everything else. Everything."

The preacher just looks across the room at the boy. You can see he's getting madder and madder. But mad or no mad, the boy ain't thinking 'bout him. He looks at that preacher just 's hard 's the preacher looks at him.

"Is this what they coming to?" the preacher says. "Is this what we educating them for?"

"You're not educating me," the boy says. "I wash dishes at night so that I can go to school in the day. So even the words you spoke need questioning."

The preacher just looks at him and shakes his head.

"When I come in this room and seen you there with your book, I said to myself, 'There's an intelligent man.' How wrong a person can be."

"Show me one reason to believe in the existence of a God," the boy says.

"My heart tells me," the preacher says.

"'My heart tells me,'" the boys says. "'My heart tells me.' Sure, 'My heart tells me.' And as long as you listen to what your heart tells you, you will have only what the white man gives you and nothing more. Me, I don't listen to my heart. The purpose of the heart is to pump blood throughout the body, and nothing else."

"Who's your paw, boy?" the preacher says.

"Why?"

"Who is he?"

"He's dead."

"And your mom?"

"She's in Charity Hospital with pneumonia. Half killed herself, working for nothing."

"And 'cause he's dead and she's sick, you mad at the world?"

"I'm not mad at the world. I'm questioning the world. I'm questioning it with cold logic sir. What do words like Freedom, Liberty, God, White, Colored mean? I want to know. That's why *you* are sending us to school, to read and to ask questions. And because we ask these questions, you call us mad. No sir, it is not us who are mad."

"You keep saying 'us'?"

"'Us.' Yes—us. I'm not alone."

The preacher just shakes his head. Then he looks at everybody in the room—everybody. Some of the people look down at the floor, keep from looking at him. I kind of look 'way myself, but soon's I know he done turn his head, I look that way again.

"I'm sorry for you," he says to the boy.

"Why?" the boy says. "Why not be sorry for yourself? Why are you so much better off than I am? Why aren't you sorry for these other people in here? Why not be sorry for the lady who had to drag her child into the dentist office? Why not be sorry for the lady sitting on that bench over there? Be sorry for them. Not for me. Some way or the other I'm going to make it."

"No, I'm sorry for you," the preacher says.

"Of course, of course," the boy says, nodding his head. "You're sorry for me because I rock that pillar you're leaning on."

"You can't ever rock the pillar I'm leaning on, young man. It's stronger than anything man can ever do."

"You believe in God because a man told you to believe in God," the boy says. "A white man told you to believe in God. And why? To keep you ignorant so he can keep his feet on your neck."

"So now we the ignorant?" the preacher says.

"Yes," the boy says. "Yes." And he opens his book again.

The preacher just looks at him sitting there. The boy done forgot all about him. Everybody else make 'tend they done forgot the squabble, too.

Then I see that preacher getting up real slow. Preacher's a great big old man and he got to brace himself to get up. He comes over where the boy is sitting. He just stands there a little while looking down at him, but the boy don't raise his head.

"Get up, boy," preacher says.

The boy looks up at him, then he shuts his book real slow and stands up. Preacher just hauls back and hit him in the face. The boy falls back 'gainst the wall, but he straightens himself up and looks right back at that preacher.

"You forgot the other cheek," he says.

The preacher hauls back and hit him again on the other side. But this time the boy braces himself and don't fall.

"That hasn't changed a thing," he says.

The preacher just looks at the boy. The preacher's breathing real hard like he just run up a big hill. The boy sits down and opens his book again.

"I feel sorry for you," the preacher says. "I never felt so sorry for a man before."

The boy makes 'tend he don't even hear that preacher. He keeps on reading his book. The preacher goes back and gets his hat off the chair.

"Excuse me," he says to us. "I'll come back some other time. Y'all, please excuse me."

And he looks at the boy and goes out the room. The boy h'ist his hand up to his mouth one time to wipe 'way some blood. All the rest of the time he keeps on reading. And nobody else in there say a word.

8 Little John Lee and his mama come out the dentist office, and the nurse calls somebody else in. Then little bit later they come out, and the nurse calls another name. But fast's she calls somebody in there, somebody else comes in the place where we sitting, and the room stays full.

The people coming in now, all of them wearing big coats. One of them says something 'bout sleeting, another one says he hope not. Another one says he think it ain't nothing but rain. 'Cause, he says, rain can get awful cold this time of year.

All round the room they talking. Some of them talking to people right by them, some of them talking to people clear 'cross the room, some of them talking to anybody'll listen. It's a little bitty room, no bigger than us kitchen, and I can see everybody in there. The little old room's full of smoke, 'cause you got two old men smoking pipes over by that side door. I think I feel my tooth thumping me some, and I hold my breath and wait. I wait and wait, but it don't thump me no more. Thank God for that.

I feel like going to sleep, and I lean back 'gainst the wall. But I'm scared to go to sleep. Scared 'cause the nurse might call my name and I won't hear her. And Mama might go to sleep, too, and she'll be mad if neither one of us heard the nurse.

I look up at Mama. I love my mama. I love my mama. And when cotton come I'm go'n get her a new coat. And I ain't go'n get a black one, either. I think I'm go'n get her a red one.

"They got some books over there," I say. "Want read one of them?"

Mama looks at the books, but she don't answer me.

"You got yourself a little man there," the lady says.

Mama don't say nothing to the lady, but she must've smiled, 'cause I seen the lady smiling back. The lady looks at me a little while, like she's feeling sorry for me.

"You sure got that preacher out here in a hurry," she says to that boy.

The boy looks up at her and looks in his book again. When I grow up I want be just like him. I want clothes like that and I want keep a book with me, too.

"You really don't believe in God?" the lady says.

"No," he says.

"But why?" the lady says.

"Because the wind is pink" he says.

"What?" the lady says.

The boy don't answer her no more. He just reads in his book.

"Talking 'bout the wind is pink," that old lady says. She's sitting on the same bench with the boy and she's trying to look in his face. The boy makes 'tend the old lady ain't even there. He just keeps on reading. "Wind is pink," she says again. "Eh, Lord, what children go'n be saying next?"

The lady 'cross from us bust out laughing.

"That's a good one," she says. "The wind is pink. Yes sir, that's a good one."

"Don't you believe the wind is pink?" the boys says. He keeps his head down in the book.

"Course I believe it, honey," the lady says. "Course I do." She looks at us and winks her eye. "And what color is grass, honey?"

"Grass? Grass is black."

She bust out laughing again. The boy looks at her.

"Don't you believe grass is black?" he says.

The lady quits her laughing and looks at him. Everybody else looking at him, too. The place quiet, quiet.

"Grass is green, honey," the lady says. "It was green yesterday, it's green today, and it's go'n be green tomorrow."

"How do you know it's green?"

"I know because I know."

"You don't know it's green," the boy says. "You believe it's green because someone told you it was green. If someone had told you it was black you'd believe it was black."

"It's green," the lady says. "I know green when I see green."

"Prove it's green," the boy says.

"Sure, now," the lady says. "Don't tell me it's coming to that."

"It's coming to just that," the boy says. "Words mean nothing. One means no more than the other."

"That's what it all coming to?" the old lady says. That old lady got on a turban and she got on two sweaters. She got a green sweater under a black sweater. I can see the green sweater 'cause some of the buttons on the other sweater's missing.

"Yes ma'am," the boy says. "Words mean nothing. Action is the only thing. Doing. That's the only thing."

"Other words, you want the Lord to come down here and show Hisself to you?" she says.

"Exactly, ma'am," he says.

"You don't mean that, I'm sure," she says.

"I do, ma'am," he says.

"Done, Jesus," the old lady says, shaking her head.

"I didn't go 'long with that preacher at first," the other lady says; "but now—I don't know. When a person say the grass is black, he's either a lunatic or something's wrong."

"Prove to me that it's green," the boy says.

"It's green because the people say it's green."

"Those same people say we're citizens of these United States," the boy says.

"I think I'm a citizen," the lady says.

"Citizens have certain rights," the boy says. "Name me one right that you have. One right, granted by the Constitution, that you can exercise in Bayonne."

The lady don't answer him. She just looks at him like she don't know what he's talking 'bout. I know I don't.

"Things changing," she says.

"Things are changing because some black men have begun to think with their brains and not their hearts," the boy says.

"You trying to say these people don't believe in God?"

"I'm sure some of them do. Maybe most of them do. But they don't believe that God is going to touch these white people's hearts and change things tomorrow. Things change through action. By no other way."

Everybody sit quiet and look at the boy. Nobody says a thing. Then the lady 'cross the room from me and Mama just shakes her head.

"Let's hope that not all your generation feel the same way you do," she says.

"Think what you please, it doesn't matter," the boy says. "But it will be men who listen to their heads and not their hearts who will see that your children have a better chance than you had."

"Let's hope they ain't all like you, though," the old lady says. "Done forgot the heart absolutely."

"Yes ma'am, I hope they aren't all like me," the boy says. "Unfortunately, I was born too late to believe in your God. Let's hope that the ones who come after will have your faith—if not in your God, then in something else, something definitely that they can lean on. I haven't anything. For me, the wind is pink, the grass is black."

9 The nurse comes in the room where we all sitting and waiting and says the doctor won't take no more patients till one o'clock this evening. My mama jumps up off the bench and goes up to the white lady.

"Nurse, I have to go back in the field this evening," she says.

"The doctor is treating his last patient now," the nurse says. "One o'clock this evening."

"Can I at least speak to the doctor?" my mama asks.

"I'm his nurse," the lady says.

"My little boy's sick," my mama says. "Right now his tooth almost killing him."

The nurse looks at me. She's trying to make up her mind if to let me come in. I look at her real pitiful. The tooth ain't hurting me at all, but Mama says it is, so I make 'tend for her sake.

"This evening," the nurse says, and goes on back in the office.

"Don't feel 'jected, honey," the lady says to Mama. "I been round them a long time—they take you when they want to. If you was white, that's something else; but we the wrong color."

Mama don't say nothing to the lady, and me and her go outside and stand 'gainst the wall. It's cold out there. I can feel that wind going through my coat. Some of the other people come out of the room and go up the street. Me and Mama stand there a little while and we start walking. I don't know where we going. When we come to the other street we just stand there.

"You don't have to make water, do you?" Mama says.

"No, ma'am," I say.

We go on up the street. Walking real slow. I can tell Mama don't know where she's going. When we come to a store we stand there and look at the dummies. I look at a little boy wearing a brown overcoat. He's got on brown shoes, too. I look at my old shoes and look at his'n again. You wait till summer, I say.

Me and Mama walk away. We come up to another store and we stop and look at them dummies, too. Then we go on again. We pass a café where the white people in there eating. Mama tells me keep my eyes in front where they belong, but I can't help from seeing them people eat. My stomach starts to growling 'cause I'm hungry. When I see people eating, I get hungry; when I see a coat, I get cold.

A man whistles at my mama when we go by a filling station. She makes 'tend she don't even see him. I look back and I feel like hitting him in the mouth. If I was bigger, I say; if I was bigger, you'd see.

We keep on going. I'm getting colder and colder, but I don't say nothing. I feel that stuff running down my nose and I sniff.

"That rag," Mama says.

I get it out and wipe my nose. I'm getting cold all over now—my face, my hands, my feet, everything. We pass another little café, but this'n for white people, too, and we can't go in there, either. So we just walk. I'm so cold now I'm 'bout ready to say it. If I knowed where we was going I wouldn't be so cold, but I don't know where we going. We go, we go, we go. We walk clean out of Bayonne. Then we cross the street and we come back. Same thing I seen when I got off the bus this morning. Same old trees, same old walk, same old weeds, same old cracked pave—same old everything.

I sniff again.

"That rag," Mama says.

I wipe my nose real fast and jugg that handkerchief back in my pocket 'fore my hand gets too cold. I raise my head and I can see David's hardware store. When we come up to it, we go in. I don't know why, but I'm glad.

It's warm in there. It's so warm in there you don't ever want to leave. I look for the heater, and I see it over by them barrels. Three white men standing round the heater talking in Creole. One of them comes over to see what my mama want.

"Got any axe handles?" she says.

Me, Mama and the white man start to the back, but Mama stops me when we come up to the heater. She and the white man go on. I hold my hands over the heater and look at them. They go all the way to the back, and I see the white man pointing to the axe handles 'gainst the wall. Mama takes one of them and shakes it like she's trying to figure how much it weighs. Then she rubs her hand over it from one end to the other end. She turns it over and looks at the other side, then she shakes it again, and shakes her head and puts it back. She gets another one and she does it just like she did the first one, then she shakes her head. Then she gets a brown one and do it that, too. But she don't like this one, either. Then she gets another one, but 'fore she shakes it or anything, she looks at me. Look like she's trying to say something to me, but I don't know what it is. All I know is I done got warm now and I'm feeling right smart better. Mama shakes this axe handle just like she did the others, and shakes her head and says something to the white man. The white man just looks at his pile of axe handles, and when Mama pass him to come to the front, the white man just scratch his head and follows her. She tells me come on and we go on out and start walking again.

We walk and walk, and no time at all I'm cold again. Look like I'm colder now 'cause I can still remember how good it was back there. My stomach growls and I suck it in to keep Mama from hearing it. She's walking right 'side me, and it growls so loud you can hear it a mile. But Mama don't say a word.

10

When we come up to the courthouse, I look at the clock. It's got quarter to twelve. Mean we got another hour and a quarter to be out here in the cold. We go and stand 'side a building. Something hits my cap and I look up at the sky. Sleet's falling.

I look at Mama standing there. I want stand close 'side her, but she don't like that. She say that's crybaby stuff. She say you got to stand for yourself, by yourself.

"Let's go back to that office," she says.

We cross the street. When we get to the dentist office I try to open the door, but I can't. I twist and twist, but I can't. Mama pushes me to the side and she twist the knob, but she can't open the door, either. She turns 'way from the door. I look at her, but I don't move and I don't say nothing. I done seen her like this before and I'm scared of her.

"You hungry?" she says. She says it like she's mad at me, like I'm the cause of everything.

"No, ma'am," I say.

"You want eat and walk back, or you rather don't eat and ride?"

"I ain't hungry," I say.

I ain't just hungry, but I'm cold, too. I'm so hungry and cold I want to cry. And look like I'm getting colder and colder. My feet done got numb. I try to work my toes, but I don't even feel them. Look like I'm go'n die. Look like I'm go'n stand right here and freeze to death. I think 'bout home. I think 'bout Val and Auntie and Ty and Louis and Walker. It's 'bout twelve o'clock and I know they eating dinner now. I can hear Ty making jokes. He done forgot 'bout getting

up early this morning and right now he's probably making jokes. Always trying
to make somebody laugh. I wish I was right there listening to him. Give anything
in the world if I was home round the fire.

"Come on," Mama says.

We start walking again. My feet so numb I can't hardly feel them. We turn
the corner and go on back up the street. The clock on the courthouse starts
hitting for twelve.

The sleet's coming down plenty now. They hit the pave and bounce like rice.
Oh, Lord; oh, Lord, I pray. Don't let me die, don't let me die, don't let me
die, Lord.

11 Now I know where we going. We going back of town where the colored
people eat. I don't care if I don't eat. I been hungry before. I can stand it. But I
can't stand the cold.

I can see we go'n have a long walk. It's 'bout a mile down there. But I don't
mind. I know when I get there I'm go'n warm myself. I think I can hold out.
My hands numb in my pockets and my feet numb, too, but if I keep moving I
can hold out. Just don't stop no more, that's all.

The sky's gray. The sleet keeps on falling. Falling like rain now—plenty,
plenty. You can hear it hitting the pave. You can see it bouncing. Sometimes it
bounces two times 'fore it settles.

We keep on going. We don't say nothing. We just keep on going, keep on
going.

I wonder what Mama's thinking. I hope she ain't mad at me. When summer
come I'm go'n pick plenty cotton and get her a coat. I'm go'n get her a red one.

I hope they'd make it summer all the time. I'd be glad if it was summer
all the time—but it ain't. We got to have winter, too. Lord, I hate the winter. I
guess everybody hate the winter.

I don't sniff this time. I get out my handkerchief and wipe my nose. My
hands's so cold I can hardly hold the handkerchief.

I think we getting close, but we ain't there yet. I wonder where everybody is.
Can't see a soul but us. Look like we the only two people moving round today.
Must be too cold for the rest of the people to move round in.

I can hear my teeth. I hope they don't knock together too hard and make
that bad one hurt. Lord, that's all I need, for that bad one to start off.

I hear a church bell somewhere. But today ain't Sunday. They must be
ringing for a funeral or something.

I wonder what they doing at home. They must be eating. Monsieur Bayonne
might be there with his guitar. One day Ty played with Monsieur Bayonne's
guitar and broke one of the strings. Monsieur Bayonne was some mad with Ty.
He say Ty wasn't go'n ever 'mount to nothing. Ty can go just like Monsieur
Bayonne when he ain't there. Ty can make everybody laugh when he starts to
mocking Monsieur Bayonne.

I used to like to be with Mama and Daddy. We used to be happy. But they took him in the Army. Now, nobody happy no more. . . . I be glad when Daddy comes home.

Monsieur Bayonne say it wasn't fair for them to take Daddy and give Mama nothing and give us nothing. Auntie say, "Shhh, Etienne. Don't let them hear you talk like that." Monsieur Bayonne say, "It's God truth. What they giving his children? They have to walk three and a half miles to school hot or cold. That's anything to give for a paw? She's got to work in the field rain or shine just to make ends meet. That's anything to give for a husband?" Auntie say, "Shhh, Etienne, shhh." "Yes, you right," Monsieur Bayonne say. "Best don't say it in front of them now. But one day they go'n find out. One day." "Yes, I suppose so," Auntie say. "Then what, Rose Mary?" Monsieur Bayonne say. "I don't know, Etienne," Auntie say. "All we can do is us job, and leave everything else in His hand . . ."

We getting closer, now. We getting closer. I can even see the railroad tracks.

We cross the tracks, and now I see the café. Just to get in there, I say. Just to get in there. Already I'm starting to feel little better.

12

We go in. Ahh, it's good. I look for the heater; there 'gainst the wall. One of them little brown ones. I just stand there and hold my hands over it. I can't open my hands too wide 'cause they almost froze.

Mama's standing right 'side me. She done unbuttoned her coat. Smoke rises out of the coat, and the coat smells like a wet dog.

I move to the side so Mama can have more room. She opens out her hands and rubs them together. I rub mine together, too, 'cause this keep them from hurting. If you let them warm too fast, they hurt you sure. But if you let them warm just little bit at a time, and you keep rubbing them, they be all right every time.

They got just two more people in the café. A lady back of the counter, and a man on this side the counter. They been watching us ever since we come in.

Mama gets out the handkerchief and count up the money. Both of us know how much money she's got there. Three dollars. No, she ain't got three dollars 'cause she had to pay us way up here. She ain't got but two dollars and a half left. Dollar and a half to get my tooth pulled, and fifty cents for us to go back on, and fifty cents worth of salt meat.

She stirs the money round with her finger. Most of the money is change 'cause I can hear it rubbing together. She stirs it and stirs it. Then she looks at the door. It's still sleeting. I can hear it hitting 'gainst the wall like rice.

"I ain't hungry, Mama," I say.

"Got to pay them something for they heat," she says.

She takes a quarter out the handkerchief and ties the handkerchief up again. She looks over her shoulder at the people, but she still don't move. I hope she don't spend the money. I don't want her spending it on me. I'm hungry, I'm almost starving I'm so hungry, but I don't want her spending the money on me.

She flips the quarter over like she's thinking. She's must be thinking 'bout us walking back home. Lord, I sure don't want walk home. If I thought it'd do any good to say something, I'd say it. But Mama makes up her own mind 'bout things.

She turns 'way from the heater right fast, like she better hurry up and spend the quarter 'fore she change her mind. I watch her go toward the counter. The man and the lady look at her, too. She tells the lady something and the lady walks away. The man keeps on looking at her. Her back's turned to the man, and she don't even know he's standing there.

The lady puts some cakes and a glass of milk on the counter. Then she pours up a cup of coffee and sets it 'side the other stuff. Mama pays her for the things and comes on back where I'm standing. She tells me sit down at the table 'gainst the wall.

The milk and the cakes's for me; the coffee's for Mama. I eat slow and I look at her. She's looking outside at the sleet. She's looking real sad. I say to myself, I'm go'n make all this up one day. You see, one day, I'm go'n make all this up. I want say it now; I want tell her how I feel right now; but Mama don't like for us to talk like that.

"I can't eat all this," I say.

They ain't got but just three little old cakes there. I'm so hungry right now, the Lord knows I can eat a hundred times three, but I want my mama to have one.

Mama don't even look my way. She knows I'm hungry, she knows I want it. I let it stay there a little while, then I get it and eat it. I eat just on my front teeth, though, 'cause if cake touch that back tooth I know what'll happen. Thank God it ain't hurt me at all today.

After I finish eating I see the man go to the juke box. He drops a nickel in it, then he just stand there a little while looking at the record. Mama tells me keep my eyes in front where they belong. I turn my head like she say, but then I hear the man coming toward us.

"Dance, pretty?" he says.

Mama gets up to dance with him. But 'fore you know it, she done grabbed the little man in the collar and done heaved him 'side the wall. He hit the wall so hard he stop the juke box from playing.

"Some pimp," the lady back of the counter says. "Some pimp."

The little man jumps up off the floor and starts toward my mama. 'Fore you know it, Mama done sprung open her knife and she's waiting for him.

"Come on," she says. "Come on. I'll gut you from your neighbo to your throat. Come on."

I go up to the little man to hit him, but Mama makes me come and stand 'side her. The little man looks at me and Mama and goes on back to the counter.

"Some pimp," the lady back of the counter says. "Some pimp." She starts laughing and pointing at the little man. "Yes sir, you a pimp, all right. Yes sir-ree."

13 "Fasten that coat, let's go," Mama says.

"You don't have to leave," the lady says. Mama don't answer the lady, and we right out in the cold again. I'm warm right now—my hands, my ears, my feet—but I know this ain't go'n last too long. It done sleet so much now you got ice everywhere you look.

We cross the railroad tracks, and soon's we do, I get cold. That wind goes through this little old coat like it ain't even there. I got on a shirt and a sweater under the coat, but that wind don't pay them no mind. I look up and I can see we got a long way to go. I wonder if we go'n make it 'fore I get too cold.

We cross over to walk on the sidewalk. They got just one sidewalk back here, and it's over there.

After we go just a little piece, I smell bread cooking. I look, then I see a baker shop. When we get closer, I can smell it more better. I shut my eyes and make 'tend I'm eating. But I keep them shut too long and I butt up 'gainst a telephone post. Mama grabs me and see if I'm hurt. I ain't bleeding or nothing and she turns me loose.

I can feel I'm getting colder and colder, and I look up to see how far we still got to go. Uptown is 'way up yonder. A half mile more, I reckon. I try to think of something. They say think and you won't get cold. I think of that poem, "Annabel Lee." I ain't been to school in so long—this bad weather—I reckon they done passed "Annabel Lee" by now. But passed it or not, I'm sure Miss Walker go'n make me recite it when I get there. That woman don't never forget nothing. I ain't never seen nobody like that in my life.

I'm still getting cold. "Annabel Lee" or no "Annabel Lee," I'm still getting cold. But I can see we getting closer. We getting there gradually.

Soon's we turn the corner, I see a little old white lady up in front of us. She's the only lady on the street. She's all in black and she's got a long black rag over her head.

"Stop," she says.

Me and Mama stop and look at her. She must be crazy to be out in all this bad weather. Ain't got but a few other people out there, and all of them's men.

"Y'all done ate?" she says.

"Just finish," Mama says.

"Y'all must be cold then?" she says.

"We headed for the dentist," Mama says. "We'll warm up when we get there."

"What dentist?" the old lady says. "Mr. Bassett?"

"Yes, ma'am," Mama says.

"Come on in," the old lady says. "I'll telephone him and tell him y'all coming."

Me and Mama follow the old lady in the store. It's a little bitty store, and it don't have much in there. The old lady takes off her head rag and folds it up.

"Helena?" somebody calls from the back.

"Yes, Alnest?" the old lady says.

"Did you see them?"

"They're here. Standing beside me."

"Good. Now you can stay inside."

The old lady looks at Mama. Mama's waiting to hear what she brought us in here for. I'm waiting for that, too.

"I saw y'all each time you went by," she says. "I came out to catch you, but you were gone."

"We went back of town," Mama says.

"Did you eat?"

"Yes, ma'am."

The old lady looks at Mama a long time, like she's thinking Mama might be just saying that. Mama looks right back at her. The old lady looks at me to see what I have to say. I don't say nothing. I sure ain't going 'gainst my mama.

"There's food in the kitchen," she says to Mama. "I've been keeping it warm."

Mama turns right around and starts for the door.

"Just a minute," the old lady says. Mama stops. "The boy'll have to work for it. It isn't free."

"We don't take no handout," Mama says.

"I'm not handing out anything," the old lady says. "I need my garbage moved to the front. Ernest has a bad cold and can't go out there."

"James'll move it for you," Mama says.

"Not unless you eat," the old lady says. "I'm old, but I have my pride, too, you know."

Mama can see she ain't go'n beat this old lady down, so she just shakes her head.

"All right," the old lady says. "Come into the kitchen."

She leads the way with that rag in her hand. The kitchen is a little bitty little old thing, too. The table and the stove just 'bout fill it up. They got a little room to the side. Somebody in there laying 'cross the bed—'cause I can see one of his feet. Must be the person she was talking to: Ernest or Alnest—something like that.

"Sit down," the old lady says to Mama. "Not you," she says to me. "You have to move the cans."

"Helena?" the man says in the other room.

"Yes, Alnest?" the old lady says.

"Are you going out there again?"

"I must show the boy where the garbage is, Alnest," the old lady says.

"Keep that shawl over your head," the old man says.

"You don't have to remind me, Alnest. Come, Boy," the old lady says.

We go out in the yard. Little old back yard ain't no bigger than the store or the kitchen. But it can sleet here just like it can sleet in any big back yard. And 'fore you know it, I'm trembling.

"There," the old lady says, pointing to the cans. I pick up one of the cans and set it right back down. The can's so light, I'm go'n see what's inside of it.

"Here," the old lady says. "Leave that can alone."

I look back at her standing there in the door. She's got that black rag wrapped round her shoulders, and she's pointing one of her little old fingers at me.

"Pick it up and carry it to the front," she says. I go by her with the can, and she's looking at me all the time. I'm sure the can's empty. I'm sure she could've carried it herself—maybe both of them at the same time. "Set it on the sidewalk by the door and come back for the other one," she says.

I go and come back, and Mama looks at me when I pass her. I get the other can and take it to the front. It don't feel a bit heavier than that first one. I tell myself I ain't go'n be nobody's fool, and I'm go'n look inside this can to see just what I been hauling. First, I look up the street, then down the street. Nobody coming. Then I look over my shoulder toward the door. That little old lady done slipped up there quiet's a mouse, watching me again. Look like she knowed what I was go'n do.

"Ehh, Lord," she says. "Children, children. Come in here, boy, and go wash your hands."

I follow her in the kitchen. She points toward the bathroom, and I go in there and wash up. Little bitty old bathroom, but it's clean, clean. I don't use any of her towels; I wipe my hands on my pants legs.

When I come back in the kitchen, the old lady done dished up the food. Rice, gravy, meat—and she even got some lettuce and tomato in a saucer. She even got a glass of milk and a piece of cake there, too. It looks so good, I almost start eating 'fore I say my blessing.

"Helena?" the old man says.

"Yes, Alnest?"

"Are they eating?"

"Yes," she says.

"Good," he says. "Now you'll stay inside."

The old lady goes in there where he is and I can hear them talking. I look at Mama. She's eating slow like she's thinking. I wonder what's the matter now. I reckon she's thinking 'bout home.

The old lady comes back in the kitchen.

"I talked to Dr. Bassett's nurse," she says. "Dr. Bassett will take you as soon as you get there."

"Thank you, ma'am," Mama says.

"Perfectly all right," the old lady says. "Which one is it?"

Mama nods toward me. The old lady looks at me real sad. I look sad, too.

"You're not afraid, are you?" she says.

"No, ma'am," I say.

"That's a good boy," the old lady says. "Nothing to be afraid of. Dr. Bassett will not hurt you."

When me and Mama get through eating, we thank the old lady again.

"Helena, are they leaving?" the old man says.

"Yes, Alnest."

"Tell them I say good-bye."

"They can hear you, Alnest."

"Good-bye both mother and son," the old man says. "And may God be with you."

Me and Mama tell the old man good-bye, and we follow the old lady in the front room. Mama opens the door to go out, but she stops and comes back in the store.

"You sell salt meat?" she says.

"Yes."

"Give me two bits worth."

"That isn't very much salt meat," the old lady says.

"That's all I have," Mama says.

The old lady goes back of the counter and cuts a big piece off the chunk. Then she wraps it up and puts it in a paper bag.

"Two bits," she says.

"That looks like awful lot of meat for a quarter," Mama says.

"Two bits," the old lady says. "I've been selling salt meat behind this counter twenty-five years. I think I know what I'm doing."

"You got a scale there," Mama says.

"What?" the old lady says.

"Weigh it," Mama says.

"What?" the old lady says. "Are you telling me how to run my business?"

"Thanks very much for the food," Mama says.

"Just a minute," the old lady says.

"James," Mama says to me. I move toward the door.

"Just one minute, I said," the old lady says.

Me and Mama stop again and look at her. The old lady takes the meat out of the bag and unwraps it and cuts 'bout half of it off. Then she wraps it up again and juggs it back in the bag and gives the bag to Mama. Mama lays the quarter on the counter.

"Your kindness will never be forgotten," she says. "James," she says to me.

We go out, and the old lady comes to the door to look at us. After we go a little piece I look back, and she's still there watching us.

The sleet's coming down heavy, heavy now, and I turn up my coat collar to keep my neck warm. My mama tells me turn it right back down.

"You not a bum," she says. "You a man."

Kay Boyle

(b. 1903) Born in Minnesota, Kay Boyle has lived in many parts of the United States and has spent twenty years in Europe. At present she makes her home in California, where she became a faculty member at San Francisco State College in 1963. She has written novels and poems but is most famous as a short story writer, focusing often on love and its problems.

His Idea of a Mother

The road wound straight on, with a small branch to the left, and there seemed no reason at all to turn and cross the stream that slid along on the other side. A queer thought it would be indeed to follow the cattle path up over the hill.

But the little boy was on his way home from school one day when he stopped at Drury's Crossing and looked up at the signpost that was insisting that the branch to the left led to Shopton and the road before him to something else again. It came into his head that the path and the way it was going had been left unmentioned. He sat down there to have a good look at the hill that was stretching away beyond.

Across the stream there seemed to be a great amount of soft, sweet turf and of greenness spread out all over. Higher, there were trees springing up, as lyrical as dancing women, though all he could see in them was the way they moved in the wind. Beside the stream there was a willow or two drying out its hair.

The path did not quite make the grade to the castle of trees that was bowing this way and that at the top. Just a minute before it got there, it threw up its two small white arms in despair and was lost forever in the blowing weeds. The little boy sat looking at what lay before him and calling upon the courage that would take him over the fence and the stream and up the hill.

The whole of the hill itself was spotted with islands of dung, and if he had summoned any courage at all, it perished at the sight of a cow making her way down. He thought she must be on her way down to drink, but when she

spied him, she stood quite still and looked at him with her soft dim eyes. He sat
hard and small against the fence, wondering if she had any young ones behind
her and watching her full sagging throat and the gentle shifting of her jaw.
Presently, another great angular cow followed the first one, and then another,
and before the little boy could get to his feet and move away, at least eight of
the beasts were stumbling down the stony path.

He stood for a while in the road, watching them lower their muzzles to
drink at the water, and the bright beads from the stream that gathered on their
sparse beards, and the long ribbons of slobber that hung from the ends of
their mouths. Every time they flung wide their rosy nostrils to drink, he could
see the clear ripples which their breath tossed across the surface of the water.
He had no great feeling of pride for himself as he stood on the other side of the
fence from them, for if men and their courage were strangers to him, at least
he knew that the delicate thing which the sight of big animals set shaking
between his ribs was fragile enough to be the ornament of any little girl. His
father had been dead eight years, and what he was like he had no idea at all.

His idea of a mother was something else again. How long she had been dead,
he did not know. He was thinking of her as he walked backward up the road.
His dragging feet were startling up fine clouds of dust in the roadway, and in the
soles of them was more than languor, as if he did not care whether he ever
found his way back to her or not. "Aunt Petoo, skee-doo," he thought. He
looked at the cows and watched their tails moving venomously across their bony
rumps. "Aunt Petoo, skee-doo."

He found her squatting down in the garden before the house. She had a
trowel in her hand, and she was prodding at her flowers. She looked up at him
and pushed her straw bonnet off her brow with the back of her hand.

"Did ye ever take a walk up the path over the hill at Drury's Crossing?" he
said to her as he swung on the gate.

She shook her head absently. "Will you get me some water in the can, there
you are," was what she said. The little boy set down his books. "Don't set
your books down there," she said. "Why do you have to swing on the gate every
time you come in like that?"

"Did ye ever take a walk on that path over the hill at Drury's Crossing?"
asked the little boy.

"Will you get me some water in the can?" said Aunt Petoo.

The little boy walked off with the can in his hand. He was looking around
about him, and up, and over, and looking at the house in its vines, and the trees
wavering and the birds flying, over his shoulder; and in this way he tripped on
a croquet wicket and fell down.

"Get up," said Reynolds.

The little boy sat rubbing his shins and looking sourly at the toes of
Reynolds' boots. Reynolds was the only man he had ever known intimately. His
vest was black and yellow, and it was his place to ride behind Aunt Petoo's
horses and to mow the grass. He could drown kittens, dispose of rabbits with one
whack of the hand, and he could swim. In the summer, he could swim the river
with the muscles of his breasts swelling and gathering like snowballs in the

water. As he stood above the little boy on the croquet lawn, he was red with anger. In one hand he held a carriage whip, and in the other an urchin.

"Look here at this urchin!" he said in contempt to Aunt Petoo. "He was come across stealing cherries!"

There in the sun shone the flushed and dripping face, the contorted mouth, and the terror of the urchin boy. The little boy himself began to whimper at the sight. When he lifted his hand to wipe off his own tears with the back of it, he could see it was shaking as if in the very teeth of cowardice.

"What are you going to do with the urchin?" said the little boy. He whispered it in terror across the grass.

"Thrash him," said Reynolds. "It's what his own father ought to be giving him, not me!" Reynolds swung about to the old lady. "I'm going to thrash him proper, Miss Petoo," he said. He held the urchin up in the sun.

"Not here," said Aunt Petoo. "The wretches squawk so." With the greatest precision she pinched off the leaves that sprang up along the stalk of a begonia. Her mouth did not relent. "Take him around by the stable," she said. "The slugs got into the very best strawberries last night. Not a sizable one for tea, Reynolds!"

"Aunt Petoo," said the little boy, "don't let him thrash the urchin." Aunt Petoo looked up from the flowers. The little boy was standing beside her. "Don't, don't, ah, please don't, Aunt Petoo!" He spoke very quietly, and the "ah" seemed a strange sound for such a small boy to be making. It was a church, a poetry sound, and to hear him using it for a moment put her out.

"But a thief," she said. "A thief who steals . . ."

The little boy's face was shaking like a small fist in her face. "Aunt Petoo, Aunt Petoo," he said. "Please, please, ah, please, please, don't let him do it!"

The garden was as soft and melting as an all-day sucker between the teeth. Aunt Petoo cracked off a great bite of it. "Oh, skee-doo," she said. "Get along with you! Let Reynolds go his own way, and you get about yours! I've been after you for water in the can . . ."

The little boy flung himself against her knees. "Ah, Aunt Petoo, Aunt Petoo," he cried. "No, no, no, no, Aunt Petoo! Let the urchin go once this time, ah, ah, ah, ah, ah, Aunt Petoo!"

A terrible look of venom crossed Aunt Petoo's face. He had made the garden go sick on her very tongue. Reynolds had walked off with the urchin under his arm, and the little boy lay on the ground at her feet, biting fiercely at the turf. "Now listen here," she said. She shook at his shoulder. "Your Uncle Dan is coming home. What do you think of a soldier hearing all this crying and this screaming?" Her voice would never give in. "It's a shame for a boy, and no soldier would bear it."

The little boy lay still.

"Who is my Uncle Dan?" he said, without lifting his head.

"Your father's brother," said Aunt Petoo. "With long whiskers and a sword."

The day had begun to fade away when the little boy started off down the road. That his father's brother was coming back was the thought that remained in his mind. He thought of this until every tree he passed became a menace to him, and his shoelace, untied and tapping at his ankle, made him skid with terror in the gloom.

When he came to Drury's Crossing, he slipped with the greatest glibness beneath the bars of the fence and leaped across the stream. His blood was singing like a harp, and he was not afraid at all. As he ran, he startled a little group of cottontails across the path. He stopped and watched them scampering off through the impenetrable grass. The water was shining like a mirror far below him, and the willows looked as soft and airy as feathers blowing along the stream.

Milkweek pods were tapping at the cups of his knees, and now and again the wing of a moth caressed his cheek. The sight of a moth in the room with him made his spine crawl, but here in the dark it was natural and left him with no fear at all. When he seated himself in the deep grass, he felt as if he were crouching on the hearth close before the fire. Even the wind that rose was as warm as a scarf around his neck.

Whether he fell asleep then or whether his eyes were open all the time he did not know. But however it was, he had not been sitting there long when he saw the cows beginning to loom out of the darkness and make their way down toward the stream. They were going slowly down, with their heads hanging like heavy copper bells between their forelegs, their jaws endlessly and softly crunching, and when they stopped at all, it was to lift their heads and call softly out through the falling night.

The deep mellow sound of the cows calling to one another was so beautiful that the little boy tried the sound of it in his own throat. He lifted his head to catch the soft shape of the cows' mouths and the turn of their velvet tongues in their jaws. His nostrils were stretched wide open, imitating the cows' rosy nostrils, which were spread full as harvest moons.

The great dark beasts seemed in no great haste to descend the hill, and they loitered here and there in the rich night. Had they been horses, thought the little boy, the least sound of him stirring would have sent them off in alarm, but here were the cows cropping at the grass and munching it almost at his feet, as though the smell of him there meant nothing to them. Any movement he made seemed natural to them, and when he put out his hand and stroked the foreleg of one cow that stood near by, she lifted her head in no dismay whatever and snuffed deeply at his neck. Such a blast of sweet meadowy odor passed across his face that he shuddered with delight.

It was then that the beast he had stroked bent her knees under her and lay down in the grass. He could not perceive her in the darkness, but from the sound and breath of her and the soft swing and crunch of her jaws, he knew that she had folded her gray, horny hoofs under her heart and was chewing gently there beside him in the grass. When he moved closer, she made no sign. Even the touch of his hand on her strong shoulder did not cause her to stir. When he stroked the stiff, sleek curve of her ear in his open hand, she flicked it solemnly back and forth.

The little boy shifted himself against her and pressed his small lean back into her strong covered bones. The endless rhythm of her cud swung easily through all her rich shoulder and bosom. Great tough ribbons of movement ran strongly through her flesh. The little boy had laid his face against her neck, and there was his ear stroked and soothed with it. He could hear the soft humming of her belly as it greeted and returned the food from her fruitful jaws. On the ground he could feel the feast of white violets and clover heads that had been spread there before her. As he lay against her he thought of the great full sack of milk that was hanging between her legs.

He was thinking what a comfort it was to have the great warm body of the cow against him in the field, and while he was drowsing, suddenly she whipped her head about so violently that she gave him a fierce blow in the ribs with the side of her horn. When he had found his senses again, he thought it must have been a fly that had disturbed her, or else she would never have struck him with such force. This was the thought that was in his head when she turned again toward him and rubbed her great bony face against his arm. Such blasts did she thrust from her nose on him, like a mother cat smelling out her young, that he thought he would be blown down the black field. But presently, when she had snuffed in enough of him, her tongue began to move rudely across his hand, lifting his fingers up and turning them over as if they were so many stalks of clover. When she had done with his hands, she licked her way up the coarse stuff of his jacket, and there was his neck and his ear and all the hairs on his head getting such a scrubbing and such a loving as would have taken his hide off had it been anyone else that was doing it to him.

It was when the half-moon was coming up from behind the trees that the mother cow, without any kind of warning at all, suddenly straightened out her legs and stood up in the grass. A terrible feeling of despair pierced the little boy's heart. But she went ambling quietly off, with her tail swinging, and the little boy himself started reluctantly down the hill. The whole world was returning again under the illumination of the moon. The trees were uncurling out of the darkness, and the grass was moving like a sea. When the little boy reached the water, he stopped for a moment. In the middle of the stream lay a little broken moon, rippling back and forth. He knelt down and put his two hands about its moving edges and tried to lift it up. In a moment the little moon was rippling back and forth again and his hands were wet and cold.

The little boy crossed the fence and started up the dusty road. The old landmarks were familiar to him in the strange light. When he came to the gate of the garden, some kind of human fear possessed him. It was a surprise to himself when he pushed the gate open and walked up the path. A man with a pipe in his mouth was turning up and down the terrace. The little boy stood still for a while and watched this sight. When the man turned again he looked down the garden, and he too stopped in his walk.

"Hullo," he remarked. He had no whiskers.

"Are you Uncle Dan?" said the little boy.

"Right you are," said the man.

"Are you going to thrash me?" said the little boy.

"Is that customary in greeting a nephew?" asked Uncle Dan.

"I ran away," explained the little boy. "If my father was here, he'd thrash me—"

"Hold on, sir," said Uncle Dan. The little boy stood staring at him in silence. Uncle Dan glanced over his shoulder. "I say," he remarked in a lower tone, "shall we walk down the road a bit so we shan't be disturbed?"

Adrienne Rich

(b. 1929) A graduate of Radcliffe College and a member of Phi Beta Kappa, Adrienne Rich has described her life as one of privilege. Her poems often reflect the anguish of her role-conflict as a wife and mother as well as a writer. Recent collections of her works include Snapshots of a Daughter-in-Law, Necessities of Life, *and* Leaflets.

Night-Pieces: For a Child

The Crib

You sleeping I bend to cover.
Your eyelids work. I see
your dream, cloudy as a negative,
swimming underneath.
You blurt a cry. Your eyes
spring open, still filmed in dream.
Wider, they fix me—
—death's head, sphinx, medusa?
You scream.
Tears lick my cheeks, my knees
droop at your fear.
Mother I no more am,
but woman, and nightmare.

Reprinted from Necessities of Life, *Poems, 1962–1965, by Adrienne Rich. By permission of W. W. Norton & Company, Inc. Copyright* ©*1966 by W. W. Norton & Company, Inc.*

III. the dominating wife: the bitch

The three stories in this section deal with violence and death. The images of guns, hunting, war, a knife, and fire are used to show the effects of an unnatural woman, one who dominates men. Mrs. Ormsby, in Wright Morris' "The Ram in the Thicket," drives her son out of the house and ultimately to his death, which becomes an occasion of self-glorification for her; she turns her husband into a "househusband," completely unmanning him. Margaret Macomber, in Hemingway's "The Short Happy Life of Francis Macomber," not only deprives her husband of pride in his courage and virility but (it is strongly implied) becomes his executioner in order to prevent his assumption of the dominant role in their relationship. Mrs. Washington, in Alice Walker's "Her Sweet Jerome," destroys the books which were her husband's only refuge from her domination and in the process destroys herself. The effects of female dominance are shown to be disastrous.

The causes of female dominance are seen as unnatural. Mrs. Ormsby, unable to nurse her baby, hires a wet-nurse for him; the humble illiterate woman is a successful mother surrogate for the learned Mrs. Ormsby who quotes Latin phrases and is an authority on birds. A fanatically clean housekeeper, she drives her husband to the basement and her son to spending most of his time outdoors. She refuses to fulfill her "natural" role as cook after her husband has given the boy a gun, which to both males is a symbol of manhood. The gulf in understanding is unbridgeable, for Mrs. Ormsby, the bird-lover, can see hunting only as destruction and death. When the boy is killed, she preens herself at the prospect of dedicating a battleship to his memory, instead of mourning as she "naturally" should.

The title of this story, "The Ram in the Thicket," reminds the reader of the Biblical story of Abraham and Isaac in which Abraham is spared having to kill his son because God provides a ram for the necessary sacrifice. Mr. Ormsby is not spared the actual death of his son; he accepts his wife's imputation that he is ultimately responsible for the boy's death. But Mr. Ormsby has what Isaac's life meant symbolically to Abraham: the continuance of his name, on the battleship *Ormsby*. The son, in dying, has given the father immortality. In focusing the story on the father as the central consciousness through whom all the characters are seen, Morris lets the reader understand more than Mr. Ormsby did; we see that it was not the father but the mother who drove the son to his death. A totally selfish, cold, unintelligent woman, she has victimized both father and son because of her refusal to let them be themselves. The husband is as dead as the son, brainwashed into a total role reversal with his wife. Neither the father nor the son is a complete person because Mrs. Ormsby is an "anal" character, in psychological terms, one who holds on to all she possesses. She will not let the males be themselves. Significantly, the only moment of human relationship between father and son comes when they share the basement toilet. Their unity is expressed through the boy's remark, "Well, Pop, I suppose one flush ought to do." Mrs. Ormsby disguises her flushings in the remote upstairs bathroom by turning on the shower. Like her sexual coldness in spite of provocative breasts, her refusal to recognize the physical is shown to be unnatural. The reader can see the irony of the title: the son has been a ram in the thicket—a substitute for the father, who is the real victim in the war between the sexes. The opening image of the story, the father's nightmare, lets us see his identification with his son. In giving the son a gun, the father was living vicariously the life he had never been able to experience for himself, and the son's death is a substitute for his own spiritual death: his name will live.

In Hemingway's story "The Short Happy Life of Francis Macomber," the war between the sexes is more overt. This is partly because the struggle of Francis Macomber for manhood, his brief achievement of a "*happy* life," is presented objectively through the eyes of a character in the story, the guide Wilson. Wilson applies his own definition of masculinity (independence and courage) to Francis Macomber and identifies Francis' assertion of his masculinity as happiness. Margaret is despised by Wilson because she rules Macomber through her beauty; he sees her as typical of American women, who are "the hardest in the world; the hardest, the cruelest, the most predatory and the most attractive." It is her love of Macomber's money which binds her to him, not any natural love; when he asserts his masculinity during the hunt, her control and possession of him are threatened. According to Wilson's view, her "accidental" shot was really intentional; she kills her husband in order to keep control over what he represented to her—his wealth. The reader, not necessarily concurring in Wilson's opinion, may see her shot as accidental; ironically, she may have wanted Francis to live because finally he has become a man to whom she can surrender. Perhaps she, too, realizes that her role as the dominant partner was "unnatural."

Both Hemingway and Morris let us see the role of dominating wife through male eyes. It is the masculine view that an "artificial" woman—one highly learned like Mrs. Ormsby, or extraordinarily beautiful but money-loving like Mrs. Macomber—is cold, selfish, and destructive. In Alice Walker's "Her Sweet Jerome" a dominating wife is revealed through a feminine central consciousness as self-destructive. Mrs. Washington significantly has no other name in the story; it is the way she plays her role as wife that leads to her death. She is big and awkward, the opposite of her "cute little" Jerome; she is not only ignorant but anti-intellectual, despised by her schoolteacher husband. Why this diverse pair should ever have married can be understood only in terms of their role reversal: the "sweet Jerome" marries a woman who is eager to provide for him all the material goods he cannot provide for himself, while she pursues and "gets" him. Like a frigid wife who marries for security, he tolerates her sexual demands; like a possessive husband, she becomes wildly jealous at the suspicion that he is unfaithful. Her frantic search for her rival turns her into a beast of prey, with wild eyes and a putrid odor.

Like Mrs. Ormsby and Mrs. Macomber, Mrs. Washington is portrayed as an unnatural woman. Her desire to play the male role, her denial that her husband beats her, and her insane jealousy leads to her total alienation from the community and to her own madness. By focusing on a female consciousness, Alice Walker emphasizes that for a woman the psychic cost of departing from a socially acceptable role is unbearable. By focusing on the male point of view, Morris and Hemingway show that a departure from the norm causes great misery for men. All three authors show that female aggressiveness, in the long run, is ineffectual in suppressing masculine goals: it does not succeed in subverting the social order. Jerome Washington continues his real concern, leading a black revolution; Roger Ormsby succeeds in showing his son how to be a man; and Francis Macomber upholds the masculine code of unflinching courage. Domination by a wife is viewed as not only unnatural but futile.

Wright Morris

*(b. 1910) Wright Morris has written
about his native Nebraska in a
novel* The Home Place *(1948);* The
Field of Vision *won the National Book
Award in 1957. One of his frequent
themes, the relationship between man
and boy, is treated in his most recent
novel,* Fire Sermon *(1971).*

The Ram in the Thicket

In this dream Mr. Ormsby stood in the yard—at the edge of the yard where
the weeds began—and stared at a figure that appeared to be on a rise. This
figure had the head of a bird with a crown of bright, exotic plumage—visible,
somehow, in spite of the helmet he wore. Wisps of it appeared at the side,
or shot through the top of it like a pillow leaking long sharp spears of yellow
straw. Beneath the helmet was the face of a bird, a long face indescribably
solemn, with eyes so pale they were like openings on the sky. The figure was
clothed in a uniform, a fatigue suit that was dry at the top but wet and dripping
about the waist and knees. Slung over the left arm, very casually, was a gun.
The right arm was extended and above it hovered a procession of birds, an
endless coming and going of all the birds he had ever seen. The figure did not
speak—nor did the pale eyes turn to look at him—although it was for this, this
alone, that Mr. Ormsby was there. The only sounds he heard were those his
lips made for the birds, a wooing call of irresistible charm. As he stared Mr.
Ormsby realized that he was pinned to something, a specimen pinned to a wall
that had quietly moved up behind. His hands were fastened over his head
and from the weight he felt in his wrists he knew he must be suspended there.
He knew he had been brought there to be judged, sentenced, or whatever—and
this would happen when the figure looked at him. He waited, but the sky-blue
eyes seemed only to focus on the birds, and his lips continued to speak to
them wooingly. They came and went, thousands of them, and there were so

Reprinted by permission of the author. From Harper's Bazaar, *May 1948; reprinted in*
Wright Morris: A Reader, *Harper & Row, 1970.*

many, and all so friendly, that Mr. Ormsby, also, extended his hand. He did this although he knew that up to that moment his hands were tied—but strange to relate, in that gesture, he seemed to be free. Without effort he broke the bonds and his hand was free. No birds came—but in his palm he felt the dull drip of the alarm clock and he held it tenderly, like a living thing, until it ran down.

In the morning light the photograph at the foot of his bed was a little startling—for the boy stood alone on a rise, and he held, very casually, a gun. The face beneath the helmet had no features, but Mr. Ormsby would have known it just by the—well, just by the stance. He would have known it just by the way the boy held the gun. He held the gun like some women held their arms when their hands were idle, like parts of their body that for the moment were not much use. Without the gun it was as if some part of the boy had been amputated; the way he stood, even the way he walked was not quite right. But with the gun—what seemed out, fell into place.

He had given the boy a gun because he had never had a gun himself and not because he wanted him to kill anything. The boy didn't want to kill anything either—he couldn't very well with his first gun because of the awful racket the beebees made in the barrel. He had given him a thousand-shot gun—but the rattle the bee-bees made in the barrel made it impossible for the boy to get close to anything. And *that* was what had made a hunter out of him. He had to stalk everything in order to get close enough to hit it, and after you stalk it you naturally want to hit something. When he got a gun that would really shoot, and only made a racket after he shot it, it was only natural that he shot it better than anyone else. He said shoot, because the boy never seemed to realize that when he shot and hit something the something was dead. He simply didn't realize this side of things at all. But when he brought a rabbit home and fried it— by himself, for Mother wouldn't let *him* touch it—he never kidded them about the meat they ate themselves. He never really knew whether the boy did that out of kindness for Mother, or simply because he never thought about such things. He never seemed to feel like talking much about anything. He would sit and listen to Mother—he had never once been disrespectful—nor had he ever once heeded anything she said. He would listen, respectfully, and that was all. It was a known fact that Mother knew more about birds and bird migration than anyone in the state of Pennsylvania—except the boy. It was clear to him that the boy knew more, but for years it had been Mother's business and it meant more to her—the business did—than to the boy. But it was only natural that a woman who founded the League for Wild Life Conservation would be upset by a boy who lived with a gun. It was only natural—he was upset himself by the *idea* of it—but the boy and his gun somehow never bothered him. He had never seen a boy and a dog, or a boy and anything any closer—and if the truth were known both the boy's dogs knew it, nearly died of it. Not that he wasn't friendly, or as nice to them as any boy, but they knew they simply didn't rate in a class with his gun. Without that gun the boy himself really looked funny, didn't know how to stand, and nearly fell over if you talked to him. It was only natural that he enlisted, and there was nothing he ever heard that surprised him less than their making a hero out of him. Nothing more natural than that they should name something after him. If the boy had had his choice it would have been a gun rather than a boat, a thousand-shot non-rattle bee-bee gun named Ormsby. But it would kill Mother if she knew—maybe it would kill nearly anybody—what he thought was the most natural thing of all. Let God strike him dead if he had known anything righter, anything more natural, than that the boy should be killed. That was something he could not explain, and would certainly never mention to Mother unless he slipped up some night and talked in his sleep.

He turned slowly on the bed, careful to keep the springs quiet, and as he lowered his feet he scooped his socks from the floor. As a precaution Mother had slept the first few months of their marriage in her corset—as a precaution and as an aid to self-control. In the fall they had ordered twin beds. Carrying his shoes—today, of all days, would be a trial for Mother—he tiptoed to the closet and picked up his shirt and pants. There was simply no reason, as he had explained to her twenty years ago, why she should get up when he could just as well get a bite for himself. He had made that suggestion when the boy was just a baby and she needed her strength. Even as it was she didn't come out of it any too well. The truth was, Mother was so thorough about everything she did that her breakfasts usually took an hour or more. When he did it himself he was out of the kitchen in ten, twelve minutes and without leaving any pile of dishes around. By himself he could quick-rinse them in a little hot water, but with Mother there was the dish pan and all of the suds. Mother had the idea that a meal simply wasn't a meal without setting the table and using half the dishes in the place. It was easier to do it himself, and except for Sunday, when they had brunch, he was out of the house an hour before she got up. He had a bite of lunch at the store and at four o'clock he did the day's shopping since he was right downtown anyway. There was a time he called her up and inquired as to what she thought she wanted, but since he did all the buying he knew that better himself. As secretary for the League of Women Voters she had enough on her mind in times like these without cluttering it up with food. Now that he left the store an hour early he usually got home in the midst of her nap or while she was taking her bath. As he had nothing else to do he prepared the vegetables, and dressed the meat, as Mother had never shown much of a flare for meat. There had been a year—when the boy was small and before he had taken up that gun—when she had made several marvelous lemon meringue pies. But feeling as she did about the gun—and she told them both how she felt about it—she didn't see why she should slave in the kitchen for people like that. She always spoke to them as *they*—or as *you* plural—from the time he had given the boy the gun. Whether this was because they were both men, both culprits, or both something else, they were never entirely separate things again. When she called *they* would both answer, and though the boy had been gone two years he still felt him *there*, right beside him, when Mother said *you*.

For some reason he could not understand—although the rest of the house was neat as a pin, too neat—the room they *lived* in was always a mess. Mother refused to let the cleaning woman set her foot in it. Whenever she left the house she locked the door. Long, long ago he had said something, and she had said something, and she had said she had wanted one room in the house where she could relax and just let her hair down. That had sounded so wonderfully human, so unusual for Mother, that he had been completely taken with it. As a matter of fact he still didn't know what to say. It was the only room in the house—except for the screened-in porch in the summer—where he could take off his shoes and open his shirt on his underwear. If the room was *clean*, it would be clean like all of the others, and that would leave him nothing but the basement and the porch. The way the boy took to the out-of-doors—he stopped looking for his cuff links, began to look for pins—was partially because he couldn't find a place in the house to sit down. They had just redecorated the house—the boy at that time was just a little shaver—and Mother had spread newspapers over everything. There hadn't been a chair in the place—except the straight-backed ones at the table—that hadn't been, that *wasn't* covered with a piece of newspaper. Anyone who had ever scrunched around on a paper knew what that was like. It was at that time that he had got the idea of having his pipe in the basement, reading in the bedroom, and the boy had taken to the out-of-doors. Because he had always wanted a gun himself, and because the boy was alone, with no kids around to play with, he had brought him home that damn gun. A thousand-shot gun by the name of Daisy—funny that he should remember the name—and five thousand bee-bees in a drawstring canvas bag.

That gun had been a mistake—he began to shave himself in tepid, lukewarm water rather than let it run hot, which would bang the pipes and wake Mother up. That gun had been a mistake—when the telegram came that the boy had been killed Mother hadn't said a word, but she made it clear whose fault it was. There was never any doubt, *any* doubt, as to just whose fault it was.

He stopped thinking while he shaved, attentive to the mole at the edge of his mustache, and leaned to the mirror to avoid dropping suds on the rug. There had been a time when he had wondered about an oriental throw rug in the bathroom, but over twenty years he had become accustomed to it. As a matter of fact he sort of missed it whenever they had guests with children and Mother remembered to take it up. Without the rug he always felt just a little uneasy, a little naked, in the bathroom, and this made him whistle or turn on the water and let it run. If it hadn't been for that he might not have noticed as soon as he did that Mother did the same thing whenever anybody was in the house. She turned on the water and let it run until she was through with the toilet, then she would flush it before she turned the water off. If you happen to have old-fashioned plumbing, and have lived with a person for twenty years, you can't help noticing little things like that. He had got to be a little like that himself: since the boy had gone he used the one in the basement or waited until he got down to the store. As a matter of fact it was more convenient, didn't wake Mother up, and he could have his pipe while he was sitting there.

With his pants on, but carrying his shirt—for he might get it soiled preparing breakfast—he left the bathroom and tiptoed down the stairs.

Although the boy had gone, was gone, that is, Mother still liked to preserve her slip covers and the kitchen linoleum. It was a good piece, well worth preserving, but unless there were guests in the house he never saw it—he nearly forgot that it was there. The truth was he had to look at it once a week, every time he put down the papers—but right now he couldn't tell you what color that linoleum was! He couldn't do it, and wondering what in the world color it was he bent over and peeked at it—blue. Blue and white, Mother's favorite colors of course.

Suddenly he felt the stirring in his bowels. Usually this occurred while he was rinsing the dishes after his second cup of coffee or after the first long draw on his pipe. He was not supposed to smoke in the morning, but it was more important to be regular that way than irregular with his pipe. Mother had been the first to realize this—not in so many words—but she would rather he did anything than not be able to do *that*.

He measured out a pint and a half of water, put it over a medium fire, and added just a pinch of salt. Then he walked to the top of the basement stairs, turned on the light, and at the bottom turned it off. He dipped his head to pass beneath a sagging line of wash, the sleeves dripping, and with his hands out, for the corner was dark, he entered the cell.

The basement toilet had been put in to accommodate the help, who had to use something, and Mother would not have them on her oriental rug. Until the day he dropped some money out of his pants and had to strike a match to look for it, he had never noticed what kind of a stool it was. Mother had picked it up secondhand—she had never told him where—because she couldn't see buying something new for a place always in the dark. It was very old, with a chain pull, and operated on a principle that invariably produced quite a splash. But in spite of that, he preferred it to the one at the store and very much more than the one upstairs. This was rather hard to explain since the seat was pretty cold in the winter and the water sometimes nearly froze. But it was private like no other room in the house. Considering that the house was as good as empty, that was a strange thing to say, but it was the only way to say how he felt. If he went off for a walk like the boy, Mother would miss him, somebody would see him, and he wouldn't feel right about it anyhow. All he wanted was a dark quiet place and the feeling that for five minutes, just five minutes, nobody would be looking for him. Who would ever believe five minutes like that were so hard to come by? The closest he had ever been to the boy—after he had given him the gun—was the morning he had found him here on the stool. It was then that the boy had said, *et tu, Brutus*, and they had both laughed so hard they had had to hold their sides. The boy had put his head in a basket of wash so Mother wouldn't hear. Like everything the boy said there were two or three ways to take it, and in the dark Mr. Ormsby could not see his face. When he stopped laughing the boy said, *Well Pop, I suppose one flush ought to do,* but Mr. Ormsby had not been able to say anything. To be called Pop made him so weak that he had to sit right down on the stool, just like he was, and support his head in his hands. Just as he had never had a name for the boy, the boy had never had a name for him—none, that is, that Mother would permit him to use. Of all the names Mother couldn't stand, Pop was the worst, and he agreed with her, it was vulgar, common, and used by strangers to intimidate old men. He agreed with her, completely—until he heard the word in the boy's mouth.

It was only natural that the boy would use it if he ever had the chance—but he never dreamed that any word, especially *that* word, could mean what it did. It made him weak, he had to sit down and pretend he was going about his business, and what a blessing it was that the place was dark. Nothing more was said, ever, but it remained their most important conversation—so important they were afraid to try and improve on it. Days later he remembered the rest of the boy's sentence, and how shocking it was but without any *sense* of shock. A blow so sharp that he had no sense of pain, only a knowing, as he had under gas, that he had been worked on. For two, maybe three minutes, there in the dark they had been what Mother called them, they were *they*—and they were there in the basement because they were so much alike. When the telegram came, and when he knew what he would find, he had brought it there, had struck a match, and read what it said. The match filled the cell with light and he saw—he couldn't help seeing—piles of tin goods in the space beneath the stairs. Several dozen cans of tuna fish and salmon, and since *he* was the one that had the points, bought the groceries, there was only one place Mother could have got such things. It had been a greater shock than the telegram—that was the honest-to-God's truth and anyone who knew Mother as well as he did would have felt the same. It was unthinkable, but there it was—and there were more on top of the water closet, where he peered while precariously balanced on the stool. Cans of pineapple, crabmeat, and tins of Argentine beef. He had been stunned, the match had burned down and actually scorched his fingers, and he nearly killed himself when he forgot and stepped off the seat. Only later in the morning—after he had sent the flowers to ease the blow for Mother—did he realize how such a thing *must* have occurred. Mother knew so many influential people, and before the war they gave her so much, that they had very likely given her all of this stuff as well. Rather than turn it down and needlessly alienate people, influential people, Mother had done the next best thing. While the war was on she refused to serve it, or profiteer in any way—and at the same time not alienate people foolishly. It had been an odd thing, certainly, that he should discover all of that by the same match that he read the telegram. Naturally, he never breathed a word of it to Mother, as something like that, even though she was not superstitious, would really upset her. It was one of those things that he and the boy would keep to themselves.

It would be like Mother to think of putting it in here, the very last place that the cleaning woman would look for it. The new cleaning woman would neither go upstairs nor down, and did whatever she did somewhere else. Mr. Ormsby lit a match to see if everything was all right—hastily blew it out when he saw that the can pile had increased. He stood up—then hurried up the stairs without buttoning his pants as he could hear the water boiling. He added half a cup, then measured three heaping tablespoons of coffee into the bottom of the double boiler, buttoned his pants. Looking at his watch he saw that it was seven-thirty-five. As it would be a hard day—sponsoring a boat was a man-size job—he would give Mother another ten minutes or so. He took two bowls from the cupboard, sat them on blue pottery saucers, and with the grapefruit knife in his hand walked to the icebox.

As he put his head in the icebox door—in order to see he had to—Mr. Ormsby stopped breathing and closed his eyes. What had been dying for some time was now dead. He leaned back, inhaled, leaned in again. The floor of the icebox was covered with a fine assortment of jars full of leftovers Mother simply could not throw away. Some of the jars were covered with little oilskin hoods, some with saucers, and some with paper snapped on with a rubber band. It was impossible to tell, from the outside, which one it was. Seating himself on the floor he removed them one at a time, starting at the front and working toward the back. As he had done this many times before, he got well into the problem, near the middle, before troubling to sniff anything. A jar which might have been carrots—it was hard to tell without probing—was now a furry marvel of green mold. It smelled only mildly, however, and Mr. Ormsby remembered that this was penicillin, the life-giver. A spoonful of cabbage—it had been three months since they had had cabbage—had a powerful stench but was still not the one he had in mind. There were two more jars of mold, the one screwed tight he left alone as it had a frosted look and the top of the lid bulged. The culprit, however, was not that at all, but in an open saucer on the next shelf—part of an egg—Mr. Ormsby had beaten the white himself. He placed the saucer on the sink and returned all but two of the jars to the icebox; the cabbage and the explosive looking one. If it smelled he took it out, otherwise Mother had to see for herself as she refused to take *their* word for these things. When he was just a little shaver the boy had walked into the living room full of Mother's guests and showed them something in a jar. Mother had been horrified—but she naturally thought it a frog or something and not a bottle out of her own icebox. When one of the ladies asked the boy where in the world he had found it, he naturally said, *In the icebox.* Mother had never forgiven him. After that she forbade him to look in the box without permission, and the boy had not so much as peeked in it since. He would eat only what he found on the table, or ready to eat in the kitchen—or what he found at the end of those walks he took everywhere.

With the jar of cabbage and furry mold Mr. Ormsby made a trip to the garage, picked up the garden spade, walked around behind. At one time he had emptied the jars and merely buried the contents, but recently, since the war that is, he had buried it all. Part of it was a question of time—he had more work to do at the store—but the bigger part of it was to put an end to the jars. Not that it worked out that way—all Mother had to do was open a new one—but it gave him a real satisfaction to bury them. Now that the boy and his dogs were gone there was simply no one around the house to eat up all the food Mother saved.

There were worms in the fork of earth he had turned and he stood looking at them—*they* both had loved worms—when he remembered the water boiling on the stove. He dropped everything and ran, ran right into Emil Ludlow, the milkman, before he noticed him. Still on the run he went up the steps and through the screen door into the kitchen—he was clear to the stove before he remembered the door would slam. He started back, but too late, and in the silence that followed the BANG he stood with his eyes tightly closed, his fists clenched. Usually he remained in this condition until a sign from Mother—a thump on the floor or her voice at the top of the stairs. None came, however, only the sound of the milk bottles that Emil Ludlow was leaving on the porch. Mr. Ormsby gave him time to get away, waited until he heard the horse walking, then he went out and brought the milk in. At the icebox he remembered the water—why it was he had come running in the first place—and he left the door open and hurried to the stove. It was down to half a cup but not, thank heavens, dry. He added a full pint, then returned and put the milk in the icebox; took out the butter, four eggs, and a Flori-gold grapefruit. Before he cut the grape-fruit he looked at his watch and seeing that it was ten minutes to eight, an hour before train time, he opened the stairway door.

"Ohhh Mother!" he called, and then he returned to the grapefruit.

Ad astra per aspera, she said, and rose from the bed. In the darkness she felt about for her corset then let herself go completely for the thirty-five seconds it required to get it on. This done, she pulled the cord to the light that hung in the attic, and as it snapped on, in a firm voice she said, *Fiat lux.* Light having been made, Mother opened her eyes.

As the bulb hung in the attic, thirty feet away and out of sight, the closet remained in an afterglow, a twilight zone. It was not light, strictly speaking, but it was all Mother wanted to see. Seated on the attic stairs she trimmed her toenails with a pearl handled knife that Mr. Ormsby had been missing for several years. The blade was not so good any longer and using it too freely had resulted in ingrown nails on both of her big toes. But Mother preferred it to scissors which were proven, along with bathtubs, to be one of the most dangerous things in the home. *Even more than the battlefield, the most dangerous place in the world. Dry feet and hands before turning on lights, dry between toes.*

Without stooping she slipped into her sabots and left the closet, the light burning, and with her eyes dimmed, but not closed, went down the hall. Locking the bathroom door she stepped to the basin and turned on the cold water, then she removed several feet of paper from the toilet paper roll. This took time, as in order to keep the roller from squeaking, it had to be removed from its socket in the wall, then returned. One piece she put in the pocket of her kimono, the other she folded into a wad and used as a blotter to dab up spots on the floor. Turning up the water she sat down on the stool—then she got up to get a pencil and pad from the table near the window. On the first sheet she wrote—

> Ars longa, vita brevis
> Wildflower club, sun. 4 pm.

She tore this off and filed it, tip showing, right at the front of her corset. On the next page—

> ROGER—
> Ivory Snow
> Sani Flush on thurs.

As she placed this on top of the toilet paper roll she heard him call "First for breakfast." She waited until he closed the stairway door, then she stood up and

turned on the shower. As it rained into the tub and splashed behind her in
the basin, she lowered the lid, flushed the toilet. Until the water closet had
filled, stopped gurgling, she stood at the window watching a squirrel cross the
yard from tree to tree. Then she turned the shower off and noisily dragged
the shower curtain, on its metal rings, back to the wall. She dampened her
shower cap in the basin and hung it on the towel rack to dry, dropping the towel
that was there down the laundry chute. This done, she returned to the basin
and held her hands under the running water, now cold, until she was awake.
With her index finger she massaged her gums—*there is no pyorrhea among the
Indians*—and then, with the tips of her fingers, she dampened her eyes.

She drew the blind, and in the half light the room seemed to be full of lukewarm water, greenish in color. With a piece of Kleenex, she dried her eyes,
then turned it to gently blow her nose, first the left side, then with a little more
blow on the right. There was nothing to speak of, nothing, so she folded the
tissue, slipped it into her pocket. Raising the blind, she faced the morning with
her eyes softly closed, letting the light come in as prescribed—gradually. Eyes
wide, she then stared for a full minute at the yard full of grackles, covered
with grackles, before she *discovered* them. Running to the door, her head in the
hall, her arm in the bathroom wildly pointing, she tried to whisper, loud-whisper
to him, but her voice cracked.

"Roger," she called, a little hoarsely. "The window—run!"

She heard him turn from the stove and skid on the newspapers, bump into
the sink, curse, then get up and on again.

"Blackbirds?" he whispered.

"Grackles!" she said, for the thousandth time she said *Grackles.*

"They're pretty!" he said.

"Family—" she said, ignoring him, "family *icteridae* American."

"Well—" he said.

"Roger!" she said, "something's burning."

She heard him leave the window and on his way back to the stove, on the
same turn, skid on the papers again. She left him there and went down the
hall to the bedroom, closed the door, and passed between the mirrors once more
to the closet. From five dresses—*any woman with more than five dresses, at
this time, should have the vote taken away from her*—she selected the navy blue
sheer with pink lace yoke and kerchief, short bolero. At the back of the closet—
but in order to see she had to return to the bathroom, look for the flashlight
in the drawer full of rags and old tins of shoe polish—were three shelves, each
supporting ten to twelve pairs of shoes, and a large selection of slippers were
piled on the floor. On the second shelf were the navy blue pumps—*we all have
one weakness, but between men and shoes you can give me shoes*—navy blue
pumps with a cuban heel and a small bow. She hung the dress from the neck of
the floor lamp, placed the shoes on the bed. From beneath the bed she pulled
a hat box—the hat was new. Navy straw with shasta daisies, pink geraniums
and a navy blue veil with pink and white fuzzy dots. She held it out where it
could be seen in the mirror, front and side, without seeing herself—*it's not every
day that one sponsors a boat.* Not every day, and she turned to the calendar

on her night table, a bird calendar featuring the natural-color male goldfinch for the month of June. Under the date of June 23rd she printed the words, *family icteridae–yardful,* and beneath it—

Met Captain Sudcliffe and gave him U. S. S. *Ormsby*

When he heard Mother's feet on the stairs Mr. Ormsby cracked her soft boiled eggs and spooned them carefully into her heated cup. He had spilled his own on the floor when he had run to look at the black—or whatever color they were—birds. As they were very, very soft he had merely wiped them up. As he buttered the toast—the four burned slices were on the back porch airing— Mother entered the kitchen and said, "Roger—*more* toast?"

"I was watching blackbirds," he said.

"Grack-les," she said, "Any bird is a *black*bird if the males are largely or entirely black."

Talk about male and female birds really bothered Mr. Ormsby. Although she was a girl of the old school Mother never hesitated, *anywhere*, to speak right out about male and female birds. A cow was a cow, a bull was a bull, but to Mr. Ormsby a bird was a bird.

"Among the birdfolk," said Mother, "the menfolk, so to speak, wear the feathers. The female has more serious work to do."

"How does that fit the blackbirds?" said Mr. Ormsby.

"Every rule" said Mother, "has an exception."

There was no denying the fact that the older Mother got the more distinguished she appeared. As for himself, what he saw in the mirror looked very much like the Roger Ormsby that had married Violet Ames twenty years ago. As the top of his head got hard the bottom tended to get a little soft, but otherwise there wasn't much change. But it was hard to believe that Mother was the pretty little pop-eyed girl—he had thought it was her corset that popped them—whose nipples had been like buttons on her dress. Any other girl would have looked like a you-know—but there wasn't a man in Media county, or anywhere else, who ever mentioned it. A man could think what he would think, but he was the only man who really knew what Mother was like. And how little she was like *that*.

"Three-seven-four east one-one-six," said Mother.

That was the way her mind worked, all over the place in one cup of coffee— birds one moment, Mrs. Dinardo the next.

He got up from the table and went after Mrs. Dinardo's letter—Mother seldom had time to read them unless he read them to her. Returning, he divided the rest of the coffee between them, unequally: three quarters for Mother, a swallow of grounds for himself. He waited a moment, wiping his glasses, while Mother looked through the window at another black bird. "Cowbird," she said, *"Molothrus ater."*

"Dear Mrs. Ormsby," Mr. Ormsby began. Then he stopped to scan the page, as Mrs. Dinardo had a strange style and was not much given to writing letters. "Dear Mrs. Ormsby," he repeated, "I received your letter and I Sure was glad to know that you are both well and I know you often think of me I often think

of you too—" He paused to get his breath—Mrs. Dinardo's style was not much
for pauses—and to look at Mother. But Mother was still with the cowbird. "Well,
Mrs. Ormsby," he continued, "I haven't a thing in a room that I know of the
people that will be away from the room will be only a week next month. But
come to See me I may have Something if you don't get Something." Mrs.
Dinardo, for some reason, always capitalized the letter S which along with everything else didn't make it easier to read. "We are both well and he is Still in the
Navy Yard. My I do wish the war was over it is So long. We are So tired of it do
come and See us when you give them your boat. Wouldn't a Street be better
than a boat? If you are going to name Something why not a Street? Here in my
hand is news of a boat Sunk what is wrong with Ormsby on a Street? Well
116 is about the Same we have the river and its nice. If you don't find Something
See me I may have something.

Best love,
Mrs. Myrtle Dinardo."

It was quite a letter to get from a woman that Mother had known, known
Mother, that is, for nearly eighteen years. Brought in to nurse the boy—he
could never understand why a woman like Mother, with her figure—but anyhow,
Mrs. Dinardo was brought in. Something in her milk, Dr. Paige said, when it
was as plain as the nose on your face it was nothing in the milk, but something in
the boy. He just refused, plain refused, to nurse with Mother. The way the little
rascal would look at her, but not a sound out of him but gurgling when Mrs.
Dinardo would scoop him up and go upstairs to their room—the only woman—
other woman, that is, that Mother ever let step inside of it. She had answered an
ad that Mother had run, on Dr. Paige's suggestion, and they had been like *that*
from the first time he saw them.
"I'll telephone," said Mother.
On the slightest provocation Mother would call Mrs. Dinardo by long
distance—she had to come down four flights of stairs to answer—and tell her she
was going to broadcast over the radio or something. Although Mrs. Dinardo
hardly knew one kind of bird from another, Mother sent her printed copies of
every single one of her bird-lore lectures. She also sent her hand-pressed flowers
from the garden.
"I'll telephone," repeated Mother.
"My own opinion—" began Mr. Ormsby, but stopped when Mother picked
up her eggcup, made a pile of her plates, and started toward the sink. "I'll
take care of that," he said. "Now you run along and telephone." But Mother
walked right by him and took her stand at the sink. With one hand—with the
other she held her kimono close about her—she let the water run into a large
dish pan. Mr. Ormsby had hoped to avoid this; now he would have to first rinse,
then dry, every piece of silver and every dish they had used. As Mother could
only use one hand it would be even slower than usual.
"We don't want to miss our local," he said. "You better run along and let me
do it."
"Cold water," she said, "for the eggs." He had long ago learned not to argue

with Mother about the fine points of washing pots, pans, or dishes with bits of egg. He stood at the sink with the towel while she went about trying to make suds with a piece of stale soap in a little wire cage. As Mother refused to use a fresh piece of soap, nothing remotely like suds ever appeared. For this purpose, he kept a box of Gold Dust Twins concealed beneath the sink, and when Mother turned her back he slipped some in.

"There now," Mother said, and placed the rest of the dishes in the water, rinsed her fingers under the tap, paused to sniff at them.

"My own opinion—" Mr. Ormsby began, but stopped when Mother raised her finger, the index finger with the scar from the wart she once had. They stood quiet, and Mrs. Ormsby listened to the water drip in the sink—the night before he had come down in his bare feet to shut it off. All of the taps dripped now and there was just nothing to do about it but put a rag or something beneath it to break the ping.

"Thrush!" said Mother. "Next to the nightingale the most popular of European songbirds."

"Very pretty," he said, although he simply couldn't hear a thing. Mother walked to the window, folding the collar of her kimono over her bosom and drawing the tails into a hammock beneath her behind. Mr. Ormsby modestly turned away. He quick-dipped one hand into the Gold Dust—drawing it out as he slipped it into the dish pan and worked up a suds.

As he finished wiping the dishes she came in with a bouquet for Mrs. Dinardo and arranged it, for the moment, in a tall glass.

"According to her letter," Mrs. Ormsby said, "she isn't too sure of having something—"

"Roger!" she said. "You're dripping."

Mr. Ormsby put his hands over the sink and said, "If we're going to be met right at the station I don't see where you're going to see Mrs. Dinardo. You're going to be met at the station and then you're going to sponsor the boat. My own opinion is that after the boat we come on home."

"I know that street of hers," said Mother. "There isn't a wildflower on it!"

On the wall above the icebox was a pad of paper and a blue pencil hanging by a string. As Mother started to write the point broke off, fell behind the icebox.

"Mother," he said, "you ever see my knife?"

"Milkman," said Mother. "If we're staying overnight we won't need milk in the morning."

In jovial tones Mr. Ormsby said, "I'll bet we're right back here before dark." That was all, that was ALL that he said. He had merely meant to call her attention to the fact that Mrs. Dinardo said—all but said—that she didn't have a room for them. But when Mother turned he saw that her mustache was showing, a sure sign that she was mad.

"Well—now," Mother said, and lifting the skirt of her kimono swished around the cabinet and then he heard her on the stairs. From the landing at the top of the stairs she said, "In that case I'm sure there's no need for *my* going. I'm sure the Navy would just as soon have you. After all," she said, "it's *your* name on the boat!"

"Now, Mother," he said, just as she closed the door, *not* slammed it, just closed it as quiet and nice as you'd pelase. Although he had been through this a thousand times it seemed he was never ready for it, never knew when it would happen, never felt anything but nearly sick. He went into the front room and sat down on the chair near the piano—then got up to arrange the doily at the back of his head. Ordinarily he could leave the house and after three or four days it would blow over, but in all his life—their life—there had been nothing like this. The Government of the United States—he got up again and called, "OHHhhhh Mother!"

No answer.

He could hear her moving around upstairs, but as she often went back to bed after a spat, just moving around didn't mean much of anything. He came back into the front room and sat down on the milk stool near the fireplace. It was the only seat in the room not protected with newspapers. The only thing the boy ever sat on when he had to sit on something. Somehow, thinking about that made him stand up. He could sit in the lawn swing, in the front yard, if Mother hadn't told everybody in town why it was that he, Roger Ormsby, would have to take the day off—not to sit in the lawn swing, not by a long shot. Everybody knew—Captain Sudcliffe's nice letter had appeared on the first page of the *Graphic,* under a picture of Mother leading a bird-lore hike in the Poconos. This picture bore the title LOCAL WOMAN HEADS DAWN BUSTERS, and marked Mother's appearance on the national bird-lore scene. But it was not one of her best pictures—it dated from way back in the twenties and those hipless dresses and round bucket hats were not Mother's type. Until they saw that picture, and the letter beneath it, some people had forgotten that Virgil was missing, and most of them seemed to think it was a good idea to swap him for a boat. The U.S.S. *Ormsby* was a permanent sort of thing. Although he was born and rasied in the town hardly anybody knew very much about Virgil, but they all were pretty familiar with his boat. "How's that boat of yours coming along?" they would say, but in more than twenty years nobody had ever asked him about *his* boy. Whose boy? Well, that was just the point. Everyone agreed Ormsby was a fine name for a boat.

It would be impossible to explain to Mother, maybe to anybody for that matter, what this U.S.S. *Ormsby* business meant to him. "The" boy and "The" *Ormsby*—it was a pretty strange thing that they both had the definite article, and gave him the feeling he was facing a monument.

"Oh Rog-gerr!" Mother called.

"Coming," he said, and made for the stairs.

From the bedroom Mother said, "However I might feel personally, I do have my *own* name to think of. I am not one of these people who can do as they please—Roger, are you listening?"

"Yes, Mother," he said.

"—with their life."

As he went around the corner he found a note pinned to the door.

> Bathroom window up
> Cellar door down
> Is it blue or brown for Navy?

He stopped on the landing and looked up the stairs.
"Did you say something?" she said.
"No, Mother—" he said, then he added, "It's blue. For the Navy, Mother, it's blue.

Ernest Hemingway

(1899–1961) Winner of both the Pulitzer and the Nobel prizes, Hemingway wrote often about boys and men who were searching for and living by a code of behavior in the masculine world of hunting, fishing, bullfighting, and war. Collections of his short stories include Men Without Women *and* Winner Take Nothing.

The Short Happy Life of Francis Macomber

It was now lunch time and they were all sitting under the double green fly of the dining tent pretending that nothing had happened.

"Will you have lime juice or lemon squash?" Macomber asked.

"I'll have a gimlet," Robert Wilson told him.

"I'll have a gimlet too. I need something," Macomber's wife said.

"I suppose it's the thing to do," Macomber agreed. "Tell him to make three gimlets."

The mess boy had started them already, lifting the bottles out of the canvas cooling bags that sweated wet in the wind that blew through the trees that shaded the tents.

"What had I ought to give them?" Macomber asked.

"A quid would be plenty," Wilson told him. "You don't want to spoil them."

"Will the headman distribute it?"

"Absolutely."

Francis Macomber had, half an hour before, been carried to his tent from the edge of the camp in triumph on the arms and shoulders of the cook, the personal boys, the skinner and the porters. The gun-bearers had taken no part in the demonstration. When the native boys put him down at the door of his tent, he had shaken all their hands, received their congratulations, and then gone into the tent and sat on the bed until his wife came in. She did not speak to him when she came in and he left the tent at once to wash his face and hands in the portable wash basin outside and go over to the dining tent to sit in a comfortable canvas chair in the breeze and the shade.

"You've got your lion," Robert Wilson said to him, "and a damned fine one too."

Mrs. Macomber looked at Wilson quickly. She was an extremely handsome and well-kept woman of the beauty and social position which had, five years before, commanded five thousand dollars as the price of endorsing, with photographs, a beauty product which she had never used. She had been married to Francis Macomber for eleven years.

"He is a good lion, isn't he?" Macomber said. His wife looked at him now. She looked at both these men as though she had never seen them before.

One, Wilson, the white hunter, she knew she had never truly seen before. He was about middle height with sandy hair, a stubby mustache, a very red face and extremely cold blue eyes with faint white wrinkles at the corners that grooved merrily when he smiled. He smiled at her now and she looked away from his face at the way his shoulders sloped in the loose tunic he wore with the four big cartridges held in loops where the left breast pocket should have been, at his big brown hands, his old slacks, his very dirty boots and back to his red face again. She noticed where the baked red of his face stopped in a white line that marked the circle left by his Stetson hat that hung now from one of the pegs of the tent pole.

"Well, here's to the lion," Robert Wilson said. He smiled at her again and, not smiling, she looked curiously at her husband.

Francis Macomber was very tall, very well built if you did not mind that length of bone, dark, his hair cropped like an oarsman, rather thin-lipped, and was considered handsome. He was dressed in the same sort of safari clothes that Wilson wore except that his were new, he was thirty-five years old, kept himself very fit, was good at court games, had a number of big-game fishing records, and had just shown himself, very publicly, to be a coward.

"Here's to the lion," he said. "I can't ever thank you for what you did."

Margaret, his wife, looked away from him and back to Wilson.

"Let's not talk about the lion," she said.

Wilson looked over at her without smiling and now she smiled at him.

"It's been a very strange day," she said. "Hadn't you ought to put your hat on even under the canvas at noon? You told me that, you know."

"Might put it on," said Wilson.

"You know you have a very red face, Mr. Wilson," she told him and smiled again.

"Drink," said Wilson.

"I don't think so," she said. "Francis drinks a great deal, but his face is never red."

"It's red today," Macomber tried a joke.

"No," said Margaret. "It's mine that's red today. But Mr. Wilson's is always red."

"Must be racial," said Wilson. "I say, you wouldn't like to drop my beauty as a topic, would you?"

"I've just started on it."

"Let's chuck it," said Wilson.

"Conversation is going to be so difficult," Margaret said.

"Don't be silly, Margot," her husband said.

"No difficulty," Wilson said. "Got a damn fine lion."

Margot looked at them both and they both saw that she was going to cry. Wilson had seen it coming for a long time and he dreaded it. Macomber was past dreading it.

"I wish it hadn't happened. Oh, I wish it hadn't happened," she said and started for her tent. She made no noise of crying but they could see that her shoulders were shaking under the rose-colored, sun-proofed shirt she wore.

"Women upset," said Wilson to the tall man. "Amounts to nothing. Strain on the nerves and one thing'n another."

"No," said Macomber. "I suppose that I rate that for the rest of my life now."

"Nonsense. Let's have a spot of the giant killer," said Wilson. "Forget the whole thing. Nothing to it anyway."

"We might try," said Macomber. "I won't forget what you did for me though."

"Nothing," said Wilson. "All nonsense."

So they sat there in the shade where the camp was pitched under some wide-topped acacia trees with a boulder-strewn cliff behind them, and a stretch of grass that ran to the bank of a boulder-filled stream in front with forest beyond it, and drank their just-cool lime drinks and avoided one another's eyes while the boys set the table for lunch. Wilson could tell that the boys all knew about it now and when he saw Macomber's personal boy looking curiously at his master while he was putting dishes on the table he snapped at him in Swahili. The boy turned away with his face blank.

"What were you telling him?" Macomber asked.

"Nothing. Told him to look alive or I'd see he got about fifteen of the best."

"What's that? Lashes?"

"It's quite illegal," Wilson said. "You're supposed to fine them."

"Do you still have them whipped?"

"Oh, yes. They could raise a row if they chose to complain. But they don't. They prefer it to the fines."

"How strange!" said Macomber.

"Not strange, really," Wilson said. "Which would you rather do? Take a good birching or lose your pay?"

Then he felt embarrassed at asking it and before Macomber could answer he went on, "We all take a beating every day, you know, one way or another."

This was no better. "Good God," he thought. "I am a diplomat, aren't I?"

"Yes, we take a beating," said Macomber, still not looking at him. "I'm awfully sorry about that lion business. It doesn't have to go any further, does it? I mean no one will hear about it, will they?"

"You mean will I tell it at the Mathaiga Club?" Wilson looked at him now coldly. He had not expected this. So he's a bloody four-letter man as well as a bloody coward, he thought. I rather liked him too until today. But how is one to know about an American?

"No," said Wilson. "I'm a professional hunter. We never talk about our clients. You can be quite easy on that. It's supposed to be bad form to ask us not to talk though."

He had decided now that to break would be much easier. He would eat, then, by himself and could read a book with his meals. They would eat by themselves. He would see them through the safari on a very formal basis—what was it the French called it? Distinguished consideration—and it would be a damn sight easier than having to go through this emotional trash. He'd insult him and make a good clean break. Then he could read a book with his meals and he'd still be drinking their whisky. That was the phrase for it when a safari went bad. You ran into another white hunter and you asked, "How is everything going?" and he answered, "Oh, I'm still drinking their whisky," and you knew everything had gone to pot.

"I'm sorry," Macomber said and looked at him with his American face that would stay adolescent until it became middle-aged, and Wilson noted his crew-cropped hair, fine eyes only faintly shifty, good nose, thin lips and handsome jaw. "I'm sorry I didn't realize that. There are lots of things I don't know."

So what could he do, Wilson thought. He was all ready to break it off quickly and neatly and here the beggar was apologizing after he had just insulted him. He made one more attempt. "Don't worry about me talking," he said. "I have a living to make. You know in Africa no woman ever misses her lion and no white man ever bolts."

"I bolted like a rabbit," Macomber said.

Now what in hell were you going to do about a man who talked like that, Wilson wondered.

Wilson looked at Macomber with his flat, blue, machine-gunner's eyes and the other smiled back at him. He had a pleasant smile if you did not notice how his eyes showed when he was hurt.

"Maybe I can fix it up on buffalo," he said. "We're after them next, aren't we?"

"In the morning if you like," Wilson told him. Perhaps he had been wrong. This was certainly the way to take it. You most certainly could not tell a damned thing about an American. He was all for Macomber again. If you could forget the morning. But, of course, you couldn't. The morning had been about as bad as they come.

"Here comes the Memsahib," he said. She was walking over from her tent looking refreshed and cheerful and quite lovely. She had a very perfect oval face, so perfect that you expected her to be stupid. But she wasn't stupid, Wilson thought, no, not stupid.

"How is the beautiful red-faced Mr. Wilson? Are you feeling better, Francis, my pearl?"

"Oh, much," said Macomber.

"I've dropped the whole thing," she said, sitting down at the table. "What importance is there to whether Francis is any good at killing lions? That's not his trade. That's Mr. Wilson's trade. Mr. Wilson is really very impressive killing anything. You do kill anything, don't you?"

"Oh, anything," said Wilson. "Simply anything." They are, he thought, the hardest in the world; the hardest, the cruelest, the most predatory and the most attractive and their men have softened or gone to pieces nervously as they have hardened. Or is it that they pick men they can handle? They can't know that much at the age they marry, he thought. He was grateful that he had gone through his education on American women before now because this was a very attractive one.

"We're going after buff in the morning," he told her.

"I'm coming," she said.

"No, you're not."

"Oh, yes, I am. Mayn't I, Francis?"

"Why not stay in camp?"

"Not for anything," she said. "I wouldn't miss something like today for anything."

When she left, Wilson was thinking, when she went off to cry, she seemed a hell of a fine woman. She seemed to understand, to realize, to be hurt for him and for herself and to know how things really stood. She is away for twenty minutes and now she is back, simply enamelled in that American female cruelty. They are the damnedest women. Really the damnedest.

"We'll put on another show for you tomorrow," Francis Macomber said.

"You're not coming," Wilson said.

"You're very mistaken," she told him. "And I want *so* to see you perform again. You were lovely this morning. That is if blowing things' heads off is lovely."

"Here's the lunch," said Wilson. "You're very merry, aren't you?"

"Why not? I didn't come out here to be dull."

"Well, it hasn't been dull," Wilson said. He could see the boulders in the river and the high bank beyond with the trees and he remembered the morning.

"Oh, no," she said. "It's been charming. And tomorrow. You don't know how I look forward to tomorrow."

"That's eland he's offering you," Wilson said.

"They're the big cowy things that jump like hares, aren't they?"

"I suppose that describes them," Wilson said.

"It's very good meat," Macomber said.

"Did you shoot it, Francis?" she asked.

"Yes."

"They're not dangerous, are they?"

"Only if they fall on you," Wilson told her.

"I'm so glad."

"Why not let up on the bitchery just a little, Margot," Macomber said, cutting the eland steak and putting some mashed potato, gravy and carrot on the down-turned fork that tined through the piece of meat.

"I suppose I could," she said, "since you put it so prettily."

"Tonight we'll have champagne for the lion," Wilson said. "It's a bit too hot at noon."

"Oh, the lion," Margot said. "I'd forgotten the lion!"

So, Robert Wilson thought to himself, she *is* giving him a ride, isn't she? Or do you suppose that's her idea of putting up a good show? How should a woman act when she discovers her husband is a bloody coward? She's damn cruel but they're all cruel. They govern, of course, and to govern one has to be cruel sometimes. Still, I've seen enough of their damn terrorism.

"Have some more eland," he said to her politely.

That afternoon, late, Wilson and Macomber went out in the motor car with the native driver and the two gun-bearers. Mrs. Macomber stayed in the camp. It was too hot to go out, she said, and she was going with them in the early morning. As they drove off Wilson saw her standing under the big tree, looking pretty rather than beautiful in her faintly rosy khaki, her dark hair drawn back off her forehead and gathered in a knot low on her neck, her face as fresh, he thought, as though she were in England. She waved to them as the car went off through the swale of high grass and curved around through the trees into the small hills of orchard bush.

In the orchard bush they found a herd of impala, and leaving the car they stalked one old ram with long, wide-spread horns and Macomber killed it with a very creditable shot that knocked the buck down at a good two hundred yards and sent the herd off bounding wildly and leaping over one another's backs in long, leg-drawn-up leaps as unbelievable and as floating as those one makes sometimes in dreams.

"That was a good shot," Wilson said. "They're a small target."

"Is it a worth-while head?" Macomber asked.

"It's excellent," Wilson told him. "You shoot like that and you'll have no trouble."

"Do you think we'll find buffalo tomorrow?"

"There's a good chance of it. They feed out early in the morning and with luck we may catch them in the open."

"I'd like to clear away that lion business," Macomber said. "It's not very pleasant to have your wife see you do something like that."

I should think it would be even more unpleasant to do it, Wilson thought, wife or no wife, or to talk about it having done it. But he said, "I wouldn't think about that any more. Any one could be upset by his first lion. That's all over."

But that night after dinner and a whisky and soda by the fire before going to bed, as Francis Macomber lay on his cot with the mosquito bar over him and listened to the night noises it was not all over. It was neither all over nor was it beginning. It was there exactly as it happened with some parts of it indelibly emphasized and he was miserably ashamed at it. But more than shame he felt cold, hollow fear in him. The fear was still there like a cold slimy hollow in all the emptiness where once his confidence had been and it made him feel sick. It was still there with him now.

It had started the night before when he had wakened and heard the lion roaring somewhere up along the river. It was a deep sound and at the end there were sort of coughing grunts that made him seem just outside the tent, and when Francis Macomber woke in the night to hear it he was afraid. He could hear his wife breathing quietly, asleep. There was no one to tell he was afraid, nor to be afraid with him, and, lying alone, he did not know the Somali proverb that says a brave man is always frightened three times by a lion; when he first sees his track, when he first hears him roar and when he first confronts him. Then while they were eating breakfast by lantern light out in the dining tent, before the sun was up, the lion roared again and Francis thought he was just at the edge of camp.

"Sounds like an old-timer," Robert Wilson said, looking up from his kippers and coffee. "Listen to him cough."

"Is he very close?"

"A mile or so up the stream."

"Will we see him?"

"We'll have a look."

"Does his roaring carry that far? It sounds as though he were right in camp."

"Carries a hell of a long way," said Robert Wilson. "It's strange the way it carries. Hope he's a shootable cat. The boys said there was a very big one about here."

"If I get a shot, where should I hit him," Macomber asked, "to stop him?"

"In the shoulders," Wilson said. "In the neck if you can make it. Shoot for bone. Break him down."

"I hope I can place it properly," Macomber said.

"You shoot very well," Wilson told him. "Take your time. Make sure of him. The first one in is the one that counts."

"What range will it be?"

"Can't tell. Lion has something to say about that. Won't shoot unless it's close enough so you can make sure."

"At under a hundred yards?" Macomber asked.

Wilson looked at him quickly.

"Hundred's about right. Might have to take him a bit under. Shouldn't chance a shot at much over that. A hundred's a decent range. You can hit him wherever you want at that. Here comes the Memsahib."

"Good morning," she said. "Are we going after that lion?"

"As soon as you deal with your breakfast," Wilson said. "How are you feeling?"

"Marvellous," she said. "I'm very excited."

"I'll just go and see that everything is ready," Wilson went off. As he left the lion roared again.

"Noisy beggar," Wilson said. "We'll put a stop to that."

"What's the matter, Francis?" his wife asked him.

"Nothing," Macomber said.

"Yes, there is," she said. "What are you upset about?"

"Nothing," he said.

"Tell me," she looked at him. "Don't you feel well?"

"It's that damned roaring," he said. "It's been going on all night, you know."

"Why didn't you wake me," she said. "I'd love to have heard it."

"I've got to kill the damned thing," Macomber said, miserably.

"Well, that's what you're out here for, isn't it?"

"Yes. But I'm nervous. Hearing the thing roar gets on my nerves."

"Well then, as Wilson said, kill him and stop his roaring."

"Yes, darling," said Francis Macomber. "It sounds easy, doesn't it?"

"You're not afraid, are you?"

"Of course not. But I'm nervous from hearing him roar all night."

"You'll kill him marvellously," she said. "I know you will. I'm awfully anxious to see it."

"Finish your breakfast and we'll be starting."

"It's not light yet," she said. "This is a ridiculous hour."

Just then the lion roared in a deep-chested moaning, suddenly gutteral, ascending vibration that seemed to shake the air and ended in a sign and a heavy, deep-chested grunt.

"He sounds almost here," Macomber's wife said.

"My God," said Macomber. "I hate that damned noise."

"It's very impressive."

"Impressive. It's frightful."

Robert Wilson came up then carrying his short, ugly, shockingly big-bored .505 Gibbs and grinning.

"Come on," he said. "Your gun-bearer has your Springfield and the big gun. Everything's in the car. Have you solids?"

"Yes."

"I'm ready," Mrs. Macomber said.

"Must make him stop that racket," Wilson said. "You get in front. The Memsahib can sit back here with me."

They climbed into the motor car and, in the gray first daylight, moved off up the river through the trees. Macomber opened the breech of his rifle and saw he had metal-cased bullets, shut the bolt and put the rifle on safety. He saw his hand was trembling. He felt in his pocket for more cartridges and moved his fingers over the cartridges in the loops of his tunic front. He turned back to where Wilson sat in the rear seat of the doorless, box-bodied motor car beside his wife, them both grinning with excitement, and Wilson leaned forward and whispered,

"See the birds dropping. Means the old boy has left his kill."

On the far bank of the stream Macomber could see, above the trees, vultures circling and plummeting down.

"Chances are he'll come to drink along here," Wilson whispered. "Before he goes to lay up. Keep an eye out."

They were driving slowly along the high bank of the stream which here cut deeply to its boulder-filled bed, and they wound in and out through big trees as they drove. Macomber was watching the opposite bank when he felt Wilson take hold of his arm. The car stopped.

"There he is," he heard the whisper. "Ahead and to the right. Get out and take him. He's a marvellous lion."

Macomber saw the lion now. He was standing almost broadside, his great head up and turned toward them. The early morning breeze that blew toward them was just stirring his dark mane, and the lion looked huge, silhouetted on the rise of bank in the gray morning light, his shoulders heavy, his barrel of a body bulking smoothly.

"How far is he?" asked Macomber, raising his rifle.

"About seventy-five. Get out and take him."

"Why not shoot from where I am?"

"You don't shoot them from cars," he heard Wilson saying in his ear. "Get out. He's not going to stay there all day."

Macomber stepped out of the curved opening at the side of the front seat, onto the step and down onto the ground. The lion still stood looking majestically and coolly toward this object that his eyes only showed in silhouette, bulking like some super-rhino. There was no man smell carried toward him and he watched the object, moving his great head a little from side to side. Then watching the object, not afraid, but hesitating before going down the bank to drink with such a thing opposite him, he saw a man figure detach itself from it and he turned his heavy head and swung away toward the cover of the trees as he heard a cracking crash and felt the slam of a .30–06 220-grain solid bullet that bit his flank and ripped in sudden hot scalding nausea through his stomach. He trotted, heavy, big-footed, swinging wounded full-bellied, through the trees toward the tall grass and cover, and the crash came again to go past him ripping the air apart. Then it crashed again and he felt the blow as it hit his lower ribs and ripped on through, blood sudden hot and frothy in his mouth, and he galloped toward the high grass where he could crouch and not be seen and make them bring the crashing thing close enough so he could make a rush and get the man that held it.

Macomber had not thought how the lion felt as he got out of the car. He only knew his hands were shaking and as he walked away from the car it was almost impossible for him to make his legs move. They were stiff in the thighs, but he could feel the muscles fluttering. He raised the rifle, sighted on the junction of the lion's head and shoulders and pulled the trigger. Nothing happened though he pulled until he thought his finger would break. Then he knew he had the safety on and as he lowered the rifle to move the safety over he moved another frozen pace forward, and the lion seeing his silhouette now clear of the silhouette of the car, turned and started off at a trot, and, as Macomber fired, he heard a whunk that meant that the bullet was home; but the lion kept on going. Macomber shot again and everyone saw the bullet throw a spout of dirt beyond the trotting lion. He shot again, remembering to lower his aim, and they all heard the bullet hit, and the lion went into a gallop and was in the tall grass before he had the bolt pushed forward.

Macomber stood there feeling sick at his stomach, his hands that held the Springfield still cocked, shaking, and his wife and Robert Wilson were standing by him. Beside him too were the two gun-bearers chattering in Wakamba.

"I hit him," Macomber said. "I hit him twice."

"You gut-shot him and you hit him somewhere forward," Wilson said without enthusiasm. The gun-bearers looked very grave. They were silent now.

"You may have killed him," Wilson went on. "We'll have to wait a while before we go in to find out."

"What do you mean?"

"Let him get sick before we follow him up."

"Oh," said Macomber.

"He's a hell of a fine lion," Wilson said cheerfully. "He's gotten into a bad place though."

"Why is it bad?"

"Can't see him until you're on him."

"Oh," said Macomber.

"Come on," said Wilson. "The Memsahib can stay here in the car. We'll go to have a look at the blood spoor."

"Stay here, Margot," Macomber said to his wife. His mouth was very dry and it was hard for him to talk.

"Why?" she asked.

"Wilson says to."

"We're going to have a look," Wilson said. "You stay here. You can see even better from here."

"All right."

Wilson spoke in Swahili to the driver. He nodded and said, "Yes, Bwana."

Then they went down the steep bank and across the stream, climbing over and around the boulders and up the other bank, pulling up by some projecting roots, and along it until they found where the lion had been trotting when Macomber first shot. There was dark blood on the short grass that the gun-bearers pointed out with grass stems, and that ran away behind the river bank trees.

"What do we do?" asked Macomber.

"Not much choice," said Wilson. "We can't bring the car over. Bank's too steep. We'll let him stiffen up a bit and then you and I'll go in and have a look for him."

"Can't we set the grass on fire?" Macomber asked.

"Too green."

"Can't we send beaters?"

Wilson looked at him appraisingly. "Of course we can," he said. "But it's just a touch murderous. You see we know the lion's wounded. You can drive an unwounded lion—he'll move on ahead of a noise—but a wounded lion's going to charge. You can't see him until you're right on him. He'll make himself perfectly flat in cover you wouldn't think would hide a hare. You can't very well send boys in there to that sort of a show. Somebody bound to get mauled."

"What about the gun-bearers?"

"Oh, they'll go with us. It's their *shauri*. You see, they signed on for it. They don't look too happy though, do they?"

"I don't want to go in there," said Macomber. It was out before he knew he'd said it.

"Neither do I," said Wilson very cheerily. "Really no choice though." Then, as an afterthought, he glanced at Macomber and saw suddenly how he was trembling and the pitiful look on his face.

"You don't have to go in, of course," he said. "That's what I'm hired for, you know. That's why I'm so expensive."

"You mean you'd go in by yourself? Why not leave him there?"

Robert Wilson, whose entire occupation had been with the lion and the problem he presented, and who had not been thinking about Macomber except to note that he was rather windy, suddenly felt as though he had opened the wrong door in a hotel and seen something shameful.

"What do you mean?"

"Why not just leave him?"

"You mean pretend to ourselves he hasn't been hit?"

"No. Just drop it."

"It isn't done."

"Why not?"

"For one thing, he's certain to be suffering. For another, some one else might run onto him."

"I see."

"But you don't have to have anything to do with it."

"I'd like to," Macomber said. "I'm just scared, you know."

"I'll go ahead when we go in," Wilson said, "with Kongoni tracking. You keep behind me and a little to one side. Chances are we'll hear him growl. If we see him we'll both shoot. Don't worry about anything. I'll keep you backed up. As a matter of fact, you know, perhaps you'd better not go. It might be much better. Why don't you go over and join the Memsahib while I just get it over with?"

"No, I want to go."

"All right," said Wilson. "But don't go in if you don't want to. This is my *shauri* now, you know."

"I want to go," said Macomber.

They sat under a tree and smoked.

"Want to go back and speak to the Memsahib while we're waiting?" Wilson asked.

"No."

"I'll just step back and tell her to be patient."

"Good," said Macomber. He sat there, sweating under his arms, his mouth dry, his stomach hollow feeling, wanting to find courage to tell Wilson to go on and finish off the lion without him. He could not know that Wilson was furious because he had not noticed the state he was in earlier and sent him back to his wife. While he sat there Wilson came up. "I have your big gun," he said. "Take it. We've given him time, I think. Come on."

Macomber took the big gun and Wilson said:

"Keep behind me and about five yards to the right and do exactly as I tell you." Then he spoke in Swahili to the two gun-bearers who looked the picture of gloom.

"Let's go," he said.

"Could I have a drink of water?" Macomber asked. Wilson spoke to the older gun-bearer, who wore a canteen on his belt, and the man unbuckled, unscrewed the top and handed it to Macomber, who took it noticing how heavy it seemed and how hairy and shoddy the felt covering was in his hand. He raised it to drink and looked ahead at the high grass with the flat-topped trees behind it. A breeze was blowing toward them and the grass rippled gently in the wind. He looked at the gun-bearer and he could see the gun-bearer was suffering too with fear.

Thirty-five yards into the grass the big lion lay flattened out along the ground. His ears were back and his only movement was a slight twitching up and down of his long, black-tufted tail. He had turned at bay as soon as he had reached this cover and he was sick with the wound through his full belly, and weakening with the wound through his lungs that brought a thin foamy red to his mouth each time he breathed. His flanks were wet and hot and flies were on the little openings the solid bullets had made in his tawny hide, and his big yellow eyes, narrowed with hate, looked straight ahead, only blinking when the pain came as he breathed, and his claws dug in the soft baked earth. All of him, pain, sickness, hatred and all of his remaining strength, was tightening into an absolute concentration for a rush. He could hear the men talking and he waited, gathering all of himself into this preparation for a charge as soon as the men would come into the grass. As he heard their voices his tail stiffened to twitch up and down, and, as they came into the edge of the grass, he made a coughing grunt and charged.

Kongoni, the old gun-bearer, in the lead watching the blood spoor, Wilson watching the grass for any movement, his big gun ready, the second gun-bearer looking ahead and listening, Macomber close to Wilson, his rifle cocked, they had just moved into the grass when Macomber heard the blood-choked coughing grunt, and saw the swishing rush in the grass. The next thing he knew he was running; running wildly, in panic in the open, running toward the stream.

He heard the *ca-ra-wong!* of Wilson's big rifle, and again in a second a crashing *carawong!* and turning saw the lion, horrible-looking now, with half his head seeming to be gone, crawling toward Wilson in the edge of the tall grass while the red-faced man worked the bolt on the short ugly rifle and aimed carefully as another blasting *carawong!* came from the muzzle, and the crawling, heavy, yellow bulk of the lion stiffened and the huge, mutilated head slid forward and Macomber, standing by himself in the clearing where he had run, holding a loaded rifle, while two black men and a white man looked back at him in contempt, knew the lion was dead. He came toward Wilson, his tallness all seeming a naked reproach, and Wilson looked at him and said:

"Want to take pictures?"

"No," he said.

That was all any one had said until they reached the motor car. Then Wilson had said:

"Hell of a fine lion. Boys will skin him out. We might as well stay here in the shade."

Macomber's wife had not looked at him nor he at her and he had sat by her in the back seat with Wilson sitting in the front seat. Once he had reached over and taken his wife's hand without looking at her and she had removed her hand from his. Looking across the stream to where the gun-bearers were skinning out the lion he could see that she had been able to see the whole thing. While they sat there his wife had reached forward and put her hand on Wilson's shoulder. He turned and she had leaned forward over the low seat and kissed him on the mouth.

"Oh, I say," said Wilson, going redder than his natural baked color.

"Mr. Robert Wilson," she said. "The beautiful red-faced Mr. Robert Wilson."

Then she sat down beside Macomber again and looked away across the stream to where the lion lay, with uplifted, white-muscled, tendon-marked naked forearms, and white bloating belly, as the black men fleshed away the skin. Finally the gun-bearers brought the skin over, wet and heavy, and climbed in behind with it, rolling it up before they got in, and the motor car started. No one had said anything more until they were back in camp.

That was the story of the lion. Macomber did not know how the lion had felt before he started his rush, nor during it when the unbelievable smash of the .505 with a muzzle velocity of two tons had hit him in the mouth, nor what kept him coming after that, when the second ripping crash had smashed his hind quarters and he had come crawling on toward the crashing, blasting thing that had destroyed him. Wilson knew something about it and only expressed it by saying, "Damned fine lion," but Macomber did not know how Wilson felt about things either. He did not know how his wife felt except that she was through with him.

His wife had been through with him before but it never lasted. He was very wealthy, and would be much wealthier, and he knew she would not leave him ever now. That was one of the few things that he really knew. He knew about that, about motor cycles—that was earliest—about motor cars, about duck-shooting, about fishing, trout, salmon and big-sea, about sex in books, many books, too many books, about all court games, about dogs, not much about horses, about hanging on to his money, about most of the other things his world dealt in, and about his wife not leaving him. His wife had been a great beauty and she was still a great beauty in Africa, but she was not a great enough beauty any more at home to be able to leave him and better herself and she knew it and he knew it. She had missed the chance to leave him and he knew it. If he had been better with women she would probably have started to worry about him getting another new, beautiful wife; but she knew too much about him to worry about him either. Also, he had always had a great tolerance which seemed the nicest thing about him if it were not the most sinister.

All in all they were known as a comparatively happily married couple, one of those whose disruption is often rumored but never occurs, and as the society columnist put it, they were adding more than a spice of *adventure* to their much envied and ever-enduring *Romance* by a *Safari* in what was known as *Darkest Africa* until the Martin Johnsons lighted it on so many silver screens where they were pursuing *Old Simba* the lion, the buffalo, *Tembo* and the elephant and as well collecting specimens for the Museum of Natural History. This same columnist had reported them *on the verge* at least three times in the past and they had been. But they always made it up. They had a sound basis of union. Margot was too beautiful for Macomber to divorce her and Macomber had too much money for Margot ever to leave him.

It was now about three o'clock in the morning and Francis Macomber, who had been asleep a little while after he had stopped thinking about the lion, wakened and then slept again, woke suddenly, frightened in a dream of the bloody-headed lion standing over him, and listening while his heart pounded, he realized that his wife was not in the other cot in the tent. He lay awake with that knowledge for two hours.

At the end of that time his wife came into the tent, lifted her mosquito bar and crawled cozily into bed.

"Where have you been?" Macomber asked in the darkness.

"Hello," she said. "Are you awake?"

"Where have you been?"

"I just went out to get a breath of air."

"You did, like hell."

"What do you want me to say, darling?"

"Where have you been?"

"Out to get a breath of air."

"That's a new name for it. You *are* a bitch."

"Well, you're a coward."

"All right," he said. "What of it?"

"Nothing as far as I'm concerned. But please let's not talk, darling, because I'm very sleepy."

"You think that I'll take anything."

"I know you will, sweet."

"Well, I won't."

"Please, darling, let's not talk. I'm so very sleepy."

"There wasn't going to be any of that. You promised there wouldn't be."

"Well, there is now," she said sweetly.

"You said if we made this trip that there would be none of that. You promised."

"Yes, darling. That's the way I meant it to be. But the trip was spoiled yesterday. We don't have to talk about it, do we?"

"You don't wait long when you have an advantage, do you?"

"Please let's not talk. I'm so sleepy, darling."

"I'm going to talk."

"Don't mind me then, because I'm going to sleep." And she did.

At breakfast they were all three at the table before daylight and Francis Macomber found that, of all the many men that he had hated, he hated Robert Wilson the most.

"Sleep well?" Wilson asked in his throaty voice, filling a pipe.

"Did you?"

"Topping," the white hunter told him.

You bastard, thought Macomber, you insolent bastard.

So she woke him when she came in, Wilson thought, looking at them both with his flat, cold eyes. Well, why doesn't he keep his wife where she belongs? What does he think I am, a bloody plaster saint? Let him keep her where she belongs. It's his own fault.

"Do you think we'll find buffalo?" Margot asked, pushing away a dish of apricots.

"Chance of it," Wilson said and smiled at her. "Why don't you stay in camp?"

"Not for anything," she told him.

"Why not order her to stay in camp?" Wilson said to Macomber.

"You order her," said Macomber coldly.

"Let's not have any ordering, nor," turning to Macomber, "any silliness, Francis," Margot said quite pleasantly.

"Are you ready to start?" Macomber asked.

"Any time," Wilson told him. "Do you want the Memsahib to go?"

"Does it make any difference whether I do or not?"

The hell with it, thought Robert Wilson. The utter complete hell with it. So this is what it's going to be like. Well, this is what it's going to be like, then.

"Makes no difference," he said.

"You're sure you wouldn't like to stay in camp with her yourself and let me go out and hunt the buffalo?" Macomber asked.

"Can't do that," said Wilson. "Wouldn't talk rot if I were you."

"I'm not talking rot. I'm disgusted."

"Bad word, disgusted."

"Francis, will you please try to speak sensibly?" his wife said.

"I speak too damned sensibly," Macomber said. "Did you ever eat such filthy food?"

"Something wrong with the food?" asked Wilson quietly.

"No more than with everything else."

"I'd pull yourself together, laddybuck," Wilson said very quietly. "There's a boy waits at table that understands a little English."

"The hell with him."

Wilson stood up and puffing on his pipe strolled away, speaking a few words in Swahili to one of the gun-bearers who was standing waiting for him. Macomber and his wife sat on at the table. He was staring at his coffee cup.

"If you make a scene I'll leave you, darling," Margot said quietly.

"No, you won't."

"You can try it and see."

"You won't leave me."

"No," she said. "I won't leave you and you'll behave yourself."

"Behave myself? That's a way to talk. Behave myself."

"Yes. Behave yourself."

"Why don't *you* try behaving?"

"I've tried it so long. So very long."

"I hate that red-faced swine," Macomber said. "I loathe the sight of him."

"He's really *very* nice."

"Oh, *shut up*," Macomber almost shouted. Just then the car came up and stopped in front of the dining tent and the driver and the two gun-bearers got out. Wilson walked over and looked at the husband and wife sitting there at the table.

"Going shooting?" he asked.

"Yes," said Macomber, standing up. "Yes."

"Better bring a woolly. It will be cool in the car," Wilson said.

"I'll get my leather jacket," Margot said.

"The boy has it," Wilson told her. He climbed into the front with the driver and Francis Macomber and his wife sat, not speaking, in the back seat.

Hope the silly beggar doesn't take a notion to blow the back of my head off, Wilson thought to himself. Women *are* a nuisance on safari.

The car was grinding down to cross the river at a pebbly ford in the gray daylight and then climbed, angling up the steep bank, where Wilson had ordered a way shovelled out the day before so they could reach the parklike wooded rolling country on the far side.

It was a good morning, Wilson thought. There was a heavy dew and as the wheels went through the grass and low bushes he could smell the odor of the crushed fronds. It was an odor like verbena and he liked this early morning smell of the dew, the crushed bracken and the look of the tree trunks showing black through the early morning mist, as the car made its way through the untracked, parklike country. He had put the two in the back seat out of his mind now and was thinking about buffalo. The buffalo that he was after stayed in the daytime in a thick swamp where it was impossible to get a shot, but in the night they fed out into an open stretch of country and if he could come between them and their swamp with the car, Macomber would have a good chance at them in the open. He did not want to hunt buff with Macomber in thick cover. He did not want to hunt buff or anything else with Macomber at all, but he was a professional hunter and he had hunted with some rare ones in his time. If they got buff today there would only be rhino to come and the poor man would have gone through his dangerous game and things might pick up. He'd have nothing more to do with the woman and Macomber would get over that too. He must have gone through plenty of that before by the look of things. Poor beggar. He must have a way of getting over it. Well, it was the poor sod's own bloody fault.

He, Robert Wilson, carried a double size cot on safari to accommodate any windfalls he might receive. He had hunted for a certain clientele, the international, fast, sporting set, where the women did not feel they were getting their money's worth unless they had shared that cot with the white hunter. He despised them when he was away from them although he liked some of them well enough at the time, but he made his living by them; and their standards were his standards as long as they were hiring him.

They were his standards in all except the shooting. He had his own standards about the killing and they could live up to them or get some one else to hunt them. He knew, too, that they all respected him for this. This Macomber was an odd one though. Damned if he wasn't. Now the wife. Well, the wife. Yes, the wife. Hm, the wife. Well he'd dropped all that. He looked around at them. Macomber sat grim and furious. Margot smiled at him. She looked younger today, more innocent and fresher and not so professionally beautiful. What's in her heart God knows, Wilson thought. She hadn't talked much last night. At that it was a pleasure to see her.

The motor car climbed up a slight rise and went on through the trees and then out into a grassy prairie-like opening and kept in the shelter of the trees along the edge, the driver going slowly and Wilson looking carefully out across the prairie and all along its far side. He stopped the car and studied the opening with his field glasses. Then he motioned to the driver to go on and the car moved slowly along, the driver avoiding wart-hog holes and driving around the mud castles ants had built. Then, looking across the opening, Wilson suddenly turned and said,

"By God, there they are!"

And looking where he pointed, while the car jumped forward and Wilson spoke in rapid Swahili to the driver, Macomber saw three huge, black animals looking almost cylindrical in their long heaviness, like big black tank cars, moving at a gallop across the far edge of the open prairie. They moved at a stiff-necked, stiff-bodied gallop and he could see the upswept wide black horns on their heads as they galloped heads out; the heads not moving.

"They're three old bulls," Wilson said. "We'll cut them off before they get to the swamp."

The car was going a wild forty-five miles an hour across the open and as Macomber watched, the buffalo got bigger and bigger until he could see the gray, hairless, scabby look of one huge bull and how his neck was a part of his shoulders and the shiny black of his horns as he galloped a little behind the others that were strung out in that steady plunging gait; and then, the car swaying as though it had just jumped a road, they drew up close and he could see the plunging hugeness of the bull, and the dust in his sparsely haired hide, the wide boss of horn and his outstretched, wide-nostrilled muzzle, and he was raising his rifle when Wilson shouted, "Not from the car, you fool!" and he had no fear, only hatred of Wilson, while the brakes clamped on and the car skidded, plowing sideways to an almost stop and Wilson was out on one side and he on the other, stumbling as his feet hit the still speeding-by of the earth, and then he was shooting at the bull as he moved away, hearing the bullets whunk into him, emptying his rifle at him as he moved steadily away, finally remembering to get his shots forward into the shoulder, and as he fumbled to re-load, he saw the bull was down. Down on his knees, his big head tossing, and seeing the other two still galloping he shot at the leader and hit him. He shot again and missed and he heard the *carawonging* roar as Wilson shot and saw the leading bull slide forward onto his nose.

"Get that other," Wilson said. "Now you're shooting!"

But the other bull was moving steadily at the same gallop and he missed, throwing a spout of dirt, and Wilson missed and the dust rose in a cloud and Wilson shouted, "Come on. He's too far!" and grabbed his arm and they were in the car again, Macomber and Wilson hanging on the sides and rocketing swayingly over the uneven ground, drawing up on the steady, plunging, heavy-necked, straight-moving gallop of the bull.

They were behind him and Macomber was filling his rifle, dropping shells onto the ground, jamming it, clearing the jam, then they were almost up with the bull when Wilson yelled "Stop," and the car skidded so that it almost swung over and Macomber fell forward onto his feet, slammed his bolt forward and fired as far forward as he could aim into the galloping, rounded black back, aimed and shot again, then again, then again, and the bullets, all of them hitting, had no effect on the buffalo that he could see. Then Wilson shot, the roar deafening him, and he could see the bull stagger. Macomber shot again, aiming carefully, and down he came, onto his knees.

"All right," Wilson said. "Nice work. That's three."

Macomber felt a drunken elation.

"How many times did you shoot?" he asked.

"Just three," Wilson said. "You killed the first bull. The biggest one. I helped you finish the other two. Afraid they might have got into cover. You had them killed. I was just mopping up a little. You shot damn well."

"Let's go to the car," said Macomber. "I want a drink."

"Got to finish off that buff first," Wilson told him. The buffalo was on his knees and he jerked his head furiously and bellowed in pig-eyed roaring rage as they came toward him.

"Watch he doesn't get up," Wilson said. Then, "Get a little broadside and take him in the neck just behind the ear."

Macomber aimed carefully at the center of the huge, jerking, rage-driven neck and shot. At the shot the head dropped forward.

"That does it," said Wilson. "Got the spine. They're a hell of a looking thing, aren't they?"

"Let's get the drink," said Macomber. In his life he had never felt so good.

In the car Macomber's wife sat very white faced. "You were marvellous, darling," she said to Macomber. "What a ride."

"Was it rough?" Wilson asked.

"It was frightful. I've never been more frightened in my life."

"Let's all have a drink," Macomber said.

"By all means," said Wilson. "Give it to the Memsahib." She drank the neat whisky from the flask and shuddered a little when she swallowed. She handed the flask to Macomber who handed it to Wilson.

"It was frightfully exciting," she said. "It's given me a dreadful headache. I didn't know you were allowed to shoot them from cars though."

"No one shot from cars," said Wilson coldly.

"I mean chase them from cars."

"Wouldn't ordinarily," Wilson said. "Seemed sporting enough to me though while we were doing it. Taking more chance driving that way across the plain full of holes and one thing and another than hunting on foot. Buffalo could have charged us each time we shot if he liked. Gave him every chance. Wouldn't mention it to any one though. It's illegal if that's what you mean."

"It seemed very unfair to me" Margot said, "chasing those big helpless things in a motor car."

"Did it?" said Wilson.

"What would happen if they heard about it in Nairobi?"

"I'd lose my licence for one thing. Other unpleasantnesses," Wilson said, taking a drink from the flask. "I'd be out of business."

"Really?"

"Yes, really."

"Well," said Macomber, and he smiled for the first time all day. "Now she has something on you."

"You have such a pretty way of putting things, Francis," Margot Macomber said. Wilson looked at them both. If a four-letter man marries a five-letter woman, he was thinking, what number of letters would their children be? What he said was, "We lost a gun-bearer. Did you notice it?"

"My God, no," Macomber said.

"Here he comes," Wilson said. "He's all right. He must have fallen off when we left the first bull."

Approaching them was the middle-aged gun-bearer, limping along in his knitted cap, khaki tunic, shorts and rubber sandals, gloomy-faced and disgusted looking. As he came up he called out to Wilson in Swahili and they all saw the change in the white hunter's face.

"What does he say?" asked Margot.

"He says the first bull got up and went into the bush," Wilson said with no expression in his voice.

"Oh," said Macomber blankly.

"Then it's going to be just like the lion," said Margot, full of anticipation.

"It's not going to be a damned bit like the lion," Wilson told her. "Did you want another drink Macomber?"

"Thanks, yes," Macomber said. He expected the feeling he had had about the lion to come back but it did not. For the first time in his life he really felt wholly without fear. Instead of fear he had a feeling of definite elation.

"We'll go and have a look at the second bull," Wilson said. "I'll tell the driver to put the car in the shade."

"What are you going to do?" asked Margaret Macomber.

"Take a look at the buff," Wilson said.

"I'll come."

"Come along."

The three of them walked over to where the second buffalo bulked blackly in the open, head forward on the grass, the massive horns swung wide.

"He's a very good head," Wilson said. "That's close to a fifty-inch spread."

Macomber was looking at him with delight.

"He's hateful looking," said Margot. "Can't we go into the shade?"

"Of course," Wilson said. "Look," he said to Macomber, and pointed. "See that patch of bush?"

"Yes."

"That's where the first bull went in. The gun-bearer said when he fell off the bull was down. He was watching us helling along and the other two buff galloping. When he looked up there was the bull up and looking at him. Gun-bearer ran like hell and the bull went off slowly into that bush."

"Can we go in after him now?" asked Macomber eagerly.

Wilson looked at him appraisingly. Damned if this isn't a strange one, he thought. Yesterday he's scared sick and today he's a ruddy fire eater.

"No, we'll give him a while."

"Let's please go into the shade," Margot said. Her face was white and she looked ill.

They made their way to the car where it stood under a single, wide-spreading tree and all climbed in.

"Chances are he's dead in there," Wilson remarked. "After a little we'll have a look."

Macomber felt a wild unreasonable happiness that he had never known before.

"By God, that was a chase," he said. "I've never felt any such feeling. Wasn't it marvellous, Margot?"

"I hated it."

"Why?"

"I hated it," she said bitterly. "I loathed it."

"You know I don't think I'd ever be afraid of anything again," Macomber said to Wilson. "Something happened in me after we first saw the buff and started after him. Like a dam bursting. It was pure excitement."

"Cleans out your liver," said Wilson. "Damn funny things happen to people."

Macomber's face was shining. "You know something did happen to me," he said. "I feel absolutely different."

His wife said nothing and eyed him strangely. She was sitting far back in the seat and Macomber was sitting forward talking to Wilson who turned sideways talking over the back of the front seat.

"You know, I'd like to try another lion," Macomber said. "I'm really not afraid of them now. After all, what can they do to you?"

"That's it," said Wilson. "Worst one can do is kill you. How does it go? Shakespeare. Damned good. See if I can remember. Oh, damned good. Used to quote it to myself at one time. Let's see. 'By my troth, I care not; a man can die but once; we owe God a death and let it go which way it will, he that dies this year is quit for the next.' Damned fine, eh?"

He was very embarrassed, having brought out this thing he had lived by, but he had seen men come of age before and it always moved him. It was not a matter of their twenty-first birthday.

It had taken a strange chance of hunting, a sudden precipitation into action without opportunity for worrying beforehand, to bring this about with Macomber, but regardless of how it had happened it had most certainly happened. Look at the beggar now, Wilson thought. It's that some of them stay little boys so long, Wilson thought. Sometimes all their lives. Their figures stay boyish when they're fifty. The great American boy-men. Damned strange people. But he liked this Macomber now. Damned strange fellow. Probably meant the end of cuckoldry too. Well, that would be a damned good thing. Damn good thing. Beggar had probably been afraid all his life. Don't know what started it. But over now. Hadn't had time to be afraid with the buff. That and being angry too. Motor car too. Motor cars made it familiar. Be a damn fire eater now. He'd seen it in the war work the same way. More of a change than any loss of virginity. Fear gone like an operation. Something else grew in its place. Main thing a man had. Made him into a man. Women knew it too. No bloody fear.

From the far corner of the seat Margaret Macomber looked at the two of them. There was no change in Wilson. She saw Wilson as she had seen him the day before when she had first realized what his great talent was. But she saw the change in Francis Macomber now.

"Do you have that feeling of happiness about what's going to happen?" Macomber asked, still exploring his new wealth.

"You're not supposed to mention it," Wilson said, looking in the other's face. "Much more fashionable to say you're scared. Mind you, you'll be scared too, plenty of times."

"But you *have* a feeling of happiness about action to come?"

"Yes," said Wilson. "There's that. Doesn't do to talk too much about all this. Talk the whole thing away. No pleasure in anything if you mouth it up too much."

"You're both talking rot," said Margot. "Just because you've chased some helpless animals in a motor car you talk like heroes."

"Sorry," said Wilson. "I have been gassing too much." She's worried about it already, he thought.

"If you don't know what we're talking about why not keep out of it?" Macomber asked his wife.

"You've gotten awfully brave, awfully suddenly," his wife said contemptuously, but her contempt was not secure. She was very afraid of something.

Macomber laughed, a very natural hearty laugh. "You know I *have*," he said. "I really have."

"Isn't it sort of late?" Margot said bitterly. Because she had done the best she could for many years back and the way they were together now was no one person's fault.

"Not for me," said Macomber.

Margot said nothing but sat back in the corner of the seat.

"Do you think we've given him time enough?" Macomber asked Wilson cheerfully.

"We might have a look," Wilson said. "Have you any solids left?"

"The gun-bearer has some."

Wilson called in Swahili and the older gun-bearer, who was skinning out one of the heads, straightened up, pulled a box of solids out of his pocket and brought them over to Macomber, who filled his magazine and put the remaining shells in his pocket.

"You might as well shoot the Springfield," Wilson said. "You're used to it. We'll leave the Mannlicher in the car with the Memsahib. Your gun-bearer can carry your heavy gun. I've this damned cannon. Now let me tell you about them." He had saved this until the last because he did not want to worry Macomber. "When a buff comes he comes with his head high and thrust straight out. The boss of the horns covers any sort of a brain shot. The only shot is straight into the nose. The only other shot is into his chest or, if you're to one side, into the neck or the shoulders. After they've been hit once they take a hell of a lot of killing. Don't try anything fancy. Take the easiest shot there is. They've finished skinning out that head now. Should we get started?"

He called to the gun-bearers, who came up wiping their hands, and the older one got into the back.

"I'll only take Kongoni," Wilson said. "The other can watch to keep the birds away."

As the car moved slowly across the open space toward the island of brushy trees that ran in a tongue of foliage along a dry water course that cut the open swale, Macomber felt his heart pounding and his mouth was dry again, but it was excitement, not fear.

"Here's where he went in," Wilson said. Then to the gun-bearer in Swahili, "Take the blood spoor."

The car was parallel to the patch of bush. Macomber, Wilson and the gun-bearer got down. Macomber, looking back, saw his wife, with the rifle by her side, looking at him. He waved to her and she did not wave back.

The brush was very thick ahead and the ground was dry. The middle-aged gun-bearer was sweating heavily and Wilson had his hat down over his eyes and his red neck showed just ahead of Macomber. Suddenly the gun-bearer said something in Swahili to Wilson and ran forward.

"He's dead in there," Wilson said. "Good work," and he turned to grip Macomber's hand and as they shook hands, grinning at each other, the gun-bearer shouted wildly and they saw him coming out of the bush sideways, fast as a crab, and the bull coming, nose out, mouth tight closed, blood dripping, massive head straight out, coming in a charge, his little pig eyes bloodshot as he looked at them. Wilson, who was ahead, was kneeling shooting, and Macomber, as he fired, unhearing his shot in the roaring of Wilson's gun, saw fragments like slate burst from the huge boss of the horns, and the head jerked, he shot again at the wide nostrils and saw the horns jolt again and fragments fly, and he did not see Wilson now and, aiming carefully, shot again with the buffalo's huge bulk almost on him and his rifle almost level with the on-coming head, nose out, and he could see the little wicked eyes and the head started to lower and he felt a sudden white-hot, blinding flash explode inside his head and that was all he ever felt.

Wilson had ducked to one side to get in a shoulder shot. Macomber had stood solid and shot for the nose, shooting a touch high each time and hitting the heavy horns, splintering and chipping them like hitting a slate roof, and Mrs. Macomber, in the car, had shot at the buffalo with the 6.5 Mannlicher as it seemed about to gore Macomber and had hit her husband about two inches up and a little to one side of the base of his skull.

Francis Macomber lay now, face down, not two yards from where the buffalo lay on his side and his wife knelt over him with Wilson beside her.

"I wouldn't turn him over," Wilson said.

The woman was crying hysterically.

"I'd get back in the car," Wilson said. "Where's the rifle?"

She shook her head, her face contorted. The gun-bearer picked up the rifle.

"Leave it as it is," said Wilson. Then, "Go get Abdulla so that he may witness the manner of the accident."

He knelt down, took a handkerchief from his pocket, and spread it over Francis Macomber's crew-cropped head where it lay. The blood sank into the dry, loose earth.

Wilson stood up and saw the buffalo on his side, his legs out, his thinly-haired belly crawling with ticks. "Hell of a good bull," his brain registered automatically. "A good fifty inches, or better. Better." He called to the driver and told him to spread a blanket over the body and stay by it. Then he walked over to the motor car where the woman sat crying in the corner.

"That was a pretty thing to do," he said in a toneless voice. "He *would* have left you too."

"Stop it," she said.

"Of course it's an accident," he said. "I know that."

"Stop it," she said.

"Don't worry," he said. "There will be a certain amount of unpleasantness but I will have some photographs taken that will be very useful at the inquest. There's the testimony of the gun-bearers and the driver too. You're perfectly all right."

"Stop it," she said.

"There's a hell of a lot to be done," he said. "And I'll have to send a truck off to the lake to wireless for a plane to take the three of us into Nairobi. Why didn't you poison him? That's what they do in England."

"Stop it. Stop it. Stop it," the woman cried.

Wilson looked at her with his flat blue eyes.

"I'm through now," he said. "I was a little angry. I'd begun to like your husband."

"Oh, please stop it," she said. "Please, please stop it."

"That's better," Wilson said. "Please is much better. Now I'll stop."

Alice Walker

(b. 1944) Born in Georgia, Alice
Walker was educated at Spelman
College and later at Sarah Lawrence.
She has published a volume of poetry
entitled Once, *a novel called* The Third
Life of Grange Copeland, *and several*
short stories. She has been a fellow
of the Radcliffe Institute and has
taught at Tougaloo College and
Wellesley College.

Her Sweet Jerome

Ties she had bought him hung on the closet door which now swung open as she hurled herself again and again into the closet. Glorious ties, some with birds and dancing women in grass skirts painted on by hand, some with little polka dots with bigger dots dispersed among them. Some red, lots red and green, and one purple, with a golden star, through the center of which went his gold mustang stickpin, which she had also given him. She looked in the pockets of the black leather jacket he had reluctantly worn the night before. Three of his suits, a pair of blue twill work pants, an old gray sweater with a hood and pockets, lay thrown across the bed. The jacket leather was sleazy and damply clinging to her hands. She had bought it for him, as well as the three suits: one light blue with side vents, one gold with green specks, and one reddish that had a silver imitation silk vest. The pockets of the jacket came softly outward from the lining like skinny milktoast rats. Empty. Slowly she sank down on the bed and began to knead, with blunt anxious fingers, all the pockets in all the clothes piled around her. First the blue suit, then the gold with green, then the reddish one that he said he didn't like most of all, but which he would some-times wear if she agreed to stay home, or if she promised not to touch him anywhere at all while he was getting dressed.

She was a big awkward woman, with big bones and a hard rubbery flesh. Her short arms ended in ham hands, and her neck was a squat roll of fat that protruded behind her head as a big bump. Her skin was rough and puffy, with plump mole-like freckles down her cheeks. Her eyes glowered from under the mountain of her brow and were circled with expensive mauve shadow. They were nervous and quick when she was flustered and darted about at nothing in particular while she was dressing hair or talking to people.

Her troubles started noticeably when she fell in love with a studious quiet school teacher, Mr. Jerome Franklin Washington III, who was ten years younger than her. She told herself that she shouldn't want him, he was so little and cute and young, but when she took into account that he was a school teacher, well, she just couldn't seem to get any rest until, as she put it, "I were Mr. and Mrs. Jerome Franklin Washington the Third, *and that's the truth!*"

She owned a small beauty shop at the back of her father's funeral home, and they were known as "colored folks with money." She made pretty good herself, though she didn't like standing on her feet so much, and her father let anybody know she wasn't getting any of his money while he was alive. She was proud to say she had never asked him for any. He started relenting kind of fast when he heard she planned to add a school teacher to the family, which consisted of funeral directors and bootleggers, but she cut him off quick and said she didn't want anybody to take care of her man but her. She had learned how to do hair from an old woman who ran a shop on the other side of town and was proud to say that she could make her own way. And much better than some. She was fond of telling school teachers (women school teachers) that she didn't miss her "eddicashion" as much as some did who had no learning and no money, both together. She had a low opinion of women school teachers because before and after her marriage to Jerome Franklin Washington III, they were the only females to whom he cared to talk.

The first time she saw him he was walking past the window of her shop with an armful of books and his coat thrown casually over his arm. Looking so neat and *cute.* What popped into her mind was that if he was hers the first thing she would get him was a sweet little red car to drive. And she worked and went into debt and got it for him too—after she got him—but then she could tell he didn't like it much because it was only a Chevy. She had started right away to save up so she could make a down payment on a brand new white Buick Deluxe with automatic drive and white wall tires.

Jerome was dapper, every inch a gentleman, as anybody with half an eye could see. That's what she told everybody before they were married. He was beating her black and blue even then, so that every time you saw her she was sporting her "shades." She could not open her mouth without him wincing and pretending he couldn't stand it, so he would knock her out of the room to keep her from talking to him. She tried to be sexy and stylish, and was, in her fashion, with a predominant taste for pastel taffetas and orange shoes. In the summertime she paid twenty dollars for big umbrella hats with bows and flowers on them and when she wore black and white together she would liven it up with elbow length gloves of red satin. She was genuinely undecided when she woke up in the morning whether she *really* outstripped the other girls in town for beauty, but could convince herself that she was equally good-looking by the time she had breakfast on the table. She was always talking with a lot of extra movement to her thick coarse mouth, with its hair tufts at the corners, and when she drank coffee she held the cup over the saucer with her little finger sticking out, while she crossed her short hairy legs at the knees.

If her husband laughed at her high heels as she teetered and minced off to church on Sunday mornings, with her hair greased and curled and her new dress bunching at the top of her girdle, she pretended his eyes were approving. Other times, when he didn't bother to look up from his books and only muttered curses if she tried to kiss him goodbye, she did not know whether to laugh or cry. However, her public manner was serene.

"I just don't know how some womens can stand it, honey," she would say slowly, twisting her head to the side and upwards in an elegant manner. "One thing my husband does not do," she would enunciate grandly, "he don't beat me!" And she would sit back and smile in her pleased oily fat way. Usually her listeners, captive women with wet hair, would simply smile and nod in sympathy and say, looking at one another or at her black eye, "You say he don't? Hummmm, well, hush your mouf." And she would continue curling or massaging or straightening their hair, fixing her face in a steamy dignified mask that encouraged snickers.

2 It was in her shop that she first heard the giggling and saw the smirks. It was at her job that gossip gave her to understand, as one woman told her, "Your cute little man is sticking his finger into somebody else's pie." And she was not and could not be surprised, as she looked into the amused and self-contented face, for she had long been aware that her own pie was going—and for the longest time had been going—strictly untouched.

From that first day of slyly whispered hints, "Your old man's puttin' something *over* on you, sweets," she started trying to find out who he was fooling around with. Her sources of gossip were malicious and mean, but she could think of nothing else to do but believe them. She searched high and she searched low. She looked in taverns and she looked in churches. She looked in the school where he worked.

She went to whorehouses and to prayer meetings, through parks and outside the city limits, all the while buying axes and pistols and knives of all descriptions. Of course she said nothing to her sweet Jerome, who watched her maneuverings from behind the covers of his vast supply of paper back books. This hobby of his she heartily encouraged, relegating reading to the importance of scanning the funnies, and besides it was something he could do at home; if she could convince him she would be completely silent for an evening, and of course, if he would stay.

She turned the whole town upside down, looking at white girls, black women, brown beauties, ugly hags of all shades. She found nothing. And Jerome went on reading, smiling smugly as he shushed her with a carefully cleaned and lustred finger. "Don't interrupt me," he was always saying, and he would read some more while she stood glowering darkly behind him, muttering swears

in her throaty voice and tramping flatfooted out of the house with her collection
of weapons.

Some days she would get out of bed at four in the morning after not sleeping
a wink all night, throw an old sweater around her shoulders and begin the
search. Her firm bulk became flabby. Her eyes were bloodshot and wild, her hair
full of lint, nappy at the roots and greasy on the ends. She smelled bad from
mouth and underarms and elsewhere. She could not sit still for a minute without
jumping up in bitter vexation to run and search a house or street she thought
she might have missed before.

"You been messin' with my Jerome?" She would ask whoever she caught in
her quivering feverish grip. And before they had time to answer she would
have them by the chin in a headlock with a long knife pressed against their necks
below the ear. Such blood chilling questioning of its residents terrified the town,
especially since her madness was soon readily perceivable from her appearance.
She had taken to grinding her teeth and tearing at her hair as she walked along.
The townspeople, none of whom knew where she lived—or anything about her
save the name of her man, "Jerome"—were waiting for her to attempt another
attack on a woman openly, or, better for them because it implied less danger to a
resident, they hoped she would complete her crack-up within the confines
of her own home, preferably while alone; in that event anyone seeing or hearing
her would be obliged to call the authorities.

She knew this in her deranged but cunning way. But she did not let it
interfere with her search. The police would never catch her, she thought; she was
too clever. She had a few disguises and a thousand places to hide. A final crack-
up in her own home was impossible, she reasoned contemptuously, for she
did not think her husband's lover bold enough to show herself on his wife's own
turf.

Meanwhile, she stopped operating the beauty shop, and her patrons were
glad, for before she left for good she had had the unnerving habit of questioning
a woman sitting underneath her hot comb, "You the one ain't you?!" and
would end up burning her no matter what she said. When her father died he
proudly left his money to "the school teacher" to share or not with his wife,
as he had "learnin' enough to see fit." Jerome had "learnin' enough" not to give
his wife one cent. The legacy pleased Jerome, though he never bought anything
with the money that his wife could see. As long as the money lasted Jerome
spoke of it as "insurance." If she asked insurance against what, he would say fire
and theft. Or burglary and cyclones. When the money was gone, and it seemed
to her it vanished overnight, she asked Jerome what he had bought. He said
something very big. She said, like what? He said, like a tank. She did not ask any
more questions after that. By that time she didn't care about the money anyhow,
as long as he hadn't spent it on some woman.

As steadily as she careened downhill, Jerome advanced in the opposite
direction. He was well-known around town as a "shrewd joker" and a scholar.
An "intellectual" some people called him, a word that meant nothing whatever
to her. Everyone described Jerome in a different way. He had friends among
the educated, whose talk she found unusually trying, not that she was ever

invited to listen to any of it. His closest friend was the head of the school he
taught in and had migrated South from some famous University in the North.
He was a small slender man with a ferociously unruly beard and large mournful
eyes. He called Jerome "brother." The women in Jerome's group wore short
kinky hair and large hoop earrings. They stuck together, calling themselves by
what they termed their "African" names, and never went to church. Along with
the men the women sometimes held "workshops" for the young toughs of
the town. She had no idea what went on in these; however, she had long since
stopped believing they had anything to do with cabinetmaking or any other
kind of wood work.

Among Jerome's group of friends, or "comrades" as he sometimes called
them jokingly, (or not jokingly for all she knew), were two or three whites from
the community's white college and university. Jerome didn't ordinarily like
white people, and she could not understand where they fit into the group. The
principal's house was the meeting place, and the whites arrived looking backwards over their shoulders after nightfall. She knew, because she had watched
this house night after anxious night trying to rouse enough courage to go inside.
One hot night, when a drink helped stiffen her backbone, she burst into the
living room in the middle of the evening. The women, whom she had grimly
"suspected," sat together in debative conversation in one corner of the room.
Every once in a while a phrase she could understand touched her ear. She
heard "slave trade" and "violent overthrow" and "off de pig," an expression
she'd never heard before. One of the women, the only one of this group to
acknowledge her, laughingly asked if she had come to "join the revolution." She
had stood shaking by the door, trying so hard to understand she felt she was
going to faint. Jerome rose from among the group of men, who sat in a circle
on the other side of the room, and, without paying any attention to her, began
reciting some of the nastiest sounding poetry she'd ever heard. She left the
room in shame and confusion, and no one bothered to ask why she'd stood so
long staring at them, or whether she needed anyone to show her out. She
had trudged home heavily, with her head down, bewildered, astonished, and
perplexed.

3 And now she hunted through her husband's clothes looking for a clue. Her
hands were shaking as she emptied and shook, pawed and sometimes even
lifted to her nose to smell. Each time she emptied a pocket she felt there was
something, *something,* some little thing that was escaping her.

Her heart pounding, she got down on her knees and looked under the bed.
It was dusty and cobwebby, the way the inside of her head felt. The house
was filthy, for she had neglected it totally since she began her search. Now it
seemed that all the dust in the world had come to rest under her bed. She
saw his shoes; she lifted them to her perspiring cheeks and kissed them. She ran
her fingers inside them. Nothing.

Then, before she got up from her knees, she thought about the intense blackness underneath the headboard of the bed. She had not looked there. On her side of the bed on the floor beneath the pillow there was nothing. She hurried around to the other side. Kneeling, she struck something with her hand on the floor under his side of the bed. Quickly, down on her stomach, she raked it out. Then she raked and raked. She was panting and sweating, her ashen face slowly coloring with the belated rush of doomed comprehension. In a rush it came to her, "It ain't no woman." Just like that. It had never occurred to her there could be anything more serious. She stifled the cry that rose in her throat.

Coated with grit, with dust sticking to the pages, she held in her crude, indelicate hands, trembling now, a sizable pile of paper back books. Books that had fallen from his hands behind the bed over the months of their marriage. She dusted them carefully one by one and looked with frowning concentration at their covers. Fists and guns appeared everywhere. "Black" was the one word that appeared consistently on each cover. *Black Rage, Black Fire, Black Anger, Black Revenge, Black Vengeance, Black Hatred, Black Beauty, Black Revolution.* Then the word "Revolution" took over. *Revolution in the Streets, Revolution from the Rooftops, Revolution in the Hills, Revolution and Rebellion, Revolution and Black People in the United States, Revolution and Death.* She looked with wonder at the books that were her husband's preoccupation; enraged that the obvious was what she had never guessed before.

How many times had she encouraged his light reading? How many times been ignorantly amused? How many times had he laughed at her when she went out looking for "his" women? With a sob she realized she didn't even know what the word "Revolution" meant, unless it meant to go round and round, the way her head was going.

With quiet care she stacked the books neatly on his pillow. With the largest of her knives she ripped and stabbed them through. When the brazen and difficult words did not disappear with the books she hastened with kerosene to set the marriage bed afire. Thirstily, in hopeless jubilation, she watched the room begin to burn. The bits of words transformed themselves into luscious figures of smoke, lazily arching toward the ceiling. "Trash!" she cried over and over, reaching through the flames to strike out the words, now raised from the dead in glorious colors. "I kill you! I kill you!" she screamed against the roaring fire, backing enraged and trembling into a darkened corner of the room, not near the open door. But the fire and the words rumbled against her together, overwhelming her with pain and enlightenment. And she hid her big wet face in her singed then sizzling arms and screamed and screamed.

IV. the seductress-goddess

Beautiful women are mysterious. When men look into their eyes, they see far more than they can understand. In Jean Toomer's story, the heroine, Fern, has strange eyes, magnetically attractive but baffling because they do not mirror any "obvious and tangible" desire. Like Freud, who asked "What do women want?" the observer is mystified because he cannot understand what she wants from him and from life. Yet he acknowledges her power over all the men who have known her; her influence makes them transcend physical desire and want to do something great and noble for her. The narrator comes to understand that her appeal is superhuman. In her eyes he sees God, who possesses her as he did the oracles of Greek myth, speaking through her tortured body paradoxical answers to existential questions.

Fern, a humble black woman, is exalted in this story. Her effect on men is beneficent and ennobling, though not a source of happiness for her. The good intentions she inspires never come to fruition; "Nothing ever came to Fern." In other literature a mysteriously beautiful woman has a deleterious effect on men; instead of inspiring them, she entices them to shame and death. Keats' "La Belle Dame sans Merci" shows a woman who may symbolize Death itself. Her wild eyes, strange language, and fairylike song have made corpses of many men. The appearance of their ghosts in a dream causes the most recent victim to realize that what he thinks is the sleep of love is really deathlike and destructive: he awakens completely disoriented. In many poems both intercourse and sleep are metaphors for death, used to express the inexpressible. Man comes close to understanding the nature of death when he compares it to the loss of power after sexual intercourse, the helplessness and oblivion of sleep. A man's love for the beautiful woman (who symbolizes Death) testifies to the strength of the death wish, which is sometimes stronger than his will to live. The beautiful woman must therefore be superhuman, like a goddess on a pedestal, to be propitiated if not worshipped.

Heine's "The Loreley" and Robert Frost's "The Pauper Witch of Grafton" emphasize the fatal power of women but also reveal that women need not have the intention of doing evil. The lovely mermaid is merely combing her hair and singing an old song when sailors crash on her rock, and Frost's witch is really a simple woman reported by a crazy countryman to have turned him into a horse. The mysterious power of these women is a fantasy of the males who have known them. So, too, in Hawthorne's "Rappaccini's Daughter" Beatrice is not responsible for the fact that her kiss is the kiss of death. It is her father's mad scientific experimentation which has turned her beauty into a trap for men. Hawthorne's allegory of a beautiful garden full of poisonous flowers, in which the gardener's daughter is the bringer of death to her lover, recalls the Garden of Eden: what might have been paradise has, through man's perverted use of it, become hell. But to the lover, beauty plus innocence is almost a fatal combination. Ailie Calhoun, in "The Last of the Belles," and Howells' "Editha" similarly cause death to their lovers as much through their innocence and lack of self-knowledge as through their charm. They do not realize the strength of their power nor understand the logical end of the path they inspire their men to take. Like Fern in Toomer's story, they are the vessels of powers they cannot understand.

Helene Davis' poem "Affair" shows that the power of love is as strong for a woman as for a man. What is demanded of the woman is not death but the loss of her identity; she must become a "velvet backdrop," a shape-changer, in order to fulfill her lover's desire as well as her own. Woman is mysterious, "a rose half-grown, a room full of music," because she wants a man to love her. What Fern's lover saw in her eyes as desire for nothing "tangible" was her need to be loved for herself, not as a symbol of the anguish of life, not as a goddess, but as one who with a beloved man becomes "one kind"—a complete human being.

Jean Toomer

*(1894–1967) Jean Toomer is known
primarily for* Cane *(1923), a collection
of short stories and poems which
focus on the dilemma of the American
Negro, male and female, who tries to
function as a full human being.*

Fern

Face flowed into her eyes. Flowed in soft cream foam and plaintive ripples,
in such a way that wherever your glance may momentarily have rested, it
immediately thereafter wavered in the direction of her eyes. The soft suggestion
of down slightly darkened, like the shadow of a bird's wing might, the creamy
brown color of her upper lip. Why, after noticing it, you sought her eyes, I
cannot tell you. Her nose was aquiline, Semitic. If you have heard a Jewish
cantor sing, if he has touched you and made your own sorrow seem trivial when
compared with his, you will know my feeling when I follow the curves of her
profile, like mobile rivers, to their common delta. They were strange eyes. In
this, that they sought nothing—that is, nothing that was obvious and tangible and
that one could see, and they gave the impression that nothing was to be denied.
When a woman seeks, you will have observed, her eyes deny. Fern's eyes desired
nothing that you could give her; there was no reason why they should withhold. Men saw her eyes and fooled themselves. Fern's eyes said to them that she
was easy. When she was young, a few men took her, but got no joy from it. And
then, once done, they felt bound to her (quite unlike their hit and run with
other girls), felt as though it would take them a lifetime to fulfill an obligation
which they could find no name for. They became attached to her, and hungered
after finding the barest trace of what she might desire. As she grew up, new
men who came to town felt as almost everyone did who ever saw her: that they
would not be denied. Men were everlastingly bringing her their bodies. Some-

thing inside of her got tired of them, I guess, for I am certain that for the life of her she could not tell why or how she began to turn them off. A man in fever is no trifling thing to send away. They began to leave her, baffled and ashamed, yet vowing to themselves that some day they would do some fine thing for her: send her candy every week and not let her know whom it came from, watch out for her wedding-day and give her a magnificent something with no name on it, buy a house and deed it to her, rescue her from some unworthy fellow who had tricked her into marrying him. As you know, men are apt to idolize or fear that which they cannot understand, especially if it be a woman. She did not deny them, yet the fact was that they were denied. A sort of super-stition crept into their consciousness of her being somehow above them. Being above them meant that she was not to be approached by anyone. She became a virgin. Now a virgin in a small southern town is by no means the usual thing, if you will believe me. That the sexes were made to mate is the practice of the South. Particularly, black folks were made to mate. And it is black folks whom I have been talking about thus far. What white men thought of Fern I can arrive at only by analogy. They let her alone.

Anyone, of course, could see her, could see her eyes. If you walked up the Dixie Pike most any time of day, you'd be most like to see her resting listless-like on the railing of her porch, back propped against a post, head tilted a little forward because there was a nail in the porch post just where her head came which for some reason or other she never took the trouble to pull out. Her eyes, if it were sunset, rested idly where the sun, molten and glorious, was pouring down between the fringe of pines. Or maybe they gazed at the gray cabin on the knoll from which an evening folk-song was coming. Perhaps they followed a cow that had been turned loose to roam and feed on cotton-stalks and corn leaves. Like as not they'd settle on some vague spot above the horizon, though hardly a trace of wistfulness would come to them. If it were dusk, then they'd wait for the search-light of the evening train which you could see miles up the track before it flared across the Dixie Pike, close to her home. Wherever they looked, you'd follow them and then waver back. Like her face, the whole countryside seemed to flow into her eyes. Flowed into them with the soft listless cadence of Georgia's South. A young Negro, once, was looking at her, spell-bound, from the road. A white man passing in a buggy had to flick him with his whip if he was to get by without running him over. I first saw her on her porch. I was passing with a fellow whose crusty numbness (I was from the North and suspected of being prejudiced and stuck-up) was melting as he found me warm. I asked him who she was. "That's Fern," was all I could get from him. Some folks already thought that I was given to nosing around; I let it go at that, so far as questions were concerned. But at first sight of her I felt as if I heard a Jewish cantor sing. As if his singing rose above the unheard chorus of a folk-song. And I felt bound to her. I too had my dreams: something I would do for her. I have knocked about from town to town too much not to know the futility of mere change of place. Besides, picture if you can, this cream-colored solitary girl sitting at a tenement window looking down on the indifferent throngs of Harlem.

Better that she listens to folk-songs at dusk in Georgia, you would say, and so would I. Or, suppose she came up North and married. Even a doctor or a lawyer, say, one who would be sure to get along—that is, make money. You and I know, who have had experience in such things, that love is not a thing like prejudice which can be bettered by changes of town. Could men in Washington, Chicago, or New York, more than the men of Georgia, bring her something left vacant by the bestowal of their bodies? You and I who know men in these cities will have to say, they could not. See her out and out a prostitute along State Street in Chicago. See her move into a southern town where white men are more aggressive. See her become a white man's concubine. . . Something I must do for her. There was myself. What could I do for her? Talk, of course. Push back the fringe of pines upon new horizons. To what purpose? and what for? Her? Myself? Men in her case seem to lose their selfishness. I lost mine before I touched her. I ask you, friend (it makes no difference if you sit in the Pullman or the Jim Crow as the train crosses her road), what thoughts would come to you— that is, after you'd finished with the thoughts that leap into men's minds at the sight of a pretty woman who will not deny them; what thoughts would come to you, had you seen her in a quick flash, keen and intuitively, as she sat there on her porch when your train thundered by? Would you have got off at the next station and come back for her to take her where? Would you have completely forgotten her as soon as you reached Macon, Atlanta, Augusta, Pasadena, Madison, Chicago, Boston, or New Orleans? Would you tell your wife or sweetheart about a girl you saw? Your thoughts can help me, and I would like to know. Something I would do for her. . .

One evening I walked up the Pike on purpose, and stopped to say hello. Some of her family were about, but they moved away to make room for me. Damn if I knew how to begin. Would you? Mr. and Miss So-and-So, people, the weather, the crops, the new preacher, the frolic, the church benefit, rabbit and possum hunting, the new soft drink they had at old Pap's store, the schedule of the trains, what kind of town Macon was, Negro's migration north, boll-weevils, syrup, the Bible—to all these things she gave a yassur or nassur, without further comment. I began to wonder if perhaps my own emotional sensibility had played one of its tricks on me. "Let's take a walk," I at last ventured. The suggestion, coming after so long an isolation, was novel enough, I guess, to surprise. But it wasn't that. Something told me that men before me had said just that as a prelude to the offering of their bodies. I tried to tell her with my eyes. I think she understood. The thing from her that made my throat catch, vanished. Its passing left her visible in a way I'd thought, but never seen. We walked down the Pike with people on all the porches gaping at us. "Doesn't it make you mad?" She meant the row of petty gossiping people. She meant the world. Through a canebrake that was ripe for cutting, the branch was reached. Under a sweet-gum tree, and where reddish leaves had dammed the creek a little, we sat down. Dusk, suggesting the almost imperceptible procession of giant trees, settled with a purple haze about the cane. I felt strange, as I always do in Georgia, particularly at dusk. I felt that things unseen to men were tangibly immediate. It would not have surprised me had I had a vision. People have them in Georgia more often than you would suppose. A black woman once saw the mother of Christ and drew her in charcoal on the courthouse wall. . . When one is on the soil of one's ancestors, most anything can come to one. . . From force of habit, I suppose, I held Fern in my arms—that is, without at first noticing it. Then my mind came back to her. Her eyes, unusually weird and open, held me. Held God. He flowed in as I've seen the countryside flow in. Seen men. I must have done something—what, I don't know, in the confusion of my emotion. She sprang up. Rushed some distance from me. Fell to her knees, and began swaying, swaying. Her body was tortured with something it could not let out. Like boiling sap it flooded arms and fingers till she shook them as if they burned her. It found her throat, and spattered inarticulately in plaintive, convulsive sounds, mingled with calls to Christ Jesus. And then she sang, brokenly. A Jewish cantor singing with a broken voice. A child's voice, uncertain, or an old man's. Dusk hid her; I could hear only her song. It seemed to me as though she were pounding her head in anguish upon the ground. I rushed to her. She fainted in my arms.

There was talk about her fainting with me in the canefield. And I got one or two ugly looks from town men who'd set themselves up to protect her. In fact, there was talk of making me leave town. But they never did. They kept a watch-out for me, though. Shortly after, I came back North. From the train window I saw her as I crossed her road. Saw her on her porch, head tilted a little forward where the nail was, eyes vaguely focused on the sunset. Saw her face flow into them, the countryside and something that I call God, flowing into them. . . Nothing ever really happened. Nothing ever came to Fern, not even I. Something I would do for her. Some fine unnamed thing. . . And, friend, you? She is still living, I have reason to know. Her name, against the chance that you might happen down that way, is Fernie May Rosen.

John Keats

*(1795–1821) John Keats, the famous
English Romantic poet, studied
medicine before embarking on his all
too brief career as a poet. His poems
reflect his love for Greek myth, for
nature, and for the supernatural, often
personified as woman.*

La Belle Dame sans Merci

Ah, what can ail thee, wretched wight,
　　Alone and palely loitering;
The sedge is wither'd from the lake,
　　And no birds sing.

Ah, what can ail thee, wretched wight,
　　So haggard and so woe-begone?
The squirrel's granary is full,
　　And the harvest's done.

I see a lilly on thy brow,
　　With anguish moist and fever dew;
And on thy cheek a fading rose
　　Fast withereth too.

I met a Lady in the meads,
　　Full beautiful, a fairy's child;
Her hair was long, her foot was light,
　　And her eyes were wild.

I set her on my pacing steed,
　　And nothing else saw all day long;
For sideways would she lean, and sing
　　A faery's song.

First published in The Indicator, *May 10, 1820.*

I made a garland for her head,
    And bracelets too, and fragrant zone,
She look'd at me as she did love,
    And made sweet moan.

She found me roots of relish sweet,
    And honey wild, and manna dew,
And sure in language strange she said,
    I love thee true.

She took me to her elfin grot,
    And there she gaz'd and sighed deep,
And there I shut her wild sad eyes—
    So kiss'd to sleep.

And there we slumber'd on the moss,
    And there I dream'd, ah woe betide
The latest dream I ever dream'd
    On the cold hill side.

I saw pale kings, and princes too,
    Pale warriors, death-pale were they all;
Who cry'd—"La belle Dame sans merci
    Hath thee in thrall."

I saw their starv'd lips in the gloom
    With horrid warning gaped wide,
And I awoke, and found me here
    On the cold hill side.

And this is why I sojourn here
    Alone and palely loitering,
Though the sedge is wither'd from the lake,
    And no birds sing.

Heinrich Heine

*(1797–1856) A well-known German
writer, Heinrich Heine voluntarily
exiled himself in Paris in 1831 to
escape the rigid political regime of his
native Prussia. His early works,
including the famous "Loreley," were
romantic; later he satirized the
Romantic movement and wrote
political and philosophical works in
prose.*

The Loreley

Ich weiss nicht, was soll es bedeuten

I cannot tell why this imagined
   Despair has fallen on me;
The ghost of an ancient legend
   That will not let me be:

The air is cool, and twilight
   Flows down the quiet Rhine;
A mountain alone in the high light
   Still holds the faltering shine.

The last peak rosily gleaming
   Reveals, enthroned in air,
A maiden, lost in dreaming,
   Who combs her golden hair.

Combing her hair with a golden
   Comb in her rocky bower,
She sings the tune of an olden
   Song that has magical power.

The boatman has heard; it has bound him
  In throes of a strange, wild love;
Blind to the reefs that surround him,
  He sees but the vision above.

And lo, hungry waters are springing—
  Boat and boatman are gone. . . .
Then silence. And this, with her singing,
  The Loreley has done.

Robert Frost

(1874–1963) One of the greatest American poets, Robert Frost wrote in a deceptively simple style about people and places in the New England he loved. His light, often humorous tone about serious existential problems results in an ironic view of life and people.

The Pauper Witch of Grafton

Now that they've got it settled whose I be,
I'm going to tell them something they won't like:
They've got it settled wrong, and I can prove it.
Flattered I must be to have two towns fighting
To make a present of me to each other.
They don't dispose me, either one of them,
To spare them any trouble. Double trouble's
Always the witch's motto anyway.
I'll double theirs for both of them—you watch me.
They'll find they've got the whole thing to do over,
That is, if facts is what they want to go by.
They set a lot (now don't they?) by a record
Of Arthur Amy's having once been up
For Hog Reeve in March Meeting here in Warren.
I could have told them any time this twelvemonth
The Arthur Amy I was married to
Couldn't have been the one they say was up
In Warren at March Meeting, for the reason
He wa'n't but fifteen at the time they say.
The Arthur Amy I was married to
Voted the only times he ever voted,

Which wasn't many, in the town of Wentworth.
One of the times was when 'twas in the warrant
To see if the town wanted to take over
The tote road to our clearing where we lived.
I'll tell you who'd remember—Heman Lapish.
Their Arthur Amy was the father of mine.
So now they've dragged it through the law courts once,
I guess they'd better drag it through again.
Wentworth and Warren's both good towns to live in,
Only I happen to prefer to live
In Wentworth from now on; and when all's said,
Right's right, and the temptation to do right
When I can hurt someone by doing it
Has always been too much for me, it has.
I know of some folks that'd be set up
At having in their town a noted witch:
But most would have to think of the expense
That even I would be. They ought to know
That as a witch I'd often milk a bat
And that'd be enough to last for days.
It'd make my position stronger, think,
If I was to consent to give some sign
To make it surer that I was a witch?
It wa'n't no sign, I s'pose, when Mallice Huse
Said that I took him out in his old age
And rode all over everything on him
Until I'd had him worn to skin and bones,
And if I'd left him hitched unblanketed
In front of one Town Hall, I'd left him hitched
In front of every one in Grafton County.
Some cried shame on me not to blanket him,
The poor old man. It would have been all right
If someone hadn't said to gnaw the posts
He stood beside and leave his trademark on them,
So they could recognize them. Not a post
That they could hear tell of was scarified.
They made him keep on gnawing till he whined.
Then that same smarty someone said to look—
He'd bet Huse was a cribber and had gnawed
The crib he slept in—and as sure's you're born
They found he'd gnawed the four posts of his bed,
All four of them to splinters. What did that prove?
Not that he hadn't gnawed the hitching posts
He said he had, besides. Because a horse
Gnaws in the stable ain't no proof to me
He don't gnaw trees and posts and fences too.

But everybody took it for a proof.
I was a strapping girl of twenty then.
The smarty someone who spoiled everything
Was Arthur Amy. You know who he was.
That was the way he started courting me.
He never said much after we were married,
But I mistrusted he was none too proud
Of having interfered in the Huse business.
I guess he found he got more out of me
By having me a witch. Or something happened
To turn him round. He got to saying things
To undo what he'd done and make it right,
Like, "No, she ain't come back from kiting yet.
Last night was one of her nights out. She's kiting.
She thinks when the wind makes a night of it
She might as well herself." But he liked best
To let on he was plagued to death with me:
If anyone had seen me coming home
Over the ridgepole, 'stride of a broomstick,
As often as he had in the tail of the night,
He guessed they'd know what he had to put up with.
Well, I showed Arthur Amy signs enough
Off from the house as far as we could keep
And from barn smells you can't wash out of ploughed ground
With all the rain and snow of seven years;
And I don't mean just skulls of Roger's Rangers
On Moosilauke, but woman signs to man,
Only bewitched so I would last him longer.
Up where the trees grow short, the mosses tall,
I made him gather me wet snow berries
On slippery rocks beside a waterfall.
I made him do it for me in the dark.
And he liked everything I made him do.
I hope if he is where he sees me now
He's so far off he can't see what I've come to.
You *can* come down from everything to nothing.
All is, if I'd a-known when I was young
And full of it, that this would be the end,
It doesn't seem as if I'd had the courage
To make so free and kick up in folks' faces.
I might have, but it doesn't seem as if.

Nathaniel Hawthorne

(1804–1864) In his masterpiece, The Scarlet Letter, *and in many other novels and stories, Hawthorne used symbol and allegory to probe the secrets of the human heart and its complex motivations. His psychological insight, long before Freud, was astonishingly prophetic of modern theories.*

Rappaccini's Daughter
(From the Writings of Aubépine)

We do not remember to have seen any transplanted specimens of the productions of M. de l'Aubépine—a fact the less to be wondered at, as his very name is unknown to many of his own countrymen as well as to the student of foreign literature. As a writer, he seems to occupy an unfortunate position between the Transcendentalists (who, under one name or another, have their share in all the current literature of the world) and the great body of pen-and-ink men who address the intellect and sympathies of the multitude. If not too refined, at all events too remote, too shadowy and unsubstantial in his modes of development to suit the taste of the latter class, and yet too popular to satisfy the spiritual or metaphysical requisitions of the former, he must necessarily find himself without an audience, except here and there an individual or possibly an isolated clique. His writings, to do them justice, are not altogether destitute of fancy and originality; they might have won him greater reputation but for an inveterate love of allegory, which is apt to invest his plots and characters with the aspect of scenery and people in the clouds, and to steal away the human warmth out of his conceptions. His fictions are sometimes historical, sometimes of the present day, and sometimes, so far as can be discovered, have little or no reference either to time or space. In any case, he generally contents himself with a very slight embroidery of outward manners—the faintest possible counterfeit of

From Democratic Review, *December 1844; collected in* Mosses from an Old Manse, *Wiley and Putnam, 1846.*

real life—and endeavors to create an interest by some less obvious peculiarity of the subject. Occasionally a breath of Nature, a raindrop of pathos and tenderness, or a gleam of humor, will find its way into the midst of his fantastic imagery, and make us feel as if, after all, we were yet within the limits of our native earth. We will only add to this very cursory notice that M. de l'Aubépine's productions, if the reader chance to take them in precisely the proper point of view, may amuse a leisure hour as well as those of a brighter man; if otherwise, they can hardly fail to look excessively like nonsense.

Our author is voluminous; he continues to write and publish with as much praiseworthy and indefatigable prolixity as if his efforts were crowned with the brilliant success that so justly attends those of Eugène Sue. His first appearance was by a collection of stories in a long series of volumes entitled *Contes deux fois racontées.* The titles of some of his more recent works (we quote from memory) are as follows: "Le Voyage Céleste à Chemin de Fer," 3 tom., 1838; "Le nouveau Père Adam et la nouvelle Mère Eve," 2 tom., 1839; "Roderic; ou le Serpent à l'estomac," 2 tom., 1840; "Le Culte du Feu," a folio volume of ponderous reserarch into the religion and ritual of the old Persian Ghebers, published in 1841; "La Soirée du Château en Espagne," 1 tom., 8vo, 1842; and "L'Artiste du Beau; ou le Papillon Mécanique," 5 tom., 4to, 1843. Our somewhat wearisome perusal of this startling catalogue of volumes has left behind it a certain personal affection and sympathy, though by no means admiration, for M. de l'Aubépine; and we would fain do the little in our power towards introducing him favorably to the American public. The ensuing tale is a translation of his "Beatrice; ou la Belle Empoisonneuse," recently published in *La Revue Anti-Aristocratique.* This journal, edited by the Comte de Bearhaven, has for some years past led the defense of liberal principles and popular rights with a faithfulness and ability worthy of all praise.

A young man, named Giovanni Guasconti, came, very long ago, from the more southern region of Italy, to pursue his studies at the University of Padua. Giovanni, who had but a scanty supply of gold ducats in his pocket, took lodgings in a high and gloomy chamber of an old edifice which looked not unworthy to have been the palace of a Paduan noble, and which, in fact, exhibited over its entrance the armorial bearings of a family long since extinct. The young stranger, who was not unstudied in the great poem of his country, recollected that one of the ancestors of this family, and perhaps an occupant of this very mansion, had been pictured by Dante as a partaker of the immortal agonies of his Inferno. These reminiscences and associations, together with the tendency to heartbreak natural to a young man for the first time out of his native sphere, caused Giovanni to sigh heavily as he looked around the desolate and ill-furnished apartment.

"Holy Virgin, signor!" cried old Dame Lisabetta, who, won by the youth's remarkable beauty of person, was kindly endeavoring to give the chamber a habitable air, "what a sigh was that to come out of a young man's heart! Do you find this old mansion gloomy? For the love of Heaven, then, put your head out of the window, and you will see as bright sunshine as you have left in Naples."

Guasconti mechanically did as the old woman advised, but could not quite agree with her that the Paduan sunshine was as cheerful as that of southern Italy. Such as it was, however, it fell upon a garden beneath the window and expended its fostering influences on a variety of plants, which seemed to have been cultivated with exceeding care.

"Does this garden belong to the house?" asked Giovanni.

"Heaven forbid, signor, unless it were fruitful of better pot herbs than any that grow there now," answered old Lisabetta. "No; that garden is cultivated by the own hands of Signor Giacomo Rappaccini, the famous doctor, who, I warrant him, has been heard of as far as Naples. It is said that he distills these plants into medicines that are as potent as a charm. Oftentimes you may see the signor doctor at work, and perchance the signora, his daughter, too, gathering the strange flowers that grow in the garden."

The old woman had now done what she could for the aspect of the chamber; and, commending the young man to the protection of the saints, took her departure.

Giovanni still found no better occupation than to look down into the garden beneath his window. From its appearance, he judged it to be one of those botanic gardens which were of earlier date in Padua than elsewhere in Italy or in the world. Or, not improbably, it might once have been the pleasure place of an opulent family; for there was the ruin of a marble fountain in the center, sculptured with rare art, but so woefully shattered that it was impossible to trace the original design from the chaos of remaining fragments. The water, however, continued to gush and sparkle into the sunbeams as cheerfully as ever. A little gurgling sound ascended to the young man's window, and made him feel as if the fountain were an immortal spirit that sung its song unceasingly and without heeding the vicissitudes around it, while one century embodied it in marble and another scattered the perishable garniture on the soil. All about the pool into which the water subsided grew various plants, that seemed to require a plentiful supply of moisture for the nourishment of gigantic leaves, and, in some instances, flowers gorgeously magnificent. There was one shrub in particular, set in a marble vase in the midst of the pool, that bore a profusion of purple blossoms, each of which had the luster and richness of a gem; and the whole together made a show so resplendent that it seemed enough to illuminate the garden, even had there been no sunshine. Every portion of the soil was peopled with plants and herbs, which, if less beautiful, still bore tokens of assiduous care, as if all had their individual virtues, known to the scientific mind that fostered them. Some were placed in urns, rich with old carving, and others in common garden pots; some crept serpent-like along the ground or climbed on high, using whatever means of ascent was offered them. One plant had wreathed itself round a statue of Vertumnus, which was thus quite veiled and shrouded in a drapery of hanging foliage, so happily arranged that it might have served a sculptor for a study.

While Giovanni stood at the window, he heard a rustling behind a screen of leaves, and became aware that a person was at work in the garden. His figure soon emerged into view, and showed itself to be that of no common laborer, but a tall, emaciated, sallow, and sickly looking man, dressed in a scholar's garb of black. He was beyond the middle term of life, with gray hair, a thin, gray beard, and a face singularly marked with intellect and cultivation, but which could never, even in his more youthful days, have expressed much warmth of heart.

Nothing could exceed the intentness with which this scientific gardener examined every shrub which grew in his path: it seemed as if he was looking into their inmost nature, making observations in regard to their creative essence, and discovering why one leaf grew in this shape and another in that, and wherefore such and such flowers differed among themselves in hue and perfume. Nevertheless, in spite of this deep intelligence on his part, there was no approach to intimacy between himself and these vegetable existences. On the contrary, he avoided their actual touch or the direct inhaling of their odors with a caution that impressed Giovanni most disagreeably; for the man's demeanor was that of one walking among malignant influences, such as savage beasts, or deadly snakes, or evil spirits, which, should he allow them one moment of license, would wreak upon him some terrible fatality. It was strangely frightful to the young man's imagination to see this air of insecurity in a person cultivating a garden, that most simple and innocent of human toils, and which had been alike the joy and labor of the unfallen parents of the race. Was this garden, then, the Eden of the present world? And this man, with such a perception of harm in what his own hands caused to grow—was he the Adam?

The distrustful gardener, while plucking away the dead leaves or pruning the too luxuriant growth of the shrubs, defended his hands with a pair of thick gloves. Nor were these his only armor. When, in his walk through the garden, he came to the magnificent plant that hung its purple gems beside the marble fountain, he placed a kind of mask over his mouth and nostrils, as if all this beauty did but conceal a deadlier malice; but, finding his task still too dangerous, he drew back, removed the mask, and called loudly, but in the infirm voice of a person affected with inward disease:

"Beatrice! Beatrice!"

"Here am I, my father. What would you?" cried a rich and youthful voice from the window of the opposite house—a voice as rich as a tropical sunset, and which made Giovanni, though he knew not why, think of deep hues of purple or crimson and of perfumes heavily delectable. "Are you in the garden?"

"Yes, Beatrice," answered the gardener, "and I need your help."

Soon there emerged from under a sculptured portal the figure of a young girl, arrayed with as much richness of taste as the most splendid of the flowers, beautiful as the day, and with a bloom so deep and vivid that one shade more would have been too much. She looked redundant with life, health, and energy; all of which attributes were bound down and compressed, as it were, and girdled tensely, in their luxuriance, by her virgin zone. Yet Giovanni's fancy must have grown morbid while he looked down into the garden; for the impression which the fair stranger made upon him was as if here were another flower, the human sister of those vegetable ones, as beautiful as they, more beautiful than the richest of them, but still to be touched only with a glove, nor to be approached without a mask. As Beatrice came down the garden path, it was observable that she handled and inhaled the odor of several of the plants which her father had most sedulously avoided.

"Here, Beatrice," said the latter, "see how many needful offices require to be done to our chief treasure. Yet, shattered as I am, my life might pay the penalty of approaching it so closely as circumstances demand. Henceforth, I fear, this plant must be consigned to your sole charge."

"And gladly will I undertake it," cried again the rich tones of the young lady, as she bent toward the magnificent plant and opened her arms as if to embrace it. "Yes, my sister, my splendor, it shall be Beatrice's task to nurse and serve thee; and thou shalt reward her with thy kisses and perfumed breath, which to her is as the breath of life."

Then, with all the tenderness in her manner that was so strikingly expressed in her words, she busied herself with such attentions as the plant seemed to require; and Giovanni, at his lofty window, rubbed his eyes and almost doubted whether it were a girl tending her favorite flower, or one sister performing the duties of affection to another. The scene soon terminated. Whether Dr. Rappaccini had finished his labors in the garden, or that his watchful eye had caught the stranger's face, he now took his daughter's arm and retired. Night was already closing in; oppressive exhalations seemed to proceed from the plants and steal upward past the open window; and Giovanni, closing the lattice, went to his couch and dreamed of a rich flower and beautiful girl. Flower and maiden were different, and yet the same, and fraught with some strange peril in either shape.

But there is an influence in the light of morning that tends to rectify whatever errors of fancy, or even of judgment, we may have incurred during the sun's decline, or among the shadows of the night, or in the less wholesome glow of moonshine. Giovanni's first movement, on starting from sleep, was to throw open the window and gaze down into the garden which his dreams had made so fertile of mysteries. He was surprised and a little ashamed to find how real and matter-of-fact an affair it proved to be, in the first rays of the sun which gilded the dewdrops that hung upon leaf and blossom, and, while giving a brighter beauty to each rare flower, brought everything within the limits of ordinary experience. The young man rejoiced that, in the heart of the barren city, he had the privilege of overlooking this spot of lovely and luxuriant vegetation. It would serve, he said to himself, as a symbolic language to keep him in communion with Nature. Neither the sickly and thought-worn Dr. Giacomo Rappaccini, it is true, nor his brilliant daughter was now visible; so that Giovanni could not determine how much of the singularity which he attributed to both was due to their own qualities and how much to his wonder-working fancy; but he was inclined to take a most rational view of the whole matter.

In the course of the day, he paid his respects to Signor Pietro Baglioni, professor of medicine in the university, a physician of eminent repute, to whom Giovanni had brought a letter of introduction. The professor was an elderly personage, apparently of genial nature, and habits that might almost be called jovial. He kept the young man to dinner, and made himself very agreeable by the freedom and liveliness of his conversation, especially when warmed by a flask or two of Tuscan wine. Giovanni, conceiving that men of science, inhabitants of the same city, must needs be on familiar terms with one another, took an opportunity to mention the name of Dr. Rappaccini. But the professor did not respond with so much cordiality as he had anticipated.

"Ill would it become a teacher of the divine art of medicine," said Professor Pietro Baglioni, in answer to a question of Giovanni, "to withhold due and well-considered praise of a physician so eminently skilled as Rappaccini; but, on the other hand, I should answer it but scantily to my conscience were I to permit a worthy youth like yourself, Signor Giovanni, the son of an ancient friend, to imbibe erroneous ideas respecting a man who might hereafter chance to hold your life and death in his hands. The truth is, our worshipful Dr. Rappaccini has as much science as any member of the faculty—with perhaps one single exception—in Padua, or all Italy; but there are certain grave objections to his professional character."

"And what are they?" asked the young man.

"Has my friend Giovanni any disease of body or heart, that he is so inquisitive about physicians?" said the professor, with a smile. "But as for Rappaccini, it is said of him—and I, who know the man well, can answer for its truth—that he cares infinitely more for science than for mankind. His patients are interesting to him only as subjects for some new experiment. He would sacrifice human life, his own among the rest, or whatever else was dearest to him, for the sake of adding so much as a grain of mustard seed to the great heap of his accumulated knowledge."

"Methinks he is an awful man indeed," remarked Guasconti, mentally recalling the cold and purely intellectual aspect of Rappaccini. "And yet, worshipful professor, is it not a noble spirit? Are there many men capable of so spiritual a love of science?"

"God forbid," answered the professor, somewhat testily, "at least, unless they take sounder views of the healing art than those adopted by Rappaccini. It is his theory that all medicinal virtues are comprised within those substances which we term vegetable poisons. These he cultivates with his own hands, and is said even to have produced new varieties of poison, more horribly deleterious than Nature, without the assistance of this learned person, would ever have plagued the world withal. That the signor doctor does less mischief than might be expected with such dangerous substances is undeniable. Now and then, it must be owned, he has effected, or seemed to effect, a marvelous cure; but, to tell you my private mind, Signor Giovanni, he should receive little credit for such instances of success—they being probably the work of chance—but should be held strictly accountable for his failures, which may justly be considered his own work."

The youth might have taken Baglioni's opinions with many grains of allowance had he known that there was a professional warfare of long continuance between him and Dr. Rappaccini, in which the latter was generally thought to have gained the advantage. If the reader be inclined to judge for himself, we refer him to certain black-letter tracts on both sides, preserved in the medical department of the University of Padua.

"I know not, most learned professor," returned Giovanni, after musing on what had been said of Rappaccini's exclusive zeal for science, "I know not how dearly this physician may love his art; but surely there is one object more dear to him. He has a daughter."

"Aha!" cried the professor, with a laugh. "So now our friend Giovanni's secret is out. You have heard of this daughter, whom all the young men in Padua are wild about, though not half a dozen have ever had the good hap to see her face. I know little of the Signora Beatrice save that Rappaccini is said to have instructed her deeply in his science, and that, young and beautiful as fame reports her, she is already qualified to fill a professor's chair. Perchance her father destines her for mine! Other absurd rumors there be, not worth talking about or listening to. So now, Signor Giovanni, drink off your glass of Lachryma."

Guasconti returned to his lodgings somewhat heated with the wine he had quaffed, and which caused his brain to swim with strange fantasies in reference to Dr. Rappaccini and the beautiful Beatrice. On his way, happening to pass by a florist's, he bought a fresh bouquet of flowers.

Ascending to his chamber, he seated himself near the window, but within the shadow thrown by the depth of the wall, so that he could look down into the garden with little risk of being discovered. All beneath his eye was a solitude. The strange plants were basking in the sunshine, and now and then nodding gently to one another, as if in acknowledgment of sympathy and kindred. In the midst, by the shattered fountain, grew the magnificent shrub, with its purple gems clustering all over it; they glowed in the air, and gleamed back again out of the depths of the pool, which thus seemed to overflow with colored radiance from the rich reflection that was steeped in it. At first, as we have said, the garden was a solitude. Soon, however—as Giovanni had half hoped, half feared would be the case—a figure appeared beneath the antique sculptured portal, and came down between the rows of plants, inhaling their various perfumes as if she were one of those beings of old classic fable that lived upon sweet odors. On again beholding Beatrice, the young man was even startled to perceive how much her beauty exceeded his recollection of it; so brilliant, so vivid, was its character, that she glowed amid the sunlight, and, as Giovanni whispered to himself, positively illuminated the more shadowy intervals of the garden path. Her face being now more revealed than on the former occasion, he was struck by its expression of simplicity and sweetness—qualities that had not entered into his idea of her character, and which made him ask anew what manner of mortal she might be. Nor did he fail again to observe, or imagine, an analogy between the beautiful girl and the gorgeous shrub that hung its gemlike flowers over the fountain—a resemblance which Beatrice seemed to have indulged a fantastic humor in heightening, both by the arrangement of her dress and the selection of its hues.

Approaching the shrub, she threw open her arms, as with a passionate ardor, and drew its branches into an intimate embrace—so intimate that her features were hidden in its leafy bosom and her glistening ringlets all intermingled with the flowers.

"Give me thy breath, my sister," exclaimed Beatrice, "for I am faint with common air. And give me this flower of thine, which I separate with gentlest fingers from the stem and place it close beside my heart."

With these words, the beautiful daughter of Rappaccini plucked one of the richest blossoms of the shrub, and was about to fasten it in her bosom. But now, unless Giovanni's draughts of wine had bewildered his senses, a singular incident occurred. A small orange-colored reptile, of the lizard or chameleon species, chanced to be creeping along the path, just at the feet of Beatrice. It appeared to Giovanni—but, at the distance from which he gazed, he could scarcely have seen anything so minute—it appeared to him, however, that a drop or two of moisture from the broken stem of the flower descended upon the lizard's head. For an instant the reptile contorted itself violently, and then lay motionless in the sunshine. Beatrice observed this remarkable phenomenon, and crossed herself, sadly, but without surprise; nor did she therefore hesitate to arrange the fatal flower in her bosom. There it blushed, and almost glimmered with the dazzling effect of a precious stone, adding to her dress and aspect the one appropriate charm which nothing else in the world could have supplied. But Giovanni, out of the shadow of his window, bent forward and shrank back, and murmured and trembled.

"Am I awake? Have I my senses?" he said to himself. "What is this being? Beautiful shall I call her, or inexpressibly terrible?"

Beatrice now strayed carelessly through the garden, approaching closer beneath Giovanni's window, so that he was compelled to thrust his head quite out of its concealment in order to gratify the intense and painful curiosity which she excited. At this moment, there came a beautiful insect over the garden wall; it had, perhaps, wandered through the city, and found no flowers or verdure among those antique haunts of men until the heavy perfumes of Dr. Rappaccini's shrubs had lured it from afar. Without alighting on the flowers, this winged brightness seemed to be attracted by Beatrice, and lingered in the air and fluttered about her head. Now, here it could not be but that Giovanni Guasconti's eyes deceived him. Be that as it might, he fancied that, while Beatrice was gazing at the insect with childish delight, it grew faint and fell at her feet; its bright wings shivered; it was dead—from no cause that he could discern, unless it were the atmosphere of her breath. Again Beatrice crossed herself and sighed heavily as she bent over the dead insect.

An impulsive movement of Giovanni drew her eyes to the window. There she beheld the beautiful head of the young man—rather a Grecian than an Italian head, with fair, regular features, and a glistening of gold among his ringlets—gazing down upon her like a being that hovered in midair. Scarcely knowing what he did, Giovanni threw down the bouquet which he had hitherto held in his hand.

"Signora," said he, "these are pure and healthful flowers. Wear them for the sake of Giovanni Guasconti."

"Thanks, signor," replied Beatrice, with her rich voice, that came forth as it were like a gush of music, and with a mirthful expression half childish and half woman-like. "I accept your gift, and would fain recompense it with this precious purple flower; but if I toss it into the air, it will not reach you. So Signor Guasconti must even content himself with my thanks."

She lifted the bouquet from the ground, and then, as if inwardly ashamed at having stepped aside from her maidenly reserve to respond to a stranger's greeting, passed swiftly homeward through the garden. But few as the moments were, it seemed to Giovanni, when she was on the point of vanishing beneath the sculptured portal, that his beautiful bouquet was already beginning to wither in her grasp. It was an idle thought; there could be no possibility of distinguishing a faded flower from a fresh one at so great a distance.

For many days after this incident, the young man avoided the window that looked into Dr. Rappaccini's garden, as if something ugly and monstrous would have blasted his eyesight had he been betrayed into a glance. He felt conscious of having put himself, to a certain extent, within the influence of an unintelligible power by the communication which he had opened with Beatrice. The wisest course would have been, if his heart were in any real danger, to quit his lodgings and Padua itself at once; the next wiser, to have accustomed himself, as far as possible, to the familiar and daylight view of Beatrice—thus bringing her rigidly and systematically within the limits of ordinary experience. Least of all, while avoiding her sight, ought Giovanni to have remained so near this extraordinary being that the proximity and possibility even of intercourse should give a kind of substance and reality to the wild vagaries which his imagination ran riot continually in producing. Guasconti had not a deep heart—or, at all events, its depths were not sounded now; but he had a quick fancy, and an ardent southern temperament, which rose every instant to a higher fever pitch. Whether or no Beatrice possessed those terrible attributes, that fatal breath, the affinity with those so beautiful and deadly flowers which were indicated by what Giovanni had witnessed, she had at least instilled a fierce and subtle poison into his system. It was not love, although her rich beauty was a madness to him; nor horror, even while he fancied her spirit to be imbued with the same baneful essence that seemed to pervade her physical frame; but a wild offspring of both love and horror that had each parent in it, and burned like one and shivered like the other. Giovanni knew not what to dread; still less did he know what to hope; yet hope and dread kept a continual warfare in his breast, alternately vanquishing one another and starting up afresh to renew the contest. Blessed are all simple emotions, be they dark or bright! It is the lurid intermixture of the two that produces the illuminating blaze of the infernal regions.

Sometimes he endeavored to assuage the fever of his spirit by a rapid walk through the streets of Padua or beyond its gates: his footsteps kept time with the throbbings of his brain, so that the walk was apt to accelerate itself to a race. One day he found himself arrested; his arm was seized by a portly personage, who had turned back on recognizing the young man and expended much breath in overtaking him.

"Signor Giovanni! Stay, my young friend!" cried he. "Have you forgotten me? That might well be the case if I were as much altered as yourself."

It was Baglioni, whom Giovanni had avoided ever since their first meeting, from a doubt that the professor's sagacity would look too deeply into his secrets. Endeavoring to recover himself, he stared forth wildly from his inner world into the outer one and spoke like a man in a dream.

"Yes; I am Giovanni Guasconti. You are Professor Pietro Baglioni. Now let me pass!"

"Not yet, not yet, Signor Giovanni Guasconti," said the professor, smiling, but at the same time scrutinizing the youth with an earnest glance. "What! did I grow up side by side with your father, and shall his son pass me like a stranger in these old streets of Padua? Stand still, Signor Giovanni; for we must have a word or two before we part."

"Speedily, then, most worshipful professor, speedily," said Giovanni, with feverish impatience. "Does not your worship see that I am in haste?"

Now, while he was speaking, there came a man in black along the street, stooping and moving feebly like a person in inferior health. His face was all overspread with a most sickly and sallow hue, but yet so pervaded with an expression of piercing and active intellect that an observer might easily have overlooked the merely physical attributes and have seen only this wonderful energy. As he passed, this person exchanged a cold and distant salutation with Baglioni, but fixed his eyes upon Giovanni with an intentness that seemed to bring out whatever was within him worthy of notice. Nevertheless, there was a peculiar quietness in the look, as if taking merely a speculative, not a human, interest in the young man.

"It is Dr. Rappaccini!" whispered the professor when the stranger had passed. "Has he ever seen your face before?"

"Not that I know," answered Giovanni, starting at the name.

"He *has* seen you! he must have seen you!" said Baglioni, hastily. "For some purpose or other, this man of science is making a study of you. I know that look of his! It is the same that coldly illuminates his face as he bends over a bird, a mouse, or a butterfly, which, in pursuance of some experiment, he has killed by the perfume of a flower; a look as deep as Nature itself, but without Nature's warmth of love. Signor Giovanni, I will stake my life upon it, you are the subject of one of Rappaccini's experiments!"

"Will you make a fool of me?" cried Giovanni, passionately. "*That,* signor professor, were an untoward experiment."

"Patience! patience!" replied the imperturbable professor. "I tell thee, my poor Giovanni, that Rappaccini has a scientific interest in thee. Thou hast fallen into fearful hands! And the Signora Beatrice—what part does she act in this mystery?"

But Guasconti, finding Baglioni's pertinacity intolerable, here broke away, and was gone before the professor could again seize his arm. He looked after the young man intently and shook his head.

"This must not be," said Baglioni to himself. "The youth is the son of my old friend, and shall not come to any harm from which the arcana of medical science can preserve him. Besides, it is too insufferable an impertinence in Rappaccini, thus to snatch the lad out of my own hands, as I may say, and make use of him for his infernal experiments. This daughter of his! It shall be looked to. Perchance, most learned Rappaccini, I may foil you where you little dream of it!"

Meanwhile Giovanni had pursued a circuitous route, and at length found himself at the door of his lodgings. As he crossed the threshold, he was met by old Lisabetta, who smirked and smiled, and was evidently desirous to attract his attention; vainly, however, as the ebullition of his feelings had momentarily subsided into a cold and dull vacuity. He turned his eyes full upon the withered face that was puckering itself into a smile, but seemed to behold it not. The old dame, therefore, laid her grasp upon his cloak.

"Signor! signor!" whispered she, still with a smile over the whole breadth of her visage, so that it looked not unlike a grotesque carving in wood, darkened by centuries. "Listen, signor! There is a private entrance into the garden!"

"What do you say?" exclaimed Giovanni, turning quickly about, as if an inanimate thing should start into feverish life. "A private entrance into Dr. Rappaccini's garden?"

"Hush! hush! not so loud!" whispered Lisabetta, putting her hand over his mouth. "Yes; into the worshipful doctor's garden, where you may see all his fine shrubbery. Many a young man in Padua would give gold to be admitted among those flowers."

Giovanni put a piece of gold into her hand.

"Show me the way," said he.

A surmise, probably excited by his conversation with Baglioni, crossed his mind that this interposition of old Lisabetta might perchance be connected with the intrigue, whatever were its nature, in which the professor seemed to suppose that Dr. Rappaccini was involving him. But such a suspicion, though it disturbed Giovanni, was inadequate to restrain him. The instant that he was aware of the possibility of approaching Beatrice, it seemed an absolute necessity of his existence to do so. It mattered not whether she were angel or demon; he was irrevocably within her sphere, and must obey the law that whirled him onward, in ever lessening circles, towards a result which he did not attempt to foreshadow; and yet, strange to say, there came across him a sudden doubt whether this intense interest on his part were not delusory; whether it were really of so deep and positive a nature as to justify him in now thrusting himself into an incalculable position; whether it were not merely the fantasy of a young man's brain, only slightly or not at all connected with his heart.

He paused, hesitated, turned half about, but again went on. His withered guide led him along several obscure passages, and finally undid a door, through which, as it was opened, there came the sight and sound of rustling leaves, with the broken sunshine glimmering among them. Giovanni stepped forth, and, forcing himself through the entanglement of a shrub that wreathed its tendrils over the hidden entrance, stood beneath his own window in the open area of Dr. Rappaccini's garden.

How often is it the case that, when impossibilities have come to pass and dreams have condensed their misty substance into tangible realities, we find ourselves calm, and even coldly self-possessed, amid circumstances which it would have been a delirium of joy or agony to anticipate! Fate delights to thwart us thus. Passion will choose his own time to rush upon the scene, and lingers sluggishly behind when an appropriate adjustment of events would seem to summon his appearance. So was it now with Giovanni. Day after day, his pulses had throbbed with feverish blood at the improbable idea of an interview with Beatrice, and of standing with her, face to face, in this very garden, basking in the Oriental sunshine of her beauty, and snatching from her full gaze the mystery which he deemed the riddle of his own existence. But now there was a singular and untimely equanimity within his breast. He threw a glance around the garden to discover if Beatrice or her father were present, and, perceiving that he was alone, began a critical observation of the plants.

The aspect of one and all of them dissatisfied him; their gorgeousness seemed fierce, passionate, and even unnatural. There was hardly an individual shrub which a wanderer, straying by himself through a forest, would not have been startled to find growing wild, as if an unearthly face had glared at him out of the thicket. Several also would have shocked a delicate instinct by an appearance of artificialness indicating that there had been such commixture and, as it were, adultery of various vegetable species that the production was no longer of God's making, but the monstrous offspring of man's depraved fancy, glowing with only an evil mockery of beauty. They were probably the result of experiment, which in one or two cases had succeeded in mingling plants individually lovely into a compound possessing the questionable and ominous character that distinguished the whole growth of the garden. In fine, Giovanni recognized but two or three plants in the collection, and those of a kind that he well knew to be poisonous. While busy with these contemplations, he heard the rustling of a silken garment, and, turning, beheld Beatrice emerging from beneath the sculptured portal.

Giovanni had not considered with himself what should be his deportment; whether he should apologize for his intrusion into the garden, or assume that he was there with the privity, at least, if not by the desire, of Dr. Rappaccini or his daughter; but Beatrice's manner placed him at his ease, though leaving him still in doubt by what agency he had gained admittance. She came lightly along the path and met him near the broken fountain. There was surprise in her face, but brightened by a simple and kind expression of pleasure.

"You are a connoisseur in flowers, signor," said Beatrice, with a smile, alluding to the bouquet which he had flung her from the window. "It is no marvel, therefore, if the sight of my father's rare collection has tempted you to take a nearer view. If he were here, he could tell you many strange and interesting facts as to the nature and habits of these shrubs; for he has spent a lifetime in such studies, and this garden is his world."

"And yourself, lady," observed Giovanni, "if fame says true, you likewise are deeply skilled in the virtues indicated by these rich blossoms and these spicy perfumes. Would you deign to be my instructress, I should prove an apter scholar than if taught by Signor Rappaccini himself."

"Are there such idle rumors?" asked Beatrice, with the music of a pleasant laugh. "Do people say that I am skilled in my father's science of plants? What a jest is there! No; though I have grown up among these flowers, I know no more of them than their hues and perfume; and sometimes methinks I would fain rid myself of even that small knowledge. There are many flowers here, and those not the least brilliant, that shock and offend me when they meet my eye. But pray, signor, do not believe these stories about my science. Believe nothing of me save what you see with your own eyes."

"And must I believe all that I have seen with my own eyes?" asked Giovanni, pointedly, while the recollection of former scenes made him shrink. "No, signora; you demand too little of me. Bid me believe nothing save what comes from your own lips."

It would appear that Beatrice understood him. There came a deep flush to her cheek; but she looked full into Giovanni's eyes, and responded to his gaze of uneasy suspicion with a queenlike haughtiness.

"I do so bid you, signor," she replied. "Forget whatever you may have fancied in regard to me. If true to the outward senses, still it may be false in its essence; but the words of Beatrice Rappaccini's lips are true from the depths of the heart outward. Those you may believe."

A fervor glowed in her whole aspect and beamed upon Giovanni's consciousness like the light of truth itself; but while she spoke, there was a fragrance in the atmosphere around her, rich and delightful, though evanescent, yet which the young man, from an indefinable reluctance, scarcely dared to draw into his lungs. It might be the odor of the flowers. Could it be Beatrice's breath which thus embalmed her words with a strange richness, as if by steeping them in her heart? A faintness passed like a shadow over Giovanni and flitted away; he seemed to gaze through the beautiful girl's eyes into her transparent soul, and felt no more doubt or fear.

The tinge of passion that had colored Beatrice's manner vanished; she became gay, and appeared to derive a pure delight from her communion with the youth not unlike what the maiden of a lonely island might have felt conversing with a voyager from the civilized world. Evidently her experience of life had been confined within the limits of that garden. She talked now about matters as simple as the daylight or summer clouds, and now asked questions in reference to the city, or Giovanni's distant home, his friends, his mother, and his sisters—questions indicating such seclusion, and such lack of familiarity with modes and forms, that Giovanni responded as if to an infant. Her spirit gushed out before him like a fresh rill that was just catching its first glimpse of the sunlight and wondering at the reflections of earth and sky which were flung into its bosom. There came thoughts, too, from a deep source, and fantasies of a gemlike brilliancy, as if diamonds and rubies sparkled upward among the bubbles of the fountain. Ever and anon there gleamed across the young man's mind a sense of wonder that he should be walking side by side with the being who had so wrought upon his imagination, whom he had idealized in such hues of terror, in whom he had positively witnessed such manifestations of dreadful attributes—that he should be conversing with Beatrice like a brother, and should find her so human and so maiden-like. But such reflections were only momentary; the effect of her character was too real not to make itself familiar at once.

In this free intercourse, they had strayed through the garden, and now, after many turns among its avenues, were come to the shattered fountain, beside which grew the magnificent shrub, with its treasury of glowing blossoms. A fragrance was diffused from it which Giovanni recognized as identical with that which he had attributed to Beatrice's breath, but incomparably more powerful. As her eyes fell upon it, Giovanni beheld her press her hand to her bosom as if her heart were throbbing suddenly and painfully.

"For the first time in my life," murmured she, addressing the shrub, "I had forgotten thee."

"I remember, signora," said Giovanni, "that you once promised to reward me with one of these living gems for the bouquet which I had the happy boldness to fling to your feet. Permit me now to pluck it as a memorial of this interview.

He made a step towards the shrub with extended hand; but Beatrice darted forward, uttering a shriek that went through his heart like a dagger. She caught his hand and drew it back with the whole force of her slender figure. Giovanni felt her touch thrilling through his fibers.

"Touch it not!" exclaimed she, in a voice of agony. "Not for thy life! It is fatal!"

Then, hiding her face, she fled from him and vanished beneath the sculptured portal. As Giovanni followed her with his eyes, he beheld the emaciated figure and pale intelligence of Dr. Rappaccini, who had been watching the scene, he knew not how long, within the shadow of the entrance.

No sooner was Guasconti alone in his chamber than the image of Beatrice came back to his passionate musings, invested with all the witchery that had been gathering around it ever since his first glimpse of her, and now likewise imbued with a tender warmth of girlish womanhood. She was human; her nature was endowed with all gentle and feminine qualities; she was worthiest to be worshiped; she was capable, surely, on her part, of the height and heroism of love. Those tokens which he had hitherto considered as proofs of a frightful peculiarity in her physical and moral system were now either forgotten, or, by the subtle sophistry of passion, transmitted into a golden crown of enchantment, rendering Beatrice the more admirable by so much as she was the more unique. Whatever had looked ugly was now beautiful; or, if incapable of such a change, it stole away and hid itself among those shapeless half ideas which throng the dim region beyond the daylight of our perfect consciousness. Thus did he spend the night, nor fell asleep until the dawn had begun to awake the slumbering flowers in Dr. Rappaccini's garden, whither Giovanni's dreams doubtless led him. Up rose the sun in his due season, and, flinging his beams upon the young man's eyelids, awoke him to a sense of pain. When thoroughly aroused, he became sensible of a burning and tingling agony in his hand—in his right hand—the very hand which Beatrice had grasped in her own when he was on the point of plucking one of the gemlike flowers. On the back of that hand there was now a purple print like that of four small fingers, and the likeness of a slender thumb upon his wrist.

Oh, how stubbornly does love—or even that cunning semblance of love which flourishes in the imagination, but strikes no depth of root into the heart—how stubbornly does it hold its faith until the moment comes when it is doomed to vanish into thin mist! Giovanni wrapped a handkerchief about his hand and wondered what evil thing had stung him, and soon forgot his pain in a reverie of Beatrice.

After the first interview, a second was in the inevitable course of what we call fate. A third; a fourth; and a meeting with Beatrice in the garden was no longer an incident in Giovanni's daily life, but the whole space in which he might be said to live; for the anticipation and memory of that ecstatic hour made up the remainder. Nor was it otherwise with the daughter of Rappaccini. She watched for the youth's appearance, and flew to his side with confidence as unreserved as if they had been playmates from early infancy—as if they were such playmates still. If, by any unwonted chance, he failed to come at the appointed moment, she stood beneath the window and sent up the rich sweetness of her tones to float around him in his chamber and echo and reverberate throughout his heart: "Giovanni! Giovanni! Why tarriest thou? Come down!" And down he hastened into that Eden of poisonous flowers.

But, with all this intimate familiarity, there was still a reserve in Beatrice's demeanor, so rigidly and invariably sustained that the idea of infringing it scarcely occurred to his imagination. By all appreciable signs, they loved; they had looked love with eyes that conveyed the holy secret from the depths of one soul into the depths of the other, as if it were too sacred to be whispered by the way; they had even spoken love in those gushes of passion when their spirits darted forth in articulated breath like tongues of long-hidden flame; and yet there had been no seal of lips, no clasp of hands, nor any slightest caress such as love claims and hallows. He had never touched one of the gleaming ringlets of her hair; her garment—so marked was the physical barrier between them—had never been waved against him by a breeze. On the few occasions when Giovanni had seemed tempted to overstep the limit, Beatrice grew so sad, so stern, and withal wore such a look of desolate separation, shuddering at itself, that not a spoken word was requisite to repel him. At such times, he was startled at the horrible suspicions that rose, monster-like, out of the caverns of his heart and stared him in the face; his love grew thin and faint as the morning mist; his doubts alone had substance. But, when Beatrice's face brightened again after the momentary shadow, she was transformed at once from the mysterious, questionable being whom he had watched with so much awe and horror; she was now the beautiful and unsophisticated girl whom he felt that his spirit knew with a certainty beyond all other knowledge.

A considerable time had now passed since Giovanni's last meeting with Baglioni. One morning, however, he was disagreeably surprised by a visit from the professor, whom he had scarcely thought of for whole weeks, and would willingly have forgotten still longer. Given up as he had long been to a pervading excitement, he could tolerate no companions except upon condition of their perfect sympathy with his present state of feeling. Such sympathy was not to be expected from Professor Baglioni.

The visitor chatted carelessly for a few moments about the gossip of the city and the university, and then took up another topic.

"I have been reading an old classic author lately," said he, "and met with a story that strangely interested me. Possibly you may remember it. It is of an Indian prince, who sent a beautiful woman as a present to Alexander the Great. She was as lovely as the dawn and gorgeous as the sunset; but what especially distinguished her was a certain rich perfume in her breath—richer than a garden of Persian roses. Alexander, as was natural to a youthful conqueror, fell in love at first sight with this magnificent stranger; but a certain sage physician, happening to be present, discovered a terrible secret in regard to her."

"And what was that?" asked Giovanni, turning his eyes downward to avoid those of the professor.

"That this lovely woman," continued Baglioni, with emphasis, "had been nourished with poisons from her birth upward, until her whole nature was so imbued with them that she herself had become the deadliest poison in existence. Poison was her element of life. With that rich perfume of her breath she blasted the very air. Her love would have been poison—her embrace death. Is not this a marvelous tale?"

"A childish fable," answered Giovanni, nervously starting from his chair. "I marvel how your worship finds time to read such nonsense among your graver studies."

"By the by," said the professor, looking uneasily about him, "what singular fragrance is this in your apartment? Is it the perfume of your gloves? It is faint, but delicious; and yet, after all, by no means agreeable. Were I to breathe it long, methinks it would make me ill. It is like the breath of a flower; but I see no flowers in the chamber."

"Nor are there any," replied Giovanni, who had turned pale as the professor spoke, "nor, I think, is there any fragrance except in your worship's imagination. Odors, being a sort of element combined of the sensual and the spiritual, are apt to deceive us in this manner. The recollection of a perfume, the bare idea of it, may easily be mistaken for a present reality."

"Ay; but my sober imagination does not often play such tricks," said Baglioni, "and, were I to fancy any kind of odor, it would be that of some vile apothecary drug wherewith my fingers are likely enough to be imbued. Our worshipful friend Rappaccini, as I have heard, tinctures his medicaments with odors richer than those of Araby. Doubtless, likewise, the fair and learned Signora Beatrice would minister to her patients with draughts as sweet as a maiden's breath; but woe to him that sips them!"

Giovanni's face evinced many contending emotions. The tone in which the professor alluded to the pure and lovely daughter of Rappaccini was a torture to his soul; and yet the intimation of a view of her character opposite to his own gave instantaneous distinctness to a thousand dim suspicions, which now grinned at him like so many demons. But he strove hard to quell them and to respond to Baglioni with a true lover's perfect faith.

"Signor professor," said he, "you were my father's friend; perchance, too, it is your purpose to act a friendly part towards his son. I would fain feel nothing towards you save respect and deference; but I pray you to observe, signor, that there is one subject on which we must not speak. You know not the Signora

Beatrice. You cannot, therefore, estimate the wrong—the blasphemy, I may even say—that is offered to her character by a light or injurious word."

"Giovanni! my poor Giovanni" answered the professor, with a calm expression of pity, "I know this wretched girl far better than yourself. You shall hear the truth in respect to the poisoner Rappaccini and his poisonous daughter; yes, poisonous as she is beautiful. Listen; for, even should you do violence to my gray hairs, it shall not silence me. That old fable of the Indian woman has become a truth by the deep and deadly science of Rappaccini and in the person of the lovely Beatrice."

Giovanni groaned and hid his face.

"Her father," continued Baglioni, "was not restrained by natural affection from offering up his child in this horrible manner as the victim of his insane zeal for science; for, let us do him justice, he is as true a man of science as ever distilled his own heart in an alembic. What, then, will be your fate? Beyond a doubt you are selected as the material of some new experiment. Perhaps the result is to be death; perhaps a fate more awful still. Rappaccini, with what he calls the interest of science before his eyes, will hesitate at nothing."

"It is a dream," muttered Giovanni to himself. "Surely it is a dream."

"But," resumed the professor, "be of good cheer, son of my friend. It is not yet too late for the rescue. Possibly we may even succeed in bringing back this miserable child within the limits of ordinary nature, from which her father's madness has estranged her. Behold this little silver vase! It was wrought by the hands of the renowned Benvenuto Cellini, and is well worthy to be a love gift to the fairest dame in Italy. But its contents are invaluable. One little sip of this antidote would have rendered the most virulent poisons of the Borgias innocuous. Doubt not that it will be as efficacious against those of Rappaccini. Bestow the vase, and the precious liquid within it, on your Beatrice, and hopefully await the result."

Baglioni laid a small, exquisitely wrought silver vial on the table and withdrew, leaving what he had said to produce its effect upon the young man's mind.

"We will thwart Rappaccini yet," thought he, chuckling to himself, as he descended the stairs. "But, let us confess the truth of him, he is a wonderful man—a wonderful man indeed; a vile empiric, however, in his practice, and therefore not to be tolerated by those who respect the good old rules of the medical profession."

Throughout Giovanni's whole acquaintance with Beatrice, he had occasionally, as we have said, been haunted by dark surmises as to her character; yet so thoroughly had she made herself felt by him as a simple, natural, most affectionate, and guileless creature, that the image now held up by Professor Baglioni looked as strange and incredible as if it were not in accordance with his own original conception. True, there were ugly recollections connected with his first glimpses of the beautiful girl; he could not quite forget the bouquet that withered in her grasp, and the insect that perished amid the sunny air, by no ostensible agency save the fragrance of her breath. These incidents, however, dissolving in the pure light of her character, had no longer the efficacy of facts, but were acknowledged as mistaken fantasies, by whatever testimony of the senses they might appear to be substantiated. There is something truer and more real than what we can see with the eyes and touch with the finger. On such better evidence had Giovanni founded his confidence in Beatrice, though rather by the necessary force of her high attributes than by any deep and generous faith on his part. But now his spirit was incapable of sustaining itself at the height to which the early enthusiasm of passion had exalted it; he fell down, groveling among earthly doubts, and defiled therewith the pure whiteness of Beatrice's image. Not that he gave her up; he did but distrust. He resolved to institute some decisive test that should satisfy him, once for all, whether there were those dreadful peculiarities in her physical nature which could not be supposed to exist without some corresponding monstrosity of soul. His eyes, gazing down afar, might have deceived him as to the lizard, the insect, and the flowers; but if he could witness, at the distance of a few paces, the sudden blight of one fresh and healthful flower in Beatrice's hand, there would be room for no further question. With this idea, he hastened to the florist's and purchased a bouquet that was still gemmed with the morning dew-drops.

It was now the customary hour of his daily interview with Beatrice. Before descending into the garden, Giovanni failed not to look at his figure in the mirror—a vanity to be expected in a beautiful young man, yet, as displaying itself at that troubled and feverish moment, the token of a certain shallowness of feeling and insincerity of character. He did gaze, however, and said to himself that his features had never before possessed so rich a grace, nor his eyes such vivacity, nor his cheeks so warm a hue of superabundant life.

"At least," thought he, "her poison has not yet insinuated itself into my system. I am no flower to perish in her grasp."

With that thought, he turned his eyes on the bouquet, which he had never once laid aside from his hand. A thrill of indefinable horror shot through his frame on perceiving that those dewy flowers were already beginning to droop; they wore the aspect of things that had been fresh and lovely yesterday. Giovanni grew white as marble, and stood motionless before the mirror, staring at his own reflection there as at the likeness of something frightful. He remembered Baglioni's remark about the fragrance that seemed to pervade the chamber. It must have been the poison in his breath! Then he shuddered—shuddered at himself. Recovering from his stupor, he began to watch with curious eye a spider that was busily at work hanging its web from the antique cornice of the apartment, crossing and recrossing the artful system of interwoven lines—as vigorous and active a spider as ever dangled from an old ceiling. Giovanni bent towards the insect, and emitted a deep, long breath. The spider suddenly ceased its toil; the web vibrated with a tremor originating in the body of the small artisan. Again Giovanni sent forth a breath, deeper, longer, and imbued with a venomous feeling out of his heart; he knew not whether he were wicked, or only desperate. The spider made a convulsive grip with his limbs and hung dead across the window.

"Accursed! accursed!" muttered Giovanni, addressing himself. "Hast thou grown so poisonous that this deadly insect perishes by thy breath?"

At that moment, a rich, sweet voice came floating up from the garden.

"Giovanni! Giovanni! It is past the hour! Why tarriest thou? Come down!"

"Yes," muttered Giovanni again. "She is the only being whom my breath may not slay! Would that it might!"

He rushed down, and in an instant was standing before the bright and loving eyes of Beatrice. A moment ago, his wrath and despair had been so fierce that he could have desired nothing so much as to wither her by a glance; but with her actual presence there came influences which had too real an existence to be at once shaken off: recollections of the delicate and benign power of her feminine nature, which had so often enveloped him in a religious calm; recollections of many a holy and passionate outgush of her heart, when the pure fountain had been unsealed from its depths and made visible in its transparency to his mental eye; recollections which, had Giovanni known how to estimate them, would have assured him that all this ugly mystery was but an earthly illusion, and that, whatever mist of evil might seem to have gathered over her, the real Beatrice was a heavenly angel. Incapable as he was of such high faith, still her presence had not utterly lost its magic. Giovanni's rage was quelled into an aspect of sullen insensibility. Beatrice, with a quick spiritual sense, immediately felt that there was a gulf of blackness between them which neither he nor she could pass. They walked on together, sad and silent, and came thus to the marble fountain and to its pool of water on the ground, in the midst of which grew the shrub that bore gemlike blossoms. Giovanni was affrighted at the eager enjoyment—the appetite, as it were—with which he found himself inhaling the fragrance of the flowers.

"Beatrice," asked he, abruptly, "whence came this shrub?"

"My father created it," answered she, with simplicity.

"Created it! created it!" repeated Giovanni. "What mean you, Beatrice?"

"He is a man fearfully acquainted with the secrets of Nature," replied Beatrice, "and, at the hour when I first drew breath, this plant sprang from the soil, the offspring of his science, of his intellect, while I was but his earthly child. Approach it not!" continued she, observing with terror that Giovanni was drawing nearer to the shrub. "It has qualities that you little dream of. But I, dearest Giovanni, I grew up and blossomed with the plant and was nourished with its breath. It was my sister, and I loved it with a human affection; for, alas!—hast thou not suspected it?—there was an awful doom."

Here Giovanni frowned so darkly upon her that Beatrice paused and trembled. But her faith in his tenderness reassured her, and made her blush that she had doubted for an instant.

"There was an awful doom," she continued, "the effect of my father's fatal love of science, which estranged me from all society of my kind. Until Heaven sent thee, dearest Giovanni, oh, how lonely was thy poor Beatrice!"

"Was it a hard doom?" asked Giovanni, fixing his eyes upon her.

"Only of late have I known how hard it was," answered she, tenderly. "Oh, yes; but my heart was torpid, and therefore quiet."

Giovanni's rage broke forth from his sullen gloom like a lightning flash out of a dark cloud.

"Accursed one!" cried he, with venomous scorn and anger. "And, finding

thy solitude wearisome, thou hast severed me likewise from all the warmth
of life and enticed me into thy region of unspeakable horror!"

"Giovanni!" exclaimed Beatrice, turning her large, bright eyes upon his face.
The force of his words had not found its way into her mind; she was merely
thunderstruck.

"Yes, poisonous thing!" repeated Giovanni, beside himself with passion.
"Thou hast done it! Thou hast blasted me! Thou has filled my veins with poison!
Thou hast made me as hateful, as ugly, as loathsome and deadly a creature as
thyself—a world's wonder of hideous monstrosity! Now, if our breath be happily
as fatal to ourselves as to all others, let us join our lips in one kiss of unutterable
hatred, and so die!"

"What has befallen me?" murmured Beatrice, with a low moan out of her
heart. "Holy Virgin, pity me, a poor heartbroken child!"

"Thou—dost thou pray?" cried Giovanni, still with the same fiendish scorn.
"Thy very prayers, as they come from thy lips, taint the atmosphere with
death. Yes, yes; let us pray! Let us to church and dip our fingers in the holy
water at the portal! They that come after us will perish as by a pestilence! Let
us sign crosses in the air! It will be scattering curses abroad in the likeness of
holy symbols!"

"Giovanni," said Beatrice, calmly, for her grief was beyond passion, "why
dost thou join thyself with me thus in those terrible words? I, it is true, am
the horrible thing thou namest me. But thou—what has thou to do, save with
one other shudder at my hideous misery to go forth out of the garden and
mingle with thy race, and forget that there ever crawled on earth such a monster
as poor Beatrice?"

"Dost thou pretend ignorance?" asked Giovanni, scowling upon her.
"Behold! this power have I gained from the pure daughter of Rappaccini."

There was a swarm of summer insects flitting through the air in search of the
food promised by the flower odors of the fatal garden. They circled round
Giovanni's head, and were evidently attracted towards him by the same influence
which had drawn them for an instant within the sphere of several of the shrubs.
He sent forth a breath among them, and smiled bitterly at Beatrice as at least
a score of the insects fell dead upon the ground.

"I see it! I see it!" shrieked Beatrice. "It is my father's fatal science! No, no,
Giovanni; it was not I! Never! never! I dreamed only to love thee and be with
thee a little time, and so to let thee pass away, leaving but thine image in mine
heart; for, Giovanni, believe it, though my body be nourished with poison,
my spirit is God's creature, and craves love as its daily food. But my father—he
has united us in this fearful sympathy. Yes; spurn me, tread upon me, kill me!
Oh, what is death after such words as thine? But it was not I. Not for a world of
bliss would I have done it."

Giovanni's passion had exhausted itself in its outburst from his lips. There
now came across him a sense, mournful, and not without tenderness, of the
intimate and peculiar relationship between Beatrice and himself. They stood, as
it were, in an utter solitude, which would be made none the less solitary by
the densest throng of human life. Ought not, then, the desert of humanity

around them to press this insulated pair closer together? If they should be cruel to one another, who was there to be kind to them? Besides, thought Giovanni, might there not still be a hope of his returning within the limits of ordinary nature, and leading Beatrice, the redeemed Beatrice, by the hand? Oh, weak, and selfish, and unworthy spirit, that could dream of an earthly union and earthly happiness as possible, after such deep love had been so bitterly wronged as was Beatrice's love by Giovanni's blighting words! No, no; there could be no such hope. She must pass heavily, with that broken heart, across the borders of Time—she must bathe her hurts in some fount of paradise, and forget her grief in the light of immortality, and *there* be well.

But Giovanni did not know it.

"Dear Beatrice," said he, approaching her, while she shrank away as always at his approach, but now with a different impulse, "dearest Beatrice, our fate is not yet so desperate. Behold! there is a medicine, potent, as a wise physician has assured me, and almost divine in its efficacy. It is composed of ingredients the most opposite to those by which thy awful father has brought this calamity upon thee and me. It is distilled of blessed herbs. Shall we not quaff it together, and thus be purified from evil?"

"Give it me!" said Beatrice, extending her hand to receive the little silver vial which Giovanni took from his bosom. She added, with a peculiar emphasis, "I will drink; but do thou await the result."

She put Baglioni's antidote to her lips; and, at the same moment, the figure of Rappaccini emerged from the portal and came slowly towards the marble fountain. As he drew near, the pale man of science seemed to gaze with a triumphant expression at the beautiful youth and maiden, as might an artist who should spend his life in achieving a picture or a group of statuary and finally be satisfied with his success. He paused; his bent form grew erect with conscious power; he spread out his hands over them in the attitude of a father imploring a blessing upon his children; but those were the same hands that had thrown poison into the stream of their lives. Giovanni trembled. Beatrice shuddered nervously, and pressed her hand upon her heart.

"My daughter," said Rappaccini, "thou art no longer lonely in the world. Pluck one of those precious gems from thy sister shrub and bid thy bridegroom wear it in his bosom. It will not harm him now. My science and the sympathy between thee and him have so wrought within his system that he now stands apart from common men, as thou dost, daughter of my pride and triumph, from ordinary women. Pass on, then, through the world, most dear to one another and dreadful to all besides!"

"My father," said Beatrice, feebly, and still as she spoke she kept her hand upon her heart, "wherefore didst thou inflict this miserable doom upon thy child?"

"Miserable!" exclaimed Rappaccini. "What mean you, foolish girl? Dost thou deem it misery to be endowed with marvelous gifts against which no power nor strength could avail an enemy—misery, to be able to quell the mightiest with a breath—misery, to be as terrible as thou art beautiful? Wouldst thou, then, have preferred the condition of a weak woman, exposed to all evil and capable of none?"

"I would fain have been loved, not feared," murmured Beatrice, sinking down upon the ground. "But now it matters not. I am going, Father, where the evil which thou hast striven to mingle with my being will pass away like a dream— like the fragrance of these poisonous flowers, which will no longer taint my breath among the flowers of Eden. Farewell, Giovanni! Thy words of hatred are like lead within my heart; but they, too, will fall away as I ascend. Oh, was there not, from the first, more poison in thy nature than in mine?"

To Beatrice—so radically had her earthly part been wrought upon by Rappaccini's skill—as poison had been life, so the powerful antidote was death; and thus the poor victim of man's ingenuity and of thwarted nature, and of the fatality that attends all such efforts of perverted wisdom, perished there, at the feet of her father and Giovanni. Just at that moment, Professor Pietro Baglioni looked forth from the window, and called loudly, in a tone of triumph mixed with horror, to the thunderstricken man of science:

"Rappaccini! Rappaccini! and is *this* the upshot of your experiment!"

F. Scott Fitzgerald

(1896–1940) Both in his life and in his fiction Fitzgerald exemplified the "Jazz Age" of the 1920's, in which a postwar generation felt it had lost all ideals and standards. The title of a volume of short stories, All the Sad Young Men, *and that of his novel* The Beautiful and Damned *describe Fitzgerald's view of his own generation. His most famous works are* The Great Gatsby *and* Tender is the Night.

The Last of the Belles

After Atlanta's elaborate and theatrical rendition of Southern charm, we all understand Tarleton. It was a little hotter than anywhere we'd been—a dozen rookies collapsed the first day in that Georgia sun—and when you saw herds of cows drifting through the business streets, hi-yaed by colored drovers, a trance stole down over you out of the hot light: you wanted to move a hand or foot to be sure you were alive.

So I stayed out at camp and let Lieutenant Warren tell me about the girls. This was fifteen years ago, and I've forgotten how I felt, except that the days went along, one after another, better than they do now, and I was empty-hearted, because up North she whose legend I had loved for three years was getting married. I saw the clippings and newspaper photographs. It was "a romantic wartime wedding," all very rich and sad. I felt vividly the dark radiance of the sky under which it took place and, as a young snob, was more envious than sorry.

A day came when I went into Tarleton for a haircut and ran into a nice fellow named Bill Knowles, who was in my time at Harvard. He'd been in the National Guard division that preceded us in camp; at the last moment he had transferred to aviation and had been left behind.

"I'm glad I met you, Andy," he said with undue seriousness. "I'll hand you on all my information before I start for Texas. You see, there're really only three girls here—"

I was interested; there was something mystical about there being three girls. "—and here's one of them now."

We were in front of a drug store and he marched me in and introduced me to a lady I promptly detested.

"The other two are Ailie Calhoun and Sally Carrol Happer."

I guessed from the way he pronounced her name that he was interested in Ailie Calhoun. It was on his mind what she would be doing while he was gone; he wanted her to have a quiet, uninteresting time.

At my age I don't even hesitate to confess that entirely unchivalrous images of Ailie Calhoun—that lovely name—rushed into my mind. At twenty-three there is no such thing as a preëmpted beauty; though, had Bill asked me, I would doubtless have sworn in all sincerity to care for her like a sister. He didn't; he was just fretting out loud at having to go. Three days later he telephoned me that he was leaving next morning and he'd take me to her house that night.

We met at the hotel and walked uptown through the flowery, hot twilight. The four white pillars of the Calhoun house faced the street, and behind them the veranda was dark as a cave with hanging, weaving, climbing vines.

When we came up the walk a girl in a white dress tumbled out of the front door, crying, "I'm so sorry I'm late!" and seeing us, added: "Why, I thought I heard you come ten minutes—"

She broke off as a chair creaked and another man, an aviator from Camp Harry Lee, emerged from the obscurity of the veranda.

"Why, Canby!" she cried. "How are you?"

He and Bill Knowles waited with the tenseness of open litigants.

"Canby, I want to whisper to you, honey," she said, after just a second. "You'll excuse us, Bill."

They went aside. Presently Lieutenant Canby, immensely displeased, said in a grim voice, "Then we'll make it Thursday, but that means sure." Scarcely nodding to us, he went down the walk, the spurs with which he presumably urged on his aeroplane gleaming in the lamplight.

"Come in—I don't just know your name—"

There she was—the Southern type in all its purity. I would have recognized Ailie Calhoun if I'd never heard Ruth Draper or read Marse Chan. She had the adroitness sugar-coated with sweet, voluble simplicity, the suggested background of devoted fathers, brothers and admirers stretching back into the South's heroic age, the unfailing coolness acquired in the endless struggle with the heat. There were notes in her voice that ordered slaves around, that withered up Yankee captains, and then soft, wheedling notes that mingled in unfamiliar loveliness with the night.

I could scarcely see her in the darkness, but when I rose to go—it was plain that I was not to linger—she stood in the orange light from the doorway. She was small and very blond; there was too much fever-colored rouge on her face, accentuated by a nose dabbed clownish white, but she shone through that like a star.

"After Bill goes I'll be sitting here all alone night after night. Maybe you'll take me to the country-club dances." The pathetic prophecy brought a laugh from Bill. "Wait a minute," Ailie murmured. "Your guns are all crooked."

She straightened my collar pin, looking up at me for a second with some-thing more than curiosity. It was a seeking look, as if she asked, "Could it be you?" Like Lieutenant Canby, I marched off unwillingly into the suddenly insufficient night.

Two weeks later I sat with her on the same veranda, or rather she half lay in my arms and yet scarcely touched me—how she managed that I don't remember. I was trying unsuccessfully to kiss her, and had been trying for the best part of an hour. We had a sort of joke about my not being sincere. My theory was that if she'd let me kiss her I'd fall in love with her. Her argument was that I was obviously insincere.

In a lull between two of these struggles she told me about her brother who had died in his senior year at Yale. She showed me his picture—it was a hand-some, earnest face with a Leyendecker forelock—and told me that when she met someone who measured up to him she'd marry. I found this family idealism discouraging; even my brash confidence couldn't compete with the dead.

The evening and other evenings passed like that, and ended with my going back to camp with the remembered smell of magnolia flowers and a mood of vague dissatisfaction. I never kissed her. We went to the vaudeville and to the country club on Saturday nights, where she seldom took ten consecutive steps with one man, and she took me to barbecues and rowdy watermelon parties, and never thought it was worth while to change what I felt for her into love. I see now that it wouldn't have been hard, but she was a wise nineteen and she must have seen that we were emotionally incompatible. So I became her confidant instead.

We talked about Bill Knowles. She was considering Bill; for, though she wouldn't admit it, a winter at school in New York and a prom at Yale had turned her eyes North. She said she didn't think she'd marry a Southern man. And by degrees I saw that she was consciously and voluntarily different from these other girls who sang nigger songs and shot craps in the country-club bar. That's why Bill and I and others were drawn to her. We recognized her.

June and July, while the rumors reached us faintly, ineffectually, of battle and terror overseas, Ailie's eyes roved here and there about the country-club floor, seeking for something among the tall young officers. She attached several, choosing them with unfailing perspicacity—save in the case of Lieutenant Canby, whom she claimed to despise, but, nevertheless, gave dates to "because he was so sincere"—and we apportioned her evenings among us all summer.

One day she broke all her dates—Bill Knowles had leave and was coming. We talked of the event with scientific impersonality—would he move her to a decision? Lieutenant Canby, on the contrary, wasn't impersonal at all; made a nuisance of himself. He told her that if she married Knowles he was going to climb up six thousand feet in his aeroplane, shut off the motor and let go. He frightened her—I had to yield him my last date before Bill came.

On Saturday night she and Bill Knowles came to the country club. They were very handsome together and once more I felt envious and sad. As they danced out on the floor the three-piece orchestra was playing *After You've Gone,* in a poignant incomplete way that I can hear yet, as if each bar were trickling off a precious minute of that time. I knew then that I had grown to love Tarleton, and I glanced about half in panic to see if some face wouldn't come in for me out of that warm, singing, outer darkness that yielded up couple after couple in organdie and olive drab. It was a time of youth and war, and there was never so much love around.

When I danced with Ailie she suddenly suggested that we go outside to a car. She wanted to know why didn't people cut in on her tonight? Did they think she was already married?

"Are you going to be?"

"I don't know, Andy. Sometimes, when he treats me as if I were sacred, it thrills me." Her voice was hushed and far away. "And then—"

She laughed. Her body, so frail and tender, was touching mine, her face was turned up to me, and there, suddenly, with Bill Knowles ten yards off, I could have kissed her at last. Our lips just touched experimentally; then an aviation officer turned a corner of the veranda near us, peered into our darkness and hesitated.

"Ailie."

"Yes."

"You heard about this afternoon?"

"What?" She leaned forward, tenseness already in her voice.

"Horace Canby crashed. He was instantly killed."

She got up slowly and stepped out of the car.

"You mean he was killed?" she said.

"Yes. They don't know what the trouble was. His motor—"

"Oh-h-h!" Her rasping whisper came through the hands suddenly covering her face. We watched her helplessly as she put her head on the side of the car, gagging dry tears. After a minute I went for Bill, who was standing in the stag line, searching anxiously about for her, and told him she wanted to go home.

I sat on the steps outside. I had disliked Canby, but this terrible, pointless death was more real to me than the day's toll of thousands in France. In a few minutes Ailie and Bill came out. Ailie was whimpering a little, but when she saw me her eyes flexed and she came over swiftly.

"Andy"—she spoke in a quick, low voice—"of course you must never tell anybody what I told you about Canby yesterday. What he said, I mean."

"Of course not."

She looked at me a second longer as if to be quite sure. Finally she was sure. Then she sighed in such a quaint little way that I could hardly believe my ears, and her brow went up in what can only be described as mock despair.

"An-dy!"

I looked uncomfortably at the ground, aware that she was calling my attention to her involuntarily disastrous effect on men.

"Good night, Andy!" called Bill as they got into a taxi.

"Good night," I said, and almost added: "You poor fool."

2 Of course I should have made one of those fine moral decisions that people make in books, and despised her. On the contrary, I don't doubt that she could still have had me by raising her hand.

A few days later she made it all right by saying wistfully, "I know you think it was terrible of me to think of myself at a time like that, but it was such a shocking coincidence."

At twenty-three I was entirely unconvinced about anything, except that some people were strong and attractive and could do what they wanted, and others were caught and disgraced. I hoped I was of the former. I was sure Ailie was.

I had to revise other ideas about her. In the course of a long discussion with some girl about kissing—in those days people still talked about kissing more than they kissed—I mentioned the fact that Ailie had only kissed two or three men, and only when she thought she was in love. To my considerable discon- certion the girl figuratively just lay on the floor and howled.

"But it's true," I assured her, suddenly knowing it wasn't. "She told me herself."

"Ailie Calhoun! Oh, my heavens! Why, last year at the Tech spring house party—"

This was in September. We were going overseas any week now, and to bring us up to full strength a last batch of officers from the fourth training camp arrived. The fourth camp wasn't like the first three—the candidates were from the ranks; even from the drafted divisions. They had queer names without vowels in them, and save for a few young militiamen, you couldn't take it for granted that they came out of any background at all. The addition to our company was Lieutenant Earl Schoen from New Bedford, Massachusetts; as fine a physical specimen as I have ever seen. He was six-foot-three, with black hair, high color and glossy dark-brown eyes. He wasn't very smart and he was definitely illiterate, yet he was a good officer, high-tempered and commanding, and with that becoming touch of vanity that sits well on the military. I had an idea that New Bedford was a country town, and set down his bumptious qualities to that.

We were doubled up in living quarters and he came into my hut. Inside of a week there was a cabinet photograph of some Tarleton girl nailed brutally to the shack wall.

"She's no jane or anything like that. She's a society girl; goes with all the best people here."

The following Sunday afternoon I met the lady at a semi-private swimming pool in the country. When Ailie and I arrived, there was Schoen's muscular body rippling out of a bathing suit at the far end of the pool.

"Hey, lieutenant!"

When I waved back at him he grinned and winked, jerking his head toward the girl at his side. Then, digging her in the ribs, he jerked his head at me. It was a form of introduction.

"Who's that with Kitty Preston?" Ailie asked, and when I told her she said he looked like a street-car conductor, and pretended to look for her transfer.

A moment later he crawled powerfully and gracefully down the pool and pulled himself up at our side. I introduced him to Ailie.

"How do you like my girl, lieutenant?" he demanded. "I told you she was all right, didn't I?" He jerked his head toward Ailie; this time to indicate that his girl and Ailie moved in the same circles. "How about us all having dinner together down at the hotel some night?"

I left them in a moment, amused as I saw Ailie visibly making up her mind that here, anyhow, was not the ideal. But Lieutenant Earl Schoen was not to be dismissed so lightly. He ran his eyes cheerfully and inoffensively over her cute, slight figure, and decided that she would do even better than the other. Then minutes later I saw them in the water together, Ailie swimming away with a grim little stroke she had, and Schoen wallowing riotously around her and ahead of her, sometimes pausing and staring at her, fascinated, as a boy might look at a nautical doll.

While the afternoon passed he remained at her side. Finally Ailie came over to me and whispered, with a laugh: "He's a following me around. He thinks I haven't paid my carfare."

She turned quickly. Miss Kitty Preston, her face curiously flustered, stood facing us.

"Ailie Calhoun, I didn't think it of you to go out and delib'ately try to take a man away from another girl."—An expression of distress at the impending scene flitted over Ailie's face—"I thought you considered yourself above anything like that."

Miss Preston's voice was low, but it held that tensity that can be felt farther than it can be heard, and I saw Ailie's clear lovely eyes glance about in panic. Luckily, Earl himself was ambling cheerfully and innocently toward us.

"If you care for him you certainly oughtn't to belittle yourself in front of him," said Ailie in a flash, her head high.

It was her acquaintance with the traditional way of behaving against Kitty Preston's naive and fierce possessiveness, or if you prefer it, Ailie's "breeding" against the other's "commonness." She turned away.

"Wait a minute, kid!" cried Earl Schoen. "How about your address? Maybe I'd like to give you a ring on the phone."

She looked at him in a way that should have indicated to Kitty her entire lack of interest.

"I'm very busy at the Red Cross this month," she said, her voice as cool as her slicked-back blond hair. "Good-by."

On the way home she laughed. Her air of having been unwittingly involved in a contemptible business vanished.

"She'll never hold that young man," she said. "He wants somebody new."

"Apparently he wants Ailie Calhoun."

The idea amused her.

"He could give me his ticket punch to wear, like a fraternity pin. What fun! If mother ever saw anybody like that come in the house, she'd just lie down and die."

And to give Ailie credit, it was fully a fortnight before he did come to her house, although he rushed her until she pretended to be annoyed at the next country-club dance.

"He's the biggest tough, Andy," she whispered to me. "But he's so sincere."

She used the word "tough" without the conviction it would have carried had he been a Southern boy. She only knew it with her mind; her ear couldn't distinguish between one Yankee voice and another. And somehow Mrs. Calhoun didn't expire at his appearance on the threshold. The supposedly ineradicable prejudices of Ailie's parents were a convenient phenomenon that disappeared at her wish. It was her friends who were astonished. Ailie, always a little above Tarleton, whose beaus had been very carefully the "nicest" men of the camp—Ailie and Lieutenant Schoen! I grew tired of assuring people that she was merely distracting herself—and indeed every week or so there was someone new—an ensign from Pensacola, an old friend from New Orleans—but always, in between times, there was Earl Schoen.

Orders arrived for an advance party of officers and sergeants to proceed to the port of embarkation and take ship to France. My name was on the list. I had been on the range for a week and when I got back to camp, Earl Schoen buttonholed me immediately.

"We're giving a little farewell party in the mess. Just you and I and Captain Craker and three girls."

Earl and I were to call for the girls. We picked up Sally Carrol Happer and Nancy Lamar, and went on to Ailie's house; to be met at the door by the butler with the announcement that she wasn't home.

"Isn't home?" Earl repeated blankly. "Where is she?"

"Didn't leave no information about that; just said she wasn't home."

"But this is a darn funny thing!" he exclaimed. He walked around the familiar dusky veranda while the butler waited at the door. Something occurred to him. "Say," he informed me—"say, I think she's sore."

I waited. He said sternly to the butler, "You tell her I've got to speak to her a minute."

"How'm I goin' tell her that when she ain't home?"

Again Earl walked musingly around the porch. Then he nodded several times and said:

"She's sore at something that happened downtown."

In a few words he sketched out the matter to me.

"Look here; you wait in the car," I said. "Maybe I can fix this." And when he reluctantly retreated: "Oliver, you tell Miss Ailie I want to see her alone."

After some argument he bore this message and in a moment returned with a reply:

"Miss Ailie say she don't want to see that other gentleman about nothing never. She say come in if you like."

She was in the library. I had expected to see a picture of cool, outraged dignity, but her face was distraught, tumultuous, despairing. Her eyes were red-rimmed, as though she had been crying slowly and painfully, for hours.

"Oh, hello, Andy," she said brokenly. "I haven't seen you for so long. Has he gone?"

"Now, Ailie—"

"Now, Ailie!" she cried. "Now, Ailie! He spoke to me, you see. He lifted his hat. He stood there ten feet from me with that horrible—that horrible woman—holding her arm and talking to her, and then when he saw me he raised his hat. Andy, I didn't know what to do. I had to go in the drug store and ask for a glass of water, and I was so afraid he'd follow in after me that I asked Mr. Rich to let me go out the back way. I never want to see him or hear of him again."

I talked. I said what one says in such cases. I said it for half an hour. I could not move her. Several times she answered by murmuring something about his not being "sincere," and for the fourth time I wondered what the word meant to her. Certainly not constancy; it was, I half suspected, some special way she wanted to be regarded.

I got up to go. And then, unbelievably, the automobile horn sounded three times impatiently outside. It was stupefying. It said as plainly as if Earl were in the room, "All right; go to the devil then! I'm not going to wait here all night."

Ailie looked at me aghast. And suddenly a peculiar look came into her face, spread, flickered, broke into a teary, hysterical smile.

"Isn't he awful?" she cried in helpless despair. "Isn't he terrible?"

"Hurry up," I said quickly. "Get your cape. This is our last night." And I can still feel that last night vividly, the candlelight that flickered over the rough board of the mess shack, over the frayed paper decorations left from the supply company's party, the sad mandolin down a company street that kept picking *My Indiana Home* out of the universal nostalgia of the departing summer. The three girls lost in this mysterious men's city felt something, too—a bewitched impermanence as though they were on a magic carpet that had lighted on the Southern countryside, and any moment the wind would lift it and waft it away. We toasted ourselves and the South. Then we left our napkins and empty glasses and a little of the past on the table, and hand in hand went out into the moonlight itself. Taps had been played; there was no sound but the far-away whinny of a horse, and a loud persistent snore at which we laughed, and the leathery snap of a sentry coming to port over by the guardhouse. Craker was on duty; we others got into a waiting car, motored into Tarleton and left Craker's girl.

Then Ailie and Earl, Sally and I, two and two in the wide back seat, each couple turned from the other, absorbed and whispering, drove away into the wide, flat darkness.

We drove through pine woods heavy with lichen and Spanish moss, and between the fallow cotton fields along a road white as the rim of the world. We parked under the broken shadow of a mill where there was the sound of running water and restive squawky birds and over everything a brightness that tried to filter in anywhere—into the lost nigger cabins, the automobile, the fastnesses of the heart. The South sang to us—I wonder if they remember. I remember—the cool pale faces, the somnolent amorous eyes and the voices:

"Are you comfortable?"

"Yes; are you?"

"Are you sure you are?"

"Yes."

Suddenly we knew it was late and there was nothing more. We turned home.

Our detachment started for Camp Mills next day, but I didn't go to France after all. We passed a cold month on Long Island, marched aboard a transport with steel helmets slung at our sides and then marched off again. There wasn't any more war. I had missed the war. When I came back to Tarleton I tried to get out of the Army, but I had a regular commission and it took most of the winter. But Earl Schoen was one of the first to be demobilized. He wanted to find a good job "while the picking was good." Ailie was noncommittal, but there was an understanding between them that he'd be back.

By January the camps, which for two years had dominated the little city, were already fading. There was only the persistent incinerator smell to remind one of all that activity and bustle. What life remained centered bitterly about divisional headquarters building with the disgruntled regular officers who had also missed the war.

And now the young men of Tarleton began drifting back from the ends of the earth—some with Canadian uniforms, some with crutches or empty sleeves. A returned battalion of the National Guard paraded through the streets with open ranks for their dead, and then stepped down out of romance forever and sold you things over the counters of local stores. Only a few uniforms mingled with the dinner coats at the country-club dance.

Just before Christmas, Bill Knowles arrived unexpectedly one day and left the next—either he gave Ailie an ultimatum or she had made up her mind at last. I saw her sometimes when she wasn't busy with returned heroes from Savannah and Augusta, but I felt like an outmoded survival—and I was. She was waiting for Earl Schoen with such a vast uncertainty that she didn't like to talk about it. Three days before I got my final discharge he came.

I first happened upon them walking down Market Street together, and I don't think I've ever been so sorry for a couple in my life; though I suppose the same situation was repeating itself in every city where there had been camps. Exteriorly Earl had about everything wrong with him that could be imagined. His hat was green, with a radical feather; his suit was slashed and braided in a grotesque fashion that national advertising and the movies have put an end to. Evidently he had been to his old barber, for his hair bloused neatly on his pink, shaved neck. It wasn't as though he had been shiny and poor, but the background of mill-town dance halls and outing clubs flamed out at you—or rather flamed out at Ailie. For she had never quite imagined the reality; in these clothes even the natural grace of that magnificent body had departed. At first he boasted of his fine job; it would get them along all right until he could "see some easy money." But from the moment he came back into her world on its own terms he must have known it was hopeless. I don't know what Ailie said or how much her grief weighed against her stupefaction. She acted quickly—three days after his arrival, Earl and I went North together on the train.

"Well, that's the end of that," he said moodily. "She's a wonderful girl, but too much of a highbrow for me. I guess she's got to marry some rich guy that'll give her a great social position. I can't see that stuck-up sort of thing." And then, later: "She said to come back and see her in a year, but I'll never go back. This aristocrat stuff is all right if you got the money for it, but—"

"But it wasn't real," he meant to finish. The provincial society in which he had moved with so much satisfaction for six months already appeared to him as affected, "dudish" and artificial.

"Say, did you see what I saw getting on the train?" he asked me after a while. "Two wonderful janes, all alone. What do you say we mosey into the next car and ask them to lunch? I'll take the one in blue." Halfway down the car he turned around suddenly. "Say, Andy," he demanded, frowning; "one thing— how do you suppose she knew I used to command a street car? I never told her that."

"Search me."

3 This narrative arrives now at one of the big gaps that stared me in the face when I began. For six years, while I finished at Harvard Law and built commercial aeroplanes and backed a pavement block that went gritty under trucks, Ailie Calhoun was scarcely more than a name on a Christmas card; something that blew a little in my mind on warm nights when I remembered the magnolia flowers. Occasionally an acquaintance of Army days would ask me, "What became of that blond girl who was so popular?" but I didn't know. I ran into Nancy Lamar at the Montmartre in New York one evening and learned that Ailie had become engaged to a man in Cincinnati, had gone North to visit his family and then broken it off. She was lovely as ever and there was always a heavy beau or two. But neither Bill Knowles nor Earl Schoen had ever come back.

And somewhere about that time I heard that Bill Knowles had married a girl he met on a boat. There you are—not much of a patch to mend six years with.

Oddly enough, a girl seen at twilight in a small Indiana station started me thinking about going South. The girl, in stiff pink organdie, threw her arms about a man who got off our train and hurried him to a waiting car, and I felt a sort of pang. It seemed to me that she was bearing him off into the lost midsummer world of my early twenties, where time had stood still and charming girls, dimly seen like the past itself, still loitered along the dusky streets. I suppose that poetry is a Northern man's dream of the South. But it was months later that I sent off a wire to Ailie, and immediately followed it to Tarleton.

It was July. The Jefferson Hotel seemed strangely shabby and stuffy—a boosters' club burst into intermittent song in the dining room that my memory had long dedicated to officers and girls. I recognized the taxi driver who took me up to Ailie's house, but his "Sure, I do, lieutenant," was unconvincing. I was only one of twenty thousand.

It was a curious three days. I suppose some of Ailie's first young lustre must have gone the way of such mortal shining, but I can't bear witness to it. She was still so physically appealing that you wanted to touch the personality that trembled on her lips. No—the change was more profound than that.

At once I saw she had a different line. The modulations of pride, the vocal hints that she knew the secrets of a brighter, finer ante-bellum day, were gone from her voice; there was no time for them now as it rambled on in the half-laughing, half-desperate banter of the newer South. And everything was swept into this banter in order to make it go on and leave no time for thinking—the present, the future, herself, me. We went to a rowdy party at the house of some young married people, and she was the nervous, glowing centre of it. After all, she wasn't eighteen, and she was as attractive in her role of reckless clown as she had ever been in her life.

"Have you heard anything from Earl Schoen?" I asked her the second night, on our way to the country-club dance.

"No." She was serious for a moment. "I often think of him. He was the—" She hesitated.

"Go on."

"I was going to say the man I loved most, but that wouldn't be true. I never exactly loved him, or I'd have married him any old how, wouldn't I?" She looked at me questioningly. "At least I wouldn't have treated him like that."

"It was impossible."

"Of course," she agreed uncertainly. Her mood changed; she became flippant: "How the Yankees did deceive us poor little Southern girls. Ah, me!"

When we reached the country club she melted like a chameleon into the—to me—unfamiliar crowd. There was a new generation upon the floor, with less dignity than the ones I had known, but none of them were more a part of its lazy, feverish essence than Ailie. Possibly she had perceived that in her initial longing to escape from Tarleton's provincialism she had been walking alone, following a generation which was doomed to have no successors. Just where she lost the battle, waged behind the white pillars of her veranda, I don't know. But she had guessed wrong, missed out somewhere. Her wild animation, which even now called enough men around her to rival the entourage of the youngest and freshest, was an admission of defeat.

I left her house, as I had so often left it that vanished June, in a mood of vague dissatisfaction. It was hours later, tossing about my bed in the hotel, that I realized what was the matter, what had always been the matter—I was deeply and incurably in love with her. In spite of every incompatibility, she was still, she would always be to me, the most attractive girl I had ever known. I told her so next afternoon. It was one of those hot days I knew so well, and Ailie sat beside me on a couch in the darkened library.

"Oh, no, I couldn't marry you," she said, almost frightened; "I don't love you that way at all. . . . I never did. And you don't love me. I didn't mean to tell you now, but next month I'm going to marry another man. We're not even announcing it, because I've done that twice before." Suddenly it occurred to her that I might be hurt: "Andy, you just had a silly idea, didn't you? You know I couldn't ever marry a Northern man."

"Who is he?" I demanded.

"A man from Savannah."

"Are you in love with him?"

"Of course I am." We both smiled. "Of course I am! What are you trying to make me say?"

There were no doubts, as there had been with other men. She couldn't afford to let herself have doubts. I knew this because she had long ago stopped making any pretensions with me. This very naturalness, I realized, was because she didn't consider me as a suitor. Beneath her mask of an instinctive thoroughbred she had always been on to herself, and she couldn't believe that anyone not taken in to the point of uncritical worship could really love her. That was what she called being "sincere"; she felt most security with men like Canby and Earl Schoen, who were incapable of passing judgments on the ostensibly aristocratic heart.

"All right," I said, as if she had asked my permission to marry. "Now, would you do something for me?"

"Anything."

"Ride out to camp."

"But there's nothing left there, honey."

"I don't care."

We walked downtown. The taxi driver in front of the hotel repeated her objection: "Nothing there now, cap."

"Never mind. Go there anyhow."

Twenty minutes later he stopped on a wide unfamiliar plain powdered with new cotton fields and marked with isolated clumps of pine.

"Like to drive over yonder where you see the smoke?" asked the driver. "That's the new state prison."

"No. Just drive along this road. I want to find where I used to live."

An old race course, inconspicuous in the camp's day of glory, had reared its dilapidated grandstand in the desolation. I tried in vain to orient myself.

"Go along this road past that clump of trees, and then turn right—no, turn left."

He obeyed, with professional disgust.

"You won't find a single thing, darling," said Ailie. "The contractors took it all down."

We rode slowly along the margin of the fields. It might have been here—

"All right. I want to get out," I said suddenly.

I left Ailie sitting in the car, looking very beautiful with the warm breeze stirring her long, curly bob.

It might have been here. That would make the company streets down there and the mess shack, where we dined that night, just over the way.

The taxi driver regarded me indulgently while I stumbled here and there in the knee-deep underbrush, looking for my youth in a clapboard or a strip of roofing or a rusty tomato can. I tried to sight on a vaguely familiar clump of trees, but it was growing darker now and I couldn't be quite sure they were the right trees.

"They're going to fix up the old race course," Ailie called from the car. "Tarleton's getting quite doggy in its old age."

No. Upon consideration they didn't look like the right trees. All I could be sure of was this place that had once been so full of life and effort was gone, as if it had never existed, and that in another month Ailie would be gone, and the South would be empty for me forever.

1929   *Taps at Reveille*

William Dean Howells

(1837–1920) Largely self-taught as a poor boy in Ohio, William Dean Howells became one of the most influential writers in America in his roles as novelist, critic, and editor of The Atlantic Monthly. *In his many works of fiction Howells tried to be completely realistic about ordinary people.*

Editha

The air was thick with the war feeling, like the electricity of a storm which has not yet burst. Editha sat looking out into the hot spring afternoon, with her lips parted, and panting with the intensity of the question whether she could let him go. She had decided that she could not let him stay, when she saw him at the end of the still leafless avenue, making slowly up towards the house, with his head down and his figure relaxed. She ran impatiently out on the veranda, to the edge of the steps, and imperatively demanded greater haste of him with her will before she called aloud to him: "George!"

He had quickened his pace in mystical response to her mystical urgence, before he could have heard her; now he looked up and answered, "Well?"

"Oh, how united we are!" she exulted, and then she swooped down the steps to him. "What is it?" she cried.

"It's war," he said, and he pulled her up to him and kissed her.

She kissed him back intensely, but irrelevantly, as to their passion, and uttered from deep in her throat, "How glorious!"

"It's war," he repeated, without consenting to her sense of it; and she did not know just what to think at first. She never knew what to think of him; that made his mystery, his charm. All through their courtship, which was contemporaneous with the growth of the war feeling, she had been puzzled by his want of seriousness about it. He seemed to despise it even more than he abhorred it. She could have understood his abhorring any sort of bloodshed; that would have been a survival of his old life when he thought he would be a minister,

From Harper's Monthly Magazine, *January 1905, pp. 214–224.*

and before he changed and took up the law. But making light of a cause so high and noble seemed to show a want of earnestness at the core of his being. Not but that she felt herself able to cope with a congenital defect of that sort, and make his love for her save him from himself. Now perhaps the miracle was already wrought in him. In the presence of the tremendous fact that he announced, all triviality seemed to have gone out of him; she began to feel that. He sank down on the top step, and wiped his forehead with his handkerchief, while she poured out upon him her question of the origin and authenticity of his news.

All the while, in her duplex emotioning, she was aware that now at the very beginning she must put a guard upon herself against urging him, by any word or act, to take the part that her whole soul willed him to take, for the completion of her ideal of him. He was very nearly perfect as he was, and he must be allowed to perfect himself. But he was peculiar, and he might very well be reasoned out of his peculiarity. Before her reasoning went her emotioning: her nature pulling upon his nature, her womanhood upon his manhood, without her knowing the means she was using to the end she was willing. She had always supposed that the man who won her would have done something to win her; she did not know what, but something. George Gearson had simply asked her for her love, on the way home from a concert, and she gave her love to him, without, as it were, thinking. But now, it flashed upon her, if he could do something worthy to *have* won her—be a hero, *her* hero—it would be even better than if he had done it before asking her; it would be grander. Besides, she had believed in the war from the beginning.

"But don't you see, dearest," she said, "that it wouldn't have come to this if it hadn't been in the order of Providence? And I call any war glorious that is for the liberation of people who have been struggling for years against the cruelest oppression. Don't you think so, too?"

"I suppose so," he returned, languidly. "But war! Is it glorious to break the peace of the world?"

"That ignoble peace! It was no peace at all, with that crime and shame at our very gates." She was conscious of parroting the current phrases of the newspapers, but it was no time to pick and choose her words. She must sacrifice anything to the high ideal she had for him, and after a good deal of rapid argument she ended with the climax: "But now it doesn't matter about the how or why. Since the war has come, all that is gone. There are no two sides any more. There is nothing now but our country."

He sat with his eyes closed and his head leant back against the veranda, and he remarked, with a vague smile, as if musing aloud, "Our country—right or wrong."

"Yes, right or wrong!" she returned, fervidly. "I'll go and get you some lemonade." She rose rustling, and whisked away; when she came back with two tall glasses of clouded liquid on a tray, and the ice clucking in them, he still sat as she had left him, and she said, as if there had been no interruption: "But there is no question of wrong in this case. I call it a sacred war. A war for liberty and humanity, if ever there was one. And I know you will see it just as I do, yet."

He took half the lemonade at a gulp, and he answered as he set the glass down: "I know you always have the highest ideal. When I differ from you I ought to doubt myself."

A generous sob rose in Editha's throat for the humility of a man, so very nearly perfect, who was willing to put himself below her.

Besides, she felt, more subliminally, that he was never so near slipping through her fingers as when he took that meek way.

"You shall not say that! Only, for once I happen to be right." She seized his hand in her two hands, and poured her soul from her eyes into his. "Don't you think so?" she entreated him.

He released his hand and drank the rest of his lemonade, and she added, "Have mine, too," but he shook his head in answering, "I've no business to think so, unless I act so, too."

Her heart stopped a beat before it pulsed on with leaps that she felt in her neck. She had noticed that strange thing in men: they seemed to feel bound to do what they believed, and not think a thing was finished when they said it, as girls did. She knew what was in his mind, but she pretended not, and she said, "Oh, I am not sure," and then faltered.

He went on as if to himself, without apparently heeding her: "There's only one way of proving one's faith in a thing like this."

She could not say that she understood, but she did understand.

He went on again. "If I believed—if I felt as you do about the war—Do you wish me to feel as you do?"

Now she was really not sure; so she said: "George, I don't know what you mean."

He seemed to muse away from her as before. "There is a sort of fascination in it. I suppose that at the bottom of his heart every man would like at times to have his courage tested, to see how he would act."

"How can you talk in that ghastly way?"

"It *is* rather morbid. Still, that's what it comes to, unless you're swept away by ambition or driven by conviction. I haven't the conviction or the ambition, and the other thing is what it comes to with me. I ought to have been a preacher, after all; then I couldn't have asked it of myself as I must, now I'm a lawyer. And you believe it's a holy war, Editha?" he suddenly addressed her. "Oh, I know you do! But you wish me to believe so, too?"

She hardly knew whether he was mocking or not, in the ironical way he always had with her plainer mind. But the only thing was to be outspoken with him.

"George, I wish you to believe whatever you think is true, at any and every cost. If I've tried to talk you into anything, I take it all back."

"Oh, I know that, Editha. I know how sincere you are, and how—I wish I had your undoubting spirit! I'll think it over; I'd like to believe as you do. But I don't, now; I don't, indeed. It isn't this war alone; though this seems peculiarly wanton and needless; but it's every war—so stupid; it makes me sick. Why shouldn't this thing have been settled reasonably?"

"Because," she said, very throatily again, "God meant it to be war."

"You think it was God? Yes, I suppose that is what people will say."

"Do you suppose it would have been war if God hadn't meant it?"

"I don't know. Sometimes it seems as if God had put this world into men's keeping to work it as they pleased."

"Now, George, that is blasphemy."

"Well, I won't blaspheme. I'll try to believe in your pocket Providence," he said, and then he rose to go.

"Why don't you stay to dinner?" Dinner at Balcom's Works was at one o'clock.

"I'll come back to supper, if you'll let me. Perhaps I shall bring you a convert."

"Well, you may come back, on that condition."

"All right. If I don't come, you'll understand."

He went away without kissing her, and she felt it a suspension of their engagement. It all interested her intensely; she was undergoing a tremendous experience, and she was being equal to it. While she stood looking after him, her mother came out through one of the long windows onto the veranda, with a catlike softness and vagueness.

"Why didn't he stay to dinner?"

"Because—because—war has been declared," Editha pronounced, without turning.

Her mother said, "Oh, my!" and then said nothing more until she had sat down in one of the large Shaker chairs and rocked herself for some time. Then she closed whatever tacit passage of thought there had been in her mind with the spoken words: "Well, I hope *he* won't go."

"And *I* hope he *will*," the girl said, and confronted her mother with a stormy exaltation that would have frightened any creature less unimpressionable than a cat.

Her mother rocked herself again for an interval of cogitation. What she arrived at in speech was: "Well, I guess you've done a wicked thing, Editha Balcom."

The girl said, as she passed indoors through the same window her mother had come out by: "I haven't done anything—yet."

In her room, she put together all her letters and gifts from Gearson, down to the withered petals of the first flower he had offered, with that timidity of his veiled in that irony of his. In the heart of the packet she enshrined her engagement ring which she had restored to the pretty box he had brought it her in. Then she sat down, if not calmly yet strongly, and wrote:

"George:—I understood when you left me. But I think we had better emphasize your meaning that if we cannot be one in everything we had better be one in nothing. So I am sending these things for your keeping till you have made up your mind.

"I shall always love you, and therefore I shall never marry anyone else. But the man I marry must love his country first of all, and be able to say to me,

> "'I could not love thee, dear, so much,
> Loved I not honor more.'

"There is no honor above America with me. In this great hour there is no other honor.

"Your heart will make my words clear to you. I had never expected to say so much, but it has come upon me that I must say the utmost.

Editha."

She thought she had worded her letter well, worded it in a way that could not be bettered; all had been implied and nothing expressed.

She had it ready to send with the packet she had tied with red, white, and blue ribbon, when it occurred to her that she was not just to him, that she was not giving him a fair chance. He said he would go and think it over, and she was not waiting. She was pushing, threatening, compelling. That was not a woman's part. She must leave him free, free, free. She could not accept for her country or herself a forced sacrifice.

In writing her letter she had satisfied the impulse from which it sprang; she could well afford to wait till he had thought it over. She put the packet and the letter by, and rested serene in the consciousness of having done what was laid upon her by her love itself to do, and yet used patience, mercy, justice.

She had her reward. Gearson did not come to tea, but she had given him till morning, when, late at night there came up from the village the sound of a fife and drum, with a tumult of voices, in shouting, singing, and laughing. The noise drew nearer and nearer; it reached the street end of the avenue; there it silenced itself, and one voice, the voice she knew best, rose over the silence. It fell; the air was filled with cheers; the fife and drum struck up, with the shouting, singing, and laughing again, but now retreating; and a single figure came hurrying up the avenue.

She ran down to meet her lover and clung to him. He was very gay, and he put his arm round her with a boisterous laugh. "Well, you must call me Captain now; or Cap, if you prefer; that's what the boys call me. Yes, we've had a meeting at the town hall, and everybody has volunteered; and they selected me for captain, and I'm going to the war, the big war, the glorious war, the holy war ordained by the pocket Providence that blesses butchery. Come along: let's tell the whole family about it. Call them from their downy beds, father, mother, Aunt Hitty, and all the folks!"

But when they mounted the veranda steps he did not wait for a larger audience; he poured the story out upon Editha alone.

"There was a lot of speaking, and then some of the fools set up a shout for me. It was all going one way, and I thought it would be a good joke to sprinkle a little cold water on them. But you can't do that with a crowd that adores you. The first thing I knew I was sprinkling hell-fire on them. 'Cry havoc, and let slip the dogs of war.' That was the style. Now that it had come to the fight, there were no two parties; there was one country, and the thing was to fight to a finish as quick as possible. I suggested volunteering then and there, and I wrote my name first of all on the roster. Then they elected me—that's all. I wish I had some ice-water."

She left him walking up and down the veranda, while she ran for the ice-pitcher and a goblet, and when she came back he was still walking up and down, shouting the story he had told her to her father and mother, who had come out more sketchily dressed than they commonly were by day. He drank goblet after goblet of the ice-water without noticing who was giving it, and kept on talking, and laughing through his talk wildly. "It's astonishing," he said, "how well the worse reason looks when you try to make it appear the better. Why, I believe I was the first convert to the war in that crowd tonight! I never thought I should like to kill a man; but now I shouldn't care; and the smokeless powder lets you see the man drop that you kill. It's all for the country! What a thing it is to have a country that *can't* be wrong, but if it is, is right, anyway."

Editha had a great, vital thought, an inspiration. She set down the ice-pitcher on the veranda floor, and ran upstairs and got the letter she had written him. When at last he noisily bade her father and mother, "Well, good-night. I forgot I woke you up: I shan't want any sleep myself," she followed him down the avenue to the gate. There, after the whirling words that seemed to fly away from her thoughts and refuse to serve them, she made a last effort to solemnize the moment that seemed so crazy, and pressed the letter she had written upon him.

"What's this?" he said. "Want me to mail it?"

"No, no. It's for you. I wrote it after you went this morning. Keep it—keep it—and read it sometime—" She thought, and then her inspiration came: "Read it if ever you doubt what you've done, or fear that I regret your having done it. Read it after you've started."

They strained each other in embraces that seemed as ineffective as their words, and he kissed her face with quick, hot breaths that were so unlike him, that made her feel as if she had lost her old lover and found a stranger in his place. The stranger said: "What a gorgeous flower you are, with your red hair, and your blue eyes that look black now, and your face with the color painted out by the white moonshine! Let me hold you under the chin, to see whether I love blood, you tiger-lily!" Then he laughed Gearson's laugh, and released her, scared and giddy. Within her wilfulness she had been frightened by a sense of subtler force in him, and mystically mastered as she had never been before.

She ran all the way back to the house, and mounted the steps panting. Her mother and father were talking of the great affair. Her mother said: "Wa'n't Mr. Gearson in rather of an excited state of mind? Didn't you think he acted curious?"

"Well, not for a man who'd just been elected captain and had set 'em up for the whole of Company A," her father chuckled back.

"What in the world do you mean, Mr. Balcom? Oh! There's Editha!" She offered to follow the girl indoors.

"Don't come, mother!" Editha called, vanishing.

Mrs. Balcom remained to reproach her husband. "I don't see much of anything to laugh at."

"Well, it's catching. Caught it from Gearson. I guess it won't be much of a war, and I guess Gearson don't think so, either. The other fellows will back down as soon as they see we mean it. I wouldn't lose any sleep over it. I'm going back to bed, myself."

Gearson came again next afternoon, looking pale and rather sick, but quite himself, even to his languid irony. "I guess I'd better tell you, Editha, that I consecrated myself to your god of battles last night by pouring too many libations to him down my own throat. But I'm all right now. One has to carry off the excitement, somehow."

"Promise me," she commanded, "that you'll never touch it again!"

"What! Not let the cannikin clink? Not let the soldier drink? Well, I promise."

"You don't belong to yourself now; you don't even belong to *me*. You belong to your country, and you have a sacred charge to keep yourself strong and well for your country's sake. I have been thinking, thinking all night and all day long."

"You look as if you had been crying a little, too," he said, with his queer smile.

"That's all past. I've been thinking, and worshipping *you*. Don't you suppose I know all that you've been through, to come to this? I've followed you every step from your old theories and opinions."

"Well, you've had a long row to hoe."

"And I know you've done this from the highest motives—"

"Oh, there won't be much pettifogging to do till this cruel war is—"

"And you haven't simply done it for my sake. I couldn't respect you if you had."

"Well, then we'll say I haven't. A man that hasn't got his own respect intact wants the respect of all the other people he can corner. But we won't go into that. I'm in for the thing now, and we've got to face our future. My idea is that this isn't going to be a very protracted struggle; we shall just scare the enemy to death before it comes to a fight at all. But we must provide for contingencies, Editha. If anything happens to me—"

"Oh, George!" She clung to him, sobbing.

"I don't want you to feel foolishly bound to my memory. I should hate that, wherever I happened to be."

"I am yours, for time and eternity—time and eternity." She liked the words; they satisfied her famine for phrases.

"Well, say eternity; that's all right; but time's another thing; and I'm talking about time. But there is something! My mother! If anything happens—"

She winced, and he laughed. "You're not the bold soldier-girl of yesterday!" Then he sobered. "If anything happens, I want you to help my mother out. She won't like my doing this thing. She brought me up to think war a fool thing as well as a bad thing. My father was in the Civil War; all through it; lost his arm in it." She thrilled with the sense of the arm round her; what if that should be lost? He laughed as if divining her: "Oh, it doesn't run in the family, as far as I know!" Then he added, gravely: "He came home with misgivings about war, and they grew on him. I guess he and mother agreed between them that I was to be brought up in his final mind about it; but that was before my time. I only knew him from my mother's report of him and his opinions; I don't know whether they were hers first; but they were hers last. This will be a blow to her. I shall have to write and tell her—"

He stopped, and she asked: "Would you like me to write, too, George?"

"I don't believe that would do. No, I'll do the writing. She'll understand a little if I say that I thought the way to minimize it was to make war on the largest possible scale at once—that I felt I must have been helping on the war somehow if I hadn't helped keep it from coming, and I knew I hadn't; when it came, I had no right to stay out of it."

Whether his sophistries satisfied him or not, they satisfied her. She clung to his breast, and whispered, with closed eyes and quivering lips: "Yes, yes, yes!"

"But if anything should happen, you might go to her and see what you could do for her. You know? It's rather far off; she can't leave her chair—"

"Oh, I'll go, if it's the ends of the earth! But nothing will happen! Nothing can! I—"

She felt herself lifted with his rising, and Gearson was saying, with his arm still round her, to her father: "Well, we're off at once, Mr. Balcom. We're to be formally accepted at the capital, and then bunched up with the rest somehow, and sent into camp somewhere, and go to the front as soon as possible. We all want to be in the van, of course; we're the first company to report to the Governor. I came to tell Editha, but I hadn't got round to it."

She saw him again for a moment at the capital, in the station, just before the train started southward with his regiment. He looked well, in his uniform, and very soldierly, but somehow girlish, too, with his clean-shaven face and slim figure. The manly eyes and the strong voice satisfied her, and his preoccupation with some unexpected details of duty flattered her. Other girls were weeping and bemoaning themselves, but she felt a sort of noble distinction in the abstraction, the almost unconsciousness, with which they parted. Only at the last moment he said: "Don't forget my mother. It mayn't be such a walk-over as I supposed," and he laughed at the notion.

He waved his hand to her as the train moved off—she knew it among a score of hands that were waved to other girls from the platform of the car, for it held a letter which she knew was hers. Then he went inside the car to read it, doubtless, and she did not see him again. But she felt safe for him through the strength of what she called her love. What she called her God, always speaking the name in a deep voice and with the implication of a mutual understanding, would watch over him and keep him and bring him back to her. If with an empty sleeve, then he should have three arms instead of two, for both of hers should be his for life. She did not see, though, why she should always be thinking of the arm his father had lost.

There were not many letters from him, but they were such as she could have wished, and she put her whole strength into making hers such as she imagined he could have wished, glorifying and supporting him. She wrote to his

mother glorifying him as their hero, but the brief answer she got was merely
to the effect that Mrs. Gearson was not well enough to write herself, and
thanking her for her letter by the hand of someone who called herself "Yrs
truly, Mrs. W. J. Andrews.".

Editha determined not to be hurt, but to write again quite as if the answer
had been all she expected. Before it seemed as if she could have written, there
came news of the first skirmish, and in the list of the killed, which was tele-
graphed as a trifling loss on our side, was Gearson's name. There was a frantic
time of trying to make out that it might be, must be, some other Gearson; but
the name and the company and the regiment and the State were too definitely
given.

Then there was a lapse into depths out of which it seemed as if she never
could rise again; then a lift into clouds far above all grief, black clouds, that
blotted out the sun, but where she soared with him, with George—George! She
had the fever that she expected of herself, but she did not die in it; she was
not even delirious, and it did not last long. When she was well enough to leave
her bed, her one thought was of George's mother, of his strangely worded
wish that she should go to her and see what she could do for her. In the
exaltation of the duty laid upon her—it buoyed her up instead of burdening
her—she rapidly recovered.

Her father went with her on the long railroad journey from Northern
New York to Western Iowa; he had business out at Davenport, and he said he
could just as well go then as any other time; and he went with her to the little
country town where George's mother lived in a little house on the edge of
the illimitable cornfields, under trees pushed to a top of the rolling prairie.
George's father had settled there after the Civil War, as so many other old soldiers
had done; but they were Eastern people, and Editha fancied touches of the
East in the June rose overhanging the front door, and the garden with early
summer flowers stretching from the gate of the paling fence.

It was very low inside the house, and so dim, with the closed blinds, that
they could scarcely see one another: Editha tall and black in her crapes which
filled the air with the smell of their dyes; her father standing decorously apart
with his hat on his forearm, as at funerals; a woman rested in a deep armchair,
and the woman who had let the strangers in stood behind the chair.

The seated woman turned her head round and up, and asked the woman
behind the chair: "*Who* did you say?"

Editha, if she had done what she expected of herself, would have gone down
on her knees at the feet of the seated figure and said, "I am George's Editha,"
for answer.

But instead of her own voice she heard that other woman's voice, saying:
"Well, I don't know as I *did* get the name just right. I guess I'll have to make a
little more light in here," and she went and pushed two of the shutters ajar.

"Then Editha's father said, in his public will-now-address-a-few-remarks
tone: "My name is Balcom, ma'am—Junius H. Balcom, of Balcom's Works, New
York; my daughter—"

"Oh!" the seated woman broke in, with a powerful voice, the voice that always surprised Editha from Gearson's slender frame. "Let me see you. Stand round where the light can strike on your face," and Editha dumbly obeyed. "So, you're Editha Balcom," she sighed.

"Yes," Editha said, more like a culprit than a comforter.

"What did you come for?" Mrs. Gearson asked.

Editha's face quivered and her knees shook. "I came—because—because George—" She could go no further.

"Yes," the mother said, "he told me he had asked you to come if he got killed. You didn't expect that, I suppose, when you sent him."

"I would rather have died myself than done it!" Editha said, with more truth in her deep voice than she ordinarily found in it. "I tried to leave him free—"

"Yes, that letter of yours, that came back with his other things, left him free."

Editha saw now where George's irony came from.

"It was not to be read before—unless—until—I told him so," she faltered.

"Of course, he wouldn't read a letter of yours, under the circumstances, till he thought you wanted him to. Been sick?" the woman abruptly demanded.

"Very sick," Editha said, with self-pity.

"Daughter's life," her father interposed, "was almost despaired of, at one time."

Mrs. Gearson gave him no heed. "I suppose you would have been glad to die, such a brave person as you! I don't believe *he* was glad to die. He was always a timid boy, that way; he was afraid of a good many things; but if he was afraid he did what he made up his mind to. I suppose he made up his mind to go; but I knew what it cost him by what it cost me when I heard of it. I had been through *one* war before. When you sent him you didn't expect he would get killed."

The voice seemed to compassionate Editha, and it was time. "No," she huskily murmured.

"No, girls don't; women don't, when they give their men up to their country. They think they'll come marching back, somehow, just as gay as they went, or if it's an empty sleeve, or even an empty pantaloon, it's all the more glory, and they're so much the prouder of them, poor things!"

The tears began to run down Editha's face; she had not wept till then; but it was now such a relief to be understood that the tears came.

"No, you didn't expect him to get killed," Mrs. Gearson repeated, in a voice which was startlingly like George's again. "You just expected him to kill some-one else, some of those foreigners, that weren't there because they had any say about it, but because they had to be there, poor wretches—conscripts, or whatever they call 'em. You thought it would be all right for my George, *your* George, to kill the sons of those miserable mothers and the husbands of those girls that you would never see the faces of." The woman lifted her powerful voice in a psalmlike note. "I thank my God he didn't live to do it! I thank my God they killed him first, and that he ain't livin' with their blood on his hands!" She dropped her eyes, which she had raised with her voice, and glared at Editha.

"What you got that black on for?" She lifted herself by her powerful arms so high that her helpless body seemed to hang limp its full length. "Take it off, take it off, before I tear it from your back!"

The lady who was passing the summer near Balcom's Works was sketching Editha's beauty, which lent itself wonderfully to the effects of a colorist. It had come to that confidence which is rather apt to grow between artist and sitter, and Editha had told her everything.

"To think of your having such a tragedy in your life!" the lady said. She added: "I suppose there are people who feel that way about war. But when you consider the good this war has done—how much it has done for the country! I can't understand such people, for my part. And when you had come all the way out there to console her—got up out of a sickbed! Well!"

"I think," Editha said, magnanimously, "she wasn't quite in her right mind; and so did papa."

"Yes," the lady said, looking at Editha's lips in nature and then at her lips in art, and giving an empirical touch to them in the picture. "But how dreadful of her! How perfectly—excuse me—how *vulgar*!"

A light broke upon Editha in the darkness which she felt had been without a gleam of brightness for weeks and months. The mystery that had bewildered her was solved by the word; and from that moment she rose from groveling in shame and self-pity, and began to live again in the ideal.

Helene Davis

*(b. 1944) Currently a student at the
University of Massachusetts at Boston,
Helene Davis was born in Providence,
Rhode Island and studied art at
Boston University. She has twice been
a member of a poetry workshop
sponsored by the Radcliffe Institute,
and at present she is working part-
time in an experimental program
teaching poetry to elementary school
children in the Boston area. This is
her first publication.*

Affair

Together our hands find no indifferent touch.
We are one kind, a dark breed who must love
for sheer breath.

> *In the old story, leaning against the lamplight,
> the woman is electric, happy,
> never cries.*

You move back into stone eyes. With your darkhaired words
you press illusion in fine volumes,
for keepsakes.

> *The woman owns no name—mistress, mother, kind
> friend or lover—a velvet backdrop
> in his quiet life.*

Without you my flesh becomes bone dry and breaks
easily, my face invisible as moss
on gravestones.

> *The woman must, like earth, be able to change
> size: a spot of dust, a rose half grown, a room
> full of music.*

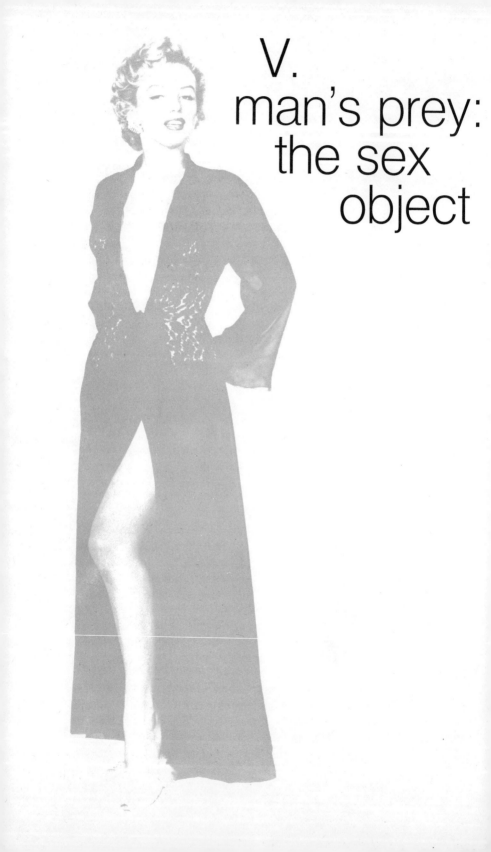

V.
man's prey:
the sex
object

A woman is confused about how to respond to wolf-calls and whistles: should she smile and accept them as efforts to humanize existence, or should she haughtily ignore them because they reduce her from person to thing, a sexual object? Often her response is ruled more by fear than reason: behind the most casual approach of a male may lurk every woman's nightmare, the rapist-murderer. Whether preceded by courtship or not, to a woman sexual intercourse is the equivalent of rape if her partner's purpose is to use her for his own pleasure, to reify or make an object of her.

In Irwin Shaw's "The Girls in Their Summer Dresses," Michael's girl-watching seems a very slight offense and his wife's anger seems possessive and out of proportion, until one realizes that he sees her just as he does the other pretty girls: to him she is an object, and he admits that probably she will be replaced by a more attractive object. Both Michael and Frances accept his roving eye as part of his nature and the unhappiness it causes as inevitable. Michael could well quote the lines of W. B. Yeats' poem "For Anne Gregory": ". . . only God, my dear, /Could love you for yourself alone." To the peasant-participants in Colette's story "The Patriarch," incest seems natural and inevitable; for a widower to impregnate each of his daughters in turn seems an acceptable and even happy solution for the loss of his wife and his daughters' need for a provider and children. The daughter newly made a mother is gay and laughing, the child is calmly asleep, the father-grandfather "impassive." Yet in making use of his daughter, even in making her happy, the father is denying her a separate life of her own. Incest is essentially rape, as the sophisticated narrator realizes.

Eudora Welty in "At the Landing" implies that sexual victimization is inevitable not only because it is natural but because a young girl, overprotected by society, cannot distinguish between sex and love. Jenny's obedience when her grandfather insists on keeping her confined to his house makes her easy

prey "to anybody, to a stranger in the street if there should be one." Her
innocence as the result of her sheltered life leads her to assume that her generous
love for Billy Floyd, the first man she encounters, is mutual—that he can sense
her desire to be fully a person as she senses his. When she is released from her
captivity by her grandfather's death and a flood which sends her out into the
world, Billy rapes her as thoughtlessly as he spears a piece of meat from the fire;
"for him it was all a taking freely of what was free," while to her his rescue
and feeding symbolized love. Even after he leaves her, her "dream of love"
makes her happy. In trying to find him, she is still smiling when a group of
fishermen rape her one at a time in a houseboat on the river. An old woman who
sees her afterwards accepts her fate as a part of life: "Is she asleep? Is she in
a spell? Or is she dead?" the woman asks—indifferent just like the other
observers.

This powerful story shows Jenny's illusions of love as all that gave meaning
to her life; even "what was done to her" leaves her with a smile. Just as the
stereotypical, submissive wife willingly assumes her role, so the sex object is
often viewed as inviting hers. In "Rima the Bird Girl," Rona Jaffe shows how a
highly educated woman can time after time give herself to a man who uses
and discards her; all her education and sophistication have told Rima what Jenny
innocently knows—that her role is to please men. As she goes from one liaison
to another, it is apparent that the price of giving herself is not to have a self;
she can only play roles. Similarly, Sergius O'Shaugnessy, in Mailer's "The Time
of Her Time," tries to find an identity for himself, a meaning to life, through
sexual conquest. His determination to bring Denise to orgasm is not because of
any pleasure that either of them might derive but from the necessity to "prove"
himself. When Denise has the last word at the end of the story, the reader is
reminded of the fate of the knife expert in the first part of the story for whom
one defeat is the end of his reign as champion. In spite of the numbers of
women Sergius' "avenger" has conquered, this one loss symbolically means the
loss of his manhood and of his attempt to find meaning in life.

The implication in all the stories in this section is that man's use of woman
is inevitable—that it is part of woman's nature to be a victim and part of man's to
prove himself by asserting his sexual power. Alberto Moravia's "The Chase"
shows that the image of man as pursuer and hunter is not universal. The parallel
between his boyhood repugnance at killing a bird and his refusal to deny his
wife her freedom emphasizes the protagonist's reluctance to play the usual
masculine role. He sees that in betraying him for a lover his wife is fulfilling her
own needs, not denying his masculinity. His decision to allow her freedom is
a denial of the double standard and an affirmation of her status as a person equal
to himself. He would find himself diminished if he asserted his will at the
expense of her freedom. Moravia's hero is quite different from the Prince of
Love in Blake's poem, who imprisons his beloved in a golden cage and mocks
her loss of liberty; but both Moravia and Blake let us see that from the woman's
point of view, sexual captivity is dehumanizing. Ultimately, to reduce women
to sex objects imperils the humanity of men as well.

Irwin Shaw

(b. 1913) Born in New York, Irwin Shaw has lived much of his adult life abroad. He has written radio and movie scripts as well as many plays, novels, and short stories. His best-known novel is The Young Lions, *and his latest collection of short stories is* Love on a Dark Street.

The Girls in Their Summer Dresses

Fifth Avenue was shining in the sun when they left the Brevoort. The sun was warm, even though it was February, and everything looked like Sunday morning—the buses and the well-dressed people walking slowly in couples and the quiet buildings with the windows closed.

Michael held Frances' arm tightly as they walked toward Washington Square in the sunlight. They walked lightly, almost smiling, because they had slept late and had a good breakfast and it was Sunday. Michael unbuttoned his coat and let it flap around him in the mild wind.

"Look out," Frances said as they crossed Eighth Street. "You'll break your neck."

Michael laughed and Frances laughed with him.

"She's not so pretty," Frances said. "Anyway, not pretty enough to take a chance of breaking your neck."

Michael laughed again. "How did you know I was looking at her?"

Frances cocked her head to one side and smiled at her husband under the brim of her hat. "Mike, darling," she said.

"O.K.," he said. "Excuse me."

Frances patted his arm lightly and pulled him along a little faster toward Washington Square. "Let's not see anybody all day," she said. "Let's just hang around with each other. You and me. We're always up to our neck in people, drinking their Scotch or drinking our Scotch; we only see each other in bed. I want to go out with my husband all day long. I want him to talk only to me and listen only to me."

"What's to stop us?" Michael asked.

"The Stevensons. They want us to drop by around one o'clock and they'll drive us into the country."

"The cunning Stevensons," Mike said. "Transparent. They can whistle. They can go driving in the country by themselves."

"Is it a date?"

"It's a date."

Frances leaned over and kissed him on the tip of the ear.

"Darling," Michael said, "this is Fifth Avenue."

"Let me arrange a program," Frances said. "A planned Sunday in New York for a young couple with money to throw away."

"Go easy."

"First let's go to the Metropolitan Museum of Art," Frances suggested, because Michael had said during the week he wanted to go. "I haven't been there in three years and there're at least ten pictures I want to see again. Then we can take the bus down to Radio City and watch them skate. And later we'll go down to Cavanaugh's and get a steak as big as a blacksmith's apron, with a bottle of wine, and after that there's a French picture at the Filmarte that everybody says—say, are you listening to me?"

"Sure," he said. He took his eyes off the hatless girl with the dark hair, cut dancer-style like a helmet, who was walking past him.

"That's the program for the day," Frances said flatly. "Or maybe you'd just rather walk up and down Fifth Avenue."

"No," Michael said. "Not at all."

"You always look at other women," Frances said. "Everywhere. Every damned place we go."

"No, darling," Michael said, "I look at everything. God gave me eyes and I look at women and men and subway excavations and moving pictures and the little flowers of the field. I casually inspect the universe."

"You ought to see the look in your eye," Frances said, "as you casually inspect the universe on Fifth Avenue."

"I'm a happily married man." Michael pressed her elbow tenderly. "Example for the whole twentieth century—Mr. and Mrs. Mike Loomis. Hey, let's have a drink," he said, stopping.

"We just had breakfast."

"Now listen, darling," Mike said, choosing his words with care, "it's a nice day and we both felt good and there's no reason why we have to break it up. Let's have a nice Sunday."

"All right. I don't know why I started this. Let's drop it. Let's have a good time."

They joined hands consciously and walked without talking among the baby carriages and the old Italian men in their Sunday clothes and the young women with Scotties in Washington Square Park.

"At least once a year everyone should go to the Metropolitan Museum of Art," Frances said after a while, her tone a good imitation of the tone she had used at breakfast and at the beginning of their walk. "And it's nice on Sunday. There're a lot of people looking at the pictures and you get the feeling maybe Art isn't on the decline in New York City, after all—"

"I want to tell you something," Michael said very seriously. "I have not touched another woman. Not once. In all the five years."

"All right," Frances said.

"You believe that, don't you?"

"All right."

They walked between the crowded benches, under the scrubby city-park trees.

"I try not to notice it," Frances said, "but I feel rotten inside, in my stomach, when we pass a woman and you look at her and I see that look in your eye and that's the way you looked at me the first time. In Alice Maxwell's house. Standing there in the living room, next to the radio, with a green hat on and all those people."

"I remember the hat," Michael said.

"The same look," Frances said. "And it makes me feel bad. It makes me feel terrible."

"Sh-h-h, please, darling, sh-h-h."

"I think I would like a drink now," Frances said.

They walked over to a bar on Eighth Street, not saying anything, Michael automatically helping her over curbstones and guiding her past automobiles. They sat near a window in the bar and the sun streamed in and there was a small, cheerful fire in the fireplace. A little Japanese waiter came over and put down some pretzels and smiled happily at them.

"What do you order after breakfast?" Michael asked.

"Brandy, I suppose," Frances said.

"Courvoisier," Michael told the waiter. "Two Courvoisiers."

The waiter came with the glasses and they sat drinking the brandy in the sunlight. Michael finished half his and drank a little water.

"I look at women," he said. "Correct. I don't say it's wrong or right. I look at them. If I pass them on the street and I don't look at them, I'm fooling you, I'm fooling myself."

"You look at them as though you want them," Frances said, playing with her brandy glass. "Every one of them."

"In a way," Michael said, speaking softly and not to his wife, "in a way that's true. I don't do anything about it, but it's true."

"I know it. That's why I feel bad."

"Another brandy," Michael called. "Waiter, two more brandies."

He sighed and closed his eyes and rubbed them gently with his fingertips. "I love the way women look. One of the things I like best about New York is the

battalions of women. When I first came to New York from Ohio that was the
first thing I noticed, the million wonderful women, all over the city. I walked
around with my heart in my throat."

"A kid," Frances said. "That's a kid's feeling."

"Guess again," Michael said. "Guess again. I'm older now. I'm a man getting
near middle age, putting on a little fat and I still love to walk along Fifth
Avenue at three o'clock on the east side of the street between Fiftieth and Fifty-
seventh Streets. They're all out then, shopping, in their furs and their crazy hats,
everything all concentrated from all over the world into seven blocks—the best
furs, the best clothes, the handsomest women, out to spend money and feeling
good about it."

The Japanese waiter put the two drinks down, smiling with great happiness.
"Everything is all right?" he asked.

"Everything is wonderful," Michael said.

"If it's just a couple of fur coats," Frances said, "and forty-five-dollar hats—"

"It's not the fur coats. Or the hats. That's just the scenery for that particular
kind of woman. Understand," he said, "you don't have to listen to this."

"I want to listen."

"I like the girls in the offices. Neat, with their eyeglasses, smart, chipper,
knowing what everything is about. I like the girls on Forty-fourth Street at lunchtime, the actresses, all dressed up on nothing a week. I like the salesgirls in the
stores, paying attention to you first because you're a man, leaving lady customers
waiting. I got all this stuff accumulated in me because I've been thinking about
it for ten years and now you've asked for it and here it is."

"Go ahead," Frances said.

"When I think of New York City, I think of all the girls on parade in the
city. I don't know whether it's something special with me or whether every man
in the city walks around with the same feeling inside him, but I feel as though
I'm at a picnic in this city. I like to sit near the women in the theatres, the
famous beauties who've taken six hours to get ready and look it. And the young
girls at the football games, with the red cheeks, and when the warm weather
comes, the girls in their summer dresses." He finished his drink. "That's the
story."

Frances finished her drink and swallowed two or three times extra. "You
say you love me?"

"I love you."

"I'm pretty, too," Frances said. "As pretty as any of them."

"You're beautiful," Michael said.

"I'm good for you," Frances said, pleading. "I've made a good wife, a good
housekeeper, a good friend. I'd do any damn thing for you."

"I know," Michael said. He put his hand out and grasped hers.

"You'd like to be free to—" Frances said.

"Sh-h-h."

"Tell the truth." She took her hand away from under his.

Michael flicked the edge of his glass with his finger. "O.K.," he said gently.
"Sometimes I feel I would like to be free."

"Well," Frances said, "any time you say."

"Don't be foolish." Michael swung his chair around to her side of the table and patted her thigh.

She began to cry silently into her handkerchief, bent over just enough so that nobody else in the bar would notice. "Someday," she said, crying, "you're going to make a move."

Michael didn't say anything. He sat watching the bartender slowly peel a lemon.

"Aren't you?" Frances asked harshly. "Come on, tell me. Talk. Aren't you?"

"Maybe," Michael said. He moved his chair back again. "How the hell do I know?"

"You know," Frances persisted. "Don't you know?"

"Yes," Michael said after a while, "I know."

Frances stopped crying then. Two or three snuffles into the handkerchief and she put it away and her face didn't tell anything to anybody. "At least do me one favor," she said.

"Sure."

"Stop talking about how pretty this woman is or that one. Nice eyes, nice breasts, a pretty figure, good voice." She mimicked his voice. "Keep it to yourself. I'm not interested."

Michael waved to the waiter. "I'll keep it to myself," he said.

Frances flicked the corners of her eyes. "Another brandy," she told the waiter.

"Two," Michael said.

"Yes, Ma'am, yes, sir," said the waiter, backing away.

Frances regarded Michael coolly across the table. "Do you want me to call the Stevensons?" she asked. "It'll be nice in the country."

"Sure," Michael said. "Call them."

She got up from the table and walked across the room toward the telephone. Michael watched her walk, thinking what a pretty girl, what nice legs.

Colette

(1873–1954) Colette is the pen name of Sidonie Gabrielle Claudine Colette, French novelist, who collaborated with her husband under the pen name Colette Willy in writing the Claudine *books. She is best known for her works about women, especially* Chéri *and* Gigi. *Many of her works have been translated into English.*

The Patriarch

Between the ages of sixteen and twenty-five, Achille, my half-brother by blood—but wholly and entirely my brother by affection, choice and likeness—was extremely handsome. Little by little, he became less so as a result of leading the hard life of a country doctor in the old days; a life which lacked all comfort and repose. He wore out his boot-soles as much as the shoes of his grey mare; he went out by day and he went out by night, going to bed too tired to want any supper. In the night he would be woken up by the call of a peasant banging his fists on the outer door and pulling the bell. Then he would get up, put on his woollen pants, his clothes and his great plaid-lined overcoat and Charles, the man-of-all-work, would harness the grey mare, another remarkable creature.

I have never known anything so proud and so willing as that grey mare. In the stable, by the light of the lantern, my brother would always find her standing up and ready for the worst. Her short, lively, well-set ears would enquire: "Chateauvieux? Montrenard? The big climb up the hill? Seventeen kilometres to get there and as many on the way back?" She would set off a little stiffly, her head lowered. During the examination, the confinement, the amputation or the dressing, she leant her little forehead against the farmhouse doors so as to hear better what *He* was saying. I could swear that she knew by heart the bits of *Le Roi d'Ys* and the Pastoral Symphony, the scraps of operas and the Schubert songs *He* sang to keep himself company.

Isolated, sacrificed to his profession, this twenty-six-year-old doctor of half a century ago had only one resource. Gradually he had to forge himself a spirit which hoped for nothing except to live and enable his family to live too. Happily, his professional curiosity never left him. Neither did that other curiosity which both of us inherited from our mother. When, in my teens, I used to accompany him on his rounds, the two of us would often stop and get out to pick a bunch of bluebells or to gather mushrooms. Sometimes we would watch a wheeling buzzard or upset the dignity of a little lizard by touching it with a finger: the lizard would draw up its neck like an offended lady and give a lisping hiss, rather like a child who has lost its first front teeth. We would carefully detach butterfly chrysalises from branches and holes in walls and put them in little boxes of fine sand to await the miracle of the metamorphosis.

The profession of country doctor demanded a great deal of a man about half a century ago. Fresh from the Medical School in Paris, my brother's first patient was a well-sinker who had just had one leg blown off by an explosion of dynamite. The brand-new surgeon came out of this difficult ordeal with honour but white-lipped, trembling all over and considerably thinner from the amount he had sweated. He pulled himself together by diving into the canal between the tall clumps of flowering rushes.

Achille taught me to fill and to stick together the two halves of antipyrine capsules, to use the delicate scales with the weights which were mere thin slips of copper. In those days, the country doctor had a licence to sell certain pharmaceutical products outside a four-kilometre radius of the town. Meagre profits, if one considers that a "consultation" cost the consultant three francs plus twenty sous a kilometre. From time to time, the doctor pulled out a tooth, also for three francs. And what little money there was came in slowly and sometimes not at all.

"Why not sue them?" demanded the chemist. "What's the law for?"

Whatever it was for, it was not for his patients. My brother made no reply but turned his greenish-blue eyes away towards the flat horizon. My eyes are the same colour but not so beautiful and not so deeply set.

I was fifteen or sixteen; the age of great devotions, of vocations. I wanted to become a woman doctor. My brother would summon me for a split lip or a deep, bleeding cut and have recourse to my slender girl's fingers. Eagerly, I would set to work to knot the threads of the stitches in the blood which leapt so impetuously out of the vein. In the morning, Achille set off too early for me to be able to accompany him. But in the afternoon I would sit on his left in the trap and hold the mare's reins. Every month he had the duty of inspecting all the babies in the region and he tried to drop in unexpectedly on their wet or dry nurses. Those expeditions used to ruin his appetite. How many babies we found alone in an empty house, tied to their fetid cradles with handkerchiefs and safety-pins, while their heedless guardians worked in the fields. Some of them would see the trap in the distance and come running up, out of breath.

"I was only away for a moment." "I was changing the goat's picket." "I was chasing the cow who'd broken loose."

Hard as his life was, Achille held out for more than twenty-five years,

seeking rest for his spirit only in music. In his youth he was surprised when he
first came up against the peaceful immorality of country life, the desire which is
born and satisfied in the depths of the ripe grass or between the warm flanks
of sleeping cattle. Paris and the Latin Quarter had not prepared him for so much
amorous knowledge, secrecy and variety. But impudence was not lacking either,
at least in the case of the girls who came boldly to his weekly surgery declaring
that they had not "seen" since they got their feet wet two months ago, pulling a
drowned hen out of a pond.

"That's fine!" my brother would say, after his examination. "I'm going to
give you a prescription."

He watched for the look of pleasure and contempt and the joyful reddening
of the cheek and wrote out the prescription agreed between doctor and chemist:
"*Mica panis*, two pills to be taken after each meal." The remedy might avert
or, at least, delay the intervention of "the woman who knew about herbs".

One day, long before his marriage, he had an adventure which was only one
of many. With a basket on one arm and an umbrella on the other, a young
woman almost as tall as himself (he was nearly six foot two) walked into his
consulting-room. He found himself looking at someone like a living statue of the
young Republic; a fresh, magnificently built girl with a low brow, statuesque
features and a calm, severe expression.

"Doctor," she said, without a smile or a shuffle, "I think I'm three months
pregnant."

"Do you feel ill, Madame?"

"Mademoiselle. I'm eighteen. And I feel perfectly all right in every way."

"Well, then, Mademoiselle! You won't be needing me for another six
months."

"Pardon, Doctor. I'd like to be sure. I don't want to do anything foolish.
Will you please examine me?"

Throwing off the skirt, the shawl and the cottom chemise that came down
to her ankles, she displayed a body so majestic, so firm, so smoothly sheathed in
its skin that my brother never saw another to compare with it. He saw too that
this young girl, so eager to accuse herself, was a virgin. But she vehemently
refused to remain one any longer and went off victorious, her head high, her
basket on her arm and her woollen shawl knotted once more over her breasts.
The most she would admit was that, when she was digging potatoes on her
father's land over by the Hardon road, she had waited often and often to see the
grey mare and its driver go past and had said "Good-day" with her hand to call
him, but in vain.

She returned for "consultation". But, far more often, my brother went and
joined her in her field. She would watch him coming from afar, put down her
hoe, and, stooping, make her way under the branches of a little plantation of
pine-trees. From these almost silent encounters, a very beautiful child was born.
And I admit that I should be glad to see, even now, what his face is like. For
"Sido" confided to me, in very few words, one of those secrets in which she was
so rich.

"You know the child of that beautiful girl over at Hardon?" she said.

"Yes."

"She boasts about him to everyone. She's crazy with pride. She's a most unusual girl. A character. I've seen the child. Just once."

"What's he like?"

She made the gesture of rumpling a child's hair.

"Beautiful, of course. Such curls, such eyes. And such a mouth."

She coughed and pushed away the invisible curly head with both hands.

"The mouth most of all. Ah! I just couldn't. I went away. Otherwise I should have taken him."

However, everything in our neighbourhood was not so simple as this warm idyll, cradled on its bed of pine-needles, and these silent lovers who took no notice of the autumn mists or a little rain, for the grey mare lent them her blanket.

There is another episode of which I have a vivid and less touching memory. We used to refer to it as "The Monsieur Binard story". It goes without saying that I have changed the name of the robust, grizzled father of a family who came over on his bicycle at dusk, some forty-eight years ago, to ask my brother to go to his daughter's bedside.

"It's urgent," said the man, panting as he spoke. His breath reeked of red wine. "I am Monsieur Binard, of X . . ."

He made a sham exit, then thrust his head round the half-shut door and declared: "In my opinion, it'll be a boy."

My brother took his instrument case and the servant harnessed the grey mare.

It turned out indeed to be a boy and a remarkably fine and well-made one. But my brother's care and attention was mainly for the far too young mother, a dark girl with eyes like an antelope. She was very brave and kept crying out loudly, almost excitedly, like a child, "Ooh! . . . Ooh! I say! . . . Ooh, I never!" Round the bed bustled three slightly older antelopes while, in the ingle-nook, the impassive Monsieur Binard superintended the mulling of some red wine flavoured with cinnamon. In a dark corner of the clean, well-polished room, my brother noticed a wicker cradle with clean starched curtains. Monsieur Binard only left the fire and the copper basin to examine the new-born child as soon as it had been washed.

"It's a very fine child," Achille assured him.

"I've seen finer," said Monsieur Binard in a lordly way.

"Oh! Papa!" cried the three older antelopes.

"I know what I'm talking about," retorted Binard.

He raised a curtain of the cradle which my brother presumed empty but which was now shown to be entirely filled by a large child who had slept calmly through all the noise and bustle. One of the antelopes came over and tenderly drew the curtain down again.

His mission over, my brother drank the warm wine which he had well and truly earned and which the little newly-confined mother was sipping too. Already she was gay and laughing. Then he bowed to the entire long-eyed troop and went out, puzzled and worried. The earth was steaming with damp but, above the low fog, the bright dancing fire of the first stars announced the coming frost.

"Your daughter seems extremely young," said my brother. "Luckily, she's come through it well."

"She's strong. You needn't be afraid," said Monsieur Binard.

"How old is she?"

"Fifteen in four months' time."

"Fifteen! She was taking a big risk. What girls are! Do you know the . . . the creature who . . ."

Monsieur Binard made no reply other than slapping the hindquarters of the grey mare with the flat of his hand but he lifted his chin with such an obvious, such an intolerable expression of fatuity that my brother hastened his departure.

"If she has any fever, let me know."

"She won't," Monsieur Binard assured him with great dignity.

"So you know more about these things than I do?"

"No. But I know my daughters. I've four of them and you must have seen for yourself that there's not much wrong with them. I know them."

He said no more and ran his hand over his moustache. He waited till the grey mare had adroitly turned in the narrow courtyard, then he went back into his house.

Sido, my mother, did not like this story which she often turned over in her mind. Sometimes she spoke violently about Monsieur Binard, calling him bitterly "the corrupt widower", sometimes she let herself go off into commentaries for which afterwards she would blush.

"Their house is very well kept. The child of the youngest one has eyelashes as long as *that*. I saw her the other day, she was suckling her baby on the doorstep, it was enchanting. Whatever am I saying? It was abominable, of course, when one knows the facts."

She went off into a dream, impatiently untwisting the entangled steel chain and black cord from which hung her two pairs of spectacles.

"After all," she began again, "the ancient patriarchs . . ."

But she suddenly became aware that I was only fifteen and a half and she went no further.

Eudora Welty

(b. 1909) Through her many novels and short stories about family life in her native Mississippi, Eudora Welty has established herself as a major American author. She writes about ordinary people often caught in absurd situations and reveals through their colloquial speech deep, often mythological meanings. Her latest work is Losing Battles *(1970).*

At the Landing

The night that Jenny's grandfather died, he dreamed of high water.

He came in his dream and stood just outside the door of her room, his little chin that was like a chicken's clean breastbone tilting upwards.

"It has come," the old man said, and he made a complaint of it.

Jenny in her bed lay still, waking more still than in the sleep of a moment before.

"The river has come back. That Floyd came to tell me. The sun was shining full on the face of the church, and that Floyd came around it with his wrist hung with a great long catfish. 'It's coming,' he said. 'It's the river.' Oh, it came then! Like a head and arm. Like a horse. A mane of cedar trees tossing over the top. It has borne down, and it has closed us in. That Floyd was right."

He reached as if to lift an obstacle that he thought was stretched there—the bar that crossed the door in her mother's time. It seemed beyond his strength, she tried to cry out, and he came in through the doorway. The cord and tassel of his brocade robe—for he had put it on—seemed to weigh upon his fragile walking like a chain, and yet it could have been by inexorable will that he wore it, so set were his little steps, in such duty he dragged it.

"Like poor people who have learned to fly at last," he said, walking, dragging, the fine deprecation in his voice, "all the people in The Landing, all kinds and conditions of people, are gliding off and upward to darkness. The little mandolin that my daughter used to play—it's rising like a bubble, and filling with water."

"Grandpa!" cried Jenny, and then she was up and taking her grandfather by his tiny adamant shoulders. It was moonlight. She saw his open eyes. "Wake up, Grandpa!"

"That Floyd's catfish has gone loose and free," he said gently, as if breaking news to someone. "And all of a sudden, my dear—my dears, it took its river life back, and shining so brightly swam through the belfry of the church, and downstream." At that his mouth clamped tight shut.

She held out both arms and he fell trembling against her. With beating heart she carried him through the dark halls to his room and put him down into his bed. He lay there in the moonlight, which moved and crept across him as it would a little fallen withered leaf, and he never moved or spoke any more, but lay softly, as if he were floating, being carried away, drawn by the passing moon; and Jenny's heart beat on and on, sharp as birdsong in the night, under her breast, until day.

Under the shaggy bluff the bottomlands lay in a river of golden haze. The road dropped like a waterfall from the ridge to the town at its foot and came to a grassy end there. It was spring. One slowly moving figure that was a man with a fishing pole passed like a dreamer through the empty street and on through the trackless haze toward the river. The town was still called The Landing. The river had gone, three miles away, beyond sight and smell, beyond the dense trees. It came back only in flood, and boats ran over the houses.

Up the light-scattered hill, in the house with the galleries, the old man and his granddaughter had always lived. They were the people least seen in The Landing. The grandfather was too old, and the girl was too shy of the world, and they were both too good—the old ladies said—to come out, and so they stayed inside.

For all her life the shy Jenny could look, if she stayed in the parlor, back and forth between her mother's two paintings, "The Bird Fair" and "The Massacre at Fort Rosalie." Or if she went in the dining room she could walk around the table or sit on one after the other of eight needlepoint pieces, each slightly different, which her mother had worked and sewn to the chairs, or she could count the plates that stood on their rims in the closet. In the library she could circle an entirely bare floor and make up a dance to a song she made up, all silently, or gaze at the backs of the books without titles—books that had been on ships and in oxcarts and through fire and water, and were singed and bleached and swollen and shrunken, and arranged up high and nearly unreachable, like objects of beauty. Wherever she went she almost touched a prism. The house was full of prisms. They hung everywhere in the shadow of the halls and in the sunlight of the rooms, stirring under the hanging lights, dangling and circling where they were strung in the window curtains. They gave off the faintest of musical notes when air stirred in any room or when only herself passed by, and they touched. It was her way not to touch them herself, but to let the touch be magical, a stir of the curtain by the outer air, that would also make them rainbows. Vases with landscapes on them stood in the halls and were reflected endlessly rising in front of her when she passed quickly between the two mirrors. She might stop and touch all things, trace their little pictures with her finger, and put them back again; it was not forbidden; but her touch that dared not break would have been transparent as a spirit's on the objects. She was calm the way a child is calm, with never the calmness of a spirit. But like distant lightning that silently bathes a whole shimmering sky, one awareness was always trembling about her: one day she would be free to come and go. Nothing now held her in her own room, with the great wardrobe in which she had sometimes longed to hide, and the great box-like canopied bed and the little picture on the wall of her mother with upturned eyes. Jenny could go from room to room, and out at the door. But at the door her grandfather would call her back, with his little murmur.

At sunset the old man and his granddaughter would take their supper in the pavilion on the knoll, that had been a gazebo when the river ran before it. There a little breeze came all the way from the river still. All about the pavilion was an ancient circling thorny rose, like the initial letter in a poetry book. The cook came out and served with exaggerated dignity, as though she scolded in the house. A little picture might be preserved then in all their heads. The old man and the young girl looked across the round table leaf-shadowed under the busy black hands, and smiled by long habit at each other. But her grandfather could not look at her without speculation in his eyes, and the gaze that went so fondly between them held and stretched tight the memory of Jenny's mother. It seemed strange that her mother had been dead now for so many years and yet the wild desire that had torn her seemed still fresh and still a small thing. It was a desire to get to Natchez. People said Natchez was a nice little town on Saturdays with a crowd filling it and moving around.

The grandfather stirred his black coffee and smiled at Jenny. He deprecated raving simply as raving, as a force of Nature and so beneath notice or mention. And yet—even now, too late—if Jenny could plead . . . ! In a heat wave one called the cook to bring a fan, and in his daughter's first raving he rang a bell and told the cook to take her off and sit by her until she had done with it, but in the end she died of it. But Jenny could not plead for her.

Her grandfather, frail as a little bird, would say when it was time to go in. He would rise slowly in the brocade gown he wore to study in, and put his weight, which was the terrifying weight of a claw, on Jenny's arm. Jenny was obedient to her grandfather and would have been obedient to anybody, to a stranger in the street if there could be one. She never performed any act, even a small act, for herself, she would not touch the prisms. It might seem that nothing began in her own heart.

Nothing ever happened, to be seen from the gazebo, except that Billy Floyd went through the town. He was almost unknown, and one to himself. If he came at all, he would come at this time of day. In the long shadows below they could see his figure with the gleaming fish he carried move clear as a candle over the road that he had to himself, and out to the blue distance. In The

Landing, every person that moved was watched out of sight, and it made a little pause in every life. And if in each day a moment of hope must come, in Jenny's day the moment was when the rude wild Floyd walked through The Landing carrying the big fish he had caught.

Under the blue sky, skirting the ravine, a half-ring of twenty cedar trees stood leading to the cemetery, their bleached trunks the colors of red and white roses. Jenny, given permission, would walk up there to visit the grave of her mother.

The cemetery was a dark shelf above the town, on the site of the old landing place when the ships docked from across the world a hundred years ago, and its brink was marked by an old table-like grave with its top ajar where the woodbine grew. Everywhere there, the hanging moss and the upthrust stones were in that strange graveyard shade where, by the light they give, the moss seems made of stone, and the stone of moss.

On one of the days, while she sat there on a stile, Jenny looked across the ravine and there was Floyd, standing still in a sunny pasture. She could watch between the grapevines, which hung and held back like ropes on either side to clear her view. Floyd had a head of straight light-colored hair and it hung over his forehead, for he never was near a comb. He stood facing her in a tall squared posture of silence and rest, while a rusty-red horse that belonged to the Lockharts cropped loudly beside him in the wild-smelling pasture.

It was said by the old ladies that he slept all morning for he fished all night. Stiff and stern, Jenny sat there with her feet planted just so on the step below, in the posture of a child who is appalled at the stillness and unsurrender of the still and unsurrendering world.

At last she sighed, and when she took up her skirt to go, as if she were dreaming she saw Floyd coming across the pasture toward her. When he reached the ravine and leaped down into it with widespread arms as though he jumped into something dangerous, she stood still on the stile to watch. He moved up near to her now, his feet on the broken ferns at the spring. The wind whipped his hair, almost making a noise.

"Go back," she said. She wanted to watch him a while longer first, before he got to her.

He stopped and looked full at her, his strong neck bending to one side as if yielding in pleasure to the wind. His arms went down and his fists opened. But for her, his eyes were as bright and unconsumed as stars up in the sky. Then she wanted to catch him and see him close, but not to touch him. He stood watching her, though, as if to prevent it. They were as still and rigid as two mocking-birds that were about to strike their beaks and dance.

She waited, but he smiled, and then knelt and cupped both hands to his face in the spring water. He drank for a long time, while she stood there with her skirt whipping in the wind, and waited on him to see how long he could drink without lifting his face. When he had drunk that much, he went back to the field and threw himself yawning down into the grass. The grass was so deep there that she could see only the one arm flung out in the torn sleeve, straight, sun-blacked and motionless.

The day she watched him in the woods, she felt it come to her dimly that her innocence had left her, since she could watch his. She could only sink down onto the step of the stile, and lay her heavy forehead in her hand. But if innocence had left, she still did not know what was to come. She would wait and see him come awake.

But he slept and slept like the dead, and defeated her. She went to her grandfather and left Floyd sleeping.

Another day, they walked for a little near together, each picking some berry or leaf to hold in the mouth, on their opposite sides of the little spring. The pasture, the sun and the grazing horse were on his side, the graves on hers, and they each looked across at the other's. The whole world seemed filled with butterflies. At each step they took, two black butterflies over the flowers were whirring just alike, suspended in the air, one circling the other rhythmically, or both moving from side to side in a gentle wave-like way, one above the other. They were blue-black and moving their wings faster than Jenny's eye could follow, always together, like each other's shadows, beautiful each one with the other. Jenny could see to start with that no kiss had ever brought love tenderly enough from mouth to mouth.

Jenny and Floyd stopped and looked for a little while at all the butterflies and they never touched each other. When Jenny did touch Floyd, touch his sleeve, he started.

He went alert in the field like a listening animal. The horse came near and when he touched it, stood with lifted ears beside him, then broke away. But over all The Landing there was not a sound that she could hear. It could only be that Floyd missed nothing in the world, and could hear innumerable outward things. He suddenly flung up his head. She knew he was smiling. And a smile was always a barrier.

She said his name, for she was so close by. It was the first time.

He stayed motionless, and she knew that he lived apart in delight. That could make a strange glow fall over the field where he was, and the world go black for her, left behind. She felt terrified, as if at a pitiless thing.

Floyd lifted his foot and stamped on the ground, and held out his careless arms to catch the horse he had excited. Then he was jumping on its bare back and riding into a gallop, shouting to frighten and amaze whoever listened. She threw herself down into the grass. Never had she known that the Lockhart horse could run like that. Floyd went at a racing speed and he seemed somehow in his tattered shirt—as she watched from beneath her arm—to stream with the wind, and he circled the steep field three times, and with flying yellow hair and a diminishing shout rode up into the woods.

If she could have followed and found him then, she would have started on foot. But she knew what she would find when she would come to him. She would find him equally real with herself—and could not touch him then. As she was living and inviolate, so of course was he, and when that gave him delight, how could she bring a question to him? She walked in the woods and around the graves in it, and knew about love, how it would have a different story in the world if it could lose the moral knowledge of a mystery that is in the other heart. Nothing in Floyd frightened her that drew her near, but at once she had the knowledge come to her that a fragile mystery was in everyone and in herself, since there it was in Floyd, and that whatever she did, she would be bound to ride over and hurt, and the secrecy of life was the terror of it. When Floyd rode the red horse, she lay in the grass. He might even have jumped across her. But the vaunting and prostration of love told her nothing—nothing at all.

The very next day Jenny waited on the stile and she saw Floyd come walking up the road in the morning, with drenched hair. He might have come and found her, but he came to the Lockhart house first.

The Lockhart house stood between two of the empty stretches along the road. It was wide, low, and twisted. Its roof, held up at the corners by the two chimneys, sagged like a hammock, and was mended with bark and small colored signs. The black high-water mark made a belt around the house and that alone seemed to tighten it and hold it together. Floyd stood gazing in at the doorway, as if what might not come out? And it was a beautiful doorway to see, with its fanlight and its sidelights, though they were blind with silt. The door was shut and the squirrels were asleep on the floor of the long cage across the front wall. Under the forward-tilting porch the clay-colored hens were sitting in twos in the old rowboat. And while Floyd looked, out came Mag.

And the next thing, he was playing with Mag Lockhart, that was an albino. Mag's short white hair would stream out from her head when she crouched nodding over her flowers in the yard, tending them with a jack-knife all day, and she would give a splitting laugh to see anyone come. Jenny from the stile watched them wrestle and play. The treadmill ran under the squirrels' quick feet.

Mag's voice came a long distance through the still day. "You are not!" "It is not!" "I am not!" she would scream, and she would jump away.

Floyd would turn on his heel and whirl old Mag off the ground. Mag ran and she snapped at him, she struggled and she crackled like a green wood fire, and he laughed and caught her. She pointed and sent him for the water, and he went and clattered and banged the buckets for her at the well until she begged him to stop. He went straight off and old Mag sat down on her front steps with the hens and rubbed at her flame-pink arms.

And then suddenly Mag was gone.

Jenny put her hands over her forehead, and then rubbed at her own arms. She believed Mag had been there, because she had felt whatever Mag had felt. If this was a vision, it was the first. And it did not frighten her; she knew it only came because she had felt what was in another heart besides her own. But it had been Mag's heart that grew clear to her, while Floyd ran away.

She lay down in the grass, which whispered in her ear. If desperation were only a country, it would be at the bottom of the well. She wanted to get there, to arrive graceful and airy in some strange other country and walk along its

level land beneath its secret sky. She thought she could see herself, fleet as a
mirror-image, rising up in a breath of astonished farewell and walking to
the well of old Mag. It was built so that it had steps like a stile. She saw herself
walk up them, stand on top, look about, and then go into the dark passage.

But my grandfather, she thought, even while she sank so deeply, will call
me back. I will have to go back. He will ask me if I have put flowers on my
mother's grave. And she looked over at the stone on the grave of her mother,
with her married name of Lockhart cut into it.

She clutched the thing in her hand, a blade of grass, and held on. There she
was, sitting up in the sun, with the blade of grass stretched between her thumbs
and held to her mouth, for the calling back that was in the world. She blew
on the grass. It made a thoughtless reedy sound, and she blew again.

2 The morning after her grandfather's death, Jenny put on a starched white
dress and went down the hill into The Landing. A little crocheted bag hung by a
ribbon over her wrist, and she had taken a nickel to put in it. Her good black
strapped slippers moved lightly in the dust. She was going to tell the news of
her grandfather, whom the old ladies had said would die suddenly—like *that*. And
looking about with every step she took, she saw what a lonesome place it was
for all of this to happen in.

She passed a house that only the mice inhabited. She passed a black boarded-
up store where an owl used to live and maintain its nocturnal habits. And there,
a young calf belonging to the Lockharts used to nose through the grassy rooms,
before the walls were carried away by the Negroes and burned in a winter for
firewood. In front of the row of Negro cabins was one long fence, made of
lumber from old boats, built there to delay the river for one more moment when
it came, the same as they would have delayed a giant bent on destruction by
some foolish pretext.

Across the end of the road, crumbling under her eyes, was a two-story
building with a remnant of gallery, and that was Jenny's destination. The store
and the postoffice were in the one used room. Across the tin awning hung the
moss icicles with which the postmaster had decorated for Christmas. Over the
door was the shriveled mistletoe, and the gun that had shot it down still
standing in the corner. Tipped back against the front wall sat five old men in
their chairs, with one holding the white cat. On the step, Son Alford was
playing his mandolin that had been Jenny's mother's and given away. He was
singing his fast song.

> Ain't she cute
> Ain't she smart
> Don't look twice
> It'll break my heart
> Everybody loves my gal.

All nodded to her, but they knew she was not supposed to speak to them.

She went inside, and the first thing she saw was Billy Floyd. He was standing in the back of the room with the postmaster saying to him, "Reckon we're going to have water this year?"

She had never seen the man between walls and under a roof and somehow it made him a different man after the one in the field. He stood in the dim and dingy store with a row of filmy glass lamps and a pair of boots behind his head, and there was something close, gathering-close, and used and worldly about him.

"That slime, that's just as slick! You know how a fish is, I expect," the postmaster was saying affably to them both, just as if they were in any way together. "That's the way a house is, been under water. It's a sight to see those niggers try to clean this place out, falling down to slide from here to the front door and back. You have to get the slime off right away too, or you never can. Sure would make the best paint in the world." He laughed.

There was something handled and used about Floyd, something strong as an odor, the odor of the old playing cards that the old men of The Landing shuffled every day over their table in the street.

"Reckon we're going to have water this year?" the postmaster asked again. He looked from one of them to the other.

Floyd said nothing, he only held a penny. For a moment Jenny thought he was going to drop his high head at being trapped in the confined place, with her between him and the door, which would be the same as telling it out, before a third person, that he could be known in time if he were caught and cornered in a little store.

"What would you like today, Miss Jenny?" asked the postmaster. "Posy seeds?"

But she could not think what she would like. She held her little bag quite still, the strings drawn tight.

All the time, Floyd was giving her a glaring look.

"Well, it makes you think sometimes, to see the water come over all the world," said the postmaster. "I took everything I could out of here last time. Then I come down from the hill and peeked in the door and what did I see? My showcases commencing to float loose. What a sight that did make! I wouldn't have thought I sold some of them things. Carried the showcases out on the hill, but nowhere much to take them. Could you believe I could carry everything out of my store in twenty minutes but my safe? Couldn't lift that. Left the door to it open and went off and left it. So as it wouldn't rust shut, Floyd, Miss Jenny. Took me a long time to scrape the river out of that thing."

All three waited a moment, and then the postmaster spoke again in a softer, intimate voice, smilingly. "Some stranger lost through here says, 'Why don't you all move away?' Move away?" He laughed, and pointed a finger at Jenny. "Did you hear that, Miss Jenny—why don't we move away? Because we live here, don't we, Miss Jenny?"

Then she knew it was a challenge Floyd made with his hard look, and she lost to him. She walked out and left him where he held his solid stand. And when the postmaster had pointed his finger at her, she remembered that she was never to speak to Billy Floyd, by the order of her grandfather.

Outside the door, she stopped still. The weight of the nickel swung in her little bag, and she felt as if she had forgotten Doomsday. She took a step back toward the challenging Floyd. Then in a kind of haste she whispered to the five old men, separately, and even to Son Alford, and each time nearer to tears for her grandfather that died in the night. Then they gathered round her, and hurried her to the old women, and so back home.

But Floyd's face glared before her eyes all the way, it was like something in her vision that kept her from seeing. It was brighter than the glare of death. He might have been buying a box of matches with his penny, which was what his going cost. He would go. The danger of flood was her grandfather's dream, and the postmaster's storekeeper wit. These were bright days and clear nights; and so Floyd would not wait long in The Landing. That was what the old ladies said, and asked that their words be marked.

But on a later day, Jenny took a walk and met Floyd by the little river that came out of the spring and went to the Mississippi beyond. She sat down and made a clover chain that would never get long because the cloverheads slipped out, and while she made it she kept looking with assuring looks into his illuminated eyes that went over the landscape and searched the sky for clouds. She could hold his look for a moment and then it would get away. She did not say a thing to him, for nobody can say, "It is a heavy heart that makes me clumsy." Nobody can say anything so true and apologetic. Nobody can say, "Forgive the heavy heart that loves more than the tongue can say or the hands can do. Look back at me everytime I look at you and never feel pity, for what my heart holds this minute is better than what you offer the least bit less." Her eyes were telling him this but if he knew it or felt a threat in it, he never gave a sign. "My heart loves more than I can say or do, but feel no pity, only have a little vision too, of all clumsiness fallen away." She guessed that all grace belongs to the future. But he never had anything to say to her thought or her guess. He stood above her with his feet planted down and looked out over the landscape from within that moment. Level with him now, all The Landing spread under his eyes. Not knowing the world around, she could not know how The Landing looked set down in it. All she knew was that he would leave it when his patience gave out, and that this little staving moment by the river would reach its limit and go first.

Her eyes descended slowly, as if adorned with flowers, from his light blowing hair and his gathering brows down, down him, past his clever hands that caught and trapped so delicately away from her side, softly down to the ground that was a sandy shore. A hidden mussel was blowing bubbles like a spring through the sand where his boot was teasing the water. It was the little pulse of bubbles and not himself or herself that was the moment for her then; and he could have already departed and she could have already wept, and it would have been the same, as she stared at the little fountain rising so gently out of the shimmering sand. A clear love is *in the world*—this came to her as insistently as the mussel's bubbles through the water. There it was, existing there where they came and were beside it now. It is in the bubble in the water in the river, and it has its own changing and its mysteries of days and nights, and it does not care how we come and go.

But when the moment ended, he went. And as soon as he left The Landing, the rain began to fall.

Each day the storm clouds were opening like great purple flowers and pouring out their dark thunder. Each nightfall, the storm was laid down on their houses like a burden the day had carried. The noise of rain, of the gullies filling, of the always the same darkness. Fires burned some where, but in the distance, red and blue.

"I . . ." she began, and stopped.

He scowled.

She knew at once that there was nothing in her life past or even now in the flood that would make anything to tell. He already knew that he had saved her life, for that had taken up his time in the time of danger. Yet she might confess it. It came to her lips. He scowled on. Still, it was not any kind of confession that she would finally wish to make. She would like to tell him some strange beautiful thing, if she could speak at all, something to make him speak. Communication would be telling something that is all new, so as to have more of the new told back. The dream of that held her spellbound, with the things possible that hung in the air like clouds over the world, and she smiled in pure belief, for they were beautiful.

"I . . ." She looked softly at him as if from a distance down a little road or a little tether he sent her on.

He took hold of her, put her out of the boat into a little place he made that was dry and green and smelled good, and she went to sleep. After a time that could have been long or short, she thought she heard him say, "Wake up."

When her eyes were open and clear upon him, he violated her and still he was without care or demand and as gay as if he were still clanging the bucket at the well. With the same thoughtlessness of motion, that was a kind of grace, he next speared a side of wild meat from an animal he had killed and had ready in his boat, and cooked it over a fire he had burning on the ground. All the water lapped around. Over its sound she whispered something, but his movement and his task went on firmly about his leaping fire. People who had been there in other floods had put their initials on the tree. Her words came a little louder and in shyness she changed them from words of love to words of wishing, but still he did not look around. "I wish you and I could be far away. I wish for a little house." But ideas of any different thing from what was in his circle of fire might never have reached his ears, for all the attention he paid to her remarks.

He had fishes ready too, wrapped and cooking in a hole scooped in the ground. When she ate it was in obedience to him, though he did not say "Eat" or say anything, he only smiled at the fire, and for him it was all a taking freely

of what was free. She knew from him nevertheless that what people ate in the
world was earth, river, wildness and litheness, fire and ashes. People took the
fresh death and the hot fire into their mouths and got their own life. She
ate greedily as long as he ate, and took what he took. She ate eagerly, looking
up at him while her teeth bit, to show him herself, her proud hunger, as if
to please and flatter him with her original and now lost starvation. But she could
make him neither sorry nor proud. When she was sick afterwards, he walked
away and waited apart from her shame, as he had left her in his delight.

The dream of love, that made her hold as still in her life as if she heard
music, had never carried her yet to the first country of which it told. But there
was a country, as surely as there was herself. When she saw the moon come up
that night and grow bright as it went above the flood and the boats in it, she
was not as sorrowful as she might have been, now that they floated so high, that
no threads hung down from the moon, no tender ladder all at once caught
light and drifted down. There was a need in all dreams for something to stay far,
far away, never to torment with the rest, and the bright moon now was that.

3 When the water was down, Jenny went back below and Floyd went down the
river in his boat. They parted with the clumsiest of touches. Down through the
exhausted and still dripping trees she made her way, again behind Mag, following
the tracks and signs of others, and the mud sticking to her. Ashes sifted through
the air and she saw them touch her skin but did not feel them. She came to
the stile where she could look at the world below. The sun was going down and
a wind blew following after the river, and the little town had turned the color
of river water and the trees in their shame of refuse rattled like yellow pebbles
and the houses sank below them scuffed and small. The smoky band of woods
that lay in the distance toward the retreating river still seemed to waver and slide.

In The Landing the houses had turned a little, like people whose skirts are
pulled. Where the front of the Lockhart house had been pulled away, the
furniture, that had been carried out of the corners by the river and rocked about,
stood in the middle of the floor and showed down its back the curly yellow
grain, like its long hair. One old store had been carried clean away, after it was
closed so long, and in its foundations were the old men standing around poking
for money with little sticks. Money could have fallen through the cracks for
many years. Fifteen cents and twenty cents and a Spanish piece were found, and
the old fellows poking with their sticks were laughing like women.

Jenny came to her house. It stood as before, except that in the yellow and
windy light it seemed to draw its galleries to itself, to return to its cave of night
and trees, crouched like a child going backwards to the womb.

But once inside, she took one step and was into a whole new ecstasy, an
ecstasy of cleaning, to wash the river out. She ran as if driven, carrying buckets
and mops. She scrubbed and pried and shook the river away. Even the pages
of books seemed to have been opened and written on again by muddy fingers.
In the long days when she stretched and dried white curtains and sheets, rubbed

the rust off knives and made them shine, and wiped the dark river from all the prisms, she forgot even love, to clean.

But the shock of love had brought a trembling to her fingers that made her drop what she touched, and made her stumble on the stair, though all the time she was driven on. And when the house was clean again she felt that there was no place to hide in it, not one room. She even opened the small door of her mother's last room, but when she looked in she thought of her mother who was kept guard on there, who struggled unweariedly and all in loneliness, and it was not a hiding place.

If in all The Landing she could have found a place to feel alone and out of sight, she would have gone there. One old lady or another would always call to her when she went by, to tell her something, and if she walked out in the road she brushed up against the old men sitting at their cards, and they spoke to her. She did not like to see faces, which were ugly, or flowers, which were beautiful and smelled sweet.

But at last the trembling left and dull strength came back, as if a wound had ceased to flow its blood. And then one day in summer she could look at a bird flying in the air, its tiny body like a fist opening and closing, and did not feel daze or pain, and then she was healed of the shock of love.

Then whenever she thought that Floyd was in the world, that his life lived and had this night and day, it was like discovery once more and again fresh to her, and if it was night and she lay stretched on her bed looking out at the dark, a great radiant energy spread intent upon her whole body and fastened her heart beneath its breath, and she would wonder almost aloud, "Ought I to sleep?" For it was love that might always be coming, and she must watch for it this time and clasp it back while it clasped, and while it held her never let it go.

Then the radiance touched at her heart and her brain, moving within her. Maybe some day she could become bright and shining all at once, as though at the very touch of another with herself. But now she was like a house with all its rooms dark from the beginning, and someone would have to go slowly from room to room, slowly and darkly, leaving each one lighted behind, before going to the next. It was not caution or distrust that was in herself, it was only a sense of journey, of something that might happen. She herself did not know what might lie ahead, she had never seen herself. She looked outward with the sense of rightful space and time within her, which must be traversed before she could be known at all. And what she would reveal in the end was not herself, but the way of the traveler.

In The Landing much was known about all kinds of love that had happened there, and wisdom traveled, when it left the porches, in the persons of three old women. The day the old women would come to see Jenny, it would be to celebrate her ruin that they trudged through the sun in their bonnets. They would come up the hill to say, "Why don't you run after him?" and to say, "Now you won't love him any more," for they always did pay a visit to say those words.

Now only Mag came sidling up, and brought a bouquet of amaryllis to present with blushes to Jenny. Jenny blushed too.

"Some people that don't speak to other people don't grow the prettiest flowers!" Mag cried victoriously as Jenny took them. Her baby hair blew down and her sharp smile cut back into her long dry cheek.

"I speak to you, Mag," said Jenny.

When she walked she heard them talk—the three old ladies. About her they said, "She'll follow her mother to her mother's grave." About Floyd they had more to say. They called him "the wild man" because they had never been told quite who he was or where he had come from. The sun had burned his skin dark and his hair light, till he was golden in the road, and they freely considered his walking by again, as if they could take his life up into their fingers with their sewing and sew it or snip it on their laps. They always went back to saying that at any rate he caught enormous fish wherever he fished in the river, and always had a long wet thing slung over his wrist when he went by, ugh! One old lady thought he was a Gipsy and had called "Gipsy!" after him when he went by her front porch once too often. One lady said she did not care what he was or if she ever knew what he was, and whether he lived or died it was all the same to her. But the third old lady had books, though she was the one that was a little crazy, and she waited till the others had done and then explained that Floyd had the blood of a Natchez Indian, though the Natchez might be supposed to be all gone, massacred. The Natchez, she said—and she nodded toward her books, "The Queen's Library," high on the shelf—were the people from the lost Atlantis, had they heard of that? and took their pride in the escape from that flood, when the island went under. And there was something all Indians knew, about never letting the last spark of fire go out. What did the other ladies think of that?

They were shocked. They had thought all the time he was really the bastard of one of the old checker-players, that had been let grow up away in the woods until he got big enough to come back and make trouble. They said he was half-wild like one family they could name, and half of the time he did not know what he was doing, like another family. All in his own right he could scent coming things like an animal and in some of his ways, just like all men, he was something of an animal. But they said it was the way he was.

"Why don't you run after him?"—"Now you won't love him any more."

Jenny wondered what more love would be like. Then of course she knew. More love would be quiet. She would never be so quiet as she wished until she was quiet with her love. In the center of everything, in the center of thunder, there was a precious piece of quiet, and into quiet her love would go. The Landing was filled with clangor, it seemed to her, until her love was filled with quiet. It seemed to her that she had been the same as in many places in the world, traveling and traveling, always with quiet to give. It had been enough to make her desperate in her heart, the long search for Billy Floyd to give quiet to.

But if Floyd had a search, what was it?

She was holding the amber beads they used to give her mother to play with. She looked at the lump of amber, and looked through to its core. Nobody could ever know about the difference between the radiance that was the surface and the radiance that was inside. There were the two worlds. There was no way at all to put a finger on the center of light. And if there were a mountain, the cloud over it could not touch its heart when it traveled over, and if there were an island out in the sea, the waves at its shore would never come over the place in the middle of the island. She looked in her very dreams at Floyd who had such clear eyes shining at her, and knew his heart lay clearer still, safe and deep in his innocence, safe and away from the outside, deeper than quiet. What she remembered was that when her hand started out to touch him in delight, he smiled and turned away—not from her, but toward something. . . .

Was it toward one thing, toward some one thing alone?

But it was when love was of the one for the one, that it seemed to hold all that was multitudinous and nothing was single any more. She had one love and that was all, but she dreamed that she lined up on both sides of the road to see her love come by in a procession. She herself was more people than there were people in The Landing, and her love was enough to pass through the whole night, never lifting the same face.

It was July when Jenny left The Landing. The grass was tall and gently ticking between the tracks of the road. The stupor of air, the quiet of the river that now went behind a veil, the sheen of heat and the gray sheen of summering trees, and the silence of day and night seemed all to touch, to bathe and administer to The Landing. The little town took a languor and a kind of beauty from the treatment of time and place. It stretched and swooned, and when two growing boys knelt in the road and caught the sun rays in a bit of glass and got fire, they seemed to tease a sleeper, and when they said "Hooray!" they sounded like adventurers in a dream.

Pears lying on the ground warmed and soured, bees gathered at the figs, birds put their little holes of possession in each single fruit in the world that they could fly to. The scent of lilies rolled sweetly from their heavy cornucopias and trickled down by shady paths to fill the golden air of the valley. The mourning dove called its three notes, kept its short silence—which was its mourning?—and called three more.

Jenny had known the most when she knew Floyd rode the horse in the field of butterflies while she was still; and she had known something when she watched him cook the meat and had eaten it for him under his eye; and now once more, in the dream of July, she knew very little, she was lost in wonder again. If she could find him now, or even find the place where he had last passed through, she would gain the next wisdom. It was a following after, now—it was too late to find any way alone.

The sun was going down when she went. The red eyes of the altheas were closing, and the lizards ran on the wall. The last lily buds hung green and glittering, pendulant in the heat. The crape-myrtle trees were beginning to fill with light for they drank the last of it every day, and gave off their white and

flame in the evening that filled with the throb of cicadas. There was an old
mimosa closing in the ravine—the ancient fern, as old as life, the tree that shrank
from the touch, grotesque in its tenderness. All nearness and darkness affected
it, even clouds going by, but for Jenny that left it no tree ever gave such
allurement of fragrance anywhere.

She looked behind her for the last time as she went down under the trees. As
if it were made of shells and pearls and treasures from the sea, the house glinted
in the sunset, tinted with the drops of light that seemed to fall slowly through
the vaguely stirring leaves. Tenderly as seaweed the long moss swayed. The
chimney branched like coral in the upper blue.

Then green branches closed it over, and with her next step trumpet and
muscadine vines and the great big-leaved vines made pillars about the trunks of
the trees and arches and buttresses all among them. Passion flowers bloomed
with their white and purple rays about her shoulders and under her feet. She
walked on into the streaming hot shade of the wilderness, and put out her hands
between the hanging vines. She feared the snakes in the sudden cool. Like
thousands of silver bells the frogs rang her through the swamp, which then
closed behind her.

All at once the whole open sky could be seen—she had come to the river.
A quiet fire burned on the bluff and moving as far outward as she could see was
the cold blur of water. A great spiraled net lay on its side and its circles twinkled
faintly on the sky. Veil behind veil of long drying nets hung on all sides, dropping softly and blue-colored in the low wind and the place was folded in by them.
All things, river, sky, fire, and air, seemed the same color, the color that is seen
behind the closed eyelids, the color of day when vision and despair are the
same thing.

Some fishermen came around her and when she named Billy Floyd they
nodded their heads. They said, what with the rains, they waited for the racing of
the waters to slow down, but that he went out on them. They said he was
out on them now, but would come back to the camp, if he did not turn over and
drown first. She asked the fishermen to let her wait there with them, since it
was to them that he would return. They said it did not matter to them how long
she waited, or where.

She stood by the nets. A little distance away men and women were cooking
and eating and she smelled the fish and the wild meat. The river went by
immeasurable under the sky, moving and dimly catching and snagging itself,
freeing itself without effort, heavy with its great waves of drift, deep with
stirring fish.

But after a certain length of time, the men that had been throwing knives at
the tree by the last light put her inside a grounded houseboat on the plank of
which chickens were standing. The willow branches hung down over and
dragged softly back and forth across the roof. There were noises and fires all
around. There were pigs in the wood.

One by one the men came in to her. She actually spoke to the first one that
entered between the dozing chickens, for now she could speak to everyone,
in a vague stir of welcome or in the humility that moved now deep in her spirit.

About them all and closer to them than their own breath was the smell of trees that had bled to the knives they wore.

When she called out, she did not call any name; it was a cry with a rising sound, as if she said "Go back," or asked a question, and then at the last protested. A rude laugh covered her cry, and somehow both the harsh human sounds could easily have been heard as rejoicing, going out over the river in the dark night. By the fire, little boys were slapped crossly by their mothers—as if they knew that the original smile now crossed Jenny's face, and hung there no matter what was done to her, like a bit of color that kindles in the sky after the light has gone.

"Is she asleep? Is she in a spell? Or is she dead?" asked a little old bright-eyed woman who went and looked in the door, and crept up to the now meditating men outside. She was so precise in her question that she even held up three rheumatic fingers when she asked.

"She's waiting for Billy Floyd," they said.

The old woman nodded, and nodded out to the flowing river, with the firelight following her face and showing its dignity. The younger boys separated and took their turns throwing knives with a dull *pit* at the tree.

Rona Jaffe

(b. 1932) A graduate of Radcliffe College, Rona Jaffe has written often about the life of career girls in New York City. Her frankness about women as sex objects in The Best of Everything *(1958) made her a fore-runner of the "second wave" of women's liberation. Her most recent book is* Fame Game.

Rima the Bird Girl

I don't remember the day we first met, but my first memory of her is of a wraithlike dark-haired girl sitting in the corner of the living room of our dormitory at college, reciting poetry—no, almost shouting it—she and a friend in unison. And it seemed to me then as if poetry should always be shouted in this inspired, almost orgiastic, way, for it was really music. "O love is the crooked thing,/-There is nobody wise enough/To find out all that is in it, . . . Ah, penny, brown penny, brown penny,/-One cannot begin it too soon."

Her name was Rima Allen, and she came from a small town in Pennsylvania which had neither the distinction of being a grimy coal town nor Main Line, but just a town. Her mother had been reading *Green Mansions* when her daughter was born, and she felt it would give her child some individuality to be named Rima. Her father was a tax accountant, a vague man who spent his life bent over records of other people's lives. He thought Rima was a silly name, but his wife overruled him, and later it was she who chose Radcliffe for Rima, and so we met.

There was a fireplace at one end of the living room in our dormitory, and beside it a nook, wood paneled and cushioned in velvet. Rima was sitting in that nook with her temporary friend, a lumpy debutante from New York who powdered her face like a Kabuki dancer and had once brought a copy of the Social Register into dinner to point out her own name in it. This frightened and graceless snob (whose registered name I have forgotten) was the last person on earth you would expect to find chanting Yeats with such obvious joy, yet Rima had made her memorize dozens of his poems. I knew at once that Rima was a special girl, a girl people gravitated toward to find their dream, their opposite, whatever it was they could not find alone.

"An aged man is but a paltry thing,/A tattered coat upon a stick, unless/Soul clap its hands and sing, and louder sing/For every tatter in its mortal dress."

Rima was a tall girl who always looked very small and fragile, until you noticed her standing next to someone else and realized with surprise that she was big. She had narrow shoulders and small bones, a delicate way of moving, and a soft, child's voice. Her face, in those years of our late teens, was a white blur, as I suppose all our faces were, for we did not yet know who we were. I have a photograph of her sitting on the library steps, a pretty, pale, no-face child of seventeen, all wonder, her arms held out to the wan New England sun.

Every one of us owned several bottles of cologne; Rima had none, but she had one bottle of perfume. We all had many party dresses; Rima had only one, but it was orange, with a swirly skirt, and it had cost a hundred dollars. I remember her always hiding in her room, the shades down, studying, or reading the poetry she loved, and then the sound of the phone bell . . . and ten minutes later she emerged—a swirl of orange skirt, a cloud of Arpege drifting after her, as if she had suddenly been told she existed.

That's all I remember of her from those days; it was, after all, fifteen years ago, and her story had not begun. When we graduated, four of us went to Washington to work in offices, share a house, and find husbands. I had been a zoology major in college, studying such unfeminine things as mollusks, but when we went to Washington I decided to become a secretary along with the others, because we were almost twenty-one and not getting any younger.Everyone knew you found nothing among the mollusks but shells and a lot of ugly old men. We had decided on Washington instead of New York because the other two girls said that was where the bright young men were. A few months after the four of us settled in rooms in a Greek Revival style mansion turned into a rooming house, the two who had brought us to this city of romance began going steady with two boys they had known back at Harvard, and I realized why we had come.

I missed zoology and hated typing and filing; but missing one's work takes an odd form in girls, I think—I was less conscious of the loss than I was of what replaced it, a ferocious need to be loved. I needed someone to inflict all that creative energy on, it didn't matter much who. Of the four of us, it was only Rima who seemed to enjoy being a secretary; who preferred staying home and listening to old Noel Coward records to going out with a new prospect; who went to bed early and got up early, eagerly, without resentment; and who went to the office in her prettiest clothes. I soon discovered it was because she was in love with someone she had met at work.

It was one of those impossibly romantic meetings that occur only in bad movies and real life. The man was attached to the State Department, one of those career diplomats whose work is so important and confidential that you can talk to him for an hour at a cocktail party and realize afterward he has not said a word about himself. He was American, forty-five years old, very attractive, totally sophisticated and, of course, married. Rima had been dispatched to take some papers to his office. There she was, in the doorway—his secretary was in the powder room—and he was alone behind the largest desk she had ever seen. She looked at him, knowing only vaguely who he was and how important he was, thinking only that he was a grownup and extraordinarily attractive. She was wearing her neat little college-girl suit, her hair tied back with a ribbon, her face all admiration and awe. She thought as girls do in the darkness of movie theaters without any sense of further reality: I'd love to go out with him! No one knows what he thought. But the next day he took her to the country for lunch.

She did not tell me who her mysterious lover was for several months, and she never told our other two roommates at all. She saved newspaper clippings about glittering Washington parties he had attended, but because diplomatic amours are very diplomatic in Washington, she had little else in the way of souvenirs, not even a matchbook from a restaurant. I did not know how they managed to meet during those first few months, but I always knew when she was meeting him because again, as in our college days, there was a swirl of brightly colored skirt running down the stairs, a faint cloud of perfume (Joy this time instead of Arpege), and the air around her was charged with life. When she finally told me his name, it was only after they had both decided they were in love.

Rima had had crushes on boys at Harvard, had even cried over a few missed phone calls, but it was nothing like this. As for him, he had played around with little interest with a few predatory wives, but he had never had a real love affair with anyone since his marriage. Rima was so young, so full of confidence in a future in which she would always be young and he would always care for her, that she never even thought of asking him to get a divorce. It was a courtship. They planned how they would meet, when they would meet, how she could see him most often, how she could get along. He could not bear for her to be poor; even the thought that she was spending part of her $60 salary on taxis to meet him appalled him, he wanted to make everything up to her, but how? She refused to go out with any of the boys (we still called them that) who phoned, and he knew it. Suddenly, one day, our freezer was full of steaks, the refrigerator was filled with splits of champagne, and our house was so filled with flowers I thought someone had died.

I went with Rima one day to help her sell her jewelry so that she could buy him a birthday present. Her charm bracelet with the gold disk that said "Sweet Sixteen," her college ring . . . whatever she could not sell she pawned. None of it meant anything to her. "I want to get him gold cuff links," she said. "He wears French cuffs." I thought of the O. Henry story about the gift of the Magi, but it was not the same, because he was not giving up anything for her, and what she was giving up for him was only bits of metal and chips of gems that belonged to an already fading past.

That summer, when our first year of independence drew to a close, our two roommates married the boys they had come to Washington to pursue, and Rima and I had two whole rooms to ourselves. Summers in Washington are very hot. An air conditioner mysteriously appeared in our bedroom window, installed by a man from the air-conditioning company whom neither of us had sent for. On the first cool fall day, for the first time, I was allowed to meet the diplomat. He came to our house for tea and sat on the edge of one of our frayed chairs, very elegant in his hand-tailored suit and Sulka tie. He even wore a vest. I thought he looked like our uncle; not our father—he was too young, too glamorous, too much from another world. But there was something fatherly in the way he looked around at our landlady's furniture with amusement and yet a little annoyance—was it clean enough, good enough, for his child?—the way he smiled with adult pride at everything Rima said, as if she were a precious being from another planet. I could hardly believe any of this was happening; I think, in a way, neither could he. Yet they were obviously in love with eath other.

He went to New York on several business trips that fall and winter and took Rima with him, meeting her as if by accident on the train, where he had taken a private bedroom for the short trip and Rima had a ticket in the parlor car. They had rooms in the same hotel on different floors. At Buccellati's he bought her a gold and emerald ring, which she wore on her left hand, but they entered and left the shop by the back door. When they returned to Washington after the last trip, his wife met him at the station, and Rima alighted from a different car and stood staring on the station platform as her love drove off in a silver-gray foreign automobile with someone who was suddenly flesh and blood, an actuality, a force, a monster.

"I saw her, the old hag," Rima said to me that night, almost in tears. "I wish I could kill her. She's very sophisticated . . . she was wearing a real Chanel suit, and the Chanel shoes and bag too . . . she's too thin, she chain-smokes and uses a holder . . . she's one of those terribly chic, tense women who knows everybody and always says and does the right things. You could tell. She's unhappy, though . . . she must know he loves someone else. Women as nervous as that always know they aren't loved. He told me he doesn't love her any more. He'd leave her if it weren't for his career; a scandal—zip!" She drew her finger across her throat. "He's so proper and old-fashioned in his way, nobody is like him any more. If it weren't for her he could marry me and we'd both be happy. I hate her, the old hag."

"She doesn't sound like an old hag," I said.

"She is!"

"All right, she is."

"And ugly, too."

"Well, at least she's ugly."

"No, she's not ugly," Rima said. "I wish she were. She must have something if he won't leave her for me. If he really didn't love her, he'd leave her, no matter what he says. How could he marry me? I couldn't be a hostess, I couldn't run two homes the way she does. I don't know anything about being a diplomat's wife. I *know* he loves me, but he won't leave *her*. . . ."

So she did want to marry him after all. It had been inevitable. The courtship had been beautiful; the five-minute meetings in hallways, the stolen afternoons and weekends—all had been part of the discovery and wonder of love. But after a year and a half the champagne of secrecy had gone flat. I suspected that Rima had wanted to marry him long before this but had never dared say the words until she saw his wife and realized bitterly that someone had married him, someone was sharing all of his life except those stolen afternoons; for someone it was possible.

All lovers make near-fatal mistakes in their relationships; it is part of the pleasure of love, illicit or not, to tempt providence. So when, one weekend when his wife was away, the diplomat took Rima to his home, it seemed to me merely one of the fatal mistakes some lovers have to make. It was not fatal in any immediate sense, for they were not caught, no one saw them, the servants were away, his wife did not return unexpectedly with a detective or a gun. On his part, it was only a further avowal of his love for Rima; he wanted her to see where and how he lived, he didn't want her to be an outsider. He wanted her to approve of him, of the beautiful things with which he filled his life. He wanted to give her a setting to picture when she dreamed of him, a background for her lonely fantasies; perhaps he also wanted to be able to imagine her in his home when she was no longer there and he was sitting through a dull diplomatic dinner party. The mistake was fatal because Rima did approve of his home . . . she approved of it too much.

She told me about it that night in detail, and I could picture her scampering through those huge rooms like a child, touching each piece of antique furniture as her lover told her what famous person might have sat in this chair, dined from that plate (now an ashtray), or what skill distinguished the weaving of this piece of cloth from any other. She peered into every closet, learning about the heirloom silver, the china, the crystal; she even tried on some of his wife's clothes. To him, Rima was a child, wistful, amusing, and filled with amazement, so he let her try on the Chanels, the Diors, stroke the furs, wave the lapis cigarette holder in the air as if it held a cigarette and she were a grownup at the ball. When she returned home to the Greek Revival rooming house, the photographic mind that had gotten *A*'s at Radcliffe was a living archive of memorabilia.

The bulging scrapbooks of souvenirs and photographs from our college days, which still amused us on Sunday afternoons, were shipped home to her parents. In their place appeared glossy magazines that looked more like books, with names like "Antiquaries," and "A History of Battersea Boxes." One of them was even in French. The diplomat collected Battersea boxes, and also tiny silver boxes with crests on them, so Rima began to scour back street antique shops for a collection exactly like his. Real Battersea boxes were too expensive, but on her twenty-third birthday the diplomat gave her one, topped with white china, on which was written in fine script: "A Trifle From a Friend."

"He wanted to give me a coat," she told me, "but this coat will go another year. I just had to have a real Battersea box."

There was a one-of-a-kind pair of Louis XV chairs in the diplomat's living room. But there turned out to be, surprisingly, an identical pair, for Rima discovered it on a trip to New York, and she began putting away part of her salary every month to buy them. "A hundred dollars a month forever . . . ." Our landlady's frayed chairs were sent to the basement, and the two Louis XV chairs took their place in front of our fireplace that December, for the diplomat had added the frighteningly large difference for a Christmas present. But he seemed disappointed with the gift she had chosen for him to give her, because he surprised her with an additional present, a beige and white fox fur coat. She looked young and rich and daring in the coat, but as for the chairs, I was afraid to sit on them.

One night Rima packed all her career-girl clothes in a large box and sent them to charity, for she was the new owner of a real Chanel suit with the shoes and bag to match. She bought a cigarette holder and began to smoke; she said it would help her lose weight, for she had suddenly decided she was too fat. When her lover told her she was getting too thin, she cried all night, but she did not stop smoking, for the excuse was it would help her stop biting her nails. The collection of tiny silver boxes with crests grew larger and covered the entire top of a spindly-legged antique table Rima had found, which was by coincidence exactly like the one in the bedroom of the diplomat and his wife. The real Chanel suit was joined, in a few months, by another, and a white Dior evening gown, which Rima wore at home in the evening, alone, while she sipped sherry from a certain crystal wineglass, chain-smoked, and wrote letters to a certain firm in Paris asking if it was possible to obtain ten yards of a certain brocaded fabric which had been specially made at one time for another American client, and a tiny sample of which she happened to have snipped from the underside of that client's sofa.

When the fabric finally arrived, the sofa it would cover had arrived too, a gift for Rima's twenty-fourth birthday. I reminded her we were still paying rent for a furnished apartment, although it now looked like a museum, and our landlady's basement looked like a warehouse. Rima looked at me with the nervous, near-tearful look she had acquired during the past year, which somehow made her look rather tragic and mysterious. "We're too old to live like pigs anymore," she said. "Don't you want a real home?"

I did, and I wanted something more, something elusive but wonderful, which I felt must surely be beyond the next corner, or at the next party, or on the threshold of our front door tomorrow night . . . . It had to be, or I felt I would disappear. So one fall evening, when the doorbell rang, announcing the arrival of perhaps the hundredth blind date I would have had in Washington, I decided: If he's anything better than a monster, whoever he is, *this one* I will fall in love with.

He was far from a monster, and he had green eyes and a sense of humor—my two fatal weaknesses—so while he sat in my living room talking and trying to make me like him he never knew he needn't have bothered, because I already loved him. He talked all night, and at dawn, when he remembered he had invited me to his apartment after dinner to make a pass at me, and now it was too late because it was day and we had to go to our offices, he decided he was in love with me, too.

"How could I not love you?" he asked (this young man who was already destined to become my first husband). "You are me. If I didn't love you, it would be like not loving myself."

My decision to marry him seemed as mad and romantic as my decision to fall in love with him. We were in his car at the curb in front of a restaurant. It was that first night, before his apartment, at our first restaurant together, the first time I had been in his car. I wanted to invent some test for destiny, something simple, arbitrary and irrevocable, therefore magic. "If he comes around to my side to open the door, I'll marry him. If he doesn't, he'll never know." He came around to open the door.

Rima gave a cocktail party for us when we announced our engagement, one of many parties she had begun to give. She had become a polished hostess, entertaining a mélange of people: minor politicians, intellectuals, an artist, a writer, an actress, a few foreigners who spoke no English at all but whose languages Rima had studied in college and perfected during the past few years of her diplomatic education. Her diplomat was not there, of course, and she had hidden her half-dozen tiny framed photographs of him in the dresser drawer, but his presence hovered in the rooms throughout the party, for it was now his home, done in his taste, filled with the objects of his pleasures, and the hostess who presided over it all with infinite charm might as well have been his wife. I had a brief irreverent fantasy of the diplomat coming here one night by accident, and panicking, not knowing which home he had come to.

At the party there was a visitor from New York, a young advertising executive. He was thirty-four, married twelve years to his high school sweetheart, and had two children. He was in Washington on business and obviously had never seen anyone like Rima at such close range. He was almost childishly infatuated with her after ten minutes. She flirted with him, named him Heathcliff (for that was rather whom he resembled), and although she obviously enjoyed playing with him, she seemed unaware of her new power. When she was moving about the room talking to her other guests he did not take his eyes off her.

"You need some more champagne, Heathcliff," Rima said, touching his arm lightly as she drifted past. "I want you to get good and drunk. 'Wine comes in at the mouth and love comes in at the eye; That's all we shall know for truth before we grow old and die.'"

"'I lift the glass to my mouth,'" he finished, "'I look at you, and I sigh.'"
She stopped dead and stared at him.

He smiled. There was something about him both boyish and wire-strong, a man who would piously refuse to deceive anyone and yet who was destined to deceive many people throughout his life because they would mistake him for someone simple. He raised his champagne glass at Rima. "'A mermaid found a swimming lad, picked him for her own, pressed her body to his body, laughed; and plunging down forgot in cruel happiness that even lovers drown.'"

"I don't think anyone could drown you," she said. "Heathcliff . . . ."
"Lady Brett Ashley . . . ." he said, transfixed.
"Me?" Rima laughed. *"Me?"*

He asked her to have dinner with him, as he was alone in this city, but she refused, explaining that she was in love with someone and never went out with anyone else.

"Where is he?" the advertising man asked, looking around the crowded room.

"He's not here."

"Oh. Married."

"Aren't you?" she replied sweetly, and drifted away to her guests.

My husband's work took him to New York, where we lived in a three-room apartment that I cleaned carefully every day. I went to the grocery store, read his magazines, his books, played his records, and waited for him to come home to eat the dinners I cooked. He did not like his work very much, and I did not work at all, so in the evenings we talked about the past, our childhoods, our friends; and when we were bored with that we talked about the future, although that seemed more like a game than reality. Sometimes we talked about Rima, who he said was neurotic. He said her life was going to end badly. "If I weren't married to you, I would save her from that man."

"Really? What makes you think she'd want you?" And at that moment, only six months after we had vowed to stay together forever, I wondered why I wanted him, either. I was beginning to look the way Rima had: nervous, lost, a bird girl who appeared out of a tree in the jungle to answer someone's dream and then disappeared at dawn . . . or was it he who disappeared, back into the real world, while the bird girl waited, invisible, for his return, for his summons, for her moments of reality?

Rima wrote to me quite regularly during those months. She had nothing else to do in the evenings, for the decorating job on her apartment was completed, and for some reason the diplomat was not seeing her as often as he used to. He was overworked, she wrote to me, and when he did manage a little time with her he usually spent it falling asleep.

"For the first time in my life," she wrote, "I feel old. I feel like a wife. But I want to marry him, and I know this isn't what our life would be like if I were really his wife. Then we'd share everything. But now he acts as if it isn't a romance any more. I don't know why. Do you remember in the beginning, when the house was full of flowers? He hasn't taken me out to lunch in four months."

They had their first serious fight. "He called me extravagant, said I cared too much about clothes," Rima wrote. "He used to tell me she was extravagant (the old hag) and I told him never to dare compare me with her. He said, 'In some ways you are like her,' and the way he said it was like an insult. He refused to explain. What more does he want from me? I can't be perfect, I need love, I can't help that. Why can't he love me enough to leave her? What's wrong with me that he can't love me enough to choose me over someone he doesn't love at all?"

The day after her fifth anniversary with the diplomat, Rima arrived at my apartment in New York. It seems they had been planning their fifth anniversary celebration for months; she had saved for and bought a new white Dior gown, had her hair done at eight in the morning in order to be at the office on time, and then at five o'clock—an hour before they were to meet to celebrate—he had phoned to say he had to go to an important dinner party, his wife would not understand if she had to attend alone, there was nothing he could do. Rima had gotten tremendously drunk on the bottle of Taittinger Blanc de Blancs 1953 she had been chilling in her refrigerator, given the Malossol caviar to the cleaning woman, thrown the white Dior on the closet floor, and taken the morning train to New York. He had promised to make it up to her, perhaps even a whole weekend away somewhere . . . but she could not wait.

"Wait!" she cried to me, tears pouring down her face as if she were a marble statue in a fountain. "Wait! Wait! All I have ever done is wait."

When my husband came home he flirted with Rima all evening—to save her?—as if I were invisible, and she took an instant dislike to it. When he started to talk about a girl he had known before he met me, Rima stood up. "If I ever get married," she said coldly, "my husband will never talk about other women in my presence. Nor will he ever flirt with other women when I am in the room. It's insulting. I am going to be the first in his life, not just something that's *there*, and if I ever find there's someone else I'm going to leave."

"Isn't that a little too much to ask of a man?" I said, wishing I had her courage.

"It's what I will ask," Rima said.

"Well, Rima," he said, cheerfully nasty, "you ought to know."

I don't remember her ever speaking to my husband again, for that was the way Rima was. She drifted in and out of rooms during the two days she stayed with us, graceful and silent as a cat, always pleasant, but whenever he began to talk she suddenly wasn't there. The afternoon of the second day, when she was feeling repentant toward the diplomat, who did not know where she had gone, I went with Rima to Gucci's where she bought him a wallet. It was elegant, expensive, and impersonal—no, thank you, she would not wait to have it initialed—the kind of gift one had to give a man whose wife noticed all his personal possessions. Coming out of the store we saw the advertising man who had been at Rima's party, or rather, he saw us, for she did not recognize him.

He was so excited he called out to stop us; he shook her gloved hand with both his hands, and then he blushed, as if he had attacked her in my presence. Rima laughed, and then he laughed, too, and invited us both for a drink.

We went to the Plaza (Rima's choice), where Heathcliff had one Scotch (his limit, he told us) and Rima had champagne. She was wearing the beige and white fox coat over a pale wool dress, she had a long gold cigarette holder, her beige alligator handbag and the little package from Gucci were on the table, and she did indeed look like Lady Brett Ashley, or someone equally golden and fictional. We sat in the dark wood-paneled room, watching the sunset through the windows that overlooked the park, laughing, happy; and I thought that people from out of town who saw her here must be thinking she was a real New Yorker, on her way somewhere exciting for the evening. The advertising man evidently thought so, too, when he got up reluctantly, almost jealously, to catch his train to Old Greenwich.

There was a row of taxis at the curb. He helped us into the first, gave her a

mischievous look and kissed her hand. When their eyes met, I had the feeling
he had done some investigating about her friend in Washington. As we watched
him walk away to the second taxi he seemed to change, grow firmer, more
stubborn, as if preparing himself for an everyday life he had momentarily
forgotten.

"He makes me feel young," Rima said wistfully. She smiled. "He makes me
want to go to the country and throw snowballs."

She went back to Washington that night, and we did not see each other
again until spring. In the meantime I had gotten what is known as a friendly
divorce, and custody of the three-room apartment. There had been only
two short letters from Rima during the intervening months. The first said, "I'm
too depressed to write, everything is lousy."

The second said, "I have begun to realize that people don't break up because
of one unforgivable incident, but rather, because of hopelessness. I used to
think love could be killed with a mortal blow, but that's not true. Love goes on
and on, until one day you wake up and realize that the hopelessness is stronger
than the love. I've done everything I could think of, and it was not enough. He
sees me once a week, for twenty minutes. How many more ways can I change?
He says he loves me, but somehow that doesn't mean anything any more;
they're just words. I hear them and I don't remember what they used to mean."

One morning Rima packed all her clothes and the collection of tiny antique
boxes, and left Washington forever. She did not say goodbye to the diplomat,
she simply disappeared into the dawn. She left every stick of antique furniture—
his, hers, theirs, whatever it was—and I imagine the rooms in the Greek Revival
style mansion must have looked very strange, as if the occupant had only
gone out for a walk. She came to stay with me, and the first thing she did was
give me her precious collection.

"I remember you used to admire them. Just consider them a house gift."

The second thing she did was get another secretarial job, because she insisted
on paying half the rent. I had decided to go back to zoology and was taking a
Master's degree at night and working days as a receptionist so I could study my
textbooks behind the potted plant that stood on my glossy desk. I was much
happier than I had expected to be. Rima surprised me by her resiliency. I had
resigned myself nervously to having to nurse a potential suicide, but what I found
was a convalescent who was grateful to have survived.

We went to a few cocktail parties, to dinner with a few old friends, and
introduced each other to the few single men we found in our respective offices
who were not nineteen. It was a restful existence, and the weeks drifted by
almost without notice. Then, one afternoon, Rima rushed back early from the
office, and when I came home the scent of bath oil filled the entire apartment.
She had put her newest Chanel suit on the bed and was washing her emerald
ring with a nail brush.

"Guess what I did today! I just felt like doing something crazy, like we used
to do when we were at college, so I called Heathcliff at his office and said,
'Here I am in New York!' He had a moment of conscience—I could hear it over
the phone, almost like a gulp—and then he asked me to dinner."

"Dinner? Where's his wife?"

"Evidently she's a Den Mother, whatever that is, and they have a meeting. He was going to stay and work late at the office. He says he works late at the office once or twice a week anyway, and he has to eat somewhere, so—oh, you should have heard the stammering, the excuses. He's terrified of me. Of *me*, the girl who never got anybody in her life!"

They went to an Italian restaurant where Rima had often gone with the diplomat, and where the advertising man had never been in his life. The head-waiter recognized her, with obvious respect. The menu was not only in Italian but in handwriting, and Rima took pains to explain innocently to the old Italian waiter what a certain simple dish consisted of, so that Heathcliff could stammer, "Make it two."

He missed the nine-o'clock train, and before the nine-forty-two he had bought her a white orchid. "An orchid," Rima laughed, showing it to me. "An *orchid!* I haven't had an orchid since the Senior prom. I didn't think they made them any more."

But she put it carefully into a glass of champagne in the refrigerator, the alchemy that we had believed in our Senior Prom days would keep an orchid fresh for a week.

She had been almost silent about her affair with the diplomat, as if the gravity of first love had stunned her, but she bubbled over with her delight in Heathcliff, and I knew she had fallen in love with him before she did. "He's so square," she would say, laughing, and then add, "But he's a fox—oh, smart— watch out! I really think I'm the only one who sees the other side of him, the humor. In the advertising business they're just afraid of him, because he's so young and shrewd and on the way up. His wife's name is Dorlee—can you imagine?—and she's the same age he is, of course, because they've known each other all their lives. The old hag."

One of Rima's casual beaus, a plump young man who was also in advertising, took her to a cocktail party where Heathcliff appeared with Dorlee. "She just stood in the corner and talked to the wives," Rima told me afterward. "She looks as if she has steel fillings in her teeth. I don't think she ever shortened a dress in her life; she just wears them the way they come from the store. I heard her telling somebody that in Old Greenwich she has a TV room decorated like the inside of a ship. When she started talking about how they had to have plastic covers on everything I had to run out of the room because I nearly choked."

Heathcliff's commuting hours were irregular, for he often worked late and his two children were old enough to stay up in the TV room decorated like a ship until the captain came home to say good night. He met Rima after work several times a week. He seemed to have a calming effect on her in one way, for she stopped smoking and gave her long gold cigarette holder to our cleaning woman, who had admired it. It was a romance confined to furtive handholding, for he was consumed by guilt and told Rima often that she was "dangerous."

"Dangerous!" she told me in delight. "Dangerous! Me, the failure, dangerous! Isn't he beautiful?"

A letter arrived from our former Washington landlady informing Rima she was not running a storage company, and then several huge crates arrived, Railway Express collect. Rima and I stared at them with dismay. "It's either storage or my own apartment," she said, "and I think at this point, an apartment of my own might be a good idea."

She found an apartment in a new, modern building, a block from Grand Central Station. "And believe me," she said, "an apartment a block from Grand Central is not easy to find." The choice of this location was logical to her—Heathcliff could stop by for a drink every evening on his way to his train. It seems several times he had mentioned, as if he were talking about an impossible dream, that such an arrangement would be the height of bliss.

The beautiful old furniture took some of the coldness away from the boxlike rooms of this glass-and-steel monstrosity, whose only redeeming feature was that it had a working fireplace; and when I went to visit her I found the rooms once again filled with flowers. The only strange note was a small bottle with a ship inside it, which perched on the center of her spindly-legged table.

"He collects them," she said. "He gave it to me. It's kind of pretty, don't you think?"

The next time I visited Rima's apartment a block from Grand Central it was a month later. There was a man's bathrobe hanging on the hook on the bathroom door, and a can of shaving cream on the tole shelf next to the sink. A small photograph of Heathcliff stood on the table beside her bed, framed in rope.

"It's so wonderful being in love with a man near my own age," she said. "He's thirty-four, I'm twenty-six—that means when I'm seventy, he'll be only seventy-eight."

"And commuting?"

"No, of course not," she said, touching his photograph reverently. "He's never been in love before, he never cheated on her in all those years, and do you know they were both virgins when they got married? Him, too. He has a very strong sense of honor. He said he wished she would find out about us so she would do something terrible to him, because he feels he deserves it; and then he said I ought to leave him, because he deserves that; and then he said if I did leave him he might as well be dead."

"He sounds happy," I said.

"It's just his sense of honor," Rima said. "It's a man like that who makes decisions. Men *do* leave their wives, you know, but only because of great love or great guilt. And he has both. I'm glad I didn't get married last time, because I was so young I mistook romance for love. This is real love: planning a life together, being able to help someone, making someone feel alive for the first time. Before he met me, his whole life was encased in plastic, just like that horrible chintz furniture of his in the country."

Men did leave their wives, as I well knew, and lovers left lovers, but it was neither for great love nor great guilt. Rima had been right the first time, in her letter to me: people part because of hopelessness. The death of love leads to the rebirth of another love, for love is a phoenix. A greater love does not kill a small one; it only adds pomp to the funeral.

During the following year, Rima and her advertising man tried to break up three times, but each time he came back to her, vowing he loved her more than ever and felt guiltier. She had already proposed to him several times, pretending it was only a joke, but at the end of their second year of afternoons before the train, she proposed to him seriously, and he answered her.

"How could I marry you?" he asked, tears in his eyes. "I'd bore you. You'd get tired of me. You're my elusive golden girl, and I'm just a husband and father."

"But that's what I *want*," Rima said.

"No. . . . I see you in front of the fire on a snowy night . . . I see you in that white fur coat, your eyes shining, going into the Plaza to meet an ambassador or a movie star. . . . I just don't see you in a gingham dress at the supermarket."

"Where do you think I get my food, out of flowers?"

"Yes," he answered. "And I will always bring them to you."

The transformation of Rima began that night. The next day, printed cotton slipcovers appeared on the Louis XV chairs. She bought a huge Early American object she informed me was called an Entertainment Center, containing a 19-inch television set, a stereo phonograph with four speakers, and a radio, with a long flat surface on top that was soon covered with a collection of ships in bottles. Her Chanels and Diors were sent to a thrift shop (tax deductible) and she replaced them with tweed skirts, cashmere sweater sets, and flowered, sleeveless cotton blouses. She had pawned her emerald ring to buy the Entertainment Center, and now she wore a single strand of imitation pearls. She learned to cook tuna fish casserole with potato chips on top, and in time even a peanut butter soufflé. She saved trading stamps and redeemed them for a hobnail glass lamp with a ruffly shade, and gave her 1850 tole lamp to the cleaning woman, who ventured she'd just as soon have had the nice new one.

She washed and set her hair herself, because it was obvious Dorlee had, and she used the money thus saved to buy books called *The Sexually Satisfied Housewife,* and *The Problems of the Adolescent Stepchild,* which she piled on top of the spindly-legged antique table until it broke and she replaced it with something that had formerly been a butter churn.

Her triumph came on Heathcliff's birthday. He had left his office early, and a light snow had begun to fall. At four-thirty, in the winter's early darkness, he arrived at Rima's apartment. There was snow on his coat, and he was carrying a gold-wrapped package that later turned out to contain champagne. Rima was sitting in front of the roaring fire, wearing blue jeans and toasting marshmallows.

He looked around the room as if he had never really noticed it before, still wearing his coat, still clutching the bottle of champagne in his arms. The air was fragrant with the scent of detergent and meat loaf.

"Happy birthday, honey," Rima said.

"Thank you. . . ." he murmured. "I'd better hang my coat in the bathroom; it's wet."

"Wait till you see your present! I made it."

When he came out of the bathroom he seemed more composed. He opened his present: a ship in a bottle. Rima had put the ship inside, herself. "You see," she said, "to get it in, the sails lie flat, and then I pull the string . . ."

"I know."

"Look at the marshmallow," she said. "When it's burned black like that, with the little red lights inside, it looks the way New York used to look to me at night, when I first came here—all dark and mysterious, with just those millions of little lights."

"Oh, Rima," Heathcliff whispered, holding the two bottles in his hands, the one with the ship and the one with the champagne, "I wish you had written me a poem."

She did write him a poem, the following summer, but she never gave it to him. Instead, she read it to me on the telephone. I had not seen very much of her during the winter and spring, because I had gotten a new job doing research (and my Master's degree), and she had spent most of her time in her apartment waiting for him to visit her, although the visits were fewer and farther between. We were both going to be thirty, but now it no longer seemed to matter that when Rima was thirty Heathcliff would be only thirty-eight.

"Send him the poem," I told her. "It's beautiful."

"No," she said. "I'm going to push it into one of his revolting little bottles and I'm going to toss it into the Greenwich Sound, or whatever the name is of that river he lives on. Then when he's walking in front of his split-level saying *Yo-Ho-Ho* he can find it, and see what he lost. Four years. . . . Well, last time it was five, so you can't say I'm not improving. At least it doesn't take me as long to find out I'm doomed, I am doomed, you know. I'm the girl they recite poetry to, and then in the mornings they always go back to their wives. It must be me, because I fell in love with two completely different men and neither of them wanted to stay with me."

"It's not you," I said. "Neither of them really knew what you were like. If they had, they would have loved you."

I don't know if she ever threw the bottle into the Sound, but she might have tossed it into the lake in Central Park, because all that Summer Rima was addicted to long, lonely walks. Perhaps she was trying to figure things out; perhaps she was only still in her fantasy of the country wife, and the streets of the summer city were her Old Greenwich roads. I felt guilty not spending more time with her, but this time I had met someone I loved. I had not met him among the mollusks and the octogenarians; I had met him at a cocktail party. He was a producer, but he did not think lady zoologists were freaks, and I certainly did not think producers were freaks, although I had never met one before, either.

While I was occupied with the extraordinary miracle of my second (and present) love, Rima became involved in what, to her, seemed only an ordinary meeting. She had been on a long walk, it was about midnight, and she was passing Grand Central Station on her way back to her apartment when she saw a man fall down in the street. The few passers-by thought he was drunk and avoided him, but Rima went closer to see if he was ill, and discovered that he was indeed drunk. She also discovered, with delight and dismay, that he was one of her favorite authors.

"What are you doing, lying there on the curb?" she said sternly. "A great writer does not lie on the curb."

"He does if he's drunk," the author answered. He was trying to go to sleep, his cheek nestled on the sidewalk.

"You get up this minute." Rima pulled him to his feet, which was not too difficult as he was a short, wiry man, about her height, quite undernourished from too much wine, women and song. He was, she remembered reading, only four years older than she was, and she felt maternal toward him.

"Have to go to Bennington," he murmured. "Where the hell is Bennington? Have to be there in the morning."

"Bennington, Vermont?"

"Little girls' school . . . college. Lecture. Where's my train?"

"You can't lecture at Bennington like this," Rima said. She inspected his soiled clothing and bleary face with distaste. "Those girls idolize you. If they see you like this, it might ruin the rest of their lives."

"I'm . . . going to be sick."

"Good."

He decided not to be sick. "Who are you?"

"A former English major at Radcliffe, and an admirer of yours—although not at the moment. Come with me, I live around the corner." She was already leading him, his arm about her shoulders.

The writer stared at the sleeveless flowered cotton blouse, the chino walking skirt, the little strand of pearls. "Funniest-looking streetwalker I ever saw . . ."

Rima slapped him.

She then took him to her apartment, a block from Grand Central, where she forced him to eat scrambled eggs and drink three cups of black coffee, and then spot-cleaned and pressed his suit while he cursed at her from a cold shower. She scanned the timetable while the writer looked around her apartment.

"You in the Waves?"

"Very funny. You can take the two-thirty train to Boston, and then there's probably a connection."

"You've even got a timetable."

"Purely for sentimental reasons," Rima said. "Here, take this aspirin and these vitamins; you'll need them later."

"You have any children?"

"No. Do you?"

"I'm not married," he said.

Suddenly, he became more than an idol or an invalid—he became a person. "You're *not?*"

"Divorced," he said.

"So am I," Rima said, "sort of."

"That's too bad. You'd make a wonderful wife. Very homey apartment. It reminds me of my mother's. You wouldn't think I had a mother, would you? Well, I do."

"You need her," Rima said. "Or a nurse. How could you possibly have gotten so drunk when you have an appointment tomorrow—or today, I should say."

"Oh!" he said, looking wildly for his jacket. "Where's the train?"

"At the station. Where are your lecture notes? Good. Your aspirin? Good. Now, take these cookies, in case you get tempted on the way."

The writer took hold firmly of Rima's arm. "You're coming with me."

"Are you crazy?"

"Yes. Come with me. I need you. I'll only be there one day, and then we'll go to St. Thomas. I live in St. Thomas; you'll like it."

Rima looked around her apartment, the cozy, chintzy, friendly room filled with its memories of love and failure. "'Be not afeard. The isle is full of noises, sounds and sweet airs, that give delight and hurt not.'"

"Come with Caliban," he said.

"No," Rima said, following him docilely to the door, "no, not Caliban . . . Shakespeare."

When she came back from Bennington she came to visit me, to bring me her collection of ships in bottles and to say goodbye. "When you marry that divine man you're going with, you'll have a little boy someday, and he'll like these."

"Are you really going away with him?" I asked stupidly.

"Imagine—St. Thomas! He can write his books, and I can keep house. I'll walk on the beach, and I'll send you shells if you like, if I find anything they don't have anywhere else. Imagine—he's not marrried—at last! He's so brilliant; I've always adored his work. I've read everything he ever wrote, and do you know what? Once, when we were in college and he had his first story published, I cut his picture out of the magazine and kept it for a year."

"Listen," I said, hating myself for it, "I read in *Time* magazine that he travels around with a Great and Good Friend. She lives in St. Thomas with him. What happened to her?"

"Oh, her!" Rima said. "He hates her. She just happens to live in St. Thomas, that's all. He says she's not a girlfriend, she's a friend girl. I saw that picture in *Time*; she looks like a squaw. She's got a braid down her back and she had this leather thong around her neck with a big tooth attached to it. I'll bet it came out of her mouth. No wonder he drank before he met me."

"He's stopped drinking?"

"One Scotch before dinner, like Heathcliff used to. Oh, I'm a reformer now." She laughed at herself, the reformer, and I wondered if life would at last be kind to her, she who could never be kind to herself.

She left the apartment, the furniture, her winter clothes, everything, and she and the writer went to St. Thomas. I went to her apartment two days before my wedding, suddenly taken by the absurdly sentimental thought that I must sell that Early American Entertainment Center and get Rima's emerald ring out of the pawn shop, if it was still there, and send it to her. I don't know why that ring seemed so important to me—perhaps because I was going to be married and I was happy, and I couldn't bear the thought of a ring Rima had worn for five years on the third finger of her left hand being misused by some stranger. But the landlord had taken possession of all the furniture in lieu of the rent she had never sent from St. Thomas, and the apartment had been sublet. Well, I thought, caught up again in my own happiness, we've both learned enough from the past, and that ring doesn't mean anything any more.

So I was married, and two years later we did have a little boy who will like the collection of ships in bottles, when he's old enough not to break them to get the ships out. Our apartment is filled with scripts, books, records, theatrical posters, an aquarium, shells, textbooks, toys; but still there is room on the piano for Rima's collection of Battersea boxes. She had written me two happy post-cards the first year, and then, nothing. I wondered if she was still in St. Thomas. Five years after she had left New York, I took a chance and wrote to her at her last address to tell her that my husband and I were going to take a winter vacation in St. Thomas, and was she still alive? She wrote back immediately.

"Yes," her letter said, "I'm still alive. Alive and single. Surprise. Look for me in the bar at your hotel any night at about ten o'clock. I'll be the one seated at the right hand of the Bard."

We arrived in St. Thomas in the afternoon. When we went down to the hotel bar that night at ten, Rima was not there. There were some pink-broiled American tourists, and a party of Italians from a large yacht that was moored in the harbor: the owner, very rich, very clean in a blue blazer, two teen-aged starlets who sat toying with the speared fruit in their drinks, two rather sinister-looking young men, and two contessas with streaks in their hair and a lot of diamonds. The Calypso trio played on a small bandstand, and the starlets got up to do whatever dance it was teen-aged starlets were doing that winter in the jet set. The contessas and their escorts looked bored because they were supposed to, and the Italian millionaire looked bored because he was. I was afraid Rima wasn't going to show up after all.

Then, at half past twelve, she arrived. She was, indeed at the right hand of the Bard, and the Bard was very, very drunk. At the left hand of the Bard, helping to support him, was a young woman the same age as Rima, with a long black braid down her back, a turtleneck T-shirt, a peasant skirt, no makeup, and a silver-and-turquoise ornament the size of a breast-plate dangling from a chain around her neck. Rima had let her hair grow to her waist and braided it, her face was scrubbed and tanned, she was dressed in an almost identical village out-fit, and the only difference between the two Squaw Twins was that Rima was the prettier one.

Rima let go the writer's hand and ran over to our table. Liberated, he pulled free of the other lady and went to the bar.

"Oh, I'm so glad to see you!" Rima said. "Look how pale you are—you'll have to come to the beach with me." She held her arm, the color of glistening walnut, against mine.

My husband was transfixed by the object dangling from a thong around Rima's neck. "Whose tooth is that?"

She shrugged. "I don't know. It's Olive's; we trade."

"How is everything?" I asked lamely.

"Don't ask that. I want to be happy tonight. No, it's all right, really. I'm content; I mean, I'm over him, I just stay with him because he needs me."

"Who's Olive?"

Rima glanced at her Squaw Twin. "Remember the girlfriend he said was only a friend girl? That's her. Actually, I'd go insane if I didn't have her to talk to. He's so drunk lately. And, do you know, in the beginning I really hated her? She has great individuality, though, and a crystalline intellect. She's above such things as jealousy and animosity, she really believes in the purity of non-thought. . . . oh, hell, she bores me to death."

The writer had taken the sticks away from the Calypso drummer and was crashing them on every cymbal, drum, and any surface in sight. The musicians and waiters ignored him as if he was a nightly fixture. Olive was watching him inscrutably. The Italians from the yacht looked amused.

"If I had his talent . . ." Rima said. "If I had *any* talent. . . . Tell me about New York! Tell me about the world, is it still there?"

We ordered drinks and told her about people she had known, and then we ordered more drinks and she made us tell her about people she didn't know. She was insatiable. The world, the world, what was happening outside this tiny island, this paradisiacal prison? The American tourists went up to bed, the Calypso trio disappeared, the writer and Olive were now sitting with the party of Italians from the yacht. The millionaire glanced over at us and bent toward him to whisper a question; the writer shook his head.

"How old is your baby?" Rima asked suddenly.

"Three years old."

"I'm thirty-five," Rima said. "Do I look it? Don't answer. Look—the sun's coming up, I'm going to walk on the beach."

She ran out of the bar, across the patio, across the sand, and was gone. I was afraid she might be going to drown herself and was going to run after her, but then I saw her again, wandering among the sea-grape trees, sad and alone. The writer had fallen asleep at the table, his head between the empty glasses. Olive was watching over him, totally still, a little smile at the corner of her mouth. The Italian millionaire excused himself to the group and went out to the beach.

I could see his silhouette in the pink-and-gold dawn, bowing slightly to Rima's silhouette, and then, after a moment, walking slowly beside it through the silhouettes of the sea-grape trees. The sea was all blue and gold and silver now, and in the distance the Italian's yacht rocked gently at anchor, all white.

We went up to our room. Then, suddenly, I felt one of those obsessive, extrasensory calls that are like a shout in the mind. "I'll be right back," I said, and ran down the stairs to the lobby.

The bar was closed, chairs piled on top of the tables. The Italians had all gone, and in a corner of the lobby Olive was asleep in a big chair. A yawning porter handed me a hotel envelope with my name on it, and went back behind the desk. The writer, despite his hangover, was milling around like twelve people. "Where is she? Where is she? *Rima. . . !*"

I tore open the envelope, and the tooth on the leather thong fell into my hand. There was a note, in Rima's impeccable script: "'When such as I cast out remorse so great a sweetness flows into the breast we must laugh and we must sing, We are blest by everything. Everything we look upon is blest.' *La donna è mobile.* Goodbye, and love."

I looked out to sea, where the yacht was only a tiny toy ship on the horizon, and then I went up to our room.

So she was gone again, with the Italian millionaire, and his starlets, and his contessas with the streaked hair. Soon, I knew, she would fall in love, and cut her braid, and toss her pueblo jewelry into the sea. She would paint her eyelids and enamel her toenails, and disappear. Once again, as always, a man who had fallen in love with a fantasy that had been created for another man would lose that fantasy, consuming it in the fire of his love. I remembered that the Rima of *Green Mansions,* for whom Rima Allen had been named, had been killed in a fire that destroyed her hiding-tree. It seemed to me, that lonely morning in St. Thomas, that the Rima I knew had been killed in many fires, rising again from the ashes of each one like a bright bird to sing the song of some wanderer's need. Had there ever been a real Rima? Born and reborn to a splendid image, she had never looked for her self, nor had anyone else. Being each man's dream of love, she had eventually failed him, and so he had failed her, and so, finally, she had failed herself.

Norman Mailer

(b. 1923) Like F. Scott Fitzgerald, Mailer has come to epitomize an age as much in his highly publicized personal life as in his fiction. A veteran of World War II, a political radical, an acknowledged addict of seconal and benzedrine, and a smoker of marijuana, he has recorded his experiences in journals such as Dissent *and* The Village Voice *as well as in his many novels, including* The Naked and the Dead *and* The Prisoner of Sex.

The Time of Her Time

1   I was living in a room one hundred feet long and twenty-five feet wide, and it had nineteen windows staring at me from three of the walls and part of the fourth. The floor planks were worn below the level of the nails which held them down, except for the southern half of the room where I had laid a rough lineoleum which gave a hint of sprinkled sand, conceivably an aid to the footwork of my pupils. For one hundred dollars I had the place whitewashed; everything; the checkerboard of tin ceiling plates one foot square with their fleurs-de-lis stamped into the metal, the rotted sashes on the window frames (it took twelve hours to scrape the calcimine from the glass), even parts of the floor had white drippings (although that was scuffed into dust as time went on) and yet it was worth it: when I took the loft it stank of old machinery and the paint was a liverish brown—I had tried living with that color for a week, my old furniture, which had been moved by a mover friend from the Village and me, showed the scars of being bumped and dragged and flung up six flights of stairs, and the view of it sprawled over twenty-five hundred feet of living space, three beat old day beds, some dusty cushions, a broken-armed easy chair, a cigarette-scarred coffee table made from a door, a kitchen table, some peeled enamel chairs which thumped like a wooden-legged pirate when one sat in them, the bookshelves of unfinished pine butted by bricks, yes, all of this, my purview, this grand vista, the New York sunlight greeting me in the morning

through the double filter of the smog-yellow sky and the nineteen dirt-frosted windows, inspired me with so much content, especially those liver-brown walls, that I fled my pad like the plague, and in the first week, after a day of setting the furniture to rights, I was there for four hours of sleep a night, from five in the morning when I maneuvered in from the last closed Village bar and the last coffee-klatsch of my philosopher friends' for the night to let us say nine in the morning when I awoke with a partially destroyed brain and the certainty that the sore vicious growl of my stomach was at least the onset of an ulcer and more likely the first gone cells of a thorough-going cancer of the duodenum. So I lived it that way for a week, and then following the advice of a bar-type who was the friend of a friend, I got myself up on the eighth morning, boiled my coffee on a hot-plate while I shivered in the October air (neither the stove nor the gas heaters had yet been bought) and then I went downstairs and out the front door of the warehouse onto Monroe Street, picking my way through the garbage-littered gutter which always made me think of the gangs on this street, the Negroes on the east end of the block, the Puerto Ricans next to them, and the Italians and Jews to the west—those gangs were going to figure a little in my life, I suspected that, I was anticipating those moments with no quiet bravery considering how hung was my head in the morning, for the worst clue to the gangs was the six-year-olds. They were the defilers of the garbage, knights of the ordure, and here, in this province of a capital Manhattan, at the southern tip of the island, with the overhead girders of the Manhattan and Brooklyn bridges the only noble structures for a mile of tenement jungle, yes here the barbarians ate their young, and any type who reached the age of six without being altogether mangled by father, mother, family or friends, was a pint of iron man, so tough, so ferocious, so sharp in the teeth that the wildest alley cat would have surrendered a freshly caught rat rather than contest the meal. They were charming, these six-year-olds, as I told my uptown friends, and they used to topple the overloaded garbage cans, strew them through the street, have summer snowball fights with orange peel, coffee grounds, soup bones, slop, they threw the discus by scaling the raw tin rounds from the tops of cans, their pillow fights were with loaded socks of scum, and a debauch was for two of them to scrub a third around the inside of a twenty-gallon pail still warm with the heat of its emptied treasures. I heard that the Olympics took place in summer when they were out of school and the streets were so thick with the gum of old detritus, alluvium and dross that the mash made by passing car tires fermented in the sun. Then the parents and the hoods and the debs and the grandmother dowagers cheered them on and promised them murder and the garbage flew all day, but I was there in fall and the scene was quiet from nine to three. So I picked my way through last night's stew of rubble on this eighth morning of my hiatus on Monroe Street, and went half down the block to a tenement on the boundary between those two bandit republics of the Negroes and the Puerto Ricans, and with a history or two of knocking on the wrong door, and with a nose full of the smells of the sick overpeppered bowels of the poor which seeped and oozed out of every leaking pipe in every communal crapper (only as one goes north does the word take on the Protestant propriety of john), I was able finally to find my man, and I was an hour ahead of him—he was still sleeping off his last night's drunk. So I spoke to his wife, a fat masculine Negress with the face and charity of a Japanese wrestler, and when she understood that I was neither a junk-peddler nor fuzz, that I sold no numbers, carried no bills, and was most certainly not a detective (though my Irish face left her dubious of that) but instead had come to offer her husband a job of work, I was admitted to the first of three dark rooms, face to face with the gray luminescent eye of the television set going its way in a dark room on a bright morning, and through the hall curtains I could hear them talking in the bedroom.

"Get up, you son of a bitch," she said to him.

He came to work for me, hating my largesse, lugging his air compressor up my six flights of stairs, and after a discussion in which his price came down from two hundred to one, and mine rose from fifty dollars to meet his, he left with one of my twenty-dollar bills, the air compressor on the floor as security, and returned in an hour with so many sacks of whitewash that I had to help him up the stairs. We worked together that day, Charley Thompson his name was, a small lean Negro maybe forty years old, and conceivably sixty, with a scar or two on his face, one a gouge on the cheek, the other a hairline along the bridge of his nose, and we got along not too badly, working in sullen silence until the hangover was sweated out, and then starting to talk over coffee in the Negro hashhouse on the corner where the bucks bridled a little when I came in, and then ignored me. Once the atmosphere had become neutral again, Thompson was willing to talk.

"Man," he said to me, "what you want all that space for?"

"To make money."

"Out of which?"

I debated not very long. The people on the block would know my business sooner or later—the reward of living in a slum is that everyone knows everything which is within reach of the senses—and since I would be nailing a sign over my mailbox downstairs for the pupils to know which floor they would find me on, and the downstairs door would have to be open since I had no bell, the information would be just as open. But for that matter I was born to attract attention; given my height and my blond hair, the barbarians would notice me, they noticed everything, and so it was wiser to come on strong than to try to sidle in.

"Ever hear of an *Escuela de Torear?*" I asked him without a smile.

He laughed with delight at the sound of the words, not even bothering to answer.

"That's a bullfighter's school," I told him. "I teach bullfighting."

"You know that?"

"I used to do it in Mexico."

"Man, you can get killed."

"Some do." I let the exaggeration of a cooled nuance come into my voice. It was true after all; some do get killed. But not so many as I was suggesting, maybe one in fifty of the successful, and one in five hundred of the amateurs like me who fought a few bulls, received a few wounds, and drifted away.

Charley Thompson was impressed. So were others—the conversation was being overheard after all, and I had become a cardinal piece on the chaotic chessboard of Monroe Street's sociology—I felt the clear bell-like adrenalins of clean anxiety, untainted by weakness, self-interest, neurotic habit, or the pure yellows of the liver. For I had put my poker money on the table, I was the new gun in a frontier saloon, and so I was asking for it, not today, not tomorrow, but come sooner, come later, something was likely to follow from this. The weak would leave me alone, the strong would have respect, but be it winter or summer, sunlight or dark, there would come an hour so cold or so hot that someone, somebody, some sexed-up head, very strong and very weak, would be drawn to discover a new large truth about himself and the mysteries of his own courage or the lack of it. I knew. A year before, when I had first come to New York, there was a particular cat I kept running across in the bars of the Village, an expert with a knife, or indeed to maintain the salts of accuracy, an expert with two knives. He carried them everywhere—he had been some sort of hophead instructor in the Marines on the art of fighting with the knife, and he used to demonstrate nice fluid poses, his elbows in, the knives out, the points of those blades capering free of one another—he could feint in any direction with either hand, he was an artist, he believed he was better with a knife than any man in all of New York, and night after night in bar after bar he sang the love-song of his own prowess, begging for the brave type who would take on his boast, and leave him confirmed or dead.

It is mad to take on the city of New York, there is too much talent waiting on line; this cat was calling for every hoodlum in every crack gang and clique who fancies himself with the blade, and one night, drunk and on the way home, he was greeted by another knife, a Puerto Rican cat who was defective in school and spent his afternoons and nights shadow-knifing in the cellar clubhouse of his clique, a real contender, long-armed for a Latin, thin as a Lehmbruck, and fast as a hungry wolf; he had practiced for two months to meet the knife of New York.

So they went into an alley, the champion drunk, a fog of vanity blanketing the point of all his artistic reflexes, and it turned out to be not too much of a fight: the Puerto Rican caught it on the knuckles, the lip, and above the knee, but they were only nicks, and the champion was left in bad shape, bleeding from the forearm, the belly, the chest, the neck, and the face: once he was down, the Puerto Rican had engraved a double oval, labium majorum and minorum on the skin of the cheek, and left him there, having the subsequent consideration or fright to make a telephone call to the bar in which our loser had been drinking. The ex-champion, a bloody cat, was carried to his pad which was not far away (a bit of belated luck) and in an hour, without undue difficulty the brother-in-law doctor of somebody or other was good enough to take care of him. There were police reports, and as our patois goes, the details were a drag, but what makes my story sad is that our ex-champion was through. He mended by sorts and shifts, and he still bragged in the Village bars, and talked of finding the Puerto Rican when he was sober and in good shape, but the truth was that he was on the alcoholic way, and the odds were that he would stay there. He had been one of those gamblers who saw his life as a single bet, and he had lost. I often thought that he had been counting on a victory to put some charge below his belt and drain his mouth of all that desperate labial libido.

Now I was following a modest parallel, and as Thompson kept asking me some reasonable if openly ignorant questions about the nature of the bullfight, I found myself shaping every answer as carefully as if I were writing dialogue, and I was speaking particularly for the black-alerted senses of three Negroes who were sitting behind me, each of them big in his way (I had taken my glimpse as I came in) with a dull, almost Chinese, sullenness of face. They could have been anything. I had seen faces like theirs on boxers and ditch diggers, and I had seen such faces by threes and fours riding around in Cadillacs through the Harlem of the early-morning hours. I was warning myself to play it carefully, and yet I pushed myself a little further than I should, for I became ashamed of my caution and therefore was obliged to brag just the wrong bit. Thompson, of course, was encouraging me—he was a sly old bastard—and he knew even better than me the character of our audience.

"Man, you can take care of yourself," he said with glee.

"I don't know about that," I answered, obeying the formal minuet of the *macho*. "I don't like to mess with anybody," I told him. "But a man messes with me—well, I wouldn't want him to go away feeling better than he started."

"Oh, yeah, ain't that a fact. I hears just what you hear." He talked like an old-fashioned Negro—probably Southern. "What if four or five of them comes on and gangs you?"

We had come a distance from the art of the *corrida*. "That doesn't happen to me," I said. "I like to be careful about having some friends." And part for legitimate emphasis, and part to fulfill my image of the movie male lead—that blond union of the rugged and the clean-cut (which would after all be *their* image as well)—I added, "Good friends, you know."

There we left it. My coffee cup was empty, and in the slop of the saucer a fly was drowning. I was thinking idly and with no great compassion that wherever this fly had been born it had certainly not expected to die in a tan syrupy ring-shaped pond, struggling for the greasy hot-dogged air of a cheap Negro hashhouse. But Thompson rescued it with a deft flip of his fingers.

"I always save," he told me seriously. "I wouldn't let nothing be killed. I'm a preacher."

"Real preacher?"

"Was one. Church and devoted congregation." He said no more. He had the dignified sadness of a man remembering the major failure of his life.

As we got up to go, I managed to turn around and get another look at the three spades in the next booth. Two of them were facing me. Their eyes were flat, the whites were yellow and flogged with red—they stared back with no love.

The anxiety came over me again, almost nice—I had been so aware of them, and they had been so aware of me.

2 That was in October, and for no reason I could easily discover, I found myself thinking of that day as I awoke on a spring morning more than half a year later with a strong light coming through my nineteen windows. I had fixed the place up since then, added a few more pieces of furniture, connected a kitchen sink and a metal stall shower to the clean water outlets in the john, and most noticeably I had built a wall between the bullfight studio and the half in which I lived. That was more necessary than one might guess—I had painted the new wall red; after Thompson's job of whitewash I used to feel as if I were going snow-blind; it was no easy pleasure to get up each morning in a white space so blue with cold that the chill of a mountain peak was in my blood. Now, when I opened my eyes, I could choose the blood of the wall in preference to the ice slopes of Mt. O'Shaugnessy, where the sun was always glinting on the glaciers of the windows.

But on this particular morning, when I turned over a little more, there was a girl propped on one elbow in the bed beside me, no great surprise, because this was the year of all the years in my life when I was scoring three and four times a week, literally combing the pussy out of my hair, which was no great feat if one knew the Village and the scientific temperament of the Greenwich Village mind. I do not want to give the false impression that I was one of the lustiest to come adventuring down the pike—I was cold, maybe by birth, certainly by environment: I grew up in a Catholic orphanage—and I had had my little kinks and cramps, difficulties enough just a few years ago, but I had passed through that, and I was going now on a kind of disinterested but developed competence; what it came down to was that I could go an hour with the average girl without destroying more of the vital substance than a good night's sleep could repair, and since that sort of stamina seems to get advertised, and I had my good looks, my blond hair, my height, build and bullfighting school, I suppose I became one of the Village equivalents of an Eagle Scout badge for the girls. I was one of the credits needed for a diploma in the sexual humanities, I was par for a good course, and more than one of the girls and ladies would try me on an off-evening like comparison-shoppers to shop the value of their boy friend, lover, mate, or husband against the certified professionalism of Sergius O'Shaugnessy.

Now if I make this sound bloodless, I am exaggerating a bit—even an old habit is livened once in a while with color, and there were girls I worked to get and really wanted, and nights when the bull was far from dead in me. I even had two women I saw at least once a week, each of them, but what I am trying to emphasize is that when you screw too much and nothing is at stake, you begin to feel like a saint. It was a hell of a thing to be holding a nineteen-year-old girl's ass in my hands, hefting those young kneadables of future power, while all the while the laboratory technician in my brain was deciding that the experiment was a routine success—routine because her cheeks looked and felt just about the way I had thought they would while I was sitting beside her in the bar earlier in the evening, and so I still had come no closer to under- standing my scientific compulsion to verify in the retort of the bed how accurately I had predicted the form, texture, rhythm and surprise of any woman who caught my eye.

Only an ex-Catholic can achieve some of the rarer amalgams of guilt, and the saint in me deserves to be recorded. I always felt an obligation—some noblesse oblige of the kindly cocksman—to send my women away with no great wounds to their esteem, feeling at best a little better than when they came in, I wanted to be friendly (what vanity of the saint!). I was the messiah of the one-night stand, and so I rarely acted like a pig in bed, I wasn't greedy, I didn't grind all my tastes into their mouths, I even abstained from springing too good a lay when I felt the girl was really in love with her man, and was using me only to give love the benefit of new perspective. Yes, I was a good sort, I probably gave more than I got back, and the only real pains for all those months in the loft, for my bullfighting classes, my surprisingly quiet time (it had been winter after all) on Monroe Street, my bulging portfolio of experiments—there must have been fifty girls who spent at least one night in the loft—my dull but doggedly advancing scientific data, even the cold wan joys of my saintliness demanded for their payment only one variety of the dead hour: when I woke in the morning, I could hardly wait to get the latest mouse out of my bed and out of my lair. I didn't know why, but I would awaken with the deadliest of depressions, the smell of the woman had gone very stale for me, and the armpits, the ammonias and dead sea life of old semen and old snatch, the sour fry of last night's sweat, the whore scent of over-exercised perfume, became an essence of the odious, all the more remarkable because I clung to women in my sleep, I was one Don John who hated to sleep alone, I used to feel as if my pores were breathing all the maternal (because sleeping) sweets of the lady, wet or dry, firm or flaccid, plump, baggy, or lean who was handled by me while we dreamed. But on awakening, hung with my head—did I make love three times that year without being drunk?—the saint was given his hour of temptation, for I would have liked nothing more than to kick the friendly ass out of bed, and dispense with the coffee, the good form, my depression and often hers, and start the new day by lowering her in a basket out of my monk-ruined retreat six floors down to the garbage pile (now blooming again in the freshets of spring), wave my hand at her safe landing and get in again myself to the blessed isolations of the man alone.

But of course that was not possible. While it is usually a creep who general- izes about women, I think I will come on so heavy as to say that the cordial tone of the morning after is equally important to the gymkhana of the night before—at least if the profit made by a nice encounter is not to be lost. I had given my working hours of the early morning to dissolving a few of the inhibitions, chilled reflexes and dampened rhythms of the corpus before me, but there is not a restraint in the world which does not have to be taken twice—

once at night on a steam-head of booze, and once in daylight with the grace of a social tea. To open a girl up to the point where she loves you or It or some tremor in her sexual baggage, and then to close her in the morning is to do the disservice which the hateful side of women loves most—you have fed their cold satisfied distrust of a man. Therefore my saint fought his private churl, and suffering all the detail of abusing the sympathetic nervous system, I made with the charm in the daylight and was more of a dear than most.

It was to be a little different this morning, however. As I said, I turned over in my bed, and looked at the girl propped on her elbow beside me. In her eyes there was a flat hatred which gave no ground—she must have been staring like this at my back for several minutes, and when I turned, it made no difference—she continued to examine my face with no embarrassment and no delight.

That was sufficient to roll me around again, my shoulder blades bare to her inspection, and I pretended that the opening of my eyes had been a false awakening. I felt deadened then with all the diseases of the dull—making love to her the night before had been a little too much of a marathon. She was a Jewish girl and she was in her third year at New York University, one of those harsh alloys of a self-made bohemian from a middle-class home (her father was a hardware wholesaler), and I was remembering how her voice had irritated me each time I had seen her, an ugly New York accent with a cultured overlay. Since she was still far from formed, there had been all sorts of Lesbian hysterias in her shrieking laugh and they warred with that excess of strength, complacency and deprecation which I found in many Jewish women—a sort of "Ech" of disgust at the romantic and mysterious All. This one was medium in size and she had dark long hair which she wore like a Village witch in two extended braids which came down over her flat breasts, and she had a long thin nose, dark eyes, and a kind of lean force, her arms and square shoulders had shown the flat thin muscles of a wiry boy. All the same, she was not bad, she had a kind of Village chic, a certain snotty elegance of superiority, and when I first came to New York I had dug girls like her—Jewesses were strange to me—and I had even gone with one for a few months. But this new chick had been a mistake—I had met her two weeks ago at a party, she was on leave from her boy friend, and we had had an argument about T. S. Eliot, a routine which for me had become the quintessence of corn, but she said that Eliot was the apotheosis of manner, he embodied the ecclesiasticism of classical and now futureless form, she adored him she said, and I was tempted to tell her how little Eliot would adore the mannerless yeasts of the Brooklyn from which she came, and how he might prefer to allow her to appreciate his poetry only in step to the transmigration of her voice from all urgent Yiddish nasalities to the few high English analities of relinquished desire. No, she would not make that other world so fast—nice society was not cutting her crumpets thus quickly because she was gone on Thomas Stearns Eeeee. Her college-girl snobbery, the pity for me of eighty-five other honey-pots of the Village aesthetic whose smell I knew all too well, so inflamed the avenger of my crotch, that I wanted to prong her then and there, right on the floor of the party, I was a primitive for a prime minute, a gorged gouge of a working-class phallus, eager to ram into all her nasty little tensions. I had the message again, I was one of the millions on the bottom who had the muscles to move the sex which kept the world alive, and I would grind it into her, the healthy hearty inches and the sweat of the cost of acquired culture when you started low and you wanted to go high. She was a woman, what! she sensed that moment, she didn't know if she could handle me, and she had the guts to decide to find out. So we left the party and we drank and (leave it to a Jewish girl to hedge the bet) she drained the best half of my desire in conversation because she was being psychoanalyzed, what a predictable pisser! and she was in that stage where the jargon had the totalitarian force of all vocabularies of mechanism, and she could only speak of her infantile relations to men, and the fixations and resistances of unassimilated penis-envy with all the smug gusto of a female commissar. She was enthusiastic about her analyst, he was also Jewish (they were working now on Jewish self-hatred), he was really an integrated guy, Stanford Joyce, he belonged to the same mountain as Eliot, she loved the doers and the healers of life who built on the foundationless prevalence of the void those islands of proud endeavor.

"You must get good marks in school," I said to her.

"Of course."

How I envied the jazzed-up grain of the Jews. I was hot for her again, I wanted the salts of her perspiration in my mouth. They would be acrid perhaps, but I would digest them, and those intellectual molecules would rise to my brain.

"I know a girl who went to your bullfighting school," she said to me. She gave her harsh laugh. "My friend thought you were afraid of her. She said you were full of narcissistic anxieties."

"Well, we'll find out," I said.

"Oh, you don't want me. I'm very inadequate as a lover." Her dark hard New York eyes, bright with appetite, considered my head as if I were a delicious and particularly sour pickle.

I paid the check then, and we walked over to my loft. As I had expected, she made no great fuss over the back-and-forth of being seduced—to the contrary. Once we were upstairs, she prowled the length of my loft twice, looked at the hand-made bullfighting equipment I had set up along one wall of the studio, asked me a question or two about the killing machine, studied the swords, asked another question about the cross-guard on the descabellar, and then came back to the living-room—bedroom—dining-room—kitchen of the other room, and made a face at the blood-red wall. When I kissed her she answered with a grinding insistence of her mouth upon mine, and a muscular thrust of her tongue into my throat, as direct and unfeminine as the harsh force of her voice.

"I'd like to hang my clothes up," she said.

It was not all that matter-of-fact when we got to bed. There was nothing very fleshy about the way she made love, no sense of the skin, nor smell, nor touch, just anger, anger at her being there, and another anger which was good for my own, that rage to achieve . . . just what, one cannot say. She made love as if she were running up an inclined wall so steep that to stop for an instant would slide her back to disaster. She hammered her rhythm at me, a hard driving rhythm, an all but monotonous drum, pound into pound against pound into pound until that moment when my anger found its way back again to that delayed and now recovered Time when I wanted to prong her at the party. I had been frustrated, had waited, had lost the anger, and so been taken by her. That finally got me—all through the talk about T. S. Eliot I had been calculating how I would lay waste to her little independence, and now she was alone, with me astride her, going through her paces, teeth biting the pillow, head turned away, using me as the dildoe of a private gallop. So my rage came back, and my rhythm no longer depended upon her drive, but found its own life, and we made love like two club fighters in an open exchange, neither giving ground, rhythm to rhythm, even to even, hypnotic, knowing neither the pain of punishment nor the pride of pleasure, and the equality of this, as hollow as the beat of the drum, seemed to carry her into some better deep of desire, and I had broken through, she was following me, her muscular body writhed all about me with an impersonal abandon, the wanton whip-thrash of a wounded snake, she was on fire and frozen at the same time, and then her mouth was kissing me with a rubbery greedy compulsion so avid to use all there was of me, that to my distant surprise, not in character for the saint to slip into the brutal, my hand came up and clipped her mean and openhanded across the face which brought a cry from her and broke the piston of her hard speed into something softer, wetter, more sly, more warm, I felt as if her belly were opening finally to receive me, and when her mouth kissed me again with a passing tender heat, warm-odored with flesh, and her body sweetened into some feminine embrace of my determination driving its way into her, well, I was gone, it was too late, I had driven right past her in that moment she turned, and I had begun to come, I was coming from all the confluences of my body toward that bud of sweetness I had plucked from her, and for a moment she was making it, she was a move back and surging to overtake me, and then it was gone, she made a mistake, her will ordered all temptings and rhythms to mobilize their march, she drove into the hard stupidities of a marching-band's step, and as I was going off in the best for many a month, she was merely going away, she had lost it again. As I ebbed into what should have been the contentments of a fine after-pleasure, warm and fine, there was one little part of me remaining cold and murderous because she had deprived me, she had fled the domination which was liberty for her, and the rest of the night was bound to be hell.

Her face was ugly. "You're a bastard, do you know that?" she asked me.

"Let it go. I feel good."

"Of course you feel good. Couldn't you have waited one minute?"

I disliked this kind of thing. My duty was reminding me of how her awakened sweets were souring now in the belly, and her nerves were sharpening into the gone electric of being just nowhere.

"I hate inept men," she said.

"Cool it." She could, at least, be a lady. Because if she didn't stop, I would give her back a word or two.

"You did that on purpose," she nagged at me, and I was struck with the intimacy of her rancor—we might as well have been married for ten years to dislike each other so much at this moment.

"Why," I said, "you talk as if this were something unusual for you."

"It is."

"Come on," I told her, "you've never made it in your life."

"How little you know," she said. "This is the first time I've missed in months."

If she had chosen to get my message, I could have been preparing now for a good sleep. Instead I would have to pump myself up again—and as if some ghost of the future laid the squeak of a tickle on my back, I felt an odd dread, not for tonight so much as for some ills of the next ten years whose first life was stirring tonight. But I lay beside her, drew her body against mine, feeling her trapped and irritable heats jangle me as much as they roused me, and while I had no fear that the avenger would remain asleep, still he stirred in pain and in protest, he had supposed his work to be done, and he would claim the wages of overtime from my reserve. That was the way I thought it would go, but Junior from New York University, with her hard body and her passion for proper poetry, gave a lewd and angry old grin as her face stared boldly into mine, and with the practical bawdiness of the Jew she took one straight utilitarian finger, smiled a deceptive girlish pride, and then she jabbed, fingernail and all, into the tight defended core of my clenched buttocks. One wiggle of her knuckle and I threw her off, grunting a sound between rage and surprise, to which she laughed and lay back and waited for me.

Well, she had been right, that finger tipped the balance, and three-quarters with it, and one-quarter hung with the mysteries of sexual ambition, I worked on her like a beaver for forty-odd minutes or more, slapping my tail to build her next, and she worked along while we made the round of the positions, her breath sobbing the exertions, her body as alive as a charged wire and as far from rest.

I gave her all the Time I had in me and more besides, I was weary of her, and the smell which rose from her had so little of the sea and so much of the armpit, that I breathed the stubborn wills of the gymnasium where the tight-muscled search for grace, and it was like that, a hard punishing session with pulley weights, stationary bicycle sprints, and ten breath-seared laps around the track. Yes, when I caught that smell, I knew she would not make it, and so I kept on just long enough to know she was exhausted in body, exhausted beyond the place where a ten-minute rest would have her jabbing that finger into me again, and hating her, hating women who could not take their exercise alone, I lunged up over the hill with my heart pounding past all pleasure, and I came, but with hatred, tight, electric, and empty, the spasms powerful but centered in my heart and not from the hip, the avenger taking its punishment even at the end, jolted clear to the seat of my semen by the succession of rhythmic blows which my heart drummed back to my feet.

For her, getting it from me, it must have been impressive, a convoluted, smashing, and protracted spasm, a hint of the death throe in the animal male which cannot but please the feminine taste for the mortal wound. "Oh, you're lucky," she whispered in my ear as I lay all collapsed beside her, alone in my athlete's absorption upon the whisperings of damage in the unlit complexities of my inner body. I was indeed an athlete, I knew my body was my future, and

I had damaged it a bit tonight by most certainly doing it no good. I disliked her for it with the simple dislike we know for the stupid.

"Want a cigarette?" she asked.

I could wait, my heart would have preferred its rest, but there was something tired in her voice beyond the fatigue of what she had done. She too had lost after all. So I came out of my second rest to look at her, and her face had the sad relaxation (and serenity) of a young whore who has finished a hard night's work with the expected lack of issue for herself, content with no more than the money and the professional sense of the hard job dutifully done.

"I'm sorry you didn't make it," I said to her.

She shrugged. There was a Jewish tolerance for the expected failures of the flesh. "Oh, well, I lied to you before," she said.

"You never have been able to, have you?"

"No." She was fingering the muscles of my shoulder, as if in unconscious competition with my strength. "You're pretty good," she said grudgingly.

"Not really inept?" I asked.

"*Sans façons,*" said the poetess in an arch change of mood which irritated me. "Sandy has been illuminating those areas where my habits make for destructive impulses."

"Sandy is Doctor Joyce?" She nodded. "You make him sound like your navigator," I told her.

"Isn't it a little obvious to be hostile to psychoanalysis?"

Three minutes ago we had been belaboring each other in the nightmare of the last round, and now we were close to cozy. I put the sole of my foot on her sharp little knee.

"You know the first one we had?" she asked of me. "Well, I wanted to tell you. I came close—I guess I came as close as I ever came."

"You'll come closer. You're only nineteen."

"Yes, but this evening has been disturbing to me. You see I get more from you than I get from my lover."

Her lover was twenty-one, a senior at Columbia, also Jewish—which lessened interest, she confessed readily. Besides, Arthur was too passive—"Basically, it's very comprehensible," said the commissar, "an aggressive female and a passive male—we complement one another, and that's no good." Of course it was easy to find satisfaction with Arthur, "via the oral perversions. That's because, vaginally, I'm anaesthetized—a good phallic narcissist like you doesn't do enough for me."

In the absence of learned credentials, she was setting out to bully again. So I thought to surprise her. "Aren't you mixing your language a little?" I began. "The phallic narcissist is one of Wilhelm Reich's categories."

"Therefore?"

"Aren't you a Freudian?"

"It would be presumptuous of me to say," she said like a seminar student working for his pee-aitch-dee. "But Sandy is an eclectic. He accepts a lot of Reich—you see, he's very ambitious, he wants to arrive at his own synthesis." She exhalted some smoke in my face, and gave a nice tough little grin which turned her long serious young witch's face into something indeed less presumptuous. "Besides," she said, "you are a phallic narcissist. There's an element of the sensual which is lacking in you."

"But Arthur possesses it?"

"Yes, he does. And you . . . you're not very juicy."

"I wouldn't know what you mean."

"I mean this." With the rich cruel look of a conquistador finding a new chest of Indian gold, she bent her head and gave one fleeting satiric half-moon of a lick to the conjugation of my balls. "That's what I mean," she said, and was out of bed even as I was recognizing that she was finally not without art. "Come back," I said.

But she was putting her clothes on in a hurry. "Shut up. Just don't give me your goddammed superiority."

I knew what it was: she had been about to gamble the reserves which belonged to Arthur, and the thought of possibly wasting them on a twenty-seven-year old connoisseur like myself was too infuriating to take the risk.

So I lay in bed and laughed at her while she dressed—I did not really want a go at things again—and besides, the more I laughed, the angrier she would be, but the anger would work to the surface, and beneath it would be resting the pain that the evening had ended on so little.

She took her leisure going to the door, and I got up in time to tell her to wait—I would walk her to the subway. The dawn had come, however, and she wanted to go alone, she had had a bellyful of me, she could tell me that.

My brain was lusting its own private futures of how interesting it would be to have this proud, aggressive, vulgar, tense, stiff and arrogant Jewess going wild on my bottom—I had turned more than one girl on, but never a one of quite this type. I suppose she had succeeded instead of me; I was ready to see her again and improve the message.

She turned down all dates, but compromised by giving me her address and the number of her telephone. And then glaring at me from the open door, she said, "I owe you a slap in the face."

"Don't go away feeling unequal."

I might have known she would have a natural punch. My jaw felt it for half an hour after she was gone and it took another thirty minutes before I could bring myself back to concluding that she was one funny kid.

All of that added up to the first night with the commissar, and I saw her two more times over this stretch, the last on the night when she finally agreed to sleep over with me, and I came awake in the morning to see her glaring at my head. So often in sex, when the second night wound itself up with nothing better in view than the memory of the first night, I was reminded of Kafka's *Castle*, that tale of the search of a man for his apocalyptic orgasm: in the easy optimism of a young man, he almost captures the castle on the first day, and is never to come so close again. Yes, that was the saga of the nervous system of a man as it was bogged into the defeats, complications, and frustrations of middle age. I still had my future before me of course—the full engagement of my will in some go-for-broke I considered worthy of myself was yet to come, but there were times in that loft when I knew the psychology of an old man, and my second night with Denise—for Denise Gondelman was indeed her name—left me racked for it amounted to so little that we could not even leave it there—the hangover would have been too great for both of us—and so we made a date for a third night. Over and over in those days I used to compare the bed to the bullfight, sometimes seeing myself as the matador and sometimes as the bull, and this second appearance, if it had taken place, in the Plaza Mexico, would have been a *fracaso* with kapok seat cushions jeering down on the ring, and a stubborn cowardly bull staying in *querencia* before the doubtful prissy overtures, the gloomy trim technique of a veteran and mediocre *torero* on the worst of days when he is forced to wonder if he has even his *pundonor* to sustain him. It was a gloomy deal. Each of us knew it was possible to be badly worked by the other, and this seemed so likely that neither of us would gamble a finger. Although we got into bed and had a perfunctory ten minutes, it was as long as an hour in a coffee shop when two friends are done with one another.

By the third night we were ready for complexities again; to see a woman three times is to call on the dialectic of an affair. If the waves we were making belonged less to the viper of passion than the worm of inquiry, still it was obvious from the beginning that we had surprises for one another. The second night we had been hoping for more, and so got less; this third night, we each came on with the notion to wind it up, and so got involved in more.

For one thing, Denise called me in the afternoon. There was studying she had to do, and she wondered if it would be all right to come to my place at eleven instead of meeting me for drinks and dinner. Since that would save me ten dollars she saw no reason why I should complain. It was a down conversation. I had been planning to lay siege to her, dispense a bit of elixir from my vast reservoirs of charm, and instead she was going to keep it *in camera*. There was a quality about her I could not locate, something independent—abruptly, right there, I knew what it was. In a year she would have no memory of me, I would not exist for her unless . . . and then it was clear . . . unless I could be the first to carry her stone of no-orgasm up the cliff, all the way, over and out into the sea. That was the kick I could find, that a year from now, five years from now, down all the seasons to the hours of her old age, I would be the one she would be forced to remember, and it would nourish me a little over the years, thinking of that grudged souvenir which could not die in her, my blond hair, my blue eyes, my small broken nose, my clean mouth and chin, my height, my boxer's body, my parts—yes, I was getting excited at the naked image of me in the young-old mind of that sour sexed-up dynamo of black-pussied frustration.

A phallic narcissist she had called me. Well, I was phallic enough, a Village stickman who could muster enough of the divine It on the head of his will to call forth more than one becoming out of the womb of feminine Time, yes a good deal more than one from my fifty new girls a year, and when I failed before various prisons of frigidity, it mattered little. Experience gave the cue that there were ladies who would not be moved an inch by a year of the best, and so I looked for other things in them, but this one, this Den-of-Ease, she was ready, she was entering the time of her Time, and if not me, it would be another—I was sick in advance at the picture of some bearded Negro cat who would score where I had missed and thus cuckold me in spirit, deprive me of those telepathic waves of longing (in which I obviously believed) speeding away to me from her over the years to balm the hours when I was beat, because I had been her psychic bridegroom, had plucked her ideational diddle, had led her down the walk of her real wedding night. Since she did not like me, what a feat to pull it off.

In the hours I waited after dinner, alone, I had the sense—which I always trusted—that tonight this little victory or defeat would be full of leverage, magnified beyond its emotional matter because I had decided to bet on myself that I would win, and a defeat would bring me closer to a general depression, a fog bank of dissatisfaction with myself which I knew could last for months or more. Whereas a victory would add to the panoplies of my ego some peculiar (but for me, valid) ingestion of her arrogance, her stubbornness, and her will— those necessary ingredients of which I could not yet have enough for my own ambition.

When she came in she was wearing a sweater and dungarees which I had been expecting, but there was a surprise for me. Her braids had been clipped, and a short cropped curled Italian haircut decorated her head, moving her severe young face half across the spectrum from the austerities of a poetess to a hint of all those practical and promiscuous European girls who sold their holy hump to the Germans and had been subsequently punished by shaved heads—how attractive the new hair proved; once punished, they were now free, free to be wild, the worst had happened and they were still alive with the taste of the first victor's flesh enriching the sensual curl of the mouth.

Did I like her this way? Denise was interested to know. Well, it was a shock, I admitted, a pleasant shock. If it takes you so long to decide, you must be rigid, she let me know. Well, yes, as a matter of fact I was rigid, rigid for her with waiting.

The nun of severity passed a shade over her. She hated men who were uncool, she thought she would tell me.

"Did your analyst tell you it's bad to be uncool?"

She had taken off her coat, but now she gave me a look as if she were ready to put it on again. "No, he did not tell me that." She laughed spitefully. "But he told me a couple of revealing things about you."

"Which you won't repeat."

"Of course not."

"I'll never know," I said, and gave her the first kiss of the evening. Her mouth was heated—it was the best kiss I had received from her, and it brought me on too quickly—"My fruit is ready to be plucked," said the odors of her mouth, betraying that perfume of the ducts which, against her will no doubt, had been plumping for me. She was changed tonight. From the skin of her face and the glen of her neck came a new smell, sweet, sweaty, and tender, the smell of a body which had been used and had enjoyed its uses. It came to me nicely, one of the nicest smells in quite some time, so different from the usual exudations of her dissatisfied salts that it opened a chain of reflexes in me, and I was off in all good speed on what Denise would probably have called the vertical foreplay. I suppose I went at her like a necrophiliac let loose upon a still-warm subject, and as I gripped her, grasped her, groped her, my breath a bellows to blow her into my own flame, her body remained unmoving, only her mouth answering my call, those lips bridling hot adolescent kisses back upon my face, the smell almost carrying me away—such a fine sweet sweat.

Naturally she clipped the rhythm. As I started to slip up her sweater, she got away and said a little huskily, "I'll take my own clothes off." Once again I could have hit her. My third eye, that athlete's inner eye which probed its vision into all the corners, happy and distressed of my body whole, was glumly cautioning the congestion of the spirits in the coils of each teste. They would have to wait, turn rancid, maybe die of delay.

Off came the sweater and the needless brassiere, her economical breasts swelled just a trifle tonight, enough to take on the convexities of an Amazon's armor. Open came the belt and the zipper of her dungarees, zipped from the front which pleased her not a little. Only her ass, a small masterpiece, and her strong thighs, justified this theatre. She stood there naked, quite psychicly clothed, and lit a cigarette.

If a stiff prick has no conscience, it has also no common sense. I stood there like a clown, trying to coax her to take a ride with me on the bawdy car, she out of her clothes, I in all of mine, a muscular little mermaid to melt on my knee. She laughed, one harsh banker's snort—she was giving no loans on my idiot's collateral.

"You didn't even ask me," Denise thought to say, "of how my studying went tonight."

"What did you study?"

"I didn't. I didn't study." She gave me a lovely smile, girlish and bright. "I just spent the last three hours with Arthur."

"You're a dainty type," I told her.

But she gave me a bad moment. That lovely flesh-spent smell, scent of the well used and the tender, that avatar of the feminine my senses had accepted so greedily, came down now to no more than the rubbings and the sweats of what was probably a very nice guy, passive Arthur with his Jewish bonanzas of mouth-love.

The worst of it was that it quickened me more. I had the selfish wisdom to throw such evidence upon the mercy of my own court. For the smell of Arthur was the smell of love, at least for me, and so from man or woman, it did not matter—the smell of love was always feminine—and if the man in Denise was melted by the woman in Arthur, so Arthur might have flowered that woman in himself from the arts of a real woman, his mother?—it did not matter—that voiceless message which passed from the sword of the man into the cavern of the woman was carried along from body to body, and if it was not the woman in Denise I was going to find tonight, at least I would be warmed by the previous trace of another.

But that was a tone poem to quiet the toads of my doubt. When Denise—it took five more minutes—finally decided to expose herself on my clumped old mattress, the sight of her black pubic hair, the feel of the foreign but brotherly liquids in her unembarrassed maw, turned me into a jackrabbit of pissy tumescence, the quicks of my excitement beheaded from the resonances of my body, and I wasn't with her a half-minute before I was over, gone, and off. I rode not with the strength to reap the harem of her and her lover, but spit like a pinched little boy up into black forested hills of motherly contempt, a passing picture of the nuns of my childhood to drench my piddle spurtings with failures of gloom. She it was who proved stronger than me, she the he to my silly she.

All considered, Denise was nice about it. Her harsh laugh did not crackle over my head, her hand in passing me the after-cigarette settled for no more than a nudge of my nose, and if it were not for the contempt of her tough grin, I would have been left with no more than the alarm to the sweepers of my brain to sweep this failure away.

"Hasn't happened in years," I said to her, the confession coming out of me with the cost of the hardest cash.

"Oh, shut up. Just rest." And she began to hum a mocking little song. I lay there in a state, parts of me jangled for forty-eight hours to come, and yet not altogether lost to peace. I knew what it was. Years ago in the air force, as an enlisted man, I had reached the light-heavyweight finals on my air base. For two weeks I trained for the championship, afraid of the other man all the way because I had seen him fight and felt he was better than me; when my night came, he took me out with a left hook to the liver which had me conscious on the canvas but unable to move, and as the referee was counting, which I could hear all too clearly, I knew the same kind of peace, a swooning peace, a clue to that kind of death in which an old man slips away—nothing mattered except that my flesh was vulnerable and I had a dim revery, lying there with the yells of the air force crowd in my ears, there was some far-off vision of green fields and me lying in them, giving up all ambition to go back instead to another, younger life of the senses, and I remember at that moment I watered the cup of my boxer's jock, and then I must have slipped into something new, for as they picked me off the canvas the floor seemed to recede from me at a great rate as if I were climbing in an airplane.

A few minutes later, the nauseas of the blow to my liver had me retching into my hands, and the tension of three weeks of preparation for that fight came back. I knew through the fading vistas of my peace, and the oncoming spasms of my nausea, that the worst was yet to come, and it would take me weeks to unwind, and then years, and maybe never to overcome the knowledge that I had failed completely at a moment when I wanted very much to win.

A ghost of this peace, trailing intimations of a new nausea, was passing over me again, and I sat up in bed abruptly, as if to drive these weaknesses back into me. My groin had been simmering for hours waiting for Denise, and it was swollen still, but the avenger was limp, he had deserted my cause, I was in a spot if she did not co-operate.

Co-operate she did. "My God, lie down again, will you," she said, "I was thinking that finally I had seen you relax."

And then I could sense that the woman in her was about to betray her victory. She sat over me, her little breasts budding with their own desire, her short hair alive and flowering, her mouth ready to taste her gentleman's defeat. I had only to raise my hand, and push her body in the direction she wished it to go, and then her face was rooting in me, her angry tongue and voracious mouth going wild finally as I had wished it, and I knew the sadness of sour timing, because this was a prize I could not enjoy as I would have on the first night, and yet it was good enough—not art, not the tease and languor of love on a soft mouth, but therapy, therapy for her, the quick exhaustions of the tension in a harsh throat, the beseechment of an ugly voice going down into the expiation which would be its beauty. Still it was good, practically it was good, my ego could bank the hard cash that this snotty head was searching me, the act served its purpose, anger traveled from her body into mine, the avenger came to attention, cold and furious, indifferent to the trapped doomed pleasure left behind in my body on that initial and grim piddle spurt, and I was ready, not with any joy nor softness nor warmth nor care, but I was ready finally to take her tonight, I was going to beat new Time out of her if beat her I must, I was going to teach her that she was only a child, because if at last I could not take care of a nineteen-year-old, then I was gone indeed. And so I took her with a cold calculation, the rhythms of my body corresponding to no more than a metronome in my mind, tonight the driving mechanical beat would come from me, and blind to nerve-raddlings in my body, and blood pressures in my brain, I worked on her like a riveter, knowing her resistances were made of steel, I threw her a fuck the equivalent of a fifteen-round fight, I wearied her, I brought her back, I drove my fingers into her shoulders and my knees into her hips, I went, and I went, and I went, I bore her high and thumped her hard, I sprinted, I paced, I lay low, eyes all closed, under sexual water, like a submarine listening for the distant sound of her ship's motors, hoping to steal up close and trick her rhythms away.

And she was close. Oh, she was close so much of the time. Like a child on a merry-go-round the touch of the colored ring just evaded the tips of her touch, and she heaved and she hurdled, arched and cried, clawed me, kissed me, even gave a shriek once, and then her sweats running down and her will weak, exhausted even more than me, she felt me leave and lie beside her. Yes, I did that with a tactician's cunning, I let the depression of her failure poison what was left of her will never to let me succeed, I gave her slack to mourn the lost freedoms and hate the final virginity for which she fought, I even allowed her baffled heat to take its rest and attack her nerves once more, and then, just as she was beginning to fret against me in a new and unwilling appeal, I turned her over suddenly on her belly, my avenger wild with the mania of the madman, and giving her no chance, holding her prone against the mattress with the strength of my weight, I drove into the seat of all stubbornness, tight as a vise, and I wounded her, I knew it, she thrashed beneath me like a trapped little animal, making not a sound, but fierce not to allow me this last of the liberties, and yet caught, forced to give up millimeter by millimeter the bridal ground of her symbolic and therefore real vagina. So I made it, I made it all the way—it took ten minutes and maybe more, but as the avenger rode down to his hilt and tunneled the threshold of sexual home all those inches closer into the bypass of the womb, she gave at last a little cry of farewell, and I could feel a new shudder which began as a ripple and rolled into a wave, and then it rolled over her, carrying her along, me hardly moving for fear of damping this quake from her earth, and then it was gone, but she was left alive with a larger one to follow.

So I turned her once again on her back, and moved by impulse to love's first hole. There was an odor coming up, hers at last, the smell of the sea, and none of the armpit or a dirty sock, and I took her mouth and kissed it, but she was away, following the wake of her own waves which mounted, fell back, and in new momentum mounted higher and should have gone over, and then she was about to hang again, I could feel it, that moment of hesitation between the past and the present, the habit and the adventure, and I said into her ear, "You dirty little Jew."

That whipped her over. A first wave kissed, a second spilled, and a third and a fourth and a fifth came breaking over, and finally she was away, she was loose in the water for the first time in her life, and I would have liked to go with her, but I was blood-throttled and numb, and as she had the first big moment in her life, I was nothing but a set of aching balls and a congested cock, and I rode with her wistfully, looking at the contortion of her face and listening to her sobbing sound of "Oh, Jesus, I made it, oh Jesus, I did."

"Compliments of T. S. Eliot," I whispered to myself, and my head was aching, my body was shot. She curled against me, she kissed my sweat, she nuzzled my eyes and murmured in my ear, and then she was slipping away into the nicest of weary sweet sleep.

"Was it good for you too?" she whispered half-awake, having likewise read the works of The Hemingway, and I said, "Yeah, fine," and after she was asleep, I disengaged myself carefully, and prowled the loft, accepting the hours it would take for my roiled sack to clean its fatigues and know a little sleep. But I had abused myself too far, and it took till dawn and half a fifth of whisky before I dropped into an unblessed stupor. When I awoke, in that moment before I moved to look at her, and saw her glaring at me, I was off on a sluggish masculine debate as to whether the kick of studying this Denise for another few nights—now that I had turned the key—would be worth the danger of deepening into some small real feeling. But through my hangover and the knowledge of the day and the week and the month it would take the different parts of all of me to repair, I was also knowing the taste of a reinforced will— finally, I had won. At no matter what cost, and with what luck, and with a piece of charity from her, I had won nonetheless, and since all real pay came from victory, it was more likely that I would win the next time I gambled my stake on something more appropriate for my ambition.

Then I turned, saw the hatred in her eyes, turned over again, and made believe I was asleep while a dread of the next few minutes weighed a leaden breath over the new skin of my ego.

"You're awake, aren't you?" she said.

I made no answer.

"All right, I'm going then. I'm getting dressed." She whipped out of bed, grabbed her clothes, and began to put them on with all the fury of waiting for me to get the pronouncement. "That was a lousy thing you did last night," she said by way of a start.

In truth she looked better than she ever had. The severe lady and the tough little girl of yesterday's face had put forth the first agreements on what would yet be a bold chick.

"I gave you what you could use," I made the mistake of saying.

"Just didn't you," she said, and was on her way to the door. "Well, cool it. You don't do anything to me." Then she smiled. "You're so impressed with what you think was such a marvelous notch you made in me, listen, Buster, I came here last night thinking of what Sandy Joyce told me about you, and he's right, oh man is he right." Standing in the open doorway, she started to light a cigarette, and then threw the matches to the floor. From thirty feet away I could see the look in her eyes, that unmistakable point for the kill that you find in the eyes of very few bullfighters, and then having created her pause, she came on for her moment of truth by saying, "He told me your whole life is a lie, and you do nothing but run away from the homosexual that is you."

And like a real killer, she did not look back, and was out the door before I could rise to tell her that she was a hero fit for me.

Alberto Moravia

(b. 1907) Alberto Moravia is the pseudonym of Alberto Pincherle, Italian novelist. Known as a realist, Moravia has written often and sympathetically about women. Among his translated works are The Time of Indifference, Woman of Rome, Two Adolescents, *and* Conjugal Love.

The Chase

I have never been a sportsman—or, rather, I have been a sportsman only once, and that was the first and last time. I was a child, and one day, for some reason or other, I found myself together with my father, who was holding a gun in his hand, behind a bush, watching a bird that had perched on a branch not very far away. It was a large, gray bird—or perhaps it was brown—with a long—or perhaps a short—beak; I don't remember. I only remember what I felt at that moment as I looked at it. It was like watching an animal whose vitality was rendered more intense by the very fact of my watching it and of the animal's not knowing that I was watching it.

At that moment, I say, the notion of wildness entered my mind, never again to leave it: everything is wild which is autonomous and unpredictable and does not depend upon us. Then all of a sudden there was an explosion; I could no longer see the bird and I thought it had flown away. But my father was leading the way, walking in front of me through the undergrowth. Finally he stooped down, picked up something and put it in my hand. I was aware of something warm and soft and I lowered my eyes: there was the bird in the palm of my hand, its dangling, shattered head crowned with a plume of already-thickening blood. I burst into tears and dropped the corpse on the ground, and that was the end of my shooting experience.

I thought again of this remote episode in my life this very day after watching

Reprinted with the permission of Farrar, Straus, & Giroux, Inc. From Command, And I Will Obey You *by Alberto Moravia, copyright © 1967 by Casa Editrice Valentino Bompiani, English translation copyright © 1969 by Martin Secker & Warburg Ltd.*

my wife, for the first and also the last time, as she was walking through the streets of the city. But let us take things in order.

What had my wife been like; what was she like now? She once had been, to put it briefly, "wild"—that is, entirely autonomous and unpredictable; latterly she had become "tame"—that is, predictable and dependent. For a long time she had been like the bird that, on that far-off morning in my childhood, I had seen perching on the bough; latterly, I am sorry to say, she had become like a hen about which one knows everything in advance—how it moves, how it eats, how it lays eggs, how it sleeps, and so on.

Nevertheless I would not wish anyone to think that my wife's wildness consisted of an uncouth, rough, rebellious character. Apart from being extremely beautiful, she is the gentlest, politest, most discreet person in the world. Rather her wildness consisted of the air of charming unpredictability, of independence in her way of living, with which during the first years of our marriage she acted in my presence, both at home and abroad. Wildness signified intimacy, privacy, secrecy. Yes, my wife as she sat in front of her dressing table, her eyes fixed on the looking glass, passing the hairbrush with a repeated motion over her long, loose hair, was just as wild as the solitary quail hopping forward along a sun-filled furrow or the furtive fox coming out into a clearing and stopping to look around before running on. She was wild because I, as I looked at her, could never manage to foresee when she would give a last stroke with the hairbrush and rise and come toward me; wild to such a degree that sometimes when I went into our bedroom the smell of her, floating in the air, would have something of the acrid quality of a wild beast's lair.

Gradually she became less wild, tamer. I had had a fox, a quail, in the house, as I have said; then one day I realized that I had a hen. What effect does a hen have on someone who watches it? It has the effect of being, so to speak, an automaton in the form of a bird; automatic are the brief, rapid steps with which it moves about; automatic its hard, terse pecking; automatic the glance of the round eyes in its head that nods and turns; automatic its ready crouching down under the cock; automatic the dropping of the egg wherever it may be and the cry with which it announces that the egg has been laid. Good-by to the fox; good-by to the quail. And her smell—this no longer brought to my mind, in any way, the innocent odor of a wild animal; rather I detected in it the chemical suavity of some ordinary French perfume.

Our flat is on the first floor of a big building in a modern quarter of the town; our windows look out on a square in which there is a small public garden, the haunt of nurses and children and dogs. One day I was standing at the window, looking in a melancholy way at the garden. My wife, shortly before, had dressed to go out; and once again, watching her, I had noticed the irrevocable and, so to speak, invisible character of her gestures and personality: something which gave one the feeling of a thing already seen and already done and which therefore evaded even the most determined observation. And now, as I stood looking at the garden and at the same time wondering why the adorable wildness of former times had so completely disappeared, suddenly my wife came into my range of vision as she walked quickly across the garden in the direction of the bus stop. I watched her and then I almost jumped for joy; in a movement she was making to pull down a fold of her narrow skirt and smooth it over her thigh with the tips of her long, sharp nails, in this movement I recognized the wildness that in the past had made me love her. It was only an instant, but in that instant I said to myself: She's become wild again because she's convinced that I am not there and am not watching her. Then I left the window and rushed out.

But I did not join her at the bus stop; I felt that I must not allow myself to be seen. Instead I hurried to my car, which was standing nearby, got in and waited. A bus came and she got in together with some other people; the bus started off again and I began following it. Then there came back to me the memory of that one shooting expedition in which I had taken part as a child, and I saw that the bus was the undergrowth with its bushes and trees, my wife the bird perching on the bough while I, unseen, watched it living before my eyes. And the whole town, during this pursuit, became, as though by magic, a fact of nature like the countryside: the houses were hills, the streets valleys, the vehicles hedges and woods, and even the passers-by on the pavements had something unpredictable and autonomous—that is, wild—about them. And in my mouth, behind my clenched teeth, there was the acrid, metallic taste of gunfire; and my eyes, usually listless and wandering, had become sharp, watchful, attentive.

These eyes were fixed intently upon the exit door when the bus came to the end of its run. A number of people got out, and then I saw my wife getting out. Once again I recognized, in the manner in which she broke free of the crowd and started off toward a neighboring street, the wildness that pleased me so much. I jumped out of the car and started following her.

She was walking in front of me, ignorant of my presence, a tall woman with an elegant figure, long-legged, narrow-hipped, broad-backed, her brown hair falling on her shoulders.

Men turned around as she went past; perhaps they were aware of what I myself was now sensing with an intensity that quickened the beating of my heart and took my breath away: the unrestricted, steadily increasing, irresistible character of her mysterious wildness.

She walked hurriedly, having evidently some purpose in view, and even the fact that she had a purpose of which I was ignorant added to her wildness; I did not know where she was going, just as on that far-off morning I had not known what the bird perching on the bough was about to do. Moreover I thought the gradual, steady increase in this quality of wildness came partly from the fact that as she drew nearer and nearer to the object of this mysterious walk there was an increase in her—how shall I express it?— of biological tension, of existential excitement, of vital effervescence. Then, unexpectedly, with the suddenness of a film, her purpose was revealed.

A fair-haired young man in a leather jacket and a pair of corduroy trousers was leaning against the wall of a house in that ancient, narrow street. He was idly smoking as he looked in front of him. But as my wife passed close to him, he threw away his cigarette with a decisive gesture, took a step forward and seized her arm. I was expecting her to rebuff him, to move away from him, but nothing happened: evidently obeying the rules of some kind of erotic ritual, she went on walking beside the young man. Then after a few steps, with a movement that confirmed her own complicity, she put her arm around her companion's waist and he put his around her.

I understood then that this unknown man who took such liberties with my wife was also attracted by wildness. And so, instead of making a conventional appointment with her, instead of a meeting in a café with a handshake, a falsely friendly and respectful welcome, he had preferred, by agreement with her, to take her by surprise—or, rather, to pretend to do so—while she was apparently taking a walk on her own account. All this I perceived by intuition, noticing that at the very moment when he stepped forward and took her arm her wildness had, so to speak, given an upward bound. It was years since I had seen my wife so alive, but alas, the source of this life could not be traced to me.

They walked on thus entwined and then, without any preliminaries, just like two wild animals, they did an unexpected thing: they went into one of the dark doorways in order to kiss. I stopped and watched them from a distance, peering into the darkness of the entrance. My wife was turned away from me and was bending back with the pressure of his body, her hair hanging free. I looked at that long, thick mane of brown hair, which as she leaned back fell free of her shoulders, and I felt that at that moment her vitality reached its diapason, just as happens with wild animals when they couple and their customary wildness is redoubled by the violence of love. I watched for a long time and then, since this kiss went on and on and in fact seemed to be prolonged beyond the limits of my power of endurance, I saw that I would have to intervene.

I would have to go forward, seize my wife by the arm—or actually by that hair, which hung down and conveyed so well the feeling of feminine passivity—then hurl myself with clenched fists upon the blond young man. After this encounter I would carry off my wife, weeping, mortified, ashamed, while I was raging and broken-hearted, upbraiding her and pouring scorn upon her.

But what else would this intervention amount to but the shot my father fired at that free, unknowing bird as it perched on the bough? The disorder and confusion, the mortification, the shame, that would follow would irreparably destroy the rare and precious moment of wildness that I was witnessing inside the dark doorway. It was true that this wildness was directed against me; but I had to remember that wildness, always and everywhere, is directed against everything and everybody. After the scene of my intervention it might be possible for me to regain control of my wife, but I should find her shattered and lifeless in my arms like the bird that my father had placed in my hand so that I might throw it into the shooting bag.

The kiss went on and on and on: well, it was a kiss of passion—that could not be denied. I waited until they finished, until they came out of the doorway, until they walked on again still linked together. Then I turned back.

William Blake

*(1757–1827) Usually considered a
Romantic poet, William Blake was
such an individual that it is hard to
label him. He was essentially a
revolutionary in politics and in
philosophy, and his long mystical
poems have had many interpretations.
His own beautiful engravings illustrate
and help to explain many of his poems.
Blake was as ardent a women's
liberationist as was his contemporary,
Mary Wollstonecraft.*

Song

How sweet I roam'd from field to field
And tasted all the summer's pride,
Till I the Prince of Love beheld
Who in the sunny beams did glide!

He show'd me lilies for my hair,
And blushing roses for my brow;
He led me through his gardens fair
Where all his golden pleasures grow.

With sweet May dews my wings were wet,
And Phoebus fir'd my vocal rage;
He caught me in his silken net,
And shut me in his golden cage.

He loves to sit and hear me sing,
Then, laughing, sports and plays with me;
Then stretches out my golden wing,
And mocks my loss of liberty.

From Poetical Sketches, *1783.*

VI. the old maid

Miss Gee, Miss Brill, and Louisa Ellis, all old maids, are presented as having missed out on life; they are observers, not participants. Miss Gee turns her head away as she passes lovers who do not ask her to stay; Miss Brill sits on a bench, vicariously living the experience of those she watches. Louisa Ellis turns with relief from the prospect of marriage, happy to see her fiancé in love with a younger woman. The cancer which consumes Miss Gee, the moth-eaten furpiece that stirs Miss Brill's maternal feelings, and the dog which Louisa keeps chained are all symbols of woman's "foiled creative fire," and they invite the reader's pity. Yet the reader is also asked to see these women as absurd. The images of Miss Gee bicycling to church as if pursued by a bull, Miss Brill thinking that her eavesdropping means sharing in the drama of life, and Louisa sweeping up after Joe are ludicrous as well as pathetic. They are regarded by the characters in the stories not with sympathy as lonely human beings but with condescension as somehow not fully human. The Oxford Groupers, members of a religious group teaching the original Christian doctrine of charity, dissect the body of Miss Gee. The callous young lovers refer to Miss Brill as an "old thing." Joe Dagget is relieved that Louisa will not marry him, and the reader is invited by images of narrowness and waste to see her decision to live alone as a refusal really to live.

Yet the reader can see that, at least for Miss Brill and Louisa, being an old maid is not totally a deprivation. Miss Brill earns her own living; she has the courage and imagination to make the most of "a diminished thing," like the ovenbird in Robert Frost's poem of that name. Like most human beings, Miss Brill must accept less of life than she had hoped to have. Yet she does so with bravery and even gaiety and should be admired, not pitied. It is the failure of the young couple's imagination that makes Miss Brill seem pathetic; it is their cruelty in stereotyping her which undermines her gallant approach to life.

Similarly, despite Mary E. Freeman's use of sunset and fading images to describe Louisa's peace of mind, Louisa's choice can be viewed as the beginning of a richer life, not a narrower one. Though she "dies to the world" as a nun does upon taking her vows, it is arrogant to conclude that being herself and living on her own terms in a world she has created for herself is a diminishment of life. Many an overworked wife living with a demanding mother-in-law might well envy Louisa Ellis her freedom. One could hardly envy Miss Gee; yet to imply that a childless woman is like a retired man, in that both are subject to cancer, is to assert that motherhood is the only means for a woman to achieve humanity—that to be flat-chested, sterile, and unwanted by men is not to live at all. Auden's attitude is a clear statement that, for women, anatomy is destiny.

W. H. Auden

*(b. 1907) Born in England, W. H.
Auden became an American citizen in
1939; for many years he has spent
his winters in New York but has
decided finally to return to Oxford to
live. Auden's early interest in Marxism
gave way to a deep commitment to
Christianity expressed most fully in*
For the Time Being. *His poems, often
light in tone, reflect a wide interest
in politics, literature, and music.*

Miss Gee

Let me tell you a little story
    About Miss Edith Gee;
She lived in Clevedon Terrace
    At Number 83.

She'd a slight squint in her left eye,
    Her lips they were thin and small,
She had narrow sloping shoulders
    And she had no bust at all.

She'd a velvet hat with trimmings,
    And a dark-grey serge costume;
She lived in Clevedon Terrace
    In a small bed-sitting room.

She'd a purple mac for wet days,
    A green umbrella too to take,
She'd a bicycle with shopping basket
    And a harsh back-pedal brake.

The Church of Saint Aloysius
    Was not so very far;
She did a lot of knitting,
    Knitting for that Church Bazaar.

Miss Gee looked up at the starlight
    And said: 'Does anyone care
That I live in Clevedon Terrace
    On one hundred pounds a year?'

She dreamed a dream one evening
    That she was the Queen of France
And the Vicar of Saint Aloysius
    Asked Her Majesty to dance.

But a storm blew down the palace,
    She was biking through a field of corn,
And a bull with the face of the Vicar
    Was charging with lowered horn.

She could feel his hot breath behind her,
    He was going to overtake;
And the bicycle went slower and slower
    Because of that back-pedal brake.

Summer made the trees a picture,
    Winter made them a wreck;
She bicycled to the evening service
    With her clothes buttoned up to her neck.

She passed by the loving couples,
    She turned her head away;
She passed by the loving couples
    And they didn't ask her to stay.

Miss Gee sat down in the side-aisle,
    She heard the organ play;
And the choir it sang so sweetly
    At the ending of the day,

Miss Gee knelt down in the side-aisle,
    She knelt down on her knees;
'Lead me not into temptation
    But make me a good girl, please.'

The days and nights went by her
    Like waves round a Cornish wreck;
She bicycled down to the doctor
    With her clothes buttoned up to her neck.

She bicycled down to the doctor,
    And rang the surgery bell;
'O, doctor, I've a pain inside me,
    And I don't feel very well.'

Doctor Thomas looked her over,
    And then he looked some more;
Walked over to his wash-basin,
    Said, 'Why didn't you come before?'

Doctor Thomas sat over his dinner,
    Though his wife was waiting to ring;
Rolling his bread into pellets,
    Said, 'Cancer's a funny thing.

'Nobody knows what the cause is,
    Though some pretend they do;
It's like some hidden assassin
    Waiting to strike at you.

'Childless women get it,
    And men when they retire;
It's as if there had to be some outlet
    For their foiled creative fire.'

His wife she rang for the servant,
    Said, 'Don't be so morbid, dear,'
He said; 'I saw Miss Gee this evening
    And she's a goner, I fear.'

They took Miss Gee to the hospital,
    She lay there a total wreck,
Lay in the ward for women
    With the bedclothes right up to her neck.

They laid her on the table,
    The students began to laugh;
And Mr. Rose the surgeon
    He cut Miss Gee in half.

Mr. Rose he turned to his students,
    Said; 'Gentlemen, if you please,
We seldom see a sarcoma
    As far advanced as this.'

They took her off the table,
    They wheeled away Miss Gee
Down to another department
    Where they study Anatomy.

They hung her from the ceiling,
    Yes, they hung up Miss Gee;
And a couple of Oxford Groupers
    Carefully dissected her knee.

Katherine Mansfield

(1888-1923) Katherine Mansfield was born in New Zealand but spent most of her life in England. She was married to the critic John Middleton Murry and was the friend of many famous writers. Her short stories show great psychological insight into children and women, whose lives she often reveals by focusing on just one incident. Major collections of her stories include Bliss, The Garden Party, *and* The Dove's Nest.

Miss Brill

Although it was so brilliantly fine—the blue sky powdered with gold and great spots of light like white wine splashed over the Jardins Publiques—Miss Brill was glad that she had decided on her fur. The air was motionless, but when you opened your mouth there was just a faint chill, like a chill from a glass of iced water before you sip, and now and again a leaf came drifting—from nowhere, from the sky. Miss Brill put up her hand and touched her fur. Dear little thing! It was nice to feel it again. She had taken it out of its box that afternoon, shaken out the moth powder, given it a good brush, and rubbed the life back into the dim little eyes. "What has been happening to me?" said the sad little eyes. Oh, how sweet it was to see them snap at her again from the red eiderdown! . . . But the nose, which was of some black composition, wasn't at all firm. It must have had a knock, somehow. Never mind—a little dab of black sealing-wax when the time came—when it was absolutely necessary . . . Little rogue! Yes, she really felt like that about it. Little rogue biting its tail just by her left ear. She could have taken it off and laid it on her lap and stroked it. She felt a tingling in her hands and arms, but that came from walking, she supposed. And when she breathed, something light and sad—no, not sad, exactly—something gentle seemed to move in her bosom.

There were a number of people out this afternoon, far more than last Sunday. And the band sounded louder and gayer. That was because the Season

313

had begun. For although the band played all the year round on Sundays, out of season it was never the same. It was like some one playing with only the family to listen; it didn't care how it played if there weren't any strangers present. Wasn't the conductor wearing a new coat, too? She was sure it was new. He scraped with his foot and flapped his arms like a rooster about to crow, and the bandsmen sitting in the green rotunda blew out their cheeks and glared at the music. Now there came a little "flutey" bit—very pretty!—a little chain of bright drops. She was sure it would be repeated. It was; she lifted her head and smiled.

Only two people shared her "special" seat: a fine old man in a velvet coat, his hands clasped over a huge carved walking-stick, and a big old woman, sitting upright, with a roll of knitting on her embroidered apron. They did not speak. This was disappointing, for Miss Brill always looked forward to the conversation. She had become really quite expert, she thought, at listening as though she didn't listen, at sitting in other people's lives just for a minute while they talked round her.

She glanced, sideways, at the old couple. Perhaps they would go soon. Last Sunday, too, hadn't been as interesting as usual. An Englishman and his wife, he wearing a dreadful Panama hat and she button boots. And she'd gone on the whole time about how she ought to wear spectacles; she knew she needed them; but that it was no good getting any; they'd be sure to break and they'd never keep on. And he'd been so patient. He'd suggested everything—gold rims, the kind that curved round your ears, little pads inside the bridge. No, nothing would please her. "They'll always be sliding down my nose!" Miss Brill had wanted to shake her.

The old people sat on the bench, still as statues. Never mind, there was always the crowd to watch. To and fro, in front of the flower beds and the band rotunda, the couples and groups paraded, stopped to talk, to greet, to buy a handful of flowers from the old beggar who had his tray fixed to the railings. Little children ran among them, swooping and laughing; little boys with big white silk bows under their chins, little girls, little French dolls, dressed up in velvet and lace. And sometimes a tiny staggerer came suddenly rocking into the open from under the trees, stopped, stared, as suddenly sat down "flop," until its small high-stepping mother, like a young hen, rushed scolding to its rescue. Other people sat on the benches and green chairs, but they were nearly always the same, Sunday after Sunday, and—Miss Brill had often noticed—there was something funny about nearly all of them. They were odd, silent, nearly all old, and from the way they stared they looked as though they'd just come from dark little rooms or even—even cupboards!

Behind the rotunda the slender trees with yellow leaves down drooping, and through them just a line of sea, and beyond the blue sky with gold-veined clouds.

Tum-tum-tum tiddle-um! tiddle-um! tum tiddley-um tum ta! blew the band.

Two young girls in red came by and two young soldiers in blue met them, and they laughed and paired and went off arm-in-arm. Two peasant women with funny straw hats passed, gravely, leading beautiful smoke-colored donkeys. A cold, pale nun hurried by. A beautiful woman came along and dropped her bunch of violets, and a little boy ran after to hand them to her, and she took them and threw them away as if they'd been poisoned. Dear me! Miss Brill didn't know whether to admire that or not! And now an ermine toque and a gentleman in gray met just in front of her. He was tall, stiff, dignified, and she was wearing the ermine toque she'd bought when her hair was yellow. Now everything, her hair, her face, even her eyes, was the same color as the shabby ermine, and her hand, in its cleaned glove, lifted to dab her lips, was a tiny yellowish paw. Oh, she was so pleased to see him—delighted! She rather thought they were going to meet that afternoon. She described where she'd been—everywhere, here, there, along by the sea. The day was so charming—didn't he agree? And wouldn't he, perhaps? . . . But he shook his head, lighted a cigarette, slowly breathed a great deep puff into her face, and, even while she was still talking and laughing, flicked the match away and walked on. The ermine toque was alone; she smiled more brightly than ever. But even the band seemed to know what she was feeling and played more softly, played tenderly, and the drum beat, "The Brute! The Brute!" over and over. What would she do? What was going to happen now? But as Miss Brill wondered, the ermine toque turned, raised her hand as though she'd seen some one else, much nicer, just over there, and pattered away. And the band changed again and played more quickly, more gayly than ever, and the old couple on Miss Brill's seat got up and marched away, and such a funny old man with long whiskers hobbled along in time to the music and was nearly knocked over by four girls walking abreast.

Oh, how fascinating it was! How she enjoyed it! How she loved sitting here, watching it all! It was like a play. It was exactly like a play. Who could believe the sky at the back wasn't painted? But it wasn't till a little brown dog trotted on solemn and then slowly trotted off, like a little "theater" dog, a little dog that had been drugged, that Miss Brill discovered what it was that made it so exciting. They were all on the stage. They weren't only the audience, not only looking on; they were acting. Even she had a part and came every Sunday. No doubt somebody would have noticed if she hadn't been there; she was part of the performance after all. How strange she'd never thought of it like that before! And yet it explained why she made such a point of starting from home at just the same time each week—so as not to be late for the performance—and it also explained why she had quite a queer, shy feeling at telling her English pupils how she spent her Sunday afternoons. No wonder! Miss Brill nearly laughed out loud. She was on the stage. She thought of the old invalid gentleman to whom she read the newspaper four afternoons a week while he slept in the garden. She had got quite used to the frail head on the cotton pillow, the hollowed eyes, the open mouth and the high pinched nose. If he'd been dead she mightn't have noticed for weeks; she wouldn't have minded. But suddenly he knew he was having the paper read to him by an actress! "An actress!" The old head lifted; two points of light quivered in the old eyes. "An actress—are ye?" And Miss Brill smoothed the newspaper as though it were the manuscript of her part and said gently: "Yes, I have been an actress for a long time."

The band had been having a rest. Now they started again. And what they played was warm, sunny, yet there was just a faint chill—a something, what was it?—not sadness—no, not sadness—a something that made you want to sing. The tune lifted, lifted, the light shone; and it seemed to Miss Brill that in another moment all of them, all the whole company, would begin singing. The young ones, the laughing ones who were moving together, they would begin, and the men's voices, very resolute and brave, would join them. And then she too, she too, and the others on the benches—they would come in with a kind of accompaniment—something low, that scarcely rose or fell, something so beautiful—moving . . . And Miss Brill's eyes filled with tears and she looked smiling at all the other members of the company. Yes, we understand, we understand, she thought—though what they understood she didn't know.

Just at that moment a boy and a girl came and sat down where the old couple had been. They were beautifully dressed; they were in love. The hero and heroine, of course, just arrived from his father's yacht. And still soundlessly singing, still with that trembling smile, Miss Brill prepared to listen.

"No, not now," said the girl. "Not here, I can't."

"But why? Because of that stupid old thing at the end there?" asked the boy. "Why does she come here at all—who wants her? Why doesn't she keep her silly old mug at home?"

"It's her fu-fur which is so funny," giggled the girl. "It's exactly like a fried whiting."

"Ah, be off with you!" said the boy in an angry whisper. Then: "Tell me, ma petite chère—"

"No, not here," said the girl. "Not *yet*."

On her way home she usually bought a slice of honeycake at the baker's. It was her Sunday treat. Sometimes there was an almond in her slice, sometimes not. It made a great difference. If there was an almond it was like carrying home a tiny present—a surprise—something that might very well not have been there. She hurried on the almond Sundays and struck the match for the kettle in quite a dashing way.

But today she passed the baker's by, climbed the stairs, went into the little dark room—her room like a cupboard—and sat down on the red eiderdown. She sat there for a long time. The box that the fur came out of was on the bed. She unclasped the necklet quickly; quickly, without looking, laid it inside. But when she put the lid on she thought she heard something crying.

Mary E. Wilkins Freeman

(1852–1930) Mary E. Wilkins Freeman wrote many novels and short stories about the frustrations of life in New England small towns, a subject she knew firsthand. Her short story collections include A Humble Romance and Other Stories, A New England Nun and Other Stories, *and* The Wind in the Rose Bush. *Many of these and several of her novels, such as* The Revolt of Mother *and* Jane Field, *depict realistically the everyday life of women.*

A New England Nun

It was late in the afternoon, and the light was waning. There was a difference in the look of the tree shadows out in the yard. Somewhere in the distance cows were lowing and a little bell was tinkling; now and then a farm-wagon tilted by, and the dust flew; some blue-shirted laborers with shovels over their shoulders plodded past; little swarms of flies were dancing up and down before the people's faces in the soft air. There seemed to be a gentle stir arising over everything for the mere sake of subsidence—a very premonition of rest and hush and night.

This soft diurnal commotion was over Louisa Ellis also. She had been peacefully sewing at her sitting-room window all the afternoon. Now she quilted her needle carefully into her work, which she folded precisely, and laid in a basket with her thimble and thread and scissors. Louisa Ellis could not remember that ever in her life she had mislaid one of these little feminine appurtenances, which had become, from long use and constant association, a very part of her personality.

Louisa tied a green apron round her waist, and got out a flat straw hat with a green ribbon. They she went into the garden with a little blue crockery bowl, to pick some currants for her tea. After the currants were picked she sat on the back door-step and stemmed them, collecting the stems carefully in her apron, and afterward throwing them into the hen-coop. She looked sharply at the grass beside the step to see if any had fallen there.

From A New England Nun and Other Stories, *1891.*

Louisa was slow and still in her movements; it took her a long time to prepare her tea; but when ready it was set forth with as much grace as if she had been a veritable guest to her own self. The little square table stood exactly in the centre of the kitchen, and was covered with a starched linen cloth whose border pattern of flowers glistened. Louisa had a damask napkin on her tea-tray, where were arranged a cut-glass tumbler full of teaspoons, a silver cream-pitcher, a china sugar-bowl, and one pink china cup and saucer. Louisa used china every day—something which none of her neighbors did. They whispered about it among themselves. Their daily tables were laid with common crockery, their sets of best china stayed in the parlor closet, and Louisa Ellis was no richer nor better bred than they. Still she would use the china. She had for her supper a glass dish full of sugared currants, a plate of little cakes, and one of light white biscuits. Also a leaf or two of lettuce, which she cut up daintily. Louisa was very fond of lettuce, which she raised to perfection in her little garden. She ate quite heartily, though in a delicate, pecking way; it seemed almost surprising that any considerable bulk of the food should vanish.

After tea she filled a plate with nicely baked thin corn-cakes, and carried them out into the back-yard.

"Caesar!" she called. "Caesar! Caesar!"

There was a little rush, and the clank of a chain, and a large yellow-and-white dog appeared at the door of his tiny hut, which was half hidden among the tall grasses and flowers. Louisa patted him and gave him the corn-cakes. Then she returned to the house and washed the tea-things, polishing the china carefully. The twilight had deepened; the chorus of the frogs floated in at the open window wonderfully loud and shrill, and once in a while a long sharp drone from a tree-toad pierced it. Louisa took off her green gingham apron, disclosing a shorter one of pink-and-white print. She lighted her lamp, and sat down again with her sewing.

In about half an hour Joe Dagget came. She heard his heavy step on the walk, and rose and took off her pink-and-white apron. Under that was still another—white linen with a little cambric edging on the bottom; that was Louisa's company apron. She never wore it without her calico sewing apron over it unless she had a guest. She had barely folded the pink and white one with methodical haste and laid it in a table-drawer when the door opened and Joe Dagget entered.

He seemed to fill up the whole room. A little yellow canary that had been asleep in his green cage at the south window woke up and fluttered wildly, beating his little yellow wings against the wires. He always did so when Joe Dagget came into the room.

"Good-evening," said Louisa. She extended her hand with a kind of solemn cordiality.

"Good-evening, Louisa," returned the man, in a loud voice.

She placed a chair for him, and they sat facing each other, with the table between them. He sat bolt-upright, toeing out his heavy feet squarely, glancing with a good-humored uneasiness around the room. She sat gently erect, folding her slender hands in her white-linen lap.

"Been a pleasant day," remarked Dagget.

"Real pleasant," Louisa assented softly. "Have you been haying?" she asked, after a little while.

"Yes, I've been haying all day, down in the ten-acre lot. Pretty hot work."

"It must be."

"Yes, it's pretty hot work in the sun."

"Is your mother well to-day?"

"Yes, mother's pretty well."

"I suppose Lily Dyer's with her now?"

Dagget colored. "Yes, she's with her," he answered slowly.

He was not very young, but there was a boyish look about his large face. Louisa was not quite as old as he, her face was fairer and smoother, but she gave people the impression of being older.

"I suppose she's a good deal of help to your mother," she said, further.

"I guess she is; I don't know how mother'd get along without her," said Dagget, with a sort of embarrassed warmth.

"She looks like a real capable girl. She's pretty-looking too," remarked Louisa.

"Yes, she is pretty fair looking."

Presently Dagget began fingering the books on the table. There was a square red autograph album, and a Young Lady's Gift-Book which had belonged to Louisa's mother. He took them up one after the other and opened them; then laid them down again, the album on the Gift-Book.

Louisa kept eying them with mild uneasiness. Finally she rose and changed the position of the books, putting the album underneath. That was the way they had been arranged in the first place.

Dagget gave an awkward little laugh. "Now what difference did it make which book was on top?" said he.

Louisa looked at him with a deprecating smile. "I always keep them that way," murmured she.

"You do beat everything," said Dagget, trying to laugh again. His large face was flushed.

He remained about an hour longer, then rose to take leave. Going out, he stumbled over a rug, and trying to recover himself, hit Louisa's work-basket on the table, and knocked it on the floor.

He looked at Louisa, then at the rolling spools; he ducked himself awkwardly toward them, but she stopped him. "Never mind," said she; "I'll pick them up after you're gone."

She spoke with a mild stiffness. Either she was a little disturbed, or his nervousness affected her, and made her seem constrained in her effort to reassure him.

When Joe Dagget was outside he drew in the sweet evening air with a sigh, and felt much as an innocent and perfectly well-intentioned bear might after his exit from a china shop.

Louisa, on her part, felt much as the kind-hearted, long-suffering owner of the china shop might have done after the exit of the bear.

She tied on the pink, then the green apron, picked up all the scattered treasures and replaced them in her work-basket, and straightened the rug. Then she set the lamp on the floor, and began sharply examining the carpet. She even rubbed her fingers over it, and looked at them.

"He's tracked in a good deal of dust," she murmured. "I thought he must have."

Louisa got a dust-pan and brush, and swept Joe Dagget's track carefully.

If he could have known it, it would have increased his perplexity and uneasiness, although it would not have disturbed his loyalty in the least. He came twice a week to see Louisa Ellis, and every time, sitting there in her delicately sweet room, he felt as if surrounded by a hedge of lace. He was afraid to stir lest he should put a clumsy foot or hand through the fairy web, and he had always the consciousness that Louisa was watching fearfully lest he should.

Still the lace and Louisa commanded perforce his perfect respect and patience and loyalty. They were to be married in a month, after a singular courtship which had lasted for a matter of fifteen years. For fourteen out of the fifteen years the two had not once seen each other, and they had seldom exchanged letters. Joe had been all those years in Australia, where he had gone to make his fortune, and where he had stayed until he made it. He would have stayed fifty years if it had taken so long, and come home feeble and tottering, or never come home at all, to marry Louisa.

But the fortune had been made in the fourteen years, and he had come home now to marry the woman who had been patiently and unquestioningly waiting for him all that time.

Shortly after they were engaged he had announced to Louisa his determination to strike out into new fields, and secure a competency before they should be married. She had listened and assented with the sweet serenity which never failed her, not even when her lover set forth on that long and uncertain journey. Joe, buoyed up as he was by his sturdy determination, broke down a little at the last, but Louisa kissed him with a mild blush, and said good-by.

"It won't be for long," poor Joe had said, huskily; but it was for fourteen years.

In that length of time much had happened. Louisa's mother and brother had died, and she was all alone in the world. But greatest happening of all—a subtle happening which both were too simple to understand—Louisa's feet had turned into a path, smooth maybe under a calm, serene sky, but so straight and unswerving that it could only meet a check at the grave, and so narrow that there was no room for any one at her side.

Louisa's first emotion when Joe Dagget came home (he had not apprised her of his coming) was consternation, although she would not admit it to herself, and he never dreamed of it. Fifteen years ago she had been in love with him—at least she considered herself to be. Just at that time, gently acquiescing with and falling into the natural drift of girlhood, she had seen marriage ahead as a reasonable feature and a probable desirability of life. She had listened with calm docility to her mother's views upon the subject. Her mother was remarkable for her cool sense and sweet, even temperament. She talked wisely to her daughter when Joe Dagget presented himself, and Louisa accepted him with no hesitation. He was the first lover she had ever had.

She had been faithful to him all these years. She had never dreamed of the possibility of marrying any one else. Her life, especially for the last seven years, had been full of a pleasant peace, she had never felt discontented nor impatient over her lover's absence; still she had always looked forward to his return and their marriage as the inevitable conclusion of things. However, she had fallen into a way of placing it so far in the future that it was almost equal to placing it over the boundaries of another life.

When Joe came she had been expecting him, and expecting to be married for fourteen years, but she was as much surprised and taken aback as if she had never thought of it.

Joe's consternation came later. He eyed Louisa with an instant confirmation of his old admiration. She had changed but little. She still kept her pretty manner and soft grace, and was, he considered, every whit as attractive as ever. As for himself, his stint was done; he had his face turned away from fortune-seeking, and the old winds of romance whistled as loud and sweet as ever through his ears. All the song which he had been wont to hear in them was Louisa; he had for a long time a loyal belief that he heard it still, but finally it seemed to him that although the winds sang always that one song, it had another name. But for Louisa the wind had never more than murmured; now it had gone down, and everything was still. She listened for a little while with half-wistful attention; then she turned quietly away and went to work on her wedding clothes.

Joe had made some extensive and quite magnificent alterations in his house. It was the old homestead; the newly-married couple would live there, for Joe could not desert his mother, who refused to leave her old home. So Louisa must leave hers. Every morning, rising and going about among her neat maidenly possessions, she felt as one looking her last upon the faces of dear friends. It was true that in a measure she could take them with her, but, robbed of their old environments, they would appear in such new guises that they would almost cease to be themselves. Then there were some peculiar features of her happy solitary life which she would probably be obliged to relinquish altogether. Sterner tasks than these graceful but half-needless ones would probably devolve upon her. There would be a large house to care for; there would be company to entertain; there would be Joe's rigorous and feeble old mother to wait upon; and it would be contrary to all thrifty village traditions for her to keep more than one servant. Louisa had a little still, and she used to occupy herself pleasantly in summer weather with distilling the sweet aromatic essences from roses and peppermint and spearmint. By-and-by her still must be laid away. Her store of essences was already considerable, and there would be no time for her to distil for the mere pleasure of it. Then Joe's mother would think it foolishness; she had already hinted her opinion in the matter. Louisa dearly loved to sew a linen seam, not always for use, but for the simple, mild pleasure which she took in it. She would have been loath to confess how more than once she had ripped a seam for the mere delight of sewing it together again. Sitting at her window during long sweet afternoons, drawing her needle gently through the dainty fabric, she was peace itself. But there was small chance of such foolish comfort in the future. Joe's mother, domineering, shrewd old matron that she was even in her old age, and very likely even Joe himself, with his honest masculine rudeness, would laugh and frown down all these pretty but senseless old maiden ways.

Louisa had almost the enthusiasm of an artist over the mere order and cleanliness of her solitary home. She had throbs of genuine triumph at the sight of the window-panes which she had polished until they shone like jewels. She gloated gently over her orderly bureau-drawers, with their exquisitely folded contents redolent with lavender and sweet clover and very purity. Could she be sure of the endurance of even this? She had visions, so startling that she half repudiated them as indelicate, of coarse masculine belongings strewn about in endless litter; of dust and disorder arising necessarily from a coarse masculine presence in the midst of all this delicate harmony.

Among her forebodings of disturbance, not the least was with regard to Caesar. Caesar was a veritable hermit of a dog. For the greater part of his life he had dwelt in his secluded hut, shut out from the society of his kind and all innocent canine joys. Never had Caesar since his early youth watched at a wood-chuck's hole; never had he known the delights of a stray bone at a neighbor's kitchen door. And it was all on account of a sin committed when hardly out of his puppyhood. No one knew the possible depth of remorse of which this mild-visaged, altogether innocent-looking old dog might be capable; but whether or not he had encountered remorse, he had encountered a full measure of righteous retribution. Old Caesar seldom lifted up his voice in a growl or a bark; he was fat and sleepy; there were yellow rings which looked like spectacles around his dim old eyes; but there was a neighbor who bore on his hand the imprint of several of Caesar's sharp white youthful teeth, and for that he had lived at the end of a chain, all alone in a little hut, for fourteen years. The neighbor, who was choleric and smarting with the pain of his wound, had demanded either Caesar's death or complete ostracism. So Louisa's brother, to whom the dog had belonged, had built him his little kennel and tied him up. It was now fourteen years since, in a flood of youthful spirits, he had inflicted that memorable bite, and with the exception of short excursions, always at the end of the chain, under the strict guardianship of his master or Louisa, the old dog had remained a close prisoner. It is doubtful if, with his limited ambition, he took much pride in the fact, but it is certain that he was possessed of considerable cheap fame. He was regarded by all the children in the village and by many adults as a very monster of ferocity. St. George's dragon could hardly have surpassed in evil repute Louisa Ellis's old yellow dog. Mothers charged their children with solemn emphasis not to go too near to him, and the children listened and believed greedily, with a fascinated appetite for terror, and ran by Louisa's house stealthily, with many sidelong glances at the terrible dog. If perchance he sounded a hoarse bark, there was a panic. Wayfarers chancing into Louisa's yard eyed him with respect, and inquired if the chain were stout. Caesar at large might have seemed a very ordinary dog, and excited no comment whatever; chained, his reputation overshadowed him, so that he lost his own proper outlines and looked darkly vague and enormous. Joe Dagget, however, with his good-humored sense and shrewdness, saw him as he was. He strode valiantly up to him and patted him on the head, in spite of Louisa's soft clamor of warning, and even attempted to set him loose. Louisa grew so alarmed that he desisted, but kept announcing his opinion in the matter quite forcibly at intervals. "There ain't a better-natured dog in town," he would say, "and it's downright cruel to keep him tied up there. Some day I'm going to take him out."

Louisa had very little hope that he would not, one of these days, when their interests and possessions should be more completely fused in one. She pictured to herself Caesar on the rampage through the quiet and unguarded village. She saw innocent children bleeding in his path. She was herself very fond of the old dog, because he had belonged to her dead brother, and he was always very gentle with her; still she had great faith in his ferocity. She always warned people not to go too near him. She fed him on ascetic fare of corn-mush and cakes, and never fired his dangerous temper with heating and sanguinary diet of flesh and bones. Louisa looked at the old dog munching his simple fare, and thought of her approaching marriage and trembled. Still no anticipation of disorder and confusion in lieu of sweet peace and harmony, no forebodings of Caesar on the rampage, no wild fluttering of her little yellow canary, were sufficient to turn her a hair's breadth. Joe Dagget had been fond of her and working for her all these years. It was not for her, whatever came to pass, to prove untrue and break his heart. She put the exquisite little stitches into her wedding-garments, and the time went on till it was only a week before her wedding-day. It was a Tuesday evening, and the wedding was to be a week from Wednesday.

There was a full moon that night. About nine o'clock Louisa strolled down the road a little way. There were harvest-fields on either hand, bordered by low stone walls. Luxuriant clumps of bushes grew beside the wall, and trees—wild cherry and old apple trees—at intervals. Presently Louisa sat down on the wall and looked about her with mildly sorrowful reflectiveness. Tall shrubs of blueberry and meadowsweet, all woven together and tangled with blackberry vines and horse-briers, shut her in on either side. She had a little clear space between them. Opposite her, on the other side of the road, was a spreading tree; the moon shone between its boughs, and the leaves twinkled like silver. The road was bespread with a beautiful shifting dapple of silver and shadow; the air was full of a mysterious sweetness. "I wonder if it's wild grapes?" murmured Louisa. She sat there some time. She was just thinking of rising, when she heard footsteps and low voices, and remained quiet. It was a lonely place, and she felt a little timid. She thought she would keep still in the shadow and let the persons, whoever they might be, pass her.

But just before they reached her the voices ceased, and the footsteps. She understood that their owners had also found seats upon the stone wall. She was wondering if she could not steal away unobserved, when the voice broke the stillness. It was Joe Dagget's. She sat still and listened.

The voice was announced by a loud sigh, which was as familiar as itself. "Well," said Dagget, "you've made up your mind, then, I suppose?"

"Yes," returned another voice; "I'm going day after to-morrow."

"That's Lily Dyer," thought Louisa to herself. The voice embodied itself in her mind. She saw a girl tall and full-figured, with a firm, fair face, looking fairer and firmer in the moonlight, her strong yellow hair braided in a close knot. A girl full of calm rustic strength and bloom, with a masterful way which might have beseemed a princess. Lily Dyer was a favorite with the village folk; she had just the qualities to arouse the admiration. She was good and handsome and smart. Louisa had often heard her praises sounded.

"Well," said Joe Dagget, "I ain't got a word to say."

"I don't know what you could say," returned Lily Dyer.

"Not a word to say," repeated Joe, drawing out the words heavily. Then there was a silence. "I ain't sorry," he began at last, "that that happened yesterday—that we kind of let on how we felt to each other. I guess it's just as well we knew. Of course I can't do anything any different. I'm going right on an' get married next week. I ain't going back on a woman that's waited for me fourteen years, an' break her heart."

"If you should jilt her to-morrow, I wouldn't have you," spoke up the girl, with sudden vehemence.

"Well, I ain't going to give you the chance," said he; "but I don't believe you would, either."

"You'd see I wouldn't. Honor's honor, an' right's right. An' I'd never think anything of any man that went against 'em for me or any other girl; you'd find that out, Joe Dagget."

"Well, you'll find out fast enough that I ain't going against 'em for you or any other girl," returned he. Their voices sounded almost as if they were angry with each other. Louisa was listening eagerly.

"I'm sorry you feel as if you must go away," said Joe, "but I don't know but it's best."

"Of course it's best. I hope you and I have got common-sense."

"Well, I suppose you're right." Suddenly Joe's voice got an undertone of tenderness. "Say, Lily," he said, "I'll get along well enough myself, but I can't bear to think—You don't suppose you're going to fret much about it?"

"I guess you'll find out I sha'n't fret much over a married man."

"Well, I hope you won't—I hope you won't, Lily. God knows I do. And—I hope—one of these days—you'll—come across somebody else—"

"I don't see any reason why I shouldn't." Suddenly her tone changed. She spoke in a sweet, clear voice, so loud that she could have been heard across the street. "No, Joe Dagget," said she, "I'll never marry any other man as long as I live. I've got good sense, an' I ain't going to break my heart nor make a fool of myself; but I'm never going to be married, you can be sure of that. I ain't that sort of a girl to feel this way twice."

Louisa heard an exclamation and a soft commotion behind the bushes; then Lily spoke again—the voice sounded as if she had risen. "This must be put a stop to," said she. "We've stayed here long enough. I'm going home."

Louisa sat there in a daze, listening to their retreating steps. After a while she got up and slunk softly home herself. The next day she did her housework methodically; that was as much a matter of course as breathing; but she did not sew on her wedding-clothes. She sat at her window and meditated. In the evening Joe came. Louisa Ellis had never known that she had any diplomacy in her, but when she came to look for it that night she found it, although meek of its kind, among her little feminine weapons. Even now she could hardly believe that she had heard aright, and that she would not do Joe a terrible injury should she break her troth-plight. She wanted to sound him without betraying too soon her own inclinations in the matter. She did it successfully, and they finally came to an understanding; but it was a difficult thing, for he was as afraid of betraying himself as she.

She never mentioned Lily Dyer. She simply said that while she had no cause of complaint against him, she had lived so long in one way that she shrank from making a change.

"Well, I never shrank, Louisa," said Dagget. "I'm going to be honest enough to say that I think maybe it's better this way; but if you'd wanted to keep on, I'd have stuck to you till my dying day. I hope you know that."

"Yes, I do," said she.

That night she and Joe parted more tenderly than they had done for a long time. Standing in the door, holding each other's hands, a last great wave of regretful memory swept over them.

"Well, this ain't the way we've thought it was all going to end, is it, Louisa?" said Joe.

She shook her head. There was a little quiver on her placid face.

"You let me know if there's ever anything I can do for you," said he. "I ain't ever going to forget you, Louisa." Then he kissed her, and went down the path.

Louisa, all alone by herself that night, wept a little, she hardly knew why; but the next morning, on waking, she felt like a queen who, after fearing lest her domain be wrested away from her, sees it firmly insured in her possession.

Now the tall weeds and grasses might cluster around Caesar's little hermit hut, the snow might fall on its roof year in and year out, but he never would go on a rampage through the unguarded village. Now the little canary might turn itself into a peaceful yellow ball night after night, and have no need to wake and flutter with wild terror against its bars. Louisa could sew linen seams, and distil roses, and dust and polish and fold away in lavender, as long as she listed. That afternoon she sat with her needle-work at the window, and felt fairly steeped in peace. Lily Dyer, tall and erect and blooming, went past; but she felt no qualm. If Louisa Ellis had sold her birthright she did not know it, the taste of the pottage was so delicious, and had been her sole satisfaction for so long. Serenity and placid narrowness had become to her as the birthright itself. She gazed ahead through a long reach of future days strung together like pearls in a rosary, every one like the others, and all smooth and flawless and innocent, and her heart went up in thankfulness. Outside was the fervid summer afternoon; the air was filled with the sounds of the busy harvest of men and birds and bees; there were halloos, metallic clatterings, sweet calls, and long hummings. Louisa sat, prayerfully numbering her days, like an uncloistered nun.

VII. the liberated woman: what price freedom?

One realization the reader must have come to by now is that the images of women in literature often serve as a justification for the continuance of traditional roles. Both for their own sakes and for the good of men and children, it is thought that women should accept their biological limitations. Some of the works in previous sections, however, indicate an undercurrent of opposition to this idea. Chekhov, for example, points out the absurdity of the social ideal of the Griselde type, and Sally Benson emphasizes its inadequacy for making men happy. Edith Wharton reveals the selfishness of a man who accepts the ideal solely on the basis of his own comfort. Alberto Moravia suggests that only freedom for women will enable men to be truly free. The images of the seductress make clear that the fear of woman is based on a myth of her "superhuman power." All of the selections, while revealing stereotypes, show that individuals may rise above them and be fully human in spite of the limiting images which others have of them.

The greatest difficulty is not in overcoming the images of others but in changing one's own self-image. Tillie Olsen's "Tell Me a Riddle" shows the anguish of a dying old woman who realizes, in looking back over her life, that she has allowed role-playing as wife and mother to cheat her of selfhood. The knowledge is so bitter that she cannot hold one of her grandchildren, nor accept the attentions of her children and of her husband. Yet painful as the self-knowledge is, in the end she is able to accept love and to allow hope for a granddaughter to mitigate her bitterness and resentment. Awareness—examining one's own life—makes life worth living. This powerful story makes the cost of achieving selfhood inescapably vivid.

Claire Booth Luce, in "A Doll's House, 1970," flippantly presents what every reader of Ibsen knows is an agonizing choice: Nora's decision to leave her husband and children in order to find herself. A reader of Tillie Olsen's story

327

realizes that Nora's decision will prevent the tragedy of self-knowledge that comes too late to act upon. Nora in 1970 can arrive at awareness with far less cost than Ibsen's Nora or Tillie Olsen's Eva because she is part of a movement. She gains support for her determination to be herself from literature she has read and from another woman who shares her feelings. Women of previous times had no such help.

The possibility that women can achieve freedom through acting together as a force is brought out in Susan Glaspell's "A Jury of Her Peers." The two women who destroy evidence that might convict Minnie of murdering her husband do so because they understand that the killing was a justifiable homicide. They judge Minnie in feminine terms, perceiving that her husband had, in effect, murdered her by making her a captive and a slave. Their decision makes certain what a male jury might well have decided, for seldom does a jury convict in crimes of passion.

In "Alraune," a chapter from *The House of Incest*, Anaïs Nin shows Lesbian lovers to be essentially like all lovers, seeking to transcend the world by losing themselves in the beloved. The woman lover, captivated by Alraune's beauty and personality, rhapsodizes upon them with imagery strikingly like that Jean Toomer uses to describe Fern: ". . . all things which had run a vertical course now turned in circles, round the face, around her face. She stared with such an ancient stare, heavy luxuriant centuries flickering in deep processions." And the lover comes to realize the danger that is inherent in all love relationships: in seeking the Other, one is seeking oneself and may thereby diminish the other. The inclusion of this episode as part of the "house" of incest—as if it were one of the zodiacal houses—emphasizes the universality and inevitability of the danger. In loving one's sister or one's brother (like Jeanne in a later episode in the book) or in loving any human being, one may be loving only the self while destroying the other. The age-old ambiguity of love is the same for Lesbians as for any other lovers: is fusion, oneness, a gain or a loss? This picture of Lesbian love as simply a kind of human love represents liberation from the narrow viewpoint that the nature of love is determined by its object.

Another limiting idea has been that a woman's sexual surrender is equivalent to self-surrender. Barbara Coles, in Doris Lessing's "One off the Short List," is free from this confusion and is able to yield to the persistent and rough Graham Spence without giving him more than physical satisfaction. Since Graham's determination to seduce Barbara has nothing to do with physical desire but rather with his need to dominate a successful woman, her bringing him to orgasm casually and scornfully is a defeat of his carefully planned strategy. Even though she acknowledges her surrender publicly in order to save his pride, she has committed nothing of herself to him—just as Denise in Mailer's "The Time of Her Time" has surrendered nothing that Sergius can value. Barbara might seem to have reversed roles with Sergius, since she "uses" a male as he uses a female; but Barbara does not need to bolster her ego as does Sergius. The incident with Graham means nothing to her, for she has a husband and children as well as her work. Her physical yielding is not an attempt to find herself but simply an acceptance of the inevitable.

Barbara is free because she is successful at a job in which she is respected by her colleagues; she has no need to prove herself. For a woman, work in a man's world, even when not so successful as Barbara's career, means a degree of freedom from traditional roles. Mary Elizabeth Vroman's "See How They Run" shows a female schoolteacher who devotes herself to her work because of her concern for others. Like her fiancé, she can find happiness in a job even though it means giving up personal happiness. In this story marriage is only postponed, whereas in "One off the Short List" Lessing shows that career and marriage can be combined successfully. Perhaps Luce's Nora and her husband's research assistant, Molly, will both manage to find the missing part of their lives and become what the liberated woman is: a complete human being. At least they will have a chance to find real fulfillment and happiness, because they possess a new dream and a new self-image.

Tillie Olsen

*(b. 1913). Tillie Olsen, born in
Nebraska, now lives in California and
teaches occasionally at Stanford. Her
short stories reflect the hardships
of the working-class life she has
experienced, and an essay "Silences,"
which appeared in Harper's Magazine
(1965), explains the difficulties
faced by a woman writer. She
received an O'Henry award for the
best American short story of 1961,
"Tell Me a Riddle," and one of her
stories appeared in The Best American
Short Stories, 1971.*

Tell Me a Riddle

1   For forty-seven years they had been married. How deep back the stubborn,
gnarled roots of the quarrel reached, no one could say—but only now, when
tending to the needs of others no longer shackled them together, the roots
swelled up visible, split the earth between them, and the tearing shook even to
the children, long since grown.

Why now, why now? wailed Hannah.

As if when we grew up weren't enough, said Paul.

Poor Ma. Poor Dad. It hurts so for both of them, said Vivi. They never had
very much; at least in old age they should be happy.

Knock their heads together, insisted Sammy; tell 'em: you're too old for this
kind of thing; no reason not to get along now.

Lennie wrote to Clara: They've lived over so much together; what could
possibly tear them apart?

Something tangible enough.

Arthritic hands, and such work as he got, occasional. Poverty all his life, and
there was little breath left for running. He could not, could not turn away from
this desire: to have the troubling of responsibility, the fretting with money,
over and done with; to be free, to be *care*free where success was not measured by
accumulation, and there was use for the vitality still in him.

There was a way. They could sell the house, and with the money join his lodge's Haven, cooperative for the aged. Happy communal life, and was he not already an official; had he not helped organize it, raise funds, served as a trustee?

But she—would not consider it.

"What do we need all this for?" he would ask loudly, for her hearing aid was turned down and the vacuum was shrilling. "Five rooms" (pushing the sofa so she could get into the corner) "furniture" (smoothing down the rug) "floors and surfaces to make work. Tell me, why do we need it?" And he was glad he could ask in a scream.

"Because I'm use't."

"Because you're use't. This is a reason, Mrs. Word Miser? Used to can get unused!"

"Enough unused I have to get used to already. . . . Not enough words?" turning off the vacuum a moment to hear herself answer. "Because soon enough we'll need only a little closet, no windows, no furniture, nothing to make work, but for worms. Because now I want room. . . . Screech and blow like you're doing, you'll need that closet even sooner. . . . Ha, again!" for the vacuum bag wailed, puffed half up, hung stubbornly limp. "This time fix it so it stays; quick before the phone rings and you get too important-busy."

But while he struggled with the motor, it seethed in him. Why fix it? Why have to bother? And if it can't be fixed, have to wring the mind with how to pay the repair? At the Haven they come in with their own machines to clean your room or your cottage; you fish, or play cards, or make jokes in the sun, not with knotty fingers fight to mend vacuums.

Over the dishes, coaxingly: "For once in your life, to be free, to have everything done for you, like a queen."

"I never liked queens."

"No dishes, no garbage, no towel to sop, no worry what to buy, what to eat."

"And what else would I do with my empty hands? Better to eat at my own table when I want, and to cook and eat how I want."

"In the cottages they buy what you ask, and cook it how you like. *You* are the one who always used to say: better mankind born without mouths and stomachs than always to worry for money to buy, to shop, to fix, to cook, to wash, to clean."

"How cleverly you hid that you heard. I said it then because eighteen hours a day I ran. And you never scraped a carrot or knew a dish towel sops. Now—for you and me—who cares? A herring out of a jar is enough. But when *I* want, and nobody to bother." And she turned off her ear button, so she would not have to hear.

But as *he* had no peace, juggling and rejuggling the money to figure: how will I pay for this now?; prying out the storm windows (there they take care of this); jolting in the streetcar on errands (there I would not have to ride to take care of this or that); fending the patronizing relatives just back from Florida (at the Haven it matters what one is, not what one can afford), he gave *her* no peace.

"Look! In their bulletin. A reading circle. Twice a week it meets."

"Haumm," her answer of not listening.

"A reading circle. Chekhov they read that you like, and Peretz. Cultured people at the Haven that you would enjoy."

"Enjoy!" She tasted the word. "Now, when it pleases you, you find a reading circle for me. And forty years ago when the children were morsels and there was a Circle, did you stay home with them once so I could go? Even once? You trained me well. I do not need others to enjoy. Others!" Her voice trembled. "Because *you* want to be there with others. Already it makes me sick to think of you always around others. Clown, grimacer, floormat, yesman, entertainer, whatever they want of you."

And now it was he who turned on the television loud so he need not hear.

Old scar tissue ruptured and the wounds festered anew. Chekhov indeed. She thought without softness of that young wife, who in the deep night hours while she nursed the current baby, and perhaps held another in her lap, would try to stay awake for the only time there was to read. She would feel again the weather of the outside on his cheek when, coming late from a meeting, he would find her so, and stimulated and ardent, sniffing her skin, coax: "I'll put the baby to bed, and you—put the book away, don't read, don't read."

That had been the most beguiling of all the "don't read, put your book away" her life had been. Chekhov indeed!

"Money?" She shrugged him off. "Could we get poorer than once we were? And in America, who starves?"

But as still he pressed:

"Let me alone about money. Was there ever enough? Seven little ones—for every penny I had to ask—and sometimes, remember, there was nothing. But always *I* had to manage. Now *you* manage. Rub your nose in it good."

But from those years she had had to manage, old humiliations and terrors rose up, lived again, and forced her to relive them. The children's needings; that grocer's face or this merchant's wife she had had to beg credit from when credit was a disgrace; the scenery of the long blocks walked around when she could not pay; school coming, and the desperate going over the old to see what could yet be remade; the soups of meat bones begged "for-the-dog" one winter. . . .

Enough. Now they had no children. Let *him* wrack his head for how they would live. She would not exchange her solitude for anything. *Never again to be forced to move to the rhythms of others.*

For in this solitude she had won to a reconciled peace.

Tranquillity from having the empty house no longer an enemy, for it stayed clean—not as in the days when it was her family, the life in it, that had seemed the enemy: tracking, smudging, littering, dirtying, engaging her in endless defeating battle—and on whom her endless defeat had been spewed.

The few old books, memorized from rereading; the pictures to ponder (the magnifying glass superimposed on her heavy eyeglasses). Or if she wishes, when he is gone, the phonograph, that if she turns up very loud and strains, she can hear: the ordered sounds and the struggling.

Out in the garden, growing things to nurture. Birds to be kept out of the pear tree, and when the pears are heavy and ripe, the old fury of work, for all must be canned, nothing wasted.

And her one social duty (for she will not go to luncheons or meetings) the boxes of old clothes left with her, as with a life-practised eye for finding what is still wearable within the worn (again the magnifying glass superimposed on the heavy glasses) she scans and sorts—this for rag or rummage, that for mending and cleaning, and this for sending away.

Being able at last to live within, and not move to the rhythms of others, as life had helped her to: denying; removing; isolating; taking the children one by one; then deafening, half-blinding—and at last, presenting her solitude.

And in it she had won to a reconciled peace.

Now he was violating it with his constant campaigning: *Sell the house and move to the Haven.* (You sit, you sit—there too you could sit like a stone.) He was making of her a battleground where old grievances tore. (Turn on your ear button—I am talking.) And stubbornly she resisted—so that from wheedling, reasoning manipulation, it was bitterness he now started with.

And it came to where every happening lashed up a quarrel.

"I will sell the house anyway," he flung at her one night. "I am putting it up for sale. There will be a way to make you sign."

The television blared, as always it did on the evenings he stayed home, and as always it reached her only as noise. She did not know if the tumult was in her or outside. Snap! she turned the sound off. "Shadows," she whispered to him, pointing to the screen, "look, it is only shadows." And in a scream: "Did you say that you will sell the house? Look at me, not at that. I am no shadow. You cannot sell without me."

"Leave on the television. I am watching."

"Like Paulie, like Jenny, a four-year-old. Staring at shadows. *You cannot sell the house.*"

"I will. We are going to the Haven. There you would not hear the television when you do not want it. I could sit in the social room and watch. You could lock yourself up to smell your unpleasantness in a room by yourself—for who would want to come near you?"

"No, no selling." A whisper now.

"The television is shadows. Mrs. Enlightened! Mrs. Cultured! A world comes into your house—and it is shadows. People you would never meet in a thousand lifetimes. Wonders. When you were four years old, yes, like Paulie, like Jenny, did you know of Indian dances, alligators, how they use bamboo in Malaya? No, you scratched in your dirt with the chickens and thought Olshana was the world. Yes, Mrs. Unpleasant, I will sell the house, for there better can we be rid of each other than here."

She did not know if the tumult was outside, or in her. Always a ravening inside, a pull to the bed, to lie down, to succumb.

"Have you thought maybe Ma should let a doctor have a look at her?" asked their son Paul after Sunday dinner, regarding his mother crumpled on the couch, instead of, as was her custom, busying herself in Nancy's kitchen.

"Why not the President too?"

"Seriously, Dad. This is the third Sunday she's lain down like that after dinner. Is she that way at home?"

"A regular love affair with the bed. Every time I start to talk to her."

Good protective reaction, observed Nancy to herself. The workings of hos-til-ity.

"Nancy could take her. I just don't like how she looks. Let's have Nancy arrange an appointment."

"You think she'll go?" regarding his wife gloomily. "All right, we have to have doctor bills, we have to have doctor bills." Loudly: "Something hurts you?"

She startled, looked to his lips. He repeated: "Mrs. Take It Easy, something hurts?"

"Nothing. . . . Only you."

"A woman of honey. That's why you're lying down?"

"Soon I'll get up to do the dishes, Nancy."

"Leave them, Mother, I like it better this way."

"Mrs. Take It Easy, Paul says you should start ballet. You should go to see a doctor and ask: how soon can you start ballet?"

"A doctor?" she begged. "Ballet?"

"We were talking, Ma," explained Paul, "you don't seem any too well. It would be a good idea for you to see a doctor for a checkup."

"I get up now to do the kitchen. Doctors are bills and foolishness, my son. I need no doctors."

"At the Haven," he could not resist pointing out, "a doctor is *not* bills. He lives beside you. You start to sneeze, he is there before you open up a Kleenex. You can be sick there for free, all you want."

"Diarrhea of the mouth, is there a doctor to make you dumb?"

"Ma. Promise me you'll go. Nancy will arrange it."

"It's all of a piece when you think of it," said Nancy, "the way she attacks my kitchen, scrubbing under every cup hook, doing the inside of the oven so I can't enjoy Sunday dinner, knowing that half-blind or not, she's going to find every speck of dirt. . . ."

"Don't, Nancy, I've told you—it's the only way she knows to be useful. What did the *doctor* say?"

"A real fatherly lecture. Sixty-nine is young these days. Go out, enjoy life, find interests. Get a new hearing aid, this one is antiquated. Old age is sickness only if one makes it so. Geriatrics, Inc."

"So there was nothing physical."

"Of course there was. How can you live to yourself like she does without there being? Evidence of a kidney disorder, and her blood count is low. He gave her a diet, and she's to come back for follow-up and lab work. . . . But he was clear enough: Number One prescription—start living like a human being. . . . When I think of your dad, who could really play the invalid with that arthritis of his, as active as a teenager, and twice as much fun. . . ."

"You didn't tell me the doctor says your sickness is in you, how you live." He pushed his advantage. "Life and enjoyments you need better than medicine.

And this diet, how can you keep it? To weigh each morsel and scrape away each bit of fat, to make this soup, that pudding. There, at the Haven, they have a dietician, they would do it for you."

She is silent.

"You would feel better there, I know it," he says gently. "There there is life and enjoyments all around."

"What is the matter, Mr. Importantbusy, you have no card game or meeting you can go to?"—turning her face to the pillow.

For a while he cut his meetings and going out, fussed over her diet, tried to wheedle her into leaving the house, brought in visitors:

"I should come to a fashion tea. I should sit and look at pretty babies in clothes I cannot buy. This is pleasure?"

"Always you are better than everyone else. The doctor said you should go out. Mrs. Brem comes to you with goodness and you turn her away."

"Because *you* asked her to, she asked me."

"They won't come back. People you need, the doctor said. Your own cousins I asked; they were willing to come and make peace as if nothing had happened. . . ."

"No more crushers of people, pushers, hypocrites, around me. No more in *my* house. You go to them if you like."

"Kind he is to visit. And you, like ice."

"A babbler. All my life around babblers. Enough!"

"She's even worse, Dad? Then let her stew a while," advised Nancy. "You can't let it destroy you; it's a psychological thing, maybe too far gone for any of us to help."

So he let her stew. More and more she lay silent in bed, and sometimes did not even get up to make the meals. No longer was the tongue-lashing inevitable if he left the coffee cup where it did not belong, or forgot to take out the garbage or mislaid the broom. The birds grew bold that summer and for once pocked the pears, undisturbed.

A bellyful of bitterness and every day the same quarrel in a new way and a different old grievance the quarrel forced her to enter and relive. And the new torment: I am not really sick, the doctor said it, then why do I feel so sick?

One night she asked him: "You have a meeting tonight? Do not go. Stay . . . with me."

He had planned to watch "This Is Your Life," but half sick himself from the heavy heat, and sickening therefore the more after the brooks and woods of the Haven, with satisfaction he grated:

"Hah, Mrs. Live Alone And Like It wants company all of a sudden. It doesn't seem so good the time of solitary when she was a girl exile in Siberia. 'Do not go. Stay with me.' A new song for Mrs. Free As A Bird. Yes, I am going out, and while I am gone chew this aloneness good, and think how you keep us both from where if you want people, you do not need to be alone."

"Go, go. All your life you have gone without me."

After him she sobbed curses he had not heard in years, old-country curses from their childhood: Grow, oh shall you grow like an onion, with your head in the ground. Like the hide of a drum shall you be, beaten in life, beaten in death. Oh shall you be like a chandelier, to hang, and to burn. . . .

She was not in their bed when he came back. She lay on the cot on the sun porch. All week she did not speak or come near him; nor did he try to make peace or care for her.

He slept badly, so used to her next to him. After all the years, old harmonies and dependencies deep in their bodies; she curled to him, or he coiled to her, each warmed, warming, turning as the other turned, the nights a long embrace.

It was not the empty bed or the storm that woke him, but a faint singing. *She* was singing. Shaking off the drops of rain, the lightning riving her lifted face, he saw her so; the cot covers on the floor.

"This is a private concert?" he asked. "Come in, you are wet."

"I can breathe now," she answered; "my lungs are rich." Though indeed the sound was hardly a breath.

"Come in, come in." Loosing the bamboo shades. "Look how wet you are." Half helping, half carrying her, still faint-breathing her song.

A Russian love song of fifty years ago.

He had found a buyer, but before he told her, he called together those children who were close enough to come. Paul, of course, Sammy from New Jersey, Hannah from Connecticut, Vivi from Ohio.

With a kindling of energy for her beloved visitors, she arrayed the house, cooked and baked. She was not prepared for the solemn after-dinner conclave, they too probing in and tearing. Her frightened eyes watched from mouth to mouth as each spoke.

His stories were eloquent and funny of her refusal to go back to the doctor; of the scorned invitations; of her stubborn silence or the bile "like a Niagara"; of her contrariness: "If I clean it's no good how I cleaned; if I don't clean, I'm still a master who thinks he has a slave."

(Vinegar he poured on me all his life; I am well marinated; how can I be honey now?)

Deftly he marched in the rightness for moving to the Haven; their money from social security free for visiting the children, not sucked into daily needs and into the house; the activities in the Haven for him; but mostly the Haven for *her:* her health, her need of care, distraction, amusement, friends who shared her interests.

"This does offer an outlet for Dad," said Paul; "he's always been an active person. And economic peace of mind isn't to be sneezed at, either. I could use a little of that myself."

But when they asked: "And you, Ma, how do you feel about it?" could only whisper:

"For him it is good. It is not for me. I can no longer live between people."

"You lived all your life *for* people," Vivi cried.

"Not with." Suffering doubly for the unhappiness on her children's faces.

"You have to find some compromise," Sammy insisted. "Maybe sell the house and buy a trailer. After forty-seven years there's surely some way you can find to live in peace."

"There is no help, my children. Different things we need."

"Then live alone!" He could control himself no longer. "I have a buyer for the house. Half the money for you, half for me. Either alone or with me to the Haven. You think I can live any longer as we are doing now?"

"Ma doesn't have to make a decision this minute, however you feel, Dad," Paul said quickly, "and you wouldn't want her to. Let's let it lay a few months, and then talk some more."

"I think I can work it out to take Mother home with me for a while." Hannah said. "You both look terrible, but especially you, Mother. I'm going to ask Phil to have a look at you."

"Sure," cracked Sammy. "What's the use of a doctor husband if you can't get free service out of him once in a while for the family? And absence might make the heart . . . you know."

"There was something after all," Paul told Nancy in a colorless voice. • "That was Hannah's Phil calling. Her gall baldder. . . . Surgery."

"Her *gall* bladder. If that isn't classic. 'Bitter as gall'—talk of psychosom—"

He stepped closer, put his hand over her mouth, and said in the same colorless, plodding voice. "We have to get Dad. They operated at once. The cancer was everywhere, surrounding the liver, everywhere. They did what they could . . . at best she has a year. Dad . . . we have to tell him."

2 Honest in his weakness when they told him, and that she was not to know. "I'm not an actor. She'll know right away by how I am. Oh that poor woman. I am old too, it will break me into pieces. Oh that poor woman. She will spit on me: 'So my sickness was how I live.' Oh Paulie, how she will be, that poor woman. Only she should not suffer. . . . I can't stand sickness, Paulie, I can't go with you."

But went. And play-acted.

"A grand opening and you did not even wait for me. . . . A good thing Hannah took you with her."

"Fashion teas I needed. They cut out what tore in me; just in my throat something hurts yet. . . . Look! so many flowers, like a funeral. Vivi called, did Hannah tell you? And Lennie from San Francisco, and Clara; and Sammy is coming." Her gnome's face pressed happily into the flowers.

It is impossible to predict in these cases, but once over the immediate effects of the operation, she should have several months of comparative well-being.

The money, where will come the money?

Travel with her, Dad. Don't take her home to the old associations. The other children will want to see her.

The money, where will I wring the money?

Whatever happens, she is not to know. No, you can't ask her to sign papers to sell the house; nothing to upset her. Borrow instead, then after. . . .

I had wanted to leave you each a few dollars to make life easier, as other fathers do. There will be nothing left now. (Failure! you and your "business is exploitation." Why didn't you make it when it could be made?—Is that what you're thinking, Sammy?)

Sure she's unreasonable, Dad—but you have to stay with her; if there's to be any happiness in what's left of her life, it depends on you.

Prop me up, children, think of me, too. Shuffled, chained with her, bitter woman. No Haven, and the little money going. . . . How happy she looks, poor creature.

The look of excitement. The straining to hear everything (the new hearing aid turned full). Why are you so happy, dying woman?

How the petals are, fold on fold, and the gladioli color. The autumn air.

Stranger grandsons, tall above the little gnome grandmother, the little spry grandfather. Paul in a frenzy of picture-taking before going.

She, wandering the great house. Feeling the books; laughing at the maple shoemaker's bench of a hundred years ago used as a table. The ear turned to music.

"Let us go home. See how good I walk now." "One step from the hospital," he answers, "and she wants to fly. Wait till Doctor Phil says."

"Look—the birds too are flying home. Very good Phil is and will not show it, but he is sick of sickness by the time he comes home."

"Mrs. Telepathy, to read minds," he answers; "read mine what it says: when the trunks of medicines become a suitcase, then we will go."

The grandboys, they do not know what to say to us. . . . Hannah, she runs around here, there, when is there time for herself?

Let us go home. Let us go home.

Musing; gentleness—*but for the incidents of the rabbi in the hospital, and of the candles of benediction.*

Of the rabbi in the hospital:

Now tell me what happened. Mother.

From the sleep I awoke, Hannah's Phil, and he stands there like a devil in a dream and calls me by name. I cannot hear. I think he prays. Go away, please, I tell him, I am not a believer. Still he stands, while my heart knocks with fright.

You scared *him*, Mother. He thought you were delirious.

Who sent him? Why did he come to me?

It is a custom. The men of God come to visit those of their religion they might help. The hospital makes up the list for them—race, religion—and you are on the Jewish list.

Not for rabbis. At once go and make them change. Tell them to write: Race, human; Religion, none.

And of the candles of benediction:

Look how you have upset yourself, Mrs. Excited Over Nothing. Pleasant memories you should leave.

Go in, go back to Hannah and the lights. Two weeks I saw candles and said nothing. But she asked me.

So what was so terrible? She forgets you never did, she asks you to light the Friday candles and say the benediction like Phil's mother when she visits. If the candles give her pleasure, why shouldn't she have the pleasure?

Not for pleasure she does it. For emptiness. Because his family does. Because all around her do.

That is not a good reason too? But you did not hear her. For heritage, she told you. For the boys, from the past they should have tradition.

Superstition! From the savages, afraid of the dark, of themselves: mumbo words and magic lights to scare away ghosts.

She told you: how it started does not take away the goodness. For centuries, peace in the house it means.

Swindler! does she look back on the dark centuries? Candles bought instead of bread and stuck into a potato for a candlestick? Religion that stifled and said: in Paradise, woman, you will be the footstool of your husband, and in life—poor chosen Jew—ground under, despised, trembling in cellars. And cremated. And cremated.

This is religion's fault? You think you are still an orator of the 1905 revolution? Where are the pills for quieting? Which are they?

Heritage. How have we come from the savages, how no longer to be savages—this to teach. To look back and learn what humanizes man—this to teach. To smash all ghettos that divide us—not to go back, not to go back—this to teach. Learned books in the house, will humankind live or die, and she gives to her boys—superstition.

Hannah that is so good to you. Take your pill, Mrs. Excited For Nothing, swallow.

Heritage! But when did I have time to teach? Of Hannah I asked only hands to help.

Swallow.

Otherwise—musing; gentleness.

Not to travel. To go home.

The children want to see you. We have to show them you are as thorny a flower as ever.

Not to travel.

Vivi wants you should see her new baby. She sent the tickets—airplane tickets—a Mrs. Roosevelt she wants to make of you. To Vivi's we have to go.

A new baby. How many warm, seductive babies. She holds him stiffly, *away* from her, so that he wails. And a long shudder begins, and the sweat beads on her forehead.

"Hush, shush," croons the grandfather, lifting him back. "You should forgive your grandmamma, little prince, she has never held a baby before, only seen them in glass cases. Hush, shush."

"You're tired, Ma," says Vivi. "The travel and the noisy dinner. I'll take you to lie down."

(A long travel from, to, what the feel of a baby evokes.)

In the airplane, cunningly designed to encase from motion (no wind, no feel of flight), she had sat severely and still, her face turned to the sky through which they cleaved and left no scar.

So this was how it looked, the determining, the crucial sky, and this was how man moved through it, remote above the dwindled earth, the concealed human life. Vulnerable life, that could scar.

There was a steerage ship of memory that shook across a great, circular sea; clustered, ill human beings; and through the thick-stained air, tiny fretting waters in a window round like the airplane's—sun round, moon round. (The round thatched roofs of Olshana.) Eye round—like the smaller window that framed distance the solitary year of exile when only her eyes could travel, and no voice spoke. And the polar winds hurled themselves across snows trackless and endless and white—like the clouds which had closed together below and hidden the earth.

Now they put a baby in her lap. Do not ask me, she would have liked to beg. Enough the worn face of Vivi, the remembered grandchildren. I cannot, cannot. . . .

Cannot what? Unnatural grandmother, not able to make herself embrace a baby.

She lay there in the bed of the two little girls, her new hearing aid turned full, listening to the sound of the children going to sleep, the baby's fretful crying and hushing, the clatter of dishes being washed and put away. They thought she slept. Still she rode on.

It was not that she had not loved her babies, her children. The love—the passion of tending—had risen with the need like a torrent; and like a torrent drowned and immolated all else. But when the need was done—oh the power that was lost in the painful damming back and drying up of what still surged, but had nowhere to go. Only the thin pulsing left that could not quiet, suffering over lives one felt, but could no longer hold nor help.

On that torrent she had borne them to their own lives, and the riverbed was desert long years now. Not there would she dwell, a memoried wraith. Surely that was not all, surely there was more. Still the springs, the springs were in her seeking. Somewhere an older power that beat for life. Somewhere coherence, transport, meaning. If they would but leave her in the air now stilled of clamor, in the reconciled solitude, to journey to her self.

And they put a baby in her lap. Immediacy to embrace, and the breath of *that* past: warm flesh like this that had claims and nuzzled away all else and with lovely mouths devoured; hot-living like an animal—intensely and now; the turning maze; the long drunkenness; the drowning into needing and being needed. Severely she looked back—and the shudder seized her again, and the sweat. Not that way. Not there, not now could she, not yet. . . .

And all that visit, she could not touch the baby.

"Daddy, is it the . . . sickness she's like that?" asked Vivi. "I was so glad to be having the baby—for her. I told Tim, it'll give her more happiness than anything, being around a baby again. And she hasn't played with him once."

He was not listening. "Aahh little seed of life, little charmer," he crooned. "Hollywood should see you. A heart of ice you would melt. Kick, kick. The future you'll have for a ball. In 2050 still kick. Kick for your grandaddy then."

Attentive with the older children; sat through their performances (command performance; we command you to be the audience); helped Ann sort autumn leaves to find the best for a school program; listened gravely to Richard tell about his rock collection, while her lips mutely formed the words to remember: *igneous, sedimentary, metamorphic;* looked for missing socks, books, and bus tickets; watched the children whoop after their grandfather who knew how to tickle, chuck, lift, toss, do tricks, tell secrets, make jokes, match riddle for riddle. (Tell me a riddle, Grammy. I know no riddles, child.) Scrubbed sills and woodwork and furniture in every room; folded the laundry; straightened drawers; emptied the heaped baskets waiting for ironing (while he or Vivi or Tim nagged: You're supposed to rest here, you've been sick) but to none tended or gave food—and could not touch the baby.

After a week she said: "Let us go home. Today call about the tickets."

"You have important business, Mrs. Inahurry? The President waits to consult with you?" He shouted, for the fear of the future raced in him. "The clothes are still warm from the suitcase, your children cannot show enough how glad they are to see you, and you want home. There is plenty of time for home. We cannot be with the children at home."

"Blind to around you as always: the little ones sleep four in a room because we take their bed. We are two more people in a house with a new baby, and no help."

"Vivi is happy so. The children should have their grandparents a while, she told to me. I should have my mommy and daddy. . . ."

"Blabber and blind. Do you look at her so tired? How she starts to talk and she cries? I am not strong enough yet to help. Let us go home."

(To reconciled solitude.)

For it seemed to her the crowded noisy house was listening to her, listening for her. She could feel it like a great ear pressed under her heart. And everything knocked: quick constant raps: let me in, let me in.

How was it that soft reaching tendrils also became blows that knocked?

C'mon, Grandma, I want to show you. . . .

Tell me a riddle, Grandma. *(I know no riddles.)*

Look, Grammy, he's so dumb he can't even find his hands. (Dody and the baby on a blanket over the fermenting autumn mould.)

I made them—for you. (Ann) (Flat paper dolls with aprons that lifted on scalloped skirts that lifted on flowered pants; hair of yarn and great ringed questioning eyes.)

Watch me, Grandma. (Richard snaking up the tree, hanging exultant, free, with one hand at the top. Below Dody hunching over in pretend-cooking.)

(Climb too, Dody, climb and look.)

Be my nap bed, Grammy. (The "No!" too late.)

Morty's abandoned heaviness, while his fingers ladder up and down her hearing-aid cord to his drowsy chant: eentsiebeentsiespider. *(Children trust.)*

It's to start off your own rock collection, Grandma. That's a trilobite fossil, 200 million years old (millions of years on a boy's mouth) and that one's obsidian, black glass.

Knocked and knocked.

Mother, I *told* you the teacher said we had to bring it back all filled out this morning. Didn't you even ask Daddy? Then tell *me* which plan and I'll check it: evacuate or stay in the city or wait for you to come and take me away. (Seeing the look of straining to hear.) It's for Disaster, Grandma. *(Children trust.)*

Vivi in the maze of the long, the lovely drunkenness. The old old noises: baby sounds; screaming of a mother flayed to exasperation; children quarreling; children playing; singing; laughter.

And Vivi's tears and memories, spilling so fast, half the words not understood.

She had started remembering out loud deliberately, so her mother would know the past was cherished, still lived in her.

Nursing the baby: My friends marvel, and I tell them, oh it's easy to be such a cow. I remember how beautiful my mother seemed nursing my brother, and the milk just flows. . . . Was that Davy? It must have been Davy. . . .

Lowering a hem: How did you ever . . . when I think how you made everything we wore . . . Tim, just think, seven kids and Mommy sewed everything . . . do I remember you sang while you sewed? That white dress with the red apples on the skirt you fixed over for me, was it Hannah's or Clara's before it was mine?

Washing sweaters: Ma, I'll never forget, one of those days so nice you washed clothes outside; one of the first spring days it must have been. The bubbles just danced while you scrubbed, and we chased after, and you stopped to show us how to blow our own bubbles with green onion stalks . . . you always. . . .

"Strong onion, to still make you cry after so many years," her father said, to turn the tears into laughter.

While Richard bent over his homework: Where is it now, do we still have it, the Book of the Martyrs? It always seemed so, well—exalted, when you'd put it on the round table and we'd all look at it together; there was even a halo from the lamp. The lamp with the beaded fringe you could move up and down; they're in style again, pulley lamps like that, but without the fringe. You know the book I'm talking about, Daddy, the Book of the Martyrs, the first picture was a bust of Socrates? I wish there was something like that for the children, Mommy, to give them what you. . . . (And the tears splashed again.)

(What I intended and did not? Stop it, daughter, stop it, leave that time. And he, the hypocrite, sitting there with tears in his eyes—it was nothing to you then, nothing.)

. . . The time you came to school and I almost died of shame because of your accent and because I knew you knew I was ashamed; how could I? . . . Sammy's harmonica and you danced to it once, yes you did, you and Davy squealing in your arms. . . . That time you bundled us up and walked us down to the railway station to stay the night 'cause it was heated and we didn't have any coal, that winter of the strike, you didn't think I remembered that, did you, Mommy? . . . How you'd call us out to see the sunsets. . . .

Day after day, the spilling memories. Worse now, questions, too. Even the grandchildren: Grandma, in the olden days, when you were little. . . .

It was the afternoons that saved.

While they thought she napped, she would leave the mosaic on the wall (of children's drawings, maps, calendars, pictures, Ann's cardboard dolls with their great ringed questioning eyes) and hunch in the girls' cupboard, on the low shelf where the shoes stood, and the girls' dresses covered.

For that while she would painfully sheathe against the listening house, the tendrils and noises that knocked, and Vivi's spilling memories. Sometimes it helped to braid and unbraid the sashes that dangled, or to trace the pattern on the hoop slips.

Today she had jacks and children under jet trails to forget. Last night, Ann and Dody silhouetted in the window against a sunset of flaming man-made clouds of jet trail, their jacks ball accenting the peaceful noise of dinner being made. Had she told them, yes she had told them of how they played jacks in her village though there was no ball, no jacks. Six stones, round and flat, toss them out, the seventh on the back of the hand, toss, catch and swoop up as many as possible, toss again. . . .

Of stones (repeating Richard) there are three kinds: earth's fire jetting; rock of layered centuries; crucibled new out of the old *(igneous, sedimentary, metamorphic)*. But there was that other—frozen to black glass, never to transform or hold the fossil memory . . . (let not my seed fall on stone). There was an ancient man who fought to heights a great rock that crashed back down eternally—eternal labor, freedom, labor . . . (stone will perish, but the word remain). And you, David, who with a stone slew, screaming: Lord, take my heart of stone and give me flesh.

Who was screaming? Why was she back in the common room of the prison, the sun motes dancing in the shafts of light, and the informer being brought in, a prisoner now, like themselves. And Lisa leaping, yes, Lisa, the gentle and tender, biting at the betrayer's jugular. Screaming and screaming.

No, it is the children screaming. Another of Paul and Sammy's terrible fights?

In Vivi's house. Severely: you are in Vivi's house.

Blows, screams, a call: "Grandma!" For her? Oh please not for her. Hide, hunch behind the dresses deeper. But a trembling little body hurls itself beside her—surprised, smothered laughter, arms surround her neck, tears rub dry on her cheek, and words too soft to understand whisper into her ear (Is this where you hide too, Grammy? It's my secret place, we have a secret now).

And the sweat beads, and the long shudder seizes.

It seemed the great ear pressed inside now, and the knocking. "We have to go home," she told him, "I grow ill here."

"It's your own fault, Mrs. Busybody, you do not rest, you do too much." He raged, but the fear was in his eyes. "It was a serious operation, they told you to take care. . . . All right, we will go to where you can rest."

But where? Not home to death, not yet. He had thought to Lennie's, to Clara's; beautiful visits with each of the children. She would have to rest first, be stronger. If they could but go to Florida—it glittered before him, the never-realized promise of Florida. California: of course. (The money, the money, dwindling!) Los Angeles first for sun and rest, then to Lennie's in San Francisco.

He told her the next day. "You saw what Nancy wrote: snow and wind back home, a terrible winter. And look at you—all bones and a swollen belly. I called Phil: he said: 'A prescription, Los Angeles sun and rest.'"

She watched the words on his lips. "You have sold the house," she cried, "that is why we do not go home. That is why you talk no more of the Haven, why there is money for travel. After the children you will drag me to the Haven."

"The Haven! Who thinks of the Haven any more? Tell her, Vivi, tell Mrs. Suspicious: a prescription, sun and rest, to make you healthy. . . . And how could I sell the house without *you?*"

At the place of farewells and greetings, of winds of coming and winds of going, they say their good-byes.

They look back at her with the eyes of others before them: Richard with her own blue blaze; Ann with the nordic eyes of Tim; Morty's dreaming brown of a great-grandmother he will never know; Dody with the laughing eyes of him who had been her springtide love (who stands beside her now); Vivi's, all tears.

The baby's eyes are closed in sleep.

Good-bye, my children.

3   It is to the back of the great city he brought her, to the dwelling places of the cast-off old. Bounded by two lines of amusement piers to the north and to the south, and between a long straight paving rimmed with black benches facing the sand—sands so wide the ocean is only a far fluting.

In the brief vacation season, some of the boarded stores fronting the sands open, and families, young people and children, may be seen. A little tasselled tram shuttles between the piers, and the lights of roller coasters prink and tweak over those who come to have sensation made in them.

The rest of the year it is abandoned to the old, all else boarded up and still; seemingly empty, except the occasional days and hours when the sun, like a tide, sucks them out of the low rooming houses, casts them onto the benches and sandy rim of the walk—and sweeps them into decaying enclosures once again.

A few newer apartments glint among the low bleached squares. It is in one of these Lennie's Jeannie has arranged their rooms. "Only a few miles north and south people pay hundreds of dollars a month for just this gorgeous air, Grandaddy, just this ocean closeness."

She had been ill on the plane, lay ill for days in the unfamiliar room. Several times the doctor came by—left medicine she would not take. Several times Jeannie drove in the twenty miles from work, still in her Visiting Nurse uniform, the lightness and brightness of her like a healing.

"Who can believe it is winter?" he asked one morning. "Beautiful it is outside like an ad. Come, Mrs. Invalid, come to taste it. You are well enough to sit in here, you are well enough to sit outside. The doctor said it too."

But the benches were encrusted with people, and the sands at the sidewalk's edge. Besides, she had seen the far ruffle of the sea: "there take me," and though she leaned against him, it was she who led.

Plodding and plodding, sitting often to rest, he grumbling. Patting the sand so warm. Once she scooped up a handful, cradling it close to her better eye; peered, and flung it back. And as they came almost to the brink and she could see the glistening wet, she sat down, pulled off her shoes and stockings, left him and began to run. "You'll catch cold," he screamed, but the sand in his shoes weighed him down—he who had always been the agile one—and already the white spray creamed her feet.

He pulled her back, took a handkerchief to wipe off the wet and the sand. "Oh no," she said, "the sun will dry," seized the square and smoothed it flat, dropped on it a mound of sand, knotted the kerchief corners and tied it to a bag—"to look at with the strong glass" (for the first time in years explaining an action of hers)—and lay down with the little bag against her cheek, looking toward the shore that nurtured life as it first crawled toward consciousness the millions of years ago.

He took her one Sunday in the evil-smelling bus, past flat miles of blister houses, to the home of relatives. Oh what is this? she cried as the light began to smoke and the houses to dim and recede. Smog, he said, everyone knows but you. . . . Outside he kept his arms about her, but she walked with hands pushing the heavy air as if to open it, whispered: who has done this? sat down suddenly to vomit at the curb and for a long while refused to rise.

One's age as seen on the altered face of those known in youth. Is this they

he has come to visit? This Max and Rose, smooth and pleasant, introducing them
to polite children, disinterested grandchildren, "the whole family, once a
month on Sundays. And why not? We have the room, the help, the food."

Talk of cars, of houses, of success: this son that, that daughter this. And
your children? Hastily skimped over, the intermarriages, the obscure work—"my
doctor son-in-law, Phil"—all he has to offer. She silent in a corner. (Car-sick
like a baby, he explains.) Years since he has taken her to visit anyone but the
children, and old apprehensions prickle: "no incidents," he silently begs, "no
incidents." He itched to tell them. "A very sick woman," significantly, indicating
her with his eyes, "a very sick woman." Their restricted faces did not react.
"Have you thought maybe she'd do better at Palm Springs?" Rose asked. "Or at
least a nicer section of the beach, nicer people, a pool." Not to have to say
"money" he said instead: "would she have sand to look at through a magnifying
glass?" and went on, detail after detail, the old habit betraying of parading the
queerness of her for laughter.

After dinner—the others into the living room in men- or women-clusters, or
into the den to watch TV—the four of them alone. She sat close to him, and did
not speak. Jokes, stories, people they had known, beginning of reminiscence,
Russia fifty-sixty years ago. Strange words across the Duncan Phyfe table:
hunger; secret meetings; human rights; spies; betrayals; prison; escape—interrupted by one of the grandchildren: "Commercial's on; any Coke left? Gee,
you're missing a real hair-raiser." And then a granddaughter (Max proudly: "look
at her, an American queen") drove them home on her way back to U.C.L.A.
No incident—except that there had been no incidents.

The first few mornings she had taken with her the magnifying glass, but he
would sit only on the benches, so she rested at the foot, where slatted bench
shadows fell, and unless she turned her hearing aid down, other voices invaded.

Now on the days when the sun shone and she felt well enough, he took her
on the tram to where the benches ranged in oblongs, some with tables for
checkers or cards. Again the blanket on the sand in the striped shadows, but she
no longer brought the magnifying glass. He played cards, and she lay in the
sun and looked towards the waters; or they walked—two blocks down to the
scaling hotel, two blocks back—past chili-hamburger stands, open-doored bars.
Next to New and Perpetual Rummage Sale stores.

Once, out of the aimless walkers, slow and shuffling like themselves, someone ran unevenly towards them, embraced, kissed, wept: "dear friends, old
friends." A friend of *hers,* not his: Mrs. Mays who had lived next door to them
in Denver when the children were small.

Thirty years are compressed into a dozen sentences; and the present, not
even in three. All is told: the children scattered; the husband dead; she lives
in a room two blocks up from the sing hall—and points to the domed auditorium
jutting before the pier. The leg? phlebitis; the heavy breathing? that, one does
not ask. She, too, comes to the benches each day to sit. And tomorrow,
tomorrow, are they going to the community sing? Of course he would have

heard of it, everybody goes—the big doings they wait for all week. They have never been? She will come to them for dinner tomorrow and they will all go together.

So it is that she sits in the wind of the singing, among the thousand various faces of age.

She had turned off her hearing aid at once they came into the auditorium—as she would have wished to turn off sight.

One by one they streamed by and imprinted on her—and though the savage zest of their singing came voicelessly soft and distant, the faces still roared—the faces densened the air—chorded into

children-chants, mother-croons, singing of the chained
love serenades, Beethoven storms, mad Lucia's scream
drunken joy-songs, keens for the dead, work-singing

> *while from floor to balcony to dome a bare-footed*
> *sore-covered little girl threaded the sound-*
> *thronged tumult, danced her ecstasy of grimace*
> *to flutes that scratched at a cross-roads village*
> *wedding*

Yes, faces became sound, and the sound became faces;
and faces and sound became weight—pushed, pressed

"Air"—her hands claw his.

"Whenever I enjoy myself. . . ." Then he saw the gray sweat on her face. "Here. Up. Help me, Mrs. Mays," and they support her out to where she can gulp the air in sob after sob.

"A doctor, we should get for her a doctor."

"Tch, it's nothing," says Ellen Mays, "I get it all the time. You've missed the tram; come to my place. Fix your hearing aid, honey . . . close . . . tea. My view. See, she *wants* to come. Steady now, that's how." Adding mysteriously: "Remember your advice, easy to keep your head above water, empty things float. Float."

The singing a fading march for them, tall woman with a swollen leg, weaving little man, and the swollen thinness they help between.

The stench in the hall: mildew? decay? "We sit and rest then climb. My gorgeous view. We help each other and here we are."

The stench along into the slab of room. A washstand for a sink, a box with oilcloth tacked around for a cupboard, a three-burner gas plate. Artificial flowers, colorless with dust. Everywhere pictures foaming: wedding, baby, party, vacation, graduation, family pictures. From the narrow couch under a slit of window, sure enough the view: lurching rooftops and a scallop of ocean heaving, preening, twitching under the moon.

"While the water heats. Excuse me . . . down the hall." Ellen Mays has gone.

"You'll live?" he asks mechanically, sat down to feel his fright; tried to pull her alongside.

She pushed him away. "For air," she said; stood clinging to the dresser. Then, in a terrible voice:

After a lifetime of room. Of many rooms.

Shhh.

You remember how she lived. Eight children. And now one room like a coffin.

She pays rent!

Shrinking the life of her   into one room   like a coffin   Rooms and rooms like this   I lie on the quilt and hear them talk

Please, Mrs. Orator-without-Breath.

Once you went for coffee   I walked   I saw   A Balzac a Chekhov to write it   Rummage   Alone   On Scraps

Better old here than in the old country!

On scraps   Yet they sang like   like   Wondrous! *Humankind one has to believe*   So strong for what? To rot not grow?

Your poor lungs beg you. They sob between each word.

Singing.   Unused the life in them. She in this poor room   with her pictures Max You   The children   Everywhere unused the life   And who has meaning?   Century after century   still all in us not to grow?

Coffins, rummage, plants: sick woman. Oh lay down. We will get for you the doctor.

"And when will it end. Oh, *the end.*" *That* nightmare thought, and this time she writhed, crumpled against him, seized his hand (for a moment again the weight, the soft distant roaring of humanity) and on the strangled-for breath, begged: "Man . . . we'll destroy ourselves?"

And looking for answer—in the helpless pity and fear for her (for *her*) that distorted his face—she understood the last months, and knew that she was dying.

4 "Let us go home," she said after several days.

"You are in training for a cross-country trip? That is why you do not even walk across the room? Here, like a prescription Phil said, till you are stronger from the operation. You want to break doctor's orders?"

She saw the fiction was necessary to him, was silent; then: "At home I will get better. If the doctor here says?"

"And winter? And the visits to Lennie and to Clara? All right," for he saw the tears in her eyes, "I will write Phil, and talk to the doctor."

Days passed. He reported nothing. Jeannie came and took her out for air, past the boarded concessions, the hooded and tented amusement rides, to the end of the pier. They watched the spent waves feeding the new, the gulls in the clouded sky; even up where they sat, the wind-blown sand stung.

She did not ask to go down the crooked steps to the sea.

Back in her bed, while he was gone to the store, she said: "Jeannie, this doctor, he is not one I can ask questions. Ask him for me, can I go home?"

Jeannie looked at her, said quickly: "Of course, poor Granny. You want your own things around you, don't you? I'll call him tonight. . . . Look I've something to show you," and from her purse unwrapped a large cookie, intricately shaped like a little girl. "Look at the curls—can you hear me well, Granny?—and the darling eyelashes. I just came from a house where they were baking them."

"The dimples, there in the knees," she marveled, holding it to the better light, turning, studying, "like art. Each singly they cut, or a mold?"

"Singly," said Jeannie, "and if it is a child only the mother can make them. Oh Granny, it's the likeness of a real little girl who died yesterday—Rosita. She was three years old. *Pan del Muerto,* the Bread of the Dead. It was the custom in the part of Mexico they came from."

Still she turned and inspected. "Look, the hollow in the throat, the little cross necklace. . . . I think for the mother it is a good thing to be busy with such bread. You know the family?"

Jeannie nodded. "On my rounds. I nursed. . . . Oh Granny, it is like a party; they play songs she liked to dance to. The coffin is lined with pink velvet and she wears a white dress. There are candles. . . ."

"In the house?" Surprised, "They keep her in the house?"

"Yes," said Jeannie, "and it is against the health law. I think she is . . . prepared there. The father said it will be sad to bury her in this country; in Oaxaca they have a feast night with candles each year; everyone picnics on the graves of those they loved until dawn."

"Yes, Jeannie, the living must comfort themselves." And closed her eyes.

"You want to sleep, Granny?"

"Yes, tired from the pleasure of you. I may keep the Rosita? There stand it, on the dresser, where I can see; something of my own around me."

In the kitchenette, helping her grandfather unpack the groceries, Jeannie said in her light voice:

"I'm resigning my job, Grandaddy."

"Ah, the lucky young man. Which one is he?"

"Too late. You're spoken for." She made a pyramid of cans, unstacked, and built again.

"Something is wrong with the job?"

"With me. I can't be"—she searched for the word—"What they call professional enough. I let myself feel things. And tomorrow I have to report a family. . . ." The cans clicked again. "It's not that, either. I just don't know what I want to do, maybe go back to school, maybe go to art school. I thought if you went to San Francisco I'd come along and talk it over with Momma and Daddy. But I don't see how you can go. She wants to go home. She asked me to ask the doctor."

The doctor told her himself. "Next week you may travel, when you are a little stronger." But next week there was the fever of an infection, and by the time that was over, she could not leave the bed—a rented hospital bed that stood beside the double bed he slept in alone now.

Outwardly the days repeated themselves. Every other afternoon and evening he went out to his newfound cronies, to talk and play cards. Twice a week, Mrs. Mays came. And the rest of the time, Jeannie was there.

By the sickbed stood Jeannie's FM radio. Often into the room the shapes of music came. She would lie curled on her side, her knees drawn up, intense in listening (Jeannie sketched her so, coiled, convoluted like an ear), then thresh her hand out and abruptly snap the radio mute—still to lie in her attitude of listening, concealing tears.

Once Jeannie brought in a young Marine to visit, a friend from high-school days she had found wandering near the empty pier. Because Jeannie asked him to, gravely, without self-consciousness, he sat himself cross-legged on the floor and performed for them a dance of his native Samoa.

Long after they left, a tiny thrumming sound could be heard where, in her bed, she strove to repeat the beckon, flight, surrender of his hands, the fluttering footbeats, and his low plaintive calls.

Hannah and Phil sent flowers. To deepen her pleasure, he placed one in her hair. "Like a girl," he said, and brought the hand mirror so she could see. She looked at the pulsing red flower, the yellow skull face; a desolate, excited laugh shuddered from her, and she pushed the mirror away—but let the flower burn.

The week Lennie and Helen came, the fever returned. With it the excited laugh, and incessant words. She, who in her life had spoken but seldom and then only when necessary (never having learned the easy, social uses of words), now in dying, spoke incessantly.

In a half-whisper: "Like Lisa she is, your Jeannie. Have I told you of Lisa who taught me to read? Of the highborn she was, but noble in herself. I was sixteen; they beat me; my father beat me so I would not go to her. It was forbidden, she was a Tolstoyan. At night, past dogs that howled, terrible dogs, my son, in the snows of winter to the road, I to ride in her carriage like a lady, to books. To her, life was holy, knowledge was holy, and she taught me to read. They hung her. Everything that happens one must try to understand why. She killed one who betrayed many. Because of betrayal, betrayed all she lived and believed. In one minute she killed, before my eyes (there is so much blood in a human being, my son), in prison with me. All that happens, one must try to understand.

"The name?" Her lips would work. "The name that was their pole star; the doors of the death houses fixed to open on it; I read of it my year of penal servitude. Thuban!" very excited, "Thuban, in ancient Egypt the pole star. Can you see, look out to see it, Jeannie, if it swings around *our* pole star that seems to *us* not to move.

"Yes, Jeannie, at your age my mother and grandmother had already buried children . . . yes, Jeannie, it is more than oceans between Olshana and you . . . yes, Jeannie, they danced, and for all the bodies they had they might as well be chickens, and indeed, they scratched and flapped their arms and hopped.

"And Andrei Yefimitch, who for twenty years had never known of it and never wanted to know, said as if he wanted to cry: but why my dear friend this malicious laughter?" Telling to herself half-memorized phrases from her few books. "Pain I answer with tears and cries, baseness with indignation, meanness with repulsion . . . for life may be hated or wearied of, but never despised."

Delirious: "Tell me, my neighbor, Mrs. Mays, the pictures never lived, but what of the flowers? Tell them who ask: no rabbis, no ministers, no priests, no speeches, no ceremonies: ah, false—let the living comfort themselves. Tell Sammy's boy, he who flies, tell him to go to Stuttgart and see where Davy has no grave. And what?" A conspirator's laugh. "And what? where millions have no graves—save air."

In delirium or not, wanting the radio on; not seeming to listen, the words still jetting, wanting the music on. Once, silencing it abruptly as of old, she began to cry, unconcealed tears this time. "You have pain, Granny?" Jeannie asked.

"The music," she said, "still it is there and we do not hear; knocks, and our poor human ears too weak. What else, what else we do not hear?"

Once she knocked his hand aside as he gave her a pill, swept the bottles from her bedside table: "no pills, let me feel what I feel," and laughed as on his hands and knees he groped to pick them up.

Nighttimes her hand reached across the bed to hold his.

A constant retching began. Her breath was too faint for sustained speech now, but still the lips moved:

> When no longer necessary   to injure others
> Pick   pick pick   Blind chicken
> As a human being   responsibility

"David!" imperious, "Basin!" and she would vomit, rinse her mouth, the wasted throat working to swallow, and begin the chant again.

She will be better off in the hospital now, the doctor said.

He sent the telegrams to the children, was packing her suitcase, when her hoarse voice startled. She had roused, was pulling herself to sitting.

"Where now?" she asked. "Where now do you drag me?"

"You do not even have to have a baby to go this time," he soothed, looking for the brush to pack. "Remember, after Davy you told me—worthy to have a baby for the pleasure of the hospital?"

"Where now? Not home yet?" Her voice mourned. "Where *is* my home?"

He rose to ease her back. "The doctor, the hospital," he started to explain, but deftly, like a snake, she had slithered out of bed and stood swaying, propped behind the night table.

"Coward," she hissed, "runner."

"You stand," he said senselessly.

"To take me there and run. Afraid of a little vomit."

He reached her as she fell. She struggled against him, half slipped from his arms, pulled herself up again.

"Weakling," she taunted, "to leave me there and run. Betrayer. All your life you have run."

He sobbed, telling Jeannie. "A Marilyn Monroe to run for her virtue. Fifty-nine pounds she weighs, the doctor said, and she beats at me like a Dempsey. Betrayer, she cries, and I running like a dog when she calls; day and night, running to her, her vomit, the bedpan. . . ."

"She needs you, Grandaddy," said Jeannie. "Isn't that what they call love? I'll see if she sleeps, and if she does, poor worn-out darling, we'll have a party, you and I: I brought us rum babas."

They did not move her. By her bed now stood the tall hooked pillar that held the solutions—blood and dextrose—to feed her veins. Jeannie moved down the hall to take over the sickroom, her face so radiant, her grandfather asked her once: "you are in love?" (Shameful the joy, the pure overwhelming joy from being with her grandmother; the peace, the serenity that breathed.) "My darling escape," she answered incoherently, "my darling Granny"—as if that explained.

Now one by one the children came, those that were able. Hannah, Paul, Sammy. Too late to ask: and what did you learn with your living, Mother, and what do we need to know?

Clara, the eldest, clenched:

Pay me back, Mother, pay me back for all you took from me. Those others you crowded into your heart. The hands I needed to be for you, the heaviness, the responsibility.

Is this she? Noises the dying make, the crablike hands crawling over the covers. The ethereal singing.

She hears that music, that singing from childhood; forgotten sound—not heard since, since. . . . And the hardness breaks like a cry: Where did we lose each other, first mother, singing mother?

Annulled: the quarrels, the gibing, the harshness between; the fall into silence and the withdrawal.

I do not know you, Mother. Mother, I never knew you.

Lennie, suffering not alone for her who was dying, but for that in her which never lived (for that which in him might never live). From him too, unspoken words: *good-bye Mother who taught me to mother myself.*

Not Vivi, who must stay with her children; not Davy, but he is already here, having to die again with *her* this time, for the living take their dead with them when they die.

Light she grew, like a bird, and, like a bird, sound bubbled in her throat while the body fluttered in agony. Night and day, asleep or awake (though indeed there was no difference now) the songs and the phrases leaping.

And he, who had once dreaded a long dying (from fear of himself, from horror of the dwindling money) now desired her quick death profoundly, for *her* sake. He no longer went out, except when Jeannie forced him; no longer laughed, except when, in the bright kitchenette, Jeannie coaxed his laughter (and

she, who seemed to hear nothing else, would laugh too, conspiratorial wisps
of laughter).

Light, like a bird, the fluttering body, the little claw hands, the beaked
shadow on her face; and the throat, bubbling, straining.

He tried not to listen, as he tried not to look on the face in which only the
forehead remained familiar, but trapped with her the long nights in that little
room, the sounds worked themselves into his consciousness, with their punctua-
tion of death swallows, whimpers, gurglings.

> *Even in reality* (swallow) *life's lack of it*
> *Slaveships deathtrains clubs eeenough*
> *The bell summons what enables*
> *78,000 in one minute* (whisper of a scream) *78,000*
> *human beings we'll destroy ourselves?*

"Aah, Mrs. Miserable," he said, as if she could hear, "all your life working,
and now in bed you lie, servants to tend, you do not even need to call to be
tended, and still you work. Such hard work it is to die? Such hard work?"

The body threshed, her hand clung in his. A melody, ghost-thin, hovered
on her lips, and like a guilty ghost, the vision of her bent in listening to it,
silencing the record instantly he was near. Now, heedless of his presence, she
floated the melody on and on.

"Hid it from me," he complained, "how many times you listened to
remember it so?" And tried to think when she had first played it, or first begun
to silence her few records when he came near—but could reconstruct nothing.
There was only this room with its tall hooked pillar and its swarm of sounds.

> *No man one except through others*
> *Strong with the not yet in the now*
> *Dogma dead war dead one country*

"It helps, Mrs. Philosopher, words from books? It helps?" And it seemed to
him that for seventy years she had hidden a tape recorder, infinitely microscopic,
within her, that it had coiled infinite mile on mile, trapping every song, every
melody, every word read, heard, and spoken—and that maliciously she was
playing back only what said nothing of him, of the children, of their intimate
life together.

"Left us indeed, Mrs. Blabbler," he reproached, "you who called others
blabbler and cunningly saved your words. A lifetime you tended and loved, and
now not a word of us, for us. Left us indeed? Left me."

And he took out his solitaire deck, shuffled the cards loudly, slapped them
down.

> *Lift high banner of reason* (tatter of an orator's voice)
> *justice freedom light*
> *Humankind life worthy capacities*
> *Seeks* (blur of shudder) *belong human being*

"Words, words," he accused, "and what human beings did *you* seek around
you, Mrs. Live Alone, and what humankind think worthy?"

Though even as he spoke, he remembered she had not always been isolated,

had not always wanted to be alone (as he knew there had been a voice before
this gossamer one; before the hoarse voice that broke from silence to lash, make
incidents, shame him—a girl's voice of eloquence that spoke their holiest
dreams). But again he could reconstruct, image, nothing of what had been before,
or when, or how, it had changed.

Ace, queen, jack. The pillar shadow fell, so, in two tracks; in the mirror
depths glistened a moonlike blob, the empty solution bottle. And it worked in
him: *of reason and justice and freedom . . . Dogma dead:* he remembered the full
quotation, laughed bitterly. "Hah, good you do not know what you say; good
Victor Hugo died and did not see it, his twentieth century."

Deuce, ten, five. Dauntlessly she began a song of their youth of belief:

> *These things shall be, a loftier race*
> *than e'er the world hath known shall rise*
> *with flame of freedom in their souls*
> *and light of knowledge in their eyes*

King, four, jack. "In the twentieth century, Hah!"

> *They shall be gentle, brave and strong*
> *to spill no drop of blood, but dare*
>
> *earth and fire and sea and air*

"To spill no drop of blood, hah! So, cadaver, and you too, cadaver Hugo,
'in the twentieth century ignorance will be dead, dogma will be dead, war will
be dead, and for all mankind one country—of fulfilment?' Hah!"

> *And every life* (long strangling cough) *shall*
> *be a song*

The cards fell from his fingers. Without warning, the bereavement and
betrayal he had sheltered—compounded through the years—hidden even from
himself—revealed itself,
>   uncoiled,
>   released,
>   *sprung*

and with it the monstrous shapes of what had actually happened in the century.

A ravening hunger or thirst seized him. He groped into the kitchenette,
switched on all three lights, piled a tray—"you have finished your night snack,
Mrs. Cadaver, now I will have mine." And he was shocked at the tears that
splashed on the tray.

"Salt tears. For free. I forgot to shake on salt?"

Whispered: "Lost, how much I lost."

Escaped to the grandchildren whose childhoods were childish, who had
never hungered, who lived unravaged by disease in warm houses of many rooms,
had all the school for which they cared, could walk on any street, stood a head
taller than their grandparents, towered above—beautiful skins, straight backs,
clear straightforward eyes. "Yes, you in Olshana," he said to the town of sixty
years ago, "they would be nobility to you."

And was this not the dream then, come true in ways undreamed? he asked.

And are there no other children in the world? he answered, as if in her harsh voice.

And the flame of freedom, the light of knowledge?

And the drop, to spill no drop of blood?

And he thought that at six Jeannie would get up and it would be his turn to go to her room and sleep, that he could press the buzzer and she would come now; that in the afternoon Ellen Mays was coming, and this time they would play cards and he could marvel at how rouge can stand half an inch on the cheek; that in the evening the doctor would come, and he could beg him to be merciful, to stop the feeding solutions, to let her die. .

To let her die, and with her their youth of belief out of which her bright, betrayed words foamed; stained words, that on her working lips came stainless.

Hours yet before Jeannie's turn. He could press the buzzer and wake her to come now; he could take a pill, and with it sleep; he could pour more brandy into his milk glass, though what he had poured was not yet touched.

Instead he went back, checked her pulse, gently tended with his knotty fingers as Jeannie had taught.

She was whimpering; her hand crawled across the covers for his. Compassionately he enfolded it, and with his free hand gathered up the cards again. Still was there thirst or hunger ravening in him.

That world of their youth—dark, ignorant, terrible with hate and disease—how was it that living in it, in the midst of corruption, filth, treachery, degradation, they had not mistrusted man nor themselves; had believed so beautifully, so . . . falsely?

"Aaah, children," he said out loud, "how we believed, how we belonged." And he yearned to package for each of the children, the grandchildren, for everyone, *that joyous certainty, that sense of mattering, of moving and being moved, of being one and indivisible with the great of the past, with all that freed, ennobled man.* Package it, stand on corners, in front of stadiums and on crowded beaches, knock on doors, give it as a fabled gift.

"And why not in cereal boxes, in soap packages?" he mocked himself. "Aah. You have taken my senses, cadaver."

Words foamed, died unsounded. Her body writhed; she made kissing motions with her mouth. (Her lips moving as she read, poring over the Book of the Martyrs, the magnifying glass superimposed over the heavy eyeglasses.) *Still she believed?* "Eva!" he whispered. "Still you believed? You lived by it? These Things Shall Be?"

"One pound soup meat," she answered distinctly, "one soup bone."

"My ears heard you. Ellen Mays was witness: 'Humankind . . . one has to believe.'" Imploringly: "Eva!"

"Bread, day-old." She was mumbling. "Please, in a wooden box . . . for kindling. The thread, hah, the thread breaks. Cheap thread"—and a gurgling, enormously loud, began in her throat.

"I ask for stone; she gives me bread—day-old." He pulled his hand away, shouted: "Who wanted questions? Everything you have to wake?" Then dully,

"Ah, let me help you turn, poor creature."

Words jumbled, cleared. In a voice of crowded terror:

"Paul, Sammy, don't fight.

"Hannah, have I ten hands?

"How can I give it, Clara, how can I give it if I don't have?"

"You lie," he said sturdily, "there was joy too." Bitterly: "Ah how cheap you speak of us at the last."

As if to rebuke him, as if her voice had no relationship with her flailing body, she sang clearly, beautifully, a school song the children had taught her when they were little; begged:

"Not look my hair where they cut. . . ."

(The crown of braids shorn.) And instantly he left the mute old woman poring over the Book of the Martyrs; went past the mother treading at the sewing machine, singing with the children; past the girl in her wrinkled prison dress, hiding her hair with scarred hands, lifting to him her awkward, shamed, imploring eyes of love; and took her in his arms, dear, personal, fleshed, in all the heavy passion he had loved to rouse from her.

"Eva!"

Her little claw hand beat the covers. How much, how much can a man stand? He took up the cards, put them down, circled the beds, walked to the dresser, opened, shut drawers, brushed his hair, moved his hand bit by bit over the mirror to see what of the reflection he could blot out with each move, and felt that at any moment he would die of what was unendurable. Went to press the buzzer to wake Jeannie, looked down, saw on Jeannie's sketch pad the hospital bed, with *her*; the double bed alongside, with him; the tall pillar feeding into her veins, and their hands, his and hers, clasped, feeding each other. And as if he had been instructed he went to his bed, lay down, holding the sketch (as if it could shield against the monstrous shapes of loss, of betrayal, of death) and with his free hand took hers back into his.

So Jeannie found them in the morning.

That last day the agony was perpetual. Time after time it lifted her almost off the bed, so they had to fight to hold her down. He could not endure and left the room; wept as if there never would be tears enough.

Jeannie came to comfort him. In her light voice she said: Grandaddy, Grandaddy don't cry. She is not there, she promised me. On the last day, she said she would go back to when she first heard music, a little girl on the road of the village where she was born. She promised me. It is a wedding and they dance, while the flutes so joyous and vibrant tremble in the air. Leave her there, Grandaddy, it is all right. She promised me. Come back, come back and help her poor body to die.

For two of that generation
Seevya and Genya

Death deepens the wonder

Clare Booth Luce

*(b. 1903) In addition to being a
writer, Clare Booth Luce has been a
Congresswoman from Connecticut and
an ambassador to Italy. She was a
newspaper columnist and editor
before writing the play* The Women
*in 1936. Her satiric style has caused
some to think of her as antifeminist,
but she seems to sympathize with
Nora in her take-off on Ibsen's* A Doll's
House, *written 91 years after the
original.*

A Doll's House, 1970

(with apologies to Henrik Ibsen)

*The scene is the Thaw Walds' cheerfully furnished middle-class living room
in New York's suburbia. There are a front door and hall, a door to the kitchen
area, and a staircase to the bedroom floor. Two easy chairs and two low hassocks
with toys on them, grouped around a television, indicate a family of four.
Drinks are on a bar cart at one end of a comfortable sofa, and an end table at
the other. There are slightly more than the average number of bookshelves.
The lamps are on, but as we don't hear the children, we know it is the Parents'
Hour.*

As the curtain rises, THAW WALD, *a good-looking fellow, about 35, is sitting
in one of the easy chairs, smoking and watching TV. His back is to the sofa
and staircase, so he does not see his wife coming down the stairs.* NORA WALD
*is a rather pretty woman of about 32. She is carrying a suitcase, handbag and an
armful of books.*

*Thaw switches channels, and lands in the middle of a panel show. During the
TV dialogue that follows Nora somewhat furtively deposits her suitcase in the
hall, takes her coat out of the hall closet, and comes back to the sofa carrying
coat, purse and books. She lays her coat on the sofa, and the books on the
end table. The books are full of little paper slips—bookmarkers. All of the above*

actions are unobserved by Thaw. We cannot see the TV screen, but we hear
the voices of four women, all talking excitedly at once.)

THAW *(to the screen and the world in general):* God, these Liberation gals! Still
at it.
MALE MODERATOR'S VOICE *(full of paternal patience wearing a bit thin):*
Ladies! Lay-deez! Can't we switch now from the question of the sex-typing of
jobs to what the Women's Liberation Movement thinks about—
OLDER WOMAN'S VOICE: May I finish! In the Soviet Union 83% of the dentists,
75% of the doctors and 37% of the lawyers are women. In Poland and Denmark—
MODERATOR: I think you have already amply made your point, Mrs. Epstein—
anything men can do, women can do better!
YOUNG WOMAN'S VOICE *(angrily):* That was *not* her point—and you know it!
What she said was, there are very few professional jobs men are doing that
women couldn't do, if only—
THAW: Well, for God's sake then, shaddup, and go do 'em—
BLACK WOMAN'S VOICE: What she's been saying, what we've all been saying, and
you men just don't want to hear us, is—things are the same for women as they
are for us black people. We try to get up, you just sit down on us, like a big
elephant sits down on a bunch of poor little mice.
MODERATOR: Well, sometimes moderators have to play the elephant, and sit
down on one subject in order to develop another. As I was about to say, ladies,
there *is one thing* a woman can do, no man can do—*(in his best holy-night-all-is-*
bright voice) give birth to a *child.*
YOUNG WOMAN'S VOICE: So what else is new?
THAW: One gets you ten, she's a Lesbo—
MODERATOR *(forcefully):* And *that* brings us to marriage! Now, if *I* may be
permitted to get in just *one* statistic, edgewise: two thirds of all adult American
females are married women. And now! *(At last he's got them where he wants*
them.) What *is* the Women's Lib view of Woman's No. 1 job—Occupation Housewife?
THAW: Ha! That's the one none of 'em can handle—
YOUNG WOMAN'S VOICE *(loud and clear):* Marriage, as an institution, is as
thoroughly corrupt as prostitution. It is, in fact, legalized and romanticized
prostitution. A woman who marries is selling her sexual services and domestic
services for permanent bed and board—
BLACK WOMAN'S VOICE: There's no human being a man can buy anymore—
except a woman—
THAW *(snapping off the TV):* Crrr-ap! Boy, what a bunch of battle-axes! *(He*
goes back to studying his TV listings.)
NORA *(raising her voice):* Thaw! I'd like to say something about what they just
said about marriage—
THAW *(in a warning voice):* Uh-uh, Nora! We both agreed months ago, you'd lay
off the feminist bit, if I'd lay off watching Saturday football—
NORA: And do something with the children . . . But Thaw, there's something
maybe, I ought to try to tell you myself—

(Thaw is not listening. Nora makes a "what's the use" gesture, then opens her purse, takes out three envelopes, carefully inserts two of them under the covers of the top two books.)

THAW: Like to hear Senators Smithers, Smethers and Smothers on "How Fast Can We Get Out of Vietnam?"

NORA *(cool mockery):* That bunch of pot-bellied, bald-headed old goats! Not one of them could get a woman—well, yes, maybe for two dollars.

THAW: You don't look at Senators, Nora. You listen to them.

NORA *(nodding):* Women are only to look at. Men are to listen to. Got it.

(Thaw snaps off the TV. He is now neither looking at her nor listening to her, as he methodically turns pages of the magazine he has picked up.)

THAW: Finished reading to the kids?

NORA: I haven't been reading to the children. I've been reading to myself—and talking to myself—for a long time now.

THAW: That's good. *(She passes him, carrying the third envelope, and goes into kitchen.)*

THAW *(Unenthusiastically):* Want some help with the dishes?

NORA'S VOICE: I'm not doing the dishes.

THAW *(enthusiastically):* Say, Nora, this is quite an ad we've got in LIFE for Stove Mountain Life Insurance.

NORA'S VOICE: Yes, I saw it. Great. *(She comes back and goes to sofa.)*

THAW: It's the kind of ad that grabs you. This sad-faced, nice-looking woman of 50, sitting on a bench with a lot of discouraged old biddies, in an employment agency. Great caption—*(reading)*

NORA and THAW *(together):* "Could this happen to *your* wife?"

NORA: I'll let you know the answer very shortly. *(A pause.)* You really don't hear me anymore, do you? *(He really doesn't. She buttons herself into her coat, pulls on her gloves.)* Well, there are enough groceries for a week. All the telephone numbers you'll need and menus for the children are in the envelope on the spindle. A girl will come in to take care of them after school—until your mother gets here.

THAW: Uh-huh. . . .

NORA *(looks around sadly):* Well, goodby dear little doll house. Goodby dear husband. You've had the best ten years of my life.

(She goes to the staircase, blows two deep kisses upstairs, just as Thaw glances up briefly at her, but returns automatically to his magazine. Nora picks up suitcase, opens the door, goes out, closing it quietly.)

THAW *(like a man suddenly snapping out of a hypnotic trance):* Nora? Nora? NOR-RA! *(He is out of the door in two seconds.)*

THAW'S and NORA'S VOICES: Nora, where're you going?—I'll miss my train—I don't understand—it's all in my letter—let me go!—You come back—

(They return. He is pulling her by the arm. He yanks the suitcase away from her, drops it in the hall.)

NORA: Ouch! You're hurting me!

THAW: Now what is this all about? *(He shoves her into the room, then stands between her and door.)* Why the hell . . . What're you sneaking out of the house . . . What's that suitcase for?

NORA: I wasn't sneaking. I told you. But you weren't listening.

THAW: I was listening . . . it just didn't register. You said you were reading to yourself. Then you started yakking about the kids and the groceries and the doll house mother sent . . . *(flabbergasted.)* Goodby?! What the hell do you mean, *goodby?!*

NORA: Just that. I'm leaving you. *(Pointing to books.)* My letter will explain everything—

THAW: Have you blown your mind?

NORA: Thaw, I've got to scoot, or I'll miss the eight-o-nine.

THAW: You'll miss it. *(He backs her to the sofa, pushes her onto it, goes and slams the door and strides back.)* Now, my girl, explain all this.

NORA: That's easy. Muscle. The heavier musculature of the male is a secondary sexual characteristic. Although that's not certain. It could be just the result of selective breeding. In primitive times, of course, the heavier musculature of the male was necessary to protect the pregnant female and the immobile young—

THAW *(his anger evaporates):* Nora, are you sick?

NORA: But what's just happened now shows that nothing has changed—I mean, fundamentally changed—in centuries, in the relations between the sexes. *You* still Tarzan, *me* still Jane.

THAW *(sits on sofa beside her, feels her head):* I've noticed you've been . . . well . . . acting funny lately. . . .

NORA: Funny?

THAW: Like there was something on your mind. . . . Tell me, what's wrong, sweetheart? Where does it hurt?

NORA: It hurts *(taps head)* here. Isn't that where thinking hurts *you?* No. You're used to it. I was, too, when I was at Wellesley. But I sort of stopped when I left. It's really hard to think of anything else when you're having babies.

THAW: Nora, isn't it about time for your period?

NORA: But if God had wanted us to think just with our wombs, why did He give us a brain? No matter what men say, Thaw, the female brain is not a vestigial organ, like a vermiform appendix.

THAW: Nora . . .

NORA: Thaw, I can just about make my train. I'll leave the car and keys in the usual place at the station. Now, I have a very important appointment in the morning. *(She starts to rise.)*

THAW: Appointment? *(Grabs her shoulders.)* Nora, look at me! You weren't sneaking out of the house to . . . get an abortion?

NORA: When a man can't explain a woman's actions, the first thing he thinks about is the condition of her uterus. Thaw, if you were leaving me and I didn't know why, would I ask, first thing, if you were having prostate trouble?

THAW: Don't try to throw me off the track, sweetie! Now, if you want another baby . . .

NORA: Thaw, don't you remember, we both agreed about the overpopulation problem—

THAW: To hell with the overpopulation problem. Let Nixon solve that. Nora, I can swing another baby—

NORA: Maybe you can. I can't. For me there are no more splendid, new truths to be learned from scanning the contents of babies' diapers. Thaw, I *am* pregnant. But not in a feminine way. In the way only men are supposed to get pregnant.

THAW: Men, pregnant?

NORA *(nodding):* With ideas. Pregnancies there *(taps his head)* are masculine. And a very superior form of labor. Pregnancies here *(taps her tummy)* are feminine—a very inferior form of labor. That's an example of male linguistic chauvinism. Mary Ellmann is *great* on that. You'll enjoy her *Thinking about Women. . . .*

THAW *(going to telephone near bookshelf):* I'm getting the doctor. *(Nora makes a dash for the door, he drops the phone.)* Oh, no you don't!

(He reaches for her as she passes, misses. Grabs her ponytail and hauls her back by it, and shoves her into the easy chair.)

NORA: Brother, Millett sure had you taped.

THAW: Milly *who? (A new thought comes to him.)* Has one of your goddam-gossipyfemale friends been trying to break up our marriage? *(He suddenly checks his conscience. It is* not *altogether pure.)* What did she tell you? That she saw me having lunch, uh, dinner, with some girl?

NORA *(nodding to herself):* Right on the button!

THAW: Now, Nora, I can explain about that girl—

NORA: You don't have to. Let's face it. Monogamy is not natural to the male—

THAW: You know I'm not in love with anybody but you—

NORA: It's not natural to the female, either. Making women think it is is man's most successful form of brainwashing—

THAW: Nora, I swear, that girl means nothing to me—

NORA: And you probably mean nothing to her. So whose skin is off whose nose?

THAW *(relieved, but puzzled):* Well, uh, I'm glad you feel that way about—uh—things.

NORA: Oh, it's not the way I *feel.* It's the way things really are. What with the general collapse of the mores, and now the Pill, women are becoming as promiscuous as men. It figures. We're educated from birth to think of ourselves just as man-traps. Of course, in my mother's day, good women thought of themselves as private man-traps. Only bad women were public man-traps. Now we've all gone public. *(Looks at watch.)* I'll have to take the eight-forty.

(She gets out of her coat, lays it, ready to slip into, on back of sofa.)

THAW *(a gathering suspicion):* Nora, are you trying to tell me . . . that *you—*

NORA: Of course, a lot of it, today, is the fault of the advertising industry. Making women think they're failures in life if they don't make like sex-pots around the clock. We're even supposed to wear false eyelashes when we're vacuuming. Betty Friedan's great on that. She says many lonely suburban house-wives, unable to identify their real problem think more sex is the answer. So they sleep with the milkman, or the delivery boy. If I felt like sleeping with anybody like that, I'd pick the plumber. When you need *him,* boy you *need* him!

THAW *(the unpleasant thought he has been wrestling with has now jelled):* Nora . . . are you . . . trying to tell me you are leaving me—for someone else?

NORA: Why, Thaw Wald! How could you even *think* such a thing? *(To herself.)* Now, how naïve can I be? What else do men think about, in connection with women, *but sex?* He is saying to himself, she's not having her period, she's not pregnant, she's not jealous: it's *got* to be another man.

THAW: Stop muttering to yourself, and answer my question.

NORA: I forgot what it was. Oh, yes. *No.*

THAW: No what?

NORA: No, I'm not in love with anybody else. I was a virgin when I married you. And intacta. And that wasn't par for the course—even at Wellesley. And I've never slept with anybody else, partly because I never wanted to. And partly because, I suppose, of our family's Presbyterian hangup. So, now that all the vital statistics are out of the way, I'll just drive around until—

(Begins to slip her arms into coat. He grabs coat, throws it on easy chair.)

THAW: You're not leaving until you tell me *why.*

NORA: But it's all in my letter. *(Points.)* The fat one sticking out of Simone de Beauvoir's *Second Sex—*

THAW: If you have a bill of particulars against me, I want it—straight. From you.

NORA: Oh, darling, I have no bill of particulars. By all the standards of our present-day society, you are a very good husband. And, mark me, you'll be president of Stove Mountain Life Insurance Company before you're 50. The point is, what will I be when I'm 50—

THAW: You'll be my wife, if I have anything to say. Okay. So you're not leaving me because I'm a bad husband, or because my financial future is dim.

NORA: No. Oh, Thaw, you just wouldn't understand.

THAW *(patiently):* I might, if you would try, for just one minute, to talk logically—

NORA: Thaw, women aren't trained to talk logically. Men don't like women who talk logically. They find them unfeminine—aggressive—

THAW: Dammit, Nora, will you talk sense . . .

NORA: But Boy! does a man get sore when a woman won't talk logically when *he* wants her to, and *(snaps fingers)* like that! And *that* isn't illogical? What women men are! Now, if you will step aside—

THAW *(grabbing her and shaking her):* You're going to tell me why you're walking out on me, if I have to *sock* you!

NORA: Thaw, eyeball to eyeball, *I am leaving you*—and not for a man. For reasons of my own I just don't think you *can* understand. And if you mean to stop me, you'll have to beat me to a pulp. But I'm black and blue already.

THAW *(seizes her tenderly in his arms, kisses her):* Nora, sweetheart! You know I couldn't really hurt you. *(Kisses, kisses.)* Ba-aaby, what do you say we call it a night? *(Scoops her up in his arms.)* You can tell me *all* about it in bed . . .

NORA: The classical male one-two. Sock 'em and screw 'em.

THAW *(dumping her on sofa):* Well, it's been known to work on a lot of occasions. Something tells me this isn't one of them. *(Pours a drink.)*

NORA: I guess I need one, too. *(He mixes them.)* Thaw?

THAW: Yes.

NORA: I couldn't help being a *little* pleased when you made like a caveman. It shows you really do value my sexual services.

THAW: Jee-zus!

NORA: Well, it can't be my domestic services—you don't realize, yet, what they're worth. *(Drinks.)* Thaw, you do have a problem with me. But you can't solve it with force. And *I* do have a problem. But I can't solve it with sex.

THAW: Could you, would you, *try* to tell me what my-you-our problem is?

NORA: Friedan's *Feminine Mystique* is very good on The Problem. I've marked all the relevant passages. And I've personalized them in my letter—

(He goes to book. Yanks out letter, starts to tear it up. Nora groans. He changes his mind, and stuffs it in his pocket.)

THAW: Look, Nora, there's one thing I've always said about you. For a woman, you're pretty damn honest. Don't you think you owe it to me to level and give me a chance to defend myself?

NORA: The trouble is, *you* would have to listen to *me*. And that's hard for you. I *understand why*. Not listening to women is a habit that's been passed on from father to son for generations. You could almost say, tuning out on women is another secondary sexual male characteristic.

THAW: So our problem is that *I* don't listen?

NORA: Thaw, you always go on talking, no matter how hard I'm interrupting.

THAW: Okay. You have the floor.

NORA: Well, let's begin where this started tonight. When you oppressed me, and treated me as an inferior—

THAW: I oppressed . . . *(Hesitates.)* Lay on, MacDuff.

NORA: You honestly don't think that yanking me around by my hair and threatening to sock me are not the oppressive gestures of a superior male toward an inferior female?

THAW: For Chrissake, Nora, a man isn't going to let the woman he loves leave him, if he can stop her!

NORA: Exactly. Domination of the insubordinate female is an almost instinctive male reflex. *In extremis*, Thaw, it is *rape*. Now, would I like it if you should say you were going to leave me? No. But could I drag you back—

THAW: You'd just have to crook your little finger.

NORA: Flattery will get you nowhere this evening. So, where was I?

THAW: I am a born rapist.

NORA: Wasn't that what you had in mind when you tried to adjourn this to our bedroom? But that's just your primitive side. There's your civilized side too. You are a patriarchal *pater familias*.

THAW: What am I now?

NORA: Thaw, you do realize we all live in a patriarchy, where men govern women by playing sexual politics?

THAW: Look, you're not still sore because I talked you into voting for Nixon? *(She gives him a withering look.)* Okay. So we all live in a patriarchy . . .

NORA: Our little family, the Walds, are just one nuclear patriarchal unit among the millions in our patriarchal male-dominated civilization, which is worldwide. It's all in that book—

THAW: Look Nora, I promise I'll read the damn book—but . . .

NORA: So who's interrupting? Well, Thaw, all history shows that the hand that cradles the *rock* has ruled the world, *not* the hand that rocks the cradle! Do you know what brutal things men have done to women? Bought and sold them like cattle. Bound their feet at birth to deform them—so they couldn't run away—like in China. Made widows throw themselves on the funeral pyres of their husbands, like in India. Cut off their clitorises, so they could be bred but not enjoy sex. Thaw, did you know that the clitoris is the only sexual organ, in either sex, solely designed by nature for sexual pleasure?

THAW: That fascinating fact, up to now, has escaped me.

NORA: Yes, it's a pity. Well . . . men who committed adultery were almost never punished. But women were always brutally punished. Why, in many countries unfaithful wives were *stoned* to death—

THAW: This is America, 1970, Nora. And here, when wives are unfaithful, *husbands* get stoned. *(Drinks.)* Mind if *I* do?

NORA: Be your guest. Oh, there's no doubt that relations between the sexes have been greatly ameliorated . . .

THAW: Now, about *our* relations, Nora. You're not holding it against *me* that men, the dirty bastards, have done a lot of foul things to women in the past?

NORA *(indignant):* What do you mean, in the *past?*

THAW *(determined to be patient):* Past, present, future—what has what other men have done to other women got to do with us?

NORA: Quite a lot. We *are* a male and a female—

THAW: That's the supposition I've always gone on. But Nora, we are a *particular* male and a *particular* female: Thaw Wald and his wife, Nora—

NORA: Yes. That's why it's so shattering when you find out you are such a typical husband and—

THAW *(a new effort to take command):* Nora, how many men do you know who are still in love with their wives after ten years?

NORA: Not many. And, Thaw, listen, maybe the reason is—

THAW: So you agree that's not typical? Okay. Now, do I ever grumble about paying the bills? So that's not typical. I liked my mother-in-law, even when she was alive. And God knows that's not typical. And don't I do every damn thing I can to keep *my* mother off your back? And that's not typical. I'm even thoughtful about the little things. You said so yourself, remember, when I bought you that black see-through nightgown for Mother's Day. That I went out and chose myself. And which *you* never wear.

NORA: I had to return it. It was too small. And do you know what the saleswoman said? She said, "Men who buy their wives things in this department are in love with them. But why do they all seem to think they are married to midgets?" That's it, Thaw, that's *it!* Men "think little"—like "thinking thin"— even about women they love. They don't think at all about women they don't love or want to sleep with. Now, I can't help it if you think of me as a midget. But don't you see, I've got to stop thinking of myself as one. Thaw, *listen . . .*

THAW: Why the devil should *you* think of yourself as a midget? *I* think you're a great woman. A *real* woman! Why, you're the dearest, sweetest, most understanding little wife—most of the time—a man ever had. And the most intelligent and wonderful little mother! Dammit, those kids are the smartest, best-behaved, most self-reliant little kids . . .

NORA: Oh, I've been pretty good at Occupation Housewife, if I do say so myself. But Thaw, *listen.* Can't you even imagine that there might be something *more* a woman needs and wants—

THAW: My God, Nora, what more can a woman want than a nice home, fine children and a husband who adores her?

NORA: *(discouraged):* You sound like old Dr. Freud, in person.

THAW: I sound like Freud? I wish I were. Then I'd know why you're so uptight.

NORA: Oh, no you wouldn't. Know what Freud wrote in his diary, when he was 77? "What do women want? My God, what do they want?" Fifty years this giant brain spends analyzing women. And he still can't find out what they want. So this makes him the world's greatest expert on feminine psychology? *(She starts to look at her watch.)* To think I bought him, in college.

THAW: You've got plenty of time. You were saying about Freud—*(He lights a cigarette, hands it to her, determined to stick with it to the end.)*

NORA: History is full of ironies! Freud was the foremost exponent of the theory of the natural inferiority of women. You know, "Anatomy is destiny"?

THAW: I was in the School of Business, remember?

NORA: Well, old Freud died in 1939. He didn't live to see what happened when Hitler adopted his theory that "anatomy is destiny." Six millions of his own people went to the gas chambers. One reason, Hitler said, that the Jews were *naturally* inferior was because they were effeminate people, with a slave mentality. He said they were full of those vices which men always identify with women—when they're feeling hostile: You know, sneakiness and deception, scheming and wheedling, whining and pushiness, oh, and materialism, sensuousness and sexuality. Thaw, what's *your* favorite feminine vice?

THAW: At this moment, feminine monologues.

NORA: I didn't think you'd have the nerve to say sneakiness. I saw you sneak a look at your watch, and egg me on to talk about Freud, hoping I'll miss my train. I won't.

THAW: So nothing I've said—what little I've had a chance to say . . . *(she shakes her head)*—you still intend to divorce me?

NORA: Oh, I never said I was divorcing you. I'm deserting you. So you can divorce me.

THAW: You do realize, Nora, that if a wife deserts her husband he doesn't have to pay her alimony?

NORA: I don't want alimony. But I do want severance pay. *(Points to books.)* There's my bill, rendered for 10 years of domestic services—the thing sticking in *Woman's Place,* by Cynthia Fuchs Epstein. I figured it at the going agency rates for a full-time cook, cleaning woman, handyman, laundress, seamstress, and part-time gardener and chauffeur. I've worked an average ten-hour day. So I've charged for overtime. Of course, you've paid my rent, taxes, clothing, medical expenses and food. So I've deducted those. Even though as a housewife, I've had no fringe benefits. Just the same, the bill . . . well, I'm afraid you're going to be staggered. I was. It comes to over $53,000. I'd like to be paid in 10 installments.

THAW *(he is staggered):* Mathematics isn't really your bag, Nora.

NORA: I did it on that little calculating machine you gave me at Christmas. If you think it's not really fair, I'll be glad to negotiate. And, please notice, I haven't charged anything for sleeping with you!

THAW: Wow! *(He is really punch drunk.)*

NORA: I'm not a prostitute. And *this* is what I wanted to say about the Lib girls. They're right about women who marry *just* for money. But they're wrong about women who marry for love. It's love makes all the difference—

THAW *(dispirited):* Well, *vive la différence.*

NORA: And, of course, I haven't charged anything for being a nurse. I've adored taking care of the children, especially when they were babies. I'm going to miss them—*awfully.*

THAW *(on his feet, with outrage):* You're deserting the children, too? My God, Nora, what kind of woman *are* you? You're going to leave those poor little kids alone in this house—

NORA: You're here. And I told you, your mother is coming. I wired her that her son needed her. She'll be happy again—and be needed again—for the first time in years—

THAW *(this is a real blow):* My *mother*! Oh, migod, you *can't*, Nora. You know how she—*swarms* over me! She thinks I'm still 12 years old . . . *(His head is now in his hands.)* You know she drives me out of my cotton-picking mind.

NORA: Yes. But you never said so before.

THAW: I love my mother. She's been a good mother, and wife. But Nora, she's a *very* limited woman! Yak, yak—food, shopping, the kids . . .

NORA: Thaw, the children love this house, and I don't want to take them out of school. And I can't give them another home. Women, you know, can't borrow money to buy a house. Besides, legally this house and everything in it, except mother's few things, are yours. All the worldly goods with which thou didst me endow seem to be in that suitcase.

THAW: Nora, you know damn well that all my life insurance is in your name. If I died tomorrow—and I may blow my brains out tonight—everything would go to you and the kids.

NORA: Widowhood is one of the few fringe benefits of marriage. But, today, all the money I have is what I've saved in the past year out of my clothes allowance —$260.33. But I hope you will give me my severance pay—

THAW: And if I don't—you know legally I don't have to—how do you propose to support yourself?

NORA: Well, if I can't get a job right away—sell my engagement ring. That's why they say diamonds are a gal's best friend. What else do jobless women *have* they can turn into ready cash—except their bodies?

THAW: What kind of job do you figure on getting?

NORA: Well, I do have a master's in English. So I'm going to try for a spot in TIME Research. That's the intellectual harem kept by the Time Inc. editors. The starting pay is good.

THAW: How do you know that?

NORA: From your own research assistant, Molly Peapack. We're both Wellesley, you know. She's a friend of the chief researcher at TIME, Marylois Vega. Also, Molly says, computer programming is a field that may open to women—

THAW *(indignant):* You told Peapack you were leaving me? Before you even told *me*? How do you like *that* for treating a mate like an inferior!

NORA: Thaw, I've told you at least three times a week for the last year that with the kids both in school, I'd like to get a job. You always laughed at me. You said I was too old to be a Playboy Bunny, and that the only job an inexperienced woman my age could get would be as a saleswoman—

THAW: Okay. Where are you going to live? That 200 won't go far—

NORA: Peapack's offered to let me stay with her until I find something.

THAW: I'm going to have a word with Miss Molly Peapack tomorrow. She's been too damned aggressive lately, anyway—

NORA: She's going to have a word with you, too. She's leaving.

THAW: Peapack is leaving? Leaving *me*?

NORA: When you got her from Prudential, you promised her, remember, you'd recommend her for promotion to office manager. So, last week you took on a man. A new man. Now she's got a job offer where she's sure she's got a 40–60 chance for advancement to management. *(Pause.)* So you've lost your home wife and your office wife.

THAW: Jesus! And *this* is a male-dominated world?

NORA: Well, I've got five minutes—

THAW: You've still not told me *why*.

NORA: Oh, Thaw darling! You poor—*man*. I have told you why: I'm leaving because I want a job. I want to do some share, however small, of the world's work, and be paid for it. Isn't the work you do in the world—and the salary you get—what makes you respect yourself, and other men respect you? Women have begun to want to respect themselves a little, too—

THAW: You mean, the real reason you are leaving is that you want a *paying* job?

NORA: Yes.

THAW: God, Nora, why didn't you say that in the beginning. All right, go get a job, if it's that important to you. But that doesn't mean you have to leave me and the kids.

NORA: I'm afraid it does. Otherwise, I'd have to do two jobs. Out there. And here.

THAW: Look, Nora, I heard some of the Lib gals say there are millions of working wives and mothers who are doing two jobs. Housework can't be all that rough—

NORA: Scrubbing floors, walls. Cleaning pots, pans, windows, ovens. Messes—dog messes, toilet messes, children's messes. Garbage. Laundry. Shopping for pounds of stuff. Loading them into the car, out of the car—*(A pause.)* Not all of it hard. But all of it routine. All of it *boring*.

THAW: Listen, Nora, what say, you work, I work. And we split the housework? How's that for a deal?

NORA: It's a deal you are not quite free to make, Thaw. You sometimes *can't* get home until very late. And you have to travel a lot, you know. Oh, it might work for a little while. But not for long. After 10 years, you still won't empty an ashtray, or pick up after yourself in the bathroom. No. I don't have the physical or moral strength to swing two jobs. So I've got to choose the one, before it's too late, that's most important for me—oh, not for me just now, but for when *I'm* 50—

THAW: When you're 50, Nora, if you don't leave me, you'll be the wife of the president of Stove Mountain Life Insurance Company. Sharing my wealth, sharing whatever status I have in the community. And with servants of your own. Now you listen to *me*, Nora. It's a man's world, out there. It's a man's world where there are a lot of women working. I see them every day. What are most of them really doing? Marking time, and looking, always looking, for a man who will offer them a woman's world . . . the world you have here. Marriage is still the best deal that the world has to offer women. And most women know it. It's always been like that. And it's going to be like that for a long, long time.

NORA: Just now I feel that the best deal I, Nora Wald, can hope to get out of life is to learn to esteem myself as a person . . . to stop feeling that every day a little bit more of my mind—and heart—is being washed down the drain with the soapsuds. . . . Thaw—listen. If I don't stop shrinking, I'll end up secretly hating you, and trying to cut you—and *your* son—down to my size. The way your poor, dear mother does you and your father. And you'll become like your father, the typical henpecked husband. Thinking of his old wife as the Ball and Chain. You know he has a mistress? *(Thaw knows.)* A smart gal who owns her own shop . . . who doesn't bore him.

THAW: Well, Nora . . . *(Pours drinks.)* One for the road?

NORA: Right. For the road.

THAW: Nora . . . I'll wait. But I don't know how long—

NORA: I've thought of that, too . . . that you might remarry . . . that girl, maybe, who means nothing—

THAW: Goddammit, a man needs a woman of his own—

NORA *(nodding):* I know. A sleep-in, sleep-with body servant of his very own. Well, that's your problem. Just now, I have to wrestle with mine. *(Goes to door, picks up suitcase.)* I'm not bursting with self-confidence, Thaw. I do love you. And I also need . . . a man. So I'm not slamming the door. I'm closing it . . . very . . . softly.

(Exits. Curtain falls.)

Susan Glaspell

(1882-1948) Susan Glaspell is perhaps best known as a dramatist and a founder of the Provincetown Players. Her play Alison's House, *based on the life of Emily Dickinson, won a Pulitzer prize in 1930. She wrote several novels and short stories, of which "A Jury of Her Peers" is the most famous; it was reprinted in* The Best Short Stories of 1917.

A Jury of Her Peers

When Martha Hale opened the storm-door and got a cut of the north wind, she ran back for her big woolen scarf. As she hurriedly wound that round her head her eye made a scandalized sweep of her kitchen. It was no ordinary thing that called her away—it was probably further from ordinary than anything that had ever happened in Dickson County. But what her eye took in was that her kitchen was in no shape for leaving: her bread all ready for mixing, half the flour sifted and half unsifted.

She hated to see things half done; but she had been at that when the team from town stopped to get Mr. Hale, and then the sheriff came running in to say his wife wished Mrs. Hale would come too—adding, with a grin, that he guessed she was getting scary and wanted another woman along. So she had dropped everything right where it was.

"Martha!" now came her husband's impatient voice. "Don't keep folks waiting out here in the cold."

She again opened the storm-door, and this time joined the three men and the one woman waiting for her in the big two-seated buggy.

After she had the robes tucked around her she took another look at the woman who sat beside her on the back seat. She had met Mrs. Peters the year before at the county fair, and the thing she remembered about her was that she didn't seem like a sheriff's wife. She was small and thin and didn't have a strong voice. Mrs. Gorman, sheriff's wife before Gorman went out and Peters

From Every Week, *March 5, 1917; collected in Edward O'Brien,* Best Short Stories of 1917.

came in, had a voice that somehow seemed to be backing up the law with every word. But if Mrs. Peters didn't look like a sheriff's wife, Peters made it up in looking like a sheriff. He was to a dot the kind of man who could get himself elected sheriff—a heavy man with a big voice, who was particularly genial with the law-abiding, as if to make it plain that he knew the difference between criminals and non-criminals. And right there it came into Mrs. Hale's mind, with a rub, that this man who was so pleasant and lively with all of them was going to the Wrights' now as a sheriff.

"The country's not very pleasant this time of year," Mrs. Peters at last ventured, as if she felt they ought to be talking as well as the men.

Mrs. Hale scarcely finished her reply, for they had gone up a little hill and could see the Wright place now, and seeing it did not make her feel like talking. It looked very lonesome this cold March morning. It had always been a lonesome-looking place. It was down in a hollow, and the poplar trees around it were lonesome-looking trees. The men were looking at it and talking about what had happened. The county attorney was bending to one side of the buggy, and kept looking steadily at the place as they drew up to it.

"I'm glad you came with me," Mrs. Peters said nervously, as the two women were about to follow the men in through the kitchen door.

Even after she had her foot on the door-step, her hand on the knob, Martha Hale had a moment of feeling she could not cross that threshold. And the reason it seemed she couldn't cross it now was simply because she hadn't crossed it before. Time and time again it had been in her mind, "I ought to go over and see Minnie Foster"—she still thought of her as Minnie Foster, though for twenty years she had been Mrs. Wright. And then there was always something to do and Minnie Foster would go from her mind. But *now* she could come.

The men went over to the stove. The women stood close together by the door. Young Henderson, the county attorney, turned around and said, "Come up to the fire, ladies."

Mrs. Peters took a step forward, then stopped. "I'm not—cold," she said.

And so the two women stood by the door, at first not even so much as looking around the kitchen.

The men talked for a minute about what a good thing it was the sheriff had sent his deputy out that morning to make a fire for them, and then Sheriff Peters stepped back from the stove, unbuttoned his outer coat, and leaned his hands on the kitchen table in a way that seemed to mark the beginning of official business. "Now, Mr. Hale," he said in a sort of semi-official voice, "before we move things about, you tell Mr. Henderson just what it was you saw when you came here yesterday morning."

The county attorney was looking around the kitchen.

"By the way," he said, "has anything been moved?" He turned to the sheriff. "Are things just as you left them yesterday?"

Peters looked from cupboard to sink; from that to a small worn rocker a little to one side of the kitchen table.

"It's just the same."

"Somebody should have been left here yesterday," said the county attorney.

"Oh—yesterday," returned the sheriff, with a little gesture as of yesterday having been more than he could bear to think of. "When I had to send Frank to Morris Center for that man who went crazy—let me tell you, I had my hands full *yesterday*. I knew you could get back from Omaha by today, George, and as long as I went over everything here myself—"

"Well, Mr. Hale," said the county attorney, in a way of letting what was past and gone go, "tell just what happened when you came here yesterday morning."

Mrs. Hale, still leaning against the door, had that sinking feeling of the mother whose child is about to speak a piece. Lewis often wandered along and got things mixed up in a story. She hoped he would tell this straight and plain, and not say unnecessary things that would just make things harder for Minnie Foster. He didn't begin at once, and she noticed that he looked queer—as if standing in that kitchen and having to tell what he had seen there yesterday morning made him almost sick.

"Yes, Mr. Hale?" the county attorney reminded.

"Harry and I had started to town with a load of potatoes," Mrs. Hale's husband began.

Harry was Mrs. Hale's oldest boy. He wasn't with them now, for the very good reason that those potatoes never got to town yesterday and he was taking them this morning, so he hadn't been home when the sheriff stopped to say he wanted Mr. Hale to come over to the Wright place and tell the county attorney his story there, where he could point it all out. With all Mrs. Hale's other emotions came the fear now that maybe Harry wasn't dressed warm enough—they hadn't any of them realized how that north wind did bite.

"We come along this road," Hale was going on, with a motion of his hand to the road over which they had just come, "and as we got in sight of the house I says to Harry, 'I'm goin' to see if I can't get John Wright to take a telephone.' You see," he explained to Henderson, "unless I can get somebody to go in with me they won't come out this branch road except for a price *I* can't pay. I'd spoke to Wright about it once before; but he put me off, saying folks talked too much anyway, and all he asked was peace and quiet—guess you know about how much he talked himself. But I thought maybe if I went to the house and talked about it before his wife, and said all the women-folks liked the telephones, and that in this lonesome stretch of road it would be a good thing—well, I said to Harry that that was what I was going to say—though I said at the same time that I didn't know as what his wife wanted made much difference to John—"

Now there he was!—saying things he didn't need to say. Mrs. Hale tried to catch her husband's eye, but fortunately the county attorney interrupted with:

"Let's talk about that a little later, Mr. Hale. I do want to talk about that, but I'm anxious now to get along to just what happened when you got here."

When he began this time, it was very deliberately and carefully:

"I didn't see or hear anything. I knocked at the door. And still it was all quiet inside. I knew they must be up—it was past eight o'clock. So I knocked

again, louder, and I thought I heard somebody say, 'Come in.' I wasn't sure—I'm
not sure yet. But I opened the door—this door," jerking a hand toward the
door by which the two women stood, "and there, in that rocker"—pointing to
it—"sat Mrs. Wright."

Everyone in the kitchen looked at the rocker. It came into Mrs. Hale's mind
that that rocker didn't look in the least like Minnie Foster—the Minnie Foster
of twenty years before. It was a dingy red, with wooden rungs up the back,
and the middle rung was gone, and the chair sagged to one side.

"How did she—look?" the county attorney was inquiring.

"Well," said Hale, "she looked—queer."

"How do you mean—queer?"

As he asked it he took out a note-book and pencil. Mrs. Hale did not like
the sight of that pencil. She kept her eye fixed on her husband, as if to keep him
from saying unnecessary things that would go into that note-book and make
trouble.

Hale did speak guardedly, as if the pencil had affected him too.

"Well, as if she didn't know what she was going to do next. And kind of—
done up."

"How did she seem to feel about your coming?"

"Why, I don't think she minded—one way or other. She didn't pay much
attention. I said, 'Ho' do, Mrs. Wright? It's cold, ain't it?'" And she said, 'Is
it?'—and went on pleatin' at her apron.

"Well, I was surprised. She didn't ask me to come up to the stove, or to sit
down, but just set there, not even lookin' at me. And so I said: 'I want to see
John.'

"And then she—laughed. I guess you would call it a laugh.

"I thought of Harry and the team outside, so I said, a little sharp, 'Can I see
John?' 'No,' says she—kind of dull like. 'Ain't he home?' says I. Then she looked
at me. 'Yes,' says she, 'he's home.' 'Then why can't I see him?' I asked her, out of
patience with her now. ''Cause he's dead,' says she, just as quiet and dull—and
fell to pleatin' her apron. 'Dead?' says I, like you do when you can't take in what
you've heard.

"She just nodded her head, not getting a bit excited, but rockin' back and
forth.

"'Why—where is he?' says I, not knowing *what* to say.

"She just pointed upstairs—like this"—pointing to the room above.

"I got up, with the idea of going up there myself. By this time I—didn't know
what to do. I walked from there to here; then I says: 'Why, what did he die of?'

"'He died of a rope round his neck,' says she; and just went on pleatin'
at her apron."

Hale stopped speaking, and stood staring at the rocker, as if he were still
seeing the woman who had sat there the morning before. Nobody spoke; it was
as if every one were seeing the woman who had sat there the morning before.

"And what did you do then?" the county attorney at last broke the silence.

"I went out and called Harry. I thought I might—need help. I got Harry in, and we went upstairs." His voice fell almost to a whisper. "There he was—lying over the—"

"I think I'd rather have you go into that upstairs," the county attorney interrupted, "where you can point it all out. Just go on now with the rest of the story."

"Well, my first thought was to get that rope off. It looked—"

He stopped, his face twitching.

"But Harry, he went up to him, and he said, 'No, he's dead all right, and we'd better not touch anything.' So we went downstairs.

"She was still sitting that same way. 'Has anybody been notified?' I asked. 'No,' says she, unconcerned.

"'Who did this, Mrs. Wright?' said Harry. He said it businesslike, and she stopped pleatin' at her apron. 'I don't know,' she says. 'You don't *know*?' says Harry. 'Weren't you sleepin' in the bed with him?' 'Yes,' says she, 'but I was on the inside.' 'Somebody slipped a rope round his neck and strangled him, and, you didn't wake up?' says Harry. 'I didn't wake up,' she said after him.

"We may have looked as if we didn't see how that could be, for after a minute she said, 'I sleep sound.'

"Harry was going to ask her more questions, but I said maybe that weren't our business; maybe we ought to let her tell her story first to the coroner or the sheriff. So Harry went fast as he could over to High Road—the Rivers' place, where there's a telephone."

"And what did she do when she knew you had gone for the coroner?" The attorney got his pencil in his hand all ready for writing.

"She moved from that chair to this one over here"—Hale pointed to a small chair in the corner—"and just sat there with her hands held together and looking down. I got a feeling that I ought to make some conversation, so I said I had come in to see if John wanted to put in a telephone; and at that she started to laugh, and then she stopped and looked at me—scared."

At sound of a moving pencil the man who was telling the story looked up.

"I dunno—maybe it wasn't scared," he hastened; "I wouldn't like to say it was. Soon Harry got back, and then Dr. Lloyd came, and you, Mr. Peters, and so I guess that's all I know that you don't."

He said that last with relief, and moved a little, as if relaxing. Every one moved a little. The county attorney walked toward the stair door.

"I guess we'll go upstairs first—then out to the barn and around there."

He paused and looked around the kitchen.

"You're convinced there was nothing important here?" he asked the sheriff. "Nothing that would—point to any motive?"

The sheriff too looked all around, as if to re-convince himself.

"Nothing here but kitchen things," he said, with a little laugh for the insignificance of kitchen things.

The county attorney was looking at the cupboard—a peculiar, ungainly structure, half closet and half cupboard, the upper part of it being built in the wall, and the lower part just the old-fashioned kitchen cupboard. As if its queerness attracted him, he got a chair and opened the upper part and looked in. After a moment he drew his hand away sticky.

"Here's a nice mess," he said resentfully.

The two women had drawn nearer, and now the sheriff's wife spoke.

"Oh—her fruit," she said, looking to Mrs. Hale for sympathetic understanding. She turned back to the county attorney and explained: "She worried about that when it turned so cold last night. She said the fire would go out and her jars might burst."

Mrs. Peters' husband broke into a laugh.

"Well, can you beat the women! Held for murder, and worrying about her preserves!"

The young attorney set his lips.

"I guess before we're through with her she may have something more serious than preserves to worry about."

"Oh, well," said Mrs. Hale's husband, with good-natured superiority, "women are used to worrying over trifles."

The two women moved a little closer together. Neither of them spoke. The county attorney seemed suddenly to remember his manners—and think of his future.

"And yet," said he, with the gallantry of a young politician, "for all their worries, what would we do without the ladies?"

The women did not speak, did not unbend. He went to the sink and began washing his hands. He turned to wipe them on the roller towel—whirled it for a cleaner place.

"Dirty towels! Not much of a housekeeper, would you say, ladies?"

He kicked his foot against some dirty pans under the sink.

"There's a great deal of work to be done on a farm," said Mrs. Hale stiffly.

"To be sure. And yet"—with a little bow to her—"I know there are some Dickson County farm-houses that do not have such roller towels." He gave it a pull to expose its full length again.

"Those towels get dirty awful quick. Men's hands aren't always as clean as they might be."

"Ah, loyal to your sex, I see," he laughed. He stopped and gave her a keen look. "But you and Mrs. Wright were neighbors. I suppose you were friends, too."

Martha Hale shook her head.

"I've seen little enough of her of late years. I've not been in this house—it's more than a year."

"And why was that? You didn't like her?"

"I liked her well enough," she replied with spirit. "Farmers' wives have their hands full, Mr. Henderson. And then—" She looked around the kitchen.

"Yes?" he encouraged.

"It never seemed a very cheerful place," said she, more to herself than to him.

"No," he agreed; "I don't think anyone would call it cheerful. I shouldn't say she had the home-making instinct."

"Well, I don't know as Wright had, either," she muttered.

"You mean they didn't get on very well?" he was quick to ask.

"No; I don't mean anything," she answered, with decision. As she turned a little away from him, she added: "But I don't think a place would be any the cheerfuler for John Wright's bein' in it."

"I'd like to talk to you about that a little later, Mrs. Hale," he said. "I'm anxious to get the lay of things upstairs now."

He moved toward the stair door, followed by the two men.

"I suppose anything Mrs. Peters does'll be all right?" the sheriff inquired. "She was to take in some clothes for her, you know—and a few little things. We left in such a hurry yesterday."

The county attorney looked at the two women whom they were leaving alone there among the kitchen things.

"Yes—Mrs. Peters," he said, his glance resting on the woman who was not Mrs. Peters, the big farmer woman who stood behind the sheriff's wife. "Of course Mrs. Peters is one of us," he said, in a manner of entrusting responsibility. "And keep your eye out, Mrs. Peters, for anything that might be of use. No telling; you women might come upon a clue to the motive—and that's the thing we need."

Mr. Hale rubbed his face after the fashion of a showman getting ready for a pleasantry.

"But would the women know a clue if they did come upon it?" he said; and, having delivered himself of this, he followed the others through the stair door.

The women stood motionless and silent, listening to the footsteps, first upon the stairs, then in the room above them.

Then, as if releasing herself from something strange, Mrs. Hale began to arrange the dirty pans under the sink, which the county attorney's disdainful push of the foot had deranged.

"I'd hate to have men comin' into my kitchen," she said testily—"snoopin' round and criticizin'."

"Of course it's no more than their duty," said the sheriff's wife, in her manner of timid acquiescence.

"Duty's all right," replied Mrs. Hale bluffly; "but I guess that deputy sheriff that come out to make the fire might have got a little of this on." She gave the roller towel a pull. "Wish I'd thought of that sooner! Seems mean to talk about her for not having things slicked up, when she has to come away in such a hurry."

She looked around the kitchen. Certainly it was not "slicked up." Her eye was held by a bucket of sugar on a low shelf. The cover was off the wooden bucket, and beside it was a paper bag—half full.

Mrs. Hale moved toward it.

"She was putting this in there," she said to herself—slowly.

She thought of the flour in her kitchen at home—half sifted, half not sifted. She had been interrupted, and had left things half done. What had interrupted Minnie Foster? Why had that work been left half done? She made a move as if to finish it,—unfinished things always bothered her,—and then she glanced around and saw that Mrs. Peters was watching her—and she didn't want Mrs. Peters to get that feeling she had got of work begun and then—for some reason— not finished.

"It's a shame about her fruit," she said, and walked toward the cupboard that the county attorney had opened, and got on the chair, murmuring: "I wonder if it's all gone."

It was a sorry enough looking sight, but "Here's one that's all right," she said at last. She held it toward the light. "This is cherries, too." She looked again. "I declare I believe that's the only one."

With a sigh, she got down from the chair, went to the sink, and wiped off the bottle.

"She'll feel awful bad, after all her hard work in the hot weather. I remember the afternoon I put up my cherries last summer."

She set the bottle on the table, and, with another sigh, started to sit down in the rocker. But she did not sit down. Something kept her from sitting down in that chair. She straightened—stepped back—and, half turned away, stood looking at it, seeing the woman who had sat there "pleatin' at her apron."

The thin voice of the sheriff's wife broke in upon her: "I must be getting those things from the front-room closet." She opened the door into the other room, started in, stepped back. "You coming with me, Mrs. Hale?" she asked nervously. "You—you could help me get them."

They were soon back—the stark coldness of that shut-up room was not a thing to linger in.

"My!" said Mrs. Peters, dropping the things on the table and hurrying to the stove.

Mrs. Hale stood examining the clothes the woman who was being detained in town had said she wanted.

"Wright was close!" she exclaimed, holding up a shabby black skirt that bore the marks of much making over. "I think maybe that's why she kept so much to herself. I s'pose she felt she couldn't do her part; and then, you don't enjoy things when you feel shabby. She used to wear pretty clothes and be lively—when she was Minnie Foster, one of the town girls, singing in the choir. But that—oh, that was twenty years ago."

With a carefulness in which there was something tender, she folded the shabby clothes and piled them at one corner of the table. She looked up at Mrs. Peters, and there was something in the other woman's look that irritated her.

"She don't care," she said to herself. "Much difference it makes to her whether Minnie Foster had pretty clothes when she was a girl."

Then she looked again, and she wasn't so sure; in fact, she hadn't at any time been perfectly sure about Mrs. Peters. She had that shrinking manner, and yet her eyes looked as if they could see a long way into things.

"This all you was to take in?" asked Mrs. Hale.

"No," said the sheriff's wife; "she said she wanted an apron. Funny thing to want," she ventured in her nervous little way, for there's not much to get you dirty in jail, goodness knows. But I suppose just to make her feel more natural.

If you're used to wearing an apron—. She said they were in the bottom drawer of this cupboard. Yes—here they are. And then her little shawl that always hung on the stair door."

She took the small gray shawl from behind the door leading upstairs, and stood a minute looking at it.

Suddenly Mrs. Hale took a quick step toward the other woman.

"Mrs. Peters!"

"Yes, Mrs. Hale?"

"Do you think she—did it?"

A frightened look blurred the other thing in Mrs. Peters' eyes.

"Oh, I don't know," she said, in a voice that seemed to shrink away from the subject.

"Well, I don't think she did," affirmed Mrs. Hale stoutly. "Asking for an apron, and her little shawl. Worryin' about her fruit."

"Mr. Peters says—." Footsteps were heard in the room above; she stopped, looked up, then went on in a lowered voice: "Mr. Peters says—it looks bad for her. Mr. Henderson is awful sarcastic in a speech, and he's going to make fun of her saying she didn't—wake up."

For a moment Mrs. Hale had no answer. Then, "Well, I guess John Wright didn't wake up—when they was slippin' that rope under his neck," she muttered.

"No, it's *strange*," breathed Mrs. Peters. "They think it was such a—funny way to kill a man."

She began to laugh; at sound of the laugh, abruptly stopped.

"That's just what Mr. Hale said," said Mrs. Hale, in a resolutely natural voice. "There was a gun in the house. He says that's what he can't understand."

"Mr. Henderson said, coming out, that what was needed for the case was a motive. Something to show anger—or sudden feeling."

"Well, I don't see any signs of anger around here," said Mrs. Hale. "I don't—"

She stopped. It was as if her mind tripped on something. Her eye was caught by a dish-towel in the middle of the kitchen table. Slowly she moved toward the table. One half of it was wiped clean, the other half messy. Her eyes made a slow, almost unwilling turn to the bucket of sugar and the half empty bag beside it. Things begun—and not finished.

After a moment she stepped back, and said, in that manner of releasing herself:

"Wonder how they're finding things upstairs? I hope she had it a little more red up up there. You know,"—she paused, and feeling gathered,—"it seems kind of *sneaking*: locking her up in town and coming out here to get her own house to turn against her!"

"But, Mrs. Hale," said the sheriff's wife, "the law is the law."

"I s'pose 'tis," answered Mrs. Hale shortly.

She turned to the stove, saying something about that fire not being much to brag of. She worked with it a minute, and when she straightened up she said aggressively:

"The law is the law—and a bad stove is a bad stove. How'd you like to cook on this?"—pointing with the poker to the broken lining. She opened the oven door and started to express her opinion of the oven; but she was swept into her own thoughts, thinking of what it would mean, year after year, to have that stove to wrestle with. The thought of Minnie Foster trying to bake in that oven—and the thought of her never going over to see Minnie Foster—.

She was startled by hearing Mrs. Peters say: "A person gets discouraged—and loses heart."

The sheriff's wife had looked from the stove to the sink—to the pail of water which had been carried in from outside. The two women stood there silent, above them the footsteps of the men who were looking for evidence against the woman who had worked in that kitchen. That look of seeing into things, of seeing through a thing to something else, was in the eyes of the sheriff's wife now. When Mrs. Hale next spoke to her, it was gently:

"Better loosen up your things, Mrs. Peters. We'll not feel them when we go out."

Mrs. Peters went to the back of the room to hang up the fur tippet she was wearing. A moment later she exclaimed, "Why, she was piecing a quilt," and held up a large sewing basket piled high with quilt pieces.

Mrs. Hale spread some of the blocks on the table.

"It's log-cabin pattern," she said, putting several of them together. "Pretty, isn't it?"

They were so engaged with the quilt that they did not hear the footsteps on the stairs. Just as the stair door opened Mrs. Hale was saying:

"Do you suppose she was going to quilt it or just knot it?"

The sheriff threw up his hands.

"They wonder whether she was going to quilt it or just knot it!"

There was a laugh for the ways of women, a warming of hands over the stove, and then the county attorney said briskly:

"Well, let's go right out to the barn and get that cleared up."

"I don't see as there's anything so strange," Mrs. Hale said resentfully, after the outside door had closed on the three men—"our taking up our time with little things while we're waiting for them to get the evidence. I don't see as it's anything to laugh about."

"Of course they've got awful important things on their minds," said the sheriff's wife apologetically.

They returned to an inspection of the block for the quilt. Mrs. Hale was looking at the fine, even sewing, and preoccupied with thoughts of the woman who had done that sewing, when she heard the sheriff's wife say, in a queer tone:

"Why, look at this one."

She turned to take the block held out to her.

"The sewing," said Mrs. Peters, in a troubled way. "All the rest of them have been so nice and even—but—this one. Why, it looks as if she didn't know what she was about!"

Their eyes met—something flashed to life, passed between them; then, as if with an effort, they seemed to pull away from each other. A moment Mrs. Hale sat there, her hands folded over that sewing which was so unlike all the rest of the sewing. Then she had pulled a knot and drawn the threads.

"Oh, what are you doing, Mrs. Hale?" asked the sheriff's wife, startled.

"Just pulling out a stitch or two that's not sewed very good," said Mrs. Hale mildly.

"I don't think we ought to touch things," Mrs. Peters said, a little helplessly.

"I'll just finish up this end," answered Mrs. Hale, still in that mild, matter-of-fact fashion.

She threaded a needle and started to replace bad sewing with good. For a little while she sewed in silence. Then, in that thin, timid voice, she heard:

"Mrs. Hale!"

"Yes, Mrs. Peters?"

"What do you suppose she was so—nervous about?"

"Oh, *I* don't know," said Mrs. Hale, as if dismissing a thing not important enough to spend much time on. "I don't know as she was—nervous. I sew awful queer sometimes when I'm just tired."

She cut a thread, and out of the corner of her eye looked up at Mrs. Peters. The small, lean face of the sheriff's wife seemed to have tightened up. Her eyes had that look of peering into something. But next moment she moved, and said in her thin, indecisive way:

"Well, I must get those clothes wrapped. They may be through sooner than we think. I wonder where I could find a piece of paper—and string."

"In that cupboard, maybe," suggested Mrs. Hale, after a glance around.

One piece of the crazy sewing remained unripped. Mrs. Peters' back turned, Martha Hale now scrutinized that piece, compared it with the dainty, accurate sewing of the other blocks. The difference was startling. Holding this block made her feel queer, as if the distracted thoughts of the woman who had perhaps turned to it to try and quiet herself were communicating themselves to her.

Mrs. Peters' voice roused her.

"Here's a bird-cage," she said. "Did she have a bird, Mrs. Hale?"

"Why, I don't know whether she did or not." She turned to look at the cage Mrs. Peters was holding up. "I've not been here in so long." She sighed. "There was a man round last year selling canaries cheap—but I don't know as she took one. Maybe she did. She used to sing real pretty herself."

Mrs. Peters looked around the kitchen.

"Seems kind of funny to think of a bird here." She half laughed—an attempt to put up a barrier. "But she must have had one—or why would she have a cage? I wonder what happened to it."

"I suppose maybe the cat got it," suggested Mrs. Hale, resuming her sewing.

"No; she didn't have a cat. She's got that feeling some people have about cats—being afraid of them. When they brought her to our house yesterday, my cat got in the room, and she was real upset and asked me to take it out."

"My sister Bessie was like that," laughed Mrs. Hale.

The sheriff's wife did not reply. The silence made Mrs. Hale turn round. Mrs. Peters was examining the bird-cage.

"Look at this door," she said slowly. "It's broke. One hinge has been pulled apart."

Mrs. Hale came nearer.

"Looks as if someone must have been—rough with it."

Again their eyes met—startled, questioning, apprehensive. For a moment neither spoke nor stirred. Then Mrs. Hale, turning away, said brusquely:

"If they're going to find any evidence, I wish they'd be about it. I don't like this place."

"But I'm awful glad you came with me, Mrs. Hale." Mrs. Peters put the bird-cage on the table and sat down. "It would be lonesome for me—sitting here alone."

"Yes, it would, wouldn't it?" agreed Mrs. Hale, a certain determined naturalness in her voice. She had picked up the sewing, but now it dropped in her lap, and she murmured in a different voice: "But I tell you what I *do* wish, Mrs. Peters. I wish I had come over sometimes when she was here. I wish—I had."

"But of course you were awful busy, Mrs. Hale. Your house—and your children."

"I could've come," retorted Mrs. Hale shortly. "I stayed away because it weren't cheerful—and that's why I ought to have come. I"—she looked around— "I've never liked this place. Maybe because it's down in a hollow and you don't see the road. I don't know what it is, but it's a lonesome place, and always was. I wish I had come over to see Minnie Foster sometimes. I can see now—" She did not put it into words.

"Well, you musn't reproach yourself," counseled Mrs. Peters. "Somehow, we just don't see how it is with other folks till—something comes up."

"Not having children makes less work," mused Mrs. Hale, after a silence, "but it makes a quiet house—and Wright out to work all day—and no company when he did come in. Did you know John Wright, Mrs. Peters?"

"Not to know him. I've seen him in town. They say he was a good man."

"Yes—good," conceded John Wright's neighbor grimly. "He didn't drink, and kept his word as well as most, I guess, and paid his debts. But he was a hard man, Mrs. Peters. Just to pass the time of day with him—." She stopped, shivered a little. "Like a raw wind that gets to the bone." Her eye fell upon the cage on the table before her, and she added, almost bitterly: "I should think she would've wanted a bird!"

Suddenly she leaned forward, looking intently at the cage. "But what do you s'pose went wrong with it?"

"I don't know," returned Mrs. Peters; "unless it got sick and died."

But after she said it she reached over and swung the broken door. Both women watched it as if somehow held by it.

"You didn't know—her?" Mrs. Hale asked, a gentler note in her voice.

"Not till they brought her yesterday," said the sheriff's wife.

"She—come to think of it, she was kind of like a bird herself. Real sweet and pretty, but kind of timid and—fluttery. How—she—did—change."

That held her for a long time. Finally, as if struck with a happy thought and relieved to get back to everyday things, she exclaimed:

"Tell you what, Mrs. Peters, why don't you take the quilt in with you? It might take up her mind."

"Why, I think that's a real nice idea, Mrs. Hale," agreed the sheriff's wife, as if she too were glad to come into the atmosphere of a simple kindness. "There couldn't possibly be any objection to that, could there? Now, just what will I take? I wonder if her patches are in here—and her things."

They turned to the sewing basket.

"Here's some red," said Mrs. Hale, bringing out a roll of cloth. Underneath that was a box. "Here, maybe her scissors are in here—and her things." She held it up. "What a pretty box! I'll warrant that was something she had a long time ago—when she was a girl."

She held it in her hand a moment; then, with a little sigh, opened it.

Instantly her hand went to her nose.

"Why—!"

Mrs. Peters drew nearer—then turned away.

"There's something wrapped up in this piece of silk," faltered Mrs. Hale.

"This isn't her scissors," said Mrs. Peters, in a shrinking voice.

Her hand not steady, Mrs. Hale raised the piece of silk. "Oh, Mrs. Peters!" she cried. "It's—"

Mrs. Peters bent closer.

"It's the bird," she whispered.

"But, Mrs. Peters!" cried Mrs. Hale. "*Look* at it! Its *neck*—look at its neck! It's all—other side *to*."

She held the box away from her.

The sheriff's wife again bent closer.

"Somebody wrung its neck," said she, in a voice that was slow and deep.

And then again the eyes of the two women met—this time clung together in a look of dawning comprehension, of growing horror. Mrs. Peters looked from the dead bird to the broken door of the cage. Again their eyes met. And just then there was a sound at the outside door.

Mrs. Hale slipped the box under the quilt pieces in the basket, and sank into the chair before it. Mrs. Peters stood holding to the table. The county attorney and the sheriff came in from outside.

"Well, ladies," said the county attorney, as one turning from serious things to little pleasantries, "have you decided whether she was going to quilt it or knot it?"

"We think," began the sheriff's wife in a flurried voice, "that she was going to—knot it."

He was too preoccupied to notice the change that came in her voice on that last.

"Well, that's very interesting, I'm sure," he said tolerantly. "He caught sight of the bird-cage. "Has the bird flown?"

"We think the cat got it," said Mrs. Hale in a voice curiously even.

He was walking up and down, as if thinking something out.

"Is there a cat?" he asked absently.

Mrs. Hale shot a look up at the sheriff's wife.

"Well, not *now*," said Mrs. Peters. "They're superstitious, you know; they leave."

She sank into her chair.

The county attorney did not heed her. "No sign at all of anyone having come in from the outside," he said to Peters, in the manner of continuing an interrupted conversation. "Their own rope. Now let's go upstairs again and go over it, piece by piece. It would have to have been someone who knew just the—"

The stair door closed behind them and their voices were lost.

The two women sat motionless, not looking at each other, but as if peering into something and at the same time holding back. When they spoke now it was as if they were afraid of what they were saying, but as if they could not help saying it.

"She liked the bird," said Martha Hale, low and slowly. "She was going to bury it in that pretty box."

"When I was a girl," said Mrs. Peters, under her breath, "my kitten—there was a boy took a hatchet, and before my eyes—before I could get there—" She covered her face an instant. "If they hadn't held me back I would have"—she caught herself, looked upstairs where footsteps were heard, and finished weakly—"hurt him."

Then they sat without speaking or moving.

"I wonder how it would seem," Mrs. Hale at last began, as if feeling her way over strange ground—"never to have had any children around?" Her eyes made a slow sweep of the kitchen, as if seeing what that kitchen had meant through all the years. "No, Wright wouldn't like the bird," she said after that—"a thing that sang. She used to sing. He killed that too." Her voice tightened.

Mrs. Peters moved uneasily.

"Of course we don't know who killed the bird."

"I knew John Wright," was Mrs. Hale's answer.

"It was an awful thing was done in this house that night, Mrs. Hale," said the sheriff's wife. "Killing a man while he slept—slipping a thing round his neck that choked the life out of him."

Mrs. Hale's hand went out to the bird cage.

"His neck. Choked the life out of him."

"We don't *know* who killed him," whispered Mrs. Peters wildly. "We don't *know.*"

Mrs. Hale had not moved. "If there had been years and years of—nothing, then a bird to sing to you, it would be awful—still—after the bird was still."

It was as if something within her not herself had spoken, and it found in Mrs. Peters something she did not know as herself.

"I know what stillness is," she said, in a queer, monotonous voice. "When we homesteaded in Dakota, and my first baby died—after he was two years old—and me with no other then—"

Mrs. Hale stirred.

"How soon do you suppose they'll be through looking for the evidence?"

"I know what stillness is," repeated Mrs. Peters, in just that same way. Then she too pulled back. "The law has got to punish crime, Mrs. Hale," she said in her tight little way.

"I wish you'd seen Minnie Foster," was the answer, "when she wore a white dress with blue ribbons, and stood up there in the choir and sang."

The picture of that girl, the fact that she had lived neighbor to that girl for twenty years, and had let her die for lack of life, was suddenly more than she could bear.

"Oh, I *wish* I'd come over here once in a while!" she cried. "That was a crime! That was a crime! Who's going to punish that?"

"We musn't take on," said Mrs. Peters, with a frightened look toward the stairs.

"I might 'a' *known* she needed help! I tell you, it's *queer*, Mrs. Peters. We live close together, and we live far apart. We all go through the same things—it's all just a different kind of the same thing! If it weren't—why do you and I *understand?* Why do we *know*—what we know this minute?"

She dashed her hand across her eyes. Then, seeing the jar of fruit on the table, she reached for it and choked out:

"If I was you I wouldn't *tell* her her fruit was gone! Tell her it *ain't.* Tell her it's all right—all of it. Here—take this in to prove it to her! She—she may never know whether it was broke or not."

She turned away.

Mrs. Peters reached out for the bottle of fruit as if she were glad to take it—as if touching a familiar thing, having something to do, could keep her from something else. She got up, looked about for something to wrap the fruit in, took a petticoat from the pile of clothes she had brought from the front room, and nervously started winding that round the bottle.

"My!" she began, in a high, false voice, "it's a good thing the men couldn't hear us! Getting all stirred up over a little thing like a—dead canary." She hurried over that. "As if that could have anything to do with—with—My, wouldn't they *laugh?*"

Footsteps were heard on the stairs.

"Maybe they would," muttered Mrs. Hale—"maybe they wouldn't."

"No, Peters," said the county attorney incisively; "it's all perfectly clear, except the reason for doing it. But you know juries when it comes to women. If there was some definite thing—something to show. Something to make a story about. A thing that would connect up with this clumsy way of doing it."

In a covert way Mrs. Hale looked at Mrs. Peters. Mrs. Peters was looking at her. Quickly they looked away from each other. The outer door opened and Mr. Hale came in.

"I've got the team round now," he said. "Pretty cold out there."

"I'm going to stay here awhile by myself," the county attorney suddenly announced. "You can send Frank out for me, can't you?" he asked the sheriff. "I want to go over everything. I'm not satisfied we can't do better."

Again, for one brief moment, the two women's eyes found one another. The sheriff came up to the table.

"Did you want to see what Mrs. Peters was going to take in?"

The county attorney picked up the apron. He laughed.

"Oh, I guess they're not very dangerous things the ladies have picked out."

Mrs. Hale's hand was on the sewing basket in which the box was concealed. She felt that she ought to take her hand off the basket. She did not seem able to. He picked up one of the quilt blocks which she had piled on to cover the box. Her eyes felt like fire. She had a feeling that if he took up the basket she would snatch it from him.

But he did not take it up. With another little laugh, he turned away, saying:

"No; Mrs. Peters doesn't need supervising. For that matter, a sheriff's wife is married to the law. Ever think of it that way, Mrs. Peters?"

Mrs. Peters was standing beside the table. Mrs. Hale shot a look up at her; but she could not see her face. Mrs. Peters had turned away. When she spoke, her voice was muffled.

"Not—just that way," she said.

"Married to the law!" chuckled Mrs. Peters' husband. He moved toward the door into the front room, and said to the county attorney:

"I just want you to come in here a minute, George. We ought to take a look at these windows."

"Oh—windows," said the county attorney scoffingly.

"We'll be right out, Mr. Hale," said the sheriff to the farmer, who was still waiting by the door.

Hale went to look after the horses. The sheriff followed the county attorney into the other room. Again—for one final moment—the two women were alone in that kitchen.

Martha Hale sprang up, her hands tight together, looking at that other woman, with whom it rested. At first she could not see her eyes, for the sheriff's wife had not turned back since she turned away at that suggestion of being married to the law. But now Mrs. Hale made her turn back. Her eyes made her turn back. Slowly, unwillingly, Mrs. Peters turned her head until her eyes met the eyes of the other woman. There was a moment when they held each other in a steady, burning look in which there was no evasion nor flinching. Then Martha Hale's eyes pointed the way to the basket in which was hidden the thing that would make certain the conviction of the other woman—that woman who was not there and yet who had been there with them all through that hour.

For a moment Mrs. Peters did not move. And then she did it. With a rush forward, she threw back the quilt pieces, got the box, tried to put it in her handbag. It was too big. Desperately she opened, started to take the bird out. But there she broke—she could not touch the bird. She stood there helpless, foolish.

There was the sound of a knob turning in the inner door. Martha Hale snatched the box from the sheriff's wife, and got it in the pocket of her big coat just as the sheriff and the county attorney came back into the kitchen.

"Well, Henry," said the county attorney facetiously, "at least we found out that she was not going to quilt it. She was going to—what is it you call it, ladies?"

Mrs. Hale's hand was against the pocket of her coat.

"We call it—knot it, Mr. Henderson."

Anaïs Nin

*(b. 1903)   Originally from France,
Anaïs Nin moved to the United States
in 1914 and now lives in California.
Recently she has lectured at the
University of California at Berkeley.
Four volumes of her* Diaries *have been
published which record her inner life
and her opinions of many famous
people she has met. She has written
a study of D. H. Lawrence as well as
short stories and several novels,
the best known of which is* A Spy in
the House of Love.

Alraune

The night surrounded me, a photograph unglued from its frame. The lining of a coat ripped open like the two shells of an oyster. The day and night unglued, and I falling in between not knowing on which layer I was resting, whether it was the cold grey upper leaf of dawn, or the dark layer of night.

Alraune's face was suspended in the darkness of the garden. From the eyes a simoun wind shrivelled the leaves and turned the earth over; all things which had run a vertical course now turned in circles, round the face, round HER face. She stared with such an ancient stare, heavy luxuriant centuries flickering in deep processions. From her nacreous skin perfumes spiralled like incense. Every gesture she made quickened the rhythm of the blood and aroused a beat chant like the beat of the heart of the desert, a chant which was the sound of her feet treading down into the blood the imprint of her face.

A voice that had traversed the centuries, so heavy it broke what it touched, so heavy I feared it would ring in me with eternal resonance, a voice rusty with the sound of curses and the hoarse cries that issue from the delta in the last paroxysm of orgasm.

Her black cape hung like black hair from her shoulders, half-draped, half-

386

floating around her body. The web of her dress moving always a moment before she moved, as if aware of her impulses, and stirring long after she was still, like waves ebbing back to the sea. Her sleeves dropped like a sigh and the hem of her dress danced round her feet.

The steel necklace on her throat flashed like summer lightning and the sound of the steel was like the clashing of swords . . . Le pas d'acier . . . The steel of New York's skeleton buried in granite, buried standing up. Le pas d'acier . . . notes hammered on the steel-stringed guitars of the gypsies, on the steel arms of chairs dulled with her breath; steel mail curtains falling like the flail of hail, steel bars and steel barrage cracking. Her necklace thrown around the world's neck, unmeltable. She carried it like a trophy wrung of groaning machinery, to match the inhuman rhythm of her march.

The leaf fall of her words, the stained glass hues of her moods, the rust in her voice, the smoke in her mouth, her breath on my vision like human breath blinding a mirror.

Talk—half-talk, phrases that had no need to be finished, abstractions, Chinese bells played on with cotton-tipped sticks; mock orange blossoms painted on porcelain. The muffled, close, half-talk of soft-fleshed women. The men she had embraced, and the women, all washing against the resonance of my memory. Sound within sound, scene within scene, woman within woman—like acid revealing an invisible script. One woman within another eternally, in a far-reaching procession, shattering my mind into fragments, into quarter tones which no orchestral baton can ever make whole again.

The luminous mask of her face waxy, immobile, with eyes like sentinels. Watching my sybaritic walk, and I the sibilance of her tongue. Deep into each other we turned our harlot eyes. She was an idol in Byzance, an idol dancing with legs parted and I wrote with pollen and honey. The soft secret yielding of woman I carved into men's brains with copper words, her image I tatooed in their eyes. They were consumed by the fever of their entrails, the indissoluble poison of legends. If the torrent failed to engulf them, or did they extricate themselves, I haunted their memory with the tale they wished to forget. All that was swift and malevolent in woman might be ruthlessly destroyed, but who would destroy the illusion on which I laid her to sleep each night? We lived in Byzance, Alraune and I, until our hearts bled from the precious stones on our foreheads, our bodies tired of the weight of brocades, our nostrils burned with the smoke of perfumes; and when we had passed into other centuries they enclosed us in copper frames. Men recognized her always: the same effulgent face, the same rust voice. And she and I, we recognized each other, I her face and she my legend.

Around my pulse she put a flat steel bracelet and my pulse beat as she willed, losing its human cadence, thumping like a savage in orgiastic frenzy. The lamentations of flutes, the double chant of wind through our slender bones, the cracking of our bones distantly remembered when on beds of down the worship we inspired turned to lust.

As we walked along, rockets burst from the street lamps; we swallowed the asphalt road with a jungle roar and the houses with their closed eyes and geranium eyelashes, swallowed the telegraph poles trembling with messages, swallowed stray cats, trees, hills, hedges, Alraune's labyrinthian smile on the key-hole. The door moaning, opening. Her smile closed. A nightingale disleafing melliferous honeysuckle. Honeysuckled. Fluted fingers. The house opened its green gate mouth and swallowed us. The bed was floating.

The record was scratched, the crooning broken. The pieces cut our feet. It was dawn and she was lost. I put back the houses on the road, aligned the telegraph poles along the river and the stray cats jumping across the road. I put back the hills. The road came out of my mouth like a velvet ribbon—it lay there serpentine. The houses opened their eyes. The keyhole had an ironic curve, like a question mark. The woman's mouth.

I was carrying her fetiches, her marionettes, her fortune teller's cards worn at the corners like the edge of a wave. The windows of the city were stained and splintered with rainlight and the blood she drew from me with each lie, each deception. Beneath the skin of her cheeks I saw ashes: would she die before we had joined in perfidious union? The eyes, the hands, the senses that only women have.

There is no mockery between women. One lies down at peace as on one's own breast.

Alraune was no longer embracing men and women. Within the fever of her restlessness the world was losing its human shape. She was losing the human power to fit body to body in human completeness. She was delimiting the horizons, sinking into planets without axis; losing her polarity and the divine knowledge of integration, of fusion. She was spreading herself like the night over the universe and found no god to lie with. The other half belonged to the sun, and she was at war with the sun and light. She would tolerate no bars of light on open books, no orchestration of ideas knitted by a single theme, she would not be covered by the sun, and half the universe belonged to him; she was turning her serpent back to that alone which might overshadow her own stature giving her the joy of fecundation.

Come away with me, Alraune, come to my island. Come to my island of red peppers sizzling over slow braseros, Moorish earthen jars catching the gold water, palm trees, wild cats, fighting; at dawn a donkey sobbing; feet on coral reefs and sea-anemones, the body covered with long seaweeds, Melisande's hair hanging over the balcony of the Opéra Comique, inexorable diamond sunlight, heavy nerveless hours in the violaceous shadows, ash-colored rocks and olive trees, lemon trees with lemons hung like lanterns at a garden party, bamboo shoots forever trembling, soft-sounding espadilles, pomegranate spurting blood, a flute-like Moorish chant, long and insistent, of the ploughmen, trilling, swearing, trilling and cursing, dropping perspiration on the earth with the seeds.

Your beauty drowns me, drowns the core of me. When your beauty burns me I dissolve as I never dissolved before man. From all men I was different, and myself, but I see in you that part of me which is you. I feel you in me, I feel my own voice becoming heavier, as if I were drinking you in, every delicate thread of resemblance being soldered by fire and one no longer detects the fissure.

Your lies are not lies, Alraune. They are arrows flung out of your orbit by the strength of your fantasy. To nourish illusion. To destroy reality. I will help you: it is I who will invent lies for you and with them we will traverse the world. But behind our lies I am dropping Ariadne's golden thread—for the greatest of all joys is to be able to retrace one's lies, to return to the source and sleep one night a year washed of all superstructures.

Alraune, you made your impression upon the world. I passed through it like a ghost. Does anyone notice the owl in the tree at night, the bat which strikes the window pane while others are talking, the eyes which reflect like water and drink like blotting paper, the pity which flickers quietly like candlelight, the understanding on which people lay themselves to sleep?

DOES ANYONE KNOW WHO I AM?

Even my voice came from other worlds. I was embalmed in my own secret vertigoes. I was suspended over the world, seeing what road I could tread without treading down even clay or grass. My step was a sentient step; the mere crepitation of gravel could arrest my walk.

When I saw you, Alraune, I chose my body.

I will let you carry me into the fecundity of destruction. I choose a body then, a face, a voice. I become you. And you become me. Silence the sensational course of your body and you will see in me, intact, your own fears, your own pities. You will see love which was excluded from the passions given you, and I will see the passions excluded from love. Step out of your role and rest yourself on the core of your true desires. Cease for a moment your violent deviations. Relinquish the furious indomitable strain.

I will take them up.

Cease trembling and shaking and gasping and cursing and find again your core which I am. Rest from twistedness, distortion, deformations. For an hour you will be me, that is, the other half of yourself. The half you lost. What you burnt, broke, and tore is still in my hands: I am the keeper of fragile things and I have kept of you what is indissoluble.

Even the world and the sun cannot show their two faces at once.

So now we are inextricably woven. I have gathered together all the fragments. I return them to you. You have run with the wind, scattering and dissolving. I have run behind you, like your own shadow, gathering what you have sown in deep coffers.

I AM THE OTHER FACE OF YOU

Our faces are soldered together by soft hair, soldered together, showing two profiles of the same soul. Even when I passed through a room like a breath, I made others uneasy and they knew I had passed.

I was the white flame of your breath, your simoun breath shrivelling the world. I borrowed your visibility and it was through you I made my imprint on the world. I praised my own flame in you.

THIS IS THE BOOK YOU WROTE AND YOU ARE THE WOMAN I AM

Only our faces must shine twofold—like day and night—always separated by space and the evolutions of time.

The smoke sent my head to the ceiling: there it hung, looking down upon frog eyes, straw hair, mouth of soiled leather, mirrors of bald heads, furred monkey hands with ham colored palms. The music whipped the past out of its tomb and mummies flagellated my memory.

Doris Lessing

(b. 1919) Born in Persia, Doris Lessing has lived in Southern Rhodesia and England. Her fiction has as its major theme the dehumanizing effects of violence in our time. The five volumes of Children of Violence *and the long novel* The Golden Notebook *focus on women as the central consciousnesses through whom society is perceived, many of them "free women" independent of men.*

One off the Short List

When he had first seen Barbara Coles, some years before, he only noticed her because someone said: "That's Johnson's new girl." He certainly had not used of her the private erotic formula: *Yes, that one.* He even wondered what Johnson saw in her. "She won't last long," he remembered thinking, as he watched Johnson, a handsome man, but rather flushed with drink, flirting with some unknown girl while Barbara stood by a wall looking on. He thought she had a sullen expression.

She was a pale girl, not slim, for her frame was generous, but her figure could pass as good. Her straight yellow hair was parted on one side in a way that struck him as gauche. He did not notice what she wore. But her eyes were all right, he remembered: large, and solidly green, square-looking because of some trick of the flesh at their corners. Emeraldlike eyes in the face of a schoolgirl, or young schoolmistress who was watching her lover flirt and would later sulk about it.

Her name sometimes cropped up in the papers. She was a stage decorator, a designer, something on those lines.

Then a Sunday newspaper had a competition for stage design and she won it. Barbara Coles was one of the "names" in the theatre, and her photograph was seen about. It was always serious. He remembered having thought her sullen.

One night he saw her across the room at a party. She was talking with a well-known actor. Her yellow hair was still done on one side, but now it looked sophisticated. She wore an emerald ring on her right hand that seemed deliberately to invite comparison with her eyes. He walked over and said: "We have met before, Graham Spence." He noted, with discomfort, that he sounded abrupt. "I'm sorry, I don't remember, but how do you do?" she said, smiling. And continued her conversation.

He hung around a bit, but soon she went off with a group of people she was inviting to her home for a drink. She did not invite Graham. There was about her an assurance, a carelessness, that he recognised as the signature of success. It was then, watching her laugh as she went off with her friends, that he used the formula: *"Yes, that one."* And he went home to his wife with enjoyable expectation, as if his date with Barbara Coles were already arranged.

His marriage was twenty years old. At first it had been stormy, painful, tragic—full of partings, betrayals and sweet reconciliations. It had taken him at least a decade to realise that there was nothing remarkable about this marriage that he had lived through with such surprise of the mind and the senses. On the contrary, the marriages of most of the people he knew, whether they were first, second or third attempts, were just the same. His had run true to form even to the serious love affair with the young girl for whose sake he had *almost* divorced his wife—yet at the last moment had changed his mind, letting the girl down so that he must have her for always (not unpleasurably) on his conscience. It was with humiliation that he had understood that this drama was not at all the unique thing he had imagined. It was nothing more than the experience of everyone in his circle. And presumably in everybody else's circle too?

Anyway, round about the tenth year of his marriage he had seen a good many things clearly, a certain kind of emotional adventure went from his life, and the marriage itself changed.

His wife had married a poor youth with a great future as a writer. Sacrifices had been made, chiefly by her, for that future. He was neither unaware of them, nor ungrateful; in fact he felt permanently guilty about it. He at last published a decently successful book, then a second which now, thank God, no one remembered. He had drifted into radio, television, book reviewing.

He understood he was not going to make it; that he had become—not a hack, no one could call him that—but a member of that army of people who live by their wits on the fringes of the arts. The moment of realisation was when he was in a pub one lunchtime near the B.B.C. where he often dropped in to meet others like himself: he understood that was why he went there—they *were* like him. Just as that melodramatic marriage had turned out to be like everyone else's—except that it had been shared with one woman instead of with two or three—so it had turned out that his unique talent, his struggles as a writer had led him here, to this pub and the half dozen pubs like it, where all the men in sight had the same history. They all had their novel, their play, their book of poems, a moment of fame, to their credit. Yet here they were, running television programmes about which they were cynical (to each other or to their wives) or writing reviews about other people's books. Yes, that's what he had become, an impresario of other people's talent. These two moments of clarity, about his marriage and about his talent, had roughly coincided: and (perhaps not by chance) had coincided with his wife's decision to leave him for a man younger than himself who had a future, she said, as a playwright. Well, he had talked her out of it. For her part she had to understand he was not going to be the T. S. Eliot or Graham Greene of our time—but after all, how many were? She must finally understand this, for he could no longer bear her awful bitterness. For his part he must stop coming home drunk at five in the morning, and starting a new romantic affair every six months which he took so seriously that he made her miserable because of her implied deficiencies. In short he was to be a good husband. (He had always been a dutiful father.) And she a good wife. And so it was: the marriage became stable, as they say.

The formula: *Yes, that one* no longer implied a necessarily sexual relationship. In its more mature form, it was far from being something he was ashamed of. On the contrary, it expressed a humorous respect for what he was, for his real talents and flair, which had turned out to be not artistic after all, but to do with emotional life, hard-earned experience. It expressed an ironical dignity, a proving to himself not only: I can be honest about myself, but also: I have earned the best in *that* field whenever I want it.

He watched the field for the women who were well known in the arts, or in politics; looked out for photographs, listened for bits of gossip. He made a point of going to see them act, or dance, or orate. He built up a not unshrewd picture of them. He would either quietly pull strings to meet her or—more often, for there was a gambler's pleasure in waiting—bide his time until he met her in the natural course of events, which was bound to happen sooner or later. He would be seen out with her a few times in public, which was in order, since his work meant he had to entertain well-known people, male and female. His wife always knew, he told her. He might have a brief affair with this woman, but more often than not it was the appearance of an affair. Not that he didn't get pleasure from other people envying him—he would make a point, for instance, of taking this woman into the pubs where his male colleagues went. It was that his real pleasure came when he saw her surprise at how well she was understood by him. He enjoyed the atmosphere he was able to set up between an intelligent woman and himself: a humorous complicity which had in it much that was unspoken, and which almost made sex irrelevant.

Onto the list of women with whom he planned to have this relationship went Barbara Coles. There was no hurry. Next week, next month, next year, they would meet at a party. The world of well-known people in London is a small one. Big and little fishes, they drift around, nose each other, flirt their fins, wriggle off again. When he bumped into Barbara Coles, it would be time to decide whether or not to sleep with her.

Meanwhile he listened. But he didn't discover much. She had a husband and children, but the husband seemed to be in the background. The children were charming and well brought up, like everyone else's children. She had affairs, they said; but while several men he met sounded familiar with her, it was hard to determine whether they had slept with her, because none directly boasted of her. She was spoken of in terms of her friends, her work, her house, a party she had given, a job she had found someone. She was liked, she was respected, and

Graham Spence's self-esteem was flattered because he had chosen her. He looked forward to saying in just the same tone: "Barbara Coles asked me what I thought about the set and I told her quite frankly. . . ."

Then by chance he met a young man who did boast about Barbara Coles; he claimed to have had the great love affair with her, and recently at that; and he spoke of it as something generally known. Graham realised how much he had already become involved with her in his imagination because of how perturbed he was now, on account of the character of this youth, Jack Kennaway. He had recently become successful as a magazine editor—one of those young men who, not as rare as one might suppose in the big cities, are successful from sheer impertinence, effrontery. Without much talent or taste, yet he had the charm of his effrontery. "Yes, I'm going to succeed, because I've decided to; yes, I may be stupid, but not so stupid that I don't know my deficiencies. Yes, I'm going to be successful because you people with integrity, etc., etc., simply don't believe in the possibility of people like me. You are too cowardly to stop me. Yes, I've taken your measure and I'm going to succeed because I've got the courage, not only to be unscrupulous, but to be quite frank about it. And besides, you admire me, you must, or otherwise you'd stop me. . . ." Well, that was young Jack Kennaway, and he shocked Graham. He was a tall, languishing young man, handsome in a dark melting way, and, it was quite clear, he was either asexual or homosexual. And this youth boasted of the favours of Barbara Coles; boasted, indeed, of her love. Either she was a raving neurotic with a taste for neurotics; or Jack Kennaway was a most accomplished liar; or she slept with anyone. Graham was intrigued. He took Jack Kennaway out to dinner in order to hear him talk about Barbara Coles. There was no doubt the two were pretty close—all those dinners, theatres, weekends in the country—Graham Spence felt he had put his finger on the secret pulse of Barbara Coles; and it was intolerable that he must wait to meet her; he decided to arrange it.

It became unnecessary. She was in the news again, with a run of luck. She had done a successful historical play, and immediately afterwards a modern play, and then a hit musical. In all three, the sets were remarked on. Graham saw some interviews in newspapers and on television. These all centered around the theme of her being able to deal easily with so many different styles of theatre; but the real point was, of course, that she was a woman, which naturally added piquancy to the thing. And now Graham Spence was asked to do a half-hour radio interview with her. He planned the questions he would ask her with care, drawing on what people had said of her, but above all on his instinct and experience with women. The interview was to be at nine-thirty at night; he was to pick her up at six from the theatre where she was currently at work, so that there would be time, as the letter from the B.B.C. had put it, "for you and Miss Coles to get to know each other."

At six he was at the stage door, but a message from Miss Coles said she was not quite ready, could he wait a little. He hung about, then went to the pub opposite for a quick one, but still no Miss Coles. So he made his way backstage, directed by voices, hammering, laughter. It was badly lit, and the group of people at work did not see him. The director, James Poynter, had his arm around

Barbara's shoulders. He was newly well-known, a carelessly good-looking young man reputed to be intelligent. Barbara Coles wore a dark blue overall, and her flat hair fell over her face so that she kept pushing it back with the hand that had the emerald on it. These two stood close, side by side. Three young men, stagehands, were on the other side of a trestle which had sketches and drawings on it. They were studying some sketches. Barbara said, in a voice warm with energy: "Well, so I thought if we did *this*—do you see, James? What do you think, Steven?" "Well, love," said the young man she called Steven, "I see your idea, but I wonder if . . ." "I think you're right, Babs," said the director. "Look," said Barbara, holding one of the sketches toward Steven, "look, let me show you." They all leaned forward, the five of them, absorbed in the business.

Suddenly Graham couldn't stand it. He understood he was shaken to his depths. He went off stage, and stood with his back against a wall in the dingy passage that led to the dressing rooms. His eyes were filled with tears. He was seeing what a long way he had come from the crude, uncompromising, admirable young egomaniac he had been when he was twenty. That group of people there—working, joking, arguing, yes, that's what he hadn't known for years. What bound them was the democracy of respect for each other's work, a confidence in themselves and in each other. They looked like people banded together against a world which they—no, not despised, but which they measured, understood, would fight to the death, out of respect for what *they* stood for, for what *it* stood for. It was a long time since he felt part of that balance. And he understood that he had seen Barbara Coles when she was most herself, at ease with a group of people she worked with. It was then, with the tears drying on his eyelids, which felt old and ironic, that he decided he would sleep with Barbara Coles. It was a necessity for him. He went back through the door onto the stage, burning with this single determination.

The five were still together. Barbara had a length of blue gleaming stuff which she was draping over the shoulder of Steven, the stagehand. He was showing it off, and the others watched. "What do you think, James?" she asked the director. "We've got that sort of dirty green, and I thought . . ." "Well," said James, not sure at all, "well, Babs, well . . ."

Now Graham went forward so that he stood beside Barbara, and said: "I'm Graham Spence, we've met before." For the second time she smiled socially and said: "Oh I'm sorry, I don't remember." Graham nodded at James, whom he had known, or at least had met off and on, for years. But it was obvious James didn't remember him either.

"From the B.B.C.," said Graham to Barbara, again sounding abrupt, against his will. "Oh I'm sorry, I'm so sorry, I forgot all about it. I've got to be interviewed," she said to the group. "Mr. Spence is a journalist." Graham allowed himself a small smile ironical of the word journalist, but she was not looking at him. She was going on with her work. "We should decide tonight," she said. "Steven's right." "Yes, I am right," said the stagehand. "She's right, James, we need that blue with that sludge-green everywhere." "James," said Barbara, "James, what's wrong with it? You haven't said." She moved forward to James, passing Graham. Remembering him again, she became contrite. "I'm sorry," she said, "we can none of us agree. Well, look"—she turned to Graham—"you advise us, we've got so involved with it that . . ." At which James laughed, and so did the stagehands. "No, Babs," said James, "of course Mr. Spence can't advise. He's just this moment come in. We've got to decide. Well I'll give you till tomorrow morning. Time to go home, it must be six by now."

"It's nearly seven," said Graham, taking command.

"It isn't!" said Barbara, dramatic. "My God, how terrible, how appalling, how could I have done such a thing. . . ." She was laughing at herself. "Well, you'll have to forgive me, Mr. Spence, because you haven't got any alternative."

They began laughing again: this was clearly a group joke. And now Graham took his chance. He said firmly, as if he were her director, in fact copying James Poynter's manner with her: "No, Miss Coles, I won't forgive you, I've been kicking my heels for nearly an hour." She grimaced, then laughed and accepted it. James said: "There, Babs, that's how you ought to be treated. We spoil you." He kissed her on the cheek, she kissed him on both his, the stage-hands moved off. "Have a good evening, Babs," said James, going, and nodding to Graham, who stood concealing his pleasure with difficulty. He knew, because he had had the courage to be firm, indeed, peremptory, with Barbara, that he had saved himself hours of maneuvering. Several drinks, a dinner—perhaps two or three evenings of drinks and dinners—had been saved because he was now on this footing with Barbara Coles, a man who could say: "No, I won't forgive you, you've kept me waiting."

She said: "I've just got to . . ." and went ahead of him. In the passage she hung her overall on a peg. She was thinking, it seemed, of something else, but seeing him watching her, she smiled at him, companionably: he realised with triumph it was the sort of smile she would offer one of the stagehands, or even James. She said again: "Just one second . . ." and went to the stage-door office. She and the stage doorman conferred. There was some problem. Graham said, taking another chance: "What's the trouble, can I help?"—as if he could help, as if he expected to be able to. "Well . . ." she said, frowning. Then, to the man: "No, it'll be all right. Goodnight." She came to Graham. "We've got ourselves into a bit of a fuss because half the set's in Liverpool and half's here and—but it will sort itself out." She stood, at ease, chatting to him, one colleague to another. All this was admirable, he felt; but there would be a bad moment when they emerged from the special atmosphere of the theatre into the street. He took another decision, grasped her arm firmly, and said: "We're going to have a drink before we do anything at all, it's a terrible evening out." Her arm felt resistant, but remained within his. It was raining outside, luckily. He directed her, authoritative: "No, not that pub, there's a nicer one around the corner." "Oh, but I like this pub," said Barbara, "we always use it."

"Of course you do," he said to himself. But in that pub there would be the stagehands, and probably James, and he'd lose contact with her. He'd become a *journalist* again. He took her firmly out of danger around two corners, into a pub he picked at random. A quick look around—no, they weren't there. At least, if there were people from the theatre, she showed no sign. She asked for a beer. He ordered her a double Scotch, which she accepted. Then, having won a dozen preliminary rounds already, he took time to think. Something was bothering him—what? Yes, it was what he had observed backstage, Barbara and James Poynter. Was she having an affair with him? Because if so, it would all be much more difficult. He made himself see the two of them together, and thought with a jealousy surprisingly strong: *Yes, that's it.* Meantime he sat looking at her, seeing himself look at her, *a man gazing in calm appreciation at a woman:* waiting for her to feel it and respond. She was examining the pub. Her white woollen suit was belted, and had a not unprovocative suggestion of being a uniform. Her flat yellow hair, hastily pushed back after work, was untidy. Her clear white skin, without any colour, made her look tired. Not very exciting, at the moment, thought Graham, but maintaining his appreciative pose for when she would turn and see it. He knew what she would see: he was relying not only on the "warm kindly" beam of his gaze, for this was merely a reinforcement of the impression he knew he made. He had black hair, a little greyed. His clothes were loose and bulky—masculine. His eyes were humorous and appreciative. He was not, never had been, concerned to lessen the impression of being settled, dependable: the husband and father. On the contrary, he knew women found it reassuring.

When she at last turned she said, almost apologetic: "Would you mind if we sat down? I've been lugging great things around all day." She had spotted two empty chairs in a corner. So had he, but rejected them, because there were other people at the table. "But my dear, of course!" They took the chairs, and then Barbara said: "If you'll excuse me a moment." She had remembered she needed make-up. He watched her go off, annoyed with himself. She was tired; and he could have understood, protected, sheltered. He realised that in the other pub, with the people she had worked with all day, she would not have thought: "I must make myself up, I must be on show." That was for outsiders. She had not, until now, considered Graham an outsider, because of his taking his chance to seem one of the working group in the theatre; but now he had thrown his opportunity away. She returned armoured. Her hair was sleek, no longer defenceless. And she had made up her eyes. Her eyebrows were untouched, pale gold streaks above the brilliant green eyes whose lashes were blackened. Rather good, he thought, the contrast. Yes, but the moment had gone when he could say: Did you know you had a smudge on your cheek? Or—my dear girl!—pushing her hair back with the edge of a brotherly hand. In fact, unless he was careful, he'd be back at starting point.

He remarked: "That emerald is very cunning"—smiling into her eyes.

She smiled politely, and said: "It's not cunning, it's an accident, it was my grandmother's." She flirted her hand lightly by her face, though, smiling. But that was something she had done before, to a compliment she had had before, and often. It was all social, she had become social entirely. She remarked: "Didn't you say it was half past nine we had to record?"

"My dear Barbara, we've got two hours. We'll have another drink or two, then I'll ask you a couple of questions, then we'll drop down to the studio and get it over, and then we'll have a comfortable supper."

"I'd rather eat now, if you don't mind. I had no lunch, and I'm really hungry."

"But my dear, of course." He was angry. Just as he had been surprised by his real jealousy over James, so now he was thrown off balance by his anger: he had been counting on the long quiet dinner afterwards to establish intimacy. "Finish your drink and I'll take you to Nott's." Nott's was expensive. He glanced at her assessingly as he mentioned it. She said: "I wonder if you know Butler's? It's good and it's rather close." Butler's was good, and it was cheap, and he gave her a good mark for liking it. But Nott's it was going to be. "My dear, we'll get into a taxi and be at Nott's in a moment, don't worry."

She obediently got to her feet: the way she did it made him understand how badly he had slipped. She was saying to herself: Very well, he's like that, then all right, I'll do what he wants and get it over with. . . .

Swallowing his own drink he followed her, and took her arm in the pub doorway. It was polite within his. Outside it drizzled. No taxi. He was having bad luck now. They walked in silence to the end of the street. There Barbara glanced into a side street where a sign said: BUTLER'S. Not to remind him of it, on the contrary, she concealed the glance. And here she was, entirely at his disposal, they might never have shared the comradely moment in the theatre.

They walked half a mile to Nott's. No taxis. She made conversation: this was, he saw, to cover any embarrassment he might feel because of a half-mile walk through rain when she was tired. She was talking about some theory to do with the theatre, with designs for theatre building. He heard himself saying, and repeatedly: Yes, yes, yes. He thought about Nott's, how to get things right when they reached Nott's. There he took the headwaiter aside, gave him a pound, and instructions. They were put in a corner. Large Scotches appeared. The menus were spread. "And now, my dear," he said, "I apologise for dragging you here, but I hope you'll think it's worth it."

"Oh, it's charming, I've always liked it. It's just that . . ." She stopped herself saying: it's such a long way. She smiled at him, raising her glass, and said: "It's one of my very favourite places, and I'm glad you dragged me here." Her voice was flat with tiredness. All this was appalling; he knew it; and he sat thinking how to retrieve his position. Meanwhile she fingered the menu. The headwaiter took the order, but Graham made a gesture which said: Wait a moment. He wanted the Scotch to take effect before she ate. But she saw his silent order; and, without annoyance or reproach, leaned forward to say, sounding patient: "Graham, please, I've got to eat, you don't want me drunk when you interview me, do you?"

"They are bringing it as fast as they can," he said, making it sound as if she were greedy. He looked neither at the headwaiter nor at Barbara. He noted in himself, as he slipped further and further away from contact with her, a cold determination growing in him; one apart from, apparently, any conscious act of will, that come what may, if it took all night, he'd be in her bed before morning. And now, seeing the small pale face, with the enormous green eyes, it was for the first time that he imagined her in his arms. Although he had said: *Yes, that one,* weeks ago, it was only now that he imagined her as a sensual experience. Now he did, so strongly that he could only glance at her, and then away towards the waiters who were bringing food.

"Thank the Lord," said Barbara, and all at once her voice was gay and intimate. "Thank heavens. Thank every power that is. . . ." She was making fun of her own exaggeration; and, as he saw, because she wanted to put him at his ease after his boorishness over delaying the food. (She hadn't been taken in, he saw, humiliated, disliking her.) "Thank all the gods of Nott's," she went on, "because if I hadn't eaten inside five minutes I'd have died, I tell you." With which she picked up her knife and fork and began on her steak. He poured wine, smiling with her, thinking that *this* moment of closeness he would not throw away. He watched her frank hunger as she ate, and thought: Sensual—it's strange I hadn't wondered whether she would be or not.

"Now," she said, sitting back, having taken the edge off her hunger: "Let's get to work."

He said: "I've thought it over very carefully—how to present you. The first thing seems to me, we must get away from that old chestnut: Miss Coles, how extraordinary for a woman to be so versatile in her work . . . I hope you agree?" This was his trump card. He had noted, when he had seen her on television, her polite smile when this note was struck. (The smile he had seen so often tonight.) This smile said: All right, if you *have* to be stupid, what can I do?

Now she laughed and said: "What a relief. I was afraid you were going to do the same thing."

"Good, now you eat and I'll talk."

In his carefully prepared monologue he spoke of the different styles of theatre she had shown herself mistress of, but not directly: he was flattering her on the breadth of her experience; the complexity of her character, as shown in her work. She ate, steadily, her face showing nothing. At last she asked: "And how did you plan to introduce this?"

He had meant to spring that on her as a surprise, something like: Miss Coles, a surprisingly young woman for what she has accomplished (she was thirty? thirty-two?) and a very attractive one. . . . "Perhaps I can give you an idea of what she's like if I say she could be taken for the film star Marie Carletta. . . ." The Carletta was a strong earthy blonde, known to be intellectual. He now saw he could not possibly say this: he could imagine her cool look if he did. She said: "Do you mind if we get away from all that—my manifold talents, et cetera. . . ." He felt himself stiffen with annoyance; particularly because this was not an accusation, he saw she did not think him worth one. She had assessed him: This is the kind of man who uses this kind of flattery and therefore. . . . It made him angrier that she did not even trouble to say: Why did you do exactly what you promised you wouldn't? She was being invincibly polite, trying to conceal her patience with his stupidity.

"After all," she was saying, "it is a stage designer's job to design what comes up. Would anyone take, let's say Johnnie Cranmore" (another stage designer) "onto the air or television and say: How very versatile you are because you did that musical about Java last month and a modern play about Irish labourers this?"

He battened down his anger. "My dear Barbara, I'm sorry. I didn't realise that what I said would sound just like the mixture as before. So what shall we talk about?"

"What I was saying as we walked to the restaurant: can we get away from the personal stuff?"

Now he almost panicked. Then, thank God, he laughed from nervousness, for she laughed and said: "You didn't hear one word I said."

"No, I didn't. I was frightened you were going to be furious because I made you walk so far when you were tired."

They laughed together, back to where they had been in the theatre. He leaned over, took her hand, kissed it. He said: "Tell me again." He thought: Damn, now she's going to be earnest and intellectual.

But he understood he had been stupid. He had forgotten himself at twenty— or, for that matter, at thirty; forgotten one could live inside an idea, a set of ideas, with enthusiasm. For in talking about her ideas (also the ideas of the people she worked with) for a new theatre, a new style of theatre, she was as she had been with her colleagues over the sketches or the blue material. She was easy, informal, almost chattering. This was how, he remembered, one talked about ideas that were a breath of life. The ideas, he thought, were intelligent enough; and he would agree with them, with her, if he believed it mattered a damn one way or another, if any of these enthusiasms mattered a damn. But at least he now had the key, he knew what to do. At the end of not more than half an hour, they were again two professionals, talking about ideas they shared, for he remembered caring about all this himself once. *When? How many years ago was it that he had been able to care?*

At last he said: "My dear Barbara, do you realise the impossible position you're putting me in? Margaret Ruyen who runs this programme is determined to do you personally, the poor woman hasn't got a serious thought in her head."

Barbara frowned. He put his hand on hers, teasing her for the frown: "No, wait, trust me, we'll circumvent her." She smiled. In fact Margaret Ruyen had left it all to him, had said nothing about Miss Coles.

"They aren't very bright—the brass," he said. "Well, never mind: we'll work out what we want, do it, and it'll be a *fait accompli.*"

"Thank you, what a relief. How lucky I was to be given you to interview me." She was relaxed now, because of the whisky, the food, the wine, above all because of this new complicity against Margaret Ruyen. It would all be easy. They worked out five or six questions, over coffee, and took a taxi through rain to the studios. He noted that the cold necessity to have her, to make her, to beat her down, had left him. He was even seeing himself, as the evening ended, kissing her on the cheek and going home to his wife. This comradeship was extraordinarily pleasant. It was balm to the wound he had not known he carried until that evening, when he had had to accept the justice of the word *journalist.* He felt he could talk forever about the state of the theatre, its finances, the stupidity of the government, the philistinism of . . .

At the studios he was careful to make a joke so that they walked in on the laugh. He was careful that the interview began at once, without conversation with Margaret Ruyen; and that from the moment the green light went on, his voice lost its easy familiarity. He made sure that not one personal note was struck during the interview. Afterwards, Margaret Ruyen, who was pleased, came forward to say so; but he took her aside to say that Miss Coles was tired and needed to be taken home at once: for he knew this must look to Barbara as if he were squaring a producer who had been expecting a different interview. He led Barbara off, her hand held tight in his against his side. "Well," he said, "we've done it, and I don't think she knows what hit her."

"Thank you," she said, "it really was pleasant to talk about something sensible for once."

He kissed her lightly on the mouth. She returned it, smiling. By now he felt sure that the mood need not slip again, he could hold it.

"There are two things we can do," he said. "You can come to my club and have a drink. Or I can drive you home and you can give me a drink. I have to go past you."

"Where do you live?"

"Wimbledon." He lived, in fact, at Highgate; but she lived in Fulham. He was taking another chance, but by the time she found out, they would be in a position to laugh over his ruse.

"Good," she said. "You can drop me home then. I have to get up early." He made no comment. In the taxi he took her hand; it was heavy in his, and he asked: "Does James slave-drive you?"

"I didn't realize you knew him—no, he doesn't."

"Well I don't know him intimately. What's he like to work with?"

"Wonderful," she said at once. "There's no one I enjoy working with more."

Jealousy spurted in him. He could not help himself: "Are you having an affair with him?"

She looked: what's it to do with you? but said: "No, I'm not."

"He's very attractive," he said, with a chuckle of worldly complicity. She said nothing, and he insisted: "If I were a woman I'd have an affair with James."

It seemed she might very well say nothing. But she remarked: "He's married."

His spirits rose in a swoop. It was the first stupid remark she had made. It was a remark of such staggering stupidity that . . . he let out a humoring snort of laughter, put his arm around her, kissed her, said: "My dear little Babs."

She said: "Why Babs?"

"Is that the prerogative of James. And of the stagehands?" he could not prevent himself adding.

"I'm only called that at work." She was stiff inside his arm.

"My dear Barbara, then . . ." He waited for her to enlighten and explain, but she said nothing. Soon she moved out of his arm, on the pretext of lighting a cigarette. He lit it for her. He noted that his determination to lay her, and at all costs, had come back. They were outside her house. He said quickly: "And now, Barbara, you can make me a cup of coffee and give me a brandy." She hesitated; but he was out of the taxi, paying, opening the door for her. The house had no lights on, he noted. He said: "We'll be very quiet so as not to wake the children."

She turned her head slowly to look at him. She said, flat, replying to his real question: "My husband is away. As for the children, they are visiting friends tonight." She now went ahead of him to the door of the house. It was a small house, in a terrace of small and not very pretty houses. Inside a little, bright, intimate hall, she said: "I'll go and make some coffee. Then, my friend, you must go home because I'm very tired."

The *my friend* struck him deep, because he had become vulnerable during their comradeship. He said gabbling: "You're annoyed with me—oh, please don't, I'm sorry."

She smiled, from a cool distance. He saw, in the small light from the ceiling, her extraordinary eyes. "Green" eyes are hazel, are brown with green flecks, are even blue. Eyes are chequered, flawed, changing. Hers were solid green, but really, he had never seen anything like them before. They were like very deep water. They were like—well, emeralds; or the absolute clarity of green in the depths of a tree in summer. And now, as she smiled almost perpendicularly up at him, he saw a darkness come over them. Darkness swallowed the clear green. She said: "I'm not in the least annoyed." It was as if she had yawned with boredom. "And now I'll get the things . . . in there." She nodded at a white door and left him. He went into a long, very tidy white room, that had a narrow bed in one corner, a table covered with drawings, sketches, pencils. Tacked to the walls with drawing pins were swatches of coloured stuffs. Two small chairs stood near a low round table: an area of comfort in the working room. He was thinking: I wouldn't like it if my wife had a room like this. I wonder what Barbara's husband . . .? He had not thought of her till now in relation to her husband, or to her children. Hard to imagine her with a frying pan in her hand, or for that matter, cosy in the double bed.

A noise outside: he hastily arranged himself, leaning with one arm on the mantelpiece. She came in with a small tray that had cups, glasses, brandy, coffeepot. She looked abstracted. Graham was on the whole flattered by this: it probably meant she was at ease in his presence. He realised he was a little tight and rather tired. Of course, she was tired too, that was why she was vague. He remembered that earlier that evening he had lost a chance by not using her tiredness. Well now, if he were intelligent . . . She was about to pour coffee. He firmly took the coffeepot out of her hand, and nodded at a chair. Smiling, she obeyed him. "That's better," he said. He poured coffee, poured brandy, and pulled the table towards her. She watched him. Then he took her hand, kissed it, patted it, laid it down gently. Yes, he thought, I did that well.

Now, a problem. He wanted to be closer to her, but she was fitted into a damned silly little chair that had arms. If he were to sit by her on the floor . . . ? But no, for him, the big bulky reassuring man, there could be no casual gestures, no informal postures. Suppose I scoop her out of the chair onto the bed? He drank his coffee as he plotted. Yes, he'd carry her to the bed, but not yet.

"Graham," she said, setting down her cup. She was, he saw with annoyance, looking tolerant. "Graham, in about half an hour I want to be in bed and asleep."

As she said this, she offered him a smile of amusement at this situation—man and woman maneuvering, the great comic situation. And with part of himself he could have shared it. Almost, he smiled with her, laughed. (Not till days later he exclaimed to himself: Lord what a mistake I made, not to share the joke with her then: that was where I went seriously wrong.) But he could not smile.

His face was frozen, with a stiff pride. Not because she had been watching him
plot; the amusement she now offered him took the sting out of that; but
because of his revived determination that he was going to have his own way, he
was going to have her. He was not going home. But he felt that he held a bunch
of keys, and did not know which one to choose.

He lifted the second small chair opposite to Barbara, moving aside the coffee
table for this purpose. He sat in this chair, leaned forward, took her two hands,
and said: "My dear, don't make me go home yet, don't, I beg you." The trouble
was, nothing had happened all evening that could be felt to lead up to these
words and his tone—simple, dignified, human being pleading with human being
for surcease. He saw himself leaning forward, his big hands swallowing her
small ones; he saw his face, warm with the appeal. And he realised he had meant
the words he used. They were nothing more than what he felt. He wanted to
stay with her because she wanted him to, because he was her colleague, a fellow
worker in the arts. He needed this desperately. But she was examining him,
curious rather than surprised, and from a critical distance. He heard himself
saying: "If James were here, I wonder what you'd do?" His voice was aggrieved;
he saw the sudden dark descend over her eyes, and she said: "Graham, would
you like some more coffee before you go?"

He said: "I've been wanting to meet you for years. I know a good many
people who know you."

She leaned forward, poured herself a little more brandy, sat back, holding
the glass between her two palms on her chest. An odd gesture: Graham felt that
this vessel she was cherishing between her hands was herself. A patient, long-
suffering gesture. He thought of various men who had mentioned her. He thought
of Jack Kennaway, wavered, panicked, said: "For instance, Jack Kennaway."

And now, at the name, an emotion lit her eyes—what was it? He went on,
deliberately testing this emotion, adding to it: "I had dinner with him last
week—oh, quite by chance!—and he was talking about you."

"Was he?"

He remembered he had thought her sullen, all those years ago. Now she
seemed defensive, and she frowned. He said: "In fact he spent most of the
evening talking about you."

She said in short, breathless sentences, which he realised were due to anger:
"I can very well imagine what he says. But surely you can't think I enjoy being
reminded that . . ." She broke off, resenting him, he saw, because he forced
her down onto a level she despised. But it was not his level either: it was all her
fault, all hers! He couldn't remember not being in control of a situation with
a woman for years. Again he felt like a man teetering on a tightrope. He
said, trying to make good use of Jack Kennaway, even at this late hour: "Of
course, he's a charming boy, but not a man at all."

She looked at him, silent, guarding her brandy glass against her breasts.

"Unless appearances are totally deceptive, of course." He could not resist
probing, even though he knew it was fatal.

She said nothing.

"Do you know you are supposed to have had the great affair with Jack

Kennaway?" he exclaimed, making this an amused expostulation against the
fools who could believe it.

"So I am told." She set down her glass. "And now," she said, standing up,
dismissing him. He lost his head, took a step forward, grabbed her in his arms,
and groaned: "Barbara!"

She turned her face this way and that under his kisses. He snatched a
diagnostic look at her expression—it was still patient. He placed his lips against
her neck, groaned "Barbara" again, and waited. She would have to do something.
Fight free, respond, something. She did nothing at all. At last she said: "For
the Lord's sake, Graham!" She sounded amused: he was again being offered
amusement. But if he shared it with her, it would be the end of this chance to
have her. He clamped his mouth over hers, silencing her. She did not fight him
off so much as blow him off. Her mouth treated his attacking mouth as a
woman blows and laughs in water, puffing off waves or spray with a laugh,
turning aside her head. It was a gesture half annoyance, half humour. He continued to kiss her while she moved her head and face about under the kisses as
if they were small attacking waves.

And so began what, when he looked back on it afterwards, was the most
embarrassing experience of his life. Even at the time he hated her for his inepti-
tude. For he held her there for what must have been nearly half an hour. She
was much shorter than he, he had to bend, and his neck ached. He held her rigid,
his thighs on either side of hers, her arms clamped to her side in a bear's hug.
She was unable to move, except for her head. When his mouth ground hers open
and his tongue moved and writhed inside it, she still remained passive. And
he could not stop himself. While with his intelligence he watched this ridiculous
scene, he was determined to go on, because sooner or later her body must soften
in wanting his. And he could not stop because he could not face the horror
of the moment when he set her free and she looked at him. And he hated her
more, every moment. Catching glimpses of her great green eyes, open and dismal
beneath his, he knew he had never disliked anything more than those "jewelled"
eyes. They were repulsive to him. It occurred to him at last that even if by
now she wanted him, he wouldn't know it, because she was not able to move at
all. He cautiously loosened his hold so that she had an inch or so leeway. She
remained quite passive. As if, he thought derisively, she had read or been told
that the way to incite men maddened by lust was to fight them. He found he was
thinking: Stupid cow, so you imagine I find you attractive, do you? You've
got the conceit to think that!

The sheer, raving insanity of this thought hit him, opened his arms, his
thighs, and lifted his tongue out of her mouth. She stepped back, wiping her
mouth with the back of her hand, and stood dazed with incredulity. The
embarrassment that lay in wait for him nearly engulfed him, but he let anger
postpone it. She said positively apologetic, even, at this moment, humorous:
"You're crazy, Graham. What's the matter, are you drunk? You don't seem
drunk. You don't even find me attractive."

The blood of hatred went to his head and he gripped her again. Now she had
got her face firmly twisted away so that he could not reach her mouth, and

she repeated steadily as he kissed the parts of her cheeks and neck that were available to him: "Graham, let me go, do let me go, Graham." She went on saying this; he went on squeezing, grinding, kissing and licking. It might go on all night: it was a sheer contest of wills, nothing else. He thought: It's only a really masculine woman who wouldn't have given in by now out of sheer decency of the flesh! One thing he knew, however: that she would be in that bed, in his arms, and very soon. He let her go, but said: "I'm going to sleep with you tonight, you know that, don't you?"

She leaned with hand on the mantelpiece to steady herself. Her face was colourless, since he had licked all the makeup off. She seemed quite different: small and defenceless with her large mouth pale now, her smudged green eyes fringed with gold. And now, for the first time, he felt what it might have been supposed (certainly by her) he felt hours ago. Seeing the small damp flesh of her face, he felt kinship, intimacy with her, he felt intimacy of the flesh, the affection and good humour of sensuality. He felt she was flesh of his flesh, his sister in the flesh. He felt desire for her, instead of the will to have her; and because of this, was ashamed of the farce he had been playing. Now he desired simply to take her into bed in the affection of his senses.

She said: "What on earth am I supposed to do? Telephone for the police, or what?" He was hurt that she still addressed the man who had ground her into sulky apathy; she was not addressing *him* at all.

She said: "Or scream for the neighbours, is that what you want?"

The gold-fringed eyes were almost black, because of the depth of the shadow of boredom over them. She was bored and weary to the point of falling to the floor, he could see that.

He said: "I'm going to sleep with you."

"But how can you possibly want to?"—a reasonable, a civilised demand addressed to a man who (he could see) she believed would respond to it. She said: "You know I don't want to, and I know you don't really give a damn one way or the other."

He was stung back into being the boor because she had not the intelligence to see that the boor no longer existed; because she could not see that this was a man who wanted her in a way which she must respond to.

There she stood, supporting herself with one hand, looking small and white and exhausted, and utterly incredulous. She was going to turn and walk off out of simple incredulity, he could see that. "Do you think I don't mean it?" he demanded, grinding this out between his teeth. She made a movement—she was on the point of going away. His hand shot out on its own volition and grasped her wrist. She frowned. His other hand grasped her other wrist. His body hove up against hers to start the pressure of a new embrace. Before it could, she said: "Oh Lord, no, I'm not going through all that again. Right, then."

"What do you mean—right, then?" he demanded.

She said: "You're going to sleep with me. O.K. Anything rather than go through that again. Shall we get it over with?"

He grinned, saying in silence: "No darling, oh no you don't, I don't care what words you use, I'm going to have you now and that's all there is to it."

She shrugged. The contempt, the weariness of it, had no effect on him, because he was now again hating her so much that wanting her was like needing to kill something or someone.

She took her clothes off, as if she were going to bed by herself: her jacket, skirt, petticoat. She stood in white bra and panties, a rather solid girl, brown-skinned still from the summer. He felt a flash of affection for the brown girl with her loose yellow hair as she stood naked. She got into bed and lay there, while the green eyes looked at him in civilised appeal: Are you really going through with this? Do you have to? Yes, his eyes said back: I do have to. She shifted her gaze aside, to the wall, saying silently: Well, if you want to take me without any desire at all on my part, then go ahead, if you're not ashamed. He was not ashamed, because he was maintaining the flame of hate for her which he knew quite well was all that stood between him and shame. He took off his clothes, and got into bed beside her. As he did so, knowing he was putting himself in the position of raping a woman who was making it elaborately clear he bored her, his flesh subsided completely, sad, and full of reproach because a few moments ago it was reaching out for his sister whom he could have made happy. He lay on his side by her, secretly at work on himself, while he supported himself across her body on his elbow, using the free hand to manipulate her breasts. He saw that she gritted her teeth against his touch. At least she could not know that after all this fuss he was not potent.

In order to incite himself, he clasped her again. She felt his smallness, writhed free of him, sat up and said: "Lie down."

While she had been lying there, she had been thinking: The only way to get this over with is to make him big again, otherwise I've got to put up with him all night. His hatred of her was giving him a clairvoyance: he knew very well what went on through her mind. She had switched on, with the determination to *get it all over with,* a sensual good humour, a patience. He lay down. She squatted beside him, the light from the ceiling blooming on her brown shoulders, her flat fair hair falling over her face. But she would not look at his face. Like a bored, skilled wife, she was: or like a prostitute. She administered to him, she was setting herself to please him. Yes, he thought, she's sensual, or she could be. Meanwhile she was succeeding in defeating the reluctance of his flesh, which was the tender token of a possible desire for her, by using a cold skill that was the result of her contempt for him. Just as he decided: Right, it's enough, now I shall have her properly, she made him come. It was not a trick, to hurry or cheat him, what defeated him was her transparent thought: Yes, that's what he's worth.

Then, having succeeded, and waited for a moment or two, she stood up, naked, the fringes of gold at her loins and in her armpits speaking to him a language quite different from that of her green, bored eyes. She looked at him and thought, showing it plainly: What sort of man is it who . . . ? He watched the slight movement of her shoulders: a just-checked shrug. She went out of the room: then the sound of running water. Soon she came back in a white dressing gown, carrying a yellow towel. She handed him the towel, looking away in politeness as he used it. "Are you going home now?" she enquired hopefully, at this point.

"No, I'm not." He believed that now he would have to start fighting her
again, but she lay down beside him, not touching him (he could feel the distaste
of her flesh for his) and he thought: Very well, my dear, but there's a lot of the
night left yet. He said aloud: "I'm going to have you properly tonight." She
said nothing, lay silent, yawned. Then she remarked consolingly, and he could
have laughed outright from sheer surprise: "Those were hardly conducive
circumstances for making love." She was *consoling* him. He hated her for it.
A proper little slut: I force her into bed, she doesn't want me, but she still has to
make me feel good, like a prostitute. But even while he hated her he responded
in kind, from the habit of sexual generosity. "It's because of my admiration
for you, because . . . after all, I was holding in my arms one of the thousand
women."

A pause. "The thousand?" she enquired, carefully.

"The thousand especial women."

"In Britain or in the world? You choose them for their brains, their beauty—
what?"

"Whatever it is that makes them outstanding," he said, offering her a
compliment.

"Well," she remarked at last, inciting him to be amused again: "I hope that
at least there's a short list you can say I am on, for politeness' sake."

He did not reply for he understood he was sleepy. He was still telling himself that he must stay awake when he was slowly waking and it was morning. It
was about eight. Barbara was not there. He thought: My God! What on earth
shall I tell my wife? Where was Barbara? He remembered the ridiculous scenes of
last night and nearly succumbed to shame. Then he thought, reviving anger:
If she didn't sleep beside me here I'll never forgive her. . . . He sat up, quietly,
determined to go through the house until he found her and, having found
her, to possess her, when the door opened and she came in. She was fully dressed
in a green suit, her hair done, her eyes made up. She carried a tray of coffee,
which she set down beside the bed. He was conscious of his big loose hairy body,
half uncovered. He said to himself that he was not going to lie in bed, naked,
while she was dressed. He said: "Have you got a gown of some kind?" She
handed him, without speaking, a towel, and said: "The bathroom's second on the
left." She went out. He followed, the towel around him. Everything in this
house was gay, intimate—not at all like her efficient working room. He wanted
to find out where she had slept, and opened the first door. It was the kitchen,
and she was in it, putting a brown earthenware dish into the oven. "The next
door," said Barbara. He went hastily past the second door, and opened (he
hoped quietly) the third. It was a cupboard full of linen. "This door," said
Barbara, behind him.

"So all right then, where did you sleep?"

"What's it to do with you? Upstairs, in my own bed. Now, if you have everything, I'll say goodbye, I want to get to the theatre."

"I'll take you," he said at once.

He saw again the movement of her eyes, the dark swallowing the light in
deadly boredom. "I'll take you," he insisted.

"I'd prefer to go by myself," she remarked. Then she smiled: "However, you'll take me. Then you'll make a point of coming right in, so that James and everyone can see—that's what you want to take me for, isn't it?"

He hated her, finally, and quite simply, for her intelligence; that not once had he got away with anything, that she had been watching, since they had met yesterday, every movement of his campaign for her. However, some fate or inner urge over which he had no control made him say sentimentally: "My dear, you must see that I'd like at least to take you to your work."

"Not at all, have it on me," she said, giving him the lie direct. She went past him to the room he had slept in. "I shall be leaving in ten minutes," she said.

He took a shower, fast. When he returned, the workroom was already tidied, the bed made, all signs of the night gone. Also, there were no signs of the coffee she had brought in for him. He did not like to ask for it, for fear of an outright refusal. Besides, she was ready, her coat on, her handbag under her arm. He went, without a word, to the front door, and she came after him, silent.

He could see that every fibre of her body signalled a simple message: Oh God, for the moment when I can be rid of this boor! She was nothing but a slut, he thought.

A taxi came. In it she sat as far away from him as she could. He thought of what he should say to his wife.

Outside the theatre she remarked: "You could drop me here, if you liked." It was not a plea, she was too proud for that. "I'll take you in," he said, and saw her thinking: Very well, I'll go through with it to shame him. He was determined to take her in and hand her over to her colleagues, he was afraid she would give him the slip. But far from playing it down, she seemed determined to play it his way. At the stage door, she said to the doorman: "This is Mr. Spence, Tom—do you remember, Mr. Spence from last night?" "Good morning, Babs," said the man, examining Graham, politely, as he had been ordered to do.

Barbara went to the door to the stage, opened it, held it open for him. He went in first, then held it open for her. Together they walked into the cavernous, littered, badly lit place and she called out: "James, James!" A man's voice called out from the front of the house: "Here, Babs, why are you so late?"

The auditorium opened before them, darkish, silent, save for an early-morning busyness of charwomen. A vacuum cleaner roared, smally, somewhere close. A couple of stagehands stood looking up at a drop which had a design of blue and green spirals. James stood with his back to the auditorium, smoking. "You're late, Babs," he said again. He saw Graham behind her, and nodded. Barbara and James kissed. Barbara said, giving allowance to every syllable: "You remember Mr. Spence from last night?" James nodded: How do you do? Barbara stood beside him, and they looked together up at the blue-and-green backdrop. Then Barbara looked again at Graham, asking silently: All right now, isn't that enough? He could see her eyes, sullen with boredom.

He said: "Bye, Babs. Bye, James. I'll ring you, Babs." No response, she ignored him. He walked off slowly, listening for what might be said. For instance: "Babs, for God's sake, what are you doing with him?" Or she might say: "Are you wondering about Graham Spence? Let me explain."

Graham passed the stagehands who, he could have sworn, didn't recognise him. Then at last he heard James's voice to Barbara: "It's no good, Babs, I know you're enamoured of that particular shade of blue, but do have another look at it, there's a good girl. . . ." Graham left the stage, went past the office where the stage doorman sat reading a newspaper. He looked up, nodded, went back to his paper. Graham went to find a taxi, thinking: I'd better think up something convincing, then I'll telephone my wife.

Luckily he had an excuse not to be at home that day, for this evening he had to interview a young man (for television) about his new novel.

Mary Elizabeth Vroman

(1925–1967) Mary Elizabeth Vroman became the first black woman accepted as a member of the Screen Writers Guild when her short story "See How They Run" was made into a movie, Bright Road, *in 1953. Her other works published before her untimely death include* Esther, Harlem Summer, *and* Shaped to Its Purpose.

See How They Run

A bell rang. Jane Richards squared the sheaf of records decisively in the large Manila folder, placed it in the right-hand corner of her desk, and stood up. The chatter of young voices subsided, and forty-three small faces looked solemnly and curiously at the slight young figure before them. The bell stopped ringing.

I wonder if they're as scared of me as I am of them. She smiled brightly.

"Good morning, children, I am Miss Richards." *As if they don't know*—the door of the third-grade room had a neat new sign pasted above it with her name in bold black capitals; and anyway, a new teacher's name is the first thing that children find out about on the first day of school. Nevertheless, she wrote it for their benefit in large white letters on the blackboard.

"I hope we will all be happy working and playing together this year." *Now why does that sound so trite?* "As I call the roll will you please stand, so that I may get to know you as soon as possible, and if you like you may tell me something about yourselves, how old you are, where you live, what your parents do, and perhaps something about what you did during the summer."

Seated, she checked the names carefully. "Booker T. Adams."

Booker stood, gangling and stoop-shouldered; he began to recite tiredly, "My name is Booker T. Adams, I'se ten years old." *Shades of Uncle Tom!* "I live on Painter's Path." He paused, the look he gave her was tinged with something very akin to contempt. "I didn't do nothing in the summer," he said deliberately.

"Thank you, Booker." Her voice was even. "George Allen." *Must remember to correct that stoop. . . . Where is Painter's Path? . . . How to go about correcting those speech defects? . . . Go easy, Jane, don't antagonize them. . . . They're clean enough, but this is the first day. . . . How can one teacher do any kind of job with a load of forty-three? . . . Thank heaven the building is modern and well built even though it is overcrowded, not like some I've seen—no potbellied stove.*

"Sarahlene Clover Babcock." *Where do these names come from? . . . Up from slavery. . . . How high is up?* Jane smothered a sudden desire to giggle. Outside she was calm and poised and smiling. Clearly she called the names, listening with interest, making a note here and there, making no corrections—not yet.

She experienced a moment of brief inward satisfaction: *I'm doing very well, this is what is expected of me* . . . Orientation to Teaching . . . Miss Murray's voice beat a distant tattoo in her memory. Miss Murray with the Junoesque figure and the moon face. . . . "The ideal teacher personality is one which, combining in itself all the most desirable qualities, expresses itself with quiet assurance in its endeavor to mold the personalities of the students in the most desirable patterns." . . . Dear dull Miss Murray.

She made mental estimates of the class. *What a cross section of my people they represent,* she thought. *Here and there signs of evident poverty, here and there children of obviously well-to-do parents.*

"My name is Rachel Veronica Smith. I am nine years old. I live at Six-oh-seven Fairview Avenue. My father is a Methodist minister. My mother is a housewife. I have two sisters and one brother. Last summer mother and daddy took us all to New York to visit my Aunt Jen. We saw lots of wonderful things. There are millions and millions of people in New York. One day we went on a ferryboat all the way up the Hudson River—that's a great big river as wide as this town, and—"

The children listened wide-eyed. Jane listened carefully. *She speaks good English. Healthy, erect, and even perhaps a little smug. Immaculately well dressed from the smoothly braided hair, with two perky bows, to the shiny brown oxford. . . . Bless you, Rachel, I'm so glad to have you.*

"—and the buildings are all very tall, some of them nearly reach the sky."

"Haw-haw"—this from Booker, cynically.

"Well, they are too." Rachel swung around, fire in her eyes and insistence in every line of her round, compact body.

"Ain't no buildings as tall as the sky, is dere, Miz Richards?"

Crisis No. 1. Jane chose her answer carefully. *As high as the sky . . . musn't turn this into a lesson in science . . . all in due time.* "The sky is a long way out, Booker, but the buildings in New York are very tall indeed. Rachel was only trying to show you how very tall they are. In fact, the tallest building in the whole world is in New York City."

"They call it the Empire State Building," interrupted Rachel, heady with her new knowledge and Jane's corroboration.

Booker wasn't through. "You been dere, Miz Richards?"

"Yes, Booker, many times. Someday I shall tell you more about it. Maybe Rachel will help me. Is there anything you'd like to add, Rachel?"

"I would like to say that we are glad you are our new teacher, Miss Richards." Carefully she sat down, spreading her skirt with her plump hands, her smile angelic.

Now I'll bet me a quarter her reverend father told her to say that. "Thank you, Rachel."

The roll call continued. . . . Tanya, slight and pinched, with the toes showing through the very white sneakers, the darned and faded but clean blue dress, the gentle voice like a tinkling bell, and the beautiful sensitive face. . . . Boyd and Lloyd, identical in their starched overalls, and the slightly vacant look. . . . Marjorie Lee, all of twelve years old, the well-developed body moving restlessly in the childish dress, the eyes too wise, the voice too high. . . . Joe Louis, the intelligence in the brilliant black eyes gleaming above the threadbare clothes. *Lives of great men all remind us—Well, I have them all . . . Frederick Douglass, Franklin Delano, Abraham Lincoln, Booker T., Joe Louis, George Washington. . . . What a great burden you bear, little people, heirs to all your parents' stillborn dreams of greatness. I must not fail you.* The last name on the list . . . C. T. Young. Jane paused, small lines creasing her forehead. She checked the list again.

"C. T., what is your name? I only have your initials on my list."

"Dat's all my name, C. T. Young."

"No, dear, I mean what does C. T. stand for? Is it Charles or Clarence?"

"No'm, jest C. T."

"But I can't put that in my register, dear."

Abruptly Jane rose and went to the next room. Rather timidly she waited to speak to Miss Nelson, the second-grade teacher, who had the formidable record of having taught all of sixteen years. Miss Nelson was large and smiling.

"May I help you, dear?"

"Yes, please. It's about C. T. Young. I believe you had him last year."

"Yes, and the year before that. You'll have him two years too."

"Oh? Well, I was wondering what name you registered him under. All the information I have is C. T. Young."

"That's all there is, honey. Lots of these children only have initials."

"You mean . . . can't something be done about it?"

"What?" Miss Nelson was still smiling, but clearly impatient.

"I . . . well . . . thank you." Jane left quickly.

Back in Room 3 the children were growing restless. Deftly Jane passed out the rating tests and gave instructions. Then she called C. T. to her. He was as small as an eight-year-old, and hungry-looking, with enormous guileless eyes and a beautifully shaped head.

"How many years did you stay in the second grade, C. T.?"

"Two."

"And in the first?"

"Two."

"How old are you?"

"'Leven."

"When will you be twelve?"

"Nex' month."

And they didn't care . . . nobody ever cared enough about one small boy to give him a name.

"You are a very lucky little boy, C. T. Most people have to take the name somebody gave them whether they like it or not, but you can choose your very own."

"Yeah?" The dark eyes were belligerent. "My father named me C. T. after hisself, Miz Richards, and dat's my name."

Jane felt unreasonably irritated. "How many children are there in your family, C. T.?"

"'Leven."

"How many are there younger than you?" she asked.

"Seven."

Very gently. "Did you have your breakfast this morning, dear?"

The small figure in the too-large trousers and the too-small shirt drew itself up to full height. "Yes'm, I had fried chicken, and rice, and coffee, and rolls, and oranges too."

Oh, you poor darling. You poor proud lying darling. Is that what you'd like for breakfast?

She asked, "Do you like school, C. T.?"

"Yes'm," he told her suspiciously.

She leafed through the pile of records. "Your record says you haven't been coming to school very regularly. Why?"

"I dunno."

"Did you eat last year in the lunchroom?"

"No'm."

"Did you ever bring a lunch?"

"No'm, I eats such a big breakfast, I doan git hungry at lunchtime."

"Children need to eat lunch to help them grow tall and strong, C. T. So from now on you'll eat lunch in the lunchroom"—an afterthought: *Perhaps it's important to make him think I believe him*—"and from now on maybe you'd better not eat such a big breakfast."

Decisively she wrote his name at the top of what she knew to be an already too-large list. "Only those in absolute necessity," she had been told by Mr. Johnson, the kindly, harassed principal. "We'd like to feed them all, so many are underfed, but we just don't have the money." Well, this was absolute necessity if she ever saw it.

"What does your father do, C. T.?"

"He work at dat big factory cross-town, he make plenty money, Miz Richards." The record said "unemployed."

"Would you like to be named Charles Thomas?"

The expressive eyes darkened, but the voice was quiet. "No'm."

"Very well." Thoughtfully Jane opened the register; she wrote firmly:

C. T. Young.

October is a witching month in the Southern United States. The richness of the golds and reds and browns of the trees forms an enchanted filigree through which the lilting voices of children at play seem to float, embodied like so many nymphs of Pan.

Jane had played a fast-and-furious game of tag with her class and now she sat quietly under the gnarled old oak, watching the tireless play, feeling the magic of the sun through the leaves warmly dappling her skin, the soft breeze on the nape of her neck like a lover's hands, and her own drowsy lethargy. *Paul, Paul my darling . . . how long for us now?* She had worshiped Paul Carlyle since they were freshmen together. On graduation day he had slipped the small circlet of diamonds on her finger. . . . "A teacher's salary is small, Jane. Maybe we'll be lucky enough to get work together, then in a year or so we can be married. Wait for me, darling, wait for me!"

But in a year or so Paul had gone to war, and Jane went out alone to teach. . . . Lansing Creek—one year . . . the leaky roof, the potbellied stove, the water from the well. . . . Maryweather Point—two years . . . the tight-lipped spinster principal with the small, vicious face and the small, vicious soul. . . . Three hard, lonely years and then she had been lucky.

The superintendent had praised her. "You have done good work, Miss—ah—Jane. This year you are to be placed at Centertown High—that is, of course, if you care to accept the position."

Jane had caught her breath. Centertown was the largest and best equipped of all the schools in the county, only ten miles from home and Paul—for Paul had come home, older, quieter, but still Paul. He was teaching now more than a hundred miles away, but they went home every other week end to their families and each other. . . . "Next summer you'll be Mrs. Paul Carlyle, darling. It's hard for us to be apart so much. I guess we'll have to be for a long time till I can afford to support you. But, sweet, these little tykes need us so badly." He had held her close, rubbing the nape of the neck under the soft curls. "We have a big job, those of us who teach," he had told her, "a never-ending and often thankless job, Jane, to supply the needs of these kids who lack so much."

They wrote each other long letters, sharing plans and problems. She wrote him about C. T. "I've adopted him, darling. He's so pathetic and so determined to prove that he's not. He learns nothing at all, but I can't let myself believe that he's stupid, so I keep trying."

"Miz Richards, please, ma'am." Tanya's beautiful amber eyes sought hers timidly. Her brown curls were tangled from playing, her cheeks a bright red under the tightly-stretched olive skin. The elbows jutted awkwardly out of the sleeves of the limp cotton dress, which could not conceal the finely chiseled bones in their pitiable fleshlessness. As always when she looked at her, Jane thought, *What a beautiful child!* So unlike the dark, gaunt, morose mother, and the dumpy, pasty-faced father who had visited her that first week. A fairy's changeling. *You'll make a lovely angel to grace the throne of God, Tanya! Now what made me think of that?*

"Please, ma'am, I'se sick."

Gently Jane drew her down beside her. She felt the parchment skin, noted the unnaturally bright eyes. *Oh, dear God, she's burning up!* "Do you hurt anywhere, Tanya?"

"My head, ma'am, and I'se so tired." Without warning she began to cry.

"How far do you live, Tanya?"

"Two miles."

"You walk to school?"

"Yes'm."

"Do any of your brothers have a bicycle?"

"No'm."

"Rachel!" *Bless you for always being there when I need you.* "Hurry, dear, to the office and ask Mr. Johnson please to send a big boy with a bicycle to take Tanya home. She's sick."

Rachel ran.

"Hush now, dear, we'll get some cool water, and then you'll be home in a little while. Did you feel sick this morning?"

"Yes'm, but Mot Dear sent me to school anyway. She said I just wanted to play hooky." *Keep smiling, Jane. Poor, ambitious, well-meaning parents, made bitter at the seeming futility of dreaming dreams for this lovely child . . . willing her to rise above the drabness of your own meager existence . . . too angry with life to see that what she needs most is your love and care and right now medical attention.*

Jane bathed the child's forehead with cool water at the fountain. *Do the white schools have a clinic? I must ask Paul. Do they have a lounge or a couch where they can lay one wee sick head? Is there anywhere in this town free medical service for one small child . . . born black?*

The boy with the bicycle came. "Take care of her now, ride slowly and carefully, and take her straight home. . . . Keep the newspaper over your head, Tanya, to keep out the sun, and tell your parents to call the doctor." But she knew they wouldn't—because they couldn't!

The next day Jane went to see Tanya.

"She's sho' nuff sick, Miz Richards," the mother said. "She's always been a puny child, but this time she's took real bad, throat's all raw, talk all out of her haid las' night. I been using a poultice and some herb brew but she ain't got no better."

"Have you called a doctor, Mrs. Fulton?"

"No'm, we cain't afford it, an' Jake, he doan believe in doctors nohow."

Jane waited till the tide of high bright anger welling in her heart and beating in her brain had subsided. When she spoke, her voice was deceptively gentle. "Mrs. Fulton, Tanya is a very sick little girl. She is your only little girl. If you love her, I advise you to have a doctor to her, for if you don't . . . Tanya may die."

The wail that issued from the thin figure seemed to have no part in reality.

Jane spoke hurriedly. "Look, I'm going into town, I'll send a doctor out. Don't worry about paying him. We can see about that later." Impulsively she put her arms around the taut, motionless shoulders. "Don't you worry, honey, it's going to be all right."

There was a kindliness in the doctor's weatherbeaten face that warmed Jane's heart, but his voice was brusque. "You sick, girl? Well?"

"No, sir. I'm not sick." *What long sequence of events has caused even the best of you to look on even the best of us as menials?* "I'm a teacher at Centertown High. There's a little girl in my class who is very ill. Her parents are very poor. I came to see if you would please go to see her."

He looked at her, amused.

"Of course I'll pay the bill, doctor," she added hastily.

"In that case . . . well . . . where does she live?"

Jane told him. "I think it's diphtheria, doctor."

He raised his eyebrows. "Why?"

Jane sat erect. *Don't be afraid, Jane! You're as good a teacher as he is a doctor, and you made an A in that course in childhood diseases.* "High fever, restlessness, sore throat, headache, croupy cough, delirium. It could, of course, be tonsillitis or scarlet fever, but that cough—well, I'm only guessing, of course," she finished lamely.

"Hmph." The doctor's face was expressionless. "Well, we'll see. Have your other children been inoculated?"

"Yes, sir. Doctor, if the parents ask, please tell them that the school is paying for your services."

This time he was wide-eyed.

The lie haunted her. She spoke to the other teachers about it the next day at recess. "She's really very sick, maybe you'd like to help?"

Mary Winters, the sixth-grade teacher, was the first to speak. "Richards, I'd like to help, but I've got three kids of my own, and so you see how it is?"

Jane saw.

"Trouble with you, Richards, is you're too emotional." This from Nelson. "When you've taught as many years as I have, my dear, you'll learn not to bang your head against a stone wall. It may sound hardhearted to you, but one just can't worry about one child more or less when one has nearly fifty."

The pain in the back of her eyes grew more insistent. "I can," she said.

"I'll help, Jane," said Marilyn Andrews, breathless, bouncy newlywed Marilyn. "Here's two bucks. It's all I've got, but nothing's plenty for me." Her laughter pealed echoing down the hall.

"I've got a dollar, Richards"—this from mousy, severe little Miss Mitchell—"though I'm not sure I agree with you."

"Why don't you ask the high-school faculty?" said Marilyn. "Better still, take it up in teachers' meeting."

"Mr. Johnson has enough to worry about now," snapped Nelson. *Why, she's mad,* thought Jane, *mad because I'm trying to give a helpless little tyke a chance to live, and because Marilyn and Mitchell helped.*

The bell rang. Wordlessly Jane turned away. She watched the children troop in noisily, an ancient nursery rhyme running through her head:

> *Three blind mice, three blind mice,*
> *See how they run, see how they run,*
> *They all ran after the farmer's wife,*

> *She cut off their tails with a carving knife.*
> *Did you ever see such a sight in your life*
> *As three blind mice?*

Only this time, it was forty-three mice. Jane giggled. *Why, I'm hysterical,* she thought in surprise. *The mice thought the sweet-smelling farmer's wife might have bread and a wee bit of cheese to offer poor blind mice, but the farmer's wife didn't like poor, hungry, dirty blind mice. So she cut off their tails. Then they couldn't run anymore, only wobble. What happened then? Maybe they starved, those that didn't bleed to death. Running round in circles. Running where, little mice?*

She talked to the high-school faculty, and Mr. Johnson. Altogether she got eight dollars.

The following week she received a letter from the doctor:

Dear Miss Richards:

I am happy to inform you that Tanya is greatly improved, and with careful nursing will be well enough in about eight weeks to return to school. She is very frail, however, and will require special care. I have made three visits to her home. In view of the peculiar circumstances, I am donating my services. The cost of the medicines, however, amounts to the sum of $15. I am referring this to you as you requested. What a beautiful child!

Yours sincerely,
Jonathan H. Sinclair, M.D.

P.S. She had diptheria.

Bless you forever and ever, Jonathan H. Sinclair, M.D. For all your long Southern heritage, "a man's a man for a' that . . . and a' that!"

Her heart was light that night when she wrote to Paul. Later she made plans in the darkness. *You'll be well and fat by Christmas, Tanya, and you'll be a lovely angel in my pageant. . . . I must get the children to save pennies. . . . We'll send you milk and oranges and eggs, and we'll make funny little get-well cards to keep you happy.*

But by Christmas Tanya was dead!

The voice from the dark figure was quiet, even monotonous. "Jake an' me, we always work so hard, Miz Richards. We didn't neither one have no schooling much when we was married—folks never had much money, but we was happy. Jake, he tenant farm. I tuk in washing—we plan to save and buy a little house and farm of our own someday. Den the children come. Six boys, Miz Richards—all in a hurry. We both want the boys to finish school, mebbe go to college. We try not to keep them out to work the farm, but sometimes we have to. Then come Tanya. Just like a little yellow rose she was, Miz Richards, all pink and gold . . . and her voice like a silver bell. We think when she grow up an' finish school she take voice lessons—be like Marian Anderson. We think mebbe by then the boys would be old enough to help. I was kinda feared for her when she get sick, but then she start to get better. She was doing so well, Miz Richards. Den it get cold, an' the fire so hard to keep all night long, an' eben the newspapers in the cracks doan keep the win' out, an' I give her all my kivver; but one night she jest tuk to shivering an' talking all out her haid—sat right up in bed, she did. She call your name onc't or twice, Miz Richards, then she say, 'Mot Dear, does Jesus love me like Miz Richards say in Sunday school?' I say, 'Yes, honey.' She say, 'Effen I die will I see Jesus?' I say, 'Yes, honey, but you ain't gwine die.' But she did, Miz Richards . . . jest smiled an' laid down—jest smiled an' laid down."

It is terrible to see such hopeless resignation in such tearless eyes. . . . One little mouse stopped running. . . . *You'll make a lovely angel to grace the throne of God, Tanya!*

Jane did not go to the funeral. Nelson and Rogers sat in the first pew. Everyone on the faculty contributed to a beautiful wreath. Jane preferred not to think about that.

C. T. brought a lovely potted rose to her the next day. "Miz Richards, ma'am, do you think this is pretty enough to go on Tanya's grave?"

"Where did you get it, C. T.?"

"I stole it out Miz Adams' front yard, right out of that li'l glass house she got there. The door was open, Miz Richards, she got plenty, she won't miss this li'l one."

You queer little bundle of truth and lies. What do I do now? Seeing the tears blinking back in the anxious eyes, she said gently, "Yes, C. T., the rose is nearly as beautiful as Tanya is now. She will like it."

"You mean she will know I put it there, Miz Richards? She ain't daid at all?"

"Maybe she'll know, C. T. You see, nothing that is beautiful ever dies as long as we remember it."

So you loved Tanya, little mouse? The memory of her beauty is yours to keep now forever and always, my darling. Those things money can't buy. They've all been trying, but your tail isn't off yet, is it, brat? Not by a long shot. Suddenly she laughed aloud.

He looked at her wonderingly. "What you laughing at, Miz Richards?"

"I'm laughing because I'm happy, C. T.," and she hugged him.

Christmas with its pageantry and splendor came and went. Back from the holidays, Jane had an oral English lesson.

"We'll take this period to let you tell about your holidays, children."

On the weekends that Jane stayed in Centertown she visited different churches, and taught in the Sunday schools when she was asked. She had tried to impress on the children the reasons for giving at Christmastime. In class they had talked about things they could make for gifts, and ways they could save money to buy them. Now she stood by the window, listening attentively, reaping the fruits of her labors.

"I got a doll and a doll carriage for Christmas. Her name is Gladys, and the carriage has red wheels, and I got a tea set and—"

"I got a bicycle and a catcher's mitt."

"We all went to a party and had ice cream and cake."

"I got—"

"I got—"

"I got—"

Score one goose egg for Jane. She was suddenly very tired. "It's your turn, C. T." *Dear God, please don't let him lie too much. He tears my heart. The children never laugh. It's funny how polite they are to C. T. even when they know he's lying. Even that day when Boyd and Lloyd told how they had seen him take food out of the garbage cans in front of the restaurant, and he said he was taking it to some poor hungry children, they didn't laugh. Sometimes children have a great deal more insight than grownups.*

C. T. was talking. "I didn't get nothin' for Christmas, because mamma was sick, but I worked all that week before for Mr. Bondel what owns the store on Main Street. I ran errands an' swep' up an' he give me three dollars, and so I bought mamma a real pretty handkerchief an' a comb, an' I bought my father a tie pin, paid a big ole fifty cents for it too . . . an' I bought my sisters an' brothers some candy an' gum an' I bought me this whistle. Course I got what you give us, Miz Richards" (she had given each a small gift) "an' mamma's white lady give us a whole crate of oranges, an' Miz Smith what live nex' door give me a pair of socks. Mamma she was so happy she made a cake with eggs an' butter an' everything; an' then we ate it an' had a good time."

Rachel spoke wonderingly. "Didn't Santa Claus bring you anything at all?"

C. T. was the epitome of scorn. "Ain't no Santa Claus," he said and sat down.

Jane quelled the age-old third-grade controversy absently, for her heart was singing. *C. T. . . . C. T., son of my own heart, you are the bright new hope of a doubtful world, and the gay new song of a race unconquered. Of them all— Sarahlene, sole heir to the charming stucco home on the hill, all fitted for gracious living; George, whose father is a contractor; Rachel, the minister's daughter; Angela, who has just inherited ten thousand dollars—of all of them who got, you, my dirty little vagabond, who have never owned a coat in your life, because you say you don't get cold; you, out of your nothing, found something to give, and in the dignity of giving found that it was not so important to receive. . . . Christ Child, look down in blessing on one small child made in Your image and born black!*

Jane had problems. Sometimes it was difficult to maintain discipline with forty-two children. Busy as she kept them, there were always some not busy enough. There was the conference with Mr. Johnson.

"Miss Richards, you are doing fine work here, but sometimes your room is a little . . . well—ah—well, to say the least, noisy. You are new here, but we have always maintained a record of having fine discipline here at this school. People have said that it used to be hard to tell whether or not there were children in the building. We have always been proud of that. Now take Miss Nelson. She is an excellent disciplinarian." He smiled. "Maybe if you ask her she will give you her secret. Do not be too proud to accept help from anyone who can give it, Miss Richards."

"No, sir, thank you, sir, I'll do my best to improve, sir." *Ah, you dear, well-*

meaning, shortsighted, round, busy little man. Why are you not more concerned about how much the children have grown and learned in these past four months than you are about how much noise they make? I know Miss Nelson's secret. Spare not the rod and spoil not the child. Is that what you want me to do? Paralyze these kids with fear so that they will be afraid to move? afraid to question? afraid to grow? Why is it so fine for people not to know there are children in the building? Wasn't the building built for children? In her room Jane locked the door against the sound of the playing children, put her head on the desk, and cried.

Jane acceded to tradition and administered one whipping. Booker had slapped Sarahlene's face because she had refused to give up a shiny little music box that played a gay little tune. He had taken the whipping docilely enough, as though used to it; but the sneer in his eyes that had almost gone returned to haunt them. Jane's heart misgave her. *From now on I positively refuse to impose my will on any of these poor children by reason of my greater strength.* So she had abandoned the rod in favor of any other means she could find. They did not always work.

There was a never-ending drive for funds. Jane had a passion for perfection. Plays, dances, concerts, bazaars, suppers, parties followed one on another in staggering succession.

"Look here, Richards," Nelson told her one day, "it's true that we need a new piano, and that science equipment, but, honey, these drives in a colored school are like the poor: with us always. It doesn't make too much difference if Suzy forgets her lines, or if the ice cream is a little lumpy. Cooperation is fine, but the way you tear into things you won't last long."

"For once in her life Nelson's right, Jane," Elise told her later. "I can understand how intense you are because I used to be like that; but, pet, Negro teachers have always had to work harder than any others and till recently have always got paid less, so for our own health's sake we have to let up wherever possible. Believe me, honey, if you don't learn to take it easy, you're going to get sick."

Jane did. Measles!

"Oh, no," she wailed, "not in my old age!" But she was glad of the rest. Lying in her own bed at home, she realized how very tired she was.

Paul came to see her that weekend, and sat by her bed and read aloud to her the old classic poems they both loved so well. They listened to their favorite radio programs. Paul's presence was warm and comforting. Jane was reluctant to go back to work.

What to do about C. T. was a question that daily loomed larger in Jane's consciousness. Watching Joe Louis' brilliant development was a thing of joy, and Jane was hard pressed to find enough outlets for his amazing abilities. Jeannette Allen was running a close second, and even Booker, so long a problem, was beginning to grasp fundamentals, but C. T. remained static.

"I always stays two years in a grade, Miz Richards," he told her blandly. "I does better the second year."

"Do you *want* to stay in the third grade two years, C. T.?"

"I don't keer." His voice had been cheerful.

Maybe he really is slow, Jane thought. But one day something happened to make her change her mind.

C. T. was possessed of an unusually strong tendency to protect those he considered to be poor or weak. He took little Johnny Armstrong, who sat beside him in class, under his wing. Johnny was nearsighted and nondescript, his one outstanding feature being his hero-worship of C. T. Johnny was a plodder. Hard as he tried, he made slow progress at best.

The struggle with multiplication tables was a difficult one, in spite of all the little games Jane devised to make them easier for the children. On this particular day there was the uneven hum of little voices trying to memorize. Johnny and C. T. were having a whispered conversation about snakes.

Clearly Jane heard C. T.'s elaboration. "Man, my father caught a moccasin long as that blackboard, I guess, an' I held him while he was live right back of his ugly head—so."

Swiftly Jane crossed the room. "C. T. and Johnny, you are supposed to be learning your tables. The period is nearly up and you haven't even begun to study. Furthermore, in more than five months you haven't even learned the two-times table. Now you will both stay in at the first recess to learn it, and every day after this until you do."

Maybe I should make up some problems about snakes, Jane mused, *but they'd be too ridiculous.... Two nests of four snakes—Oh, well, I'll see how they do at recess.* Her heart smote her at the sight of the two little figures at their desks, listening wistfully to the sound of the children at play, but she busied herself and pretended not to notice them. Then she heard C. T.'s voice:

"Lissen, man, these tables is easy if you really want to learn them. Now see here. Two times one is two. Two times two is four. Two times three is six. If you forgit, all you got to do is add two like she said."

"Sho' nuff, man?"

"Sho'. Say them with me ... two times one—" Obediently Johnny began to recite. Five minutes later they came to her. "We's ready, Miz Richards."

"Very well. Johnny, you may begin."

"Two times one is two. Two times two is four. Two times three is.... Two times three is—"

"Six," prompted C. T.

In sweat and pain, Johnny managed to stumble through the two-times table with C. T.'s help.

"That's very poor, Johnny, but you may go for today. Tomorrow I shall expect you to have it letter perfect. Now it's your turn, C. T."

C. T.'s performance was a fair rival to Joe Louis's. Suspiciously she took him through in random order.

"Two times nine?"

"Eighteen."

"Two times four?"

"Eight."

"Two times seven?"

"Fourteen."

"C.T., you could have done this long ago. Why didn't you?"

"I dunno. . . . May I go to play now, Miz Richards?"

"Yes, C. T. Now learn your three-times table for me tomorrow."

But he didn't, not that day, or the day after that, or the day after that. . . . *Why doesn't he? Is it that he doesn't want to? Maybe if I were as ragged and deprived as he I wouldn't want to learn either.*

Jane took C. T. to town and bought him a shirt, a sweater, a pair of dungarees, some underwear, a pair of shoes, and a pair of socks. Then she sent him to the barber to get his hair cut. She gave him the money so he could pay for the articles himself and figure up the change. She instructed him to take a bath before putting on his new clothes, and told him not to tell anyone but his parents that she had bought them.

The next morning the class was in a dither.

"You seen C. T.?"

"Oh, boy ain't he sharp!"

"C. T., where'd you get them new clothes?"

"Oh, man, I can wear new clothes any time I feel like it, but I can't be bothered with being a fancypants all the time like you guys."

C. T. strutted in new confidence, but his work didn't improve.

Spring came in its virginal green gladness and the children chafed for the out-of-doors. Jane took them out as much as possible on nature studies and excursions.

C. T. was growing more and more mischievous, and his influence began to spread throughout the class. Daily his droll wit became more and more edged with impudence. Jane was at her wit's end.

'You let that child get away with too much, Richards," Nelson told her. "What he needs is a good hiding."

One day Jane kept certain of the class in at the first recess to do neglected homework, C. T. among them. She left the room briefly. When she returned C. T. was gone.

"Where is C. T.?" she asked.

"He went out to play, Miz Richards. He said couldn't no ole teacher keep him in when he didn't want to stay."

Out on the playground C. T. was standing in a swing, gently swaying to and fro, surrounded by a group of admiring youngsters. He was holding forth.

"I gets tired of stayin' in all the time. She doan pick on nobody but me, an' today I put my foot down. 'From now on,' I say, 'I ain't never goin' to stay in, Miz Richards.' Then I walks out." He was enjoying himself immensely. Then he saw her.

"You will come with me, C. T." She was quite calm except for the telltale veins throbbing in her forehead.

"I ain't comin'." The sudden fright in his eyes was veiled quickly by a nonchalant belligerence. He rocked the swing gently.

She repeated, "Come with me, C. T."

The children watched breathlessly.

"I done told you I ain't comin', Miz Richards." His voice was patient, as though explaining to a child. "I ain't . . . comin' . . . a . . . damn . . . tall!"

Jane moved quickly, wrenching the small but surprisingly strong figure from the swing. Then she bore him bodily, kicking and screaming, to the building.

The children relaxed and began to giggle. "Oh, boy! Is he goin' to catch it!" they told one another.

Panting, she held him, still struggling, by the scruff of his collar before the group of teachers gathered in Marilyn's room. "All right, now *you* tell me what to do with him!" she demanded. "I've tried everything." The tears were close behind her eyes.

"What'd he do?" Nelson asked.

Briefly she told them.

"Have you talked to his parents?"

"Three times I've had conferences with them. They say to beat him."

"That, my friend, is what you ought to do. Now he never acted like that with me. If you'll let me handle him, I'll show you how to put a brat like that in his place."

"Go ahead," Jane said wearily.

Nelson left the room, and returned with a narrow but sturdy leather thong. "Now, C. T."—she was smiling, tapping the strap in her open left palm—"go to your room and do what Miss Richards told you to."

"I ain't gonna, an' you can't make me." He sat down with absurd dignity at a desk.

Still smiling, Miss Nelson stood over him. The strap descended without warning across the bony shoulders in the thin shirt. The whip became a dancing demon, a thing possessed, bearing no relation to the hand that held it. The shrieks grew louder. Jane closed her eyes against the blurred fury of a singing lash, a small boy's terror, and a smiling face.

Miss Nelson was not tired. "Well, C. T.?"

"I won't. Yer can kill me but I *won't!*"

The sounds began again. Red welts began to show across the small arms and through the clinging sweat-drenched shirt.

"Now will you go to your room?"

Sobbing and conquered, C. T. went. The seated children stared curiously at the little procession. Jane dismissed them.

In his seat C. T. found pencil and paper.

"What's he supposed to do, Richards?"

Jane told her.

"All right, now write!"

C. T. stared at Nelson through swollen lids, a curious smile curving his lips. Jane knew suddenly that come hell or high water, C. T. would not write. *I musn't interfere. Please, God, don't let her hurt him too badly. Where have I failed so miserably? . . . Forgive us our trespasses.* The singing whip and the shrieks became a symphony from hell. Suddenly Jane hated the smiling face with an almost unbearable hatred. She spoke, her voice like cold steel.

"That's enough, Nelson."

The noise stopped.

"He's in no condition to write now anyway."

C. T. stood up. "I hate you. I hate you all. You're mean and I hate you."
Then he ran. No one followed him. *Run, little mouse!* They avoided each other's
eyes.

"Well, there you are," Nelson said as she walked away. Jane never found
out what she meant by that.

The next day C. T. did not come to school. The day after that he brought
Jane the fatal homework, neatly and painstakingly done, and a bunch of wild
flowers. Before the bell rang, the children surrounded him. He was beaming.

"Did you tell yer folks you got a whipping, C. T.?"

"Naw! I'd 'a' only got another."

"Where were you yesterday?"

"Went fishin'. Caught me six cats long as your haid, Sambo."

Jane buried her face in the sweet-smelling flowers. *Oh, my brat, my wonderful resilient brat. They'll never get your tail, will they?*

It was seven weeks till the end of term when C. T. brought Jane a model
wooden boat.

Jane stared at it. "Did you make this? It's beautiful, C. T."

"Oh, I make them all the time . . . an' airplanes an' houses too. I do 'em in
my spare time," he finished airily.

"Where do you get the models, C. T.?" she asked.

"I copies them from pictures in the magazines."

Right under my nose . . . right there all the time, she thought wonderingly.
"C. T., would you like to build things when you grow up? Real houses and
ships and planes?"

"Reckon I could, Miz Richards," he said confidently.

The excitement was growing in her. "Look, C. T. You aren't going to do
any lessons at all for the rest of the year. You're going to build ships and houses
and airplanes and anything else you want to."

"I am, huh?" He grinned. "Well, I guess I wasn't goin' to get promoted
nohow."

"Of course, if you want to build them the way they really are, you might
have to do a little measuring, and maybe learn to spell the names of the parts
you want to order. All the best contractors have to know things like that,
you know."

"Say, I'm gonna have real fun, huh? I always said lessons wussent no good
nohow. Pop say too much study eats out yer brains anyway."

The days went by. Jane ran a race with time. The instructions from the
model companies arrived. Jane burned the midnight oil planning each day's
work:

*Learn to spell the following words: ship, sail, steamer—boat, anchor, airplane
wing, fly.*

Write a letter to the lumber company, ordering some lumber.

The floor of our model house is ten inches wide and fourteen inches long. Multiply the length by the width and you'll find the area of the floor in square inches.

Read the story of Columbus and his voyages.

Our plane arrives in Paris in twenty-eight hours. Paris is the capital city of a country named France across the Atlantic Ocean.

Long ago sailors told time by the sun and the stars. Now, the earth goes around the sun—

Work and pray, work and pray!

C. T. learned. Some things vicariously, some things directly. When he found that he needed multiplication to plan his models to scale, he learned to multiply. In three weeks he had mastered simple division.

Jane bought beautifully illustrated stories about ships and planes. He learned to read.

He wrote for and received his own materials.

Jane exulted.

The last day! Forty-two faces waiting anxiously for report cards. Jane spoke to them briefly, praising them collectively, and admonishing them to obey the safety rules during the holidays. Then she passed out the report cards.

As she smiled at each childish face, she thought, *I've been wrong. The long arm of circumstance, environment, and heredity is the farmer's wife that seeks to mow you down, and all of us who touch your lives are in some way responsible for how successful she is. But you aren't mice, my darlings. Mice are hated, hunted pests. You are normal, lovable children. The knife of the farmer's wife is double-edged for you because you are Negro children, born mostly in poverty. But you are wonderful children, nevertheless, for you wear the bright protective cloak of laughter, the strong shield of courage, and the intelligence of children everywhere. Some few of you may indeed become as the mice—but most of you shall find your way to stand fine and tall in the annals of men. There's a bright new tomorrow ahead. For every one of us whose job it is to help you grow that is insensitive and unworthy there are hundreds who daily work that you may grow straight and whole. If it were not so, our world could not long endure.*

She handed C. T. his card.

"Thank you, ma'am."

"Aren't you going to open it?"

He opened it dutifully. When he looked up, his eyes were wide with disbelief. "You didn't make no mistake?"

"No mistake, C. T. You're promoted. You've caught up enough to go to the fourth grade next year."

She dismissed the children. They were a swarm of bees released from a hive. "'By, Miss Richards." . . . "Happy holidays, Miss Richards."

C. T. was the last to go.

"Well, C. T.?"

"Miz Richards, you remember what you said about a name being important?"

"Yes, C. T."

"Well, I talked to mamma, and she said if I wanted a name it would be all right, and she'd go to the courthouse about it."

"What name have you chosen, C. T.?" she asked.

"Christopher Turner Young."

"That's a nice name, Christopher," she said gravely.

"Sho'nuff, Miz Richards?"

"Sure enough, C. T."

"Miz Richards, you know what?"

"What, dear?"

"I love you."

She kissed him swiftly before he ran to catch his classmates.

She stood at the window and watched the running, skipping figures, followed by the bold mimic shadows. *I'm coming home, Paul. I'm leaving my forty-two children, and Tanya there on the hill. My work with them is finished now.* The laughter bubbled up in her throat. *But Paul, oh Paul. See how straight they run!*

suggestions for further reading

introduction

Beauvoir, Simone de. *The Second Sex.* New York: Knopf, 1953. Also in paperback (Bantam).

Ellman, Mary. *Thinking About Women.* New York: Harcourt Brace Jovanovich, 1968.

Fiedler, Leslie A. *Love and Death in the American Novel.* rev. ed. New York: Stein and Day, 1966. Also in paperback (Dell).

Friedan, Betty. *The Feminine Mystique.* New York: Norton, 1963. Also in paperback (Dell).

Greer, Germaine. *The Female Eunuch.* New York: McGraw-Hill, 1971. Also in paperback (Bantam).

Janeway, Elizabeth. *Man's World, Woman's Place: A Study in Social Mythology.* New York: Morrow, 1971.

Mailer, Norman. *The Prisoner of Sex.* Boston: Little, Brown, 1971.

Mead, Margaret. "Witch, Bitch, Goddess, or Human Being?" Review of *Man's World, Woman's Place* by Elizabeth Janeway. *The New York Times Book Review,* June 20, 1971, pp. 7, 18–19.

Millett, Kate. *Sexual Politics.* Garden City: Doubleday, 1970.

Reeves, Nancy. *Womankind: Beyond the Stereotypes.* Chicago: Aldine-Atherton, 1971. (An original paperback.)

Rogers, Katharine M. *The Troublesome Helpmate: A History of Misogyny in Literature.* Seattle: University of Washington Press, 1966. (A paperback.)

Trilling, Diana. "The Image of Women in Contemporary Literature." In *The Woman in America.* Edited by Robert J. Lifton. Boston: Beacon Press, 1967. (A paperback.)

I.   the submissive wife

Bawden, Nina. *A Woman of My Age.* New York: Lancer, 1967.

Chaucer, Geoffrey. "The Clerk's Prologue and Tale." In *The Works of Geoffrey Chaucer.* 2nd ed. Edited by F. N. Robinson. Boston: Houghton Mifflin, 1961. See the character Griselde.

Didion, Joan. *Play It As It Lays.* New York: Farrar, Straus & Giroux, 1970. Also in paperback (Bantam).

Dostoevsky, Fyodor. "A Gentle Creature." In *A Gentle Creature and Other Stories.* Translated by David Magarshack. London: John Lehmann, 1950.

Hochman, Sandra. *Walking Papers.* New York: Viking, 1971.

Kaufman, Sue. *The Diary of a Mad Housewife.* New York: Random House, 1967. Also in paperback (Bantam).

Lawrence, D. H. *The Rainbow & Women in Love.* Edited by Colin Clarke. Nashville: Aurora, 1970.

Lessing, Doris. "To Room 19." In *A Man and Two Women.* New York: Simon & Schuster, 1963.

Lopata, Helena Z. *Occupation Housewife.* New York: Oxford University Press, 1971. Nonfiction.

Martinerie, Andree. *A Life's Full Summer.* New York: Harcourt Brace Jovanovich, 1971.

Oates, Joyce Carol. "Pastoral Blood." In *By the North Gate.* New York: Vanguard, 1963. Also in paperback (Fawcett).

Roiphe, Anne R. *Up the Sandbox!* New York: Simon & Schuster, 1971.

Tolstoy, Leo. *Anna Karenina.* Translated by Joel Carmichael. New York: Bantam, 1960. (A paperback.) Originally published in 1876.

Weingarten, Violet. *A Loving Wife.* New York: Knopf, 1969. Also in paperback (Signet).

II.   the mother

Betts, Doris, "Still Life with Fruit." In *Red Clay Reader 7.* Charlotte, N.C.: Southern Review, 1970

Howard, Sidney. *The Silver Cord: A Comedy in three acts.* New York: French, 1928. Originally published in 1913.

Lawrence, D. H. *Sons and Lovers.* New York: Viking, 1958. (A paperback.)

—— *The Virgin and the Gipsy.* New York: Knopf, 1930. Also in paperback (Bantam).

Nin, Anaïs. "Birth." In *Under a Glass Bell and Other Stories.* Chicago: Swallow Press, 1968.

O'Neill, Eugene. *Desire Under the Elms.* In *Three Plays by Eugene O'Neill.* New York: Random House, 1968. (A Vintage paperback.) Originally published in 1924.

Rechy, John. *This Day's Death.* New York: Grove Press, 1970.

Roth, Philip. *Portnoy's Complaint.* New York: Random House, 1969. Also in paperback (Bantam).

Wylie, Philip. *Generation of Vipers.* New York: Holt, Rinehart and Winston, 1942.

III.   the dominating wife

Albee, Edward. *Who's Afraid of Virginia Woolf?* New York: Atheneum, 1962. (A paperback.)

Chaucer, Geoffrey. "The Prologue and Tale of the Wife of Bath," *The Works of Geoffrey Chaucer.* 2nd ed. Edited by F. N. Robinson. Boston: Houghton Mifflin, 1961.

Chrêtien de Troyes. "The Knight of the Cart." In *Arthurian Romances.* Translated by W. W. Comfort. New York: Dutton, 1956. (Everyman's Library.) This romance of the 12th century concerns Lancelot.

Flaubert, Gustave. *Madame Bovary.* Translated by Eleanor Marx-Aveling. New York: Dutton, 1953. (A paperback.) Originally published in 1846.

Ibsen, Henrik. *Hedda Gabler.* Translated by Max Faber. New York: Theatre Arts, 1966. Originally published in 1890.

Kopit, Arthur. *Oh Dad, Poor Dad, Mamma's Hung You in the Closet and I'm Feelin' So Sad.* New York: Hill and Wang, 1960.

Mailer, Norman. *An American Dream.* New York: Dial, 1964. Also in paperback (Dell).

Shakespeare, William. *The Taming of the Shrew.* Edited by Alfred Harbage & Richard Hosley. Baltimore: Penguin, 1963- . (A Pelican paperback.) Originally published in 1954.

—— *Macbeth.* Edited by Alfred Harbage. Baltimore: Penguin, 1963- . (A Pelican paperback.) Originally published in 1606.

Strindberg, August. *The Father.* Somerville, Mass.: Humphries, 1964. (A paperback.) Originally published in 1886.

—— *Married.* Translated by Ellie Schleussner. London: Palmer, 1913. Originally published in 1884. See especially "A Doll's House," Strindberg's answer to Ibsen.

Thurber, James. "The Secret Life of Walter Mitty." In *The Thurber Carnival.* New York: Harper & Row, 1945. Also in paperback (Dell).

IV. the seductress-goddess

Hays, H. Q. *The Dangerous Sex: the Myth of Feminine Evil.* New York: G. P. Putnam's Sons, 1964.

Miller, Arthur. *After the Fall.* New York: Viking, 1964. (A paperback.)

Rougemont, Denis de. *Love in the Western World.* New York: Pantheon, 1956. Also in paperback (Fawcett).

Segal, Erich. *Love Story.* New York: Harper & Row, 1970. Also in paperback (Signet).

V. the sex object

Crane, Stephen. *Maggie: A Girl of the Streets.* New York: Fawcett, 1964. (A paperback.) Originally published in 1892.

Gorky, Maxim. "The Woman with the Blue Eyes." In *Selected Short Stories, 1892–1901.* Translated by Margaret Wettlin. New York: Ungar, 1959.

Lawrence, D. H. *Lady Chatterley's Lover.* New York: Grove Press, 1962. (A paperback.) Originally published in 1926.

——— *The Woman Who Rode Away and Other Stories.* New York: Knopf, 1928. See the title story.

Lessing, Doris. "Notes for a Case History" and "A Woman on a Roof." In *A Man and Two Women.* New York: Simon & Schuster, 1963.

Millett, Kate. "Quartet." In *Woman in Sexist Society.* Edited by Vivian Gornick and Barbara Moran. New York: Basic Books, 1971. Soon to be in paperback.

Murdoch, Iris. *A Severed Head.* New York: Viking, 1961. (A paperback.)

Nabokov, Vladimir. *Lolita.* New York: G. P. Putnam's Sons, 1958. Also in paperback (Medallion).

Nin, Anaïs. "The Mouse." In *Under a Glass Bell and Other Stories.* Chicago: Swallow Press, 1966. (A paperback.) Originally published in 1948.

Réage, Pauline. *Story of O.* New York: Grove Press, 1965. (A paperback.)

Wakefield, Dan. *Going All the Way.* New York: Delacorte, 1970. Also in paperback (Dell).

VI. the old maid

Anderson, Sherwood. "Adventure." In *Winesburg, Ohio.* New York: Viking, 1958. (A paperback.) Originally published in 1919.

Deegan, Dorothy. *The Stereotype of the Single Woman in American Novels.* New York: Octagon Books, 1969. (A paperback.) Originally published in 1951.

Faulkner, William. "A Rose for Emily." In *The Portable Faulkner.* New York: Viking, 1946. Originally published in 1924.

Flaubert, Gustave. "The Simple Heart." In *Three Tales.* New York: Knopf, 1924. Originally published in 1877.

James, Henry. "Four Meetings." In *The Portable Henry James.* New York: Viking, 1951. Originally published in 1877.

Lessing, Doris. "Our Friend Judith." In *A Man and Two Women.* New York: Simon & Schuster, 1963.

Moore, Brian. *The Lonely Passion of Judith Hearne.* Boston: Little, Brown, 1955. Also in paperback (Dell).

Spark , Muriel. *The Prime of Miss Jean Brodie.* Philadelphia: Lippincott, 1961. Also in paperback (Dell).

Welty, Eudora. "Clytie" and "June Recital." In *Selected Short Stories of Eudora Welty.* New York: Modern Library, 1954. Originally published in 1941 and 1949, respectively.

VII.   the liberated woman

Autobiographies:
Angelou, Maya. *I Know Why the Caged Bird Sings.* New York: Random House, 1969. Also in paperback (Bantam).

Devlin, Bernadette. *The Price of My Soul.* London: Deutsch, 1969.

Giovanni, Nikki. *Gemini.* Indianapolis: Bobbs-Merrill, 1972.

Glasgow, Ellen. *The Woman Within.* New York: Harcourt Brace Jovanovich, 1954.

Jackson, Shirley. *Life Among the Savages.* New York: Farrar, Straus & Giroux, 1953. Also in paperback (Scholastic Books Star Line).

Knef, Hildegarde. *The Gift Horse.* New York: McGraw-Hill, 1971.

McCarthy, Mary. *Memories of a Catholic Girlhood.* New York: Harcourt Brace Jovanovich, 1957. Also in paperback (Medallion).

Moody, Anne. *Coming of Age in Mississippi.* New York: Dial, 1968. Also in paperback (Dell).

Nin, Anaïs. *Diary.* New York: Harcourt Brace Jovanovich, 1966- . (An original paperback.) Four volumes to date.

Woolf, Virginia. *A Writer's Diary.* New York: Harcourt Brace, 1954. Also in paperback (Signet).

Fiction:
Cather, Willa. *My Antonia.* Boston: Houghton Mifflin, 1961. (A paperback.) Originally published in 1928.

Chopin, Kate. *The Awakening.* New York: Capricorn Books, 1964. (A paperback.) Originally published in 1899.

Glasgow, Ellen. *Barren Ground.* New York: Hill and Wang, 1957. (A paperback.) Originally published in 1925.

—— *Vein of Iron.* New York: Harcourt Brace, 1935.

Hall, Radclyffe. *The Well of Loneliness.* Maplewood, N.J.: Hammond, 1944. Also in paperback (Pocket Books). Originally published in 1928.

James, Henry. *The Bostonians.* New York: Dial, 1945. Also in paperback (Modern Library). Originally published in 1886.

Lessing, Doris. *The Golden Notebook.* New York: Simon & Schuster, 1962. Also in paperback (Ballantine).

Marshall, Paule. "Reena." In *American Negro Short Stories.* Edited by John H. Clarke. New York: Hill and Wang, 1966. (A paperback.)

Undset, Sigrid. *Kristin Lavransdatter.* New York: Knopf, 1923.

index of authors

photo credits